CULTURE AND MANAGEMENT
text and readings in comparative management

THE IRWIN SERIES IN MANAGEMENT

CONSULTING EDITOR   JOHN F. MEE   *Indiana University*

AMMER   *Materials Management*   rev. ed.

BRENNAN   *Wage Administration: Plans, Practices, and Principles*   rev. ed.

BROOM   *Production Management*   rev. ed.

CHAMPION & BRIDGES   *Critical Incidents in Management*   rev. ed.

EELLS & WALTON   *Conceptual Foundations of Business*

FARMER & RICHMAN   *Comparative Management and Economic Progress*

GREENE   *Production Control: Systems and Decisions*

HANEY   *Communication and Organizational Behavior: Text and Cases*   rev. ed.

HOUSTON   *Manager Development: Principles and Perspectives*

JONES   *Executive Decision Making*   rev. ed.

JUCIUS   *Personnel Management*   6th ed.

JUCIUS & SCHLENDER   *Elements of Managerial Action*   rev. ed.

LING   *The Management of Personnel Relations: History and Origins*

MCDONOUGH & GARRETT   *Management Systems: Working Concepts and Practices*

MEGGINSON   *Personnel: A Behavioral Approach to Administration*

MOORE   *Manufacturing Management*   5th ed.

MOORE & KIBBEY   *Manufacturing: Materials and Processes*

MORRIS   *The Analysis of Management Decisions*   rev. ed.

NADLER   *Work Design*

NIEBEL   *Motion and Time Study*   4th ed.

PATTON, LITTLEFIELD, & SELF   *Job Evaluation: Text and Cases*   3d ed.

PRINCE   *Information Systems for Management Planning and Control*

REED   *Plant Layout: Factors, Principles, and Techniques*

RICHARDS & GREENLAW   *Management Decision Making*

ROSCOE   *Organization for Production: An Introduction to Industrial Management*   4th ed.

ROSCOE   *Project Economy*

SCOTT   *Organization Theory: A Behavioral Analysis for Management*

SEIMER   *Cases in Industrial Management*

SHULL & DELBECQ (eds.)   *Selected Readings in Management: Extensions and Modifications*   2d Series

SIEGEL   *Industrial Psychology*

SIMONDS & GRIMALDI   *Safety Management: Accident Cost and Control*   rev. ed.

SPRIEGEL & MYERS (eds.)   *The Writings of the Gilbreths*

TERRY   *Principles of Management*   5th ed.

THAYER   *Communication and Communication Systems: In Organization Management and Interpersonal Relations*

TIMMS   *The Production Function in Business: Fundamentals and Analysis for Management*   rev. ed.

VORIS   *Production Control: Text and Cases*   3d ed.

WEBBER   *Culture and Management: Text and Readings in Comparative Management*

CULTURE AND MANAGEMENT

text and readings in comparative management

by ROSS A. WEBBER
Wharton School of Finance and Commerce
University of Pennsylvania

1969
Richard D. Irwin, Inc. · Homewood, Illinois
Irwin-Dorsey Limited · Nobleton, Ontario

658.008
W 372

To my parents: Richard and Muriel Webber

Preface

From art to politics, business to war, the United States has entered the world to a degree approximated only by 19th century Britain and Imperial Rome. This book reflects a judgment that the American business manager of tomorrow will have to know more about why he manages as he does and why others manage as they do. The destinies of organizations the world over are becoming interdependent. Management education is awakening to these developments. Curricula are notoriously slow to change, but already the International Business program is one of the largest concentrations at the graduate level, and comparative approaches to management are being developed. We hope that this book will assist in this expansion of managerial perspectives.

The volume may be helpful in a variety of ways:

1. The readings comprise much of the content of a Wharton graduate course in comparative management open to MBA and Ph.D. candidates majoring in industrial administration and international business. Recently, there has been a significant increase in such courses in comparative management.
2. The materials can be used as supplementary readings in basic undergraduate and graduate management or organizational behavior courses.
3. These readings are particularly appropriate to courses in conceptual and historical foundations of business, or business and society.
4. Many of the authors deal explicitly with issues that are the substance of courses in anthropology and sociology.
5. The comparative and cross-cultural orientation of this book should make it particularly helpful in international executive programs such as those being held in Switzerland, France, and other nations.
6. Finally, the various articles are intrinsically interesting and important. The practising manager may find much here that will intrigue, frighten, and inform him.

However this volume is used, it is apparent that these "foreign" materials have pertinence to the education of managers in the United States. And, as J. Boddewyn has pointed out, a comparative approach may be introduced in a variety of ways:

In teaching, it should be made apparent that the comparative study of business administration does not have to be considered as a separate branch of knowledge but as a point of view . . . as such it can be incorporated into any course which can at least implicitly be made "comparative" through the inclusion of "foreign" data. Some schools may want special foreign courses; others may prefer to integrate comparative findings into existing advanced theory courses; all can include comparisons in the content of basic introductory courses once suitable publications have become more readily available.[1]

---

[1] Jean Boddewyn, "The Comparative Approach to the Study of Business Administration," *Academy of Management Journal,* December 1965, p. 267.

It is hoped that this book brings together such materials.

An outline of the volume and a description of chapter contents are included in Chapter One, "The Expanding World of Management." I do want to point out here that each chapter includes a sizable, although not exhaustive, list of references. In addition, a list of student research topics is provided in the appendix. I have assigned these topics both for oral and written reports with excellent results.

Herbert Northrup, Chairman of the Industry Department at the Wharton School of Finance and Commerce, University of Pennsylvania, provided funds for research and clerical assistance. For this I am grateful. My secretaries Loretta Hentz and Helen White courageously attacked my mumbled voice tapes and barely legible notes—and produced a typed manuscript. My sincerest thanks to them. Professors Herbert Northrup, William Gomberg, John Mee, and Richard Farmer all have commented on various portions of this volume. Their observations have been very helpful. I have not always followed their advice, but I have learned from their criticism. Special gratitude is due my wife Mary Lou who has read the manuscript many times and assisted me on numerous decisions about what to exclude and include.

Additional thanks go to my three research assistants who, over the past two years, helped me in canvassing many books and journals—first, to initiate a new course; and second, to put this book together. They are Philip Patrick McGrath, now with Towers, Perrin, Forster & Crosby; Edward R. Silansky, now with Morgan Stanley & Co., and Eric J. Walter, now with McKinsey and Company. Finally, I am grateful to the numerous authors and publishers who have graciously permitted me to select and edit the articles and excerpts appearing in this volume.

Cherry Hill, N.J.   Ross A. Webber
December, 1968

Table of Contents

chapter one: The Expanding World of Management 1

chapter two: Culture and Management: An Overview 9

    1. Culture and Work, *William F. White,* 30

chapter three: Management in the United States: The Historical Setting . . . 41

chapter four: Culture and Attitudes Affecting Economic Activities 55

    2. The Meaning of Culture, *Ruth Benedict,* 56
    3. Culture and Personality, *Victor Barnouw,* 67
    4. Ideological Preparation: The Wish before the Fact, *Lewis Mumford,* 82
    5. The Protestant Ethic and the Spirit of Capitalism, *Max Weber and Kemper Fullerton,* 91
    6. Mahatma Gandhi's Views on Machines and Technology, *D. P. Mukerji,* 112
    7. A Chinese Philosopher Prefers the Material Civilization of the West, *Hu Shih,* 120
    Additional References, 124

chapter five: Business Managers and Economic Development 127

    8. Business in Western Europe, *Richard Eells and Clarence Walton,* 128
    9. The Shackles of Backwardness, *Robert Heilbroner,* 145
    10. The Stages of Economic Growth, *W. W. Rostow,* 157
    11. The Critical Role of the High Achiever, *David C. McClelland,* 163
    12. Cross-Cultural Studies of Technical Change, *Margaret Mead,* 182
    Additional References, 196

chapter six: Origins of Managers 199

    13. The Industrializing Elites, *Clark Kerr, John T. Dunlop, Frederick Harbison, and Charles A. Myers,* 200
    14. Social Class Background of Managers in Various Countries, *David C. McClelland,* 214
    15. Business and Class in Europe, *David Granick,* 218

16. The Dilemma of an Elite Group: The Industrialist in Latin America, *John D. Harbron,* 233
Additional References, 246

chapter seven: Education and Management 247

17. Industrialization and Fundamental Education, *Margaret Mead,* 248
18. Higher Education and the Level of Economic Development, *Frederick Harbison and Charles A. Myers,* 257
19. Heroes, Homework, and Industrial Growth, *William F. Whyte and Robert R. Braun,* 286
20. The Renaissance of Foreign Business Schools, *Alan B. Coleman and Dan Throop Smith,* 295
21. Europe's Business Schools: A Good Start, But . . . , *John G. Hutchinson,* 299
Additional References, 307

chapter eight: Managerial Philosophies and Practices 309

22. Social and Cultural Factors in Management Development, *Editors, International Labour Review,* 311
23. The Interplay of Culture and Management in a Guatemalan Textile Plant, *Manning Nash,* 317
24. Cultural Patterns in the Role of the Manager, *Mason Haire, Edwin E. Ghiselli, and Lyman W. Porter,* 325
25. Contrasting Motives and Attitudes of Managers in More and Less Developed Countries, *David C. McClelland,* 341
26. American vs. European Management Philosophy, *Otto H. Nowotny,* 346
27. Group Management, European Style, *F. Newton Parks,* 356
28. An Aspect of Management Philosophy in the United States and Latin America, *Eugene C. McCann,* 366
29. Management Aims and Development Needs in Latin America, *Albert Lauterbach,* 370
Additional References, 392

chapter nine: Examples of Management in Specific Countries 393

30. The Socio-Cultural Setting of Management in the United Kingdom, *Rosemary Stewart,* 395
31. I Was a Soviet Manager, *Gregory Ryapolov,* 416
32. Japanese Management—the Cultural Background, *William Brown,* 428
33. Social and Cultural Factors in Management Development in India, *Kamla Kapur Chowdhry,* 442

34. The Manager in the Polish Enterprise: A Study of Accommodation under Conditions of Role Conflict, *Solomon John Rawin,* 453
35. Capitalists and Managers in Communist China, *Barry M. Richman,* 467
36. The Egyptian Executive: A Study in Conflict, *Harold Q. Langenderfer,* 488
37. Business Management in French Canada, *Gaston Pelletier,* 501
Additional References, 509

— **chapter ten: Convergence in Managerial Philosophy and Practice?** 517

38. The Road to Similarity, *Clark Kerr, John T. Dunlop, Frederick Harbison, and Charles A. Myers,* 529
39. Evolving Organizations, *Chadwick J. Haberstroh,* 538
40. The New Industrial State, *John Kenneth Galbraith,* 547
41. Creeping Capitalism in the Soviet Union? *Harry Landreth,* 557
42. Are Industrial Societies Becoming Alike? *Arnold S. Feldman and Wilbert E. Moore,* 567
Additional References, 572

chapter eleven: Conclusion: American Students and Foreign Management . . 573

appendix: Suggested Topics for Independent Research 587

index 593

chapter one

The Expanding World of Management

Bikini-clad blondes with water skis invite us. Equally daring alpinists with snow skis beckon. On numerous travel posters and airline advertisements they tell us the world is shrinking. It is getting smaller as streaking jet aircraft and orbiting communications satellites decrease the time and effort between men. But, they are wrong. The world is not shrinking; for the individual it is expanding. And time is not being saved; it is being consumed by more events. As Marshall McLuhan points out,[1] communications and travel media are the extensions of man, and they are not making the world smaller and simpler, but larger and more complex.

Robert Heilbroner shows us that the scope of history has virtually exploded in recent times.

To the West, the chain of happenings leading up to World War II seemed to reach around the entire world. Yet what strikes us now is not how large, but how circumscribed and restricted was the theatre of history of those days. While Europe and America hovered at the brink of a supreme historic involvement, at least to Western eyes, the far larger and more populous areas of the East and South mainly slumbered. India, plucking feebly at its British bonds, resembled a drugged Gulliver, China, in itself comprising a quarter of the world's population, suffered military rape in a surrender of total exhaustion, Latin America, aside from its dreary chronicle of coup and exploitation, was to all intents and purposes an historic zero. Africa languished in oblivion. The Near East rotted amid general indifference.

. . . Insofar as "history" consists of a shared political and social and economic self-consciousness which becomes part of the biographies of millions of human beings, helping to shape these biographies and to give them a common purpose, it can fairly be said that most of the world had no history.[2]

[1] See H. Marshall McLuhan, *Understanding Media—the Extension of Man* (New York: McGraw-Hill Book Co., Inc., 1964).

[2] Robert L. Heilbroner, *The Great Ascent* (New York: Harper & Row, Publishers, 1963), pp. 16–17.

1

No longer is this true, however. Life in America is not so insular; it can be shaken by events in far-removed places. The historian E. H. Carr has written: "It is only today that it has become possible for the first time even to imagine a whole world consisting of peoples who have in the fullest sense entered history and become the concern, no longer of the colonial administrator or the anthropologist, but of the historian."[3]

Simply put, more things that affect us—or could affect us—are going on across the Atlantic or below the equator or over the horizon. The world of interest and relevant events is becoming larger, and this is as true for the business manager as for the historian or statesman.

AMERICAN PROVINCIALISM

The great problem for the American manager in thinking about this expanding world is that he looks at it from a narrow perspective—a perspective of ethnocentralism. After watching a television commercial in which a French foreign legionnaire orders an American legionnaire off his sand dune because the American had stolen his family deodorant, my younger daughter asked, "Daddy, why does that man speak so funny?" Before I could reply, her 10-year-old sister explained, "Because Frenchmen speak American with French accents, Englishmen speak American with English accents, and we speak American without any accent." Her profundity silenced me.

Such provincialism, however, is one of the reasons for the preparation of this volume. On no subject are Americans (even that term is wrong in referring to citizens of the United States, for, after all, Brazilians or Peruvians are Americans, too) more self-centered and ethnocentric than on the management of economic enterprise. Thus, with some justification we observe that the United States is the most advanced and productive society in the world, and we conclude that our business management must be the best. In addition, since we have probably written more books and held more classes on management than all other countries put together, many foreign administrators and educators turn to the United States when they begin to think about the practice and teaching of management. Nonetheless, our own success in economic affairs and business management may blind us to others. Perhaps more than most people, we tend to delude ourselves that we are different—harder working, broader in our views, less self-interested, and so on.[4] As a result, we are constantly responding to the foreign environment from an American value system base. Walter Ong, a long-time observer of overseas Americans, describes it this way.

Our own great American achievement has somehow become a positive psychological handicap. The United States has become a vast and successful working machine for converting into ourselves persons from every nation of the world. . . . We cannot make ourselves over, even imaginatively, into other people. . . . Our thoughtlessness is caught in our assumption that what we do is never chauvinistic or nationalistic, though what others may

---

[3] E. H. Carr, *What Is History* (New York: Alfred A. Knopf, Inc., 1962), p. 199.
[4] See Charles Frankel, "Four Illusions that Beset Us," *New York Times Magazine*, September 22, 1963, p. 31.

do may well be. Thus for British missionaries to teach cricket or Canadian missionaries to teach lacrosse would be chauvinistic, but for American missionaries to teach baseball is not spreading American culture but merely enabling the benighted natives to be human beings.[5]

To this, we might add our assumption that what the world needs is more American managerial know-how. Just as many would suggest that European and South American soccer is a better sport than U.S. baseball, so might there be some things that foreign managers do better than Americans. Whatever advantage the United States may have in scientific and rational management, however, history has repeatedly shown us that we neglect foreign practices to our own peril. For all its faults, socialism is succeeding in many places, and there are numerous excellent managers in Russia. Similarly, with all its backwardness in rational management thought, Japan—or even Italy—has made enormous strides in business. We may be better, but are we better in everything? Is there nothing we can learn from foreign managers?

Obviously, the questions are rhetorical. The existence of this volume implies that we Americans can learn about management even from less advanced countries. At the national level, we believe, then, that the United States can learn more in its strongest area from others who lag or are pursuing different paths.

For example, in the education of managers: Soviet Russia's are virtually all engineering graduates; Great Britain's are mostly trained in the humanities. In the United States, we are apparently moving from liberal arts to engineering as a background for top executives. At the moment, we are about balanced. By looking at the United Kingdom and the U.S.S.R., we may be able to see the strengths and weaknesses of each background.

Another example, in the practice of management: Japanese companies apparently get remarkable loyalty and effort out of their employees, while in the United States some managers are concerned about the decline in American youth's willingness to work. Aside from cultural factors, other differences in management policies and procedures may be pertinent.

At the level of the individual company and the individual manager there is also need to expand awareness and interest in foreign management. Many authors have been concerned with international business and the management of American interests abroad. Most of this literature deals with the utilization of U.S. management philosophies and techniques abroad. This is not our purpose. We want to consider some matters that should *precede* consideration of how U.S. managers should manage abroad. That is, we want to consider how foreign managers manage in their own countries. "Domestic Management Abroad" or "Native Management at Home" might be other titles of this volume from an American perspective.

Although we do not consider Americans overseas, studies of foreign management should be helpful in overcoming the naïve ethnocentricity that has so often impaired both the business and political effectiveness of American executives

---

[5] Walter J. Ong, "That American Way," *America,* November 22, 1958. Quoted in Harlan Cleveland *et al., The Overseas American* (New York: McGraw-Hill Book Co., 1960), pp. 30–31.

in their work abroad. It is not clear whether the future will bring more or less overseas positions for U.S. citizens. A recent survey of the literature suggests that foreign posts are increasingly being filled by nationals of the countries involved.[6] Nonetheless, the age of the multinational firm is on us. Isolated in their steel and glass towers on Madison Avenue, American executives may need a *better* understanding of how cultural factors affect their foreign operations than they would need if they were themselves in Paris or New Delhi. As our relationships with other countries and foreign managers become both closer and more important, it is more than ever necessary that American business leaders generally, and not merely those with specialized international responsibilities, learn to transcend their limited backgrounds and adopt a world view. Michael Haider, chairman of New Jersey Standard Oil, states that tomorrow's manager must be "A Man for All Countries."[7]

PLAN OF THE BOOK

The subject of this volume, then, is managerial philosophy and practice in other countries. But management does not exist in a vacuum. Four intermeshing systems impinge on managers—technical, political, economic, and cultural. Exhibit 1 summarizes these variables.

Certainly, managerial behavior is influenced by the technological characteristics of business, the attitudes and policies of government, and the type and level of economic development. The relationship between management and each of these systems is important. The emphasis of this volume, however, is on management and how it is related to cultural factors. Even the most ardent universalist advocating application of "principles of management" in all countries recognizes that cultural factors such as class structure, attitudes toward money and work, or the meaning of authority influence how management is actually conducted. These historical and cultural factors also influence who actually become managers.

In exploring management in a variety of cultural settings, we shall proceed as follows.

Chapter Two. Culture and Management: An Overview. In this chapter, we shall introduce the concept of culture, how cultural values and attitudes affect individual needs and aspirations, and what this implies for management.

Chapter Three. Management in the United States: The Historical Setting. Before we study management abroad, we should briefly examine the United States. Accordingly, in this chapter we consider management's unique position here, for nowhere else have management and managers—even with current college student problems and past politician problems—enjoyed such legitimacy, attention, and prestige.

---

[6] Arthur G. Houghton, "Management for the Worldwide Enterprise" (unpublished M.B.A. thesis, Wharton School of Finance and Commerce, University of Pennsylvania, 1968).

[7] Michael Haider, "Tomorrow's Executive: A Man for All Countries," *Columbia Journal of World Business*, Vol. 1, No. 1 (Winter, 1966), p. 107.

EXHIBIT 1-1
Four Intermeshing Systems Which Influence Managerial Philosophy and Practice*

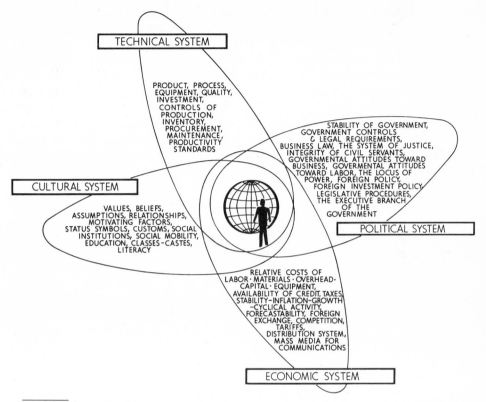

TECHNICAL SYSTEM

PRODUCT, PROCESS,
EQUIPMENT, QUALITY,
INVESTMENT,
CONTROLS OF
PRODUCTION,
INVENTORY,
PROCUREMENT,
MAINTENANCE,
PRODUCTIVITY
STANDARDS

STABILITY OF GOVERNMENT,
GOVERNMENT CONTROLS
& LEGAL REQUIREMENTS,
BUSINESS LAW, THE SYSTEM OF JUSTICE,
INTEGRITY OF CIVIL SERVANTS,
GOVERNMENTAL ATTITUDES TOWARD
BUSINESS, GOVERMENTAL ATTITUDES
TOWARD LABOR, THE LOCUS OF
POWER, FOREIGN POLICY,
FOREIGN INVESTMENT POLICY,
LEGISLATIVE PROCEDURES,
THE EXECUTIVE BRANCH
OF THE
GOVERNMENT

CULTURAL SYSTEM

VALUES, BELIEFS,
ASSUMPTIONS, RELATIONSHIPS,
MOTIVATING FACTORS,
STATUS SYMBOLS, CUSTOMS, SOCIAL
INSTITUTIONS, SOCIAL MOBILITY,
EDUCATION, CLASSES–CASTES,
LITERACY

POLITICAL SYSTEM

RELATIVE COSTS OF
LABOR· MATERIALS · OVERHEAD·
CAPITAL· EQUIPMENT,
AVAILABILITY OF CREDIT, TAXES,
STABILITY–INFLATION–GROWTH
–CYCLICAL ACTIVITY,
FORECASTABILITY, FOREIGN
EXCHANGE, COMPETITION,
TARIFFS,
DISTRIBUTION SYSTEM,
MASS MEDIA FOR
COMMUNICATIONS

ECONOMIC SYSTEM

*From C. Wickham Skinner, "Management of International Production," *Harvard Business Review,* September–October, 1964, p. 132. © 1964 by the President and Fellows of Harvard College; all rights reserved.

Chapter Four. Culture and Attitudes Affecting Economic Activities.   The selected readings in this chapter will examine cultural values and desirability of economic pursuits for the society and for the individual. Attitudes toward time and the role of religion are considered.

Chapter Five. Business Managers and Economic Development.   Selected readings discuss the key role of managers with their high achievement needs in promoting business and economic development. With the broad range of factors examined in Chapters Four and Five, the readings are necessarily eclectic. Anthropologists, psychologists, economists, historians, and even theologians are represented.

Chapter Six. Origins of Managers.   The readings here will consider the socio-economic backgrounds of managers in a variety of settings.

Chapter Seven. Education and Management.   Industrialization and general education have long been closely related. In recent years, there has been rapid expansion in professional training for managers. These readings survey these developments.

Chapter Eight. Managerial Philosophies and Practices. The interrelationships between culture and management introduced in Chapter Two are discussed in greater depth with examples from several cultural settings.

Chapter Nine. Examples of Management in Specific Countries. Management philosophies and practices in a cross section of developed and less developed nations are considered in these selected readings.

Chapter Ten. Convergence in Managerial Philosophy and Practice? In this chapter, we examine suggestions, from a variety of disciplines, that our modern world is characterized by convergence in economics, management, and even politics—for example, that management in the United States, Russia, and even Tanzania will gradually become more and more similar. Cases for convergence and some counter arguments are presented.

Chapter Eleven. American Students and Foreign Management. In the final chapter we return to our discussion of what foreign philosophy and practice offers to the United States. Students' responses to the study of comparative management are analyzed to reveal what they perceive as problems in American management.

In any work of comparative scope there is always the danger of degeneration into a series of unconnected case examples. One way to organize this volume simply would be to provide reports on a series of countries. However, no one can hope to learn about management everywhere. If this book is to have any value to the reader, it must consider the relationships between management and the important factors that influence philosophy and practice in order to provide some conceptual tools to apply to specific countries and situations. We try to do this by providing integrated readings that consider a variety of countries to illustrate the respective subjects: attitudes toward economic development and material goods, the desirability of direction versus persuasion in management, the education associated with different styles of management, and so on. At various places in Chapters Four through Eight, a reading will consider a specific country to clearly illustrate a point. For the most part, however, these readings are integrated and comparative, not single, isolated cases.

Regardless of the desirability for comparative and analytical materials, we do need to consider some country examples. Only in this way can we get a feeling for the interrelatedness of culture, history, economics, and management. The problem for the author and editor (and ultimately the reader) is that we must limit the number of countries considered and the depth devoted to each. Consequently, there is danger that we oversimplify complex reality. In Chapter Nine, we present several readings that deal with management in the United Kingdom, Russia, Japan, and other nations. These selections are by no means exhaustive. To facilitate further investigation of specific countries, a list of additional references is included.

So let us begin our survey of management and its cultural settings. I assume that American readers know something about management theory and practice in the United States, and I hope they have some awareness of how business fits into our society. If so, as one progresses through these readings about management in other societies, one cannot fail to learn about the distinctness of American culture.

Additional References

Barnes, William S. "Guides to International Operations," *Harvard Business Review,* Vol. 43, No. 6 (November–December, 1965).

Boddewyn, J. "The Comparative Approach to the Study of Business Administration," *Academy of Management Journal,* Vol. 8, No. 4 (December, 1965).

Brohi, Allah Baksh K. "Dynamic Management in a Changing World," *Management International,* No. 4 (1965).

The Changing Role of the International Executive. NICB Pamphlet on Business Policy #119.

Farmer, R., and Richman, B. "Economic Progress, Management Theory and Comparative Management," *Comparative Management and Economic Progress,* chap. 1, pp. 1–10. Homewood, Ill.: Richard D. Irwin, Inc., 1965.

Kircher, Donald P. "Now the Transnational Enterprise," *Harvard Business Review,* March–April, 1964.

"These American Managers Don't Impress Europe," *Fortune* (December, 1964).

"U.S. Managers Overseas," *University of Michigan Graduate School of Business Journal,* Autumn, 1965.

Wilkins, Mira. "The Businessman Abroad," *Annals of the American Academy of Political and Social Science,* Vol. 368 (November, 1966), pp. 83–94.

Yoshino, M. Y. "Administrative Attitudes and Relationships in a Foreign Culture," *Business Topics,* Michigan State University, Vol. 16, No. 1 (Winter, 1968), pp. 59–72.

chapter two

Culture and Management: An Overview

Two students are playing. In this game of interpersonal conflict, each contestant has two strategies from which he may choose, with the following results. If both choose strategy A, each receives $3; if both choose strategy B, each receives $2; if they split on strategies AB or BA, each receives $1.

Player 1

		A	B
	A	$3	$1
Player 2			
	B	$1	$2

Given this matrix, on repeated plays American M.B.A. candidates at the Wharton School tend to stabilize on strategy A. Both earn $3. Such is not the case for students from Korea. Playing the same game under similar conditions, Korean students attending the University of Pennsylvania tend to select strategy B. Both earn $2.[1] Why?

Perhaps cultural factors cause the difference. It appears that the Koreans cannot cooperate. Either they distrust each other, or they want to minimize the earnings of their competitors even more than to maximize their own. Relative status seems to be more important than individual gain, in contrast to the Americans.

Of course, this experiment does not prove that personal noncooperativeness

---

[1] For this information, we are indebted to Professor David Conrath of the Wharton School of Finance and Commerce. Research is being conducted under the auspices of the Management Science Center of the University of Pennsylvania.

9

is characteristic of Korean society. If it did, however, it would have implications for management. Organization size may have to be limited to facilitate central control, since unsupervised cooperation is not likely, or top management may be afraid to delegate authority because it is not sure that subordinate managers will work in the organization's interest. Whatever the actual situation, cultural factors influence organizational management.

In the decision game, cultural factors probably affected the behavior of our American and Korean students—in this situation, cooperative or uncooperative behavior. Behavior, of course, results from motivation, the desire to satisfy certain needs. The relative importance of these needs and the wants that satisfy them are, in turn, culturally influenced. In short, culture, behavior (especially in business and at work), and motivation are the subjects of this chapter and this volume. Briefly, we shall first consider the concept of culture, then how culture may affect business behavior. Finally, and most important, we shall examine a general model of human needs and the impact of culture on the model.

Culture influences managerial philosophy and practice mainly through motivation. It is a truism that management is working through people. However tautological, this is a vital idea to remember when managing in a foreign culture; for culture affects people, their needs, wants, and aspirations—and it is these that the manager must tap. An understanding of the dominant needs that motivate behavior in a society is essential if the manager is to be successful in his primary function of influencing behavior.

THE MEANING OF CULTURE

We are immersed in a sea. It is warm, comfortable, supportive, and protecting. Most of us float below the surface; some bob about, catching glimpses of land from time to time; a few emerge from the water entirely. The sea is our culture.

Most of us act, think, and dream in terms of the norms and standards we have absorbed from the culture in which we are reared. What our culture values, we value; what our culture abhors, we abhor. By education or experience, some of us become aware that there are other values and beliefs that make sense, too—as much or more sense than our own. But we see them hazily, and all too often with age the awareness slips away. A few, very few, are able to escape, overcome parochialism, and see the world more objectively. But escape is by no means entirely desirable. We can feel alone and unsure when the comfortable values of our old culture fall away and become irrelevant, and are replaced by nothing. The great Irish expatriot writer James Joyce showed us that it is not easy or pleasant to escape from the warm sea of culture.[2]

Anxiety may seize the adventurous who attempt to flee their native culture.

---

[2] See James Joyce, *Portrait of the Artist as a Young Man* (New York: Random House, Inc., 1916).

Culture is a great source of security that frequently tells us what is right and good. The problem, as numerous anthropologists have pointed out, is that what is right and good to one society appears irrational and unpredictable to another. Take kissing, for example. In Micronesia, the idea of putting mouth on mouth is unthinkable. In a recent book, *Gluttons and Libertines: Human Problems of Being Natural,*[3] Marston Bates (a University of Michigan professor) wonders what antioral Micronesians would think of the display near a women's dormitory at an American university just before check-in time. Still worse, for the non-kissing Micronesians the "female breast has no sexual significance; it is an organ for providing food for the nursing infant." Americans, Bates writes of our mammary culture, "must seem very queer to non-breast loving cultures."

Anthropologists and psychologists have recorded sex perversion to the ultimate quirk and oddity, but, Bates asks, what of food perversion? Maybe "we are surrounded by food perverts, undetected and unclassified, undermining the fiber of our civilization, infiltrating our diplomatic service, influencing our mass media, corrupting our youth . . . who knows, how many people in this country put sugar in their salad dressing . . . ?" The point of Bates' excursion into the bizarre realms of sex and food is that nothing is natural to man. "There is no natural man," he asserts; and we cannot "talk about artificial manners . . . because all manners are artificial."

Culture therefore influences what human needs are emphasized and what behavior is approved or disapproved. It used to be thought feasible to describe whole cultures in terms of limited characterizations. For example, three categories of cultures have been suggested—Apollonian, Faustian, and Dionysian.

The Apollonian society stresses security and friendship. Relationships are based upon equality, and all people engage in mutual efforts to help one another. They attempt to adapt to nature, even to fit into it rather than to overcome it. (For example, in their art they stress the commonplace; painting and decoration is used only on common houseware items, etc.) The Apollonian culture would distrust the individual who attempts to satisfy egoistic drives for prestige, achievement, or power. The big man on campus would seem odd in this context. In a Zuni Indian town, the local oddity might have just those egoistic characteristics that are valued elsewhere—perhaps on Madison Avenue.

A Dionysian society also values low-level needs for security and affiliation, but it emphasizes different behavior. Rather than passive acceptance of the world, the misery of existence is stressed. The self is encouraged to escape the confines of nature and society by seeking the gaudy, the sensual, and the forbidden. Art becomes free of the need to be utilitarian or representative. Realism is obliterated in a riot of form and color.[4] To other societies, behavior desirable in a Dionysian culture is considered immoral, but it serves a purpose. The lack of discipline and the spontaneous expression of emotion are honest, and a paradoxical means of self-expression and escape.

---

[3] New York: Random House, Inc., 1968.
[4] See C. W. Ceram, *Graves, Gods and Scholars* (New York: Alfred A. Knopf, Inc., 1967).

Finally, the Faustian society glorifies the individual and his egocentric behavior. He must compete. Life is a challenge to the individual and every man's salvation is primarily his to decide. Intense drives for prestige and power are viewed with respect if not affection. In such a society, the noncompetitor is odd. The loving, altruistic individual who seeks only to help others may be tolerated and even liked, but he is not accorded honor, for he does not conform to the society's highest values. In such a culture, art is less expression of emotion or utilitarian decoration than a means to reflect the glory of man or his god.

Modern societies are too complex to summarize under these three cultural rubrics; they are not so pure. Even labeling the simple Zuni, Dobu, and Kwakiutl societies with these terms, as Ruth Benedict did in her pathbreaking *Patterns of Culture,*[5] is an oversimplification. The same themes exist everywhere in varying degrees. Thus, the dominant theme in the United States has been the ego-centered Faustian orientation, with strong—and probably increasing—Dionysian characteristics. Within particular subgroups in the United States—until recently, the Negro in the South—the culture has approximated the Apollonian.

We should not think that any one culture is right and others are wrong. Bates asks, "What is natural?" The Faustian culture with its individual drive for achievement seems most familiar to us, but certainly we value some characteristics of the Apollonian, and we demonstrate some of the behavior of the Dionysian. All the human needs that are appealed to by these different cultures reside in all individuals, but physical reality and historical events shape specific development.

CULTURE AND MANAGERIAL BEHAVIOR

Let us introduce the interrelationship between culture and management by discussing two questions often raised by American executives who do business abroad. I am not repeating them to express criticism, nor to imply that American behavior is better. Rather, the questions point out cultural differences: (1) Why are foreign managers so late for business appointments? (2) When Americans and foreigners do meet, why are foreigners so slow in getting down to business?[6] Whether these two questions reflect truth or perceptual distortion is not known, but they are frequently expressed. Let us consider what cultural factors may be involved.

Appointment Punctuality

Tardiness may reflect the individual's and society's conception of time. Is it a scarce commodity to be saved and used carefully? Or is it an endless resource to be consumed carelessly? There has been some research on the meaning of

---

5 (Boston: Houghton Mifflin Co., 1934).
6 These questions suggested by James A. Lee in "Cultural Analysis in Overseas Operations," *Harvard Business Review,* March–April, 1966, pp. 106–14.

time;[7] here are two of the tests used. First, what is the closest metaphor of time for you: (1) a galloping horseman, or (2) a quiet motionless ocean? Second, which set of words do you associate with time: (1) clear, young, sharp, action or (2) empty, soothing, sad, cold, deep? Probably you chose the first response in both tests. And probably most Americans and Europeans would pick similarly. But in a steamy village in India or out in the remote Chinese countryside, people might respond with that empty, deep, motionless ocean. Why? Because of the different culturally influenced conceptions of time.

To portray the matter schematically, time may be seen as either a circle or a straight line. The circle suggests repetition and continuity. Time is measured by natural events—the movement of the sun, the phases of the moon, the seasons, life and death. Measurement tends to be gross; minutes and hours have no meaning. If the present is wasted, it will come around again. Today will return tomorrow; life and time are endless repetition. With such a view, life can appear unhurried and even serene.[8]

How different is the linear view! Yesterday is gone forever, today is here but a moment, and tomorrow depends on what you do now. In a selected reading in Chapter Four, Lewis Mumford points out that time becomes less associated with natural phenomena, more with the artificial movement of a mechanical clock. Time becomes measured; times are not ranges but precise points. So life may appear cluttered and hectic as we respond to time's demands.

These conceptions of time have moral implications. The hustle and bustle of time-conscious occidentals is often denigrated by orientals, while the oriental's slowness and passivity are criticized by the occidental. These attitudes are also reflected in religion. Thus, for many oriental sects life is a long, repetitive series of reincarnations in which lives are lived under various guises, depending on the spiritual worthiness of the past life—a crab becomes the new form for the cheat, an eagle for the prudent, and so on. Salvation is not the achievement of a specific life form, however; it is relief from the never-ending circle of time. It is the escape from time into a dimensionless Nirvana where time is irrelevant.

Salvation for the Westerner is different. Whether it be the Judeo-Christian or Marxist version, time is going somewhere—not to nothingness but to a utopia here or in Heaven. Time and life thus share a mission. They have purpose and they should be lived correctly. The importance of time is epitomized in the old American minihomilies: "Waste of time is the worst of sins." "Time is money." "Idle hands are the devil's workshop." Similarly, after he took power Lenin preached to the Russians that time was to be preserved and to be used effectively. The old superfluity of time that the peasants enjoyed (or found monotonous) on the steppes did not exist for the citizen in the new worker's state.

---

7 R. H. Knapp and J. T. Garbutt, "Time Imagery and the Achievement Motive," *Journal of Personality,* Vol. 26 (1958), pp. 426–34. See also the discussion in David C. McClelland, *The Achieving Society* (Princeton, N.J.: D. Van Nostrand Co., Inc., 1961), pp. 324–29.

8 See Robert Heilbroner, *The Future as History* (New York: Harper & Row, Publishers, 1959).

Here is part of the text from a leaflet distributed by the Soviet Time League, whose members were obliged to protest against and report every waste of time they encountered.

> Measure your time, control it!
> Do everything on time! exactly on the minute!
> Save time, make time count, work fast!
> Divide your time correctly, time for work and time for leisure! [9]

So the American (and I suppose the contemporary Russian) may be correct when he complains about foreign managers who are late for appointments. For them, time just may be less precious. And practice makes perfect, as the old cliché goes. Concern with time utilization, and subsequent practice in using it, making appointments and meeting them, and so on, simply makes the U.S. manager more skilled in planning to be on time, arranging transportation, and all the other requirements of a time-conscious society.

A class discussion of these matters once was interrupted at this point by a Spanish student who observed that this consideration of time is irrelevant. The foreign manager may, indeed, value time highly, but not for business. Enjoying a social visit with a colleague, or sampling the delicacies at the local *ristorante* may be more important. Not that business is unimportant, nor that social engagements are scheduled to interfere, but when they inevitably conflict, social matters may have priority over business.

Finally, we have overlooked the most obvious reason for tardiness, at least in the less-developed nations. Transportation facilities are lacking. It simply may be much harder to schedule meetings to very close limits if transportation is unpredictable.

We could go on, but the discussion illustrates the cultural factors that may affect simple business punctuality. Underlying philosophies toward life, attitudes toward time, behavioral experience—all are relevant. As a result, in Saudi Arabia one may be on time anywhere within a three-hour span. In New York, the acceptable span may be just five minutes.

Delays in Doing Business

The question about delays in getting down to business reflects similar factors. At the most superficial level, it may be behavioral habit—thought to be good manners. Perhaps because of attitudes toward time, haste is to be avoided. There are, however, more rational reasons. The American is more willing to accept impersonal relations in his business dealings. Ideally (for business), agreements and decisions should be made on the basis of objective information, not social relations or subjective feelings. Reality in American business is not so emotionless, but the impersonality compared with less developed and more traditional countries is striking. Where the prevalent social teaching is to distrust all strang-

---

9 Distributed in 1923; quoted in Reinhard Bendix, *Work and Authority in Industry* (New York: John Wiley & Sons, Inc., 1956), p. 208.

ers and favor friends or relatives, a manager is reluctant to do business until he has established personal relations. Friendship may not be essential, but mutual exchange of sentiment is.

This is not pure emotion. Where the ethical system includes a double standard—one set of rules for insiders, another for outsiders—it is logical to be wary of impersonal business arrangements. The prudent manager in this culture gets to know those with whom he does business in order to judge what ethics are being extended to him. On a more abstract level, this reflects the nature of the ethical system—particular or general. In the Judeo-Christian tradition, one is supposed to extend the same ethics to everyone, as the parable of the Good Samaritan suggests. Whether you do or do not know your customer, like or dislike your associate, the ethics of business should be unchanging. But only a minority of the world's cultures share this generalized and impersonal ethical system. For most people, your friend or relative should be favored in business dealings. Not to do so would be disloyal. Not that you need to cheat the stranger, but *caveat emptor.*

Once again, we see how a rather trivial business practice can be related to complex cultural values, attitudes, and behavior. What is involved here, of course, is motivation. Culture influences motivation which, in turn, influences business behavior. Culture's impact on the needs that men strive to satisfy is the core of the affect of cultural variables on management. Therefore, we must examine the interrelation between culture and human needs in greater detail.

CULTURE AND HUMAN NEEDS

In the early 1800's, a group of courageous pioneers sought a passage west across the American continent. With their ox-drawn covered wagons, the Donner party traversed the western plains and climbed the mountains that blocked their way. Many never made it. Some years ago, a diary of one of this party was published.[10] At the beginning of their journey, the writer described his compatriots as the salt of the earth—God-fearing, individualistic, but cooperative and socially concerned for one another's welfare. For many, however, the trip ended high in the mountains. Marooned by enormous snow drifts, they were unable to move forward or go back. Exhausting their supply of food and slowly freezing on the wind-swept slopes of the Rocky Mountains, the people gradually deteriorated. They withdrew into themselves; concern shifted from the larger group to the immediate family, then to the individual, and finally emerged the ultimate horror—cannibalism. As in MacKinlay Kantor's terrifying description of the Civil War prison camp at Andersonville, the strong played on the weak for personal survival.[11]

This tragedy is an unpleasant illustration of the hierarchy of human needs. To the survivors of the Donner party, food became all-important and all-motivating.

---

10 Homer Croy, *Wheels West* (New York: Hastings House, Publishers, Inc., 1955).
11 MacKinlay Kantor, *Andersonville* (Cleveland: World Publishing Co., 1955).

Therefore, when Abraham Maslow described a need hierarchy [12] he put physiological needs at the bottom, because satisfaction of these drives is essential for the maintenance of life; they are prepotent for the motivation of behavior. If one is long without food, one is presumably reduced to a sort of human piranha fish who thinks food, dreams food, and hunts food without any other concern. [13] Such a food-seeking monster is not interested in building monuments, wearing fine clothes, or even worshipping his god.

Happily, the hierarchical model suggests that as physical necessities are met (at least at a minimum level), new needs emerge to motivate behavior. We have seen that man is a wanting creature, striving to satisfy many different needs. Maslow described these needs and their order of potency as follows.

- self-actualization
- esteem
- love
- safety
- physiological

In the 25 years since this hierarchical model was advanced, there has been substantial research on the nature and impact of these needs on human behavior. Of special concern have been the upper levels of the hierarchy—the so-called higher needs for competence, power, and achievement. Proceeding up the hierarchy, let us consider the following needs: safety and security, affiliation, social esteem, self-esteem and competence, power, and achievement. Then we shall examine how culture influences the order of needs. The Maslow model has not been proven (and probably cannot be tested), but it has been influential in shaping the thinking and behavior of many researchers and managers. It is very helpful for thinking about how culture affects management.

The Hierarchy of Needs

Safety and Security.   Assuming that the individual has relative satisfaction of physiological requirements, there emerges a new set of needs—for safety or security. If one has food and shelter now, one may be concerned about securing the sources of these satisfactions. This is a very rational, prudent, and conscious security drive. There is also a more subtle, pervasive, and unconscious security drive—a vague anxiety concerning the satisfaction of a wide range of higher needs.

The need for safety or security is perhaps most apparent in the child. At certain stages in their development, all of my children have been upset by changes in the routine of daily life. They have preferred a safe, orderly, predictable, organized world. Unexpected events have been upsetting. In U.S. society,

---

[12] Abraham Maslow, "A Theory of Human Motivation," *Psychological Review,* Vol. L (1943), pp. 370–96. See also *Motivation and Personality* (New York: Harper & Bros., 1954).
    [13] For a classic literary example of this, see the recently published translation of Knut Hamsun, *Hunger* (New York: Alfred A. Knopf, Inc., first published 1899).

safety needs usually are met quite easily, but certainly the concern in the late 1960's about safety in urban areas and the political impact of this concern are indications of the potent power of the need. Some people are guided predominantly by security motives throughout their lives, commencing long before they could make any rational analysis of the hazards of life, which persist throughout their careers. The hazards they seek to protect themselves against are vague, pervasive, and fearsome; usually these people have an underlying conviction that the environment is, at best, capricious and, at worst, malicious. Their overriding need, therefore, is to find some measure of safety, usually achieved by entering into relationships with people or organizations who seem able to guarantee them a reasonably unruffled life.

Many of us, and successful businessmen in particular, tend to snicker at security motives, as if they were somehow less manly or less respectable than some of the higher-level drives for power and achievement that we shall discuss. It is true that excessive security motivation probably prevents many people from fully utilizing their abilities. But all of us have a security drive. Life is seldom so clear-cut or simple as to exclude influences that contribute to the need for security. A strong security motive is simply one that begins to manifest itself when only a modest amount of peril is present in the environment; therefore, even a weak security motive could begin to show its influence if the individual were placed under enough stress. Most of us, fortunately, are able to satisfy this need rather easily, so that we may move on to other things.

Affiliation. The Bible is right; man does not live by bread alone. Even with secure sources of food and shelter, he is not satisfied. Further needs emerge. The first, perhaps, is a need for social belonging, affection, membership, or affiliation. A complex need, the basis of affiliation ranges from simple enjoyment of other human beings (psychologists tell us man is a social animal) to more complex desires for group affirmation of an individual's self-conception. Thus, affiliation can be either a means to an end or an end in itself.

Stress is explicit in most observations of this need. For example, chimpanzees were the subject of an epic natural science research effort over the past decade. Perhaps as much was learned about man. On a recent television show, the National Geographic Society presented films on an observation of apes in their natural habitat. One sequence showed a chimp stranger entering the domain of an established tribe. Fear, anxiety, and longing were evident in the stranger's face. She wanted to be accepted, perhaps because she needed the protection and companionship afforded by the group. A poetic moment occurred when an old ape touched the newcomer's hand, signifying acceptance. Relief and gratitude were immediately reflected.

Now, men are not chimpanzees, but the rewards of affiliation may be as great. In a description of his prisoner-of-war experience during the Korean war, General Dean indicated how much he missed human companionship[14] — so much

---

[14]William Friske Dean, *General Dean's Story* (As told to William L. Worden) (New York: Viking Press, 1954).

so that he talked extensively to a Communist interrogator who acted warmly toward him. Desires for companionship flowed virtually automatically from the human relationship, even between the prisoner and his keeper. Similarly, veteran soldiers comment on the tendency of new recruits to herd together for friendship and support when under stress, even though they know intellectually that grouping increases the danger. Finally, American songs, miniskirts, and haircuts reflect the teenager's efforts to define himself in terms of his companions. Self-image derives from social image.

Many empirical researchers corroborate these observations. As Stanley Schachter has demonstrated, people under stress especially tend to socialize.[15] When there is apparent threat to an important belief, people are relieved to find their thinking shared by many others, almost as if this agreement confirms the rightness and therefore the safety of one's own ideas. The most important element in the pattern is the reassuring effect of sharing an opinion.

More than just company is provided by this affiliation. Socializing, in this instance, serves to make life seem a little more manageable, a little less inexplicable. Nonetheless, even if the others one seeks out cannot assist him, even psychologically, they are apparently still sought out, especially if they are under similar stress. If people are upset, they do not seek out just any company indiscriminately; they prefer people who are in a similar predicament. Misery definitely loves company, particularly if the company has the same misery. Merely being in the presence of others—above all, unhappy others—seems to reduce unhappiness.

Social Esteem, Prestige, and Status. Most men have this need for affiliation and membership. Yet, once they have established mutual relationships, paradoxically, many individuals want to be a little different than their companions. Everyone wants to be equal, but as George Orwell put it in *Animal Farm,* "some want to be more equal than others." With affiliation, a new need emerges—desire for social esteem, prestige, or status—that is, some social position differentiation from associates and peers.

Prestige is frequently defined as a set of unwritten rules about the kind of conduct people are expected to show in one's presence—what degree of respect or disrespect, familiarity or unfamiliarity, reserve or frankness. However, with our habits of social informality, prestige in U.S. society is more subtle (or gross, depending on your value position). That is, one's desires for prestige are mainly satisfied not by how people behave toward you but how much they knowingly or secretly envy you.

Thus, the desire for social esteem is more a psychological than a behavioral phenomenon. "The grass is always greener . . ." goes the old cliché. Most of us, however, are happier when others think the grass is greener on our side of the street.

---

15 Stanley Schachter, *The Psychology of Affiliation* (Stanford, Calif.: Stanford University Press, 1959).

Social observers and Europeans have long satirized and criticized American status-seeking, especially when it takes the form of conspicuous consumption. But prestige-seeking is not a 20th-century phenomenon. Mankind has apparently always created social structures differentiating between the power and glory of his fellows. "Like it or not," Saul Gellerman tells us, "people have evidently been sorting themselves out into chiefs and Indians, nobles and peasants, executives and hourly workers from time immemorial, and they show no signs of stopping."[16] The classless society has yet to appear, and as the Yugoslav Milovan Diljias courageously affirmed, even Communist societies acquire and develop a class or prestige system.[17]

People seek prestige throughout their lives in countless ways, some subtle, others blatant, because there is widespread need to have one's relative importance clarified and to set that importance at a level the individual feels he deserves. Hence, prestige is not a matter of absolutes but of relatives—relative to what others have and relative to what one thinks one merits. As such, prestige can be a potent motivator for people of both low and high absolute status.

Ego satisfaction is the positive goal of such a drive, avoidance of ridicule, perhaps, the negative. Man likes to be looked up to but fears being dismissed as inferior or irrelevant. And it has even been suggested that fear of ridicule is the most potent of all human motivations. An anthropologist provides an interesting example of this motivation, and how education is seen as the answer.

A great chief from New Guinea attended a South Pacific conference and was laughed at by educated people from other islands. After introducing himself, his speech was short. "I come from the bush. I have no English. I cannot read or write. My tongue is thick. My head is a stone. In my country I am a big man, yet I stand before you as a child. I have been a leader in battle with bow and arrow and spear, but today I am a baby feeding at its mother's breast. Soon I will die and in a little while my son will come here in my place and sit among you and speak English and write his name and be a leader among you, and you will not laugh at him."[18]

Self-Esteem and Competence.   Innumerable novelists have suggested that for many of us social esteem is necessary but not sufficient. In the long run, we are told, what we think of ourselves is more important. So emerges the need for self-esteem, competence, and the feeling that one is capable of meeting challenge. We are dealing now with a complex need, and perhaps we shall lump disparate needs into one package. But the thrust of the set of needs referred to as self-esteem, or competence, is clear. The individual is more than just a vehicle for instincts; he is also an active observer and shaper of his environment.

Robert White suggests that one of the mainsprings of human motivation is an interest in getting to know what the world is like and in learning to get what one

---

[16] Saul W. Gellerman, *Motivation and Productivity* (New York: American Management Association, 1963), p. 151.

[17] Milovan Diljias, *The New Class* (New York: Frederick A. Praeger, Inc., 1957).

[18] Maslyn Williams, *The Stone Age Island: New Guinea Today* (New York: Doubleday & Co., Inc., 1964.

wants from it.[19] He calls this a competence motive. The teacher hopes this drive is reflected in a desire to master a discipline and to expand intellectually. Obviously, the competence motive may also take other directions. Self-esteem may be derived from competence in a wide variety of vocational and avocational activities.

Even in very young infants this competence motive can be seen in the fun of random fingering of objects, poking around, and feeling whatever is in reach. Later, it is exploring, tinkering, taking things apart, putting them together, and the like. Whether an adult's competence is strong or weak depends on the balance of successes and failures he has experienced in these and later encounters with the world.

Implicit in this need for self-esteem, and related to the need for social esteem, is a further desire: most men want to feel they are doing something important, that their activities have social purpose. We want to feel that we are contributing members of society. There is ego satisfaction in awareness of the dependence and gratitude of others. Nonetheless, the drive for competence is mainly internal. In order to satisfy ourselves, we strive to understand, explore, and, as the mountain climber declares, to conquer the peak because it is there.

David Riesman gave us the terms to describe an old American view. The "other-directed man" is driven by desires for recognition and status from others; the more mature and independent "inner-directed" individual, however, strives to satisfy only himself.[20] Of course, the distinction is a simplification. Most men are both types. The need hierarchy suggests that as we obtain *some* social esteem we should shift from being other-directed to inner-directed in the effort to satisfy ourselves.

Notice that we lose some people as we move up the hierarchy of needs. Not everyone advances to new needs for competence, power or achievement as the lower needs are relatively satisfied. Also, as we have moved up the hierarchy the reader has probably grown more restive about the order. The relative importance of higher-level needs is simply less clear, and the distinction among needs becomes more ambiguous. This is especially true of the next two needs to be considered—power and achievement. For both are powerful drives to exceptional performance.

Power.   Many years ago, Alfred Adler maintained that power is the best explanation for the behavior of exceptional people.[21] Freud was right in suggesting that virtually everybody has pleasure-seeking and life-sustaining drives— needs much lower on the hierarchy. Nonetheless, his contemporary, Adler, emphasized the importance of power to the leaders of mankind. By power, we mean the ability to influence others to behave in ways that suit our purposes.

---

19 Robert W. White, "Motivation Reconsidered: The Concept of Competence," *Psychological Review,* Vol. 66 (1959).

20 David Riesman, with N. Glazer and R. Denny, *The Lonely Crowd* (New Haven, Conn.: Yale University Press, 1950).

21 H. L. Ansbacher and R. R. Ansbacher (eds.), *The Individual Psychology of Alfred Adler* (New York: Basic Books, Inc., Publishers, 1956).

David McClelland explains that it is measured by the individual's concern about control of the means for influencing other people.[22] Such concern may be inferred from emotional reaction to a dominance situation—for example, pleasure in winning or anger in losing an argument, statements about wanting to avoid weakness, concern with disputing a position, trying to put across a point, giving a command.

As with social esteem, most of us have mixed feelings about the drive for power. Adler pointed out that the process of influencing and controlling other people is intrinsically enjoyable. "Power and glory" wrote Bertrand Russell, "are chief among the infinite desires of man."[23] Friedrich Nietzsche declared: "All life desires above all is to express its power. Life is itself will to power. The impulse of survival is only an indirect consequence of this will."[24] But for Lord Acton, power corrupts.[25] And in the views of Protestant theologian Reinhold Niebuhr, the need for power may reflect man's inherent weakness or basic sinfulness.[26] Power emphasizes the I at the expense of the thou. Most of us (Adler included) feel that the drive for power is healthier when it is power over nature and environment rather than control of human beings.

The inverse of personal power is freedom from the power of others. Freedom from arbitrary and unilateral authority, even from the benevolent ruler, is a persistent theme in history. Indeed, Adler suggested that the power drive has its roots in the helplessness of childhood, when the child is dependent on and controlled by adults. The child wants to gain power over these superiors in order to ensure that they will meet his requirements. With maturity, he attempts to develop his abilities to gain autonomy from these power figures. The drive for autonomy reflects both fear of dependence on others for satisfaction of physiological necessities and desire for freedom to pursue higher needs.

Achievement. Finally, we have reached what may be the apex of human needs. At the top of the hierarchy emerge drives for achievement, creativity, or self-actualization. Again, as with the competence need, we are perhaps inappropriately combining some distinct motives, but they all point in the same direction. The idea is what a man can be, he must be; one should create and achieve everything one is capable of. Overcoming challenging, difficult, and novel problems, creating new institutions and objects, developing one's attributes and capabilities — all are sources of satisfaction for this need. Such drives would characterize the most healthy and mature individuals—those who have moved beyond lower-level needs.

The achievement need, as McClelland and his associates show, is manifest in efforts to achieve a standard of excellence—that is, the high achiever commits

22 David C. McClelland, *The Achieving Society, op. cit.*
23 Bertrand R. Russell, *Power, A New Social Analysis* (New York: W. W. Norton & Co., Inc., 1938), p. 12.
24 Friedrich Nietzsche, *The Will To Power,* trans. A. M. Ludovici (New York: Macmillan Co., 1929), p. 41.
25 Lord Acton, *Essays on Freedom and Power* (New York: Noonday Press, 1948).
26 Reinhold Niebuhr, *The Nature and Destiny of Man* (New York: Charles Scribner's Sons, 1949).

himself emotionally to the accomplishment of tasks he considers worthwhile and difficult.[27] What we are talking about is a basic attitude toward life; when challenged, the individual with a high achievement need tries harder and demands more of himself. Consequently, he accomplishes more.

Thus, the most fascinating aspect of the achievement motive is that it seems to make accomplishment an end in itself. If anything, it is the person with little achievement motivation who expects a tangible reward for greater effort. While the achievement-motivated person does not spurn tangible rewards, they are not really essential to him either. He takes a special joy in winning, in competing successfully with a difficult standard; this means more to him than money or a public pat on the back. He is not an altruist; he simply finds enough delight in doing difficult things so that he does not need to be bribed to do them.

In general, people with a high degree of achievement motivation are more consistent, realistic, and action-minded than are people with other kinds of motivational patterns. But this does not necessarily make them more productive; that seems to depend on whether the task requires some degree of personal initiative or inventiveness. If it does, the achievement-motivated person is very likely to leave his competitors far behind. But if it does not, he is likely to turn in a very ordinary, uninspired performance.

This drive is especially relevant to managers in business organizations. Indeed, in a selected reading David McClelland maintains that the need for achievement is *the* factor in managerial success.

The hierarchy of needs is not so rigid or fixed as this description implies. The hierarchy suggests that lower-level needs must be satisfied before upper needs become motivating. Before one becomes concerned about social esteem, one must have sufficient food and shelter. Before most of us become concerned about achievement, we must have some affiliation, and so on. Still, only relative, not complete, satisfaction is necessary. We don't know what the proportions are, but we may assume 70–80 percent satisfaction of a lower need before the next higher need becomes motivating. Of course, with physiological needs some minimal level is necessary to sustain life, but even here the level of needs among Americans will be higher than the level in some other nations.

Culture and the Order of Needs

But is the hierarchy a good model of man? We are all familiar, at least through literature, with the artist who apparently devotes virtually all his energy to creativity at the expense of his social prestige, status, and perhaps even love and physiological satisfaction. Just as individuals vary in their structure of needs, so do subcultural groups and whole societies. We have seen that concepts of normality and rightness vary with cultures (and also with groups and individuals). The medial need structure may differ from culture to culture.

---

[27] David C. McClelland, J. W. Atkinson, R. A. Clock, and E. L. Lowell, *The Achievement Motive* (New York: Appleton-Century-Crofts, 1953).

Even within our national society there will be some subcultural groups that are rather different in their values. Hospital orderlies provide an interesting example. Burling, Lentz, and Wilson describe the self-contained culture of orderlies.[28] Men who have withdrawn from competitive striving for status and power drift in a world jointly devoted to helpfulness and alcoholic companionship. The social climber or power seeker is deplored and rejected.

The meaning of the hierarchical organization of needs, as we have suggested, is that lower-level needs must be satisfied before upper-level needs become motivating. Leavitt suggests that if there is continued, long-lasting deprivation of lower-level need satisfaction, behavior will continue to be motivated by these lower-level needs; the individual will not move on to higher needs.[29] In effect, his need structure becomes truncated.

In a report issued during his tenure as assistant secretary of labor (1965), Daniel Moynihan discussed the role of the family in the urban Negro's plight. Initially, the report was warmly received, later was rejected, and Moynihan was accused of being a racist because he attributed much of the problem to the fragmented Negro family. Moynihan's thesis was that the inability of the father to support and lead a family has led to a matriarchal society (such male inadequacy had its roots in the slave society). Thus, the father's role disappears or is filled by a series of men on a rotating basis. What he is suggesting is that the need hierarchy of some Negro youths is permanently truncated. Inability to satisfy needs for status, prestige, love, safety, or security, and in many cases even physiological needs, means that future behavior of these Negro youths is mainly to satisfy the lower-level drives. Consequently, the needs for self-esteem, competence, and achievement never become motivating. Apparently, aspiration level becomes permanently low because of these early experiences.

The opposite of dominance by lower-level needs is also possible. When lower needs have been satisfied without effort for a long time, they may become undervalued. The upper middle-class white youth who has always enjoyed the satisfaction of his needs—physiological, security, affiliation, and status—may be motivated only by higher needs. Hence, the idealism of some youths who aspire only for service, creativity, and achievement, while perhaps being cynical of pursuit of lower needs. Such a situation partly explains the critical view of business careers that characterize present college students. Marriage, however, has a way of dramatically lowering the need structure of an individual, or at least of motivating him to act on some lower-level needs—"realism" to middle-aged adults, "compromise" to youths.

On a larger scale, culture influences the modal need hierarchy of large masses of people. These cultural factors especially influence child training practices, and the values and standards held by the family and transmitted to the child. As a

---

28 Temple Burling, Edith Lentz, and Robert Wilson, *The Give and Take in Hospitals* (New York: G. P. Putnam's Sons, 1956), pp. 101–92.

29 Harold Leavitt, *Managerial Psychology* (2d ed.; Chicago: University of Chicago Press, 1964).

person grows up, he learns the values, attitudes, and assumptions about life that are characteristic of the culture he was born to. He is taught the traditions of his society, its religious concepts, ethical doctrines, and metaphysical assumptions. These may vary a great deal from one society to another. As we have seen, some cultural historians and anthropologists have attempted to categorize the implicit world views of different cultures. These people suggest that cultures have a characteristic spirit, prevalent tone, or sentiment of a people or community. Among the Zuni Indians, in the earlier examples from Ruth Benedict's *Patterns of Culture,* the man with the drive for power or achievement, or perhaps even social prestige, was considered odd, if not insane. Even if one had physical well-being, love, and acceptance, higher-level drives simply were not accepted by the society. Behavior was concentrated on lower needs. In contrast, the Kwakiutl Indians of the Northwest Pacific Coast demonstrated fantastic drive for status and power. Social satisfaction and affiliation were valued much less. A brave who rejected the pursuit of prestige in favor of affiliation and love was thought to be insane within the definition of their society—as well he might in the United States.

What about modern societies? Haire, Ghiselli, and Porter have studied needs cross-culturally among some 3,600 managers in 14 countries.[30] They report basic similarity, but with differences. Remember that the order of needs in the original Maslow model of the need hierarchy was physiological, security, social, esteem, self-actualization. Since all men obviously must satisfy the first need, Haire and his associates eliminated it from their research. Among the remaining needs, the hierarchical arrangement implies that the degree of satisfaction existing on each need decreases as we proceed up the hierarchy. That is, security needs should be most satisfied, social next, and so on; self-actualization should be least satisfied.

Is this true? It is in the United States and the United Kingdom only. Figure 2-1 presents the findings on need satisfaction, grouped by clusters of countries, that the researchers found in their data. Only in the Anglo-American countries does the line slope upward to the right, from satisfaction to dissatisfaction, as we would expect from the need hierarchy. In all the other clusters, the data suggest a different order of needs. For example, in the Latin-European countries (Spain, Italy, France, and Belgium) and the developing countries (Argentina, India, and Chile), social needs apparently are of great importance when compared with the other countries.

We can investigate this more directly. Haire and his fellow researchers asked questions about the importance of needs to the managers sampled. Figure 2-2 compares each of the country clusters with the importance attached to each need by the average of all responses. Points above the mean line indicate that the nation's managers consider a need more important than the average manager does; points below the line indicate less importance. Thus, managers in the

---

[30] Mason Haire, Edwin E. Ghiselli, and Lyman W. Porter, *Managerial Thinking* (New York: John Wiley & Sons, Inc., 1966).

developing nations attribute more importance to all needs; the Nordic-Europeans (Denmark, Germany, Norway, and Sweden) attribute less importance.

The sharpest differences among managers in the more industrialized countries are: (1) the high importance attached to social needs in Japan versus the low importance by the Nordic-Europeans and even the Anglo-Americans; (2) the

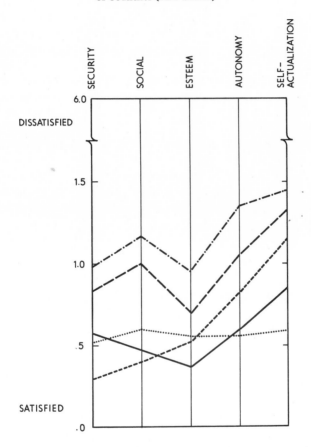

FIGURE 2-1
Need Satisfaction: By Clusters
of Countries (Raw Scores)*

―――――― NORDIC-EUROPEAN COUNTRIES (GERMANY, DENMARK, SWEDEN & NORWAY)
― ― ― ― LATIN-EUROPEAN COUNTRIES (SPAIN, FRANCE, BELGIUM, ITALY)
- - - - - - ANGLO-AMERICAN COUNTRIES (U.S. AND U.K.)
―·―·― DEVELOPING COUNTRIES (ARGENTINA, CHILE, AND INDIA)
················· JAPAN

*From Mason Haire, Edwin Ghiselli, and Lyman Porter, *Managerial Thinking* (New York: John Wiley & Sons, Inc., 1966), p. 90. By permission.

FIGURE 2-2
Need Importance: By Clusters of
Countries (Standard Scores)*

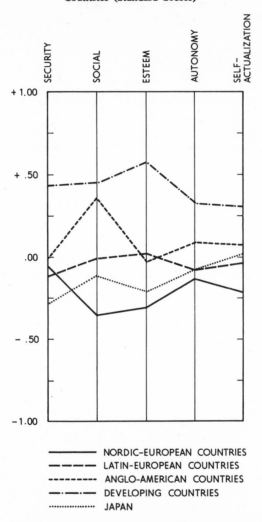

NORDIC–EUROPEAN COUNTRIES
LATIN-EUROPEAN COUNTRIES
ANGLO-AMERICAN COUNTRIES
DEVELOPING COUNTRIES
JAPAN

Note: Positive values indicate greater importance
attached to a need than for the average manager;
negative values indicate lesser importance.

From Haire, Ghiselli, and Porter, *Managerial
Thinking* (New York: John Wiley & Sons, Inc., 1966),
p. 103. By permission.

relatively low importance of esteem needs by Anglo-Americans and Nordic-Europeans compared with the Japanese and the Latin-Europeans.

The most striking similarities are: (1) the relatively lower importance of security in the United States and United Kingdom and the similarity of responses among the other managers on this need; (2) the similarity of the importance attached to needs for autonomy and self-actualization.

It is apparent, then, that the order in the need hierarchy for managers is largely the same at the two ends—physiological–security at one end and autonomy–self-actualization at the other. The importance attributed to social and esteem needs varies more widely. The managers in this research study are, of course, not typical citizens. Because of greater cosmopolitanism and knowledge about the world, their responses on need importance and satisfaction are probably more homogeneous than would be the responses of most people in these countries. The impact of culture on human needs is probably greater than this study suggests.

Culture also affects the specific wants that people have, the occupations, goods, and services that satisfy various needs. Seaweed and grasshoppers may be desirable as food in Korea but unthinkable in western Europe. The need is the same; the want differs. Many wives is a want, a source of social esteem in Basutoland. Nonetheless, however desirable multiple wives seem to the American male, it is not a real want because society (and the law) frowns on it. Similarly, in modern Africa an ambitious young man with high need for achievement is likely to view a professional career as the only acceptable life for a college graduate; in Japan, however, business is a desirable and honorable career for the same kind of person.

SUMMARY

Culture influences what we want and believe, and how we behave. For management, the appropriate questions are the following.

1. Do we want wealth and material gain? Is this considered socially desirable?
2. Do we want to satisfy achievement, confidence, or power needs at work? Are workers and managers more concerned with security and social needs?
3. Do young men want to become managers? What is the dominant social attitude toward management?
4. Do young people want to climb the social ladder? Are they status seekers? And is social mobility possible? If so, is business employment a way of climbing?
5. Is it good to hold authority? What is the dominant social attitude toward authority and persons in subordinate positions?
6. What is the attitude toward achievement and work? What is the attitude toward scientific method? Is rational thinking considered desirable or is a spontaneous intuitive process more valuable?
7. What is the attitude toward risk-taking? Is the taking of various kinds of personal, collective, or national risk generally considered acceptable?
8. Finally, what are the dominant attitudes toward change? Is change feared, avoided, and resisted, or is change associated with progress?

Culture, of course, is not the sole determinant of these basic aspects of man and society. For the individual, physical factors (age, energy, appearance), family (the particular wants, beliefs, and behavior of his parents), physical environment

EXHIBIT 2-1. The Cultural System as It Affects Production Management*

Differences in these cultural factors—	... affect a people's values and habits relating to—	For example, the local employee might feel that—	... and this would tend to affect approaches in these (and other) areas of manufacturing management—
I. Assumptions and attitudes	Time	Time is not measured in minutes, but in days and years.	Production control, scheduling, purchasing
	One's proper purpose in life	The only purpose which makes sense is to enjoy each day.	Management development
	The future	The future is not in man's hands.	Short- and long-range planning
	This life vs. the hereafter	Life and death are completely ordained and predetermined.	Safety programs
	Duty, responsibility	Your job is completed when you give an order to a subordinate.	Executive techniques of delegation and follow-up
II. Personal beliefs and aspirations	Right and wrong	I give the boss inventory counts which please him.	Inventory control system
	Sources of pride	A college degree places one higher in society for life.	Selection of supervisors
	Sources of fear and concern	Jobs are hard to get for a man laid off, regardless of the cause of layoff.	Layoff policy
	Extent of one's hopes	Without the right education and social class, advancement is limited.	Incentives, motivation
	The individual vs. society	The individual's wants and needs must be subordinated to the whole group.	Labor relations
III. Interpersonal relationships	The source of authority	My men don't like the new process. It won't work.	Quality control
	Care or empathy for others	I'd rather give my salary raise to my foreman than have to tell him he is not to receive one.	Merit reviews
	Importance of family obligations	I had to stay home because my father was sick.	Absenteeism
	Objects of loyalty	Friendship is more important than business.	Work-group relationships
	Tolerance for personal differences	If you don't agree with your boss, he will be insulted.	The decision-making process
IV. Social structure	Interclass mobility	I'd refuse to work for a man without a trade school certificate.	Promotion from within
	Class or caste systems	Men with my standing don't move heavy objects such as typewriters.	Job descriptions — flexibility of job assignments
	Urban-village-farm origins	The company must take the place of the village in caring for its people.	Fringe-benefit programs
	Determinants of status	Elderly people have wisdom. They deserve the most important jobs on big machines.	Equipment selection

*From C. Wickham Skinner, "Management of International Production," *Harvard Business Review,* September–October, 1964, p. 129. © 1964 by the President and Fellows of Harvard College; all rights reserved.

(weather, terrain), his education and experience, and even chance—all play their roles. Nonetheless, his family, the subcultural group in which he lives, and his education are affected by the greater cultural values of his society. Even the response to his physical characteristics (whether tall people will be respected or mocked, or whether fat women are considered beautiful or ugly) depends on cultural values.

Intuitively we feel that cultural values, characteristic wants, and behavior patterns influence management. Thus, our illustrative examples suggest that: (1) the apparent attitudes and behavior toward other people demonstrated by U.S. and Korean students in the two-person competitive game affect motivation, delegation of authority, and cooperation in business; (2) attitudes toward time and social needs versus achievement drives affect managerial punctuality, at least; (3) social needs and achievement drives, and impersonal versus personal ethics also seem to affect business transactions with strangers and the rapidity of getting down to business after meeting.

Our discussion of culture and human needs indicates that a manager must be aware of the relevant needs—and the specific wants these needs focus on—of those whom he wants to influence. The hierarchical theory about needs implies that as lower level needs are relatively satisfied, they become less motivating for behavior. The research of Haire, Ghiselli, and Porter shows that the security need tends to stretch out, retaining its importance after substantial satisfaction. Nonetheless, other gratified needs, in a sense, disappear. They become less motivating. A person is motivated mainly by the next level of unsatisfied need. For the Chilean manager, it is security; for the Italian, it is apparently affiliation; for the German, it is autonomy. Since every manager attempts to influence human behavior, he must consider what needs are relatively unsatisfied and hence can serve as motivational levers. More broadly, Exhibit 2-1 summarizes how the cultural system influences management—in this case, production management. Differences in cultural factors such as (1) attitudes and assumptions, (2) personal beliefs and aspirations, (3) interpersonal relationships, and (4) social structure are shown to affect such traditional management functions as motivation, recruitment and development, organizing, planning and decision making, and controlling.

In the selected readings in subsequent chapters we shall explore in greater depth the interrelationships between cultural factors, personal aspirations, managerial philosophy and practice, and national economic development. In Chapter Three, however, let us take a closer look at the United States. For, as we pointed out in Chapter One, "nowhere else have management and managers—even with current college student problems and past politician problems—enjoyed such legitimacy, attention, and prestige."

selection 1
Culture and Work*

William F. Whyte

Why does Joe behave as he does? He behaves that way, in part, because he is an American—because he has grown up in the culture of the United States.

Ask Joe to describe the culture of the United States, and he won't know how to begin. His difficulties will not be due entirely to the technical term, "culture." Even when we define the term—as we shall shortly—his difficulties are not resolved. He has trouble because he is trying to talk about things he takes for granted.

It is said that the most important things to know about a group of people are the things they themselves take for granted. Yet it is precisely those things that the people find most difficult to discuss. . . .

What do we mean by culture? We must first recognize that the word is used in several senses.

In the sense often encountered in conversation, culture refers particularly to music, art, and literature. A cultured individual is one who knows what is supposedly best in music, art, and literature—and also behaves according to the social customs of other "cultured" (or "cultivated") people. A man who does not have these attributes can be said to be "uncultured."

I shall use the word in quite a different sense—the technical meaning that it has in anthropology and sociology. This refers to the patterns of belief and behavior of a given society. It includes music, art, and literature, but these are only a small part of the concern of the anthropologist as he studies the culture of a given group. In this sense, every human group has its own culture. We cannot say that one group or individual has more or less culture than another group or individual. We can, however, compare cultures from group to group, noting their similarities and differences.

The individual is not born with culture. He learns the culture of his own particular group in the process of growing up. When we say that culture is learned, we also note that it is subject to change. In fact, cultures are constantly changing all over the world. In some cases, changes come quite rapidly, but rare indeed is the situation in such a state of flux that the student is unable to provide a coherent description of the culture of the people in question.

---

*From *Men at Work* (Homewood, Ill.: Richard D. Irwin, Inc. and The Dorsey Press, 1961), pp. 57–67.

Culture is often thought of in esoteric terms. A given people have a religion very different from ours, they have food habits that seem strange to us, and they also dress quite differently. These are indeed matters of culture, and they are not without importance. However, such differences are so obvious that they can hardly escape attention. We shall be concerned here with the way culture influences the day-to-day behavior of people in organizations and even the way in which they build their own organizations.

THE MEANING OF WORK

This is what work meant to a highly successful U.S. inventor and business-man:

> I often tell my people that I don't want any fellow who has a job working for me; what I want is a fellow whom a job has. I want the job to get the fellow and not the fellow to get the job. And I want that job to get hold of this young man so hard that no matter where he is the job has got him for keeps. I want that job to have him in its clutches when he goes to bed at night, and in the morning I want that same job to be sitting on the foot of his bed telling him it's time to get up and go to work. And when a job gets a fellow that way, he's sure to amount to something.[1]

Ponder carefully this statement by Charles F. Kettering. It was made in America, and indeed there are few other countries in the world where such a statement could be made and given wide currency.

This is not to suggest that Kettering's is a typical U.S. view of the meaning of work. When I first came upon this gem of wisdom, I posted it on the bulletin board outside of my university office. Within a short time it had accumulated penciled comments from graduate students and secretaries—all derogatory. The critics did not seem to take the advice seriously.

Even as we recognize the Kettering statement to be extreme, let us not dis-count it altogether. It represents the pure, distilled essence of what the eminent German sociologist, Max Weber, has called the Protestant ethic.[2] In this view, work is not only a means of getting ahead, but it is considered to be of positive moral value. Note that Kettering is not simply saying, "If you work hard, you will have a better chance of getting ahead than if you don't work hard." Such a statement could conceivably be subjected to a scientific test which would prob-ably prove it to be true more often than not. But one doesn't test moral prin-ciples scientifically, and the Kettering statement bears the stamp of a strong moral admonition on the intrinsic value of work.

Weber called this view the Protestant ethic because it seemed to gain cur-rency in the Western world at the time of the Reformation and grew out of the views of some of the leaders of the Protestant movement. The view is no longer exclusively associated with one church. In the United States today few Protes-tants would subscribe to such an extreme view, although there may be some

---

[1] Charles F. Kettering, quoted in *Coronet*, September, 1949, p. 72.

[2] See Talcott Parsons' translation of *The Protestant Ethic and the Spirit of Capitalism* (Glencoe, Ill.: The Free Press, 1948).

broad differences between average Protestants and Catholics in their feelings on the value of work. . . .

In our own country, we should expect to find that views on the value of work vary with class differences. Workers are not as likely to place the same value on work in itself as might management people. In fact, many management people are concerned with giving more meaning to the work workers do. . . . Some factory jobs seem to offer little inherent interest to the workers and the moral value of work is not a strong motivating force for them.

If we compare individual to individual and group to group in our society, we will find a wide range of sentiments regarding work, but this should not obscure the fact that there are more important differences between our culture and some others regarding the value of work.

All over the world most people must work for a living. But in some societies work is regarded as simply a means to an end. If one has enough money to live in the style of his own social group without working, then he doesn't work. He has others do the work for him.

Not so in the United States. The millionaire playboy may be a familiar phenomenon in the newspapers, but he is also the butt of strong public censure. We wonder how he can justify his existence if he doesn't work. In fact, most millionaires keep right on working, piling up more money or giving it away—or both. Even when we criticize some of the causes to which the millionaire gives his money, we recognize that he is working hard at giving it away and we respect him for that.

In other countries there are culturally determined sentiments regarding the type of organization in which the individual may work and the type of position he may hold. In most of Latin America, at least until recent years, it has not been considered appropriate for the son of an upper-class family to have his career within a large company. At most, he may work for a short time in a large company—perhaps a U.S. concern—in order to learn something about modern business methods. He will then leave the company to take up the position of running or helping to run the family business. "The organization man," as we know him here, just does not fit into the upper-class pattern of life in such countries. This means that companies cannot go beyond the stage of a small family organization without recruiting children of middle and lower class parents for managerial positions. Thus on the one hand, these upper class sentiments regarding organizational membership may retard progress in economic development. On the other hand, as industrialization nevertheless does proceed, it tends to raise up to social prominence people who could never have risen except through such organizations.

Culture also creates sentiments regarding the appropriate type of economic enterprise for a given individual. In parts of Latin America as well as a number of other countries, the traditional aristocracy is based upon land ownership. For example, in the family which owns a large hacienda devoted to cattle raising or farming, the owner is traditionally expected to do little work. He employs a manager or overseer to run the hacienda for him, and his own managerial functions are limited to inspections of progress. In fact, the owner often does not live on the land. He prefers to live the life of leisure in the capital city and make only occasional trips to the hacienda.

As long as his land holdings are large and provide him with an income adequate to maintain his family's style of life, the owner has no incentive to increase the productivity of his enterprise. In fact, most such enterprises are probably highly inefficient according to current U.S. standards of agricultural methods and productivity of workers.

How do new economic enterprises develop in a country where the social leadership is tied to the traditional exploitation of land and labor? Everett Hagen, of the Center for International Studies at Massachusetts Institute of Technology, provides us with a case study that helps to answer this question.[3]

In his studies of personalities and social backgrounds of economic innovators in Colombia, Hagen found that a disproportionately large number of these men came from in and around the city of Medellin in the valley of Antioquia. As he traced the history of Colombia back to the era of first settlement, he gained some clues as to the preponderant influence of Antioqueños in Colombian economic life.

Medellin and the valley of Antioquia were among the first areas settled by the Spaniards. Other areas that were settled early were appropriate for large-scale farming and cattle raising. The Spanish settlers in these areas were able to take over lands and become landed aristocracy, with Indians and other servants or slaves doing the work for them. In this way, the hacienda pattern was established.

Not so in Antioquia. In that valley, the land was not suitable for large-scale agriculture or cattle raising. The valley did, however, possess one important resource: gold. With Indian slaves, the Antioqueños began exploiting the mines. The Indians could not stand the rigors of this new type of work and the treatment they received, and so this particular labor force died out. The Antioqueños then imported slaves from Africa, but this again was no solution. Importation was expensive, and the mines were not so rich as to cover the continuing costs of importation of slaves and constant replacement of those who died out. So at last the Antioqueños faced a most unhappy decision. They would either have to abandon the mines—their only source of wealth—or else they would have to go in and dig out the gold themselves. They chose to dig. In this way, over several generations, the Antioqueños were able to gain themselves a reasonably good living.

This experience naturally conditioned their sentiments regarding work. While the landed aristocrats from the other towns regarded them as an inferior people

---

[3] "The Entrepreneur as Rebel Against Traditional Society: A Research Note," *Human Organization*, Vol. 19, No. 3 (Winter, 1960–61).

grubbing the ground, the Antioqueños began to gain some appreciation of the dignity of hard work and of the values of building up industrial enterprises. These sentiments have carried over to this day, so that the sons of the social leaders of Antioquia have an outlook regarding work and industrial organizations that is quite different from that of the landed aristocracy.

This is not to say that only the Antioqueños built the thriving industry now to be found in Colombia. Many others have participated in that development. However, Hagen argues that where these others have been of upper class origin, they have also been, for one reason or another, rebels against their class. They have not accepted the traditional standards. Somehow they have believed that there was indeed dignity in industrial and commercial enterprise.

The same points can be illustrated historically. In England, it was not the landed aristocracy which ushered in the Industrial Revolution. With few exceptions, members of this class looked down upon the new industrial pursuits and upon those who engaged in them. That revolution depended upon new groups of people coming forward from lower status levels.

Culture also has a strong influence upon the way in which work at lower levels of the organization is viewed. We find a distinction between white collar and blue collar jobs, between office jobs primarily involving the handling of papers and shop jobs involving the handling of machines and other physical objects.

While some distinction is universally observed, the magnitude of the status distinction between the two classes of jobs varies greatly from society to society. Our own society tends to minimize this distinction. From earliest times, most of our forefathers had to work with their hands to some extent in order to establish homes and gain a living. A landed aristocracy, with servants or slaves to do the manual work, developed only in a few sections of the country. This background helped to clothe working by hand with dignity, even when office workers were recognized as superior in status.

It seems likely that the status difference between the two classes of work has declined further in recent years with the relative gain in earnings of blue collar workers and improvements in the physical conditions of the factory. The blurring of lines between the types of jobs may be carried further by the progress of automation which creates new classes of jobs, located in factory-like areas, which involve no real handwork but require instead the observation of a highly technical process.

In Latin America, the line between white collar and blue collar workers is much more sharply drawn. This is illustrated even in the two languages, English and Spanish. We can use the one word, "employees," to refer to office and factory workers alike. The other common word, "workers," does not make the distinction explicit either. It is more generally used to apply to factory workers, but when a person uses that word, it is not clear that he is referring only to factory workers. To make the distinction in English, we have to use rather cumbersome language. The terms "office workers" and "factory workers" will serve in some situations, but what about the cases where the men who work with their hands don't work in factories? Perhaps the most useful terms are "white collar workers" and "blue collar workers"—but note that we have to use three words in each case to make the distinction clear. Not so in Spanish. That language offers one word for each of the categories. A white collar worker is an *empleado* and a blue collar worker is an *obrero*.

Along with this linguistic difference go important differences in the handling of these classes of people. In countries such as Peru, the distinction is basic to the labor laws of the country and the *empleados* have substantial government protection, whereas the *obreros* are given little attention at all.

This distinction is constantly reflected in daily behavior in Latin America. For example, consider the case of a U.S. professor who was teaching in a Venezuelan university. He had just received a shipment of supplies from the United States and was eager to open up the wooden crate as soon as possible. He called upon the janitor to bring him a hammer. When the janitor returned, the professor, without thinking, reached for the hammer. The janitor did not give it to him. The professor then asked for the hammer, but again the janitor refused to give it to him. The crate was opened only when the professor stepped back and allowed the janitor to open it. The work involved lasted only for a moment and involved a minimum of physical effort. The janitor responded quickly to any *appropriate* order the professor gave him, but he felt strongly that it was not fitting that a man with the status of a professor should do the slightest bit of work suitable for an *obrero*.

In the United States, a middle-class man may shine his own shoes, wash his own car, paint his own house, and so on if he feels inclined to do so. He may have various reasons for not undertaking such tasks, but the fear of losing social status will not be one of them. Doing physical work on one's own house and possessions is not considered beneath the dignity of a middle-class man in this country. He may even enhance his personal reputation by doing a good job in these fields. However, there are many countries in which a middle-class man who can ill afford to pay to get such tasks done will still feel that he cannot undertake them himself. He will not feel right himself about doing the jobs, and he will fear losing status in the eyes of others.

A sharp line of social distinction between white collar and blue collar jobs can be a very serious obstacle to the economic development of a country. In underdeveloped countries, with broadening educational opportunities and new job openings in industry, most young men and women who have learned to read and write want to become office workers. Thus these countries are faced with an oversupply of clerks and a critical shortage of skilled workers. This presents a problem not only to management people and government officials concerned with economic development, but also to the employees themselves. In many of these situations of early industrialization, most clerical jobs will be dead end jobs, whereas a good man starting in the plant or field may move up steadily to the top skill classifications and then perhaps a step or two beyond this into the lower ranks of supervision. However, wherever there is a sharp distinction between office and shop, even those people who see the advantages of potential progress in the shop job will hesitate to forsake the job classification which establishes them as respectable people from the outset.

COMMUNICATION AT WORK

Culture also affects the pattern of communication among individuals.

If you disagree with someone, do you thrash it out with him face-to-face? Do you keep it to yourself? Or do you take it up with some third party?

In union-management relations, the grievance procedure as we know it is rare inside Latin American plants. To a much greater extent than in the United States, the government becomes involved in the handling of all kinds of labor problems.

These differences seem to be clearly related to the culture and social organization of Latin America. There we find that society has been much more rigidly stratified than it has with us. As a corollary, we find a greater emphasis upon authority in family and community.

This emphasis upon status differences makes it difficult for people at varying status levels to express themselves freely in discussion and argument. In the past, the pattern has been for the man of lower status to express deference to his superior in any face-to-face contact. This has been the case even when everyone knows that the subordinate dislikes the superior. In fact, the culture of Latin America seems to place a great premium upon keeping personal relations harmonious on the surface.

In the United States, we feel that it is not only desirable but natural to speak up to your superior, to tell the boss exactly what you think, even when you disagree with him. Of course, we don't always do this, but the important thing is that we think we should do it, and we feel guilty if we fail to speak our minds frankly. When workers in our factories are newly elected to local union office, they may find themselves quite self-conscious about speaking up to the boss and arguing grievances, but many of them quickly learn to do it—and enjoy the experience. As our culture emphasizes thrashing out differences of opinion in face-to-face contact and de-emphasizes the importance of status differences, we find ourselves in a cultural environment which makes it possible to build our institutions for the handling of industrial disputes on the basis of the local situation and direct discussion by the parties immediately involved.

In Latin America, where it is exceedingly difficult for people to express their differences face-to-face, and where status differences and authority are much more strongly emphasized than here, it is quite natural for workers to look for some third party—the government—to take care of their problems. If they have difficulty in thrashing out their problems with management, they find no difficulty in telling government people how they feel about management.

Consider the case of a Venezuelan drilling foreman with a large U.S. oil company in Venezuela. A man of very little formal education but substantial ability, he had worked himself up to the position of supervisor over a drilling crew. His classification was higher than that of the first-line foreman, who was a member of the "junior staff." This man had reached a "senior staff" position and so had "arrived" as a bona fide member of the management.

I found the Venezuelan supervisor highly satisfied with his job on all points except one, which involved communication. He said he had advanced much higher in the company than he had ever expected. He spoke of his North American superior with real enthusiasm. He described the superior as an able, sympathetic, and understanding person, and added, "He actually speaks better Spanish than I do." How then could there be a problem of communication between the two individuals?

The Venezuelan described his problem. No sooner would he have the men on his crew trained so that he had a good team working for him than one or another of them would be transferred to some other crew. His superior made the decisions on these transfers, and the Venezuelan didn't understand why the transfers were made so frequently.

I asked, "Have you ever complained to your superior?"

The Venezuelan seemed startled at the very idea: "Oh, no, no!"

"Well," I tried again, "perhaps I put it the wrong way. Have you ever discussed the matter with your superior?"

He said he had not.

"Have you ever thought that some time you might bring it to his attention?"

The Venezuelan paused to give that question some thought. Finally, he answered, "Well, maybe some time when we are talking about something else, I might indirectly bring it in." But then a happy thought struck: "But Mr. Jones has the same job I have and he has exactly the same problem. I think he is going to bring it up to the boss."

We might say that when a man fails to speak up to his boss, it is because he is afraid of what the boss will do to him. Certainly, fear played a part in establishing the culture pattern in the society as a whole. In a highly stratified society where all powers are concentrated in the hands of the superior, the subordinate learns that it can be dangerous to question a decision of the superior. In this type of situation, people learn to behave submissively—at least in the presence of the boss. They do not learn to thrash things out with him, face-to-face. Then, when there is no reason to fear, they still do not feel that it is natural to speak up.

In this case, the Venezuelan spoke most cordially of his boss and gave not the slightest indications of fear. Furthermore, as he well recognized, his position in the organization was completely secure. Nevertheless, it somehow did not seem natural for him to speak up even to a sympathetic and understanding superior. He did not even have to make his criticism direct. He might simply have asked the superior to explain the reasons behind his decisions on transfer of workers. But even that was too much.

We can sum up the difference in this way. In the United States, subordinates do not just automatically speak up to their superiors. The superior needs to behave in such a way as to make it clear that he will not retaliate in response to criticism. If he gets that point across, he can be confident that real communication will flow upward, because people in our society are primed to speak up to the boss whenever the situation seems right. In Latin America and in other more highly stratified societies, it is not enough simply to remove the fear of retaliation. The manager who wants his subordinates to speak up to him must provide incentives to help them to learn this type of communication.

In the United States, the pressure for upward communication is always present. The superior needs only to take the cork out of the channel of communication. In Latin America, the superior, in addition to removing the cork, must provide some sort of suction to bring this sort of communication up to him. . . .

For a final example of the impact of culture upon organizational life, let us consider a case entirely outside of Western civilization, *The Japanese Factory,* as discussed by James Abegglen.[4]

The impact of cultural differences does not seem to pass away before advancing industrialization. Japan is a highly industrialized nation, and yet as Abegglen points out, her factories are organized according to a social logic quite different from ours.

Japanese workers are hired for life. They are practically never fired. Promotions go largely by seniority even at managerial levels. The incompetent executive moves up with advancing years to positions with titles appropriate to his age—even when this means devising types of duties that will keep him from interfering with the progress of the firm. The pay of workers bears no relation to their productivity. The pay envelope is the sum of a complex set of factors, in which length of service and number of dependents figure prominently. All management decisions are made on a group basis—at least nominally. If an individual were credited with a certain decision that turned out to be unwise, then the individual would lose face. To spare management people from such humiliation, to all appearances the group as a whole shares responsibility in all decisions.

If we were to see such a system being established in a company in the United States, we would confidently predict that it would not work. No doubt that prediction would prove correct, because the Japanese system would not fit into our own culture. However, the important point to note is that the system does work in Japan. That is not to say that there are no sources of inefficiency in the system. Indeed, Abegglen points out some of the inherent difficulties. At the same time, however, he points out that Japan's industry has advanced just as rapidly as ours in the last century.

Clearly, a United States management expert attempting to advise Japanese industrialists would have to make sure that his recommendations fitted into the

---

[4] Glencoe, Ill.: The Free Press, 1958.

culture and social organization of Japan and were not simply homemade United States recipes, automatically applied.

In conclusion, the individual brings part of his culture with him into the workplace. A knowledge of the culture will therefore be helpful in understanding his behavior.

Since culture is, in part, learned behavior, and since there are differences among the parts of a large and complex society, we should expect to find individual differences in what people within the same society learn from their culture. At the same time, we should expect to find similarities in beliefs and behavior within a given culture and contrasts when we compare it with another culture. . . .

Additional References

Blake, Robert R., and Mouton, Jane S. "International Managerial Grids," *Training Directors Journal,* May, 1965.

Bonaparte, Tony H. "Management in the Cultural Setting," *Advanced Management Journal,* October, 1966.

Brand, W. "Social and Cultural Factors in Management Development," *Management International Review,* No. 3 (1966).

Dichter, Ernest. "The World Customer," *Harvard Business Review,* July–August, 1962.

Gonzalez, R. F., and McMillan, C. "The University of American Management Philosophy," *Journal of the Academy of Management,* Vol. 4, No. 1 (1961), pp. 34–37.

Kerr, C.; Dunlop, J.; Harbison, F.; and Myers, C. *Industrialism and Industrial Man.* New York: Oxford University Press, 1964.

Lee, James. "Cultural Analysis in Overseas Operations," *Harvard Business Review,* Vol. 44, No. 2 (March–April, 1966).

Negandhi, Anant F., and Estafen, Bernard D. "A Research Model to Determine the Applicability of American Management Know-How in Differing Cultures and/or Environments," *Academy of Management Journal,* December, 1965, pp. 309–18.

Oberg, W. "Cross Cultural Perspectives on Management Principles," *Journal of the Academy of Management,* Vol. 6, No. 2 (1963), pp. 129–43.

Prasad, S. B. (ed.). *Management in International Perspective.* New York: Appleton-Century-Crofts, 1966.

Priceman, Mark. "Inter-Cultural Competence and the American Businessman," *Training Directors Journal,* Vol. 19, No. 3 (March, 1965), p. 4.

Richman, Barry M. "Significance of Cultural Variables," *Academy of Management Journal,* Vol. 8, No. 4 (December, 1965).

"Social and Cultural Factors in Management Development," *International Labour Review,* Vol. 94, No. 2 (August, 1966), pp. 101–7.

Vayda, Andrew P. "On the Anthropological Study of Economics," *Journal of Economic Issues* (Association for Evolutionary Economics), Vol. 1, Nos. 1 and 2 (June, 1967), pp. 86–90.

chapter three

Management in the United States: The Historical Setting

"All history is bunk," Henry Ford is reputed to have announced. What Henry was suggesting is that the manager is concerned with the future. His thoughts should be about future returns, future events, and future market conditions. Thus, we learn in accounting and financial management that past costs are gone; they do not play a role in decisions about the future. We learn in evaluating human performance that the control system should not emphasize punishment for past deeds, but should be future-oriented toward motivating improved organizational performance. Ultimately, our concern in comparative management is with present and future managerial practices. Nonetheless, such practices reflect cultural history. The past can be vital for understanding the present and visualizing the future.

Ironically, the Ford Motor Company dramatically illustrates the relevance of the past to present decisions.[1] Henry Ford's inadequate understanding of history contributed directly to the late 1920's decline in the Ford Motor Company's fortunes. In his memoirs,[2] Alfred P. Sloan, Jr., long-time chief executive of General Motors, points out that Ford did not recognize the historical development of the public's taste, the people's desire for increased choice and luxury. Sloan understood this, and General Motors responded to it in their product policy. Ford did not, so sales of the model-T declined as precipitously as had sales of horse-drawn buggies a generation before. In 1927, almost none were sold, and Ford had nothing else to offer until a year later when the model-A was introduced—a model that Sloan thought to be old-fashioned even at its

---

[1] See Allan Nevins, with collaboration of Frank E. Hill, *Ford* (3 vols.; New York: Charles Scribner's Sons, 1954–1963), esp. vol. 3, *Decline and Rebirth.*

[2] Alfred P. Sloan, Jr., *My Years with General Motors,* ed. John McDonald with Catharine Stevens (Garden City, N.Y.: Doubleday & Co., Inc., 1964).

introduction. A favorite saying of the late John F. Kennedy (borrowed from George Santayana) is appropriate: "Those who do not know history are doomed to relive it."

In Robert Heilbroner's apt phrase, we need a historical view in order to conceive "the future as history."[3] Therefore, we have included a number of historical readings in the following chapters. But before we look at management development elsewhere, we need to review the history of management in the United States. As we indicated in Chapter One, we assume that the reader has a general familiarity with contemporary American managerial philosophy and practice. A short survey of the growth of professional management here would be helpful, nonetheless. We do not intend a comprehensive description of the historical development of modern business and management, but several themes seem relevant to our concerns here. To investigate the historical antecedents of management in America, however, we need to take a quick trip to ancient Israel, Greece, and Rome.

BUSINESS IN HISTORY

Murder, plunder, and destruction have characterized the historical debate over the proper role of the businessman. The ancient conflicts on this issue predate by many centuries the day when Matthew recorded his version of the Sermon on the Mount, bidding us not to be anxious in our quest for material goods.

See how the lilies of the field grow; they neither toil nor spin, yet I say to you that not even Solomon in all his glory was arrayed like one of these. . . . But if God so clothes the grass of the field, which today is alive and tomorrow is thrown into the oven, how much more you, O you of little faith! Therefore do not be anxious, saying "What shall we eat?" or "What shall we drink?" or "What shall we put on?"[4]

But man is anxious, always has been, and probably always will be. His effort to improve his standard of living and free himself from the vicissitudes of fickle nature have been persistent historical themes. Yet, he has always seemed guilty about it. Then and now, this debate about business ultimately raises questions about the purpose of society. In most societies, there has been frequent difficulty in reconciling business values with other cultural values—whether these were democracy, spiritualism, or militarism.

Business versus "Higher Values"

In the Homeric Age, there was confrontation between warrior Greek and merchant Lydian.[5] The Athenians denigrated economic labor. A man lowered

[3] Robert Heilbroner, *The Future as History* (New York: Harper & Bros., Inc., 1960).
[4] Gospel according to St. Matthew, chap. 6, vs. 25–31.
[5] Miriam Beard, *A History of the Businessman* (Ann Arbor: University of Michigan paperback, 1961).

himself by economic activities; these jobs were delegated to slaves. Not just the expected mundane, hard, and dirty functions were so delegated, but also the intellectual work associated with running a business. Thus, planning, accounting, and merchandizing were handled by slaves. A slave could rise to some affluence and prominence in ancient Athens by running his owner's business. He might even be allowed a home for himself—not, of course, in the restricted areas of Athens, but in the ghetto of Pireaus. Nonetheless, a slave was not a citizen (nor were most of the poorer freemen), and a true citizen did not concern himself with economic activities. To be truly free, the citizen should devote his time to the higher pursuits of art, philosophy, athletics, or political justice.

To attain these higher honors, the Greeks (theoretically, at least) advocated austerity, commitment, and manliness. To these sons of Olympus, the trading Lydians appeared effete and ridiculous in their "purple robes pompously stalking about with their beautifully dressed hair reeking with ointments."[6] To the Spartans, and even the Athenians, the business activities of the Lydians emphasized comfort at the expense of preparedness, weakness and debauchery at the expense of strength and purity. Whether or not such comparisons were valid is perhaps unimportant now, except that the Greeks did slaughter the Lydians.

In the era of the Roman Republic, the sons of Romulus and Remus did battle with the businessmen of Carthage. Of course, it was a struggle for power and command of the Mediterranean, but it was also conflict over the proper style of life. The militarily and agriculturally oriented Romans emphasized the glory and power (and economic gain) to be obtained through plunder and tribute; they manufactured and traded little. The Carthaginians, in contrast, traded from Cornwall to Malabar in pearls, purple dye, ivory, and precious metals. Carthage was one of the largest and richest cities in the ancient world. To the Roman, however, it symbolized more than just a competing power. Carthage stood for decadent, soft, feministic living, which seemed morally wrong and dangerous to the austere and unsophisticated early Romans. So Carthage was destroyed.

Private Business versus Public Interest

The cheers and jeers for business, as Henri Pirenne pointed out years ago, have alternated in successive eras for many centuries.[7] The monarchs of the mercantilist national states of the 16th, 17th, and 18th centuries placed severe restraints on the freedom of business. International commerce was emphasized because the mercantilist-political powers believed business should exist to serve the interests of the state. Of course, there were various ways of seeing that the nation's interest did not conflict too sharply with the private interests of powerful individuals. But, theoretically at least, private business interests were subservient to the state. The evolutionary revolution of the new middle classes in

---

[6] *Ibid.*, p. 19.

[7] Henri Pirenne, "The Stages in the Social History of Capitalism," *American Historical Review*, Vol. 19 (April, 1914), pp. 494–515.

the early 19th century ushered in a new era of private managerial independence, which was followed by new regulations, and so on.

So the struggle went for centuries—struggle essentially over the role of individual, business, and state. Does business exist to meet minimum individual needs, with surplus to be devoted to the greater glory of the collective people as the state decrees? Or does the state exist to foster the stability and environment to allow individuals and businesses to pursue their own ends? The Greeks and Romans were disposed to believe in state supremacy—not only because they glorified the state and denigrated the individual, but also because they believed that business independence and ascendency meant decadent, dangerous, and perhaps immoral living. The Carthaginians and Lydians, in contrast, saw the city-state as only a means toward economic and business power—not only because they valued stability and comfort, but also because they saw the Greeks and Romans as rude and uncivilized.

Attitudes toward Profits

Implicit in much of this conflict over the role of business was a distrust of profits. Uneasiness about profits is an old theme in human history; it is not a recent communist plot nor a reflection of creeping socialism. Ambivalence about profits stems from a problem of reconciling business ends and other higher human values and, perhaps even more fundamentally, from a historical dichotomy between matter and spirit. Aristotle felt that profit making on luxury goods was immoral. In a business venture, one should deal only in the necessities of life. Cicero, in contrast, justified profits on luxury goods if the business manager also supplied necessities. Later, Thomas Aquinas added the requirement that to justify profits one had to give some of the funds to charity or use them in the public interest, as in public works.

Under the influence of Renaissance humanism, individualism, Calvinism, and the later secularized version of the Protestant ethic, and buttressed by rationalism and scientific thought, we have become more sympathetic to economic activity and the role of the business manager. However, the remnants of the old debate remain to varying extents in different countries. Students should recognize that these ancient dialogues have played a profound role in economic development, in the position of the manager, and in theorizing about management. In most civilizations, the business manager has never quite made it to the top of the social or power ladder. He has been subservient to the politician, the military hero, the churchman, or landed aristocracy. Cassius aspired to leadership in ancient Rome, but he never got beyond being a power behind the scenes.

BUSINESS IN AMERICA

Depending on one's perspective, the conflicts between economic values and other values have been reconciled for good or evil to a greater extent in the

United States than in any other place. In America, the businessman and the manager have occupied what is perhaps a unique position. A British observer once remarked, "America has a secular religion of progress, and businessmen are the high priests of that religion."[8] What Christopher Dawson was referring to was the status and the prestige that business managers historically have held in American society. Of course, there have been ups and downs; the businessman's prestige nose-dived in the 1930's, climbed again in the fifties, perhaps is decreasing in the sixties. But if we compare with most other cultures and most other societies, business management has had a respected place in American life.

Through most of our history, the son of the successful family, the son of the well born, the son of the upper middle-class and upper-class family could enter business as a respectable and honorable career. Many did. Contrast this with even the present situation in the United Kingdom where we are only just beginning to see the entrance of the best-educated and the best-born people into the economic sphere. Contrast the United States with the more traditional societies of South America, where a business career is simply not a desirable alternative for the upper class, not a possibility for the lower class, and where not much middle class exists. Let us consider why the business manager is unique in America. The reasons are many and complex.

The Colonies and Colonists

While we glorify the early settlers of New England and are proud of the religious principles on which we like to think our country was founded, we sometimes neglect to examine who those people really were. They were not the poor, downtrodden masses later immortalized by Emma Lazarus in her poem engraved on the Statue of Liberty.[9] They were not, for the most part, prisoners and indentured servants fleeing from the Hogarthian slums of London. Most were middle class, fairly well educated, and familiar with the calculus of profit and loss.

We think of the Puritans and the Pilgrims as disciplined and austere. In today's terms, undoubtedly this is true. But from the very beginning, these people had consumer desires that required the importation of finished goods from the old country. They had desires for tableware, for clothing, and for a variety of household and educational needs that were among the most advanced in the world. Their consumption needs were more advanced than those of the typical present-day African native in Nigeria or Ghana. These people in the early American colonies considered necessary a variety of goods that then and even now most people in the world would consider luxuries. Our forefathers wanted these things

---

[8] Christopher H. Dawson, *Progress and Religion: An Historical Inquiry* (New York: Sheed & Ward, 1938).

[9] The concluding lines of Emma Lazarus' sonnet, "The New Colossus," written in 1882, are inscribed on the base of the Statue of Liberty: "Send Me Your Tired, Your Poor, Your Huddled Masses Yearning To Be Free. . . ."

and were willing to work for them. Hence, in New England there were jobs for the businessman from the very beginning.

In addition, Samuel Eliot Morison points out, many of these early colonies were businesses themselves.[10] Investors in the old country had set up these colonies for the purpose of making a profit. The settlers knew they were expected to produce a surplus—a surplus that could be used to provide necessities and limited luxuries, and to pay a return to the project's investors. They were familiar, as we have observed, with the calculus of profit and loss. Since many had operated businesses in England and France, the colonials were familiar with the process of managing and investing for economic advantage—concepts that still remain foreign to most of the world. From the very beginning, then, business considerations, even in the religious communities, had an acceptable place.

Religious commitments also played a role, of course. In recent years, David McClelland has given corroborative evidence for Max Weber's thesis on the role of the Protestant ethic.[11] Work was intrinsically good and honorable—and it kept the Devil at arm's length. In the words of Poor Richard, Benjamin Franklin's fictitious observer of American life, "a waste of time is the worst of sins." In the new colonies, no social stigma was attached to economic work or to manual work. The people were willing to work—and to reinforce this helpful attitude, in the Massachusetts Bay Colony one could be thrown into the stockade for refusing to work on Christmas day. What better way to honor the Lord on his birthday than to work?

The Absent Nobility

The merchant businessman was needed in the New World, so his role had legitimacy from the beginning. With time, the prestige and power of the businessman grew—especially since there was no nobility above him. In general, neither the English nobility nor the wealthy investors in the colonies came over. Life was easier and more pleasant for the establishment at home than in the rude settlements of North America. Consequently, there was no simple transference of the old nobility to the new land.

In addition, a widespread indigenous aristocracy did not develop. Only in parts of South Carolina, Louisiana, and the old South, the Hudson Valley in New York, and perhaps the eastern shore of Maryland did a feudal structure begin to develop. Such areas had a limited availability of highly profitable land. Not all soil was suited to the profitable crops of cotton, indigo, rice, or tobacco. In these areas where good land was limited and the early families obtained and maintained control, a nobility of sorts did start to develop. In the rest of the

---

10 Samuel Eliot Morison, *The Oxford History of the American People* (New York: Oxford University Press, 1965).

11 David C. McClelland, *The Achieving Society* (Princeton, N.J.: D. Van Nostrand Co., Inc., 1961). See also Max Weber, *The Protestant Ethic and the Spirit of Capitalism,* trans. Talcott Parsons (New York: Charles Scribner's Sons, 1958, originally published in 1904–5), and the reading selection by Weber and Fullerton in Chapter Four.

new colonies, however, there were almost unlimited acres of land. If one was dissatisfied with conditions in one area, one could move on. The British effort to limit such free movement was one of the earliest issues of conflict with the colonials. Because of land conditions and social and religious attitudes, opposition to formal nobility was strong, and such an institution never developed.

Such hinderance to a landed aristocracy can be contrasted with many South American nations, where the Spanish nobility actually moved to the New World, imposing the social and class structure of the old society. We don't imply that from the beginning no class distinctions existed in the original colonies and the early United States, but the class system tended to be dependent on factors other than simple ownership of land or bloodlines. More important, the social system was fluid enough that the early businessman was able to rise within its structure to become one of the highest ranking members of the developing social structure in the 19th and early 20th centuries.

Of course, American literature is full of stories of the nouveau riche, showing that the new businessman was not fully accepted in the traditional southern community nor the old New England town. Nonetheless, perhaps more than any other country, money earned social success. It became the passport to social ranking. Whether one criticizes America for being materialistic or praises it for being open and democratic, the fact remains that the absence of a landed nobility and the ability of the successful manager to climb the social ladder were major motivating forces for economic development.

Politics and Business

We have mentioned that many of the early colonies, in effect, were businesses. They were also political entities, and the distinction between political and economic was indistinct. Governor Bradford was a political leader, but he was also the resident manager of the Massachusetts Company's interests. The people in government and business were the same; their interests were the same; there was no simple dichotomy between public and private affairs. We sometimes let our ideology interfere with our perceptions on this subject. The call for separation of government and business came much later in American life. In the early years, the two spheres were inescapably intertwined. Even after the formal founding of the United States, the debate between Hamilton and Jefferson reiterated this point.[12] For Hamilton, business and government were interdependent, and decisions in each area should be made with the other in mind. His view prevailed in the early years. Perhaps we should remember this when we become too critical of the developing nations and the role of central government in economic development.

Arthur M. Schlesinger, Jr., has incisively summarized the unique development of the American economy.

---

[12] See Louis Hacker, *The Triumph of American Capitalism* (New York: Columbia University Press, 1947).

The economic experience of the United States provides a compact example of the growth of an underdeveloped country into a great and rich industrial state. When the thirteen colonies gained their independence toward the end of the eighteenth century, they joined together to form a weak and diffuse nation of some 4 million people, living in a confederation of states straggling along the Atlantic seaboard. Contemporary students of economic development would find the pattern of 1790 familiar enough: Four-fifths of the American labor force were farmers; capital, technology, and finished goods came predominantly from overseas; and the prevailing vision of the nation's economic future was (except for improvements in agricultural productivity) essentially static. Today, a century and three-quarters later, the United States is a vast continental nation, with a population of nearly 170 million living in an opulent industrial society, ceaselessly generating its own capital and its own technology, dedicated to the objective of an ever-expanding economy.

One must hastily add that this experience offers little comfort in the middle of the twentieth century to the new nations of Asia and Africa struggling to overcome the torpor of centuries and to achieve economic and social modernization in a single generation. While America in 1790 possessed certain features of what we call in 1960 an underdeveloped country, it also enjoyed certain advantages denied to most underdeveloped countries today — advantages that enormously facilitated the processes of economic growth on the North American continent.

Some of these advantages derived from America's natural situation. The new nation had available for exploitation a fertile subcontinent well supplied with resources. A brisk and temperate climate preserved health and stimulated energy. A wide ocean provided relative freedom from foreign aggression; national defense did not have to become a consuming preoccupation of the new state. But what was perhaps the decisive advantage lay in the character of America's population and in the ideas and institutions that this population brought with them.

The first conspicuous fact about the American people was that there were not many of them. The young republic had no problem of overpopulation; it was free from the curse of Malthus. Hungry masses were not pressing on available resources and preventing the accumulation of capital. Public health was a spur, not a threat, to economic growth. Indeed, the relative scarcity of labor hastened development by creating a need for technological advances to render labor unnecessary.

Not only was the population scant in relation to land and resources; it was also fairly advanced, culturally, politically, and morally. The legacy of Calvinism and the rising faith of democracy joined in producing respect for learning and reason. Most Americans could read and write. They understood about the role of law and had had significant experience in self-government. They believed in education and were prepared to invest a tolerable share of resources in schools and libraries. Calvinism had instilled in them the determination to work and to save; democracy was developing in them the capacity to consume and to enjoy. The combination made economic progress almost irresistible.

American society, moreover, having skipped the feudal stage of development, escaped many of the social rigidities and economic inequalities that bottled up talent and energy in contemporary Europe. The decision of the ex-colonies to federate after independence meant the beginning of an internal market and thus a developing stimulus to economic growth. Here was a nation where opportunity prompted men to develop latent abilities, where social mobility became the vehicle of economic energy. The ever-beckoning, ever-receding western frontier confirmed the inherent social mobility, intensified the instinct for swift adaptation to novel problems and circumstances, and promised a continental fulfillment of the American destiny. Americans were thus endowed by birthright with a spontaneous and spacious belief in opportunity and equality as the ends of society and in social, political, and technological invention as the means.

Work, democracy, innovation, education — these were particular sources of the national talent for economic growth. The commitment to work beyond the need for subsistance (a rarer thing in history than one might imagine) made it possible for individuals to begin the long labor of capital accumulation. The commitment to democracy, with the "pursuit of happiness" formally avowed as the national goal, expressed and encouraged the national passion for individual economic betterment. The commitment to innovation, the never-ending fascination with new methods, new materials, and new machines, provided the methodology for national abundance. The commitment to education, enlarging both the common fund of knowledge and the individual's access to it, assured the efficient use and the steady improvement of human resources. The mobility of American life thus stimulated the productive ambitions of millions of individual Americans, and egalitarian democracy assured a wide diffusion of the resulting benefits. The consequence of this fortunate alliance of ideas and institutions was a release of social energy which remade a continent and which has not yet been exhausted.[13]

BUSINESS EDUCATION AND PROFESSIONALISM

Our discussion so far gives some feel for the reasons business management and business managers in America historically have enjoyed an honorable place in American society—if not at the top, at least well thought of and justified in most times. Given this status for the businessman, it is perhaps not surprising that so much of the writing on management theory and practice has come from the United States. Probably the majority of articles and books published on the process of management have come from America.

Even where Americans have elaborated on the writings of others, it has been in the United States that the foreign writer's influence has been most felt. Recently, I was explaining management study in the United States to a group of visiting French students. In order to be polite and politic, I attempted to explain how much of the traditional aspect of the American approach to management stems from the work of a French businessman, Henri Fayol, who wrote about 60 years ago.[14] I was flabbergasted to find that none of the students had ever even heard of Fayol, and they were business majors at a French university! Similarly, the work of later Englishmen such as Colonel Urwick and, more recently, Wilfred Brown generated greater interest and comment in the United States than in Great Britain.[15] Why has the intellectual development of management been so much an American development? And why has business education been emphasized in the United States? Several answers have been advanced. Let us consider them.

Business schools began to appear in the United States in the late 19th century, with the founding of the Wharton School in 1881; others followed. Although the study of managerial theory in these early schools was subordinated to the traditional accounting and finance functions, management gradually became an important part of the curriculum, and books on management became more common. Of course, the study of management reflects the growth of the American economy and the important role of the businessman and manager in American society. Nonetheless, other factors help to explain why management as a profes-

---

[13] Arthur Schlesinger, Jr., "Ideas and Economic Process," in Seymour Harris (ed.), *American Economic History* (New York: McGraw-Hill Book Co., Inc., 1961), pp. 3–5.

[14] Henri Fayol, *General and Industrial Management* (London: Pitman & Sons, 1949, first published 1916).

[15] See Lyndall Urwick, *Management of Tomorrow* (London: Nisbet, 1933); and Wilfred B. Brown, *Explorations in Management* (New York: John Wiley & Sons, Inc., 1960).

sional field of study developed in the United States, while even in the rapidly developing western European nations such study still lags.

Corporations and the Separation of Ownership from Management

One of the keys may be the pattern of ownership and control of business. In early 19th-century United States, dominant control of business organizations was vested in the owner-manager. In these circumstances, there tended to be relatively little concern about the internal management processes of the organization. Presumably, the organization was understood by understanding the motivation of the owner-manager. He was interested in profit, and he made his decisions accordingly. In addition, given our respect for private property, the policies and directives of the manager were legitimate and justified. He was the owner; he controlled the property; therefore, he issued orders to the people who operated the property.

Corporations, however, developed early in the United States. Perhaps reflecting Alexis de Tocqueville's early observation on the American disposition to form organizations,[16] but more fundamentally reflecting the nature of the economic task to be performed in America, groups of entrepreneurs incorporated. America was large. Much capital was required to undertake communication and transportation development. Since the wealth of the United States was widely distributed and a wealthy traditional aristocracy did not exist, the funds for such undertakings had to come from many sources. Foreign investment and the investments of relatively large groups of Americans were pooled to form corporations.

The decentralization of U.S. politics facilitated the obtaining of corporate charters, and contributed to the growth of a wide variety of mixed public and private interest organizations in these early years. In addition, the growth of freely marketable ownership shares in these fledgling corporations suited the needs of a migratory society and the need to have some liquidity in investments. For these reasons, at a relatively early time the corporation owned by a rather large number of people became an important economic factor in America.

The growth of corporate business tended to dilute the owner's control over management of the organization. It was not so much that the owners were absent or had no interest in their businesses. Indeed, in the 19th century many if not most owners actually participated in management. But as they grew, the organizations began to need a bureaucracy. In short, businesses required administrators and managers who were not owners or who had only relatively small financial investments in the organization. When the manager is an owner, his qualifications for the job are not much questioned. But when that owner must hire someone, he becomes concerned about such qualifications. Thus, the need

---

[16] See Alexis de Tocqueville, *Democracy in America* (New York: Alfred A. Knopf, Inc., 1945, originally published 1835.

for salaried managers encouraged the development of business schools that could teach the necessary technical information.

These ownership and control trends have led to the differing perspectives on business that still exist between the United States and western Europe. We Americans like to think of our country as one of private property and private enterprise. Nonetheless, there are substantial distinctions between the private ownership and operation of the means of production in the United States compared with Europe. David Granick points out that although there are growing publicly held businesses in western Europe, the dominant ideological orientation is toward the owner-managed private concern.[17] Family ownership and management is far more pervasive than in the United States. This leads to a striking difference, for example, in managers' pay. In the typical French company, a manager's income is heavily dependent on his ownership interest. Salary is only part of his income. Because of his membership in the controlling family, funds from interests, rents, or profits account for a major part of his money. In contrast, the typical American manager's income consists mainly of salary. In the large publicly owned American corporation, although the manager may share in profits through a bonus plan his ownership interest tends to be small.

Decentralized Education

The schools in America responded to these developments and demands to a larger extent, perhaps, than those in Europe. This again is a reflection of decentralization of American politics, especially decentralization of control over schools. Harbison and Myers observe:

> Control of education (including higher education) is centralized in such countries as France, Germany, and the Soviet Union. Educational planning for expansion is particularly notable in France. Great Britain and Sweden have had various Royal Commissions and special committees concerned with various aspects of secondary and higher education, and the University Grants Commission was established in Great Britain in 1919 to guide and help finance expansion of higher education. For example, over three-fourths of university income in Great Britain came from government grants in 1960–1961, as compared to less than a fourth from the Federal government and a third from the state governments in the United States.
>
> Both financing and control of education in the United States have been more decentralized and localized than in most other advanced countries. This is deeply rooted in the tradition of community responsibility for elementary and secondary schools, assisted to varying degrees by the states in which they are located. States have also supported higher education, as we have seen, initially through the stimulus of the Morrill Act with national land grants. This was an early example of Federal government financing, but there was no evidence of the "Federal interference" in education so feared in some quarters in the United States today. Many American colleges and universities are now partially financially dependent on Federally financed research programs, and students in some fields (particularly science) are supported by government scholarships. But Federal financial aid to education is still a controversial issue in the United States.[18]

---

[17] David Granick, *The European Executive* (New York: Doubleday Anchor Books, 1962).

[18] Frederick Harbison and Charles A. Myers, *Education, Manpower, and Economic Growth* (New York: McGraw-Hill Book Co., Inc., 1964), pp. 158–59.

With the exception of agriculture, federal influence in American education has been slight; indeed, there was almost none until the 1954 creation of the office of the Commissioner of Education and some scholarship and building acts. But even today there are no national standards of education, and the federal government's role in curriculum has been only peripheral in terms of research grants in the sciences and so forth. This may be good or bad, but as a result curricula have been developed by local authorities and privately owned institutions. The state, of course, has played a role in the state universities, but even here business interests were able to influence policies.

This influence in both private and public schools was economic. Through their contributions, businessmen have played a major role in the development of American universities. Andrew Carnegie, the Rockefellers, George Eastman (who built much of the M.I.T. and University of Rochester campuses), and others played major roles in the development of institutional facilities and endowments. The first collegiate business school suggests the business orientation of the local community. David McClelland points out that the Quakers were among the most successful businessmen in American history,[19] and it is no coincidence that the University of Pennsylvania, a Quaker founded institution, was the site of the first business school.

Finally, at a more philosophical level, the development of business education and, more importantly, the attempt to rationalize management reflects the American tendency to codify and organize laws and professions. The development of professional management as a discipline and a philosophy is another result of American faith in education and rationality as vehicles for social and economic progress.

In short, the status of the American businessman or manager has been unique. Accepted, often honored, his career was open to the best in United States society, if not to all. His education and that of his subordinates was responsive to the needs of business more than elsewhere. He studied the process of management more, and his subsidized professors thought and wrote more about managerial theory.

With this short review of the United States, let us turn to management elsewhere, not to corroborate our feeling of superiority, but to learn and question and understand others as well as ourselves.

Additional References

"American Managers as Australians See Them," *Training and Development Journal*, June, 1966.

Beard, Miriam. *A History of Business,* Vols. 1 and 2. Ann Arbor: University of Michigan Press, 1962.

---

19 David McClelland, *op. cit.*

Bendix, R. "The American Experience," *Work and Authority in Industry,* chap. 2, pp. 254–340. New York: Harper Torchbook, 1963.

Berg, Ivar. *The Business of America.* New York: Harcourt, Brace & World, 1967.

Berle, Adolf A., Jr. *The 20th Century Capitalist Revolution.* New York: Harcourt, Brace & World, 1954.

Cheit, Earl F. (ed.). *The Business Establishment.* New York: John Wiley & Sons, Inc., 1964.

Cochran, Thomas. *The American Business System.* New York: Harper & Bros., 1955.

George, Claude S., Jr. *The History of Management Thought.* Englewood Cliffs, N.J.: Prentice-Hall, Inc., 1968.

Hof, Robert T. "Contemporary American Management," *Business Perspectives,* Vol. 3, No. 2 (Winter, 1967), pp. 5–10.

Lamb, H. B. "The Indian Merchant," *Journal of American Folklore,* Vol. 71 (1958), pp. 231–40.

Lewis, David. "Heroes and Heels in Business History," *Management of Personnel Quarterly,* Vol. 5, No. 4 (Winter, 1967), pp. 10–21.

Monsen, R. Joseph, Jr. *Modern American Capitalism – Ideologies and Issues.* Houghton Mifflin Co., 1963.

Warner, Lloyd W., and Abegglen, James C. *Big Business Leaders in America.* Harper & Bros., 1955.

Warner, Lloyd W.; Unwalla, Darab; and Trimin, John H. *The Emergent American Society, Vol. 1, Large Scale Organizations.* New Haven, Conn.: Yale University Press, 1967.

chapter four

Culture and Attitudes Affecting Economic Activities

In this first chapter of readings in our survey of world management, we consider interrelationship between cultural values and the society's views on economic activity. These perspectives and attitudes influence the origins, status, and behavior of managers.

Selection: "The Meaning of Culture," Ruth Benedict

Our first reading is taken from *Patterns of Culture,* a classic of anthropological literature, published in 1934. Benedict gives us a survey of the meaning of culture, its diversity, and its impact on human life. This selection will convey feeling for the way culture affects people and influences their attitudes toward economic pursuits and business, which we will examine in later readings. Most important, Benedict suggests that our system is not the only (nor necessarily the best) way to organize economic activities.

Selection: "Culture and Personality," Victor Barnouw

An idea common to many of the readings in this volume is that cultural values influence personal ambitions for management and social attitudes toward business. Is it right to strive for leadership and power? Is it right to pursue economic or materialist goals? Even more fundamentally, as Benedict showed, culture influences the development of individual personality, shaping the needs that tend to characterize a nation of people. Do they emphasize security, or affection, or prestige, or achievement? In this selection, a professor of anthropology examines the interplay between culture and personality.

Selection: "Ideological Preparation: The Wish before the Fact," Lewis Mumford

In a number of books, Lewis Mumford has shown us (contrary to Karl Marx) that human history reflects ideological change before material advancement. That is, changes in human thinking and values must precede economic development. Perspectives on time, space, and motion are perhaps the most important of these factors. This selection from Mumford's *Technics and Civilization* considers these ideas.

**Selection: "The Protestant Ethic and the Spirit of Capitalism,"
Max Weber and Kemper Fullerton**

A famous argument for the success of economic development in the Western world was offered by Max Weber in his theory on the relation between Protestantism and capitalism. A short passage from Weber defines his purpose, and the article by Fullerton, an Oberlin theology professor for many years, explains the Weber thesis.

**Selection: "Mahatma Gandhi's Views on Machines and Technology,"
D. P. Mukerji**

In contrast to the philosophies that characterize the preceding selection are the reservations about economic development expressed by India's revered leader Mahatma Gandhi. This selection gives the reader insight into less enthusiastic attitudes toward business and industrialization.

**Selection: "A Chinese Philosopher Prefers the Material Civilization of the West,"
Hu Shih**

In a fascinating comment on the nonmaterialist views of the Orient, Hu Shih expresses a positive conception of economic and business development.

selection 2

*The Meaning of Culture**

Ruth Benedict

Anthropology is the study of human beings as creatures of society. It fastens its attention upon those physical characteristics and industrial techniques, those

---

*From *Patterns of Culture* by Ruth Benedict. Copyright 1934 by Ruth Benedict. Copyright renewed 1962 by Ruth Valentine. Reprinted by permission of the publisher, Houghton Mifflin Company. Pp. 1–18, 32–33.

conventions and values, which distinguish one community from all others that belong to a different tradition.

The distinguishing mark of anthropology among the social sciences is that it includes for serious study other societies than our own. For its purposes any social regulation of mating and reproduction is as significant as our own, though it may be that of the Sea Dyaks, and have no possible historical relation to that of our civilization. To the anthropologist, our customs and those of a New Guinea tribe are two possible social schemes for dealing with a common problem, and in so far as he remains an anthropologist he is bound to avoid any weighting of one in favour of the other. He is interested in human behaviour, not as it is shaped by one tradition, our own, but as it has been shaped by any tradition whatsoever. He is interested in the great gamut of custom that is found in various cultures, and his object is to understand the way in which these cultures change and differentiate, the different forms through which they express themselves, and the manner in which the customs of any peoples function in the lives of the individuals who compose them.

Now custom has not been commonly regarded as a subject of any great moment. The inner workings of our own brains we feel to be uniquely worthy of investigation, but custom, we have a way of thinking, is behaviour at its most commonplace. As a matter of fact, it is the other way around. Traditional custom, taken the world over, is a mass of detailed behaviour more astonishing than what any one person can ever evolve in individual actions, no matter how aberrant. Yet that is a rather trivial aspect of the matter. The fact of first-rate importance is the predominant rôle that custom plays in experience and in belief, and the very great varieties it may manifest.

No man ever looks at the world with pristine eyes. He sees it edited by a definite set of customs and institutions and ways of thinking. Even in his philosophical probings he cannot go behind these stereotypes; his very concepts of the true and the false will still have reference to his particular traditional customs. John Dewey has said in all seriousness that the part played by custom in shaping the behaviour of the individual as over against any way in which he can affect traditional custom, is as the proportion of the total vocabulary of his mother tongue over against those words of his own baby talk that are taken up into the vernacular of his family. When one seriously studies social orders that have had the opportunity to develop autonomously, the figure becomes no more than an exact and matter-of-fact observation. The life history of the individual is first and foremost an accommodation to the patterns and standards traditionally handed down in his community. From the moment of his birth the customs into which he is born shape his experience and behaviour. By the time he can talk, he is the little creature of his culture, and by the time he is grown and able to take part in its activities, its habits are his habits, its beliefs his beliefs, its impossibilities his impossibilities. Every child that is born into his group will share them with him, and no child born into one on the opposite side of the globe can ever achieve the thousandth part. There is no social problem it is more incumbent upon us to understand than this of the rôle of custom. Until we are intelligent as to its laws and varieties, the main complicating facts of human life must remain unintelligible.

The study of custom can be profitable only after certain preliminary propositions have been accepted, and some of these propositions have been violently opposed. In the first place any scientific study requires that there be no preferential weighting of one or another of the items in the series it selects for its consideration. In all the less controversial fields like the study of cacti or termites or the nature of nebulae, the necessary method of study is to group the relevant material and to take note of all possible variant forms and conditions. In this way we have learned all that we know of the laws of astronomy, or of the habits of the social insects, let us say. It is only in the study of man himself that the major social sciences have substituted the study of one local variation, that of Western civilization.

Anthropology was by definition impossible as long as these distinctions between ourselves and the primitive, ourselves and the barbarian, ourselves and the pagan, held sway over people's minds. It was necessary first to arrive at that degree of sophistication where we no longer set our own belief over against our neighbour's superstition. It was necessary to recognize that these institutions which are based on the same premises, let us say the supernatural, must be considered together, our own among the rest.

In the first half of the nineteenth century this elementary postulate of anthropology could not occur to the most enlightened person of Western civilization. Man, all down his history, has defended his uniqueness like a point of honour. In Copernicus' time this claim to supremacy was so inclusive that it took in even the earth on which we live, and the fourteenth century refused with passion to have this planet subordinated to a place in the solar scheme. By Darwin's time, having granted the solar system to the enemy, man fought with all the weapons at his command for the uniqueness of the soul, an unknowable attribute given by God to man in such a manner that it disproved man's ancestry in the animal kingdom. No lack of continuity in the argument, no doubts of the nature of this "soul," not even the fact that the nineteenth century did not care in the least to defend its brotherhood with any group of aliens—none of these facts counted against the first-rate excitement that raged on account of the indignity evolution proposed against the notion of man's uniqueness.

Both these battles we may fairly count as won—if not yet, then soon; but the fighting has only massed itself upon another front. We are quite willing to admit now that the revolution of the earth about the sun, or the animal ancestry of man, has next to nothing to do with the uniqueness of our human achievements. If we inhabit one chance planet out of a myriad solar systems, so much the greater glory, and if all the ill-assorted human races are linked by evolution with the animal, the provable differences between ourselves and them are the more extreme and the uniqueness of our institutions the more remarkable. But *our* achievements, *our* institutions are unique; they are of a different order from those of lesser races and must be protected at all costs. So that today, whether it is a question of imperialism, or of race prejudice, or of a comparison between Christianity and paganism, we are still preoccupied with the uniqueness, not of the human institutions of the world at large, which no one has ever cared about anyway, but of our own institutions and achievements, our own civilization.

Western civilization, because of fortuitous historical circumstances, has spread itself more widely than any other local group that has so far been known. It has standardized itself over most of the globe, and we have been led, therefore, to accept a belief in the uniformity of human behaviour that under other circumstances would not have arisen. Even very primitive peoples are sometimes far more conscious of the rôle of cultural traits than we are, and for good reason. They have had intimate experience of different cultures. They have seen their religion, their economic system, their marriage prohibitions, go down before the white man's. They have laid down the one and accepted the other, often uncomprehendingly enough, but they are quite clear that there are variant arrangements of human life. They will sometimes attribute dominant characteristics of the white man to his commercial competition, or to his institution of warfare, very much in the fashion of the anthropologist.

The white man has had a different experience. He has never seen an outsider, perhaps, unless the outsider has been already Europeanized. If he has traveled, he has very likely been around the world without ever staying outside a cosmopolitan hotel. He knows little of any ways of life but his own. The uniformity of custom, of outlook, that he sees spread about him seems convincing enough, and conceals from him the fact that it is after all an historical accident. He accepts without more ado the equivalence of human nature and his own culture standards.

Yet the great spread of white civilization is not an isolated historical circumstance. The Polynesian group, in comparatively recent times, has spread itself from Ontong, Java, to Easter Island, from Hawaii to New Zealand, and the Bantu-speaking tribes spread from the Sahara to southern Africa. But in neither case do we regard these peoples as more than an overgrown local variation of the human species. Western civilization has had all its inventions in transportation and all its far-flung commercial arrangements to back up its great dispersion, and it is easy to understand historically how this came about.

The psychological consequences of this spread of white culture have been out of all proportion to the materialistic. This world-wide cultural diffusion has protected us as man had never been protected before from having to take seriously the civilizations of other peoples; it has given to our culture and massive universality that we have long ceased to account for historically, and which we read off rather as necessary and inevitable. We interpret our dependence, in our civilization, upon economic competition, as proof that this is the prime motivation that human nature can rely upon, or we read off the behaviour of small children as it is moulded in our civilization and recorded in child clinics, as child psychology or the way in which the young human animal is bound to behave. It is the same whether it is a question of our ethics or of our family organization. It is the inevitability of each familiar motivation that we defend, attempting always to identify our own local ways of behaving with Behaviour, or our own socialized habits with Human Nature.

Now modern man has made this thesis one of the living issues in his thought and in his practical behaviour, but the sources of it go far back into what appears to be, from its universal distribution among primitive peoples, one of the earliest of human distinctions, the difference in kind between "my own" closed group and the outsider. All primitive tribes agree in recognizing this category of the outsiders, those who are not only outside the provisions of the moral code which holds within the limits of one's own people, but who are summarily denied a place anywhere in the human scheme. A great number of the tribal names in common use, Zuñi, Déné, Kiowa, and the rest, are names by which primitive peoples know themselves, and are only their native terms for "the human beings," that is, themselves. Outside of the closed group there are no human beings. And this is in spite of the fact that from an objective point of view each tribe is surrounded by peoples sharing in its arts and material inventions, in elaborate practices that have grown up by a mutual give-and-take of behaviour from one people to another.

Primitive man never looked out over the world and saw "mankind" as a group and felt his common cause with his species. From the beginning he was a provincial who raised the barriers high. Whether it was a question of choosing a wife or of taking a head, the first and important distinction was between his own human group and those beyond the pale. His own group, and all its ways of behaving, was unique.

So modern man, differentiating into Chosen People and dangerous aliens, groups within his own civilization genetically and culturally related to one another as any tribes in the Australian bush are among themselves, has the justification of a vast historical continuity behind his attitude. The Pygmies have made the same claims. We are not likely to clear ourselves easily of so fundamental a human trait, but we can at least learn to recognize its history and its hydra manifestations.

One of these manifestations, and one which is often spoken of as primary and motivated rather by religious emotions than by this more generalized provincialism, is the attitude that has universally held in Western civilizations so long as religion remained a living issue among them. The distinction between any closed group and outside peoples, becomes in terms of religion that between the true believers and the heathen. Between these two categories for thousands of years there were no common meeting-points. No ideas or institutions that held in the one were valid in the other. Rather all institutions were seen in opposing terms according as they belonged to one or the other of the very often slightly differentiated religions: on the one side it was a question of Divine Truth and the true believer, of revelation and of God; on the other it was a matter of mortal error, of fables, of the damned and of devils. There could be no question of equating the attitudes of the opposed groups and hence no question of understanding from objectively studied data the nature of this important human trait, religion.

We feel a justified superiority when we read a description such as this of the standard religious attitude. At least we have thrown off that particular absurdity, and we have accepted the study of comparative religion. But considering the scope a similar attitude has had in our civilization in the form of race prejudices, for example, we are justified in a little scepticism as to whether our sophistication in the matter of religion is due to the fact that we have outgrown naïve childishness, or simply to the fact that religion is no longer the area of life in which the important modern battles are staged. In the really live issues of our civilization we seem to be far from having gained the detachment that we have so largely achieved in the field of religion.

There is another circumstance that has made the serious study of custom a late and often a half-heartedly pursued discipline, and it is a difficulty harder to surmount than those of which we have just spoken. Custom did not challenge the attention of social theorists because it was the very stuff of their own thinking: it was the lens without which they could not see at all. Precisely in proportion as it was fundamental, it had its existence outside the field of conscious attention. There is nothing mystical about this blindness. When a student has assembled the vast data for a study of international credits, or of the process of learning, or of narcissism as a factor in psychoneuroses, it is through and in this body of data that the economist or the psychologist or the psychiatrist operates. He does not reckon with the fact of other social arrangements where all the factors, it may be, are differently arranged. He does not reckon, that is, with cultural conditioning. He sees the trait he is studying as having known and inevitable manifestations, and he projects these as absolute because they are all the materials he has to think with. He identifies local attitudes of the [present] with Human Nature, the description of them with Economics or Psychology.

Practically, it often does not matter. Our children must be educated in our pedagogical tradition, and the study of the process of learning in our schools is of paramount importance. There is the same kind of justification for the shrug of the shoulders with which we often greet a discussion of other economic systems. After all, we must live within the framework of mine and thine that our own culture institutionalizes.

That is true, and the fact that the varieties of culture can best be discussed as they exist in space gives colour to our nonchalance. But it is only limitation of historical material that prevents examples from being drawn rather from the succession of cultures in time. That succession we cannot escape if we would, and when we look back even a generation we realize the extent to which revision has taken place, sometimes in our most intimate behaviour. So far these revisions have been blind, the result of circumstances we can chart only in retrospect. Except for our unwillingness to face cultural change in intimate matters until it is forced upon us, it would not be impossible to take a more intelligent and directive attitude. The resistance is in large measure a result of our misunderstanding of cultural conventions, and especially an exaltation of those that happen to belong to our nation and decade. A very little acquaintance with other conventions, and a knowledge of how various these may be, would do much to promote a rational social order.

The study of different cultures has another important bearing upon present-day thought and behaviour. Modern existence has thrown many civilizations into close contact, and at the moment the overwhelming response to this situation is nationalism and racial snobbery. There has never been a time when civilization stood more in need of individuals who are genuinely culture-conscious, who can see objectively the socially conditioned behaviour of other peoples without fear and recrimination.

Contempt for the alien is not the only possible solution of our present contact of races and nationalities. It is not even a scientifically founded solution. Traditional Anglo-Saxon intolerance is a local and temporal culture-trait like any other. Even people as nearly of the same blood and culture as the Spanish have not had it, and race prejudice in the Spanish-settled countries is a thoroughly different thing from that in countries dominated by England and the United States. In this country it is obviously not an intolerance directed against the mixture of blood of biologically far-separated races, for upon occasion excitement mounts as high against the Irish Catholic in Boston, or the Italian in New England mill towns, as against the Oriental in California. It is the old distinction of the in-group and the out-group, and if we carry on the primitive tradition in this matter, we have far less excuse than savage tribes. We have travelled, we pride ourselves on our sophistication. But we have failed to understand the relativity of cultural habits, and we remain debarred from much profit and enjoyment in our human relations with peoples of different standards, and untrustworthy in our dealings with them.

The recognition of the cultural basis of race prejudice is a desperate need in present Western civilization. We have come to the point where we entertain race prejudice against our blood brothers the Irish, and where Norway and Sweden speak of their enmity as if they too represented different blood. The so-called race line, during a war in which France and Germany fight on opposite sides, is held to divide the people of Baden from those of Alsace, though in bodily form they alike belong to the Alpine sub-race. In a day of footloose movements of people and of mixed marriages in the ancestry of the most desirable elements of the community, we preach unabashed the gospel of the pure race.

To this anthropology makes two answers. The first is as to the nature of culture, and the second is as to the nature of inheritance. The answer as to the nature of culture takes us back to prehuman societies. There are societies where Nature perpetuates the slightest mode of behaviour by biological mechanisms, but these are societies not of men but of the social insects. The queen ant, removed to a solitary nest, will reproduce each trait of sex behaviour, each detail of the nest. The social insects represent Nature in a mood when she was taking no chances. The pattern of the entire social structure she committed to the ant's instinctive behaviour. There is no greater chance that the social classes of an ant society, or its patterns of agriculture, will be lost by an ant's isolation from its group than that the ant will fail to reproduce the shape of its antennae or the structure of its abdomen.

For better or for worse, man's solution lies at the opposite pole. Not one item of his tribal social organization, of his language, of his local religion, is carried in his germ cell. In Europe, in other centuries, when children were occasionally found who had been abandoned and had maintained themselves in forests apart from other human beings, they were all so much alike that Linnaeus classified them as a distinct species, *Homo ferus,* and supposed that they were a kind of gnome that man seldom ran across. He could not conceive that these half-witted brutes were born human, these creatures with no interest in what went on about them, rocking themselves rhythmically back and forth like some wild animal in a zoo, with organs of speech and hearing that could hardly be trained to do service, who withstood freezing weather in rags and plucked potatoes out of boiling water without discomfort. There is no doubt, of course, that they were children abandoned in infancy, and what they had all of them lacked was association with their kind, through which alone man's faculties are sharpened and given form.

We do not come across wild children in our more humane civilization. But the point is made as clearly in any case of adoption of an infant into another race and culture. An Oriental child adopted by an Occidental family learns English, shows toward its foster parents the attitudes current among the children he plays with, and grows up to the same professions that they elect. He learns the entire set of the cultural traits of the adopted society, and the set of his real parents' group plays no part. The same process happens on a grand scale when entire peoples in a couple of generations shake off their traditional culture and put on the customs of an alien group. The culture of the American Negro in northern cities has come to approximate in detail that of the whites in the same cities. A few years ago, when a cultural survey was made of Harlem, one of the traits peculiar to the Negroes was their fashion of gambling on the last three unit figures of the next day's stock turnover. At least it cost less than the whites' corresponding predilection for gambling in the stocks themselves and was no less uncertain and exciting. It was a variation on the white pattern, though hardly a great departure. And most Harlem traits keep still closer to the forms that are current in white groups.

All over the world, since the beginning of human history, it can be shown that peoples have been able to adopt the culture of peoples of another blood. There is nothing in the biological structure of man that makes it even difficult. Man is not committed in detail by his biological constitution to any particular variety of behaviour. The great diversity of social solutions that man has worked out in different cultures in regard to mating, for example, or trade, are all equally possible on the basis of his original endowment. Culture is not a biologically transmitted complex.

What is lost in Nature's guaranty of safety is made up in the advantage of greater plasticity. The human animal does not, like the bear, grow himself a polar coat in order to adapt himself, after many generations, to the Arctic. He learns to sew himself a coat and put up a snow house. From all we can learn of the history of intelligence in prehuman as well as human societies, this plasticity has been the soil in which human progress began and in which it has maintained itself. In the ages of the mammoths, species after species without plasticity arose, overreached itself, and died out, undone by the development of the very traits it had biologically produced in order to cope with its environment. The beasts of prey and finally the higher apes came slowly to rely upon other than biological adaptations, and upon the consequent increased plasticity the foundations were laid, bit by bit, for the development of intelligence. Perhaps, as is often suggested, man will destroy himself by this very development of intelligence. But no one has suggested any means by which we can return to the biological mechanisms of the social insect, and we are left no alternative. The human cultural heritage, for better or for worse, is not biologically transmitted.

The corollary in modern politics is that there is no basis for the argument that we can trust our spiritual and cultural achievements to any selected hereditary germ plasms. In our Western civilization, leadership has passed successively in different periods to the Semitic-speaking peoples, to the Hamitic, to the Mediterranean sub-group of the white race, and lately to the Nordic. There is no doubt about the cultural continuity of the civilization, no matter who its carriers were at the moment. We must accept all the implications of our human inheritance, one of the most important of which is the small scope of biologically transmitted behaviour, and the enormous rôle of the cultural process of the transmission of tradition.

The second answer anthropology makes to the argument of the racial purist concerns the nature of heredity. The racial purist is the victim of a mythology. For what is "racial inheritance"? We know roughly what heredity is from father to son. Within a family line the importance of heredity is tremendous. But heredity is an affair of family lines. Beyond that it is mythology. In small and static communities like an isolated Eskimo village, "racial" heredity and the heredity of child and parent are practically equivalent, and racial heredity therefore has meaning. But as a concept applied to groups distributed over a wide area, let us say, to Nordics, it has no basis in reality. In the first place, in all Nordic nations there are family lines which are represented also in Alpine or Mediterranean communities. Any analysis of the physical make-up of a European population shows overlapping: the dark-eyed, dark-haired Swede represents family lines that are more concentrated farther south, but he is to be understood in relation to what we know of these latter groups. His heredity, so far as it has any physical reality, is a matter of his family line, which is not confined to Sweden. We do not know how far physical types may vary without intermixture. We know that inbreeding brings about a local type. But this is a situation that in our cosmopolitan white civilization hardly exists, and when "racial heredity" is invoked, as it usually is, to rally a group of persons of about the same economic status, graduating from much the same schools, and reading the same weeklies, such a category is merely another version of the in- and the out-group and does not refer to the actual biological homogeneity of the group.

What really binds men together is their culture—the ideas and the standards they have in common. If instead of selecting a symbol like common blood heredity and making a slogan of it, the nation turned its attention rather to the culture that unites its people, emphasizing its major merits and recognizing the different values which may develop in a different culture, it would substitute realistic thinking for a kind of symbolism which is dangerous because it is misleading.

A knowledge of cultural forms is necessary in social thinking, and the present volume is concerned with this problem of culture. As we have just seen, bodily form, or race, is separable from culture, and can for our purposes be laid to one side except at certain points where for some special reason it becomes relevant. The chief requirement for a discussion of culture is that it should be based on a wide selection of possible cultural forms. It is only by means of such facts that we can possibly differentiate between those human adjustments that are culturally conditioned and those that are common and, so far as we can see, inevitable in mankind. We cannot discover by introspection or by observation of any one society what behaviour is "instinctive," that is, organically determined. In order to class any behaviour as instinctive, much more is necessary than that it should be proved to be automatic. The conditioned response is as automatic as the organically determined, and culturally conditioned responses make up the greater part of our huge equipment of automatic behaviour.

Therefore the most illuminating material for a discussion of cultural forms and processes is that of societies historically as little related as possible to our own and to one another. With the vast network of historical contact which has spread the great civilizations over tremendous areas, primitive cultures are now the one source to which we can turn. They are a laboratory in which we may study the diversity of human institutions. With their comparative isolation, many primitive regions have had centuries in which to elaborate the cultural themes they have made their own. They provide ready to our hand the necessary information concerning the possible great variations in human adjustments, and a critical examination of them is essential for any understanding of cultural processes. It is the only laboratory of social forms that we have or shall have. . . .

Such a bird's-eye survey of human cultural forms makes clear several common misconceptions. In the first place, the institutions that human cultures build up upon the hints presented by the environment or by man's physical necessities do not keep as close to the original impulse as we easily imagine. These hints are, in reality, mere rough sketches, a list of bare facts. They are pin-point potentialities, and the elaboration that takes place around them is dictated by many alien considerations. Warfare is not the expression of the instinct of pugnacity. Man's pugnacity is so small a hint in the human equipment that it may not be given any expression in inter-tribal relations. When it is institutionalized, the form it takes follows other grooves of thought than those implied in the original impulse. Pugnacity is no more than the touch to the ball of custom, a touch also that may be withheld.

Such a view of cultural processes calls for a recasting of many of our current arguments upholding our traditional institutions. These arguments are usually based on the impossibility of man's functioning without these particular traditional forms. Even very special traits come in for this kind of validation, such as the particular form of economic drive that arises under our particular system of property ownership. This is a remarkably special motivation and there are evidences that even in our generation it is being strongly modified. At any rate, we do not have to confuse the issue by discussing it as if it were a matter of biological survival values. Self-support is a motive our civilization has capitalized. If our economic structure changes so that this motive is no longer so potent a drive as it was in the era of the great frontier and expanding industrialism, there are many other motives that would be appropriate to a changed economic organization. Every culture, every era, exploits some few out of a great number of possibilities. Changes may be very disquieting, and involve great losses, but this is due to the difficulty of change itself, not to the fact that our age and country has hit upon the one possible motivation under which human life can be conducted. Change, we must remember, with all its difficulties, is inescapable. Our fears over even very minor shifts in custom are usually quite beside the point. Civilizations might change far more radically than any human authority has ever had the will or the imagination to change them, and still be completely workable. The minor changes that occasion so much denunciation today, such as the increase of divorce, the growing secularization in our cities, the prevalence of the petting party, and many more, could be taken up quite readily into a slightly different pattern of culture. Becoming traditional, they would be given the same richness of content, the same importance and value, that the older patterns had in other generations.

The truth of the matter is rather that the possible human institutions and motives are legion, on every plane of cultural simplicity or complexity, and that wisdom consists in a greatly increased tolerance toward their divergencies. No man can thoroughly participate in any culture unless he has been brought up and has lived according to its forms, but he can grant to other cultures the same significance to their participants which he recognizes in his own.

selection 3
*Culture and Personality**

Victor Barnouw

Culture-and-personality is an area of research where anthropology and psychology come together—more particularly where the fields of cultural and social anthropology relate to the psychology of personality. Ethnologists, or cultural anthropologists, are students of culture—of the different ways of living that have developed in human societies in different parts of the world, while psychiatrists and (at least some) psychologists are analysts of human personality whose work involves an effort to understand why and how individuals differ from one another as they do. The work of the early anthropologists had little to do with personality, and it is only in recent years that psychiatrists and personality-psychologists have concerned themselves much with culture. But obviously the two are closely related. Culture-and-personality is the area of research concerned with this mutual relationship. . . .[1]

An initial difficulty is that the terms "culture" and "personality," which give the field its name, are hard to define in clear-cut unambiguous fashion. Both are associated in popular usage with older colloquial meanings which differ from those given in social science literature. ("He has a lot of culture," we might say, "but she's the one with the personality.") We must first consider these two terms in some detail.

THE DEFINITION OF CULTURE

E. B. Tylor, in 1871, was the first to use the word "culture" in English in the sense now accepted by anthropologists and sociologists.[2] Following the lead of

---

*From *Culture and Personality* (The Dorsey Press, Inc., 1963), pp. 3–17, 20–26.

1 Kluckhohn and Murray have expressed some dissatisfaction with the phrase "culture and personality," partly because of the dualism implied by it. They feel that "culture *in* personality" or "personality *in* culture" would serve as better conceptual models. The usual phrase ignores other determinants of personality beside culture. " 'Culture and personality' is as lopsided as 'biology and personality.' " (Clyde Kluckhohn and Henry A. Murray, *Personality in Nature, Society, and Culture* [New York: Alfred A. Knopf, 1948], p. 44.) Francis L. K. Hsu has suggested the term "psychological anthropology" to designate this field. The word "psychoethnography" has also been used, i.e., as a book review heading in the *American Anthropologist.* However, the most usual designation continues to be "culture and personality." I prefer to hyphenate this phrase to emphasize its unity.

2 A. L. Kroeber and Clyde Kluckhohn, "Culture: A Critical Review of Concepts and Definitions," *Papers of the Peabody Museum of American Archeology and Ethnology,* Vol. 47, No. 1 (Cambridge, Mass.: Harvard University Press, 1952), p. 9.

some German writers who used *Kultur* in this sense, he named his pioneer work *Primitive Culture* and defined the term on page one as "that complex whole which includes knowledge, belief, art, law, morals, custom, and any other capabilities and habits acquired by man as a member of society."[3]

This may be called an omnibus or sum-total definition, in that it lumps together a number of different categories which serve to make up the term defined. One weakness of such a definition is that it omits the element of integration found in every culture, although that is hinted at in the phrase "complex whole." Another weakness is that the list of categories cannot be complete. However, Tylor's definition was an important achievement in its time, for it set forth the subject matter of the then new science of cultural anthropology.

Under this view, culture could be studied as a sphere apart from psychology or biology, because cultural phenomena were believed to have their own laws.

Years later, Ralph Linton offered a definition of culture which stressed the factor of integration: "A culture is the configuration of learned behavior and results of behavior whose component elements are shared and transmitted by the members of a particular society."[4] Here some might object to the inclusion of "results of behavior" in the definition, for opinions are divided as to whether objects—"material culture," so called—are to be regarded as culture.[5] Note that Linton has defined *a* culture and not culture in general. The broader term is useful in clarifying how man's behavior differs from that of other animals, which do not have a language and which cannot, therefore, transmit culture in the human sense. But anthropologists more frequently speak of particular cultures— of "Blackfoot culture," for example, meaning the way of life characteristic of the Blackfoot Indians of Montana in the early nineteenth century.

Here is a definition which I think most anthropologists would accept: *A culture is the way of life of a group of people, the configuration of all of the more or less stereotyped patterns of learned behavior which are handed down from one generation to the next through the means of language and imitation.* The nub of this definition is the first clause: "the way of life of a group of people." This way of life has some integration and cohesion to it—hence the term "configuration." It consists of patterns of learned behavior which are transmitted through language and imitation—not through instinct or any direct action of the genes. These patterns are only relatively fixed. For example, in our culture it has long been the custom for men to wear trousers and women to wear skirts. But this pattern is amenable to change and is only "more or less"

---

[3] Edward B. Tylor, *Primitive Culture. Researches into the Development of Mythology, Philosophy, Religion, Language, Art, and Customs* (New York: Henry Holt & Co., 1877), Vol. 1, p. 1.

[4] Ralph Linton, *The Cultural Background of Personality* (New York: Appleton-Century Co., 1945), p. 32.

[5] For statements by those who oppose including "material culture," see E. A. Hoebel, "The Nature of Culture," in Harry L. Shapiro (ed.), *Man, Culture and Society* (New York: Oxford University Press, 1956), p. 176; Walter W. Taylor, *A Study of Archeology* (American Anthropological Association Memoir No. 69, 1948), pp. 98–102; and Ralph L. Beals and Harry Hoijer, *An Introduction to Anthropology* (New York: Macmillan Co., 1961), p. 229.

stereotyped; for women often wear slacks nowadays, and some Scotsmen wear kilts. Culture, then, is marked by plasticity and change; although some societies have gone through centuries, even millennia, with very little change.

The culture of a society provides a number of ready-made answers to the problems of life. The child learns these as he grows up and comes to see the world through the particular spectacles of his culture. The culture provides him with means for coping with the world; mastery of these methods increases his sense of confidence. The culture also has a body of doctrines about the world—religious traditions and folklore—which give some orientation and reassurance to the individual. But the culture may also provide threatening influences such as beliefs in evil spirits, malevolent gods, sorcery, and so forth, which may structure a view of the world as dangerous.

From a logical point of view, it is surprising how seldom people come to question the tenets of the culture into which they are born. But usually they do not have the perspective to do so. In some ways cultural behavior is like that of persons under posthypnotic suggestion, who perform actions without realizing why they do so. Man would be lost without his culture—hardly different from the apes. But while he gains so much from culture, man is also brainwashed, to some extent, by the culture to which he is exposed from birth. Equipped with a collection of stereotypes with which to face the world, man is apt to lose sight of possible alternative modes of behavior and understanding.

THE DEFINITION OF PERSONALITY

The definition of "personality" is an even more vexed question than that of culture, and there are many types of definition to choose from.[6] For example, there are omnibus definitions, like this one from Morton Prince: "*Personality* is the sum-total of all the biological innate dispositions, impulses, tendencies, appetites, and instincts of the individual, and the acquired dispositions and tendencies—*acquired* by experience."[7]

Such definitions are open to the same objection as is Tylor's definition of culture—the omission of an element of integration. Another type of definition puts the emphasis on just this factor—the integrative nature of personality, which gives some consistency to the behavior of the individual. Allport's definition may be cited as an example: "Personality is the dynamic organization within the individual of those psychophysical systems that determine his unique adjustments to his environment."[8]

Not all psychologists would accept such a definition. Those influenced by positivistic and behaviorist traditions might regard it as an unwarranted reification or even as an effort to reintroduce soul or psyche into psychology. Avoiding

---

[6] For a brief history of this term, from its beginnings in the Greek word *persona*, meaning mask, see Gordon W. Allport, *Personality, A Psychological Interpretation* (New York: Henry Holt & Co., 1937).

[7] Morton Prince, *The Unconscious* (rev. ed.; New York: Macmillan Co., 1929), p. 532.

[8] Allport, *op. cit.*, p. 48.

such dangers, Watson refers to personality as "the sum of activities that can be discovered by actual observation over a long enough period of time to give reliable information,"[9] while, for McClelland, personality is "the most adequate conceptualization of a person's behavior in all its detail that the scientist can give at a moment of time."[10]

Parallel problems appear in defining "culture" and "personality." As we have seen, each term has been given "sum-total" definitions and also definitions which emphasize configuration or integration. For both terms, some definitions include and some exclude behavior. McClelland's definition, which stresses that personality is an abstraction in the mind of the scientist, has its counterpart in Osgood's definition of culture: "Culture consists of all ideas of the manufactures, behavior, and ideas of the aggregate of human beings which have been directly observed or communicated to one's mind and of which one is conscious."[11]

One's definition of culture or personality, then, evidently reflects one's central assumptions. A behaviorist's definition of personality will differ from a psychoanalyst's. American academic psychology has been much influenced by the behaviorist viewpoint. However, the American anthropologists who have done the most research in culture-and-personality have, for better or worse, been influenced more by psychological and psychiatric schools of European origin, such as the Gestalt and psychoanalytic schools; and they have tended, at least implicitly, to accept a view of personality which stresses its integrative, configurational character. I think that they have also tended to think of personality as something which influences behavior, rather than equating it with behavior itself.

A statement about personality with which I agree, though with some reservations, is one given by the authors of *The Authoritarian Personality:* ". . . personality is a more or less enduring organization of forces within the individual. These persisting forces of personality help to determine response in various situations, and it is thus largely to them that consistency of behavior—whether verbal or physical is attributable. But behavior, however consistent, is not the same thing as personality; personality lies *behind* behavior and *within* the individual. The forces of personality are not responses but *readinesses for response. . . .*"[12]

An objection that can be raised here is that consistency of behavior might be ascribed to culture or to the social role of the individual, rather than to personality. Consistency of verbal behavior, if we mean speaking English or Chinese, is certainly a matter of culture, not of personality. Consistency of physical behavior (sitting on chairs in our culture, or squatting in a primitive tribe) may also be more readily ascribed to culture. If a man is consistent in going to work

9 John B. Watson, *Behaviorism* (rev. ed.; New York: W. W. Norton & Co., Inc., 1930). Italics in original.

10 D. C. McClelland, *Personality* (William Sloan Associates, 1951), p. 69.

11 Cornelius Osgood, "Culture, Its Empirical and Non-Empirical Character," *Southwestern Journal of Anthropology,* Vol. 7 (1951), p. 208. Italics in original.

12 T. W. Adorno, Else Frenkel-Brunswik, D. J. Levinson, and R. Nevitt Sanford, *The Authoritarian Personality* (New York: Harper & Bros., 1950), p. 5. Italics as in the original.

every morning at a certain hour by subway and returning home at a predictable time in late afternoon, this consistency is the product of a particular sociocultural system and the man's role within it, although the performance of this dull routine may well require a particular kind of personality organization. But this is not what the author of the statement in *The Authoritarian Personality* had in mind.

With the reservations noted, their view of personality is one which I share. Moreover, I believe that part of the consistency inherent in personality relates to the acquisition of values and attitudes by the individual. The analysis of a Thematic Apperception Test, for example, or of a life history document, brings to light the characteristic attitudes and values of the subject, and it is assumed that there is some degree of stability in these patterns. Personality is also characterized by certain patterns of perception and cognition, as may be manifest in a subject's Rorschach protocol. In modifying the statement in *The Authoritarian Personality*, let me conclude with this suggested definition: *Personality is a more or less enduring organization of forces within the individual associated with a complex of fairly consistent attitudes, values, and modes of perception which account, in part, for the individual's consistency of behavior.*

CONSISTENCY IN PERSONALITY

Those who hold a view of personality along some such lines as these are apt to see everything that a person does, or the way in which he does it, as expressive of his personality to some degree. Experiments have shown that individuals have characteristic and consistent patterns of walking, gesturing, and even of sleeping. We recognize that our friends have certain predictable styles of behavior and modes of expression—something well illustrated by the works of composers and painters. A music lover may correctly identify a piece of music as being by Mozart even if he hasn't heard that particular piece before, just as one can recognize a painting as the work of Rembrandt or van Gogh, or a passage of prose as being by Hemingway or Henry James on the basis of style. But is there a general consistency in such matters as posture, gait, vocal expression, and so forth? That is to say, did Mozart, for example, have a particularly Mozartian way of walking or writing? Did Hemingway put out a cigarette very differently from Henry James, and would that way of putting it out express something of the writer's inner nature?

Werner Wolff has approached this sort of problem through some ingenious matching experiments. He showed a group of twenty subjects three specimens of musical notations, one by Bach, one by Beethoven, and one by Mozart; and asked them to guess which musician wrote which. Sixteen of the subjects made correct matchings, the four mistakes being made with the samples of Mozart and Bach.[13] While this experiment turned out successfully, it raises some questions.

---

[13] Werner Wolff, *The Expression of Personality. Experimental Depth Psychology* (New York: Harper & Bros., 1943), pp. 20–21.

One wonders if Beethoven in his earlier years, when his music was more like Mozart's, had a more Mozartian calligraphy and style of writing notations? And did Mozart, in his later years, when his music became more like Beethoven's, write in a more Beethovenish handwriting? Such second thoughts show how intricately culture and personality are interrelated. A particular literary or musical style may come to be imitated by people of very different personality characteristics. Yet, as one may see in the impressionist school of painting (or any other), individual differences still persist. All the children in a particular class may have learned how to write from the same teacher; nevertheless, each soon develops idiosyncratic peculiarities of style, a characteristic handwriting, which friends and relatives can recognize at once. . . .

. . . If one can speak of a hierarchy of realities, I would say that personality is more "real" than culture. Personalities existed before culture came into being. Our earliest hominid forebears had personalities before speech or the use of tools were developed. But while personality in the distant past must have existed without culture, culture can only be mediated through individual personalities. The reality of personality is indicated by the difficulty which psychotherapists encounter when they try to bring about character changes in their patients. It must be admitted that there is something tough and consistent about personality.

INTERNAL PERSONALITY CONFLICTS

To affirm that personality is characterized by consistency is not to deny that a personality may have its internal conflicts and inconsistencies. A man given to swagger and boastfulness is not necessarily a person with a deep sense of confidence in himself; perhaps quite the contrary. A boy who feels himself to be physically inferior may develop overcompensating tendencies and "act tough"; but inconsistencies of this sort are not basic. Such a mechanism may be seen as part of the total personality. There are also apparent inconsistencies stemming from situational conditions of status and role; a boy may behave differently with his parents than with his friends at school. But the playing of different roles does not negate an underlying consistency of personality. We must grant that personality may change over time. Despite much carry-over, the adult is a different person from the child. Gordon Allport, who has done so much to demonstrate the consistency of personality, has also emphasized the "functional autonomy" of adult life. According to him, adult motives may grow out of antecedent childhood systems, but are functionally independent of them.[14] Thus, there are both consistency and change in personality, just as there are both consistency and change in culture.

Most of the foregoing discussion has emphasized the uniqueness of the individual personality. We turn now to the question of whether there may be similarities in personality characteristics among people sharing the same culture.

-----
[14] Gordon W. Allport, *Personality, A Psychological Interpretation* (New York: Henry Holt & Co., 1937), p. 194.

It is this notion which underlies such concepts as "basic personality structure" and "national character." Do Hopi Indians, for example, have some personality traits in common, and do they differ from the Navaho in these respects? Further, if there are differences in personality patterns in these two groups, what has brought them about? What are the significant determinants affecting personality in these societies? It is with problems of this sort that the field of culture-and-personality is concerned.

THE AYMARA INDIANS

Let us consider, for a moment, a particular group of people—the Aymara Indians of Bolivia and Peru, who live in the Andes mountains around Lake Titicaca. A number of anthropologists and travelers have visited and described these highlanders—David Forbes in the mid-nineteenth century; E. G. Squier and Adolf Bandelier, two early American anthropologists; and, more recently, Edgar L. Hewett, Weston LaBarre, and Harry Tschopik. All of these writers, and others as well, have described the Aymara in very similar terms. From their accounts we get a general picture of these Indians as being submissive, gloomy, anxious and mistrustful, dirty and slovenly in personal habits, quarrelsome and capable of cruelty and malice. The Aymara seem to have little in the way of aesthetic interests; and Tschopik has characterized them as "utilitarian," meaning by this that they stress the useful and practical, although the term does not imply any special resourcefulness or ingenuity on their part.[15] Tschopik tells that the Aymara, brought up to be submissive to authority, are reluctant to assume leadership. Hostility is suppressed or repressed among them, but may break through in drunken acts of violence.[16] Above all, in Tschopik's view, the Aymara are an anxious people:

> . . . among the Aymara anxiety is so general and intense, so ever-present and all-pervading, that it has left its particular mark on virtually every individual and has colored the entire fabric of the culture. . . . Anxiety is, in fact, the keystone of Aymara "modal" personality, the central principle in terms of which other personality characteristics become intelligible. . . . Diffuse anxiety is revealed by their pessimistic outlook as well as by fits of depression and gloom for which they have a name. In addition, flight from anxiety is indicated by the inordinate use of alcohol and coca. On the cultural level the presence of anxiety is reflected in the elaborate pharmacopoeia, the vast number of omens, most of them boding ill, and the proliferation of divinatory techniques.[17]

If only one writer had described the Aymara in these terms, one might suspect exaggeration in this picture—at least some degree of personal projection

---

[15] Harry Tschopik, Jr., *The Aymara of Chucuito, Peru: I. Magic* (Anthropological Papers of the American Museum of Natural History, Vol. 44, Part 2) (1951), p. 185. For quotations about the Aymara by the above-mentioned writers and others, see Tschopik, *ibid.*, pp. 172–73; and Weston LaBarre, *The Aymara Indians of the Lake Titicaca Plateau, Bolivia* (Memoir of the American Anthropological Association, No. 68) (1948), p. 39.

[16] Tschopik, *op. cit.,* pp. 182–83.

[17] *Ibid.,* p. 174.

or subjectivity. But all the published accounts, while differently expressed, re-flect the same state of affairs—and one apparently persisting over a period of time. The picture would no doubt be strengthened if some cross-checking devices had been employed—for example, projective tests like the Rorschach and Thematic Apperception Test, and the documentation of life histories. But even lacking these, the descriptions by various writers present such a consistent consensus that it is hard not to concede that the Aymara must be much as Tschopik, LaBarre, and others have described them. We need not assume that *all* Aymara have the traits mentioned, or in the same degree; there may well be many to whom the description does not apply. But as a group picture it prob-ably has much validity.

Thinking about the Aymara, then, in these terms, one can't help but wonder why they have come to be such anxious, unhappy people. A number of possible reasons—indeed, a whole battery of them—appear in the accounts of Tschopik and LaBarre. There is first the matter of adjustment to high altitudes. *Sorroche* is a native term for high altitude sickness, brought about by lack of oxygen. Among the symptoms are headache, nausea, a sense of oppression and fatigue, and sometimes even temporary psychosis. Commercial pilots who are often exposed to anoxemia are said to suffer from grouchiness, as an almost standard occupational disease.[18] Perhaps, then, high altitude is one of the contributing factors to the Aymara personality picture.

We learn from LaBarre that intoxication at high altitudes has more drastic effects than at sea level, and that "The Aymara are a notoriously drunken group. . . . All travellers have remarked on the quantities of alcohol the Aymara can consume, and the states of intoxication to which they can attain, and I can only confirm that I have never anywhere seen American Indians more thor-oughly intoxicated than at the usual Aymara fiesta."[19] Alcohol, then, must be another contributory factor, as well as being an indicator of the degree of anxiety among the Aymara.

In addition to liquor, the Aymara are widely addicted to the chewing of coca, from which the narcotic cocaine is derived. Frequent coca chewing, as medical experiments have shown, may lead to pallor and muscular weakness. Gutierrez and von Hagen state that ". . . coca chewers present emotional dullness or apathy, indifference, lack of will power, and low capacity for attention. They are mistrustful, shy, unsociable, and indecisive."[20] Perhaps, then, this is the source, or one of the sources, of the observed Aymara traits.

Moreover, we learn from Tschopik that the houses of these highlanders give poor protection. They are crowded, unheated, dirty, and unhygienic. Their clothing is inadequate too, and men often walk without sandals in subfreezing weather. The children are poorly clad. According to a medical survey in Ichu,

---

18 LaBarre, *op. cit.*, p. 174.
19 *Ibid.*, pp. 48, 65.
20 Quoted by Tschopik, *op. cit.*, p. 187.

the diet of at least some Aymara groups is inadequate—low in fats, vitamins A and C, iron, and calcium, and energy-producing foods.[21]

Little wonder that there is a good deal of sickness, especially respiratory and heart ailments, but also skin diseases, smallpox, scarlet fever, typhus, and venereal disease, among others. The Aymara, indeed, are said to have the highest infant mortality rate in the New World—one in seven during the first year.[22]

High altitude, excessive drinking and coca chewing, combined with unsanitary homes, inadequate clothing, poor diet, and much sickness—is there any wonder that the Aymara are unhappy? Yet these are not the only factors that may be responsible for their alleged character traits. There is also the historical background of these people and their social relationships with the Mestizos toward whom they play a submissive role.

During the Spanish colonial period, the Aymara were made to work in the mines at forced labor. The Spaniards treated them brutally, and it has been estimated that eight million natives, the majority of them Aymara, died during this time.[23] The Aymara rebelled repeatedly, but with little success, and they have remained in a subordinate position for the past five centuries. Their present overlords, the Mestizos, now command all the important political offices, own the best farm lands and better houses, and are, in general, much better off than the Aymara, who tip their hats submissively to the Mestizos as they pass, and who kiss the hands or garments of the Mestizos in gratitude for favors conferred.[24]

Among the Aymara, to consider another aspect, there is a growing shortage of land. Ideally, members of an extended family are expected to cooperate with one another, but the land shortage leads to individualistic self-assertive behavior and to conflicts within the extended family. According to Tschopik, this results in more uneasiness and anxiety. Moreover, there is a good deal of tension within the average family. Marriages are unstable, infidelity and divorce common. The children born to such families are given relatively little affection.[25]

There are, then, a multitude of possible causes for the alleged character traits of the Aymara—climatic, toxicological, historical, and sociological. We might say that Aymara personality has been overdetermined. A number of factors have driven it, so to speak, in the same direction, so that we have as end-product the anxious, submissive and gloomy Aymara character with its repressed rage and its obsession with magic and divination.

Further reflection about this general picture leads to another question. Granted that all the factors cited have played a role in the shaping of Aymara personality, have they all been equally important? Have not some exerted a more telling influence than others? How could we weigh their relative importance?

How significant, for example, is the factor of high altitude? If the Aymara

---

21 *Ibid.*, pp. 157–58.
22 LaBarre, *op. cit.*, pp. 47, 126.
23 *Ibid.*, p. 31.
24 Tschopik, *op. cit.*, p. 159.
25 *Ibid.*, pp. 162–63.

lived at lower levels, would they be different? Are all mountaineers and high-landers anxious and grouchy? We have no intensive personality study of the Nepalese or Tibetans, but judging from the accounts of travelers, the high-dwelling Himalayan peoples seem to be quite different from the Aymara, often being pictured as cheerful, cooperative, and self-reliant. For example, C. J. Morris has written:

> The most striking element in the character of the Gurkhas [Nepalese] is their unfailing cheerfulness even in the most adverse circumstances; and this, more perhaps than any other single factor, distinguishes them so markedly from the peoples of India proper. This essential difference is very apparent to the foreign traveller who has the good fortune to be allowed to enter Nepal. There is at once a sense of something utterly different, but a sense so subtle that it is difficult to define in *words*. I think it is due to this pervading cheerfulness of the people more than to anything else; they are happy and contented—on good terms with life—and the stranger who is prepared to accept them as they are cannot help but feel the same. Their sense of humor and especially of the ridiculous is highly developed, and no Gurkha can remain for long without a joke, even though it be against himself.[26]

Yet some Nepalese live at even higher levels than the Aymara. Moreover, both LaBarre and Tschopik claim that the depressing personality picture of the Aymara which they present applies more specifically to the Aymara of towns and haciendas than to the more independent Indians who live in *ayllus*, the traditional social units of the highland region.[27] This is not a difference in alti-tude, but in the texture of social life. Social and cultural factors may therefore be the more important determinants in this respect. . . .

CHILDHOOD DETERMINISM

Under this heading may be grouped those approaches which consider person-ality to be largely fixed by the age of five or six, as the result of experiences undergone during the early years of life. Although the Freudians stress the biological basis for developments in this period, it would seem appropriate to classify them here. According to this school of thought, weaning, toilet training, and sexual disciplines significantly affect the personality of a growing child, and the Oedipus complex, the "primal scene" (the child's witnessing of its parents' intercourse), and real or imagined castration threats may establish attitudes and reactions of lifelong importance. Later influences on the individual, such as status and occupation, are seen as playing only a relatively minor role in the shaping of personality.

From a Freudian point of view a sociable disposition would not be accounted for by an individual's plump constitution (if he has one). Rather, such patterns would be traced to the "oral optimism" established in the subject's infancy through adequate suckling and maternal care. The reserved, cold individual, on the other hand, might be seen as an "anal pessimist" whose toilet training was

---

26 Charles John Morris, "Some Aspects of Social Life in Nepal," *Journal of the Royal Central Asian Society*, Vol. 22 (1935), p. 437. See also Ella Maillart, *The Land of the Sherpas* (London: Hodder & Stoughton, 1955), p. 12.

27 LaBarre, *op. cit.*, pp. 39, 40, 156; Tschopik, *op. cit.*, p. 173.

too rigid. Character attitudes, according to Freud, represent compromises between instinctual impulses and the controlling forces of the ego.[28] "The permanent character traits," he wrote, "are either unchanged perpetuations of the original impulses, sublimations of them, or reaction formations against them."[29]

Freud believed that the individual passes through certain stages of libido development: oral, anal, and genital. If he meets with sufficient frustration at some point in this development, he may regress to an earlier level, thus becoming neurotic or psychotic. The type of neurosis or psychosis would be determined, not by constitutional type, but by the strength and nature of the frustration met with and the degree of security previously known.

Some "criminal" behavior, if not all, may be explained in Freudian terms. For example, Franz Alexander and Hugo Staub have described a type of "neurotic criminal" who compulsively acts out antisocial impulses which stem from an unresolved Oedipus complex. Punishment is no deterrent to criminals of this sort, for they have an unconscious desire for punishment.[30]

Childhood determinist approaches to the study of national character have been made by Geoffrey Gorer and Weston LaBarre, among others. . . .

The Freudians are not the only childhood determinists. A number of writers have drawn attention to the importance of early mother–child relationships and to the damaging consequences of early maternal separation for the development of personality.[31] Some of these reports may, however, have been too alarmist. A recent study reports that "statements implying that children who experience institutionalization and similar forms of severe privation and deprivation in early life *commonly* develop psychopathic or affectionless characters are incorrect."[32] Other recent studies have reached similar conclusions.[33]

At the other extreme from maternal deprivation, David M. Levy has discussed the damaging consequences of maternal overprotection, which may also have lasting effects upon personality.[34]

---

[28] Otto Fenichel, *The Psychoanalytic Theory of Neurosis* (New York: W. W. Norton & Co., Inc., 1945), p. 470.

[29] S. Freud, *Character and Anal Erotism* (Collected Papers, II) (London: The Hogarth Press, 1950), p. 50.

[30] Franz Alexander and Hugo Staub, *The Criminal, the Judge, and the Public; A Psychological Analysis*, trans. from the German by Gregory Zilboorg (New York: Macmillan Co., 1931).

[31] John Bowlby, *Child Care and the Growth of Love*, abridged and edited by Margery Fry (London and Tonbridge: Penguin Books, 1953); Margaret Ribble, *The Rights of Infants: Early Psychological Needs and Their Satisfaction* (New York: Columbia University Press, 1943); Rene A. Spitz, "Hospitalism. An Inquiry into the Genesis of Psychiatric Conditions in Early Childhood," *The Psychoanalytic Study of the Child*, Vol. 1 (New York: International Universities Press, 1945), pp. 53–74; Jenny Roudinesco, "Severe Maternal Deprivation and Personality Development in Early Childhood," *Understanding the Child, A Magazine for Teachers*, 21 (1952), pp. 104–8.

[32] John Bowlby, Mary Ainsworth, Mary Boston, and Dina Rosenbluth, "The Effects of Mother–Child Separation: A Follow-up Study," *British Journal of Medical Psychology*, 29 (1956), p. 242.

[33] Hilda Lewis, *Deprived Children. The Mersham Experiment. A Social and Clinical Study* (London: Oxford University Press, 1954); J. W. B. Douglas and J. M. Blomfield, *Children Under Five* (London: George Allen and Unwin, 1958).

[34] David M. Levy, *Maternal Overprotection* (New York: Columbia University Press, 1943).

THE SITUATIONAL APPROACH

In this group belong those who stress the more immediate contemporary scene in which the individual finds himself—the roles which he has learned to play, his "reference groups," his current interpersonal relationships. Although the individual may have been considerably shaped by past events, he is seen as having a good measure of "functional autonomy," in Allport's words. The neo-Freudians, Fromm and Horney, share this emphasis on the present situation; so do psychologists of the "field theory" school, and many sociologists and anthropologists. In discussing "the culture of poverty," Oscar Lewis has emphasized the conditioning factors of poverty, while David M. Potter has drawn attention to the influence of an economy of abundance upon American national character. Some of the psychological consequences of modern business organization are explored by William H. Whyte, Jr. The writings of Riesman and his associates about the changing American character may, I think, be characterized as "situational."[35] The abundant writings about the American class system by such sociologists as the Lynds and W. L. Warner also embody an implicit situational approach.

Studies of class and caste in the deep South, like those of Dollard and of Davis and the Gardners, emphasize the influence of sociological factors, such as the maintenance of social distance.[36] This approach has also been applied in the study of American Indian groups; Bernard J. James, for example, interprets Ojibwa personality in terms of the "reservation situation" and the nature of the self-image developed by Indians through their contacts with whites.[37]

Some writers have examined the effects that assuming a particular profession may have upon personality. Thus, Willard Waller has discussed what teaching does to teachers, and how experienced teachers differ from those just starting in the profession. Robert K. Merton has dealt with the influence of bureaucratic occupation upon personality, and William E. Henry has delineated the personality characteristics of the successful business executive.[38] In these studies reference is made to relatively late events in the individual's life and to the role of a profession or status in bringing about modification in character.

A boy living in the slums might develop antisocial behavior in somewhat the

---

[35] Oscar Lewis, *The Children of Sanchez. Autobiography of a Mexican Family* (New York: Random House, 1961); David M. Potter, *People of Plenty. Economic Abundance and the American Character* (Chicago: University of Chicago Press, 1954); William H. Whyte, Jr., *The Organization Man* (New York: Doubleday & Co., Inc., 1956); David Riesman, with Nathan Glazer and Reuel Denney, *The Lonely Crowd. A Study of the Changing American Character* (New York: Doubleday & Co., Inc., 1953).

[36] John Dollard, *Caste and Class in a Southern Town* (New York: Harper & Bros., 1949); Allison Davis, Burleigh B. Gardner, and Mary R. Gardner, *Deep South; A Social Anthropological Study of Caste and Class* (Chicago: University of Chicago Press, 1941).

[37] Bernard J. James, "Social-Psychological Dimensions of Ojibwa Acculturation," *American Anthropologist*, 63 (1961), pp. 721–46.

[38] Willard Waller, *The Sociology of Teaching* (New York: John Wiley & Sons, Inc., 1932), pp. 381–436; Robert K. Merton, "Bureaucratic Structure and Personality," *Social Forces*, 18 (1940), pp. 560–68; William E. Henry, "The Business Executive: The Psychodynamics of a Social Role," *American Journal of Sociology*, 54 (1949), pp. 286–91.

same way, through membership in a gang and exposure to its way of life. He comes to accept a criminal "culture," let us say, much as an Eskimo child assumes the patterns of Eskimo culture. We need not assume that there is any inborn criminal streak in him or that he has been maimed by some early childhood trauma.

A situational approach to mental disorders has been made by Robert Faris and H. W. Dunham in their study of Chicago. The authors found that schizophrenic patients in Chicago generally come from the poor rooming-house districts in the center of the city, while patients suffering from manic-depression tend to come from more peripheral and higher-rental residence areas. The authors interpret the high incidence of schizophrenia in central Chicago as being due to the absence of close, rewarding social relationships in the disorganized migrant population. Social isolation, they claim, makes for mental breakdown, although a different kind of etiology is seen in manic-depression.[39] A recent large-scale investigation of the relationship between social class and mental illness in New Haven has been made by A. B. Hollingshead and F. O. Redlich. These authors find a significant relationship between social class and the prevalence and nature of mental disorder. In general, the lower the class, the higher the rate of mental disorder. This is not due to a downward "drift" of the maladjusted, nor to any biological differences between rich and poor.[40]

Another situational factor affecting mental health is migration. Many studies have reported a high incidence of mental disorders for migrants. In some areas rapid culture change seems to be a source of mental disorder. . . .

Some studies have tried to trace the psychological consequences of certain drastic experiences, such as slavery, concentration camp internment, and combat experience.[41] The term "situational" thus covers a wide variety of studies. Most contemporary work in the field of social psychology seems to be of a situational character.

THE CONCEPT OF WORLD VIEW

To the foregoing approaches or sets of assumptions about personality formation—the physiological, the childhood determinist, and the situational—a fourth may be added. This one ascribes an important influence to the values, attitudes, and assumptions about life which are characteristic of the culture into which one is born. As a person grows up, he comes to learn the traditions of his society, its religious concepts, ethical doctrines, and metaphysical assumptions. These may vary a great deal from one society to another. Some culture historians and

---

[39] Robert L. K. Faris and H. Warren Dunham, *Mental Disorders in Urban Areas* (Chicago: University of Chicago Press, 1939).

[40] August B. Hollingshead and Frederick O. Redlich, *Social Class and Mental Illness, A Community Study* (New York: John Wiley & Sons, Inc., 1958).

[41] Stanley Elkins, "Slavery and Personality," in Bert Kaplan (ed.), *Studying Personality Cross-Culturally* (Evanston, Ill.: Row, Peterson & Co., 1961), pp. 243–67; Elie A. Cohen, *Human Behavior in the Concentration Camp* (New York: W. W. Norton & Co., Inc., 1953); Roy Grinker and John Spiegel, *Men Under Stress* (Philadelphia: Blakiston, 1945).

anthropologists have delineated the implicit world views of different cultures—as in Spengler's picture of the "Faustian" view of life of the Western world, Ruth Benedict's of the "Apollonian" character of Pueblo society, A. I. Hallowell's analysis of the "behavioral environment" of the Canadian Ojibwa, and Robert Redfield's discussion of the world view of peasant societies. . . .

The term "ethos" has been used in some studies, notably by Gregory Bateson and John J. Honigmann. The Oxford English Dictionary defines "ethos" as "the characteristic spirit, prevalent tone of sentiment of a people or community, the 'genius' of an institution or system." This concept . . . would seem to cover only part of the concept of world view, which also includes values and conceptions about the nature of things. Some aspects of world view may be inculcated simply through the language spoken by a society's members. Different concepts of space and time, as Benjamin Lee Whorf has argued, may be implicit in different languages. . . .

The concept of world view differs from some of the approaches previously discussed in that it is not usually invoked to account for all aspects of personality. Ruth Benedict, like Margaret Mead, wrote about the deviants in the cultures she described—people who did not altogether accept the traditional viewpoint of the society in which they lived. She claimed a great deal for the moulding force of culture, but not everything. This, I think, has generally been true of those who have discussed "world view," "ethos," and similar concepts.

INTERRELATIONS OF THE DETERMINANTS

The different approaches which have been reviewed—the physiological, the childhood determinist, the situational and that of the world view—are not, of course, mutually exclusive. Hollingshead and Redlich, for instance, suggest some childhood determinist hypotheses in a study which I have labeled "situational,"— that is, that a loveless infancy is more likely to occur in the lowest socio-economic class than in the upper-middle class.[42]

Many combinations are possible. However, it is not my purpose in this book to promote a particular theoretical scheme or school of thought, and there seems to be no reason to rely upon any one of these approaches to the exclusion of the others. One approach may work best in one situation, another in another. Clearly, the sluggish personality traits of a cretin are most readily explained in terms of endocrine deficiency, but a physiological explanation would probably not be the best way to account for the fanaticism of a convinced Nazi.

It is often difficult to assess the relative significance of the various determinants of personality, since they are all constantly at work. A human being is always in a particular situation, but he sees that situation in a manner determined by his past experience. A person's physical makeup and his culture are always with him. Moreover, physiological functions are related in complex ways

---

[42]Hollingshead and Redlich, *op. cit.,* p. 361.

to early social relationships. This has been indicated by Harry Harlow's experiments with rhesus monkeys. Harlow has shown that monkeys deprived of their mothers and raised with surrogate cloth or wire "mothers" fail to develop normal patterns of heterosexual behavior in later years. Females brought up in this way and who have, despite their lack of interest, been impregnated by normal male monkeys, fail to develop maternal feelings toward their offspring.[43]

It is difficult to relate Harlow's findings in any direct way to human beings, since, fortunately, people are never brought up in caged isolation from birth. However, a study by Spitz and Wolf has pointed to differences in auto-erotic behavior among institutionalized infants and infants in homes with good maternal care, there being much more genital self-stimulation in the latter group.[44] Physiological and social determinants of personality seem to be closely interrelated, as may be seen in psychosomatic and hysterical disorders and in the development of a self-concept. One's self-image is compounded partly of one's own bodily consciousness and awareness of one's appearance; it is also influenced by the experiences that one has with other persons and by the attitudes manifested towards oneself.

Although physiological, social, and cultural determinants of personality are closely intermeshed, this book will not deal with the physiological or constitutional aspects of man. The reason for this limitation is that culture-and-personality studies have focused on social and cultural factors rather than on biological ones. There must be limits to any field of investigation. . . .

The field of culture-and-personality has come in for some severe criticism in recent years, much of it well deserved. It is necessary to correct past mistakes and to improve methods of research. Yet, while mistakes have been made, a great deal has been learned as well. The relationship between culture and personality is full of puzzles, but it is marked by regularities too. This is what makes it a suitable and challenging area of research.

---

[43] Harry Harlow, "The Heterosexual Affectional System in Monkeys," *American Psychologist,* Vol. 17 (1962), pp. 1–9.

[44] René A. Spitz and Katherine M. Wolf, "Autoerotism. Some Empirical Findings and Hypotheses on Three of Its Manifestations in the First Year of Life," *The Psychoanalytic Study of the Child* (New York: International Universities Press, 1949), Vols. 3-4, pp. 85-120.

selection 4

*Ideological Preparation: The Wish before the Fact**

Lewis Mumford

During the last thousand years the material basis and the cultural forms of Western Civilization have been profoundly modified by the development of the machine. How did this come about? Where did it take place? What were the chief motives that encouraged this radical transformation of the environment and the routine of life: what were the ends in view; what were the means and methods: what unexpected values have arisen in the process? These are some of the questions that the present study seeks to answer.

While people often call our period the "Machine Age," very few have any perspective on modern technics or any clear notion as to its origins. Popular historians usually date the great transformation in modern industry from Watt's supposed invention of the steam engine; and in the conventional economics textbook the application of automatic machinery to spinning and weaving is often treated as an equally critical turning point. But the fact is that in Western Europe the machine had been developing steadily for at least seven centuries before the dramatic changes that accompanied the "industrial revolution" took place. Men had become mechanical before they perfected complicated machines to express their new bent and interest; and the will-to-order had appeared once more in the monastery and the army and the counting-house before it finally manifested itself in the factory. Behind all the great material inventions of the last century and a half was not merely a long internal development of technics; there was also a change of mind. Before the new industrial processes could take hold on a great scale, a reorientation of wishes, habits, ideas, goals was necessary.

To understand the dominating role played by technics in modern civilization, one must explore in detail the preliminary period of ideological and social preparation. Not merely must one explain the existence of the new mechanical instruments: one must explain the culture that was ready to use them and profit by them so extensively. For note this: mechanization and regimentation are not new phenomena in history: what is new is the fact that these functions have been projected and embodied in organized forms which dominate every aspect of

*Abridged from *Technics and Civilization* by Lewis Mumford, copyright, 1934, by Harcourt, Brace & World, Inc.; renewed 1962, by Lewis Mumford. Reprinted by permission of the publishers.

our existence. Other civilizations reached a high degree of technical proficiency without, apparently, being profoundly influenced by the methods and aims of technics. All the critical instruments of modern technology—the clock, the printing press, the water-mill, the magnetic compass, the loom, the lathe, gunpowder, paper, to say nothing of mathematics and chemistry and mechanics—existed in other cultures. The Chinese, the Arabs, the Greeks, long before the Northern European had taken most of the first steps toward the machine. And although the great engineering works of the Cretans, the Egyptians, and the Romans were carried out mainly on an empirical basis, these peoples plainly had an abundance of technical skill at their command. They had machines; but they did not develop "the machine." It remained for the peoples of Western Europe to carry the physical sciences and the exact arts to a point no other culture had reached, and to adapt the whole mode of life to the pace and the capacities of the machine. How did this happen? How in fact could the machine take possession of European society until that society had, by an inner accommodation, surrendered to the machine?

Plainly, what is usually called *the* industrial revolution, the series of industrial changes that began in the eighteenth century, was a transformation that took place in the course of a much longer march.

· ·

. . . Technics and civilization as a whole are the result of human choices and aptitudes and strivings, deliberate as well as unconscious, often irrational when apparently they are most objective and scientific: but even when they are uncontrollable they are not external. Choice manifests itself in society in small increments and moment-to-moment decisions as well as loud dramatic struggles; and he who does not see his choice in the development of the machine merely betrays his incapacity to observe cumulative effects until they are bunched together so closely that they seem completely external and impersonal. No matter how completely technics relies upon the objective procedures of the sciences, it does not form an independent system, like the universe: it exists as an element in human culture and it promises well or ill as the social groups that exploit it promise well or ill. The machine itself makes no demands and holds out no promises: it is the human spirit that makes demands and keeps promises. In order to reconquer the machine and subdue it to human purposes, one must first understand it and assimilate it. So far, we have embraced the machine without fully understanding it, or, like the weaker romantics, we have rejected the machine without first seeing how much of it we could intelligently assimilate.

· ·

THE MONASTERY AND THE CLOCK

Where did the machine first take form in modern civilization? There was plainly more than one point of origin. Our mechanical civilization represents the convergence of numerous habits, ideas, and modes of living, as well as technical instruments; and some of these were, in the beginning, directly opposed to the civilization they helped to create. But the first manifestation of the new order took place in the general picture of the world: during the first seven centuries of the machine's existence the categories of time and space underwent an extraordinary change, and no aspect of life was left untouched by this transformation. The application of quantitative methods of thought to the study of nature had its first manifestation in the regular measurement of time; and the new mechanical conception of time arose in part out of the routine of the monastery. Alfred Whitehead has emphasized the importance of the scholastic belief in a universe ordered by God as one of the foundations of modern physics; but behind that belief was the presence of order in the institutions of the Church itself.

The technics of the ancient world were still carried on from Constantinople and Baghdad to Sicily and Cordova: hence the early lead taken by Salerno in the scientific and medical advances of the Middle Ages. It was, however, in the monasteries of the West that the desire for order and power, other than that expressed in the military domination of weaker men, first manifested itself after the long uncertainty and bloody confusion that attended the breakdown of the Roman Empire. Within the walls of the monastery was sanctuary: under the rule of the order surprise and doubt and caprice and irregularity were put at bay. Opposed to the erratic fluctuations and pulsations of the worldly life was the iron discipline of the rule. Benedict added a seventh period to the devotions of the day, and in the seventh century, by a bull of Pope Sabinianus, it was decreed that the bells of the monastery be rung seven times in the twenty-four hours. These punctuation marks in the day were known as the canonical hours, and some means of keeping count of them and ensuring their regular repetition became necessary.

According to a now discredited legend, the first modern mechanical clock, worked by falling weights, was invented by the monk named Gerbert who afterwards became Pope Sylvester II near the close of the tenth century. This clock was probably only a water clock, one of those bequests of the ancient world either left over directly from the days of the Romans like the water-wheel itself, or coming back again into the West through the Arabs. But the legend, as so often happens, is accurate in its implications if not in its facts. The monastery was the seat of a regular life, and an instrument for striking the hours at intervals or for reminding the bell-ringer that it was time to strike the bells, was an almost inevitable product of this life. If the mechanical clock did not appear until the cities of the thirteenth century demanded an orderly routine, the habit of order itself and the earnest regulation of time-sequences had become almost second nature in the monastery. Coulton agrees with Sombart in looking upon the Benedictines, the great working order, as perhaps the original founders of modern capitalism: their rule certainly took the curse off work and their vigorous engineering enterprises may even have robbed warfare of some of its glamor. So one is not straining the facts when one suggests that the monasteries—at one time there were 40,000 under the Benedictine rule—helped to give human enterprise the regular collective beat and rhythm of the machine; for the clock is not merely a means of keeping track of the hours, but of synchronizing the actions of men.

Was it by reason of the collective Christian desire to provide for the welfare of souls in eternity by regular prayers and devotions that timekeeping and the habits of temporal order took hold of men's minds: habits that capitalist civilization presently turned to good account? One must perhaps accept the irony of this paradox. At all events, by the thirteenth century there are definite records of mechanical clocks, and by 1370 a well-designed "modern" clock had been built by Heinrich von Wyck at Paris. Meanwhile, bell towers had come into existence, and the new clocks, if they did not have, till the fourteenth century, a dial and a hand that translated the movement of time into a movement through space, at all events struck the hours. The clouds that could paralyze the sundial, the freezing that could stop the water clock on a winter night, were no longer obstacles to timekeeping: summer or winter, day or night, one was aware of the measured clank of the clock. The instrument presently spread outside the monastery; and the regular striking of the bells brought a new regularity into the life of the workman and the merchant. The bells of the clock tower almost defined urban existence. Timekeeping passed into time-serving and time-accounting and time-rationing. As this took place, Eternity ceased gradually to serve as the measure and focus of human actions.

The clock, not the steam-engine, is the key-machine of the modern industrial age. For every phase of its development the clock is both the outstanding fact and the typical symbol of the machine: even today no other machine is so ubiquitous. Here, at the very beginning of modern technics, appeared prophetically the accurate automatic machine which, only after centuries of further effort, was also to prove the final consummation of these technics in every department of industrial activity. There had been power-machines, such as the water-mill, before the clock; and there had also been various kinds of automata, to awaken the wonder of the populace in the temple, or to please the idle fancy of some Moslem caliph: machines one finds illustrated in Hero and Al-Jazari. But here was a new kind of power-machine, in which the source of power and the transmission were of such a nature as to ensure the even flow of energy throughout the works and to make possible regular production and a standardized product. In its relationship to determinable quantities of energy, to standardization, to automatic action, and finally to its own special product, accurate timing, the clock has been the foremost machine in modern technics: and at each period it has remained in the lead: it marks a perfection toward which other machines aspire. The clock, moreover, served as a model for many other kinds of mechanical works, and the analysis of motion that accompanied the perfection of the clock, with the various types of gearing and transmission that were elaborated, contributed to the success of quite different kinds of machine. Smiths could have hammered thousands of suits of armor or thousands of iron cannon, wheelwrights could have shaped thousands of great water-wheels or crude gears, without inventing any of the special types of movement developed in clockwork, and without any of the accuracy of measurement and fineness of articulation that finally produced the accurate eighteenth century chronometer.

The clock, moreover, is a piece of power-machinery whose "product" is seconds and minutes: by its essential nature it dissociated time from human events and helped create the belief in an independent world of mathematically measurable sequences: the special world of science. There is relatively little foundation for this belief in common human experience: throughout the year the days are of uneven duration, and not merely does the relation between day and night steadily change, but a slight journey from East to West alters astronomical time by a certain number of minutes. In terms of the human organism itself, mechanical time is even more foreign: while human life has regularities of its own, the beat of the pulse, the breathing of the lungs, these change from hour to hour with mood and action, and in the longer span of days, time is measured not by the calendar but by the events that occupy it. The shepherd measures from the time the ewes lambed; the farmer measures back to the day of sowing or forward to the harvest; if growth has its own duration and regularities, behind it are not simply matter and motion but the facts of development: in short, history. And while mechanical time is strung out in a succession of mathematically isolated instants, organic time—what Bergson calls duration—is cumulative in its effects. Though mechanical time can, in a sense, be speeded up or run backward, like the hands of a clock or the images of a moving picture, organic time moves in only one direction—through the cycle of birth, growth, development, decay, and death—and the past that is already dead remains present in the future that has still to be born.

Around 1345, according to Thorndike, the division of hours into sixty minutes and of minutes into sixty seconds became common: it was this abstract framework of divided time that became more and more the point of reference for both action and thought, and in the effort to arrive at accuracy in this department, the astronomical exploration of the sky focused attention further upon the regular, implacable movements of the heavenly bodies through space. Early in the sixteenth century a young Nuremberg mechanic, Peter Henlein, is supposed to have created "many-wheeled watches out of small bits of iron" and by the end of the century the small domestic clock had been introduced in England and Holland. As with the motor car and the airplane, the richer classes took over the new mechanism and popularized it: partly because they alone could afford it, partly because the new bourgeoisie were the first to discover that, as Franklin later put it, "time is money." To become "as regular as clockwork" was the bourgeois ideal, and to own a watch was for long a definite symbol of success. The increasing tempo of civilization led to a demand for greater power: and in turn power quickened the tempo.

Now, the orderly punctual life that first took shape in the monasteries is not native to mankind, although by now Western peoples are so thoroughly regimented by the clock that it is "second nature" and they look upon its observance as a fact of nature. Many Eastern civilizations have flourished on a loose basis in time: the Hindus have in fact been so indifferent to time that they lack even an authentic chronology of the years. Only yesterday, in the midst of the industrialization of Soviet Russia, did a society come into existence to further the carrying of watches there and to propagandize the benefits of punctuality. The popularization of timekeeping, which followed the production of the cheap standardized watch, first in Geneva, then in America around the middle of the last century, was essential to a well-articulated system of transportation and production.

To keep time was once a peculiar attribute of music: it gave industrial value to the workshop song or the tattoo or the chantey of the sailors tugging at a rope. But the effect of the mechanical clock is more pervasive and strict: it presides over the day from the hour of rising to the hour of rest. When one thinks of the day as an abstract span of time, one does not go to bed with the chickens on a winter's night: one invents wicks, chimneys, lamps, gaslights, electric lamps, so as to use all the hours belonging to the day. When one thinks of time, not as a sequence of experiences, but as a collection of hours, minutes, and seconds, the habits of adding time and saving time come into existence. Time took on the character of an enclosed space: it could be divided, it could be filled up, it could even be expanded by the invention of labor-saving instruments.

Abstract time became the new medium of existence. Organic functions themselves were regulated by it: one ate, not upon feeling hungry, but when prompted by the clock; one slept, not when one was tired, but when the clock sanctioned it. A generalized time-consciousness accompanied the wider use of clocks: dissociating time from organic sequences, it became easier for the men of the Renascence to indulge the fantasy of reviving the classic past or of reliving the splendors of antique Roman civilization: the cult of history, appearing first in daily ritual, finally abstracted itself as a special discipline. In the seventeenth century journalism and periodic literature made their appearance: even in dress, following the lead of Venice as fashion-center, people altered styles every year rather than every generation.

The gain in mechanical efficiency through co-ordination and through the closer articulation of the day's events cannot be overestimated: while this increase cannot be measured in mere horsepower, one has only to imagine its absence today to foresee the speedy disruption and eventual collapse of our entire society. The modern industrial regime could do without coal and iron and steam easier than it could do without the clock.

SPACE, DISTANCE, MOVEMENT

. . . .
Between the fourteenth and the seventeenth century a revolutionary change in the conception of space took place in Western Europe. Space as a hierarchy of values was replaced by space as a system of magnitudes. One of the indications of this new orientation was the closer study of the relations of objects in space and the discovery of the laws of perspective and the systematic organi-

zation of pictures within the new frame fixed by the foreground, the horizon and the vanishing point. Perspective turned the symbolic relation of objects into a visual relation: the visual in turn became a quantitative relation. In the new picture of the world, size meant not human or divine importance, but distance. Bodies did not exist separately as absolute magnitudes: they were co-ordinated with other bodies within the same frame of vision and must be in scale. To achieve this scale, there must be an accurate representation of the object itself, a point for point correspondence between the picture and the image: hence a fresh interest in external nature and in questions of fact. The division of the canvas into squares and the accurate observation of the world through this abstract checkerboard marked the new technique of the painter, from Paolo Uccello onward.

The new interest in perspective brought depth into the picture and distance into the mind. In the older pictures, one's eye jumped from one part to another, picking up symbolic crumbs as taste and fancy dictated: in the new pictures, one's eye followed the lines of linear perspective along streets, buildings, tessellated pavements whose parallel lines the painter purposely introduced in order to make the eye itself travel. Even the objects in the foreground were sometimes grotesquely placed and foreshortened in order to create the same illusion. Movement became a new source of value: movement for its own sake. The measured space of the picture re-enforced the measured time of the clock.

Within this new ideal network of space and time all events now took place; and the most satisfactory event within this system was uniform motion in a straight line, for such motion lent itself to accurate representation within the system of spatial and temporal co-ordinates. One further consequence of this spatial order must be noted: to place a thing and to time it became essential to one's understanding of it. In Renascence space, the existence of objects must be accounted for: their passage through time and space is a clue to their appearance at any particular moment in any particular place. The unknown is therefore no less determinate than the known: given the roundness of the globe, the position of the Indies could be assumed and the time-distance calculated. The very existence of such an order was an incentive to explore it and to fill up the parts that were unknown.

What the painters demonstrated in their application of perspective, the cartographers established in the same century in their new maps. The Hereford Map of 1314 might have been done by a child: it was practically worthless for navigation. That of Uccello's contemporary, Andrea Banco, 1436, was conceived on rational lines, and represented a gain in conception as well as in practical accuracy. By laying down the invisible lines of latitude and longitude, the cartographers paved the way for later explorers, like Columbus: as with the later scientific method, the abstract system gave rational expectations, even if on the basis of inaccurate knowledge. No longer was it necessary for the navigator to hug the shore line: he could launch out into the unknown, set his course toward an arbitrary point, and return approximately to the place of departure. Both Eden and Heaven were outside the new space; and though they lingered on as the ostensible subjects of painting, the real subjects were Time and Space and Nature and Man.

Presently, on the basis laid down by the painter and the cartographer, an interest in space as such, in movement as such, in locomotion as such, arose. In back of this interest were of course more concrete alterations: roads had become more secure, vessels were being built more soundly, above all, new inventions—the magnetic needle, the astrolabe, the rudder—had made it possible to chart and to hold a more accurate course at sea. The gold of the Indies and the fabled fountains of youth and the happy isles of endless sensual delight doubtless beckoned too: but the presence of these tangible goals does not lessen the importance of the new schemata. The categories of time and space, once practically dissociated, had become united: and the abstractions of measured time and measured space undermined the earlier conceptions of infinity and eternity, since measurement must begin with an arbitrary here and now even if space and time be empty. The itch to *use* space and time had broken out: and once they were co-ordinated with movement, they could be contracted or expanded: the conquest of space and time had begun. (It is interesting, however, to note that the very concept of acceleration, which is part of our daily mechanical experience, was not formulated till the seventeenth century.)

The signs of this conquest are many: they came forth in rapid succession. In military arts the cross-bow and the ballista were revived and extended, and on their heels came more powerful weapons for annihilating distance—the cannon and later the musket. Leonardo conceived an airplane and built one. Fantastic projects for flight were canvassed. In 1420 Fontana described a velocipede: in 1589 Gilles de Bom of Antwerp apparently built a man-propelled wagon: restless preludes to the vast efforts and initiatives of the nineteenth century. As with so many elements in our culture, the original impulse was imparted to this movement by the Arabs: as early as 880 Abû l-Qâsim had attempted flight, and in 1065 Oliver of Malmesbury had killed himself in an attempt to soar from a high place: but from the fifteenth century on the desire to conquer the air became a recurrent preoccupation of inventive minds; and it was close enough to popular thought to make the report of a flight from Portugal to Vienna serve as a news hoax in 1709.

The new attitude toward time and space infected the workshop and the counting house, the army and the city. The tempo became faster: the magnitudes became greater: conceptually, modern culture launched itself into space and gave itself over to movement. . . .

THE INFLUENCE OF CAPITALISM

. . . .
. . . While the feudal families, with their command over the land, often had a monopoly over such natural resources as were found in the earth, and often retained an interest in glass-making, coal-mining, and iron-works right down to

modern times, the new mechanical inventions lent themselves to exploitation by the merchant classes. The incentive to mechanization lay in the greater profits that could be extracted through the multiplied power and efficiency of the machine.

Thus, although capitalism and technics must be clearly distinguished at every stage, one conditioned the other and reacted upon it. The merchant accumulated capital by widening the scale of his operations, quickening his turnover, and discovering new territories for exploitation: the inventor carried on a parallel process by exploiting new methods of production and devising new things to be produced. Sometimes trade appeared as a rival to the machine by offering greater opportunities for profit: sometimes it curbed further developments in order to increase the profit of a particular monopoly: both motives are still operative in capitalist society. From the first, there were disparities and conflicts between these two forms of exploitation: but trade was the older partner and exercised a higher authority. It was trade that gathered up new materials from the Indies and from the Americas, new foods, new cereals, tobacco, furs: it was trade that found a new market for the trash that was turned out by eighteenth century mass-production: it was trade—abetted by war—that developed the large-scale enterprises and the administrative capacity and method that made it possible to create the industrial system as a whole and weld together its various parts.

Whether machines would have been invented so rapidly and pushed so zealously without the extra incentive of commercial profit is extremely doubtful: for all the more skilled handicraft occupations were deeply entrenched, and the introduction of printing, for example, was delayed as much as twenty years in Paris by the bitter opposition of the guild of scribes and copyists. But while technics undoubtedly owes an honest debt to capitalism, as it does likewise to war, it was nevertheless unfortunate that the machine was conditioned, at the outset, by these foreign institutions and took on characteristics that had nothing essentially to do with the technical processes or the forms of work. Capitalism utilized the machine, not to further social welfare, but to increase private profit: mechanical instruments were used for the aggrandizement of the ruling classes. It was because of capitalism that the handicraft industries in both Europe and other parts of the world were recklessly destroyed by machine products, even when the latter were inferior to the thing they replaced: for the prestige of improvement and success and power was with the machine, even when it improved nothing, even when technically speaking it was a failure. It was because of the possibilities of profit that the place of the machine was overemphasized and the degree of regimentation pushed beyond what was necessary to harmony or efficiency. It was because of certain traits in private capitalism that the machine—which was a neutral agent—has often seemed, and in fact has sometimes been, a malicious element in society, careless of human life, indifferent to human interests. The machine has suffered for the sins of capitalism; contrariwise, capitalism has often taken credit for the virtues of the machine.

By supporting the machine, capitalism quickened its pace, and gave a special incentive to preoccupation with mechanical improvements: though it often failed to reward the inventor, it succeeded by blandishments and promises in stimulating him to further effort. In many departments the pace was over-accelerated, and the stimulus was over-applied: indeed, the necessity to promote continual changes and improvements, which has been characteristic of capitalism, introduced an element of instability into technics and kept society from assimilating its mechanical improvements and integrating them in an appropriate social pattern. As capitalism itself has developed and expanded, these vices have in fact grown more enormous, and the dangers to society as a whole have likewise grown proportionately. Enough here to notice the close historical association of modern technics and modern capitalism, and to point out that, for all this historical development, there is no necessary connection between them. . . .

selection 5

The Protestant Ethic and the Spirit of Capitalism

Max Weber and Kemper Fullerton†*

The impulse to acquisition, pursuit of gain, of money, of the greatest possible amount of money, has in itself nothing to do with capitalism. This impulse exists and has existed among waiters, physicians, coachmen, artists, prostitutes, dishonest officials, soldiers, nobles, crusaders, gamblers, and beggars. One may say that it has been common to all sorts and conditions of men at all times and in all countries of the earth, wherever the objective possibility of it is or has been given. It should be taught in the kindergarten of cultural history that this naive idea of capitalism must be given up once and for all. Unlimited greed for gain is not in the least identical with capitalism, and is still less its spirit. Capitalism *may* even be identical with the restraint, or at least a rational tempering, of this irrational impulse. But capitalism is identical with the pursuit of profit, and forever *renewed* profit, by means of continuous, rational, capitalistic enterprise. For it must be so: in a wholly capitalistic order of society, an individual capitalistic enterprise which did not take advantage of its opportunities for profit-making would be doomed to extinction.

*Reprinted with the permission of Charles Scribner's Sons from *The Protestant Ethic and the Spirit of Capitalism* by Max Weber, translated by Talcott Parsons, pp. 16–27. Also used by permission from George Allen & Unwin, Ltd.

†From Kemper Fullerton, "Calvinism and Capitalism," *The Harvard Theological Review*, Vol. 21 (1928), pp. 163–91.

Let us now define our terms somewhat more carefully than is generally done. We will define a capitalistic economic action as one which rests on the expectation of profit by the utilization of opportunities for exchange, that is on (formally) peaceful chances of profit. Acquisition by force (formally and actually) follows its own particular laws, and it is not expedient, however little one can forbid this, to place it in the same category with action which is, in the last analysis, oriented to profits from exchange. Where capitalistic acquisition is rationally pursued, the corresponding action is adjusted to calculations in terms of capital. This means that the action is adapted to a systematic utilization of goods or personal services as means of acquisition in such a way that, at the close of a business period, the balance of the enterprise in money assets (or, in the case of a continuous enterprise, the periodically estimated money value of assets) exceeds the capital, i.e. the estimated value of the material means of production used for acquisition in exchange. It makes no difference whether it involves a quantity of goods entrusted *in natura* [in kind] to a travelling merchant, the proceeds of which may consist in other goods *in natura* acquired by trade, or whether it involves a manufacturing enterprise, the assets of which consist of buildings, machinery, cash, raw materials, partly and wholly manufactured goods, which are balanced against liabilities. The important fact is always that a calculation of capital in terms of money is made, whether by modern bookkeeping methods or in any other way, however primitive and crude. Everything is done in terms of balances: at the beginning of the enterprise an initial balance, before every individual decision a calculation to ascertain its probable profitableness, and at the end a final balance to ascertain how much profit has been made. . . . That a really accurate calculation or estimate may not exist, that the procedure is pure guesswork, or simply traditional and conventional, happens even today in every form of capitalistic enterprise where the circumstances do not demand strict accuracy. But these are points affecting only the *degree* of rationality of capitalistic acquisition.

For the purpose of this conception all that matters is that an actual adaptation of economic action to a comparison of money income with money expenses takes place, no matter how primitive the form. Now in this sense capitalism and capitalistic enterprises, even with a considerable rationalization of capitalistic calculation, have existed in all civilized countries of the earth, so far as economic documents permit us to judge—in China, India, Babylon, Egypt, Mediterranean antiquity, and the Middle Ages, as well as in modern times. These were not merely isolated ventures, but economic enterprises which were entirely dependent on the continual renewal of capitalistic undertakings, and even continuous operations. However, trade especially was for a long time not continuous like our own, but consisted essentially in a series of individual undertakings. Only gradually did the activities of even the large merchants acquire an inner cohesion (with branch organizations, etc.). In any case, the capitalistic enterprise and the capitalistic entrepreneur, not only as occasional but as regular entrepreneurs, are very old and were very widespread.

Now, however, the Occident has developed capitalism both to a quantitative extent, and (carrying this quantitative development) in types, forms, and directions which have never existed elsewhere. All over the world there have been merchants, wholesale and retail, local and engaged in foreign trade. Loans of all kinds have been made, and there have been banks with the most various functions, at least comparable to ours of, say, the sixteenth century. . . . Whenever money finances of public bodies have existed, money-lenders have appeared, as in Babylon, Hellas, India, China, Rome. They have financed wars and piracy, contracts and building operations of all sorts. In overseas policy they have functioned as colonial entrepreneurs, as planters with slaves, or directly or indirectly forced labour, and have farmed domains, offices, and, above all, taxes. They have financed party leaders in elections and *condottieri* in civil wars. And, finally, they have been speculators in chances for pecuniary gain of all kinds. This kind of entrepreneur, the capitalistic adventurer, has existed everywhere. With the exception of trade and credit and banking transactions, their activities were predominantly of an irrational and speculative character, or directed to acquisition by force, above all the acquisition of booty, whether directly in war or in the form of continuous fiscal booty by exploitation of subjects.

The capitalism of promoters, large-scale speculators, concession hunters, and much modern financial capitalism even in peace time, but, above all, the capitalism especially concerned with exploiting wars, bears this stamp even in modern Western countries, and some, but only some, parts of large-scale international trade are closely related to it, today as always.

But in modern times the Occident has developed, in addition to this, a very different form of capitalism which has appeared nowhere else: the rational capitalistic organization of (formally) free labour. Only suggestions of it are found elsewhere. . . . Even real domestic industries with free labour have definitely been proved to have existed in only a few isolated cases outside the Occident. The frequent use of day labourers led in a very few cases—especially State monopolies, which are, however, very different from modern industrial organization—to manufacturing organizations, but never to a rational organization of apprenticeship in the handicrafts like that of our Middle Ages. . . .

Hence in a universal history of culture the central problem for us is not, in the last analysis, even from a purely economic viewpoint, the development of capitalistic activity as such, differing in different cultures only in form: the adventurer type, or capitalism in trade, war, politics, or administration as sources of gain. It is rather the origin of this sober bourgeois capitalism with its rational organization of free labour. Or in terms of cultural history, the problem is that of the origin of the Western bourgeois class and of its peculiarities, a problem which is certainly closely connected with that of the origin of the capitalistic organization of labour, but is not quite the same thing. For the bourgeois as a class existed prior to the development of the peculiar modern form of capitalism, though, it is true, only in the Western hemisphere.

Now the peculiar modern Western form of capitalism has been, at first sight, strongly influenced by the development of technical possibilities. Its rationality is today essentially dependent on the calculability of the most important technical factors. But this means fundamentally that it is dependent on the peculiarities of modern science, especially the natural sciences based on mathematics and exact and rational experiment. On the other hand, the development of these sciences and of the technique resting upon them now receives important stimulation from these capitalistic interests in its practical economic application. It is true that the origin of Western science cannot be attributed to such interests. Calculation, even with decimals, and algebra have been carried on in India, where the decimal system was invented. But it was only made use of by developing capitalism in the West, while in India it led to no modern arithmetic or book-keeping. Neither was the origin of mathematics and mechanics determined by capitalistic interests. But the *technical* utilization of scientific knowledge, so important for the living conditions of the mass of people, was certainly encouraged by economic considerations, which were extremely favourable to it in the Occident. But this encouragement was derived from the peculiarities of the social structure of the Occident. We must hence ask, from *what* parts of that structure was it derived, since not all of them have been of equal importance?

Among those of undoubted importance are the rational structures of law and of administration. For modern rational capitalism has need, not only of the technical means of production, but of a calculable legal system and of administration in terms of formal rules. Without it adventurous and speculative trading capitalism and all sorts of politically determined capitalisms are possible, but no rational enterprise under individual initiative, with fixed capital and certainty of calculations. Such a legal system and such administration have been available for economic activity in a comparative state of legal and formalistic perfection only in the Occident. We must hence inquire where that law came from. Among other circumstances, capitalistic interests have in turn undoubtedly also helped, but by no means alone nor even principally, to prepare the way for the predominance in law and administration of a class of jurists specially trained in rational law. But these interests did not themselves create that law. Quite different forces were at work in this development. And why did not the capitalistic interests do the same in China or India? Why did not the scientific, the artistic, the political, or the economic development there enter upon that path of rationalization which is peculiar to the Occident?

For in all the above cases it is a question of the specific and peculiar rationalism of Western culture. Now by this term very different things may be understood, as the following discussion will repeatedly show. There is, for example, rationalization of mystical contemplation, that is of an attitude which, viewed from other departments of life, is specifically irrational, just as much as there are rationalizations of economic life, of technique, of scientific research, of military training, of law and administration. Furthermore, each one of these fields may be rationalized in terms of very different ultimate values and ends, and what is rational from one point of view may well be irrational from another. Hence rationalizations of the most varied character have existed in various departments of life and in all areas of culture. To characterize their differences from the viewpoint of cultural history it is necessary to know what departments are rationalized, and in what direction. It is hence our first concern to work out and to explain genetically the special peculiarity of Occidental rationalism, and within this field that of the modern Occidental form. Every such attempt at explanation must, recognizing the fundamental importance of the economic factor, above all take account of the economic conditions. But at the same time the opposite correlation must not be left out of consideration. For though the development of economic rationalism is partly dependent on rational technique and law, it is at the same time determined by the ability and disposition of men to adopt certain types of practical rational conduct. When these types have been obstructed by spiritual obstacles, the development of rational economic conduct has also met serious inner resistance. The magical and religious forces, and the ethical ideas of duty based upon them, have in the past always been among the most important formative influences on conduct. . . .

MAX WEBER

Perhaps in nothing, not even in scientific outlook, is the contrast between the Modern Age and the Middle Ages more striking than in the changed attitude toward money and money-making. In the Middle Ages trade was frowned upon and the money-lender despised. In this attitude church and society generally agreed. The church was always castigating the sin of avarice. The making of money was designated by Thomas Aquinas as "turpitudo," even though he admitted its necessity. The thesis that the shop-keeper could only with difficulty please God was introduced into canon law. Usury, which meant not only extortionate interest but interest of any kind, was prohibited by several councils of the church, and to a usurer the privileges of the sacraments were often denied. Even in those days there were, to be sure, practical qualifications of these theoretical judgments, due to the need of money—a need often as keenly felt by the lords spiritual as by the lords temporal. Nevertheless the generalization is safe that money-making was regarded as socially degrading and morally and religiously dangerous. Today all this is changed. Money-making has become the chief aim of modern civilization. In countless ways, gross or subtle, it determines our lives and thinking. It entices into its service many of the best minds of our college graduates. Even our professions, law, medicine, the ministry (witness the vast development of ecclesiastical advertising), are more and more entangled in its net, while the commercialization of amusements, including our college sports, is notorious.

But at this point a distinction is necessary. The change between the present and the past is not primarily in the greater love of money in the present. In all ages avarice has been found in all classes. Whether it is now more widespread than heretofore is not the important question. That difference, if it exists, would be only quantitative, not qualitative. Nor is the change in the method of money-making, its technology, the distinguishing characteristic. Capitalism has existed in one form or another in every age. The real difference, which it is Professor Max Weber's aim to point out and more closely examine in the essay which the present article discusses, is found in what he calls "the spirit of modern capitalism." The difference is psychological, or, more precisely formulated, it is found in a new "ethos" of money-making. What is meant by this spirit of modern capitalism and, an even more interesting question, what is its origin?

Before attempting to answer these questions Weber makes a preliminary historical observation of great interest. He notes that the great trading-classes of the bourgeoisie have been chiefly found in the ranks of Protestantism. The proportion of leading industrialists, traders, financiers, technical experts, is greater among Protestants than among Catholics. The latter have always been more inclined to the handicrafts. The Spaniards early recognized this. They said that heresy (that is, the Calvinism of the Netherlands) furthers the spirit of trade. More specifically, these same classes in the sixteenth and seventeenth centuries were mainly found not merely among the Protestants, but among the Protestants of Calvinistic or Calvinistically allied churches—the Huguenots of France, the great Dutch traders, the Puritans of England. In other words, the growth of capitalism in its modern expression coincided to a remarkable degree with that form of Protestantism which, as contrasted with Lutheranism, Weber calls the "ascetic" form. Montesquieu seems to have recognized this singular coincidence when he said of the Protestant English that "they are superior to all other peoples in three things, piety, trade, and liberty." Is this coincidence merely an historical accident, or is there some inner organic connection between these two phenomena, the rise of modern capitalism (or rather of the spirit of modern capitalism) and the great Protestant "ascetic" movement, dominated very largely by the Calvinistic theology? At first sight the two seem quite unlike each other and in their existing forms they really are unlike. In order to answer this question Weber next seeks to define more nearly what he means by the spirit of modern capitalism.

He chooses as the starting-point in his analysis of the spirit of modern capitalism Benjamin Franklin's "Advice to a Young Tradesman":

> Remember that time is money. He who could make ten shillings a day through his work, but goes walking half the day or idles in his room, even if he spends for his amusement only a sixpence, may not count this alone [as a loss], but he has, in addition, given up five shillings, or rather thrown it away. Remember that credit is money. If anyone leaves money with me after it falls due, he makes me a present of the interest. This amounts to a considerable sum if a man has good credit and makes good use of it. Remember that money can beget money [a theory the reverse of Aristotle's!]. Five shillings turned over become six . . . and so on till they are a hundred pounds sterling. He who kills a sow destroys its progeny till the thousandth generation. He who wastes five shillings murders [note the unconscious choice of an ethical term here!], all that might have been produced by it, whole columns of pounds sterling.

It is not simply the saving of money for the use to which it can afterwards be put that Franklin has in mind. The idea which really lies back of it is that of making money as an end in itself, as a profession, as a "calling," in which all one's best capacities are to be engaged. Franklin quotes Prov. 22, 29, "Seest thou a man diligent [note the word!] in business? he shall stand before kings." Here it is not so much the reward of efficiency as diligence, or the duty of efficiency, in which Franklin is interested. He means to enjoin not the love of money but the obligation to make money. But where an obligation exists, there an ethical element enters in. It is this feeling of responsibility to make money which Weber finds the most significant difference between modern capitalism and the forms of capitalism current in past ages. In other words, the difference lies in the spirit, the peculiar ethos of modern capitalism, defined as a sense of obligation in money-making. When one seriously examines this sense of obligation, the question at once arises, Why does it exist? A reason can be seen for making money in order to provide for a man's family, or to secure prestige and power, or even to lead a life of self-indulgence. But there would seem to be something irrational in a ceaseless drive to make money and ever more money. It is not a native instinct in man. In fact, it has to assert itself against his native instincts. One of the greatest difficulties which capitalism in its modern forms has had to contend with is the frequent lack of this feeling of responsibility among workmen. For the intensification of production a sense of responsibility on the part of workmen is absolutely necessary. But if in an emergency higher wages are offered for increased exertion, workmen will indeed work harder, but are apt to work for only half the time; they prefer to halve their time rather than double their wages. The opposite method, that of starving workmen into harder work by reducing their wages, is even less successful in stimulating productivity. (But Weber notices, in passing, that among working-people of pietistic circles in Germany this feeling of obligation is often highly developed!) This indifference to the obligation to make all the money a workman possibly can is called by Weber "traditionalism," as opposed to the spirit of modern capitalism. Before the modern era this traditionalism prevailed not only among the working classes but among the employing classes as well, and Weber draws a picture of the easy-going life of the trader in earlier times. He felt no particular obligation to increase his trade. He felt no anxiety lest, if his trade did not increase, it would dry up. He did not feel it necessary to turn most of his profits back into his business instead of enjoying himself. An excellent example of the spirit of traditionalism is a bazaar-keeper in Damascus of whom I was told when I was in the Near East. My informant said he always liked to trade with this particular dealer. But there was one difficulty. You never could tell when he would be in his shop. It was his custom in the morning to go to his little booth, but he would shut up shop, no matter what the hour, whenever he thought he had made enough metallik for the day, and would then go home to smoke his narghile and enjoy himself. The mediaeval man, even a man engaged in capitalistic enterprises, would have understood this Damascene shop-keeper's intermittent trading far better than he would the ceaseless drive of my poor friend. He would probably have thought the oriental mode of life much the more rational of the two.

But there is another element in the spirit of modern capitalism upon which Weber comments, besides this feeling of obligation to make more profits. Those who are most permanently successful in modern business life are usually marked by a certain quality of self-discipline or "asceticism." They are not the spenders and wastrels of the world. They live moderate and abstemious lives. They do not seek display. They must, if they are to be permanently successful, win the confidence of their workmen and customers. They must be trustworthy. Though Weber does not refer to them, John D. Rockefeller and Russell Sage are excellent examples of the type he has in mind. Such men must pass self-denying ordinances upon themselves. Free indulgence in ordinary pleasures and recreations is not for them. A measure of rigid self-discipline is necessary to ultimate success. Thus, in addition to the feeling of obligation, Weber's analysis of the spirit of modern capitalism includes this tinge of "asceticism." Sacrifices are entailed. And for what? In order to make ever larger and larger profits! Again the question must be raised: Is there not an element of irrationality in all this, if it be judged by the usual standards of what makes life worth living? How can this curious phenomenon be explained?

It might be thought that because this spirit of capitalism is at present so necessary in carrying on the capitalistic processes it is therefore a result of these processes, and the explanation might be given that this feeling of obligation is an adjustment of men's minds to the new economic era that was ushered in by the great discoveries of the fifteenth and sixteenth centuries with their stimulation of trade. But Weber points out that capitalistic forms and capitalistic spirit, which so naturally go together, by no means always coincide. The capitalistic spirit, the feeling of obligation in one's business or calling, was prevalent in seventeenth-century New England, which was founded by preachers and university men in the interest of religion, but wanting in the Southern states, which were developed in the interests of business. The same spirit was wanting in Florence in the fourteenth and fifteenth centuries, in spite of a highly developed form of capitalism, but present in the Pennsylvania backwoods of the eighteenth century amid such primitive economic conditions that, because of the lack of gold, trade was almost reduced to barter and banks were in their infancy. Under such conditions Franklin emphasized the moral obligation of making money. Could there be a greater contrast than in this differing attitude toward money-making? Instead of being "turpitudo," money-making is now itself almost a religion. A religion! Might it be that this strange irrational feeling of obligation to make money, though now unconnected with any religious interest, once had a religious sanction which gave it meaning and support?

The reader will recall the observation that the great trading classes arose and became most fully developed among Protestants rather than Catholics. Is there not here a hint of some strange elusive connection between the Protestant form of religion and money-making?

We have now reached a point where we must embark with Weber on a voyage of rediscovery to a world that for most of us has sunk as completely as Atlantis beneath the waves of the sea. His account of this rediscovered world, and the connection which he establishes between it and the life of our capitalistic culture today, form the most fascinating part of his essay.

In casting about for a clue to the possible solution of the interesting question just raised, Weber lights upon a curious philological fact. He notes that Luther used the German word *Beruf* ("calling") in a sense which it had never before possessed. Nor is there any precise equivalent for it either in antiquity or Catholicism. It appears in Luther's translation of Ecclesiasticus 11, 21, "Trust in the Lord and abide in thy *Beruf.*" From this translation and from Luther's use of the word elsewhere it became a standing word in the vocabulary of the Protestant peoples. . . . What did Luther mean by it? From his use of the term elsewhere it is clear that he is here thinking of the labor of the secular, everyday life as a God-appointed task, a calling. By means of this word a religious significance thus comes to be attached to the secular life, even down to its humblest details. "God accomplishes all things through you," he tells us, "through you he milks the cow and does the most servile works." But more especially still, this conception of the secular life as a God-appointed task necessarily involves the idea that the proper performance of such a secular task is a religious obligation; and the idea of the obligation to live a religious life within the sphere of the secular which is found in Luther's use of the word "calling" is one of the most momentous contributions which the Reformation made to social theory. How significant it is can be fully appreciated only when the Catholic theory is understood which Luther was attacking through the use of this word. One of the fundamental doctrines of Roman Catholicism is the sharp distinction between the laity and "secular" clergy on the one hand and "religious" orders on the other. The adjective, "religious," was applied, not to the former but to the monks and the nuns. The latter were "religious" in a sense in which others could not be. A different standard of morals was enjoined upon them. The general obligations of a Christian were comprised in what were known as *praecepta evangelica,* or the morals of the Decalogue, which were in turn practically identified with natural-law morality, or the law written upon the conscience of mankind of which St. Paul speaks in the first chapter of Romans. The religious orders, on the other hand, were obligated to follow the *consilia evangelica,* the higher morality of the gospels, specially expressed in the vows of obedience, poverty, and chastity. This latter morality was impossible of fulfilment in the secular life; in order to practise it, men must withdraw from the world. "Come out from among them and be ye separate," is the motto of monasticism. Thus what may be called a double standard of morality came to exist within the church itself.

Luther's conception of the secular life as a "calling" involved a complete break with this theory. For him no distinction was permissible between two standards of morality, *praecepta evangelica,* to be performed within the world, and *consilia evangelica,* which can be fulfilled only apart from the world. All men are equally obligated to fulfil both the commands and the "advices" of the gospel. And this fulfilment is to be accomplished, not in the cloister, apart from the world, but in the sphere of the secular life itself. This does not mean that Luther's attitude was essentially a "world-affirming" attitude. It was not. He was to a very large degree inwardly estranged from the world. His view, as distinguished from the monastic view, may be summed up in the words, "Be ye in the world but not of it." Nevertheless Luther's conception of "calling" was the first and most important step toward a new appraisal of the secular life. For the Catholic, "calling," or "vocation," was to live the religious life apart from the world. "Calling" for Luther was to live the secular life religiously, to serve God within one's calling *(in vocatione).* The final step remained to be taken, namely, to serve God by one's calling *(per vocationem).* This step Luther does not seem to have taken in any decisive way. In his earlier writings he had a Pauline indifference to the secular life; it was morally and religiously neutral like eating and drinking. Later, through his opposition to monasticism, which he repudiated as egoistic and an evasion of the duties of love to one's neighbor, he came to look upon the secular life as affording opportunities to express this love. Through the various secular activities of our lives we are to serve others.

But as Luther came more and more under the domination of the predestinarian idea, he began to look on "calling" as an opportunity given to man primarily for the purpose of obeying God by humbly and cheerfully acquiescing in that lot in life to which God had assigned him. Not what a man could accomplish through his calling *(per vocationem)* but the spirit of obedience or resignation which he could exhibit within it *(in vocatione)* was Luther's controlling thought in his conception of the secular life. Thus it came to pass that while Luther opened the way for a new appraisal of the secular life by breaking down the Catholic distinction between it and the religious life, he did not himself develop the vast economic possibilities latent in this new appraisal. As a matter of fact he remained a "traditionalist" in his attitude toward money-making, untouched by the spirit of modern capitalism. Through this new estimate of the secular life we begin dimly, though only dimly, to see how it may possibly have come about that Protestants rather than Catholics have been the chief traders and industrialists; the Protestant religion begins to invade the sphere of the secular. But it is yet a far cry from the religious value which Luther set on the sphere of the secular and the utterly irreligious spirit of modern capitalism. Is there any middle term between these two extremes? The Protestants of Calvinistic origin have been the most conspicuous exponents of successful trade. Is the middle term to be found in this branch of Protestantism? To the examination of the great Calvinistic movement, or, more generally stated, of the disciplinary, or "ascetic," movement in Protestantism as distinct from Lutheranism, we must now turn.

While Luther started from the experience of justification by faith, that is, from the human side of experience, Calvin's attempt to restate the Christian religion as against Rome starts from the conception of God. In his view God is absolute Will, and the only absolute that exists. Hence God is the only being who is perfectly free. Therefore what God wills is right, and must be accepted whether we can understand it or not (which is a fundamentally irrational conception of God). This free and righteous will of God expresses itself in Scripture, according to Calvin, in the double decree of election and reprobation. Calvin's treatment of this doctrine is thoroughly intellectualized; its implications are drawn out by logical processes; experience and emotion play little part in his deductions. In other words, Calvinism as a system, though it starts from an irrational conception of God, is worked out in a thoroughly rationalistic way, and this rationalistic note in the system must be constantly borne in mind as we study its practical consequences.

The first great consequence is what may be called an intellectual as well as practical other-worldliness. Man is not the centre of the system, nor is even Christ, but God. In the words of the famous answer to the first question of the Westminster Shorter Catechism, "Man's chief end is to glorify God and enjoy him forever." This aim gives to life its reason, its *rationale*. Anything that diverts the mind from this one supreme aim is a species of idolatry, a worship of the creature rather than the creator. Out of this suspicion of the creature arises the "ascetic" view of life, so characteristic of Calvinism and of the Puritan movement generally, which continued to prevail even after the dogmatic system of Calvinism became seriously impaired. Again, since the individual is elected by the eternal decree of God, all intermediaries between God and man are, at least theoretically, excluded. No sacramental grace, no priesthood which controls it, no church, no human help of any kind avails here. The soul stands in the presence of its God in awful isolation. Weber calls this the "dis-enchantment of the world," that is, its emancipation from sacramental magic, begun by Old Testament prophecy, supported by the scientific movement of Hellenism, and now culminating in the Calvinistic polemic against Rome. It is at this point that Calvinism distinguishes itself most sharply from Rome.

Because of the elimination of all intermediaries between God and man there arises at the very heart of the Calvinistic system a tremendous emphasis upon individualism. That this individualism has played a noble part in the cause of human liberty is too often forgotten, but logically it is anti-social. It concentrates the attention upon the self, even at times to the extent of avoiding too intimate friendships as a worship of, or reliance upon, the creature. The gentle Baxter warns us that "it is an *irrational* act and not fit for a *rational* creature to love any one farther than *reason* will allow us. . . . It very often taketh up men's minds so as to hinder their love of God." This intense preoccupation with oneself is effectively illustrated in the opening chapter of the *Pilgrim's Progress,* where the Pilgrim's flight from the City of Destruction is described:

> So I saw in my dream that the man began to run. Now he had not run far from his own door when his wife and children, perceiving it, began to cry after him to return; but the man put his fingers in his ears and ran on, crying, "Life! life! eternal life!"

On the other hand, in sharp contrast with this emphasis upon the individual, Calvinism has shown a much greater genius for social organization than Lutheranism, and with its intense individualism has been able to combine an equally intense social activity. The Pilgrim, in order to get to heaven, does not flee to the desert as an anchorite. His way lies, as Weber points out, through *Vanity Fair.* Not withdrawal from the world, as in monasticism, but struggle with the world is the Calvinistic idea of life. Not, "Come out from among them and be ye separate," but, "Be ye in the world but not of it," is the new battle cry. Weber points out the striking contrast between the *Divine Comedy,* which closes with the contemplation of the vision of God, and *Paradise Lost,* at the end of which Adam and Eve go forth, in a kind of triumphant resignation, to battle with the world. In the Puritan poem, what has been called the "mysticism of action" has been substituted for the mysticism of contemplation. And this action is within the world, within society. But how can the intense individualism of Calvinism and its equally intense social activity be combined? The middle term is here the glory of God. That is the aim of society as well as of the individual. Through the improvement of society God is also glorified. And how is this improvement to be accomplished? Through faithfulness in one's calling. This world of ours was so arranged by God as to serve the needs of mankind. In our calling we too are to follow this cosmic hint of God and serve our fellow men.

But at this point Luther's conception of "calling" undergoes in Calvinism a significant transformation. It will be remembered that Luther considered our calling to be the means of expressing either love to our neighbor or our acquiescence in the divine will concerning our lives. In the former case a personal, humane interest in our neighbor was the natural result; in the latter case there develops a rather quietistic attitude toward life. But by the introduction of the greater glory of God as the supreme and absorbing motive of all human endeavor, both these consequences of Luther's conception of calling become modified in very important ways. In the first place, since the work for the regeneration of society is now to be done primarily for the glory of God, the emotional, humanitarian element in what we today call the "social-service ideal" is largely eliminated. The general good of the many takes the place of personal interest in the individual. Social service becomes, to use Weber's term, "depersonalized." It is social only because it is performed within society. It ministers, indeed, to the good of society, but it is not done primarily for the sake of society. It is done for the glory of God. If it were done for the sake of the individual alone, that would set the creature in place of the creator, and so be a species of idolatry. Two illustrations will make clear what Weber means by a depersonalized social activity. In the life of Adoniram Judson his reflections are recorded after he had tried to evangelize the city of Proom in Burmah and was stoned out of town. His sad comment was that its inhabitants would have the chains of hell fastened upon them more tightly because they had heard the gospel message and refused it. If the purely personal and humanitarian interest had been uppermost, it would probably have prevented Judson from exposing the people of Proom to such a dreadful risk. But as it was, he felt that he was discharging the will of God: "Go ye into all the world, and preach the gospel to every creature." In 1915 the present writer was ordered out of Palestine by the Turks and left the country in company with many members of the religious orders and Protestant missionaries. One of these, a member of the Christian and Missionary Alliance, was asked if he expected to return after the war. He was doubtful about it, and gave as his reason that he had already preached the gospel in all the villages of Palestine and had thus fulfilled the will of God. The heroic but in fact absurd slogan of the Student Volunteer Movement in its earlier stages, "The Evangelization of the World in this Generation," springs from the same depersonalized conception of the social activity of the missionary. The evangelization of the world because God wills it takes the place of the salvation of the world for its own sake. Contrast the appealing close of the book of Jonah.

In the next place, though work for the good of mankind is in a certain measure depersonalized when the motive of love to our neighbor is modulated into the motive of God's glory, there is no lessening of the pressure of work. If God has ordered and arranged this great physical universe for the good of man and through this manifests his glory, it is supremely important to correlate society to the same great end, and this is done through the fulfilment of such duties in our calling as are imposed by the laws of nature. No mere quietistic acceptance of the universe is possible here. The tremendous drive of God's will and God's glory lies back of all work in our calling. The normal result is a tense and ceaseless activity. Thus the new motive of life, to glorify God and enjoy him forever, this completely other-worldly orientation of our existence, leads to a rationalized and a quasi-ascetic view of life in general (we are to enjoy forever God, not creature-pleasures), a depersonalized and therefore rationalized view of love to our neighbor, and ceaseless activity within the sphere of the secular in order to bring the secular within the final aim of life, the glory of God. But this drive toward activity in one's calling which, along with the rationalizing of life, Weber wishes especially to emphasize, is intensified even more directly by another consideration which originates in the heart of the Calvinistic system, namely in the doctrine of election.

The great question for every non-sacramental religion is, How can I be sure that I am saved? or, in the Calvinistic formula, How can I be sure that I am one of the elect? In Roman Catholicism the church could mediate to the believer this assurance through the sacraments, especially the sacrament of penance, but in Calvinism, as we have seen, all authoritative intermediaries are swept aside and the soul is left alone in the presence of its Maker. And its Maker's will is inscrutable. How, then, is the soul to be assured of its election? At first the question was not so insistent in Calvin's own thinking. The promises of God in Scripture and Calvin's own unwavering faith in Christ made doubt impossible. But as Calvinism developed, the question pressed more and more for an answer. Two answers were given. Assurance can be obtained either from the *testimonium*

Spiritus Sancti, the inner consciousness of the individual that the power of God is *in* him, or from the ability consistently to perform good works, the consciousness of the individual that the power of God is working *through* him. In the first case he is conscious that he is a vessel, in the second that he is an instrument. While the first method of assurance was undoubtedly emphasized by Calvin himself and always played, at least theoretically, a part in Calvinistic theology, the second method became the more important in practice. And it is at this point that one of the main differences between Calvinism and Lutheranism emerges. Lutheran piety is more of the passive, contemplative, mystical type. It shares with Catholic mystics the idea of the mystical union with God, in which God enters into the soul, or, rather, in which the soul becomes absorbed in God and thus finds assurance. But Calvinism had a highly transcendentalized conception of God to which the idea of the mystical union was inwardly alien, and, as a highly rationalized system of thought, it was suspicious of the emotional life favored by the idea of the mystical union. Emotions can deceive. For these reasons both the logic and the philosophy of Calvinism worked more and more away from the idea of assurance based upon inward experience, in which there was an important point of contact with the Lutheran conception of the mystical union, and came to rest for the assurance of election upon the outward sensible signs of a pious life. Certitude is to be preserved not so much through the feelings as in action. . . . Objective, recognizable signs in the Christian's mode of life are now required in addition to inward feeling in order to give assurance. The great spiritual support for this idea is 1 John 2, 3: "Hereby we do know that we know him, if we keep his commandments." Thus once more we arrive at the emphasis upon action which is so characteristic of Calvinism. The will of God, God's own glory which is at the same time the chief end of man, combined with the soul's necessity of gaining an assurance of election, produces a tremendous drive toward action, as contrasted with the contemplative life.

We have now reached the point where the bearing of all this upon the peculiar Calvinistic conception of "calling" may be seen, and at the same time the similarities and differences between Calvinism on the one hand and Roman Catholicism and Lutheranism on the other are most clearly revealed.

(1) Both Calvinism and Catholicism lay great emphasis upon works. Lutheran theologians often twitted the Calvinists with this romanizing insistence upon works. But there was a sharp distinction between the Romanist and the Calvinist doctrine of works. In the former, works are the means of salvation; in the latter, the means of assurance. By faith alone could men be saved—the Calvinist held fast to this great Reformation principle.

(2) But Calvinism followed Luther in ignoring the Catholic distribution of good works between *praecepta evangelica* and *consilia evangelica.* The former, as we have seen, furnished the standards for the laity and secular clergy, the latter for the religious orders. In the case of the laity, Mother Church mercifully took account of the weakness of the flesh. Any defective performance of the "pre-

cepts," due to the corruption of man's nature, could be made good by sacramental grace (penance). The consequence was that Catholic lay morality took on, in the Protestant view, a certain casualness. Lapses were easily made good. It was far otherwise with the performance of the *consilia*. Within the secular life these could be performed only to a limited degree; and so life withdrawn from the world now becomes necessary. But within this withdrawn life itself the sternest self-discipline is required. The whole of it is subjected to the strictest and most constant regulation. The "ascetic" ideal, the necessity of which was waived for the laity, is reserved for the religious orders, and for them not even the sacraments could ameliorate its severity. It is true that here also lapses could be made good by the sacraments, but if "merit" were to be gained, the number of lapses must be reduced as much as possible. Hence the whole monastic life had to be rationalized upon the basis of the "ascetic" ideal. Now when Luther broke down the distinction between the life of the laity and the life of the monks, and contended that the full Christian life could be lived within the sphere of the secular, he did not work out the final consequences of his new position. He did not introduce the rationalized, "ascetic" ideal of monasticism into the secular life. We have seen how in Luther's idea of "calling," that is of the Christian life in the secular sphere, there is expressed either a quietistic acquiescence in the will of God or love to our neighbor. He laid little emphasis on works, much less on a systematized and rationalized life of action. "Tears," he said, "precede works and suffering surpasses doing." His experience of forgiveness and of justification by faith led him to emphasize the inner life of the Christian rather than his outer life. Thus Lutheranism in its main tendency was never ascetic. The piety of the Lutheran was more like the casual piety of the Catholic layman. It was a piety dominated by emotion rather than by reason, and this characteristic was favored also by the considerable measure of sacramentarianism which Luther took over from Catholicism. But in Calvinism all this is reversed. By the ideal of man's chief end as the glorification of God, an ideal that is God-willed, and by the practical necessity of having some means of assurance, a necessity that springs from the doctrine of election when the sacramental approach to God is abandoned, the basis is furnished for a new conception of the secular life. The ideal of discipline, or "asceticism," proper to Catholic monasticism is now transferred to the secular life. Within the sphere of this life lies one's calling (so Luther), but calling now becomes the means of moral discipline (so Calvin). Just as the monk apart from the world must subject the whole of his life to the severest regulation, so now the Calvinist within the world must rigorously discipline himself. His life is to be a rationalized life of systematic self-control. The monk did this to secure a reward. It was a work of supererogation. The Calvinist did it not for reward—that would be to deny the grace of God in election, but in order to secure the sense of assurance that he was elect. Yet this statement is not quite exact. The Calvinist practised self-discipline not even to secure assurance; he practised it for the glory of God, and in the practice of it assurance came. Assurance itself was not the aim but the consequence of this discipline, a kind of by-product, though a by-product of immense importance.

(3) But further, as merit was not secured by the Catholic except through extraordinary effort, through works of supererogation, so *full* assurance did not come to the Calvinist except through perseverance. He must continue in good works if he is to continue in assurance. Thus the Calvinist, as contrasted with the Lutheran, was led again to transfer the Catholic monastic ideal of strict discipline to the secular life, the life of "calling." According to Sebastian Franck the significance of the Reformation is just this, that "every Christian must be a monk *his whole life long."* Instead of the spiritual aristocracy of the monks apart from the world, we now have, as Weber puts it, "a spiritual aristocracy of the elect within the world." We can now understand what the Calvinistic or, more generally, the Puritan conception of "calling" is, and in what respects it resembles or differs from Catholicism and Lutheranism. It is the life of strict discipline (an idea borrowed from Catholic monasticism) lived in the secular sphere (an idea borrowed from Luther) with the sole intent of glorifying God and with the blessed sense of assurance of election as its reward (the special contribution of Calvinism). We have thus finally arrived at the idea of the service of God through one's calling *(per vocationem)* as contrasted with Luther's idea of this service in one's calling *(in vocatione).* This life of calling must be quasi-ascetic, for the secular life tempts to the worship of the creature and so would detract from God's glory. This "asceticism" takes the form of the strictest regulation of the whole of life, as in monasticism. Assurance is attained only through perseverance. Life thus becomes thoroughly rationalized, Calvinistic piety at this point contrasting with Lutheran piety. It is rationalized by its aim, the glory of God, and by its method, a life of ceaseless watchful self-control. All this led practically to the development of an immensely intensified moral activity within the sphere of the secular life as the most noticeable characteristic of the Calvinistic churches and of similar Protestantism generally, a moral activity which has probably never been equalled before or since. It is (a) this rationalized theory of life, (b) this intensified mood for work, and (c) the quasi-ascetic discipline which accompanies both theory and mood that have immediate interest for Weber. Such an immense output of spiritual energy could not fail profoundly to influence subsequent generations. Can it be that these three factors, which grew directly out of the Calvinistic theology in its distinction from Rome on the one hand and from Lutheranism on the other, furnish the key to the development of the spirit of modern capitalism? Do these aspects of Calvinism furnish the middle term between Luther's conception of "calling" performed in the secular life and that conception of money-making as in itself a "calling" which in part constitutes the spirit of modern capitalism?

In the last main section of his essay Weber undertakes to show how this rationalized, strenuously active, methodically "ascetic" mode of life, represented by the Puritan conception of "calling," furnishes the religious basis of capitalism, without which capitalism would never have attained the control which it now exercises over the minds of men. After all, however blind economists may be to the fact, metaphysical convictions are the only ones which have the power absolutely to dominate men's lives. Economic reasons alone cannot account for the extraordinary power in the western civilization of today which the money-making motive exerts. The whole point of Weber's essay is to show that something deeper, more transcendental, more idealistic, is at work here, and must be reckoned with if the psychology of capitalism, its spirit or temper, is to be adequately explained.

If one looks into Baxter's "The Saints' Everlasting Rest" or his "Christian Directory" or similar pastoral works of the Puritan divines (and it is such practical works rather than the more theoretical dogmatic discussions which reflect the real moral interests of the masses), one is at first sight struck by the suspicious attitude toward riches expressed in all these writings, in full harmony with the similar warnings of the mediaeval church. The possession of riches is regarded as dangerous, and equally so the pursuit of them. Riches tempt to confidence and contentment therein, to laziness and sensuality. The pursuit of them diverts from the main object of life, the glory of God. But in conjunction with all these warnings, and unconsciously confusing them, another note is sounded by these writers. They are constantly exhorting to industry. The saints' everlasting rest is a rest in the next life, not in this one. Here it behooves man to work, and ever more to work.

There are two chief motives given for work. Work is still, as it always has been in the western church, a means of discipline. It is the best prophylactic against what the Puritan called the "unclean life," against the sloth and sensuality which riches so often engender. Work in one's calling is Baxter's prescription against sexual temptation as well as against religious doubts. Again, work is to be done because God commanded it, in other words for his glory. This meant that utilitarian motives were disregarded or at least subordinated. So far as this life is concerned, work becomes an end in itself. It gains a meaning beyond itself only when looked at *sub specie aeternitatis,* from a religious and other-worldly point of view.

> It is for action [says Baxter] that God maintaineth us and our activities. Work is the moral as well as the natural end of power. . . . It is action that God is most served and honored by. . . . The public welfare or the good of many is to be valued above our own.

This last sentence sounds like an expression of our own social-service ideal. It must be understood in the light of what has already been said as to the religious, depersonalized interest in public welfare, yet it does form, as Weber suggests, the point of transition from the motive of the glory of God to the utilitarianism of the later liberal theology. Again Baxter says:

> Will not wealth excuse [from work]? Answer: It may excuse you from some sordid sort of work, by making you more serviceable to another, but you are no more excused from the service of work . . . than the poorest man. . . . Though they [the rich] have no outward want to urge them, they have as great a necessity to obey God. . . . God has strictly commanded it [work] to all.

Even Zinzendorf says: "One does not work simply to live, but one lives to work." The great scriptural warrant for the exhortation to work is 2 Thess. 3, 10, "that if any would not work, neither shall he eat." This passage emphasizes not the reward, but the duty, of work. The Puritan will make the most of his calling. A bee-like industriousness is enjoined.

> God hath commanded you [urges Baxter] some way or other to labor for your daily bread and not to live as drones of the sweat of others.

And again:

> Be wholly taken up in diligent business of your lawful callings when you are not exercised in the more immediate service of God. . . . Labor hard in your calling. . . . See that you have a calling which will find you employment for all the time which God's immediate service spareth.

The terrific Puritan drive toward intense activity is illustrated in various ways in Baxter's writings. For example, it leads him to elaborate the reasons for various callings. Specialization in callings educates and trains the skill of the laborer, and so enables him to increase his output quantitatively and to better it qualitatively. It thus makes for the common good, which is the good of the most people—ideas these which, as Weber reminds us, strikingly resemble the economic principles of Adam Smith. But it cannot be too often repeated that this apparent utilitarianism of Baxter is not in his case real utilitarianism. It springs out of religious interests, not out of humanitarian or economic interests. It is, so to speak, the "ascetic" rather than the economic use of "calling." Industry in one's calling is the expression of the methodically disciplined life devoted to the glory of God. But, and this is to be remembered in view of what follows, the mood for work in such an "ascetic" Protestantism, although engendered by religious considerations, may easily become diverted to a purely economic interest when once the other-worldly point of view is abandoned.

Again, the emphasis upon activity is indicated by what is said by Baxter and others on the use of time:

> Keep up a high esteem of time and be every day more careful that you lose none of your time than you are that you lose none of your gold and silver. And if vain recreations, dressings, feastings, idle talk, unprofitable company or sleep be any of them temptations to rob you of your time, accordingly heighten your watchfulness.

With these warnings of Baxter may be compared that of Matthew Henry: "Those who are prodigal of their time despise their own souls." Sloth becomes one of the deadly sins. It is, so to speak, a continuous sin, and thus interferes in the most dangerous way with the methodically disciplined life. To sleep more than six or at most eight hours is, according to Baxter, morally reprehensible. "Sloth," he says, "destroys the state of grace." We have not yet reached Franklin's "Time is money," but we have arrived at its religious counterpart. Time is infinitely valuable, for every lost hour detracts from the glory of God.

Now all this emphasis upon industry and efficiency in a man's calling insensibly leads to a new attitude toward riches, in sharp contrast with the warnings against them already cited. As a matter of fact, the religious and disciplinary use of one's calling has much the same result as the directly economic exploitation of it. It inevitably leads to the accumulation of riches. It is permissible to change one's calling if the glory of God can be better subserved. Practically this means, if the new calling is a more useful one; and the standards for judging its usefulness are first, its moral character, secondly, the importance of the goods to be produced, and thirdly, its profitableness, for if God who orders our lives provides a chance for profit, he has his own purposes in this, and therefore the chance of profit must be accepted. Thus Baxter says:

> When God shows you a way in which you can lawfully make more without danger to your soul or to others than you can in some other way, and when you reject this way and follow the way that brings in less, then you cross one of the purposes of your calling. You refuse to be God's steward and to accept his gifts in order to use them for others when he so demands. Of course [Baxter continues, as though aware of the danger of this advice] you are not to labor to be rich for the purposes of fleshy indulgence, but for God's sake.

To strive for riches as an exercise in one's calling is thus not only permissible, but commendable.

> You may labor in that manner that tendeth most to success and lawful gain. You are bound to improve your talents.

It was frequently argued that to wish to be poor was as absurd as to wish to be sick. As scriptural warrant for all this the parable of the talents did yeoman's service. Thus arises the strange anomaly that the pursuit of riches, which is such a danger to the soul, since it tends to divert it from doing all things to the glory of God, has become, from the standpoint of magnifying one's calling, not only permissible but a duty, and the possession of riches, which tempts to sensuality and sloth, has become a mark of faithfulness in the discharge of one's calling. It is clear that in this whole development the decisive thing is the idea of "calling," that is, of the methodically disciplined mode of life within the sphere of the secular. The more intense the life of calling, the more God is honored; the more consistently such a life is lived, the more sure one can be of salvation. All this works out into an intensified industriousness, into the mood for work, and the natural economic result is riches. The most earnest adherents of the disciplinary ideal of Protestantism thus come to serve the interests of Capitalism. This result must now be studied more in detail.

The direct economic effects of the Puritan mode of life in calling are manifested in two ways. In the first place the "ascetic" mode of life worked powerfully toward the limitation of consumption. The Puritan looked, for example, with suspicion upon fine clothes. He looked with suspicion upon all the enjoyments of the senses as inclining to the worship of the creature. As a protest against the extravagant life of the feudal nobility the Puritan exalted the idea of stewardship. Enjoyment must not cost anything. To spend money upon one's self leads to unfaithfulness in stewardship. Frugality comes to be a cardinal virtue. Baxter says:

Every penny which is paid upon yourselves or your children or your friends must be done by God's own appointment, and to serve and please him [the glory of God motive]. Watch narrowly, or else that thievish, carnal self will leave God nothing.

Accordingly, what is spent upon oneself must be strictly limited. It also follows that the more property one has, the greater the sense of stewardship. It must be kept unimpaired and even increased, as Jesus taught in the parable of the talents, for this redounds to the glory of God.

In the second place, the intensified activity in one's calling which Puritanism encouraged led to a vastly increased production. Money-making was now freed from the traditional opprobrium which had attached to it. Profits had already been legalized. Calvin himself had seen to that, when, for the first time in history, he had advocated the permissibility of usury (interest). But now profits were looked upon as willed by God, as a mark of his favor and a proof of success in one's calling. The Puritans continued to wage war against the dangers of riches, yet this was not in opposition to rational business, but, as Weber puts it, to irrational consumption, to the extravagance and dissipation which wealth might encourage. Their attack was directed against indulgence in all the external forms of luxury which characterized the feudal aristocracy as a worship of the creature and as opposed to the rational, God-willed use of possessions for the good of the individual and the community. The limit of the permissible in consumption is defined by the word comfort. It was extravagance, display, that was sinful. The ideal of the home takes the place of the feudal ideal of the palace. So far as production was concerned, Puritanism fought against injustice in money-making, against hoarding, against mammonism, the love of riches for their own sake.

But at this point Puritanism found itself in a dilemma. On the one hand the pursuit of wealth for its own sake was sinful. On the other the religious value set upon constant, systematic, efficient work in one's calling as the readiest means of securing the certainty of salvation and of glorifying God became a most powerful agency in economic expansion. The rigid limitations of consumption on the one hand and the methodical intensification of production on the other could have but one result—the accumulation of capital. But the Puritan attitude to calling, with its almost automatic result in accumulation of riches, was destined to become more influential than the Puritan fear of riches. To a very large extent the disciplinary rationalization of life as "calling" accounts for the spirit of modern capitalism. It is not the accumulation of capital in itself that is the decisive thing, but rather a methodical accumulation of it which is a chief characteristic of modern capitalism. And this methodical accumulation has at least one of its main motives in the Calvinistic conception of life as calling. Wherever the Puritan theory of life was held, it strengthened the tendency toward a rationalized, bourgeois, economic mode of life. The Puritan, as Weber expresses it, "stood at the cradle of the economic man." Weber clinches his argument by the following remarkable paragraph from one of John Wesley's sermons:

I fear whenever riches have increased, the essence of religion has decreased in the same proportion. Therefore I do not see how it is possible in the nature of things for any revival of true religion to continue long. For religion must necessarily produce both industry and frugality, and these cannot but produce riches. But as riches increase, so will pride, anger, and love of the world in all its branches. How then is it possible that Methodism, that is, a religion of the heart, though it flourishes now like a green bay tree, should continue in this state? For the Methodists in every place grow diligent and frugal. Consequently they increase in goods. Hence they proportionately increase in pride, in anger, in the desire of the flesh, the desire of the eyes, and the pride of life. So, although the form of religion remains, the spirit is swiftly vanishing away. Is there no way to prevent this continued decay of pure religion? We ought not to prevent people from being diligent and frugal; we must exhort all Christians to gain all they can and to save all they can, that is, in effect, to grow rich. What way can we take that our money-making may not sink us to the nethermost hell? There is one way, and there is no other under heaven. If those who gain all they can and save all they can will also give all they can [the 'ascetic' motive], then, the more they gain the more they will grow in grace and the more treasure they will lay up in heaven.

To this passage I would add another taken from one of the last sermons preached by Wesley before his death:

After you have gained all you can and saved all you can, spend not one pound, one shilling, one penny, to gratify either the desire of the flesh, the desire of the eyes, or the pride of life, or for any other end than to please and glorify God [note the usual motive]. Having avoided this rock on the right hand, beware of that on the left. Hoard nothing. Lay up no treasure on earth; give all you can, that is, all you have. I defy all men upon earth, yea all angels in heaven, to find any other way to extract the poison from riches. . . . You who receive 500 pounds a year and spend only 200, do you give back 300 to God? If not, you certainly rob God of that 300. . . . Nay, may I not do what I will with my own? Here lies the ground of your mistake. It is not your own. It cannot be, unless you are lord of heaven and earth.

In these citations we have in a nutshell most of those fundamental ideas of Protestant "asceticism" which Weber has been describing. Wesley correctly foresaw the dangers which would befall the church through the very virtues which Puritanism emphasized. What he did not foresee was the cosmic extent of these dangers. He did not foresee a world so dominated by money-making that its whole organization is determined by this one great aim. And now we are prepared to understand the way in which Protestant "asceticism" became transformed into the spirit of modern capitalism.

As the great economic movements of the seventeenth, eighteenth, and nineteenth centuries developed through the increasing exploitation of the New World, Africa, and Asia, through the consequent growth of foreign trade, and through the rise of industrialism, the making of profits became an end in itself. *But before this was accomplished religion had consecrated money-making.* As Weber says, "What the great religious epoch of the seventeenth century bequeathed to its utilitarian heir was above all else a gloriously, one might even say a pharisaically, good conscience in money-making."

Is it merely a coincidence [asks the Quaker Rowntree] or is it a consequence that the lofty profession of spirituality made by the Friends has gone hand in hand with shrewdness and tact in the transaction of mundane affairs? Real piety favors the success of the trader by insuring his integrity [faithfulness in calling] and fostering habits of prudence and forethought, important items in obtaining that standing and credit in the commercial world which are requisite for the steady accumulation of wealth.

The relationship of the Puritan self-disciplined and methodical life, as seen in the words "integrity," "prudence," "forethought," to the methodical life of business, as seen in the phrase, "the steady accumulation of wealth," could not be more tellingly, because unconsciously, expressed. Every vestige of the old ecclesiastical theory that a tradesman could scarcely please God now disappeared, and the specifically bourgeois ethic represented in Franklin's maxims arose. No longer was money-making a means, by which the assurance of salvation could be secured or God be glorified. It had become an end in itself. The methodical "asceticism" of the Puritan, his thrift and frugality, are now employed in a business interest. Baxter and Wesley exhorted their hearers to save in order not to rob God, and the habit of frugality was established; Franklin exhorts his young tradesman to save in order to accumulate capital. Puritanism had led to the rationalization of life as calling. Then a tragic thing happened. Capitalism saw the business significance of calling, removed the transcendental, otherworldly motive, and transformed "calling" into a job. . . .

KEMPER FULLERTON

selection 6

*Mahatma Gandhi's Views on Machines and Technology**

D. P. Mukerji

This paper comes out of the conviction that any study of the social changes brought about by technology should be based primarily on an understanding of the conditions of both the society which introduces technology and the society to which it is introduced. If these conditions are crystallized in two systems of values, one which has accepted, and the other which has not accepted "technical progress" as desirable or technological advance as "a self-evident good" . . . ; and further, if the strains of technological advance, which any scheme of technological assistance brings in its wake, must be reduced or eliminated so as to render the assistance genuinely effective, then one of the chief concerns of the sociologist as well as of the technical administrator is the discovery of the terms of the normative system of both countries concerned. . . .

*From *International Social Science Bulletin*, Vol. 6, No. 3, UNESCO, Paris, 1954. Reprinted in Charles R. Walker, *Modern Technology and Civilization* (McGraw-Hill Book Co., Inc., 1962), pp. 379–90.

It is disheartening that no formulation of the Eastern value-system has been made by an Eastern sociologist. One reason for this may be that Eastern people are still too deeply involved in their system and, therefore, the technological impact on their basic values is as yet superficial. Another reason may be that those who could formulate and compare the value-systems are the very people who believe in technical advance as a "self-evident good" and, therefore, do not worry about the problem beyond the stage of annoyance with temporary mal-adjustments which, in their view, a welfare state, or a similar agency or agencies, would benevolently remove sooner or later. . . . [Mahatma Gandhiji] was deeply and primarily concerned with the value-systems, . . . and he put his views very sharply indeed. One may not like his manner of posing the problem, one may consider it as partial, one may dismiss it, if one chooses, as many "educated" men and industrialists of India have chosen. But his statements remain a challenge to the entire problem of technological change and schemes of technical assistance. . . . From them one might infer that the term "underdeveloped economy," which is the excuse of technical assistance, was inappropriate insofar as it confused the co-existence of two different value-systems by placing them on the assembly-line of historical development in which economic growth, being the supreme value, was subservient to and dependent only upon technological advance. Perhaps, Gandhiji was unfair to the European civilization; it may also be that he did not subscribe to the unilinear concept of history. But it is certain that he had other values and his understanding of India, at least, was unerring. We Indians love to think that Gandhiji's views correctly represent the unformu- lated values of the vast majority of the Indian population towards social changes. They, as he would say, would welcome change on their own human terms. . . .

Let us follow the development of Gandhiji's ideas. In October 1924, soon after he had broken one of his famous fasts, he gave an interview to a student from Santiniketan, Sir Ramchandran, who questioned him on his views on the place of Art in national regeneration and on machinery. Ramchandran asked (*Mahatma*, vol. 2, p. 212)

R. Are you against all machinery?

G. How can I be when I know that even this body is a delicate piece of machinery? The spinning wheel itself is a machine; a little tooth-pick is a machine. What I object to is the craze for machinery, not machinery as such. The craze is for what they call labour-saving machinery. Men go on "saving labour" till thousands are without work and thrown on the streets to die of starvation. I want to save time and labour, not for a fraction of mankind, but for all. I want the concentration of wealth, not in the hands of a few, but in the hands of all. Today machinery helps a few to ride on the backs of millions. The impetus behind it is not the philanthropy to save labour, but greed. It is against this constitution of things that I am fighting with all my might.

R. Then you are fighting not against machinery as such, but against its abuses, which are so much in evidence today?

G. I would unhesitatingly say yes; but I would add that scientific truths and discoveries should first cease to be mere instruments of greed. Then labourers will not be overworked and machinery instead of becoming a hindrance will be a help. I am aiming not at eradica- tion of all machinery, but limitation.

R. When logically argued out, that would imply that all complicated power-driven machinery should go.

G. It might have to go, but I must make one thing clear. The supreme consideration is man. The machine should not tend to keep atrophied the limbs of man. For instance, I would make intelligent exceptions. Take the case of the Singer Sewing Machine.

R. But, in that case, there would have to be a factory for making these Singer Sewing Machines, and it would have to contain power-driven machinery of ordinary type.

G. Yes, surely. But I am Socialist enough to say that such factories should be nationalized or state-controlled. They ought only to be working under the most attractive and ideal conditions, not for profit, but for the benefit of humanity, love taking on the place of greed as the motive. It is an alteration in the conditions of labour that I want. This mad rush for wealth must cease and the labourer must be assured not only of a living wage but a daily task that is not a mere drudgery. The machine will, under these conditions, be as much a help to the man working it as to the state, or the man who owns it. The present mad rush will cease and the labourer will work, as I have said, under attractive and ideal conditions. This is but one of the exceptions I have in mind. The sewing machine had love at its back. The individual is the one supreme consideration. The saving of labour of the individual should be the object and honest humanitarian considerations, and not greed the motive. . . . Therefore, replace greed by love and everything will come right.

Next morning the interview was continued. Ramchandran persisted:

R. If you make an exception of the Singer Sewing Machine and your spindle, where would these exceptions end?

G. Just where they cease to help the individual and encroach upon his individuality. The machine should not be allowed to cripple the limbs of man.

R. But I was not thinking just now of the practical side. Ideally would you not rule out all machinery? When you except the sewing machine, you will have to make exceptions of the bicycle, the motor-car, etc.

G. No, I don't, because they do not satisfy any of the primary wants of man; . . . Ideally, however, I would rule out all machinery, even as I would reject this very body, which is not helpful to salvation and seek the absolute liberation of the soul. From that point of view, I would reject all machinery, but machines will remain because, like the body, they are inevitable. The body itself, as I told you, is the *purest piece* of mechanism; but if it is a hindrance to the highest flights of the soul, it has to be rejected. . . .

The "ideal" pattern of Hindu values was never forsaken by Gandhiji. It was woven round "wantlessness." How could technology and machines geared to the production of goods for the satisfaction of wants, which created more wants, joint wants, derived wants, the infinite hyperbola of wants, be consonant with the pattern of Indian norms? How could such norms square for that matter, with Economics, grounded as it was on wants and their satisfaction? If absolute liberation of the soul from the body be the utter sum of existence, then Gandhiji, and with him, every Hindu who was aware of his ancestry, would raise the eternal query: Why this craze for machinery? Why machine-civilization at all? Other problems such as machines helping a few to ride on the back of millions, the concentration of power and wealth, of justice for the labourer as man, securing attractive conditions of life for him and of giving him security of employment, etc. etc. would be subsidiary. These latter, in Gandhiji's opinion, ultimately hinged upon non-possession, wantlessness, subordination of body and bodily wants to the need of the soul's liberation from its physical encasement, which was *the* end.

These subsidiary problems, however, were far from socially insignificant. In the Gandhian view of life, they were related to the means. To many "educated"

Indians they were the ends, or the primary values. Gandhiji had many opportunities of discussing them with those who were more sensitive to the needs and
ideas of the day. Rabindranath Tagore's objection was of a different type, but it
was met by the logic of means. The poet had written in 1925 against the charkha
(the spinning wheel), because he felt that it would bring about a deathlike
sameness in the nation. Gandhiji met this argument on the highest level. Taking
his cue from the Hindu philosophical conception of oneness, identity, or sameness, which Sankar had carried to its logical extreme, Gandhiji held that "behind
a variety of occupations there is an indispensable sameness also of occupation."
After inveighing for a while against exploitation both by European and Indian
manufacturers, Gandhiji conceded:

> Machinery has its place; it has come to stay. But it must not be allowed to displace the
> necessary human labour. An important plough is a good thing. But if by some chance one
> man could plough up by some mechanical invention of his the whole of the land of India
> and control all the agricultural produce and if the millions had no other occupation, they
> would starve, and being idle, they would become dunces, as many have already become.
> There is hourly danger of many more being reduced to that unenviable state. I would
> welcome every improvement in the cottage machine but I know that it is criminal to
> displace the hand labour by the introduction of power-driven spindles unless one is at the
> same time ready to give millions of farmers some other occupation in their homes. (*Young
> India*, 5 Nov. 1925; *Mahatma*, vol. 2, p. 283.)

Here was argument on the purely economic level of means, that is, of employment and unemployment. (Also, vol. 4, 34, p. 238-9.) To a modern Western
economist it may appear to be old-fashioned. He thinks that he has devised
excellent measures against various types of unemployment, cyclical, structural,
frictional, seasonal, and all that, and he is not worried if even under full employment two to five per cent are unemployed. But Gandhiji was not to be deluded
by such theories and measures emerging out of the practices of countries that
had been wedded to industrial and technical civilization, that had colonies to
exploit and accepted competitive values in production, trade and commerce.
The essence of Gandhiji's concession in this open letter to Tagore is, however,
historical. That is to say, so long as "some other occupation in their homes" was
not available—and it was not likely to be available in that historical context, or
in the near future, because imperialist exploitation would not allow India to
create alternative occupations—Gandhiji would stick to the spinning wheel and
be against the displacement of labour by machinery. In other words, India in
her present context should have labour-intensive economy for the sake of full
employment.

Gandhiji was very respectful towards Tagore, and as we have seen met the
poet's cultural charge with economic arguments. But he was not so soft towards
the Indian Communist M. P. Mr. Saklatwala. . . .

He wrote:

> For unlike Saklatwala, I do not believe that multiplication of wants and machinery con-
> trived to supply them is taking the world a single step nearer its goal. Comrade Saklatwala
> swears by the modern rush. I wholeheartedly detest this mad desire to destroy distance and

time, to increase animal appetites and go to the ends of the earth in search of their satis-faction. If modern civilization stands for all this, and I have understood it to do so, I call it satanic and with it the present system of government, its best exponent.

Then follow some sentences which would remind one of the wrath of proph-ets, but with a difference.

I would destroy that system today, if I had the power. I would use the most deadly weapons, if I believed that they would destroy it. I refrain only because the use of such weapons could only perpetuate the system though it may destroy its present administration. Those, who seek to destroy men rather than their manners, adopt the latter and become worse than those whom they destroy under the mistaken belief that the manners will die with the men. They do not know the root of the evil.

The last paragraph seems to retain its pertinence today in spheres wider than the Indian. The points to be noticed in Gandhiji's reply to Saklatwala's appeal are Gandhiji's firm faith in wantlessness as a cardinal human virtue, and his objection only to the "modern rush," in which he included both the Western and the Indian values of the day. We may further note his association of modernism with the British Government in India. Strictly from the point of view of the propagation of an unswerving faith, this mixture of basic values with nationalism was excellent. A sociologist would not cavil at it. Technological values are usually associated with the nationalist values, particularly in the Eastern countries in the period of their anti-imperialist struggle which centres in their opposition to the obstacles that imperialism places in their economic growth, and also in the period of economic advance which is held to be possible only with the help of technology. But it is equally understandable that national-ist, antisubjectionist motives and attitudes should be integrated with the basic values which are, or are interpreted to be, specific to the culture of the nation. While it is true that in this extract no reference is made to the Indian-ness of the objection to the modern rush and the argument appears to rest on the personal level, it is apparent, as it certainly was to the Indian of 1925, that it was a typically Indian argument securely grounded on the Indian philosophy of life,... non-possession, enjoyment through giving away.

We must repeat that Gandhiji collected other arguments round this basic objection to machines. They were mainly what we would call sociological argu-ments on the score of excessive population on land, of idle labour, of bad distribution of wealth, benefit to the nation, that is to say, the welfare of the people. He referred to unemployment again and again, to bad health, unwhole-some food, and to the decay of art. He categorically stated that labour had a unique place in swaraj, or independence, and formed its content. Each argument depended on another and the whole formed a pattern of positive values. In 1935, on 23 April, he said after opening the first All-India Village Industries Exhibition at Indore:

The reason why our average life-rate is deplorably low, the reason why we are getting more and more impoverished is that we have neglected our 100,000 villages. We have indeed thought of them, but only to the extent of exploiting them. We read thrilling accounts of the "glory that was India," of the land that was flowing with milk and honey; but today it is a land of starving millions. We are sitting in this fine pandal under a blaze of electric lights, but we do not know that we are burning these lights at the expense of the poor. We have no right to use the lights if we forget that we owe these to them.

Gandhiji would seldom forget to remind his audience of their responsibility towards the people. . . .

On 22 October 1937 he inaugurated the Educational Conference at Wardha and developed his ideas of education through handicrafts. It was a new setting for his constructive programme—an integration of living in love, with efficiency and independence, without exploitation, conflict and poverty, and with education of the body and mind. In expounding his thesis, he said:

> Then, take the question of machinery. I think that machinery is not necessary for us at all. We should use khadi (home-spun cloth); and, therefore, we do not require mills. We should try to produce all the necessary cloth in villages, and we need not be the slaves of machines. I am afraid, by working with machines we have become machines ourselves, having lost all sense of art and handwork. If you still think that we cannot do without machines, the scheme (of new education) I have placed before you will be futile. You wish to keep our village alive by means of machines and think of imparting education to the village children through them. Machines will only help in making all the thirty-five crores of people unemployed. If you think that machines are really indispensable, you must reject the scheme and suggest a new one. (*Mahatma,* vol. 4, p. 238-9.)

In 1946 India was passing through a severe food crisis. Gandhiji offered advice to those who sought it. There were suggestions and counter-suggestions. Even in those dire days he would not move from his fundamental ground. In one of his replies he said:

> I regard the existence of power wheels for the grinding of corn in thousands of villages as the limit of our helplessness. I suppose India does not produce all the engines and grinding machines. . . . The planting of such machinery and engines on a large scale in villages (a suggestion made by a correspondent for resolving the food crisis) is also a sign of greed. Is it proper to fill one's pockets in this manner at the expense of the poor? Every such machinery puts thousands of hand *chakkis* (grindstones for corn) out of work, and takes away employment from thousands of housewives and artisans who make these *chakkis.* Moreover, the process is infective and spreads to every village industry. The decay of the latter spells too the decay of art. If it meant the replacement of the old crafts by the new ones, one might not have much to say against it. But this is not what is happening. In the thousands of villages, where power-machinery exists, one misses the sweet music in the early morning of the grinders at work. But to come to the main point. Whilst I hold that these power engines are, at present, being put to wrong use, it would be some compensation if these engines, in addition to their present use, were also used to pump water out of the rivers, tanks and wells for irrigation. (*Mahatma,* vol. 7, p. 71-2.)

Probably the most comprehensive and yet succinct account of the place of machinery in the context of independence was written by Gandhiji in the *Harijan* of 15 July 1946. It was a clarification for the benefit of Congressmen of his concept of independence. He painted a glorious picture of self-sufficient villages, giving free and voluntary play to mutual forces, highly cultured in the sense that there every man and woman knows what he or she wants and, what is more, knows that no one should want anything that the others cannot have with equal labour, a society based on the living force of truth and nonviolence, a society not like a pyramid but like "an oceanic circle."[1]

We have traced the development of Gandhiji's ideas on machines, and on machine-civilization and found that despite many concessions to the "proper" use of machines his values were definitely opposed to those which make for technological civilization and are made by it. By "proper" he meant, positively, that which was prompted by love and good for humanity, and negatively, what did not lead to concentration of wealth in a few hands and inequality, to centralization of power, to urbanization, to unemployment, to political, economic and social exploitation. These evils, which in his view, were the characteristics of the modern society, with its American apogee, were the consequences of the large scale use of machines, and they had to be fought with vigour. To that extent he was placing Indian (Eastern) against Western (Euro-American, modern) values. It was certainly not a case of revivalism, but a clear statement of a principle of social organization which was different from the one that had succeeded in imposing itself on the strength of political suzerainty. His minimal idea was to establish co-existence of different social systems, on the basis of equality, though the prophetic strain that came to him in the course of his experiments with Truth led him to think that the values he propagated would also be good for the Western world. We will leave it to the Western sociologist to ponder over this issue. An Indian sociologist can only mention that Gandhiji's protagonism of Indian values was not a manifestation of the romantic agony of nationalist historians, nor was it a reactionary, obscurantist throw-back. It is submitted here that he was a revolutionary and what a revolutionary in India should be, viz., an Indian revolutionary, that is, one who would first be steeped in Indian realities and then evaluate the nature of changes in social realities in order to create fresh norms. Gandhiji did not go to the past: in fact, he was not an Indologist; he only went to the roots and the sources. And "the deeper you go to the root the more radical you become."...

Thus the Gandhian conclusion in regard to machines and technology is logical if one accepts the postulates that India has a separate norm of values—with the hidden assumption that values determine conduct—that she has a separate principle of social organization which would be disturbed and even destroyed by large-scale use of machinery for greed and profit, and that a proper use would presuppose certain attitudes, some traditional and others not, but all working in alliance, and also a type of State that would own and control large machineries, if they were indispensable for defined purposes. Otherwise, the machineries to

---

1 "I may be taunted with the retort that this is all Utopian and, therefore, not worth a single thought. If Euclid's point, though incapable of being drawn by any human agency, has an imperishable value, my picture has its own for mankind to live. Let India live for this true picture, though never realizable in its completeness. . . . In it, there is no room for machines that would displace human labour and that would concentrate power in a few hands. Labour has its unique place in a cultured human family. Every machine that helps every individual has a place. But I must confess that I have never sat down to think out what that machine can be. I have thought of Singer's Sewing Machine. But even that is perfunctory. I do not need it to fill in my picture." (*Mahatma*, vol. 7, p. 201-2.)

be used would be of a special type suitable for removing drudgery of handi-craft and improving its quality, if possible. They would operate in the general context of de-centralized economy, in close alliance with agriculture. Gandhiji would thus remove the stings of Capitalism and Socialism alike.

In this author's opinion, Gandhiji's views have to be carefully studied before any scheme of technical assistance and large-scale technological development is initiated. While it is very true that among certain strata and sections of the Indian people these views appear strange, even though lip-service is paid to them, and that such people would want to initiate rapid technological change in the name of economic advance, evolution and progress, it is also clear that an unintelligent injection of technology would so disturb the existing social pattern of human relations that work would cease to be associated with joy and work-manship, that skill would be replaced by efficiency, that "the public identity of the job" would be lost, that scientific management and discipline would squeeze the labourer of all humaneness, and that a new instrument of social power would "teach docility" or "break the intransigence of workers," all the time keeping greed, profit and more profit in the background, beyond the sight of those who are to be immediately benefited by higher wages, better conditions of living, welfare-measures and the like (*Social Theory and Social Structure*, R. K. Merton, p. 318–22).

In other words, the sociologist would do well to study the sociology of the demand for technology in India and the sociology of its supply. Fortunately, the Indian masses are not yet fully taken in by the technological values. They are being acted upon by technology, and they are showing healthy, normal reactions to the injection by absenteeism, inattentiveness, a sort of lackadaisical attitude towards work in the factories, unpunctuality, the so-called absence of pride in work and workmanship, but unfortunately, quite often in accidents and ill-health. Even strikes, which are bemoaned as symptoms of industrial conflict, can be traced to the search of the soil-bound peasantry of India for mental and social peace in holiday, away from the scene of work, the din of factories and technology, to the villages where the pattern which they know and instinctively feel to be right, rules even today.

An Indian sociologist cannot thus help questioning the manner and the possi-ble hidden motivations of a technological advance, of those who want it and those who supply it. He can, at least, categorically state, with Gandhiji, that if change is inevitable, let it come in the shape of certain types of machines, at the proper time, in the proper context; and that if large-scale use of machinery is unavoidable, let it be owned and managed by the State, a new form of State. Judging from experience, he cannot share Gandhiji's hope of an interim trustee-ship by the fortunate few. In short, the whole problem of technological advance in India, which, let it be repeated, is undeveloped only in the purely technologi-cal sense, and therefore, in the sense of being more socially integrated and less fragmentized, has to be studied from the points of view of both the types of machinery to be introduced and of the types of people who would accept them with due regard to the motivations of introduction. In India, human beings are not yet atomistic, so that no functional specification in the most common productive processes, which are those of agriculture, is possible. Nor has it occurred in many industries. In India, no productive section of society is "universalistic," that is, only very few "criteria possibly present in any segment of the population without regard to previous social relationships or membership in irrelevant groups" are available. In India, human relations are affective rather than rational and impersonal. The normative system suitable for the industrial mode of production through large-scale use of machines is thus not the normative system of India. A matter of additional importance is the fact that this normative system has combined with nationalism, anti-imperialism, and Gandhiji's interpretation of independence to convince some people that it is still valuable. So change must take account of these facts in order not to produce the same evils to which the West has been an heir.[2]

---

[2] Most of the quotations from Gandhiji's writings have been taken from D. G. Tendulkar's monumental biography, *Mahatma*, seven volumes of which are available at the time of writing, the eighth being in press.

selection 7

A Chinese Philosopher Prefers the Material Civilization of the West*

Hu Shih

As a true Chinese, I must begin with Confucius. According to Confucius, all implements of civilization are spiritual in origin: they all come from "ideas." "When conceived, they are called ideas. When materially embodied, they are called implements. When instituted for general use, they are called forms or patterns. When wrought into the everyday life of all the people, they marvel at them and call them the work of the gods." Confucius cited many examples to illustrate this point of view. Man saw wood floating on water and invented ships; he saw wood submerged under water and, caring for the preservation of the bodies of his dead parents, invented coffins and tombs. He saw rain fall from

---

* From "The Civilizations of the East and the West," in *Whither Mankind*, ed. Charles A. Beard (Longmans, Green and Co., 1928), pp. 25–31. Reprinted in *The World of Business*, ed. Edward Bursk, Donald Clark, and Ralph Hidy (Simon and Schuster, Inc., 1962), pp. 1505–10.

the heavens and, thinking probably of the work of time obliterating all traces of human memory, invented writing to take the place of knotted cords.

Needless to say, this view of Confucius was supported by Plato and Aristotle in the West. Human tools and institutions had their origin in the "ideas" or ideal patterns which Aristotle called the "formal causes." Confucius and Plato and Aristotle lived in those good old days when the human mind was not yet troubled by the medieval dualism of matter and spirit and was therefore able to recognize the ideality underlying the material embodiment of human inventions.

Indeed there is no such thing as a purely material civilization. Every tool of civilization is produced by human intelligence making use of the matter and energy in the natural world for the satisfaction of a want, a desire, an esthetic feeling or an intellectual curiosity. A clay pot is no more material than a love lyric; nor is St. Paul's Cathedral less material than the Woolworth Building. Indeed when man first made fire by accidentally drilling wood, the invention was regarded as such a spiritual thing as to be attributed to one of the greatest gods. In the East, all the legendary kings of China were not priest-philosophers, but inventors. Such, for example, were Sui-jen, the discoverer of fire, You-tsao, the first builder of houses, and Shen-nung, the first teacher of agriculture and medicine.

Our forefathers were quite right in deifying the creators of tools. Man is a tool-making animal, and it is tool-making which constitutes civilization. The invention of fire created a new epoch in the history of human civilization; agriculture, another; the invention of writing, a third; printing, a fourth. It was the invention of the telescope and the steam engine and the discovery of electricity and radioactivity that have made the modern world what it is today. And if the priests of the Medieval Age were justly canonized as saints, Galileo, Watt, Stephenson, Morse, Bell, Edison, and Ford certainly deserve to be honored as gods and enshrined with Prometheus and Cadmus. They represent that which is most divine in man, namely, that creative intelligence which provides implements and makes civilization possible.

The civilization of a race is simply the sum total of its achievement in adjusting itself to its environment. Success or failure in that adjustment depends upon the ability of the race to use intelligence for the invention of necessary and effective tools. Advancement in civilization depends upon the improvement of tools. Such terms as the Stone Age, the Bronze Age, the Iron Age and the Steam and Electricity Age tell the tale of the development of civilization. And what is true of the historical development of civilization is no less true of the geographical distribution of the different civilizations. The difference between the Eastern and Western civilizations is primarily a difference in the tools used. The West has during the last two hundred years moved far ahead of the East merely because certain Western nations have been able to devise new tools for the conquest of nature and for the multiplication of the power to do work. The East, whence have come a number of the epoch-making tools of ancient civilizations, has failed to carry on that great tradition and is left behind in the stage of manual labor while the Western world has long entered the age of steam and electricity.

This, then, is the real difference between the Oriental and the Western civilizations. The Oriental civilization is built primarily on human labor as the source of power whereas the modern civilization of the West is built on the basis of the power of machinery. . . . The modern city of Harbin [in Manchuria] was formerly a Russian Concession which grew up from a small trading center into what is now called the "Shanghai of North China." With the development of the Russian Concession, there grew up, a few miles away, the native city of Harbin which was once only a group of peasant villages. While I was touring through the city, I was struck by one interesting fact: whereas practically all the vehicles of locomotion in the native city were jinrikshas, or carriages pulled by human power, no riksha was allowed to operate in the former Russian city which, though now under Chinese administration, still retained much of Russian influence and tradition. Transportation and traveling in the modern city of Harbin were by tramways and taxicabs; rikshas carrying passengers from the native city must leave without a fare.

Here I made my great discovery in modern geography—I discovered the borderline between the Eastern and Western civilizations. The city of Harbin separates the East from the West by separating the jinriksha (man-power-carriage) civilization from the motorcar civilization!

Let all apologists for the spiritual civilization of the East reflect on this. What spirituality is there in a civilization which tolerates such a terrible form of human slavery as the riksha coolie? Do we seriously believe that there can be any spiritual life left in those poor human beasts of burden who run and toil and sweat under the peculiar bondage of slavery which knows neither the minimum wage nor any limit of working hours? Do we really believe that the life of a riksha coolie is more spiritual or more moral than that of the American workman who rides to and from his work in his own motorcar, who takes his whole family out picnicking on Sundays in distant parks and woods, who listens to the best music of the land on the radio for almost no cost, and whose children are educated in schools equipped with the most modern library and laboratory facilities?

It is only when one has fully realized what misery and acute suffering the life of riksha-pulling entails and what effects it produces on the bodily health of those human beasts of burden—it is only then that one will be truly and religiously moved to bless the Hargreaveses, the Cartwrights, the Watts, the Fultons, the Stephensons, and the Fords who have devised machines to do the work for man and relieve him from much of the brutal suffering to which his Oriental neighbor is still subject.

Herein, therefore, lies the real spirituality of the material civilization, of mechanical progress *per se*. Mechanical progress means the use of human intelligence to devise tools and machines to multiply the working ability and productivity of man so that he may be relieved from the fate of toiling incessantly with his unaided hands, feet and back without being able to earn a bare subsistence, and so that he may have enough time and energy left to seek and enjoy the higher values which civilization can offer him. Where man has to sweat blood in order to earn the lowest kind of livelihood, there is little *life* left, let alone civilization. A civilization to be worthy of its name must be built upon the foundation of material progress. As the Chinese statesman Kuan Chung (died 645 B.C.) said twenty-six centuries ago, "When food and clothing are sufficiently provided for, honor and disgrace can be distinguished; and when granaries are full, the people will know good manners." This is not to drag in the so-called economic interpretation of history: it is simple common sense. Picture a civilization where boys and girls and old women with bamboo baskets tied to their backs and with pointed sticks in hand flock to every dumping place of refuse and search for a possible torn piece of rag or a half-burnt piece of coal. How can we expect a moral and spiritual civilization to grow up in such an atmosphere?

Then people may point to the religious life in those regions where the material civilization is low. What spirituality is there, let us say, in the old beggar-woman who dies in the direst destitution, but who dies while still mumbling, *"Namo Amita Buddha!"*[1] and in the clear conviction that she will surely enter that blissful paradise presided over by the Amita Buddha? Do we earnestly think it moral or spiritual to inculcate in that beggar-woman a false belief which shall so hypnotize her as to make her willingly live and die in such dire conditions where she ought not to have been had she been born in a different civilization?

No! All those hypnotic religions belong to an age when man had reached senility and felt himself impotent in coping with the forces of nature. Therefore he gave up the fight in despair and, like the disappointed fox in the ancient fable who declared the grapes sour because he could not reach them, began to console himself and teach the world that wealth and comfort are contemptible and that poverty and misery are something to be proud of. From this it was only a step to the idea that life itself was not worth living and that the only desirable thing was the blissful existence in the world beyond. And when wise men calmly taught these ideas, fanatics went further and practiced self-denial, self-torture, and even suicide. In the West, saints prayed, fasted, slept on pillars, and whipped themselves at regular intervals. In medieval China, monks prayed, fasted, and, feeding themselves daily with fragrant oil and tying their bodies with oiled cloth, gladly burned themselves to death as offerings to some deity of Mahayana Buddhism.

It took over a thousand years for a portion of mankind to emerge from the civilization which glorifies poverty and sanctifies disease, and slowly build up a new civilization which glorifies life and combats poverty as a crime. As we look around today, the religions of the Middle Ages are still there, the churches and

---

[1] This sentence, meaning "Homage to the Amita Buddha," is daily recited by followers of the Paradise (Pure Land) Sect of Buddhism.

cathedrals are still there, the monasteries and nunneries are still there. How is it that the outlook upon life has so radically changed? The change has come because in the last two centuries men have hit upon a few key inventions out of which a vast number of tools and machines have been constructed for the control of the resources and powers in nature. By means of these machines men have been able to save labor and reduce distance, to fly in the air, tunnel the mountains and sail underneath the deep seas, to enslave lightning to pull our carriages and employ "ether" to deliver our messages throughout the world. Science and machinery seem to meet no resistance from nature. Life has become easier and happier, and man's confidence in his own powers has greatly increased. Man has become the master of himself and of his own destiny.

Additional References

Ayal, Eliezar, B. "Nationalist Ideology and Economic Development," *Human Organization*, Vol. 25, No. 3 (Fall, 1966), pp. 230–39.

Campos, Robert de Oliveira. "Rising Expectations: With or Without Revolution," *Columbia Journal of World Business*, Vol. 3, No. 3 (May–June, 1968), pp. 9–16.

Fanfani, Amintore. *Catholicism, Protestantism and Capitalism.* New York: Sheed & Ward, 1955.

Farmer, R., and Richman, B. "Environmental Constraints: Sociological-Cultural" and "Sociological-Cultural Constraints: External," *Comparative Management and Economic Progress*, chaps. 7 and 8, pp. 109–237. Homewood, Ill.: Richard D. Irwin, Inc., 1965.

Finney, Ben. "Money Work, Fast Money, and Prize Money: Aspects of the Tahitian Labor Commitment," *Human Organization*, Vol. 26, No. 4 (Winter, 1967), pp. 195–99.

Gellerman, Saul. "Passivity, Paranoia, and Pakikisama," *Columbia Journal of World Business*, September–October, 1967.

Hajime, Nakanura. "Modern Trend in Religious Thoughts," *The Developing Economies*, Vol. 3, No. 4 (December, 1965), p. 573.

Hanna, Willard. "The Magical-Mystical Syndrome in the Indonesian Mentality," American Universities Field Staff Reports Service, Southeast Asia Series, Vol. 15, Nos. 5–9 (1967).

———. "Cushioning and Conditioning the Pioneer: How Indigent Settlers Achieve Self-sufficiency" (Malaysia), American Universities Field Staff Reports Service, Southeast Asia Series, Vol. 13, No. 2 (September, 1965).

Heilbroner, Robert L. *The Worldly Philosophers.* New York: Simon and Schuster, Inc., 1961.

Linton, Ralph. *The Cultural Background of Personality.* Appleton-Century-Crofts, 1945.

McClelland, David. *The Achieving Society.* Princeton, N.J.: D. Van Nostrand Co., Inc., 1961, especially "Value Attitudes of Entrepreneurs and Professionals," pp. 281–87.

———. "The Urge to Achieve," *New Society* (U.K.), February 16, 1967, pp. 227–29.

Meadows, Paul. "Traditional Motivations in an Age of Rapid Change," *Business and Society*, Vol. 8, No. 1 (Autumn, 1967), pp. 19–29.

Polanyi, Karl. *The Great Transformation.* Boston: Beacon Press, 1957.

Ravenholt, Albert. "India's Bovine Burden—Dairy Cooperatives in a Tradition-ridden Society," American Universities Field Staff Reports Service, South Asia Series, Vol. 10, No. 12 (December, 1966).

Rosen, B. C. "Race, Ethnicity and the Achievement Syndrome," *American Sociological Review,* Vol. 24 (1959), pp. 47–60.

Sanford, Edward. "The Influence of Values and Attitudes on Economic Changes in Western Culture," *Business and Society,* Vol. 8, No. 2 (Spring, 1968), pp. 32–43.

Smith, Rolland F. "Christian Idea of Work," *Carroll Business Bulletin,* Vol. 9, No. 4 (Winter, 1967), pp. 3–8.

Tawney, R. H. *Religion and the Rise of Capitalism.* New York: New American Library, Mentor Book, 1954, original 1926.

Walker, Charles R. "Perspectives: Time, Space and History," *Technology, Industry, and Man,* chap. 2. New York: McGraw-Hill Book Co., Inc., 1968.

chapter five

Business Managers and Economic Development

Whether socialist or capitalist, government appointee or private citizen, managers of economic enterprises play a crucial role in industrial development. The process of economic growth and the contributions of management are considered in these reading selections.

Selection: "Business in Western Europe," Richard Eells and Clarence Walton

In an earlier selection, Lewis Mumford described psychological changes in attitudes that preceded and accompanied economic development, primarily in Europe. This reading from Eells' and Walton's *Conceptual Foundations of Business* describes the development of business philosophies in Western Europe from ancient times to the 19th century.

Selection: "The Shackles of Backwardness," Robert Heilbroner

The problem in much of the rest of the world has been the difficulty in changing attitudes and fostering economic development because of the limits that underdeveloped societies impose on people. In this selection from *The Great Ascent,* Heilbroner discusses the ideological, social, and economic conditions of backward societies.

Selection: "The Stages of Economic Growth," W. W. Rostow

With varying degrees of success, countries attempt to overcome the shackles that Heilbroner describes and to expand their economic capacity. In this reading

127

from Rostow's well known and influential book, *The Stages of Economic Growth,* we consider this process, especially the critical role played by entrepreneurs and managers.

Selection: "The Critical Role of the High Achiever," David C. McClelland

Elaborating on entrepreneurs' contributions to economic growth, McClelland shows us how psychologists have identified the need for achievement, which apparently is vital for economic development. In this selection from McClelland's article, "Business Drive and National Achievement," we get empirical evidence for Lewis Mumford's suggestion that ideology is the energizing factor.

Selection: "Cross-Cultural Studies of Technical Change," Margaret Mead

In the 1950's, the United Nations commissioned a large scale research project to examine the impact of industrialization on culture. An eminent anthropologist reports on its conclusions.

selection 8

*Business in Western Europe**

Richard Eells and Clarence C. Walton

Werner Sombart, the great historian of capitalism, held that "all culture, and consequently all economy, is historical. As there is in the abstract no religion, no language, no state, but merely a certain religion, a certain art, a certain language, a certain state, so there is no economy [or business] in the abstract, but a particularly constituted, historically distinguishable economic life."[1]

By abstracting from selected phases of business history—ancient to modern— those characteristics that give adequate explanation of the meaning of business, we shall attempt here to answer with concrete examples such questions as: How was business actually carried out? What promoted business and what hindered it? What were the relationships of other cultural institutions to business? Perhaps the businessman, so often castigated for a myopic historical sense, can discover from even a limited and cursory examination of the past some valuable clues to these questions. Unlike other ages, ours has been characterized as an era of

---

**Conceptual Foundations of Business* (Homewood, Ill.: Richard D. Irwin, Inc., 1961), pp. 17–38.

[1] Werner Sombart, "Capitalism," *Encyclopaedia of the Social Sciences,* Vol. 3, p. 196.

accelerating change. Even so, twentieth-century business has an ancestry, and its nature is the product of many centuries of evolution and creative adaptation, however unprecedented its pace today.

THE ANCIENT WORLD

The Greek Ideal

The Greek ideal of the self-sufficient household managed by those skilled in animal husbandry and in agriculture had little place for the merchant. But reality has a way of distorting ideals. Mountainous terrain and a scarcity of fertile soil forced Greece to import from other Mediterranean peoples the foodstuffs and raw materials it lacked. These imports were paid for through the export of specialized farm products, like olive oil and wine, and specialized industrial goods, like iron tools, pots, and works of art. Indeed, the Greeks offer testimony to a proposition that has almost universal applicability: trade implies the existence of surplus in one area and of demand for this surplus in another. It also implies the willingness and availability of people to carry the goods. Such carriers are more apt to be found in areas where there are groups of people who cannot find employment either in agriculture or in existing industries.

The growth of commerce in Ancient Greece was painfully uneven, but grow it did, and Greek exchange during the later Hellenic period exhibits remarkable vigor. Improvements in the systems of roads, the increasing use of money as a medium of exchange, the diffusion of a common language and a common system of law, and the consequent development of similar forms of business procedure promoted a lively commerce within the various Hellenic city-states. The great lawgiver Solon (c. 639–559 B.C.) even persuaded his fellow Athenians to adopt the Euboic standard of weights and measures so as to facilitate commerce with the prosperous communities of Asia Minor.[2] And there existed a rather sophisticated group of bankers (the *trapezitae*) who served the business community in an honest and skillful manner.

Yet there were important deterrents to the expansion of Greek trade. Hostility to the trader, political insecurity, lack of progress in nautical sciences, the drive toward self-sufficiency on the part of each city-state, the absence of vigorous mass markets, and a business class that was losing vitality all plagued the Greek business community.

Notwithstanding these limitations, the growth of Greek commerce and banking is indicative of the existence and use of business devices that have become familiar. There is also ample evidence that trade and finance were controlled by a profit motive. One writer notes that "it is sad to see how often Athenian genius was wronged, and Greek love of freedom betrayed by greed and the desire for profit making."[3] M. L. W. Laistner states that "the enterprising [merchants]

---

[2] M. L. W. Laistner (ed. and trans.), *Greek Economics* (New York: E. P. Dutton, 1923), pp. xv–xvi.

[3] Helen Corke, *Toward Economic Freedom* (London: Methuen & Co., 1937), p. 28.

made great efforts to keep themselves informed of prices and the state of the markets in different ports, but the absence of modern 'facilities' greatly restricted the possibilities of carrying out a successful 'coup.'"[4] Perhaps the most telling evidence of the existence of the profit motive is Aristotle's condemnation of wealth-getting as an overriding life goal: ". . . some men turn every quality or art into a means of getting wealth; this they conceive to be the end and to the promotion of the end they think all things must contribute."[5]

The Roman Version

After the Punic Wars, the economic rationale for Roman trade was identical with that of the Greek city-states. The needs of the Imperial City's great population for food far exceeded what the Italian fields could provide, and her sophisticated classes craved adornments as much as her ruling classes craved conquest. The story of Rome is, in important respects, the tale of a sordid affair between two ruthless self-seekers, each bent on exploiting the other. One, the government, dedicated itself to systematic military expansion and political annexation; the other, business, pledged itself to provide the money for such conquests—always at handsome profits! It might be said in truth that pre-Augustan Rome was ruled by a warrior-aristocratic class that had neither interest in nor ability for the necessary arts of revenue raising, and this goes a long way toward explaining its profligate use of resources. Eagle and vulture shared the same nest!

The Roman state contracted out mining and coinage, road building and tax collecting;[6] it relied on the despised business community to provide moneys for war and for the disposal of loot and captives. Naturally, the businessman took care of himself. If titles were denied, profits were not, and Atticus, the elegant friend of Cicero, provides a striking illustration of the times. Atticus was honored with a statue from grateful debtors of one of the distressed municipalities because he was content with a 48 per cent interest rate when he might easily have exacted 73 per cent!

For troubled centuries, until the Augustan compromise, the patrician fought the trader. The genius of Augustus was to deny to a rapacious business group some of the time-honored tricks for getting rich at the public expense. Tax collecting was returned to the state, and with this and similar devices in other areas, Augustus turned many businessmen into salaried civil servants. Here the experience of the past has considerable meaning for the present. The price exacted for greater justice and orderliness was uncreativeness and dullness—a moral not missed by Arnold Toynbee and given interesting modern applications

---

[4] Laistner, *op. cit.*, p. xxvi.

[5] Aristotle, *Politics* (Modern Library ed., 1943), pp. 69–70.

[6] Contracting out has been, historically, a device that created problems. In our own day it remains an issue. It was a major issue in 1960 behind the first national strike in the history of the Pennsylvania Railroad. See the study by Margaret Chandler and Leonard Sayles, *Contracting Out: A Study of Management Decision Making* (New York: Columbia University Graduate School of Business, 1959).

by David McCord Wright.[7] In the long duel for control of Rome, the business-man "captured plains and foothills, but, despite his millions, he remained barred from the last high peaks of power, . . ."[8] a history that he was to repeat with singular monotony until modern times.

The attitude of other social classes in Greece and Rome toward the business-man deserves some further elaboration. The most casual sampling of works by the best-known spokesmen for Greek and Roman philosophy reveals a persistent current of mistrust of the merchant. In the fourth century B.C., Plato voiced suspicion of the merchant who, although performing certain useful functions, was prone to seek inordinate profits.[9] To Plato the only reasonable solution was to impose severe restrictions, even to the point of prohibiting resident citizens from engaging in business, lest they, too, become contaminated. Aristotle, dis-tinguishing between acquisition of goods and management of the household economy, proceeded to make refinements on the former pursuit. If a man's acquisitive instincts led him toward "natural" occupations, such as fishing or hunting, this was all well and good; but once exchange (indirect business) entered into the picture, caveats were in order. If commerce was intended to provide for necessities, it was legitimate, but if the merchant sought simply to amass riches from it, then it became reprehensible.

According to the Greek ideal, the literally "dirty" work of transforming raw materials into goods designed for human needs was to be done by the majority of men, mainly slaves, in order that the elite might engage in pure exercises of the mind—art, philosophy, and politics—the pursuits of leisure.

> Deep-rooted in Hellenic thought was the conviction that the external world of material things is an endless recurrence of phenomena which spring up and die down, are born and pass away, are generated and become corrupted, turning continually in a circle on them-selves, without beginning or end, in an incessant change, ceaseless and vain. To save oneself from the stormy ocean of the exterior world, to retire into the depths of one's own soul, secure from change, concentrated in an unalterable identity: this was, for the Greeks the goal of life.
>
> Hence any activity which brings the spirit into close contact with the material world seemed to them a painful and humiliating necessity, to be reduced to the lowest pos-sible minimum, if possible to be eliminated altogether. Truth alone is the only worthy concern. . . .[10]

Rome maintained much of the Greek tradition. In the first century B.C., Cicero saw the need of the businessman but distinguished between the whole-sale merchant who was performing a praiseworthy function and the small retailer who conducted his operations on the basis of fraud and lies.[11] To these specu-

---

[7] Arnold Toynbee, "Where are we going—and How did we get this way?" in D. H. Fenn (ed.), *Management's Mission in a New Society* (New York: McGraw-Hill Book Co., Inc., 1959), pp. 75-84; David McCord Wright, "Thinking Ahead," *Harvard Business Review*, Vol. 37 (May-June, 1959), pp. 23-32; and "Adventure or Routine," *Harvard Business Review*, Vol. 33 (September–October, 1955), pp. 33-40.

[8] Miriam Beard, *A History of the Business Man* (New York: Macmillan Co., 1938), p. 38.

[9] Plato, *Laws*, Book XI, chap. iii.

[10] Adriano Tilgher, *Work*, trans. Dorothy C. Fisher (New York: Harcourt, Brace & Co., 1930), pp. 5-6.

[11] Cicero, *De officiis*, Book I, chap. xlii.

lations were added, as previously noted, the fierce hatreds of the Roman patrician for the merchant.

THE MEDIEVAL SCENE

When Roman legions no longer struck terror in enemy hearts and when the Empire itself had become obscured in forgotten glory, the lively arts of making, trading, and gaining perished as well. For a century or two the character of Roman trade along the Mediterranean was maintained by Rome's conquerors, the Latinized barbarians, who came in prior to the conquering Teutonic tribes; but in the seventh century, the Islamic Arabs took control and western Europe became virtually landlocked. Although Islam was not intrinsically opposed to commerce, it viewed the foreign trader with contempt, as an importer of the debilitating cultural and religious germs of other lands into the pure body of Moslemism. Trade between East and West, therefore, was not to be countenanced.

From the ninth to the eleventh century, the West was literally bottled up. Commerce stagnated, towns declined, poverty spread, public authority disintegrated. Land became the only real symbol of wealth, and the Roman Catholic Church alone retained economic and moral ascendancy. (The influence of feudalism on contemporary European industrial organization should not be underestimated. There is a strong tendency for the modern European businessman to identify himself with the medieval *signore* and adopt a strongly paternalistic attitude toward his employees. In Italy an owner-manager is still commonly referred to by his employees as *padrone*—the "big father"—a phrase dating back to medieval and even Roman times.)

In the early stages of the eleventh century the Italian city-states regained a measure of trade with Byzantium, and when this southern movement was joined to the trade efforts in the north, linking the Low Countries with England, the stage was set for revival. Yet it took centuries, as Henri Pirenne reminds us in his *Economic and Social History of Medieval Europe*,[12] to fashion practices adapted to the economic revival and to accept as legitimate the notions of commercial profits and interest.

By the time the Middle Ages reached this apogee in the thirteenth century town life had regained much of its vigor. Yet a distinction has to be made. In one type of town medieval commerce lived off itself, while in a second type the town traded with other parts of the world. Only in this latter type do we find the more developed forms of capitalism, with letters of credit, money exchange, loans at interest, and gold coinage being widely employed.

There are three points worthy of special mention in any assessment of business in the Middle Ages, and these relate respectively to attitudes toward business, the philosophy of trade, and the evolution of the capitalist.

---

[12] Henri Pirenne, *Economic and Social History of Medieval Europe* (New York: Harcourt, Brace & Co., 1937), esp. pp. 1–15 and 162–68. See also Bede Jarrett, *Social Theories of the Middle Ages* (Westminster, Md.: Newman Book Shop, 1942), pp. 154–62.

Attitudes toward Business

Since the Church was the dominant medieval institution, its influence on the times was great. As the Church Fathers of Christian antiquity found little systematic treatment of mercantile activity in either the Old or the New Testament, they may have turned, almost instinctively, to the pagans whom they knew most intimately: Plato, Aristotle, and Cicero. Yet this conclusion must be accepted cautiously, since the New Testament abounds with Christ's injunctions against the corrupting influences of wealth, and the writings of the Apostle Paul, and of Basil the Great and Jerome, in the Greek and Latin traditions, faithfully mirror these admonitions. Yet these were mainly exhortations against riches per se; and the trading function was far less frequently mentioned.

Those Fathers who turned their attention toward commerce invariably reflected the same Platonic and Ciceronian hostility toward the merchant. In the third century A.D., Tertullian asserted that greed was the root of all evil and that greed motivated the merchant; in the following century, St. Ambrose, Bishop of Milan, mirrored this thought by depicting the merchant as one who labored day and night against the principles of justice and honesty. And Ambrose's famous contemporary, St. Augustine, shared these same views, although to a lesser degree. To the early Fathers, as to the Greek and Roman philosophers, farming, mining, and fishing were worthy pursuits, but the exploitative merchant turned the industry of nature into a fraud. These views of the Church Fathers were, in the main, inherited by the medievalists, who continued to look at riches and their acquisition through commerce with jaundiced eyes. St. Augustine was the best-known figure, and his cautious views on trade were generally well known and accepted. Yet Augustine provided some essential distinctions, on which the medievalists built a more elaborate theoretical structure, which, in turn, provided the basis for some reorientations of attitudes toward business.

The Philosophy of Trade

If the prevailing medieval attitude was one of abiding mistrust of business, there was also a clear recognition that commerce was an essential feature of the social order. The task of theorists was to explain with great precision how commerce might be legitimately carried out. In ancient and medieval times the concern was largely with the quality of the goods and the price exacted for the product. Of the two problems, the latter attracted the greater attention largely because the selling price involved a host of complicated market factors including supply and demand and changes in goods caused by interspatial or intertemporal factors.

From the very beginning of Roman law the sovereignty of the wills of the buyer and seller was recognized as the ultimate arbiter of price. Buyers and sellers were permitted, therefore, to outwit one another in bargaining. In the earliest form of sales, such as the *mancipatio* of the Law of the Twelve Tables in the fifth century B.C., the price agreed upon by seller and buyer was valid without further consideration of the "true" value of the goods. In the Theodosian code there are several imperial rescripts refusing to annul contracts because the seller had alleged a low selling price. Freedom of bargaining was as fundamental to Roman law as was the assumption that good faith must prevail.

There was one exception. In the sale of land if a parcel was sold by the father at less than half the market value the son had the right under law to repurchase the property at the original sale price or to exact from the buyer the other half of the market value. This right was called the *laesio enormis* and since it was a device similar to the *onaah* in the *Talmudic Mishnah* there is reason to assume a strong Jewish influence on Roman trade practices. Yet the basic principle of free bargaining was retained throughout the Middle Ages—so much so that efforts were made in certain regions (such as the Lower Languedoc in France) to remove altogether the remedies traditionally provided under *laesio enormis*.

It is a common error to equate the entire Middle Ages with feudalism and to ignore the significant evolutions in business practices during the later medieval period. As business became more active, there was need for refinement and reformulation of some of the cherished tenets of its social philosophy. These refinements were undertaken by St. Thomas Aquinas, who found in Aristotelianism a useful intellectual tool kit. Like his precursor, Aquinas felt there was something degrading in trade and in the haggling over goods and prices; like Aristotle, he justified profits acquired in the effort to make a living. More significantly, Aquinas went beyond Aristotle to introduce the notion of profit for other purposes—notably for charity or for public needs. And his idea that a just price was determined by the public's evaluation of the commodity went far beyond Aristotle.

There is a short tale in the *Summa* [13] that is especially revealing. Here Aquinas tells of a merchant who had been earlier discussed by Cicero in his *De officiis*. The merchant had an opportunity and a problem. He was carrying grain to a famine-stricken town, and he knew that other merchants were following him with more grain. Is the merchant obliged to tell the townsmen that more grain is on its way? Or could he maintain silence and sell grain at the higher rate that a desperate and hungry people would pay? Cicero recalled the Stoic philosopher who replied that the merchant was duty-bound to tell the whole story and to sell at a lower price. Aquinas, on the other hand, argued that the merchant was not obliged to tell the story of more grain in the offing, since this was a future event and therefore uncertain. If grain failed to arrive, the merchant lost a just opportunity for reasonable gain. One might argue that the merchant would be more virtuous to tell of the coming caravans, but this virtue exceeded the bounds

[13] Aquinas, *Summa theologicae,* II–II, qu. 77. 9. 3., obj. 4, as quoted by J. W. Baldwin, *The Medieval Theories of the Just Price* (Philadelphia: American Philosophical Society, 1959), p. 78. Benjamin Nelson shows how the original prohibitions against interest taking yielded to a permissive stage during which lenders were allowed to take interest from strangers. *The Idea of Usury: From Tribal Brotherhood to Universal Brotherhood* (Princeton, N.J.: Princeton University Press, 1949).

of simple justice. This tale represents Aquinas' last word on the subject of just price and excludes any explicit theory of cost-of-producing prices.

In his *Commentary on Ethics* Aquinas considered both cost of production and current market price as possible determinants of the just price, but in the *Secunda-secundae,* finished five years later, he definitely favored the latter. Shortly after Aquinas, Duns Scotus (d. 1308) made an explicit connection between market price and cost-of-production pricing theory and received credit for an economic solution that approximated the "law of costs" of the nineteenth century.

On the basis of extensive studies, Schumpeter, in his classic *History of Economic Analysis,* has concluded that the later medievalists (notably St. Antonine of Florence in the fifteenth century and Lessius, Molina, and de Lugo, Jesuits of the sixteenth century) clearly anticipated many of the economic theories elaborated during the eighteenth and nineteenth centuries.

One other point must be mentioned. There was a substantial body of medieval social doctrine that took into account the needs and structures of a stratified society subsisting at marginal levels. During the Middle Ages canon law had the universality of an acknowledged public authority. The standard text in all the law centers of Christendom was the *Decretum,* prepared and issued around 1140 by Gratian, a monk of Bologna. But since the *Decretum* drew its descriptive materials from the early centuries of the Christian Era, the canonists were constantly forced to make adaptations to changing conditions. As the lawyers of the medieval world, the canonists drew sharp distinctions between voluntary poverty and idle begging, between holy and accepted asceticism and squalid impoverishment. Yet the attitude was far different from that expressed in the majority report of a 1909 English royal commission—that poverty implied a defect in citizen character. Poverty was no crime in the Middle Ages.

There was, further, a general acceptance of the notion that riches involved obligations to the poor and that the latter had a *right* to charity, even as the former had a duty to extend it. The underprivileged—whether wanting property, health, or education—were presumed to have claims against society, and here again there is a vast difference between, for example, Innocent IV's commentary of 1250 insisting on free schooling for the indigent and the 1847 mandate by the Poor Law Commissioners of England that prohibited the use of public money for the education of poor children.[14]

Finally, the Middle Ages accepted the pre-eminence of the small group, and it discerned a clear and precise relationship existing between the individual and the group to which he belonged; indeed, one fulfilled oneself only through the group, and this meant the Church, the village, and the family. Taxes and fines were often levied on the group rather than on the individual. In Italian business enterprises, for example, lone-wolf operations were the exception, and the typical operation was the *casa,* a term used to indicate the family business. It was

---

[14] Brian Tierney, *Medieval Poor Law* (Berkeley: University of California Press, 1959).

the *casa* that bore the burdens of duties that its members assumed in civic life, paid the initiation fees for admission to the guilds, met charitable obligations, provided the expenses for entertaining visiting dignitaries, sustained the onus of the forced loans or patriotic subscriptions, and passed on bribes for great concessions and the like.[15]

The foregoing discussion takes on great relevance when it is realized that much of our own economic theory has held that its only province was the rather narrow one of the market place. Failure to develop an adequate social philosophy for an industrialized society has been a constant source of tension since the nineteenth century. Working conditions and status are today as relevant to business as is the issue of equitable distribution of profits among various claimants.

The Evolution of the Capitalist

Henri Pirenne has argued that there is a distinct and separate class of capitalists for each major period of history.[16] These men arise from the lower strata of society and, having nothing, are prepared to undertake the exciting risk ventures occasioned by changes in the social order. Further, these new businessmen are not related to the previous capitalists but emerge in answer to unmet needs; invariably they enjoy the widest possible freedoms during the early stages of their development. As they entrench themselves, two things happen: they become more regulated by the public authorities, and they become more interested in status and security. Consequently, the "mature" business group fails to maintain contact with changing business conditions and is replaced by the new entrepreneurs, who then repeat the cycle in a sort of Spenglerian rise-and-fall rhythm.

A discontinuous development in business is thus a characteristic of history. A further characteristic, but ancillary to it, is the concept of recurring cycles of freedom and control. The following diagram suggests the way Pirenne categorizes the great epochs of business evolution:

Freedom (Laissez Faire)	*Public Control (Regulation)*
Eleventh and twelfth centuries	
	Thirteenth-fourteenth centuries
Fifteenth century	
	Sixteenth-eighteenth (mercantilism)
Nineteenth century	
	Twentieth century

This hypothesis—and such it must remain until more definitive evidence has been garnered by historians—has the merit of inviting critical and reflective inquiry into the drifts of our own society. There is need to know much more

---

15 R. L. Reynolds, "Origins of Modern Business Enterprise: Medieval Italy," *Journal of Economic History*, Vol. 12 (Fall, 1952), pp. 350-65.

16 "The Stages in the Social History of Capitalism," *American Historical Review*, Vol. 19 (April, 1914), pp. 494-515.

about technology as a determinant of the business order. There is a necessity to appraise centralizing trends in decision making as facilitated by electronic data processing on one hand, and on the other, by boards of directors which in reality determine policy for companies within companies. It is equally urgent to learn whether risk taking — which Pirenne has posited as the essential element of genuine entrepreneurship — is as understood and as willingly assumed by professional managers today as it was understood and practiced by earlier generations of businessmen. These observations are simply suggestive of some of the things that must be done before we can generate sufficient hypotheses for testing and explaining our modern industrial and business order.[17]

On the basis of the foregoing analysis of the ancient and medieval worlds we might essay certain conclusions and hypotheses which, together, form a basis for fruitful applications to today's problems.

1. Business has always been suspect in the eyes of other value-forming institutions whether we look to the Greek city-state, the Roman Empire, or the Catholic Church.

2. Theories of pricing and markets have been more sophisticated than the attitudes. These theories have reflected the almost uneasy recognition that business was a necessary adjunct to every healthy social order.

3. Political and financial stability are necessary conditions to thriving business activity but when desire for stability has been carried to extremes—as evidenced by the Augustan peace in Rome—creativity and innovation have been stifled.

4. Every major historical epoch produces a new class of business leadership. Whether he evolves from previous business leaders or whether he emerges from a totally new class in society (as Pirenne suggests) the need for creative adaptation has been a constant challenge to the business community.

5. There appears to be a persistent cycle of "freedom-control — freedom-control" in the history of business enterprise. Clearly, this process has relevance to twentieth-century business.

6. A thriving middle class, living in a vigorous urban atmosphere, appears to be both cause and effect of effective business operation.

THE EARLY MODERN PERIOD: 1500–1750

The shifting focus of trade from the Mediterranean to the Atlantic favored nations like Portugal, Spain, England, France, and Holland. And overseas trade made tremendous demands for new capital, which, in turn, made demands on business organization. From medieval practice it was apparent that money men could be brought together as the active participants in the enterprise, or they could be brought together simply as investors, with no policy-making prerogatives. When recourse was had to the first alternative, the resulting organization was the regulated company, such as the English Merchant Company, which exercised monopoly rights over trade in certain regions. As time went on, the other approach, of combining investors' capital, became more common. Entrepreneurs issued stock to the public at a specified price and simply returned

---

[17] For an ambitious effort to develop a theory of industrialized societies see Clark Kerr, John T. Dunlop, Frederick Harbison, and Charles A. Myers, *Industrialism and Industrial Man: The Problem of Labor and Management and Economic Growth* (Cambridge, Mass.: Harvard University Press, 1960).

dividends if and when success yielded profits. The joint-stock company was one of the major innovations of all time in business organization, and the successes of the British East India Company, chartered on the very last day of 1600, brought a train of emulators.

Acceptance of the Profit Principle

These changes—when added to a new spirit of individualism encouraged by humanism and Protestantism—were complemented by advances in the use of coal, in mining, and in manufacturing techniques during the eighteenth century. Luther's emphasis on individual enterprise, on biblical interpretation, and on the importance of work was reinforced and expanded by Calvin, who placed frugality, thrift, and industry—virtues dear to those earlier businessmen—high in his schema of values. Furthermore, by focusing on the notion that worldly success and prosperity might be construed as signs of God's approval for the elect, Calvin provided a religious incentive that harmonized effectively with the spread of the profit motive in Western society. The fusion of these various innovations resulted in analogous changes in the economic system. Under the industrial system, surpluses were built from the performances of machines, creating new wealth through large-scale production at unprecedented rates, and through the acceptance of the profit principle as the legitimate quest and reward for business effort. Money permeated every aspect of economic life and served as a prime regulator for business activity; banks grew and flourished; credit expanded. John A. Hobson, in his book *The Evolution of Modern Capitalism,* enumerates what are to him the essential conditions for a system of industrial capitalism:

First, a production of wealth not required to satisfy the current wants of its owners, and therefore saved.

Second, the existence of a proletariat or laboring class deprived of the means of earning an independent livelihood.

Third, such a development of the industrial arts as enables indirect methods of production to afford profitable employment to organized group-labor using tools or machinery.

Fourth, the existence of large, accessible markets with populations willing and economically able to consume the products of capitalist industry.

Fifth, the capitalist spirit, or the desire and the capacity to apply accumulated wealth to profit making by the organization of industrial enterprise.[18]

These are not, of course, wholly independent conditions. On the contrary, they are closely interrelated. But by comparing these conditions with earlier business ventures, one can discern that this concept of capitalism is a special case in the broader concept of business. R. H. Tawney summarizes the change in this manner:

The rise of a naturalistic science of society, with all its magnificent promise of fruitful action and of intellectual light; the abdication of the Christian Churches from departments of economic conduct and social theory long claimed as their province; the general acceptance by thinkers of a scale of ethical values, which turned the desire for pecuniary gain from a

---

[18] Hobson, *The Evolution of Modern Capitalism* (new ed.; London: Walter Scott Publishing Co., 1917), p. 2.

perilous, if natural, frailty into the idol of philosophers and the mainspring of society—such movements are written large over the history of the tempestuous age which lies between the Reformation and the full light of the eighteenth century.[19]

Economic life is one aspect of a total culture. In previous historical periods—Greek, Roman, medieval—there was a tendency for other aspects of cultural life, such as politics, religion, the arts, and philosophy, to be dominant in the hierarchy of human achievements and satisfactions. Economic life was subordinated to these other arts and sciences as a means of achieving or realizing the purpose of life. Moreover, within the realm of economic activity itself, business was not dominant. So long as people are dependent for their livelihood upon the direct consumption of all they produce, business cannot exist, because there is no place for profit making. Both in antiquity and in the Middle Ages, the bulk of mankind was occupied with agriculture, either of a subsistence nature or, where a surplus was obtained, paid to or expropriated by a small minority of large landowners or by the state. Business was an activity of the minority, and it always took a second place to the procurement of food from the soil.

What distinguishes the early modern era from past historical periods is not the existence of business but the emerging dominance of the profit-and-loss calculus in the economic life of society and the acceptance of the pursuit of profit as one of the major and legitimate purposes of life. The unanswered question is whether, by means of continuous, rational business enterprise, profits can be harnessed to larger social purposes.

The Theory of Mercantilism

As medievalists had struggled to develop a theory which would accommodate the facts of business life to the values cherished by their society, so were modern economists challenged by business changes to make a similar effort. The theory was called mercantilism, developed around 1500, and designed to make private business interests an arm of the nation-state. Hecksher,[20] among others, has pointed out that mercantilism does not describe accurately a compact and consistent system but provides a concept that enables us to assess the period more accurately than might otherwise be the case.

Confronted by the sorry lessons of medieval particularisms (in the form of controls by independent feudal lords, on the one hand, and independent towns, on the other, each of which levied its own taxes and coined its own money), the new nation-state moved logically and determinedly to correct the abuses. Protectionism, bureaucracy, and autarchy were hallmarks of the mercantile state. But, if the government subordinated business to its national purposes, the real question of who controlled the governors remained wrapped in enigma. The zenith of French mercantilism was reached during the ministry of Jean Baptiste

---

[19] R. H. Tawney, *Religion and the Rise of Capitalism* (New York: Harcourt, Brace & Co., 1926), p. 277.

[20] Eli F. Hecksher, *Mercantilism*, trans. Mendel Shapiro (London: Allen and Unwin, 1935).

Colbert (1619–83), son of a Rheims cloth merchant, who was no theorist but a hardheaded businessman interested in a thriving French economy. In England, Thomas Mun was as influential as any man in persuading his countrymen that a protected trade was the nation's greatest asset. Mun himself was a director of the English East India Company and another realistic businessman.

But mercantilism could not survive the onslaughts of the advocates of *laissez faire*. David Hume launched attacks against mercantilism in essays published in 1752 and 1753, but it remained for Adam Smith's *Wealth of Nations* to deliver in 1776 what eventually became the *coup de grâce*. Smith argued eloquently for business freedom on grounds that with this liberty would come specialization, division of labor, and increased production of goods and services. Smith argued that the "invisible hand" of the competitive free market would necessarily convert the self-interested actions of individuals into socially beneficial employments. But it was not until the nineteenth century—when England had little to fear from foreign competition—that the nation freely prepared to heed his voice.

THE MODERN PERIOD: 1750 TO THE PRESENT

Events of the last two centuries constitute the most dramatic epoch of material advance in the history of man. To speak of *the* modern period, however, as if it were all of one piece, is to suggest a consistency that is not borne out by history. There are radical differences between the pre-1914 and post-1914 worlds. We must also reckon with a difference in the productive techniques employed at even the most mature stage of the first Industrial Revolution and those new technologies (atomic power, electronics, and automation) that have heralded the second Industrial Revolution. Still in its infancy, this new revolution dates back only to this century's late twenties or early thirties, but, in the opinion of C. P. Snow, "it is in cardinal respects different in kind from anything that has gone before, and will change the world much more." [21]

When emphasis turns to how money is provided to sustain expanding production facilities, three other stages in this evolution are discernible. There is initially the period running primarily throughout the second half of the nineteenth century that was dominated by the "industrial" capitalist—the man whose ultimate skill at mass production and mass marketing gave him an ascendant role; the second period, covering the years from 1900 to 1930, equated the "finance capitalist" of Wall Street with effective control in American business; finally, there is the current stage, coinciding with the scientific revolution previously noted, wherein dominance is held by the "professional" manager—the man whose skills in organization and administration, broadly conceived, have made him the indispensable figure. Because of his appearance, a conviction has developed that modern business is undergoing specific stresses that are changing its basic *modus operandi*.

---

21 C. P. Snow, *The Two Cultures and the Scientific Revolution* (London: Cambridge University Press, 1959), p. 31.

Professor N. S. B. Gras of Harvard, in his book, *Business and Capitalism,* developed the thesis that the administrator was the key figure in business history and that his role was changing significantly. James Burnham, following shortly with his famous *The Managerial Revolution,* argued that those new administrators (required by a new society markedly different from anything we have hitherto experienced) will constitute the new ruling class. But our concern here is with how industrial society has worked over the last hundred and fifty years.

Practices and Achievements of the First Industrial Revolution

Stripped to its essentials, the Industrial Revolution refers to that historical period starting in the mid-eighteenth century, when man freed himself from primary dependence on animal power. It was the age when old king coal shared regal prerogatives with iron. The earth disgorged coal, iron, and other treasures at stupendous rates, and these, in turn, moved to the factory, where they were transformed into articles of consumption. The zest of the new age has been caught up in the imagery of Paul Mantoux's description:

The characteristic monument containing within its walls the raw material, and embodying in a visible form the very principle of modern production, is the factory. Within are vast workshops through which run belts or transmission wires by which power is distributed. Each workshop is fitted with powerful and delicate machinery, which fills the place with its clatter, aided by the frenzied labour of its disciplined population, which the machines seem to sweep along with them in their panting rhythm.

The one object of all this is the production of commodities as quickly as possible in unlimited quantities. Here are woven goods unrolling themselves in yards and yards of cloth, or piling up in mountains of cylindrical bales; there steel is boiling in gigantic retorts and flinging up showers of dazzling sparks. Continuous production has become the rule for all industrial undertakings, unless it is limited in consequence of a definite agreement between producers. Left entirely to itself, production would rush on to excess, until it became ruinous overproduction; a paradoxical result of the instinctive tendency of capital, which ends in self-destruction.

Once manufactured, these quantities of goods must be sold. Sale, resulting in profit, is the final goal of all industrial production. The immense stimulus given to production by the factory system immediately affects the distribution of commodities. The increased amount of goods on the market lowers prices, lower prices mean increased demand, and more business. Competition becomes more intense. As improvements in transport open an ever wider field to its activities, it extends from individuals to regions and to nations, more eager than ever in the pursuit of their material interests. Conflicts and economic wars are let loose, and the winner is he who succeeds in enlarging, in spite of his competitors, his sphere of operations, and in finding more and ever more new markets. The ambition of producers makes them more daring, and the most distant countries, continents hardly yet explored, become their prey. The whole world henceforward is nothing but one immense market, where the great industries of all countries contend as on a battlefield.

A special method of distributing wealth goes with this great productivity, with its enlarged circulation reacting to the confines of the inhabited world. Obviously the consumer is now in a much more favourable position than he was before the Industrial Revolution took place. Goods have greatly increased in quantity, while prices have been, on the whole, considerably reduced. Many things, formerly expensive and hard to come by, are obtainable in localities and in circles where previously they were unknown. Nevertheless the optimistic view with which such a spectacle inspired the classical economist is profoundly changed when the condition of the producers is examined. The whole structure of the factory system is built up on the power furnished by machinery, together with an immense accumulation of human labour, supporting, at the top, the towering and ever-growing force of capital. Producers are divided into two classes. The first gives its labour and possesses nothing else, selling the strength of its arms and the hours of its life for a wage. The second commands capital, owns the factories, the raw materials, the machinery, and reaps the profits and dividends. At its head are the great leaders, the captains of industry, as Carlyle called them, organizers, rulers and conquerors.

From this has grown up the social system characteristic of our modern civilization, which forms a whole as complete and as coherent as the feudal system of the tenth century can have been. But whilst the latter was the consequence of military necessity and of the dangers which threatened human life in a Europe given over to anarchical barbarism, the former has been produced by a concatenation of purely economic forces, grouped around the central fact of the factory system.[22]

This kind of industrialism, with its socioeconomic dislocations, continued until man's ingenuity unharnessed the secrets of the atom in practically useful ways and, at the same time, turned electronics into a mighty servant of industry and business. By happy fortune, the development came none too soon, since supplies of coal and oil are dwindling, and fossil fuels will soon provide inadequate supports for the American economy. Heavy labor is being lifted from man's back, and repetitive routine work from man's mind, at such a rate that the least skilled may become a new leisure class.

Modern transportation systems have brought most major population centers within half an hour of each other, and probes into outer space suggest that before the end of the century man will be visiting other planets and perhaps planting human colonies. Accomplishments in the half-millennium between 1492 and 1992 promise to stagger the wildest imagination.[23] How will man *relate* his vast accomplishments to the universe of other values?

The New Philosophy of Business

In many respects the refinements and adaptations built into Adam Smith's theories by classical economists represent an achievement in intellectual history. Both as description and prescription, *laissez faire* served eminently well. The theory posited an equation between private interest and public good that seemed in accord with the facts; it trusted to the automatic operation of unrestricted market forces to assure equity, and it rejoiced in the disciplines provided by competition *inter pares*. Indeed, the nineteenth century was an epoch of rising production, rising population, rising living standards, and rising educational levels for the Western world.

Yet the facts began to get out of hand. Invariably, competition between industrial and agricultural countries, between the have and the have-not nation, between the cartel and the small, privately owned firm, between employer and employee, worked to the advantage of the former in each of the cases cited.

Reactions set in—and quickly! In point of origin, the first was born of revul-

---

22 Paul J. Mantoux, *The Industrial Revolution in the Eighteenth Century*, trans. Marjorie Vernon (rev. ed.; London: J. Cape, 1928), pp. 26–27.
23 See, e.g., the report by John Ray Dunning, *Science, Engineering, and the Liberal Arts* (New York: Columbia University, School of Engineering, 1960).

sion against an economic order that imposed its costs so brutally on the worker and returned its rewards so handsomely to the owner. Karl Marx and Friedrich Engels issued the *Manifesto* in 1848, and Marx issued the first volume of his monumental *Das Kapital* in 1867.[24] Borrowing his model from the "dialectic" developed at the University of Berlin by Georg Wilhelm Friedrich Hegel, Marx posited a formula of *thesis* (existing capitalist order), *antithesis* (proletarian opposition), and eventual *synthesis* (the classless society). Explicit in the dialectic was the notion of matter as the only reality, necessary struggle, and inexorable progress leading to victory by the proletariat.

Just a decade after the appearance of the *Manifesto,* Charles Darwin published his classic *Origin of Species,* in which he enunciated the theory of evolution of matter from lower to higher forms through a struggle for survival. His caution in restricting the theory to the biological world imposed no similar restraint on social scientists, who saw in Darwinism both the explanation and the defense of the highly competitive order of the nineteenth century. If England gave Darwin to the world, the United States gave Darwinism its most articulate expression by accepting almost as an article of faith the writings of Herbert Spencer, the English sociologist who extended biological determinism to the social order. Singularly attuned for rationalizing the *status quo,* this social Darwinism gave to competition the force of a natural law.[25] Thus Marxism and Darwinism arrived at diametrically opposed conclusions and were used for contradictory purposes. One stressed revolution, and the other evolution. Yet interestingly enough—and insufficiently noted—were the similarities in the two doctrines. The common ingredients included emphasis on the universe of matter, acceptance of ruthless conflict as the natural disciplinarian over human affairs, emergence of a "better" class, and the gospel of inevitable progress.

In the face of remarkable transformations in today's society, where stands twentieth-century theory? The whole modern period has borne eloquent witness to the influence of certain scientific advances on social philosophy; the Copernican revolution required major revisions in cosmology and adjustment to the fact that this magnificent earth was a puny fraction of a mighty universe; the Newtonian and post-Newtonian eras spawned mechanical models as explanations of society; and Darwinism—as we have seen—provided the basis for lively intellectual reformulations for scholars in the late nineteenth century. There are even now certain signs that Heisenberg's law of indeterminacy, Planck's quantum theory, and the advances outlined by Einstein are being paralleled by economic theory as it turns away from Newtonian molds and into new patterns.

Economic theory in the West is always market oriented. It feeds on supply

---

24 Volumes II and III of the German edition were posthumously printed, edited by Engels (1885–94); English translation, 1901–9. Brilliant background sketches of some of Engels' major revolutionaries are given by Edmund Wilson in *To the Finland Station* (New York: Doubleday & Co., 1940), Part II.

25 Darwinism has been studied intensively in its many phases. One of the best inquiries is that of Richard Hofstadter, *Social Darwinism in American Thought* (rev. ed.; Boston: Beacon Press, 1955), esp. chap. i.

and demand, on competition, on value and exchange theories, for its daily bread. And in this respect it provides sustenance for business institutions. Yet, in the still unformulated theory of business, the frontiers go beyond those provided by conventional economic theory. The whole world of production involves concern with a philosophy of work, as such, with status for the laborer, with functions and incentives for the managers. And beyond that is the *troisième force* represented by the various publics with which business must deal. Here the dynamic is equity, and in the present climate a clash between efficiency and equity is likely to result in the emergence of efficiency as the tarnished ideal. Indeed, one might hazard the speculation that in firms and nations at early stages of economic development, the drive for efficiency will outrun the drive for equity. As productive capacity increases relative to demand, the pendulum begins its slow and laborious swing until finally, in conditions approximating affluence, the weight of emphasis shifts to justice.

In the contemporary scene, business is no longer the institution playing a subordinate role in the mighty drama of events. It has achieved in the secular societies of the West some stature of partnership with other value-forming institutions. Perhaps business has the potential of becoming for our time a *force civilisatrice.* For, as it provides the goods and services that make possible the good life for a greater number of people, it crosses, in peace, those frontiers where religious differences (Moslemism versus Christianity) or political differences (communism versus democracy) have hitherto made any neutral amity impossible.

Whatever the ultimate verdict—whether business has too much influence or too little, whether it wields its power for good or for evil—the necessity remains for business to understand itself in terms of potentialities and restrictions, to discipline itself with restraints when appropriate and with courage when opportune. Having achieved both understanding and discipline, business then must articulate its theory. But understanding must come first. . . .

selection 9

The Shackles of Backwardness*

Robert L. Heilbroner

It is well that we begin our examination of economic development with a recognition of this diversity of problems, for it inculcates a healthy skepticism against panaceas. More than that, it begins to indicate, from country to country, what is feasible and what is not: in this diversity of underdevelopment are the hard facts of life for a development economist, a UN committee weighing the merits of a request for technical assistance, or the governments of the one hundred nations themselves.

Yet it would be as misleading to stop our analysis of underdevelopment here as to have concluded it with our first composite picture of its poverty. For despite their critical differences, all of the one hundred countries also display important resemblances. If they face physical and natural obstacles of the greatest variety, they are nonetheless hobbled in the first instance by common shackles of a social and economic kind. Heretofore we have paid attention to the characteristics which differentiate one underdeveloped country from another. Now we must study even more closely the problems which are common and central to all of them.

THE PROBLEM OF PRODUCTIVITY

Once we start to look for resemblances in the various areas of the underdeveloped world, one common handicap springs to sight immediately. It is the fact that human labor in all of these nations is so pitifully unproductive—that a day's toil, often far more back-breaking than the equivalent day's work in the West, produces so heartbreakingly little.

We see this particularly in the sector which is the very foundation of all the underdeveloped economies: agriculture. In the United States one farmer typically supports about twenty-four non-food-producing citizens. Compare this with the situation in Africa: "The productivity of African agriculture is still so low," writes Dr. Kimble, "that it takes anywhere from two to ten people—men, women and children—to raise enough food to supply their own needs and those of *one* additional—non-food-growing—adult."[1]

Or take the situation in that life-and-death crop of the East: rice. The table below shows the difference between the productivity of rice fields in the main Asiatic countries and those of the United States and Australia:

RICE YIELD PER HECTARE[2]
(100 kilograms)

	1955
United States	34.3
Australia	45.9
Burma	14.8
China (1954)	24.7
India	12.6
Indonesia	16.5
Thailand	14.3
Philippines	11.9
Vietnam	12.3

What is true of rice can be found true of nearly every crop. In soybeans, for instance, the United States is roughly twice as productive per acre as China or Indonesia; in tobacco it is nearly three times as productive as the Philippines. "One of the most distressing shocks to the foreign economic advisor when he first goes on mission to an underdeveloped country," writes Professor Higgins, "is the discovery that the most important local agricultural product . . . cannot compete in the free market with imports from advanced countries. Thus one finds Louisiana rice competing with native rice in the Philippines, imported dates underselling the inferior homegrown dates in Libya, California oranges competing with the small, bitter native citrus fruits in the Riau Archipelago of Indonesia."[3]

And if we compare the relative productivities, not of hectares of land, but of human labor, the contrast is even more striking. An American farmer spreads his labor over 50 to 200 acres of land; an Asian or South American farmer pours all his energies into two or three. Thus human productivity may be as little as one two-hundredth of that in an economically advanced country.

Why is agricultural labor in the underdeveloped world so unproductive? The very discrepancies in the scale of agriculture in the advanced and backward nations provide an answer.

What has been called "postage stamp cultivation" marks the pattern of farming throughout Asia and the Near East, and in much of South America and Africa. Not the farm, but the plot, is the standard unit of cultivation. Even when large landlord estates exist, they are typically subdivided into a crossword

---

[1] George Kimble, *Tropical Africa* (New York: Twentieth Century Fund, 1960), Vol. 1, p. 572 (italics added).
[2] From Benjamin Higgins, *Economic Development* (New York: W. W. Norton, 1959), p. 16.
[3] *Ibid.*, p. 17.

puzzle of miniscule holdings cropped by tenants. John Gunther, writing of India twenty years ago, describes the situation vividly:

> There is no primogeniture in India as a rule, and when the peasant dies his land is sub-divided among all his sons, with the result that most holdings are infinitesimally small. In one district in the Punjab, following fragmentation through generations, 584 owners culti-vate no less than 16,000 fields; in another 12,800 acres are split into actually 63,000 holdings. Three quarters of the holdings in India as a whole are under ten acres. In many parts of India the average holding is less than an acre.[4]

That was twenty years ago, but the situation is not significantly remedied today, and it is mirrored in many other underdeveloped lands.

Many causes contribute to this terrible division and subdivision of land. In some countries it is the custom of inheritance which Gunther mentions. In others it is attributable to feudal landlord systems in which peasants cannot legally own or accumulate their own land. In still larger part it is due to the pressure of too many people on too little arable soil, aggravated by enormous concentrations of landholdings in the hands of the upper classes. To many of these causal factors we shall have reason to turn again. But at this stage what we must notice is that, whatever the causes, the result is the same: agriculture suf-fers from a devastating lack of productivity brought about by grotesque man–land ratios.

Thus the overcrowding of the land gives rise to a *technical* condition which tragically curtails the output of crops from a given area of soil. For peasants working their tiny strips cannot efficiently utilize—nor could they possibly afford—the physical, mechanical, and chemical means by which agriculture in the West attains its rich returns. On the miniscule farms of the backward lands reapers and binders and sowers are totally uneconomic. Worse yet, because the peasant earns no investable surplus he cannot even exchange his wooden plow for a steel one, or substitute chemical fertilizer for animal or human dung. Indeed, even animal fertilizer is seldom applied; it is used instead as the slow-burning fuel over which the peasant cooks his bowl of rice. Nor is assistance available in the form of draft animals; a grim joke used to be that the Indian villager hitched his plow to the village bull, the Chinese hitched his to his wife. We can summarize all these paralyzing and debilitating lacks in a single con-cept: the low level of agricultural productivity is largely due to an inability to apply capital to the productive process.

This impoverishing absence of capital is by no means confined to agriculture. On the contrary, the problem pervades every underdeveloped economy from top to bottom. It is for lack of capital of every sort, not just for lack of capital on the land, that the underdeveloped nations are unable to produce adequate incomes. What these nations lack is not a supply of human labor or, in most cases, at least some resources which could be turned to account. Rather, what lacks are the machines, the power lines, the engines, the cranes, warehouses, factories, generators by which men and resources can be given the capacity to

---

[4] *Inside Asia* (New York: Harper & Bros., 1939), p. 385.

produce more than the tiny flow of output which nature yields to bare hands and primitive equipment. This is one principal reason why in 1959, for instance, when an average American worker produced $3.90 worth of goods in an hour, his Japanese counterpart produced only 40 cents' worth. And Japan is, by the standards of the underdeveloped countries, a capital-rich, highly productive economy.

This deep and ubiquitous problem of the insufficiency of capital is a matter on which we shall later dwell at some length, for clearly here lies a vital element in the prescription for economic development. But at this juncture, while we are seeking only to identify the common defects of the underdeveloped continents, it is enough that we identify the problem. If a low level of productivity is the universal economic attribute of underdevelopment, a fearful shortage of capital is its well-nigh invariable cause.

THE PROBLEM OF SOCIAL ATTITUDES

And yet this economic handicap is not the ultimate cause of underdevelopment. For the shortage of capital itself testifies to a still deeper problem. This is the absence of those social attitudes and institutions which create capital. That is, the lack of capital directs our attention to the all-important fact that the economies of the underdeveloped world are not capital-generating. In some important structural way these economies must be different from the economies of the West, capitalist and communist alike.

What is that difference? We begin to find it when we now examine not the physical but the social attributes of the underdeveloped lands. Let us commence by considering the predominant social type of these lands—the peasant cultivator who comprises 70 to 80 percent of the populations of all the backward areas.

What do we mean by a "peasant cultivator"? Emphatically we do not mean a farmer. A farmer, particularly as we meet him in the United States, is essentially a businessman of the land. He is price and cost conscious, quick to adjust his output to the signals of the marketplace. He is technically minded and ready to alter his practices if something demonstrably better comes along. He is, for all his traditional ties to the land, very much an economic man.

The peasant presents a sharp contrast to the farmer. He does not normally reckon in terms of the plus and minus of balance sheets. He does not readily shift from this crop to that as prices change. He is not technically trained or innovation-minded. To him, the world of nature is fixed and immutable; it is to be propitiated rather than vanquished.

Thus Dr. Alvin Hansen writes of such peasant attitudes in India:

> Often village opinion is hostile to . . . new developments, and unless there is continual prodding, a relapse back to traditional practices is likely. This is certainly not surprising. An illiterate community with traditional cultural and religious convictions, firmly implanted from generation to generation, cannot easily be shunted over to a modern view of social values. Innovations that run counter to established dogmas and beliefs are feared lest they

might anger various deities. . . . Innovations might bring upon the helpless villagers scourges, pestilence, floods and droughts. . . .

Agricultural practices are controlled by custom and tradition. A villager is fearful of science. For many villagers insecticide is taboo because all life is sacred. A new and improved seed is suspect. To try it is a gamble. Fertilizers, for example, are indeed a risk unless scientifically applied and with just the right amount of moisture. To adopt these untried methods might be to risk failure. And failure could mean starvation.[5]

This does not mean that the peasant is forever tied to the past. When he is convinced of success, he will change his ways. As Dr. Arthur Lewis has pointed out, Gold Coast farmers, reputed to have been the laziest in the world, switched over en masse from subsistence agriculture to cocoa production when it was profitable to do so, and other economists have emphasized the response of Malayan and Ceylonese cultivators to changes in the relative prices of crops available to them. Thus it would be wrong to picture the peasant as devoid of business incentives or locked in an unshakable embrace with tradition.

But the testimony of endless teams of technical assistance workers, of agricultural experts and anthropologists warns us that the pace of peasant change in the ordinary instance is painfully slow.[6] And here Dr. Hansen's observations provide an insight into the peasant's motivations. The cultivator of the soil is not just mulish or stupid. He is operating in a world in which there is no margin for error, no room for maneuver. Against the logic of a science he does not understand, he opposes the logic of the past which has permitted him to stay alive. And sometimes he is right. In a study of the impact of innovations prepared by UNESCO we read of the unexpected vindication of old ways in the face of efforts to bring change and growth:

In Burma, deep ploughing introduced by European agricultural experts broke up the hardpan that held the water in the rice fields. The weeding of rubber plantations reduced the sap. The new tomato, which the Burmese were persuaded to grow because it was more productive, had a flavor they did not like. In Turkey experts trained abroad persuaded some of the younger peasants to remove the stones from their tilled land; when the grain sprouted, the fields of the old men had a better crop, since in that dry climate, the stones served the function of retaining moisture.[7]

Such wry miscarriages of advice should not be magnified out of proportion. In the vast majority of cases, when the peasant refuses to change his ways, he is tragically mistaken. Yet it makes more understandable the fact that change comes slowly in the peasant world, much more slowly than is needed if the Great Ascent is to move at more than a snail's pace.

WORKERS, ENTREPRENEURS, AND BUREAUCRATS

It is not only in a reluctance to change agricultural ways that we find social attitudes constituting an impediment to economic change. In the industrial sec-

---

[5] *Economic Issues of the 1960s* (New York: McGraw-Hill Book Co., Inc., 1960), pp. 157–58.

[6] Cf. *Cultural Patterns and Technical Change*, ed. Margaret Mead (New York: New American Library, 1955), pp. 177–94.

[7] *Ibid.*, p. 186.

tor—among those who work in and direct the enterprise of the underdeveloped nations—we find similar obstacles.

Take, for instance, the raw working force with which the new factories must be run. Eugene Black, President of the World Bank, has described their situation graphically:

> The migrant to the city is perhaps the most cruelly treated by the historic transformation going on in the underdeveloped world. Away from the familiar ways of his native village, he is plunged into a bewildering, formless, insecure life, requiring a whole new set of attitudes towards life and work. If he is lucky enough to get a factory job, he is likely to find factory discipline irksome and pointless. If it is no great problem to teach him to operate a machine, often there is no common language with which to introduce him to such sophisticated ideas as quality control or the terms of a labor contract. Away from work he is more often than not herded into a wretched slum and exploited by the large, permanent world of beggars, vagrants, refugees, petty criminals, and the like who manage somehow to survive on the fringe economies of the cities of the underdeveloped world.[8]

Hence the worker, like the peasant, is not easily transformed into a member of a modern economic system. Unused to thinking of factory work as a permanent way of life, certainly unused to the idea that it might offer the prospect of a slowly rising standard of living, he accepts the often noisome conditions of factory labor as one might accept a temporary prison sentence. "In the least developed areas," reads a recent UNESCO report, "the worker's attitude toward labour may entirely lack time perspective, let alone the concept of productive investment. For example, the day labourer in a rural area on his way to work, who finds a fish in the net he placed in the river the night before, is observed to return home, his needs being met. The worker in an urban area who receives an increase in pay works less and goes back to his native village so much the sooner."[9]

These attitudes of inertia and resistance before the demands of an industrial society are by no means confined to the humbler classes of society. "A common psychological obstacle to economic achievement," continues the UNESCO report, "is the fact that much higher status tends to be associated with landownership or government position or professional or intellectual activity than is enjoyed by the business-man, engineer, mechanic, agronomist or some other type of person concerned directly with material production."[10] Thus in the least developed lands the more privileged classes frequently display as much obduracy before economic development as do the peasant and simple laborer. The rich have always counted their assets in terms of gold, jewels, houses, land, and do not easily learn to count as "wealth" an ugly factory or printed stock certificates. The able have always gravitated to the law, to letters, to the ministries of government, and do not take quickly to the idea of making their careers in "vulgar" undertakings. Significantly, of the many students from underdeveloped lands studying in the United States, only 4 percent are interested in that funda-

[8] *The Diplomacy of Economic Development* (Cambridge, Mass.: Harvard University Press, 1960), pp. 10–11.
[9] *Report on World Social Situation,* UNESCO, March 9, 1961, p. 79.
[10] *Ibid.,* p. 80.

mental problem of their homelands—agriculture.[11] More than that, in societies in which power and status are based on land, the rise of a mercantile or industrial class is viewed with suspicion. Let us recall the bitter fight between the old aristocracy and the new manufacturers in France in the eighteenth century and in England in the early nineteenth century when we blandly assume that "wealth is wealth" and that landowners can easily metamorphize into or identify their interests with industrial capitalists.

And then, too, even among the small industrial class, the prevalent orientation toward money-making itself is different in a typical Asian or African or Latin-American nation from our own. The psychology of most businessmen is not that of the Western entrepreneur. It is more that of the bazaar merchant. Not large-scale production and long-term return, but fast trading and quick profit are the usual objectives. Nor is this surprising in an economic environment in which much business tends to be petty and transient, and in which even big business depends for its profits more on the vagaries of international commodity fluctuations than on the slow improvement of the domestic market.

Yet another difference in social attitudes is to be found in that critically important sector, government officialdom. In the West, by and large, we associate the idea of government personnel with that of a civil service bureaucracy. And this is particularly true as we go into the larger agencies and higher branches of government. We expect to find there, not only an incorruptible judiciary and legislature, but an impersonal hierarchy of technical experts.

Quite different traditional attitudes characterize the majority of the underdeveloped lands. Here "squeeze," nepotism, petty and large-scale graft are taken as the norm for government operation rather than as the occasional exception. In Latin America, for example, as Albert Hirschman writes, "Frequently the state is compared to the organized bandits of the backlands exacting their tribute and leading a purely parasitic existence. The idea that economic development takes place in spite of, rather than because of, state action is well expressed in the Brazilian saying, 'Our country grows by night when the politicians sleep.' "[12]

To be sure, there is always a danger that generalizations such as these will distort a would-be portrait into a caricature. It need hardly be said that in most underdeveloped lands there exist some modern farmers, some skilled and disciplined workers, some highly efficient business executives and dedicated government officials. Yet the existence of these "Western" types is more apt to be the exception than the rule. One need examine only the history of one of the most advanced underdeveloped nations, such as Mexico, to encounter in living reality the social types we have described: inert peasants, undisciplined workers, gouging businessmen, and rapacious government officials.[13]

Let us complete this survey of social types by pointing up two conclusions.

---

11 *Ibid.*, p. 81.

12 *Latin American Issues* (New York: Twentieth Century Fund, 1961), p. 24.

13 Some of these stereotypes take on added reality in that extraordinary document of Mexican life, *The Children of Sanchez*, by Oscar Lewis (New York: Random House, 1961). See also his *Five Families* (New York: Basic Books, Inc., 1959).

The first is that we find ourselves, in the typical underdeveloped country, facing a structure of social stratification unlike any we know from our own historic experience. Not only is the social distance between classes incomparably greater than that which separates upper and lower classes in the West, but class consciousness is also far more pronounced. An awareness of enormous social differences, a feeling of "belonging" to a certain class and of having little or nothing in common with a higher or lower class, is very much a part of the underdeveloped scene, whether in India, in Latin America, in the Near East, or in Africa.

This does not mean a *militant* class consciousness. On the contrary, the prevalent attitude of both upper and lower ends of the social spectrum is one of acquiescence in the existing social stratification. But the existence of huge differentials within society has its important political consequences nonetheless. It implies—perhaps it necessitates—a traditional structure of power based upon the maintenance of the profound inertia of the lower classes. When the gulf which divides rich and poor is as impassable as that of a backward nation, we cannot expect to find on the part of the favored classes an interest in change, in ferment, in "progress." The *anciens régimes* of the poor nations—many of which are still current *régimes*—find their natural self-interest in the preservation of accepted ways, or, at most, in the most cautious introduction of new social outlooks and opportunities.

Second, it is apparent these social types and social structures do not tend to produce economic systems which are capital-creating. Peasants do not and cannot create for themselves large surpluses which can be reapplied to their lands. A ragged and casual labor force does not generate so much as a trickle of savings. The middle classes are weak and small. And most important, while the upper classes do amass a very considerable flow of investable profits, they do not find their traditional interests directed toward investing those profits into the channels required for development.

Thus the societies of underdevelopment suffer from an economic inertia which springs in the final analysis from social institutions and attitudes. In place of the culture of striving so characteristic of the West, a culture of acceptance weakens the determination and action necessary for the Great Ascent. While only someone unacquainted with the never-ending labors of the backward lands could claim that their populations "do not work," nonetheless it is true that work does not carry the freight of hope, and therefore the psychological attraction, of the West. Hopelessness breeds dispiritedness; resignation feeds upon and justifies itself. An enormous gulf of motives as well as of institutions and productive capabilities separates the poor lands from the rich. "The underdeveloped countries are not simply less prosperous models of the wealthy nations," said a lecturer at the University College of Ghana recently. "There are embedded in their structure factors which make for inertia and even retrogression." [14]

---

[14] Inaugural Lecture, Dr. Adam Curle, February 15, 1961.

THE GREAT TRANSFORMATION

All these ways of thought and behavior are capable of change. The traditional suspiciousness of the peasant can give way—as it did in postfeudal Europe—to a "commercial" approach to farming. A raw labor force can become disciplined into the industrial army of a modern state. Merchants can become businessmen; government sinecurists can turn into civil servants. But a focus on the obstacles raised by social attitudes begins to make us aware of how inadequate a description of the Great Ascent is contained in the words "economic development."

For *economic* development—that is, the deepening flow of incomes and the widening flow of production—is itself dependent on the presence of an "economic" population: of production-minded farmers, industrial workers, enterprising factory managers, helpful government officials. So long as these do not exist, economic development cannot commence on a broad base.

True, a few showplaces of industrialism can be erected; steel mills can rise next to paddy fields; even a small industrial complex can take shape. Yet, as is shown by the juxtaposition of a prosperous São Paulo with a desperate Brazilian northeast, or the existence of an immense mining operation in Katanga with a totally underdeveloped hinterland, or a heavily industrialized Damodar Valley within sight of primitive Indian hillsmen, the mere laying-in of a core of capital equipment, indispensable as that is for further economic expansion, does not yet catalyze a tradition-bound society into a modern one. For that catalysis to take place, nothing short of a pervasive social transformation will suffice: a wholesale metamorphosis of habits, a wrenching reorientation of values concerning time, status, money, work; an unweaving and reweaving of the fabric of daily existence itself. And as we have seen, for such a social reorientation to take place, a precondition must be the replacement of regimes based on a perpetuation of the *status quo* by regimes audacious enough to unleash social change.

. . . Let us emphasize only the fact that in any society such a transformation is a profoundly dislocating experience. We have but to think of the painful struggles which accompanied the evolution of our Western "modern" society out of its feudal matrix to remind ourselves that the habits of thought and action acquired over generations are not lightly shed. The process takes time—even in the West, after several centuries, when we look at the peasants of southern Italy, or the government of Spain, it is clearly not yet complete. How long it may take in the underdeveloped nations cannot be foretold. What is certain is that economic development, in the sense of a broadly based and shared upward climb, must wait on the establishment of social change on the grand scale.

THE QUICKSAND OF POPULATION GROWTH

But we have not yet completed our survey of the endemic problems of the underdeveloped lands. There still remains to be considered the hurdle which, by virtue of its immediate impact, may well pose the most formidable of all the barriers to progress. This is the overwhelming problem of population growth.

No one who looks for very long into the question of population growth in the underdeveloped areas can refrain from a feeling of impending catastrophe. A few figures are all that are needed to make the point.

Let us begin with our southern neighbor, Mexico. Today Mexico has a population equal to that of New York, Pennsylvania, New Jersey, and Connecticut—36 million in all. Forty years from now, if Mexico's present rate of population increase continues, it will have 123 million people—as many as the present population of the four states above, *plus* the rest of New England, *plus* the entire South Atlantic seaboard, *plus* the entire West Coast, *plus* Ohio, Indiana, Illinois, Michigan, and Wisconsin. Or take the Caribbean and the Central American area. Today that relatively small area has a population of 66 million. In forty years, at its present rate of growth, its population will outnumber by thirty million the entire population of the United States today. By that year South America, now 20 percent less populous than we, is likely to be 200 percent larger than our present population. At current rates of increase, India will then number a billion souls, China 1.5 billion.

It is possible that these cancerous rates of growth will decelerate, although no such trend is as yet evident. If they do not, their impending impact on development is all too obvious. Take, for instance, the case of the Aswan High Dam in Egypt—one of the most colossal engineering undertakings in any underdeveloped nation. The dam, which will be as high as a thirty-story building and three miles long, will make available approximately two million acres of new land for crops. It will generate three times the total amount of electricity now produced in Egypt. Its over-all impact on increased agricultural production may run as high as 45 percent. Meanwhile, however, that figure happens to be the percentage by which Egyptian population is estimated to rise in the ten-year period during which the dam will be under construction. Hence, despite the long-term gain in power, the near-term effect in raising per-capita living standards will be zero. So far as immediate results are concerned, the entire gigantic enterprise will only succeed in preventing the Egyptian economy from suffocating under its proliferating human mass.

And the same bleak outlook is found on the other continents. Calculations show that Asia, merely to *maintain* her present low level of living standards, must *increase* her aggregate product by 60 percent between now and 1975, and by an additional 75 percent between 1975 and 2000. Thus the bulk of any gains from increased productivity is used up merely in sustaining the ever-threatened level of subsistence.

We have already seen one result of the relentless proliferation of people in the fragmentation of landholdings. But the problem soon goes beyond mere fragmentation. In India, Eugene Black tells us, already a population equivalent to that of all Great Britain has been squeezed out of *any* landholding whatsoever—even though they still dwell in rural areas. Hence population pressure generates massive and widespread rural poverty, and a push from the countryside into the already teeming and overcrowded cities. In Indonesia, where population density has reached the fantastic figure of 1,100 per square mile (compare American population density of 50.4 people per square mile), five hundred families a day move into Jakarta from the surrounding fields. Two hundred and fifty families a day move into Bangkok and Rangoon. The crowd of beggars, street-livers, and scavengers grows.

It is an ironic commentary that the population explosion is a fairly recent phenomenon, and attributable, largely, to the incursion of Western medicine and public health into the underdeveloped areas. Prior to World War II, the poorer countries were generally marked by high birth rates, but their population increase was held in check by comparable death rates. Since then, the birth rates have continued high, but the death rates have plunged dramatically—and with unexpectedly tragic consequences. In Ceylon, for example, the death rate dropped 30 percent in the single year 1946 following the adoption of malaria control and other health measures. In Taiwan, in Malaya, in vast areas of Africa and the Near East, comparable extensions in the span of life—and in the ensuing bulge of population—have taken place. And the explosion of populations is not over. In tropical Africa today infant mortality runs between 200 and 800 per thousand, and averages 300 to 500 per thousand. There is an enormous source of future population growth as these ghastly rates begin to fall (as they will) toward the American infant death rate of twenty-six per thousand.

. . . It is well to conclude our brief survey of the problem with the somber words of Eugene Black: "Unless population growth can be restrained, we may have to abandon for this generation our hopes for economic progress in the crowded lands of Asia and the Middle East."

VICIOUS CIRCLES

. . . The problems we have itemized in the last few pages are, of course, by no means a complete catalogue of the common handicaps of underdevelopment. Moreover, as we have already noted, we must not suppose that all underdeveloped nations suffer from these handicaps in precisely the same way. In each the mix of the ingredients differs; in each there may be additional factors no less deeply rooted or intransigent: caste barriers in India, a disdain for work among the men of certain tribes of Africa, uneconomic notions of "fairness" in Java.

And then we have not even mentioned as yet the problems of health or of ignorance—problems which in every underdeveloped land produce a sucking undertow against the force of development. Take, for instance, malaria. More than 100 million people are today threatened by malaria; in a country like India, a fifth or more of the population may be unable to work for some period of each year because it is down with malarial fever. In Afghanistan, wide sections of arable lands around Kunduz are uncultivated for the same reason; the Afghan saying is, "If you want to die, go to Kunduz." In Mexico, malaria costs the nation an estimated $175 million a year in crops lost because their cultivators are unable to tend them.

Malaria is, of course, only one part of the health problem which undermines economic development. Yaws, a horrible, erosive disease which can be totally cured by five cents' worth of penicillin, until recently afflicted an estimated fifty million people a year. TB, "the quiet killer," has taken five million victims a year; leprosy claims up to twelve million sufferers; trachoma, the blinder, impairs the eyesight of some 400 million. All of these diseases are the target of WHO and UNICEF programs; and all of them have begun to yield before the first international medical crusade in history, but they still constitute a major stumbling block to development: in Africa, for instance, malaria kills off about 12 percent of all Africans before they reach maturity. In other words, over fifteen million Africans live only long enough to consume their share of the continent's meager output, but not long enough to contribute to it.

Sickness is not the only developmental block to which we have paid inadequate attention. There is hunger, which can be equally crippling to human energy; ignorance, which can serve even more tellingly to hinder development; isolation—roadless villages, totally insulated communities—which can underlie ignorance. The list could be many times lengthened.

This complex multi-casuality of underdevelopment can be summarized in the often-used expression "vicious circles." It is not "just" a lack of capital, or "just" backward ways, or "just" a population problem, or even "just" a political problem, which weighs upon the poorer nations. It is a combination of all of these, each aggravating the other. The troubles of underdevelopment feed upon themselves; one cannot easily attack one of the shackles of underdevelopment without contending with them all.

These are the hard—the brutally hard—difficulties of underdevelopment. An interlocking of evil conditions, a self-generating tendency toward defeat, are the overwhelming realities which greet anyone who looks into the conditions of existence of most of mankind today and the prospects which stare it in the face for tomorrow. Nothing is gained by minimizing this grim condition. It is only by coming to grips with the problem in its full magnitude that we can begin to formulate plans adequate to deal with it. . . .

selection 10

The Stages of Economic Growth*

W. W. Rostow

It is possible to identify all societies, in their economic dimensions, as lying within one of five categories: the traditional society, the preconditions for take-off, the take-off, the drive to maturity, and the age of high mass-consumption.

THE TRADITIONAL SOCIETY

First, the traditional society. A traditional society is one whose structure is developed within limited production functions, based on pre-Newtonian science and technology, and on pre-Newtonian attitudes towards the physical world. Newton is here used as a symbol for that watershed in history when men came widely to believe that the external world was subject to a few knowable laws, and was systematically capable of productive manipulation.

The conception of the traditional society is, however, in no sense static; and it would not exclude increases in output. Acreage could be expanded; some *ad hoc* technical innovations, often highly productive innovations, could be introduced in trade, industry and agriculture; productivity could rise with, for example, the improvement of irrigation works or the discovery and diffusion of a new crop. But the central fact about the traditional society was that a ceiling existed on the level of attainable output per head. This ceiling resulted from the fact that the potentialities which flow from modern science and technology were either not available or not regularly and systematically applied.

Both in the longer past and in recent times the story of traditional societies was thus a story of endless change. The area and volume of trade within them and between them fluctuated, for example, with the degree of political and social turbulence, the efficiency of central rule, the upkeep of the roads. Population—and, within limits, the level of life—rose and fell not only with the sequence of the harvests, but with the incidence of war and of plague. Varying degrees of manufacture developed; but, as in agriculture, the level of productivity was limited by the inaccessibility of modern science, its applications, and its frame of mind.

---

*From *The Stages of Economic Growth* (Cambridge University Press, 1960), pp. 4–12.

Generally speaking, these societies, because of the limitation on productivity, had to devote a very high proportion of their resources to agriculture; and flowing from the agricultural system there was an hierarchical social structure, with relatively narrow scope—but some scope—for vertical mobility. Family and clan connexions played a large role in social organization. The value system of these societies was generally geared to what might be called a long-run fatalism; that is, the assumption that the range of possibilities open to one's grandchildren would be just about what it had been for one's grandparents. But this long-run fatalism by no means excluded the short-run option that, within a considerable range, it was possible and legitimate for the individual to strive to improve his lot, within his lifetime. In Chinese villages, for example, there was an endless struggle to acquire or to avoid losing land, yielding a situation where land rarely remained within the same family for a century.

Although central political rule—in one form or another—often existed in traditional societies, transcending the relatively self-sufficient regions, the centre of gravity of political power generally lay in the regions, in the hands of those who owned or controlled the land. The landowner maintained fluctuating but usually profound influence over such central political power as existed, backed by its entourage of civil servants and soldiers, imbued with attitudes and controlled by interests transcending the regions.

In terms of history then, with the phrase "traditional society" we are grouping the whole pre-Newtonian world: the dynasties in China; the civilization of the Middle East and the Mediterranean; the world of medieval Europe. And to them we add the post-Newtonian societies which, for a time, remained untouched or unmoved by man's new capability for regularly manipulating his environment to his economic advantage.

To place these infinitely various, changing societies in a single category, on the ground that they all shared a ceiling on the productivity of their economic techniques, is to say very little indeed. But we are, after all, merely clearing the way in order to get at . . . the post-traditional societies, in which each of the major characteristics of the traditional society was altered in such ways as to permit regular growth: its politics, social structure, and (to a degree) its values, as well as its economy.

THE PRECONDITIONS FOR TAKE-OFF

The second stage of growth embraces societies in the process of transition; that is, the period when the preconditions for take-off are developed; for it takes time to transform a traditional society in the ways necessary for it to exploit the fruits of modern science, to fend off diminishing returns, and thus to enjoy the blessings and choices opened up by the march of compound interest.

The preconditions for take-off were initially developed, in a clearly marked way, in Western Europe of the late seventeenth and early eighteenth centuries as the insights of modern science began to be translated into new production functions in both agriculture and industry, in a setting given dynamism by the lateral expansion of world markets and the international competition for them. But all that lies behind the break-up of the Middle Ages is relevant to the creation of the preconditions for take-off in Western Europe. Among the Western European states, Britain, favoured by geography, natural resources, trading possibilities, social and political structure, was the first to develop fully the preconditions for take-off.

The more general case in modern history, however, saw the stage of pre-conditions arise not endogenously but from some external intrusion by more advanced societies. These invasions—literal or figurative—shocked the traditional society and began or hastened its undoing; but they also set in motion ideas and sentiments which initiated the process by which a modern alternative to the traditional society was constructed out of the old culture.

The idea spreads not merely that economic progress is possible, but that economic progress is a necessary condition for some other purpose, judged to be good: be it national dignity, private profit, the general welfare, or a better life for the children. Education, for some at least, broadens and changes to suit the needs of modern economic activity. New types of enterprising men come forward—in the private economy, in government, or both—willing to mobilize savings and to take risks in pursuit of profit or modernization. Banks and other institutions for mobilizing capital appear. Investment increases, notably in trans-port, communications, and in raw materials in which other nations may have an economic interest. The scope of commerce, internal and external, widens. And, here and there, modern manufacturing enterprise appears, using the new meth-ods. But all this activity proceeds at a limited pace within an economy and a society still mainly characterized by traditional low-productivity methods, by the old social structure and values, and by the regionally based political institu-tions that developed in conjunction with them.

In many recent cases, for example, the traditional society persisted side by side with modern economic activities, conducted for limited economic purposes by a colonial or quasi-colonial power.

Although the period of transition—between the traditional society and the take-off—saw major changes in both the economy itself and in the balance of social values, a decisive feature was often political. Politically, the building of an effective centralized national state—on the basis of coalitions touched with a new nationalism, in opposition to the traditional landed regional interests, the colo-nial power, or both, was a decisive aspect of the preconditions period; and it was, almost universally, a necessary condition for take-off. . . .

THE TAKE-OFF

We come now to the great watershed in the life of modern societies: the third stage in this sequence, the take-off. The take-off is the interval when the old blocks and resistances to steady growth are finally overcome. The forces making for economic progress, which yielded limited bursts and enclaves of modern activity, expand and come to dominate the society. Growth becomes its normal condition. Compound interest becomes built, as it were, into its habits and institutional structure.

In Britain and the well-endowed parts of the world populated substantially from Britain (the United States, Canada, etc.) the proximate stimulus for take-off was mainly (but not wholly) technological. In the more general case, the take-off awaited not only the build-up of social overhead capital and a surge of technological development in industry and agriculture, but also the emergence to political power of a group prepared to regard the modernization of the economy as serious, high-order political business.

During the take-off, the rate of effective investment and savings may rise from, say, 5% of the national income to 10% or more; although where heavy social overhead capital investment was required to create the technical preconditions for take-off the investment rate in the preconditions period could be higher than 5%, as, for example, in Canada before the 1890's and Argentina before 1914. In such cases capital imports usually formed a high proportion of total investment in the preconditions period and sometimes even during the take-off itself, as in Russia and Canada during their pre-1914 railway booms.

During the take-off new industries expand rapidly, yielding profits a large proportion of which are reinvested in new plant; and these new industries, in turn, stimulate, through their rapidly expanding requirement for factory workers, the services to support them, and for other manufactured goods, a further expansion in urban areas and in other modern industrial plants. The whole process of expansion in the modern sector yields an increase of income in the hands of those who not only save at high rates but place their savings at the disposal of those engaged in modern sector activities. The new class of entrepreneurs expands; and it directs the enlarging flows of investment in the private sector. The economy exploits hitherto unused natural resources and methods of production.

New techniques spread in agriculture as well as industry, as agriculture is commercialized, and increasing numbers of farmers are prepared to accept the new methods and the deep changes they bring to ways of life. The revolutionary changes in agricultural productivity are an essential condition for successful take-off; for modernization of a society increases radically its bill for agricultural products. In a decade or two both the basic structure of the economy and the social and political structure of the society are transformed in such a way that a steady rate of growth can be, thereafter, regularly sustained.

. . . One can approximately allocate the take-off of Britain to the two decades after 1783; France and the United States to the several decades preceding 1860; Germany, the third quarter of the nineteenth century; Japan, the fourth quarter of the nineteenth century; Russia and Canada the quarter-century or so preceding 1914; while during the 1950's India and China have, in quite different ways, launched their respective take-offs.

THE DRIVE TO MATURITY

After take-off there follows a long interval of sustained if fluctuating progress, as the now regularly growing economy drives to extend modern technology over the whole front of its economic activity. Some 10–20% of the national income is steadily invested, permitting output regularly to outstrip the increase in population. The make-up of the economy changes unceasingly as technique improves, new industries accelerate, older industries level off. The economy finds its place in the international economy: goods formerly imported are produced at home; new import requirements develop, and new export commodities to match them. The society makes such terms as it will with the requirements of modern efficient production, balancing off the new against the older values and institutions, or revising the latter in such ways as to support rather than to retard the growth process.

Some sixty years after take-off begins (say, forty years after the end of take-off) what may be called maturity is generally attained. The economy, focused during the take-off around a relatively narrow complex of industry and technology, has extended its range into more refined and technologically often more complex processes; for example, there may be a shift in focus from the coal, iron, and heavy engineering industries of the railway phase to machine-tools, chemicals, and electrical equipment. This, for example, was the transition through which Germany, Britain, France, and the United States had passed by the end of the nineteenth century or shortly thereafter. . . .

Formerly, we can define maturity as the stage in which an economy demonstrates the capacity to move beyond the original industries which powered its take-off and to absorb and to apply efficiently over a very wide range of its resources—if not the whole range—the most advanced fruits of (then) modern technology. This is the stage in which an economy demonstrates that it has the technological and entrepreneurial skills to produce not everything, but anything that it chooses to produce. It may lack (like contemporary Sweden and Switzerland, for example) the raw materials or other supply conditions required to produce a given type of output economically; but its dependence is a matter of economic choice or political priority rather than a technological or institutional necessity.

Historically, it would appear that something like sixty years was required to move a society from the beginning of take-off to maturity. Analytically the explanation for some such interval may lie in the powerful arithmetic of compound interest applied to the capital stock, combined with the broader consequences for a society's ability to absorb modern technology of three successive generations living under a regime where growth is the normal condition. But, clearly, no dogmatism is justified about the exact length of the interval from take-off to maturity.

THE AGE OF HIGH MASS-CONSUMPTION

We come now to the age of high mass-consumption, where, in time, the leading sectors shift towards durable consumers' goods and services: a phase from which Americans are beginning to emerge; whose not unequivocal joys

Western Europe and Japan are beginning energetically to probe; and with which Soviet society is engaged in an uneasy flirtation.

As societies achieved maturity in the twentieth century two things happened: real income per head rose to a point where a large number of persons gained a command over consumption which transcended basic food, shelter, and clothing; and the structure of the working force changed in ways which increased not only the proportion of urban to total population, but also the proportion of the population working in offices or in skilled factory jobs—aware of and anxious to acquire the consumption fruits of a mature economy.

In addition to these economic changes, the society ceased to accept the further extension of modern technology as an overriding objective. It is in this post-maturity stage, for example, that, through the political process, Western societies have chosen to allocate increased resources to social welfare and security. The emergence of the welfare state is one manifestation of a society's moving beyond technical maturity; but it is also at this stage that resources tend increasingly to be directed to the production of consumers' durables and to the diffusion of services on a mass basis, if consumers' sovereignty reigns. The sewing-machine, the bicycle, and then the various electric-powered household gadgets were gradually diffused. Historically, however, the decisive element has been the cheap mass automobile with its quite revolutionary effects—social as well as economic—on the life and expectations of society.

For the United States, the turning point was, perhaps, Henry Ford's moving assembly line of 1913–14; but it was in the 1920's, and again in the post-war decade, 1946–56, that this stage of growth was pressed to, virtually, its logical conclusion. In the 1950's Western Europe and Japan appear to have fully entered this phase, accounting substantially for a momentum in their economies quite unexpected in the immediate post-war years. The Soviet Union is technically ready for this stage, and, by every sign, its citizens hunger for it; but Communist leaders face difficult political and social problems of adjustment if this stage is launched.

BEYOND CONSUMPTION

Beyond, it is impossible to predict, except perhaps to observe that Americans, at least, have behaved in the past decade as if diminishing relative marginal utility sets in, after a point, for durable consumers' goods; and they have chosen, at the margin, larger families—behaviour in the pattern of Buddenbrooks dynamics.[1] Americans have behaved as if, having been born into a system that provided economic security and high mass-consumption, they placed a lower valuation on acquiring additional increments of real income in the conventional

---

[1] In Thomas Mann's novel of three generations, the first sought money; the second, born to money, sought social and civic position; the third, born to comfort and family prestige, looked to the life of music. The phrase is designed to suggest, then, the changing aspirations of generations, as they place a low value on what they take for granted and seek new forms of satisfaction.

form as opposed to the advantages and values of an enlarged family. But even in this adventure in generalization it is a shade too soon to create—on the basis of one case—a new stage-of-growth, based on babies, in succession to the age of consumers' durables: as economists might say, the income-elasticity of demand for babies may well vary from society to society. But it is true that the implications of the baby boom along with the not wholly unrelated deficit in social overhead capital are likely to dominate the American economy over the next decade rather than the further diffusion of consumers' durables.

Here then, in an impressionistic rather than an analytic way, are the stages-of-growth which can be distinguished once a traditional society begins its modernization: the transitional period when the preconditions for take-off are created generally in response to the intrusion of a foreign power, converging with certain domestic forces making for modernization; the take-off itself; the sweep into maturity generally taking up the life of about two further generations; and then, finally, if the rise of income has matched the spread of technological virtuosity (which, as we shall see, it need not immediately do) the diversion of the fully mature economy to the provision of durable consumers' goods and services (as well as the welfare state) for its increasingly urban—and then suburban—population. Beyond lies the question of whether or not secular spiritual stagnation will arise, and, if it does, how man might fend it off. . . .

selection 11

The Critical Role of the High Achiever*

David C. McClelland

What accounts for the rise in civilization? Not external resources (i.e., markets, minerals, trade routes, or factories), but the entrepreneurial spirit which exploits those resources—a spirit found most often among businessmen.

Who is ultimately responsible for the pace of economic growth in poor countries today? Not the economic planners or the politicians, but the executives whose drive (or lack of it) will determine whether the goals of the planners are fulfilled.

Why is Russia developing so rapidly that—if it continues its present rate of growth—it will catch up economically with the most advanced country in the world, the United States, in 25 or 30 years? Not, as the U.S.S.R. claims, because

---

*From "Business Drive and National Achievement," *Harvard Business Review,* July–August, 1962, pp. 92–112. © 1962 by the President and Fellows of Harvard College; all rights reserved.

of the superiority of its Communist system, but because—by hook or by crook—it has managed to develop a stronger spirit of entrepreneurship among executives than we have today in the U.S.

How can foreign aid be most efficiently used to help poor countries develop rapidly? Not by simply handing money over to their politicians or budget makers, but by using it in ways that will select, encourage, and develop those of their business executives who have a vigorous entrepreneurial spirit or a strong drive for achievement. In other words: *invest in a man, not just in a plan.*

What may be astonishing about some of these remarks is that they come from a college professor, and not from the National Association of Manufacturers. They are not the defensive drum rattlings of an embattled capitalist, but are my conclusions, based on nearly 15 years of research, as a strictly academic psychologist, into the human motive that appears to be largely responsible for economic growth—research which has recently been summarized in my book, entitled *The Achieving Society.*[1]

Since I am an egghead from way back, nothing surprises me more than finding myself rescuing the businessman from the academic trash heap, dusting him off, and trying to give him the intellectual respectability that he has had a hard time maintaining for the last 50 years or so. For the fact is that the businessman has taken a beating, not just from the Marxists, who pictured him as a greedy capitalist, and the social critics, who held him responsible for the Great Depression of the 1930's, but even from himself, deep in his heart.

One of the queerest ironies of history, as John Kenneth Galbraith points out in *The Affluent Society,*[2] is that in a sense Marx won his case with his sworn enemies, the capitalists. Marx loudly asserted that they were selfish and interested only in profits. In the end many agreed. They accepted the Marxist materialistic view of history. The modern businessman, says Galbraith, "suspects that the moral crusade of reformers, do-gooders, liberal politicians, and public servants, all their noble protestations notwithstanding, are based ultimately on self-interest. 'What,' he inquires, 'is their gimmick?' "[3]

If not only the Marxists, but Western economists, and even businessmen themselves, end up assuming that their main motive is self-interest and a quest for profit, it is small wonder that they have had a hard time holding their heads high in recent years.

But now the research I have done has come to the businessman's rescue by showing that everyone has been wrong, that it is *not* profit per se that makes the businessman tick but a strong desire for achievement, for doing a good job. Profit is simply one measure among several of how well the job has been done, but it is not necessarily the goal itself.

---

[1] David C. McClelland, *The Achieving Society* (Princeton, N.J.: D. Van Nostrand Co., Inc., 1961).

[2] John Kenneth Galbraith, *The Affluent Society* (Boston: Houghton Mifflin Co., 1958).

[3] *Ibid.,* p. 71.

THE ACHIEVEMENT GOAL

But what exactly does the psychologist mean by the "desire for achievement"? How does he measure it in individuals or in nations? How does he know that it is so important for economic growth? Is it more important for businessmen to have this desire than it is for politicians, bishops, or generals? These are the kinds of questions which are answered at great length and with as much scientific precision as possible in my book. Here we must be content with the general outline of the argument, and develop it particularly as it applies to businessmen.

To begin with, psychologists try to find out what a man spends his time thinking and daydreaming about when he is not under pressure to think about anything in particular. What do his thoughts turn to when he is by himself or not engaged in a special job? Does he think about his family and friends, about relaxing and watching TV, about getting his superior off his back? Or does he spend his time thinking and planning how he can "sell" a particular customer, cut production costs, or invent a better steam trap or toothpaste tube?

If a man spends his time thinking about doing things better, the psychologist says he has a concern for achievement. In other words, he cares about achievement or he would not spend so much time thinking about it. If he spends his time thinking about family and friends, he has a concern for affiliation; if he speculates about who is boss, he has a concern for power, and so on. What differs in my approach from the one used by many psychologists is that my colleagues and I have not found it too helpful simply to *ask* a person about his motives, interests, and attitudes. Often he himself does not know very clearly what his basic concerns are—even more often he may be ashamed and cover some of them up. So what we do is to try and get a sample of his normal waking thoughts by asking him just to tell a few stories about some pictures.

Stories within Stories

Let us take a look at some typical stories written by U.S. business executives. These men were asked to look briefly at a picture—in this case, a man at a worktable with a small family photograph at one side—and to spend about five minutes writing out a story suggested by the picture. Here is a very characteristic story:

The engineer is at work on Saturday when it is quiet and he has taken time to do a little daydreaming. He is the father of the two children in the picture—the husband of the woman shown. He has a happy home life and is dreaming about some pleasant outing they have had. He is also looking forward to a repeat of the incident which is now giving him pleasure to think about. He plans on the following day, Sunday, to use the afternoon to take his family for a short trip.

Obviously, no achievement-related thoughts have come to the author's mind as he thinks about the scene in the picture. Instead, it suggests spending time pleasantly with his family. His thoughts run along *affiliative* lines. He thinks readily about interpersonal relationships and having fun with other people. This, as a matter of fact, is the most characteristic reaction to this particular picture. But now consider another story:

> A successful industrial designer is at his "work bench" toying with a new idea. He is "talking it out" with his family in the picture. Someone in the family dropped a comment about a shortcoming in a household gadget, and the designer has just "seen" a commercial use of the idea. He has picked up ideas from his family before—he is "telling" his family what a good idea it is, and "confidentially" he is going to take them on a big vacation because "their" idea was so good. The idea will be successful, and family pride and mutual admiration will be strengthened.

The author of this story maintains a strong interest in the family and in affiliative relationships, but has added an achievement theme. The family actually has helped him innovate—get a new idea that will be successful and obviously help him get ahead. Stories which contain references to good new ideas, such as a new product, an invention, or a unique accomplishment of any sort, are scored as reflecting a concern for achievement in the person who writes them. In sum, this man's mind tends to run most easily along the lines of accomplishing something or other. Finally, consider a third story:

> The man is an engineer at a drafting board. The picture is of his family. He has a problem and is concentrating on it. It is merely an everyday occurrence—a problem which requires thought. How can he get that bridge to take the stress of possible high winds? He wants to arrive at a good solution of the problem by himself. He will discuss the problem with a few other engineers and make a decision which will be a correct one—he has the earmarks of competence.

The man who wrote this story—an assistant to a vice president, as a matter of fact—notices the family photograph, but that is all. His thoughts tend to focus on the problem that the engineer has to solve. In the scant five minutes allowed, he even thinks of a precise problem—how to build a bridge that will take the stress of possible high winds. He notes that the engineer wants to find a good solution by himself, that he goes and gets help from other experts and finally makes a correct decision. These all represent different aspects of a complete achievement sequence—defining the problem, wanting to solve it, thinking of means of solving it, thinking of difficulties that get in the way of solving it (either in one's self or in the environment), thinking of people who might help in solving it, and anticipating what would happen if one succeeded or failed. Each of these different ideas about achievement gets a score of +1 in our scoring system so that the man in the last incident gets a score of +4 on the scale of concern or need for achievement (conventionally abbreviated to *n* Achievement). Similarly, the first man gets a score of –1 for his story since it is completely unrelated to achievement, and the second man a score of +2 because there are two ideas in it which are scorable as related to achievement.

Each man usually writes six such stories and gets a score for the whole test. The coding of the stories for "achievement imagery" is so objective that two expert scorers working independently rarely disagree. In fact, it has recently been programed for a high-speed computer that does the scoring rapidly, with complete objectivity, and fairly high accuracy. What the score for an individual represents is the frequency with which he tends to think spontaneously in achievement terms when that is not clearly expected of him (since the instructions for the test urge him to relax and to think freely and rapidly).

Thinking Makes It So

What are people good for who think like this all the time? It doesn't take much imagination to guess that they might make particularly good business executives. People who spend a lot of their time thinking about getting ahead, inventing new gadgets, defining problems that need to be solved, considering alternative means of solving them, and calling in experts for help should also be people who in real life *do* a lot of these things or at the very best are readier to do them when the occasion arises.

I recognize, of course, that this is an assumption that requires proof. But, as matters turned out, our research produced strong factual support. . . . In three countries representing different levels and types of economic development [United States, Italy, and Poland], managers or executives scored considerably higher on the average in achievement thinking than did professionals or specialists of comparable education and background.

Take the two democratic countries. In the United States the comparison was between matched pairs of unit managers and specialists of the same position level, age, educational background, and length of service in the General Electric Company. The managers spent more of their time in the test writing about achievement than the specialists did. The same was true of middle-level executives from various companies in Italy when contrasted with students of law, medicine, and theology who were roughly of the same intelligence level and social background.

In other words it takes a concern for achievement to be a manager in a foreign country like Italy, for instance, just as it does in the United States. It is worth noting in passing, however, that the level of achievement thinking among Italian managers is significantly lower than it is among American managers—which, as will be shown later, quite probably has something to do with the lower level and rate of economic development in Italy.

What about a Communist country? The figures for Poland are interesting, because (1) the level of concern for achievement is about what it is in the United States, and (2) even in businesses owned and operated by the state, as in Poland, managers tend to have a higher concern for achievement than do other professionals.

Another even more striking result . . . is the fact that there is *no real difference* between the average *n* Achievement score of managers working for the U.S. government and those in U.S. private business generally. Apparently, a manager working for the Bureau of Ships in the Department of the Navy spends as much time thinking about achievement as his counterpart in Ford or Sears, Roebuck; government service does not weaken his entrepreneurial spirit. Whether he is able to be as effective as he might be in private business is another matter, not touched on here.

Careful quantitative studies of the prevalence of achievement concern among various types of executives also yield results in line with what one would expect. Thus, sales managers score higher than other types of managers do.

In general, more successful managers tend to score higher than do less successful managers (except in government service where promotion depends more on seniority). The picture is clear in small companies, where the president tends to score higher than his associates. In large companies, the picture is a little more complicated. Men in the lowest salary brackets (earning less than $20,000 a year) definitely have the lowest average n Achievement scores, while those in the next bracket up ($20,000 to $25,000 a year) have the highest average n Achievement level. Apparently an achievement concern helps one get out of the ranks of the lowest paid into the higher income bracket. But from there on, the trend fades. Men in the highest income brackets have a somewhat lower average concern for achievement, and apparently turn their thoughts to less achievement-oriented concerns. Possibly these men are doing well enough to relax a little.

BUSINESSMEN & ACHIEVEMENT

Businessmen usually raise either one of two questions at this point:

1. "Where can I get this test for n Achievement? It sounds like a good way of picking young executives!"

2. "Why is this concern for achievement specific to being a success as a business manager? What about other types of achievement? Why isn't the entrepreneurial spirit necessary for success as an opera star, a preacher, a great teacher, or a great scientist?"

The answer to the first question, unfortunately, is simple: no practicable, marketable test for assessing achievement concern exists as yet. The method of measurement we have been using is too sensitive, too easily influenced by the social atmosphere surrounding the people who take the test, to give reliable individual results. Under carefully controlled conditions it works adequately to distinguish large groups of people like managers versus professionals, but it is not yet useful for individual selection. What we have here is a theoretical, scientific "breakthrough," not a practicable working device.

The second question is harder to answer but it takes us further in the direction of understanding exactly what kind of a person it is who spends a lot of his time thinking about achievement. To begin with, the facts are clear: many important types of professionals (doctors, lawyers, priests, or research scientists) fail to score on the average as high as business executives, yet clearly their work is in every sense as much of an achievement as the businessman's. How come?

Let us consider a particular case for a moment—that of the research scientist. Certainly his work represents an important achievement, for he is the one who often makes the breakthrough on which new technological and economic advances depend. Shouldn't he be thinking about defining a problem, doing a good job of solving it, getting help from experts, etc.?

Yet, when we tested a number of such scientists—including several outstanding Nobel prize winners—we found, somewhat to our surprise, that they were not unusually high in *n* Achievement but rather tended to be average. Then it occurred to us that having a very high concern for achievement might make a person unsuitable for being a research scientist. Why? Simply because in research a man must often work for what may become very long periods of time without any knowledge of how well he is doing. He may not even know if he is on the right track for as much as five or ten years. But a man with a high need for achievement likes to know quickly whether he is accomplishing anything and quite possibly would become frustrated by the lack of feedback in basic science as to whether he is getting anywhere. He would then more likely move into an area such as management where results are more tangible. On the other hand, the research scientist obviously needs *some* achievement concern, or he is not likely to want to engage in his occupation at all.

Characteristics of Achievers

Considerations like these focus attention on what there is about the job of being a business entrepreneur or executive that should make such a job peculiarly appropriate for a man with a high concern for achievement. Or, to put it the other way around, a person with high *n* Achievement has certain characteristics which enable him to work best in certain types of situations that are to his liking. An entrepreneurial job simply provides him with more opportunities for making use of his talents than do other jobs. Through careful empirical research we know a great deal by now about the man with high *n* Achievement, and his characteristics do seem to fit him unusually well for being a business executive. Specifically:

1. *To begin with, he likes situations in which he takes personal responsibility for finding solutions to problems.* The reason is obvious. Otherwise, he could get little personal achievement satisfaction from the successful outcome. No gambler, he does not relish situations where the outcome depends not on his abilities and efforts but on chance or other factors beyond his control. For example:

Some business school students in one study played a game in which they had to choose between two options, in each of which they had only one chance in three of succeeding. For one option they rolled a die and if it came up, say, a 1 or a 3 (out of six possibilities), they won. For the other option they had to work on a difficult business problem which they knew only one out of three people had been able to solve in the time allotted.

Under these conditions, the men with high *n* Achievement regularly chose to work on the business problem, even though they knew the odds of success were statistically the same as for rolling the dice.

To men strong in achievement concern, the idea of winning by chance simply does not produce the same achievement satisfaction as winning by their own personal efforts. Obviously, such a concern for taking personal responsibility is useful in a business executive. He may not be faced very often with the alternative of rolling dice to determine the outcome of a decision, but there are many other ways open to avoid personal responsibility, such as passing the buck, or trying to get someone else (or a committee) to take the responsibility for getting something done.

The famed self-confidence of a good executive (which actually is related to high achievement motivation) is also involved here. He thinks it can be done if *he* takes responsibility, and very often he is right because he has spent so much time thinking about how to do it that he does it better.

2. *Another characteristic of a man with a strong achievement concern is his tendency to set moderate achievement goals and to take "calculated risks."* Again his strategy is well suited to his needs, for only by taking on moderately difficult tasks is he likely to get the achievement satisfaction he wants. If he takes on an easy or routine problem, he will succeed but get very little satisfaction out of his success. If he takes on an extremely difficult problem, he is unlikely to get any satisfaction because he will not succeed. In between these two extremes, he stands the best chance of maximizing his sense of personal achievement.

The point can be made with the children's game of ring toss, some variant of which we have tried out at all ages to see how a person with high *n* Achievement approaches it. To illustrate:

The child is told that he scores when he succeeds in throwing a ring over a peg on the floor, but that he can stand anywhere he pleases. Obviously, if he stands next to the peg, he can score a ringer every time; but if he stands a long distance away, he will hardly ever get a ringer.

This curious fact is that the children with high concern for achievement quite consistently stand at moderate distances from the peg where they are most apt to get achievement satisfaction (or, to be more precise, where the decreasing probability-of-success curve crosses the increasing satisfaction-from-success curve). The ones with low *n* Achievement, on the other hand, distribute their choices of where to stand quite randomly over the entire distance. In other words, people with high *n* Achievement prefer a situation where there is a challenge, where there is some real risk of not succeeding, but not so great a risk that they might not overcome it by their own efforts.

Again, such a characteristic would seem to suit men unusually well for the role of business entrepreneur. The businessman is always in a position of taking calculated risks, of deciding how difficult a given decision will be to carry out. If he is too safe and conservative, and refuses to innovate, to invest enough in research or product development or advertising, he is likely to lose out to a more aggressive competitor. On the other hand, if he invests too much or overextends himself, he is also likely to lose out. Clearly, then, the business executive should be a man with a high concern for achievement who is used to setting moderate goals for himself and calculating carefully how much he can do successfully.

Therefore, we waste our time feeling sorry for the entrepreneur whose constant complaints are that he is overworking, that he has more problems than he knows how to deal with, that he is doomed to ulcers because of overwork, and so on. The bald truth is that if he has high *n* Achievement, he loves all those challenges he complains about. In fact, a careful study might well show that he creates most of them for himself. He may talk about quitting business and living on his investments, but if he did, he might then *really* get ulcers. The state of mind of being a little overextended is precisely the one he seeks, since overcoming difficulties gives him achievement satisfaction. His real problem is that of keeping the difficulties from getting *too* big for him, which explains in part why he talks so much about them because it is a nagging problem for him to keep them at a level he can handle.

3. *The man who has a strong concern for achievement also wants concrete feedback as to how well he is doing.* Otherwise how could he get any satisfaction out of what he had done? And business is almost unique in the amount of feedback it provides in the form of sales, cost, production, and profit figures. It is really no accident that the symbol of the businessman in popular cartoons is a wall chart with a line on it going up or down. The businessman sooner or later knows how well he is doing; salesmen will often know their success from day to day. Furthermore, there is a concreteness in the knowledge of results which is missing from the kind of feedback professionals get.

Take, for example, the teacher as a representative professional. His job is to transmit certain attitudes and certain kinds of information to his students. He does get some degree of feedback as to how well he has done his job, but results are fairly imprecise and hardly concrete. His students, colleagues, and even his college's administration may indicate that they like his teaching, but he still has no real evidence that his students have *learned* anything from him. Many of his students do well on examinations, but he knows from past experience that they will forget most of that in a year or two. If he has high *n* Achievement and is really concerned about whether he has done his job well, he must be satisfied with sketchy, occasional evidence that his former pupils did absorb some of his ideas and attitudes. More likely, however, he is not a person with high *n* Achievement and is quite satisfied with the affection and recognition that he gets for his work which gratify other needs that he has.

The case of the true entrepreneur is different. Suppose he is a book publisher. He gets a manuscript and together with his editors decides that it is worth publication. At time of issuance, everyone is satisfied that he is launching a worthwhile product. But then something devastatingly concrete happens—something far more definite than ever happens to a teacher—namely, those monthly sales figures.

Obviously not everyone likes to work in situations where the feedback is so concrete. It can prove him right, but it also can prove him wrong. Oddly enough, the person with high *n* Achievement has a compelling interest to know whether he was right or wrong. He thrives and is happier in this type of situation than he is in the professional situation.

Two further examples from our research may make the point clearer. Boys with high *n* Achievement tend to be good with their hands, to like working in a shop or with mechanical or electrical gadgets. What characterizes such play again is the concrete feedback it provides as to how well a person is doing. If he wires up an electric circuit and then throws the switch, the light either goes on or it does not. Knowledge of results is direct, immediate, and concrete. Boys with high *n* Achievement like this kind of situation, and while some may go on to become engineers, others often go into business where they can continue getting this kind of concrete feedback.

What Money Means

In business, this feedback comes in the form of money, in costs and profits that are regularly reported. It is from this simple fact that the confusion between the so-called profit motive and the achievement motive has arisen in the minds of both Marxist and classical economists. For, in the typical case, a concern for profit in a capitalist economy does *not* mean that the businessman is primarily interested in money for its own sake. Rather, this concern is merely the *symptom* of a strong achievement concern, since profitability in a capitalist economy provides the best and simplest measure of success. It provides the same sort of concrete knowledge of achievement that a person with high *n* Achievement seeks all the time. Research findings clearly support this analysis. If you simply offer a person with high *n* Achievement a larger money reward for doing a certain task, he doesn't do any better than he did without the prize. In fact, he tends to do a little worse because the money makes him nervous. Not so the person with low *n* Achievement; he works harder when he has a chance of taking some money away from a situation. The money in and of itself means more to him than it does to the person with high *n* Achievement.

Of course, it follows that concrete measures of achievement other than money could be devised by other types of economic systems to satisfy the entrepreneurial spirit. Something like this has apparently happened in Communist states like Poland and Russia, where plant managers work under a fairly rigid quota system which demands that they make their quotas—or else! In the free enterprise system a businessman must make his profit—or else. The psychological effects, so far as the achievement motive is concerned, are apparently pretty much the same. In both systems the manager gets feedback in concrete terms as to how well he is doing. If he has high *n* Achievement, he is more likely to live and survive under such a challenge.

While these three characteristics of people with a strong concern for achievement – the desire for personal responsibility, the tendency to set moderate achievement goals, and the need for concrete feedback of results—are the most important, there are some other minor characteristics possessed by these people which tend to suit them for an entrepreneurial job. They like to travel, they are willing to give up one bird in the hand to get two in the bush, and they prefer experts to friends as working partners. But to discuss any of these in detail would take us far afield.

ACHIEVING NATIONS

If the theory underlying the experiments with determining n Achievement in individuals is correct, then what is true for groups of individuals might well prove true for nations. Does a high achievement concern herald a nation's rise? Let's take a look at the facts.

Naturally, tests of individual businessmen in particular countries would not prove very much about the influence of achievement concern on the nation's success. However, we figured that by coding popular literature of past and present, we could get a rough estimate of the strength of the concern for achievement in a given country at a given time period. So we took samples from various time periods of a wide variety of the most popular imaginative literature we could find—poems, songs, plays—and scored them for n Achievement just as we had scored the simple stories written by individuals.

When we plotted the number of achievement ideas per hundred lines sampled in a given time period against economic indexes for the same time period, we got two curves that showed a very interesting relationship to each other. Normally, we found, a high level of concern for achievement is followed some 50 years or so later by a rapid rate of economic growth and prosperity. Such was certainly the case in ancient Greece and in Spain in the late Middle Ages. Furthermore, in both cases a decline in achievement concern was followed very soon after by a decline in economic welfare. . . . [During] the 300-year time span from Tudor times to the Industrial Revolution in England:

> There were two waves of economic growth in this time period, one smaller one around 1600 and a much larger one around 1800 at the beginning of the Industrial Revolution. Each wave was preceded by a wave of concern for achievement reflected in popular literature, a smaller one prior to the growth spurt around 1600 and a larger one prior to the Industrial Revolution.

What clearer evidence could one ask for? What people are concerned about determines what they do, and what they do determines the outcome of history!

Present Confirms Past

In modern nations, too, the picture is very much the same. Children's stories used in public school textbooks proved to be the most standardized form of popular literature that we could get from a large number of different countries. As a matter of fact, the simple imaginative stories that every country uses to teach its children to read are very similar in format to the stories produced by individuals when we test them as described earlier, particularly if one concentrates as we did on second-, third-, and fourth-grade readers, where normally political influences are quite unimportant. The stories could be coded quite easily by the standard n Achievement scoring system.

Growth rates had to be estimated from the only figures available that could be trusted on such a wide variety of countries—namely, the figures showing electric power consumption—but there is ample evidence to show that electricity consumed is probably the best single available index of gross national income in modern times.

The *n* scores, when compared with the subsequent rates of economic growth for various countries, confirm the findings of the historical studies to a surprising extent. The higher the *n* Achievement level in the children's readers around 1925, the more rapid the subsequent rate of economic growth. (For 22 countries, the correlation was actually a substantial .53.) Furthermore, the higher the *n* Achievement level in a country's children's readers around 1950, the more rapid its rate of growth between 1952–1958. In fact, of 20 countries above average in *n* Achievement in 1950, 13 (or 65%) showed a rapid rate of economic growth in 1952–1958. Whereas, of 19 low in *n* Achievement, only 5 (or 26%) achieved a rapid rate of growth.

Prediction Possibilities

How meaningful are these findings, especially when one realizes the crudity of the data? In a certain sense, the cruder one admits the data to be, the more remarkable the findings appear. After all, the data suggest that one could have got a pretty good line on the economic future of various countries by studying its stories for children in 1925—regardless of a major depression, a World War, and a host of other political and economic factors.

Is it possible that we have stumbled on a way of predicting the future course of history? And from such an almost laughable source—stories for children— rather than the serious pronouncements of statesmen, generals, and economists? How is it possible?

The best interpretation of such findings would appear to run something as follows. The stories tell us what is on the minds of significant elites in the country, what these influential persons tend to think about most naturally, when they are "off guard," so to speak, and not under any particular pressure to think one thing or another. In this sense, the stories are exactly analogous to the ones written for us by individuals. If you ask a man whether he is interested in achievement, the chances are that he will tell you that of course he is. Similarly, if you were to ask a country's leaders whether they wanted their nation to forge ahead, they would find it unpatriotic to say no. But, regardless of what such leaders say in public, the stories in the children's readers of many nations will show whether their peoples' thoughts turn naturally to achievement or to matters other than achievement.

Here is an illustration. Take a simple story theme like one in which some children are building a boat. Such themes are frequently borrowed by one culture from another and appear in several different readers, but the way they are embroidered may be quite different and quite revealing. For example:

In Country A, an *achievement*-oriented country, the emphasis is on making the boat, on constructing something that will work, and not sink or tip over in a strong wind.

In Country B, the emphasis may be on *affiliation,* on the fun that the children have in playing together to sail their boat. Here little may be said about the details of constructing a seaworthy craft and much about the personal interaction of the children.

In Country C, the story may center on *power,* and describe how the children were organized to produce the boat. One boy might set himself up as a leader, coordinating the work of the other children and telling them what to do.

Apparently, what comes most readily to the minds of these authors—whether concepts of achievement, affiliation, or power—reflects sufficiently well what is on the minds of key people in the country. And not only will these concepts seem natural and pleasing to the readers of these stories but will determine what they spend their time doing in the years to come. Thus, if the stories stress achievement, it means that an entrepreneurial spirit is abroad in the land. It indicates that many key people are thinking in achievement terms even when they do not need to.

In a nation, a strong achievement orientation affects particularly the business or economic sector of the population. And if the entrepreneurial types are strongly motivated to do well, they apparently succeed in getting the economy moving at a faster rate. So the children's stories are a symptom of the quality or "drive" of the entrepreneurial sector of an economy.

Rising & Falling Nations

With this in mind it is interesting to look at scores for particular countries—if only to make a better guess as to where to invest one's money! A generation ago, the North European countries, particularly Sweden and England, were very high in *n* Achievement, but both have fallen in the 1950's to well below average. Is it just a coincidence that one hears reports of stagnation or "maturity" in both economies? Are England's present difficulties the fault of outside circumstances, or do these difficulties stem from the fact that its citizens have lost their achievement drive? For some reason, the Central European countries—France, Germany, and Russia—were all low in achievement concern in 1925, but by the 1950's all had increased sharply.

The case of Russia is particularly critical for us. How does the United States stand in achievement motivation as compared to the U.S.S.R.? According to a historical study, achievement concern in the United States increased regularly from 1800 to around 1890 but has decreased more or less regularly since, although there is a possibility that the decline has leveled off in the past 30 years. We are still above average and, in fact, were at approximately the same level as Russia in 1950, although we were probably on the way down while they were certainly on the way up.

From the point of view of this analysis, the argument as to whether a socialist or a free enterprise system is the better way of stimulating an economy has been based on a false premise all along. Americans claimed that the success of their economy resulted, naturally, from the free enterprise system. Then, when the Soviet Union scored successes in outer space and in other fields, the Russians immediately claimed these great economic and technological achievements stemmed from the superiority of their system.

Both contentions may well be wrong. Economic success and technological development depend on achievement motivation, and the rapid rate of Russian economic growth is due to an increase in her achievement concern just as ours was a generation or so earlier. There are other issues involved in comparing the two social systems, of course, but so far as this particular issue is concerned it has been misunderstood by both sides.

Need for Acceptance

There is one final question that must be answered before we move on. Is it possible that achievement motivation will be aroused in *any* nation which comes in contact with modern technology and sees vividly the opportunity for a better life? Can't achievement motivation be "borrowed" or assimilated from one nation to another? Are there not good illustrations of countries in which need for achievement has risen as they see more and more clearly the possibilities of growing and developing into modern, economically advanced nations? Are we just describing the "revolution of rising expectations" in fancy psychological jargon?

Opportunity is part of the story, of course. It does arouse people to act, but it arouses precisely those who have some need for achievement *already*. The soil must be ready for the seeds, if they are to grow. After all, many countries have been in touch with Western technology for generations—for example, the Islamic nations around the Mediterranean; yet they have been very slow to respond to the possibilities of a better life clearly presented to them all this time.

Consider, for example, a nation like Nigeria, which provides a good illustration of how opportunity and motivation must interact. Nigeria is essentially a federation of three regions, each of which is dominated by a different cultural group. Only one of these groups—the Yoruba—is known to be very high in need for achievement. In fact, long before the Yoruba had much contact with the West, this tribe was noted for its skill and interest in trade and native financial transactions. An indication of the validity of the achievement theory is shown by the fact that the Yoruba tribe, when exposed to new opportunities, produced a much stronger and more successful economic response than did the other tribes—as would be predicted. The regional bank operated by the Yoruba is in a much sounder position, for example, than the other two regional banks in Nigeria.

Opportunity challenges those who are achievement-oriented. Like two other groups high in *n* Achievement, American Jews and American Catholics between the ages of 35 and 45 (President Kennedy, for instance), the Yoruba reacted vigorously to develop economic opportunities as they became available. Exposure to economic and technological opportunities did not produce as vigorous a response from groups lower in *n* Achievement in Nigeria any more than a similar exposure has done through the years to similar low *n* Achievement groups in the United States.

WHAT CAN WE DO?

Is it inevitable that the achievement concern shown by U.S. citizens should continue to decline? Must we fade out in time as all other civilizations have in the past? Not if we understand what is happening and take steps to change it. Not if we move decisively and quickly to influence the sources of achievement concern in individuals and in our nation.

What are those sources? Clearly, not race or climate—those traditional external explanations of the superior energies of some nations. For Russia's *n* Achievement level has increased decisively since 1925, while Sweden's and England's have dropped. Certainly there have been no equally decisive changes in the gene pools or the climates of those nations in that time period.

In fact, external factors are usually unimportant, though occasionally they may play a role, as they have in helping to create generally high levels of *n* Achievement in immigrant countries like the United States, Canada, and Australia. Such nations tended to attract immigrants higher in *n* Achievement, because:

1. They drew their population initially from countries that were higher in achievement concern than those from which the Latin American countries drew.

2. They provided a haven for many persecuted religious minorities whose achievement concern was very strong.

3. They did not provide as many opportunities for getting rich quick as did Mexico and Peru, for example, with their plentiful supplies of gold and silver.

In short, countries like the United States were lucky. The barrier to migration was so formidable that primarily those with high *n* Achievement climbed it.

Historians have sometimes claimed that it was the great frontier in the United States that provided the challenge and stimulus to development. Nonsense. Great frontiers have existed and still exist in many South American countries without eliciting a similar response. It was the achievement-oriented immigrants to America who regarded the frontier as a challenge to be overcome. It was not the frontier that made them achievement-oriented. Opportunities, like new frontiers, always exist, but it takes a certain kind of person to see them and believe he can exploit them.

While our distance from Europe, our tolerance for religious minorities, our good fortune in drawing immigrants initially from countries high in *n* Achievement tended to ensure that we got more citizens with high achievement motivation, our later restrictive immigration policies have drastically reduced our chances of continuing to receive such people. These policies continue to give preference to immigrants from the North European countries, whose achievement drive has dropped significantly, and to restrict immigration from other countries where the *n* Achievement has been rising sharply. It would be a tragic irony of history if in an endeavor to protect ourselves, we managed to shut off the supply of that entrepreneurial spirit that made our country great!

Sources of Achievement

Where does strong achievement motivation come from? Values, beliefs, ideology—these are the really important sources of a strong concern for achievement in a country. Studies of the family have shown, for instance, that for a boy three factors are important in producing high *n* Achievement—parents' high standards of achievement, warmth and encouragement, and a father who is not dominating and authoritarian. Here is a typical study that reveals this fact:

> A group of boys were blindfolded and asked to stack irregularly shaped blocks on top of each other with their left hands, at home in front of their parents. Separately, the mothers and fathers were asked how high they thought their sons could stack the blocks. Both parents of a boy with high *n* Achievement estimated that their boys should do better; they expected more of him than did the parents of a boy with low *n* Achievement. They also encouraged him more and gave him more affection and reward while he was actually doing the task. Finally, the fathers of boys with high *n* Achievement directed the behavior of their sons much less when they were actually stacking the blocks; that is, they told them less often to move their hands this way or that, to try harder, to stop jiggling the table, and so forth, than did the fathers of boys with low *n* Achievement.

Other studies have shown that fathers must be respected by their sons; but after the boy is capable of achieving something for himself, his father must stop directing every step he takes if the boy is to develop a strong concern for achievement.

In a sense, however, these family studies only push the question further back. Where did the parents get their standards? Why do some emphasize achievement and affectionately reward self-reliance? Because, very simply, they themselves believe in achievement for their family or for their political, social, or religious group. For one reason or another they are caught up in some great wave of achievement ideology.

One of the paradoxes of history is that often the achievement concern was not itself initially directed toward business or economics. For instance, the two great waves of achievement concern in the history of England . . . were each associated with waves of Protestant reform or revival, whose explicit aims were not secular but strictly religious. The Methodists, for example, in the second wave of the English Protestant revival, stressed religious perfection in this life; yet even John Wesley recognized with some puzzlement that devout Methodists tended to get rich, a fact which he considered a handicap in attaining religious perfection.

But now we can understand what happened. The strong concern for Christian perfection in this world tended to produce an achievement orientation in Methodist parents and their sons that turned the boys toward business because, as we have shown above, an achievement concern is most easily satisfied in business. In our day, it is the secular religions of nationalism and communism that have placed the highest emphasis on achievement and tended to create higher levels of *n* Achievement in underdeveloped and Communist countries. Communism lays the same claims to superiority as a means of salvation that Christianity once did. However wrong we may feel it to be, we must recognize that it tends to create a strong atmosphere of achievement that has important consequences for economic growth.

THE ACHIEVEMENT CHALLENGE

If we are to compete successfully with Russia in the economic sphere, we must develop an achievement ideology at least as strong as hers. If we are to help poor countries develop rapidly and become self-reliant, we must recognize that the first order of priority lies in fostering the entrepreneurial spirit in those countries, not in simply providing them with material capital or in meeting their physical needs.

Oddly enough, a businessman knows this about his own company. He knows that in the final analysis it is the spirit in the company that counts most—the entrepreneurial drive of the executives, the feeling of all that they are working together to achieve a common goal; it is not "hardware" that counts in the long run—the size and slickness of the plant, or the money in the bank. These assets will melt away like snow in a hot sun without the proper achievement orientation in the company. Knowing this, the wise executive acts accordingly. He is concerned to keep the achievement orientation of the company alive by talking about its aims, by setting moderate but realizable goals for himself and his associates, by assigning personal responsibility, by making sure that people know how well they are doing, by selecting executives with high *n* Achievement or by developing it in those who need it.

What is true for a business is also true for a country, but this is not widely recognized. And we must realize that it is important to foster the achieving spirit not only at home but abroad if we are to be effective as a nation. American foreign policy is currently based on two main strategies: (a) the provision of political freedom and (b) material aid. Both are excellent goals, but they are not enough. How long would a company last if its chief goals were freedom from interference by others and freedom from want? It needs positive, specific goals such as a more effective marketing program, or a strict cost reduction program; something dynamic is necessary to keep a company—and a country—alive and growing.

Over and over again we have failed to learn the lesson that political freedom without a strong drive for progress is empty and impossible to maintain for long. China was politically free under Chiang Kai-shek, but it lacked the dynamic of a really self-sacrificing achievement effort until it was taken over by the Communists. Unless we learn our lesson and find ways of stimulating that drive for achievement under freedom in poor countries, the Communists will go on providing it all around the world. We can go on building dikes to maintain freedom and impoverishing ourselves to feed and arm the people behind those dikes, but only if we develop the entrepreneurial spirit in those countries will we have a sound foreign policy. Only then can they look after their own dikes and become economically self-sufficient.

Compare India and China, for example. Despite newspaper reports to the contrary, economic experts assure us that China is developing much more rapidly economically today than is India. Why? Is it because the West has given less material help to India than the Communist world has to China? Probably not. Is it because there is less political freedom in India than in China? Certainly not. Yet if the keystones of our foreign aid policy are the ensuring of political freedom and the granting of economic aid, these measures are clearly not doing very well as far as developing India is concerned. Russia has apparently exported something more important to China—namely, an achievement dynamic that has galvanized the whole country. There is absolutely no evidence that this dynamic needs to be associated with regimentation and lack of personal freedom as it is in China, for the United States had this dynamic once, still has quite a lot of it, and could export it more effectively—if we really tried.

Hard to Export

Actually, we have been hampered in exporting our achievement dynamic, not only by a misguided emphasis on material as opposed to motivational factors, but also by a laudable desire to avoid appearing superior. When Americans travel and discover how poor people are in many countries and how inferior their political institutions appear to be to ours, they often either withdraw in horror into their own American enclaves and become "ugly Americans" or they remember their college anthropology and become cultural relativists, deciding that after all there is some good in all ways of life and we must not impose ours on other people. Neither of these reactions is very intelligent. For the fact is that all poor countries are going to modernize and want to modernize. They refuse to remain quaint, impoverished specimens for the anthropologist to study.

How can we help provide such countries with an achievement dynamic without seeming to impose it on them? One simple way is to sell them on *their own country* and *its* possibilities, not on *ours*. It may sound absurd to say that our job is to help sell the Tanganyikans on Tanganyika or the Mexicans on Mexico, but the fact is that in many of these countries most of the people have never even heard of the nation of which they are citizens, and know little or nothing about the possibilities for a better life that they may have at home.

In other words, our job really is to do what Americans have been so good at doing—creating wants, selling a people on their future, making them believe in their own achievement.

Our other difficulty is organizational. Somewhere along the line we decided that federal funds for foreign aid must be spent by federal employees, usually in the form of grants or loans to be doled out by federal employees in other countries. This is a natural enough policy, because foreign relations are sensitive matters, but there is nothing inevitable about it. In fact, there is considerable evidence that aid channeled through nonofficial or private agencies is much more welcome in many countries and also less expensive.

Private organizations in the U.S. have had a long record of useful service abroad. Why should their resources not be increased by federal grants so that they can do their job even more effectively and on a larger scale? Why do new federal agencies have to be created all the time to try to hire people away from such groups when they are already organized to do a good job? Why must the Peace Corps compete for scarce specialists, whom it is currently having trouble recruiting? Why couldn't it make grants to organizations which already have such specialists on their staffs and instruct them to expand their efforts abroad?

Often such organizations can do a better job because they are not official representatives of Uncle Sam. They would certainly be more welcome in countries like Mexico, which will not accept Peace Corps volunteers because as U.S. employees they have political significance. What if some of these organizations are religious, when we believe in the separation of church and state? This is true, of course, but *all* Russians sent abroad are "religious" Communists. Can we really object to helping a few Christians go abroad, particularly if they are not official representatives of our government?

CONCLUSION

Our biggest challenge is to find some way to harness the enormous potential of American business to help develop poor countries. Why should creeping federalism continue to spawn new agencies for providing economic assistance to foreign countries when such agencies already exist under private ownership in the United States? For example, if Brazil needs a new electric power system somewhere, why should our government not help by working out a contract, complete with all the necessary credits or loans, with one of our own light and power companies? Aid, in other words, would be on a company-to-company basis rather than on a government-to-government basis. In the long run, it would probably prove to be cheaper and more efficient. More important, the achievement orientation of our business executives could make itself felt in various ways in the newly developing companies abroad.

This idea has many complexities which need to be worked out—some of which are dealt with in *The Achieving Society*—but basically it is designed to harness some of the enormous reserves of achievement ideology and skill in American business to the gargantuan task of developing poor countries. Money is not enough. Drive and enthusiasm are needed. Ways of locating and exporting these resources must be found.

If there is one thing that all this research has taught me, it is that men can shape their own destiny, that external difficulties and pressures are not nearly so important in shaping history as some people have argued. It is how people respond to those challenges that matters, and how they respond depends on how strong their concern for achievement is. So the question of what happens to our civilization or to our business community depends quite literally on how much time tens of thousands or even millions of us spend thinking about achievement, about setting moderate achievable goals, taking calculated risks, assuming personal responsibility, and finding out how well we have done our job. The answer is up to us.

selection 12

Cross-Cultural Studies of Technical Change*

Margaret Mead

Civilization in the last century has meant increasing industrialization in Europe as well as in the United States, and in the countries with which they came in contact, and which, courted or coerced into commerce with them, also became progressively industrialized. In both West and East the process was, for long, unplanned. The people in responsible positions had, as a rule, no view of the total picture, and no suspicion of the eventual results and their ramifications. Those who did either hailed the increase in material goods as an increase in human welfare, or offered romantic escapism. Even now, after long experience, and with all our awareness and intensive investigation of the concomitants of industrialization, we are astounded when we see the far-reaching results of the introduction of money into a barter economy, or of a new tool as simple as the kerosene lamp or a wooden-wheeled wagon.

Industrialization is with us to stay. We may decry its effects, as did a Venezuelan editor recently, appalled at the hidden poverty of rich, industrialized Caracas.[1] Yet, "The demographic consequences of industrialization constitute a powerful propulsive toward further industrialization. . . . It is not a reversible process."[2] And other countries, still primarily agrarian, are now drawn into the process of industrialization as a result of contact with Western civilization. Some-

---

*From *Cultural Patterns and Technical Change* by Margaret Mead, pp. 236–62. Reprinted by permission of UNESCO.

[1] *Time*, Vol. 57, No. 8 (1951), p. 39.

[2] Irene B. Taeuber, 1950, p. 292.

times, in introducing a programme of industrialization or the building of great public works and large factories, such countries have introduced radical change in the standard of living, drastically curtailing consumers' goods.[3] Usually the effects have been much more far-reaching and costly in human welfare than this statement implies.

The areas of agricultural change and industrialization overlap in certain respects. Large plantations, usually owned and operated by people of Western origin, use large numbers of labourers, as does industry, and seeing the process merely as one of money-making, often exploit land and people.[4] In Africa, plantations are often near the labourers' native villages, so that there is no accompanying disruption of the family and village life, as there is in connexion with industry; but in New Guinea, where labourers were brought from great distances, there was such disruption, as well as demoralization, among the large groups of men living without women and without families or villages.[5] In addition, mechanization itself, whether in agriculture or in industry, separates man from the traditional processes and techniques of his social unit, from the skills which he learned as an aspect of his belongingness with his family, or of his identification with his father and his line of ancestors. Finally, even on small farms, where cash crops have been introduced, the effects of the new money economy have often been of the same kind as with the introduction of industrial wages.

Governments throughout the world have done away with the more obvious ills of industrial labour. Women may no longer be allowed to work 14 hours a day, as they did in Turkey in 1914, or in rooms where no fresh air is allowed to enter lest the humidity shrink the cotton, as they did in Bombay at that time. But neither are they any longer allowed to bring their children to sleep or play at their feet.[6] The new laws have given workers protection, but the efficiency measures, and measures undertaken honestly for the protection of children, have worked toward breaking up the family unit during the day.[7]

The implications of industrialization for mental health are not covered by the new laws. For example, when it was proposed to a group of fellahin that a village pump be installed as a labour-saving device for the women, they said, "You say that the pump will save our women effort and time. If that happens, what are they going to do with themselves all day long?"[8] And it is not merely a question of occupying time. This is one of the components of womanhood; a woman carries water from the fountain. When Arab pictures are made for the tourist trade, they often portray a woman with a water pitcher. So also, among the Tiv, as well as the Burmese, women were identified with the pounding mortar;

---

3 Horace Belshaw, 1950, p. 50.

4 Candido M. de Silva Rondon, 1943, p. 23.

5 William Malcolm Hailey, 1938, p. 699; S. M. Lambert, 1941, p. 21; Richard C. Thurnwald, 1935, p. 118.

6 Janet Harvey Kelman, 1923, p. 83.

7 Lo-Chun, 1938, pp. 241–42.

8 Edmund de S. Brunner and others, 1945, p. 99.

and the wife whom the Tiv, Akiga, pictures, was one who spun and wove for her husband. What happens to the woman, and to the man's relation with her, when she ceases to fulfil her role, to fit the picture of womanhood and wife-hood? When work is neither virtue nor necessity, but merely a way of life, what happens when "labour" is saved? what happens when industriousness is one of the highest virtues, as it is with some American Indians?

Such factors must be taken into account when and if industrialization is to be introduced without undue destruction. For example, the FAO mission fund found that Greece must be industrialized and must change to a predominantly cash-crop economy if it is to be able to support its growing population and to raise its standard of living. There is a practical problem here of how best to reconcile cultural patterns with technical change. It is suggested that women in the villages be persuaded to buy factory-woven cloth, and to send their clothes to the laundry, and to support processing industries in general. Yet the launder-ing on the slab by the village fountain, or on the rocks by the stream, is a time of enjoyable social intercourse; one of the beloved songs of the round dance tells of such a laundering group. Again, visitors bring away a happy picture of the mother weaving under the grape-arbor in the spring, now and then stirring the cooking-pot, while her children play about. Good mothers start weaving for their daughters almost from birth. Factory-woven cloth is in use to some extent, but can all home weaving disappear without impoverishing the life of the indi-vidual and of the family? And if it does, can industry provide an equally mean-ingful occupation to take up the released time? Again, the FAO report suggests that Greeks be persuaded to invest their money in industry, so as to make industrialization possible; but this runs counter to the Greek attitude of trusting only a sure thing, the known present. One speculates *about* the future, not *in* the future. A Greek traditionally likes his money in the form of a lump under the mattress, not as so many figures on a chart, or a number of shares of stock. And when people love their life on the land so much that the greatest gift of gratitude they can send to the United Nations is a jar of Peloponnesian earth, the displacement of the individual or the family from the village to the industrial centre could bring much distress. All these difficulties are not insurmountable, but to effect technological change with the least human destruction, these prob-lems and others of their kind must be taken into account.

Actually, there are patterns in Greek life that allow for continuity in spite of radical change of occupation. When Greek men first emigrated to the United States, they brought with them the construct of the family and the village; in one sense they never left home. They did not become part of the community around them and barely recognized its existence. They were working for the family they had left behind, spending on themselves only what was absolutely necessary, since they were earning family money, money for a sister's dowry or a brother's education, or an additional family field. With this background to give them stability, and with the strong feeling for personal freedom, they could take up a completely non-traditional occupation, that of restaurateurs, without dis-ruption, an occupation that did not demand obedience to the external authority of an employer, and in which the structured relationships of the family could be reproduced. This was also true of Chinese emigrants who, sustained by family continuity, could safely be away from home for many years and take on the non-traditional occupation of laundry-men.

MONEY ECONOMY

Here we must distinguish between the presence of money in a community and a money economy. For example, Burma traditionally had essentially a subsistence and barter economy, although money was in use. Money was not used to create more money, or to found a fortune, or to make the individual independent of the family; and the earning of money was incidental to living, it was not an end. Linton reports trying to buy the entire stock of pieces of raffia cloth from a trader in a Madagascar market-town, and of being refused on the ground that the trader would be bored through the rest of the day if he had nothing to sell. In addition, the buyer being a poor bargainer, was actually paying too high a price; yet bargaining is often considered the spice of social intercourse, and this too may have caused the trader to refuse to give up a day's bargaining for the sake of extra profit.[9] This is not what the Western world means by a money economy.

Technological change in agriculture, as well as in industrialization, has introduced a money economy in many regions. For example, the Navaho, who were established by the United States Government on farms in an unusually fertile strip, learned to neglect their farms so as to work for cash wages. Mothers left their children untended, gave up time-consuming preparation of their traditional foods for makeshift, processed store foods. The health of the Navaho children, it was found, had been maintained at a higher level under the conditions of a subsistence economy. In Africa, the introduction of a money economy has usually meant atomization of the individuals within the family, complete destruction of the structuring of family relationships, and of the social and economic system of the group. Where wealth lay in herds of cattle under the head of the family or the extended family, who had "earned" the right to this position organically, the growing boy had an established place within the scheme, and was dependent upon the head until he himself reached the position of headship organically. Now a boy can go and earn money to buy a cow. The money economy has meant secession and revolt, the undermining of parental authority and the authority of tradition, and this has resulted in the rise of the "younger generation" as a class apart. Marriage is often no longer a contract between two families but, particularly in the cities, one between a man and a woman. The traditional *lobola,* the bride-price, which cemented two families in interdependence and maintained strongly structured continuities within the family, is now frequently handed by the boy to the girl, closely imitating the pattern of prostitution which is prevalent in the cities.[10] Where a traveller always knew he could

---

[9] Ralph Linton, 1936, p. 144.
[10] Hailey, *op. cit.,* p. 605; Thurnwald, *op. cit.,* p. 111.

find ready hospitality, he now often has to pay for food and shelter, even to his relatives; or he may find that his friend, seeing a traveller arriving, has conveniently disappeared, to spare himself the expense of entertaining with bought food, or food he could sell for cash.[11] In China also, industrialization has meant that "family relations are more and more disregarded in property ownership."[12] Where a money economy has not been accepted or understood by people living in the midst of this industrial society, there is frequently a tendency toward exploitation.[13]

INTRODUCTION OF NEW TOOLS

New tools are being introduced, whether in agriculture or industry, to save labour or to increase production, or to improve a product, but the change they effect often involves much more than this. Where technology is simple, the tool is an extension of the body; the shuttle elongates and refines the finger, the mallet is a harder and more powerful fist. The tool follows the rhythm of the body; it enhances and intensifies; but it does not replace and does not introduce anything basically different. But the machine is not body-patterned. It has its own existence, its own rhythm, to which man must submit. The woman at her hand-loom controls the tension of the weft by the feeling in her muscles and the rhythm of her body motion; in the factory she watches the loom, and acts at externally stated intervals, as the operations of the machine dictate them. When she worked at home, she followed her own rhythm, and ended an operation when she felt—by the resistance against the pounding mallet or the feel between her fingers—that the process was complete. In the factory she is asked to adjust her rhythm to that of the rhythm prescribed by the factory; to do things according to externally set time limits. The changes of processes and tools involved in industrialization have often brought a shattering break between the living and the all-important, sustaining dead members of the family unit. "To the Chinese the introduction of power machinery meant (that) he had to throw over not only habits of work but a whole ideology; for, dissatisfaction with the ways of his fathers in one particular meant doubt of the father's way of life in all its aspects. If the old loom must be discarded, then 100 other things must be discarded with it, for there are somehow no adequate substitutes."[14]

The suggested technological changes are sometimes uneconomical, as the labour they save is cheaper than the purchase and upkeep of the new tool. Sometimes they are resisted precisely because they do save labour, threatening to deprive workers of their maintenance. A Puerto Rican company which delayed importation and use of mechanical and chemical means of lowering production costs is much admired by the workers, partly because it does not displace them, partly on the ground that "the cane needs the human touch to grow well," and

11 Thurnwald, *op. cit.,* p. 133.
12 Wong Yin-seng, Chang Hsi-chang, and others, 1938, pp. 21–25.
13 Charles Wagley and Eduardo Galvão, 1949, p. 169.
14 H. D. Fong, 1937, pp. 3–4.

because of a feeling that herbicide is evil.[15] Sometimes machines are introduced without plan and fail because no provision is made for upkeep or replacement of parts, as when outboard motors were introduced in Brazil without parts for repair, and without, or with exorbitantly expensive, oil for fueling. Agricultural machinery is demonstrated to farmers far too poor to afford its purchase and upkeep and with farms too small for its effective use, when what they need is an improved hoe or plough.[16] In sections of Africa, the sewing-machine and manufactured cloth have been introduced without the use of the needle. Africans buy clothing made on sewing-machines by Indians, but they have no way of mending them, or having them mended, since machine mending has not been introduced.

The introduction of a new tool which is completely accepted may have unimagined results. In certain sections of Uganda, the introduction of lamps meant an added fire hazard to thatched roofs and provided, in turn, fire-proof roofing: kerosene tins, which, flattened, took the place of the thatching materials which were rapidly decreasing because of the increasing use of land for cash crops. This affected the health picture, since the old roofing had harboured rats which were a plague hazard. However, the next step in efficiency has resulted in the sale of kerosene in the bulk, and people now carry it home in Coca Cola or beer bottles; the new roofing material has disappeared, and the administration of Uganda now has to experiment with suitable roofing materials.[17]

In Africa railroads were built as a measure in the campaign against slavery, particularly the slavery encouraged by the need for porters. But until contact with the West, the need for porterage had been non-existent. Slavery had been merely a form of agricultural or domestic service. The West, in an attempt to eradicate an evil of its own making, built a railroad by compulsory labour at the expense of a very high toll of life, supporting the introduction of cash crops and a money economy for its own uses, destroying traditional patterns of family living, marriage, and parental authority. Ultimately the public works were perhaps "instruments of world welfare" at best. They have yet, however, to be made instruments of African welfare.[18]

An interesting example comes from the Papago Indians, among whom a wooden wagon was introduced by the United States Government around 1900. The men quickly taught their horses to pull the wagon, and one man learned to work iron, so that they could shoe the horses and repair the metal parts of the wagon. The women had been carrying water for household needs in earthen *ollas,* from a distance. Now the wagon could be used for this, and the water used in the household increased. The *ollas* were found to break easily in the wagon, so they were replaced by wooden, and later by metal, barrels; only a few *ollas* were kept for holding the drinking-water, since their porous walls kept

15 Sidney W. Mintz, 1951.
16 Brunner, *op. cit.,* p. 129; Charles P. Loomis, 1950, pp. 117, 124.
17 George Gillanders, 1940, pp. 233–37.
18 J. S. Furnivall, 1948, pp. 320–22.

the water cool. The wagon was then used to transport the family to its summer camp; and in order to do this, a road had to be built. Soon the traditional practice of having the women gather small pieces of fuel (a wide-spread Indian custom, defining the role of the woman) was changed by the presence of the wagon. Now men undertook the bringing of wood, cutting instead of merely gathering, and presently they hauled wood to the nearest towns for sale, introducing a money economy, which eventually meant that the villagers began to grow cash crops to add to the loads of wood going into town.[19] What we do not know, of course, was what had been present in the culture to guide the change in this particular direction, and what hidden benefit or harm came with it.

EFFECTS ON HEALTH AND NUTRITION

The attention paid to the health of workers limits itself, as a rule, to what is considered physical health, and varies in different countries. Where the conquered peoples under Western jurisdiction have been considered an inferior species of humanity, legislation protecting the welfare of workers has often been weak. In Kenya, for example, there has been the practice of "payment by pigment"; and the wages of the Africans are permitted to be so low that they do not assure an adequate subsistence for one, discouraging the workers from bringing their families or from getting married, and encouraging prostitution. There is malnutrition, and a lowering of efficiency, which need not worry the employer when labour can be had at such low recompense. Where wages are to be paid partly in food, often only poor food is given; and during World War II employers cheated freely, since rations were fixed, thus making extra money for themselves. And when employers break the law not deliberately, but in ignorance, the effect is the same.[20] Basic to this condition is not merely industrialization but an expression of disrespect for, and exploitation of, one section of humanity by another, and it is encouraging to know that now the government shows concern over the condition of its wards. Here and in other parts of Africa, there are sometimes industrial centres surrounded by tribes where wage employment is not countenanced. To reach these centres, people from distant reserves may walk as much as 700 miles.[21] They arrive worn-out from their exertion as well as from poor nutrition along the way. Companies often bring such people up to par with rest and good food before putting them to work.[22] This is good practice from the financial standpoint. However, these same companies are ready to release these people during a period of seasonal slackness, jobless and penniless, hundreds of miles away from home.

Where workers are considered full citizens or full members of the society, conditions are usually better. A government such as that of Egypt, for example,

19 John Adair and Edward H. Spicer, n.d.
20 S. and K. Aaronovitch, 1947, pp. 106–12; Kenya Colony and Protectorate, 1939.
21 *The Industrialization of the African,* 1937, p. 4f.
22 Hailey, *op. cit.,* pp. 1120–21.

sees the welfare of the country as a totality, recognizes that the solution of the continuing increase in population lies in industrialization, and prepares for this by planning adequate housing for workers near urban centres.[23]

In general, the effect of a cash-crop or wage economy on nutrition has been one of lowering the level by disturbing the balance achieved under subsistence economy, introducing processed foods as prestige foods, limiting the amount and quality of subsistence crops in favour of cash crops, or the amount of time spent in preparation and preservation of food for home consumption.

ATTITUDES AFFECTING INDUSTRIALIZATION

Obstacles to the establishment of an industry are often encountered, arising from the values of the culture involved. The Masai, for example, will not work for wages, since tending cattle is the only valued occupation,[24] and cattle themselves are the highest good. In many parts of Africa the relationship of obedience to someone without traditional authority is lacking. The Zulus, considering themselves a dominant warrior race, think it degrading to accept the discipline of industrial labour; they are ready, however, to accept domestic service, since this falls within a differently structured relationship.[25] The Tiv say that only boys who are asocial and who do not fit into the group are ready to live away from home earning wages; that is, boys who are essentially maladjusted. On the other hand, when the railroad went through Tiv country, groups of people from the district concerned worked happily for wages, and revealed qualities much liked by their employers.

The assumption that all peoples have an incentive to improve the standard of living, and therefore of taking on employment, is not justified. Puerto Rican workers may express a desire to earn enough money to pay the first installment on the installation of electric light or the purchase of a radio; yet this desire often does not counterbalance the distaste for working for wages, so that payments may not be completed, or an individual may leave his employment if he has some money accumulated.[26] This is essentially true also of the Spanish Americans of New Mexico, as well as of many Mexican wage-earners. The incentive to improve subsistence by wage-earning is reported lacking in many parts of Africa.[27] In the Anglo-Egyptian Sudan, when peasant proprietors found their incomes increased to unaccustomed amounts, they did not know what to do with the surplus, and spent it hiring others to do their work. Their incomes had been increased through external aid, not through internal motivation such as desire for new goods and services. Or the incentive may be present, but not as an incentive to improve subsistence. For example, in China: "One large employer of a highly skilled class of labour, not long ago, was moved by the obvious

---

23 René Francis, 1948, p. 24.
24 Hailey, *op. cit.*, pp. 604–5.
25 *Ibid.*, p. 694.
26 Mintz, *op. cit.*
27 Hailey, *op. cit.*, pp. 604–5.

physical inefficiency of many of his employees and the large incidence of sickness among them to raise wages of his own accord. The only result, as he was able to discern not long afterwards, was that each of these men was now supporting an even larger number of relatives than a person in his position was expected to look after."[28] In Puerto Rico, where the pattern of supporting a large number of dependent relatives is present along with changing values making for individualism, men prefer to emigrate alone to the United States for wagework, so that, if they are single, they can save or spend their money as they please with no relatives to claim a share, and if they are married, they can send money home to their wives knowing that it will be used for the immediate family, since women living without men are not supposed to support dependents.[29]

In Annam it is difficult to get the original inhabitants to work in the mines, as they fear to disturb the mountain spirits; and their fears are supported by the high mortality in the mining occupation.[30]

In many parts of the world we find that one works as necessity calls; this may be the need for the day's food, or for preparation for a ceremonial, or it may be the need of the land or the growing plant which must be attended to on that particular day. But the machine has no such insistent need; so if the worker has enough food or money for his needs, he does not see why he has to go to his job. In fact, if he also has a garden, or if the fish are running in the stream, he has a valid reason for not going. This is part of a general attitude which we find also in connexion with school attendance. And it is an aspect of the different conception of time as a process rather than as programmatic. People may operate in terms of mechanical "time-saving" tools—automobiles, radios, telegraph— but this does not mean that they accept the need for speed which these implements represent; they may be only modern conveniences to these people. The exact minute may be unimportant, and the time "saved" using such devices may nevertheless be spent in inactivity; people "stand or sit doing very little for hours at a time." Industrialization, in the interest of good results and human welfare, must take account of such basic patterns, either working within them, or else educating people in an understanding of the Western framework of industrial work.[31]

Cultural attitudes often determine the composition and quality of the personnel in an industrial establishment. Where familial values are of paramount importance, as in Greece, China, and Japan, a man has to give jobs to relatives, choosing them neither according to ability nor according to merit. And even when the employees are not all relatives, the structure of the organization may follow the lines of the kinship unit. In China, for example, there was reluctance to discharge a delinquent employee (as one punished one's own son for wrongdoing, but did not expel him from the family)[32] there was a decided preference

28 Fong, *op. cit.,* pp. 6–7, 38.
29 Mintz, *op. cit.*
30 Virginia Thompson, 1937, pp. 456–66.
31 John F. Embree, 1950.
32 Fong, *op. cit.,* p. 7; C. L. Nieh, 1933, p. 7.

for punishment, and therefore businesses in China and Japan were found to be losing money. In Japan, when a business was losing money and there was not enough work for all the employees, the employer did not therefore dismiss them; he was responsible for them. (This was termed "feather-bedding" by the *New York Times,* when a financial adviser from the United States discovered that it was the pattern in government offices.) The practice was accorded unqualified condemnation; Western methods were then applied by employers in private firms, and caused upheaval and indignation on all sides.[33] In addition, when authority was part of the structure of the family or extended family, the employee did not know how to obey a foreman, and the employer did not know how to treat the employee. And people to whom honesty was a matter of personal family relations acted with dishonesty in terms of the industrial organization the validity of which as a unit they did not recognize.[34]

In Burma, the attitude against the accumulation of capital, the tendency to spend much money for religious purposes, the tenet that a Buddhist cannot make a valid will, all militate against the creation of capital needed for industrial enterprise of any major scope. However, small mills and small plants in rural areas have been increasing and fit into the Burmese pattern. Under British administration, machinery for agriculture was regarded with suspicion as another device to raise taxable capacity, but agricultural shows, where they were exhibited, were attended, since they fit into the pattern of "convivial celebration, with a few side-shows such as exhibitions of fertilizers and insect pests, matters to which the government attaches superstitious importance."[35] In Turkey, there was a shortage in qualified labour, and low efficiency of unskilled labour, because the worker simply did not like industry, and did not remain long enough to be trained, preferring to go back to his agriculture.

INDUSTRY AND THE SOCIAL UNIT

Industrialization affects the social unit in a variety of ways. Even in changing its tools, it makes a change within the structure, re-aligning roles in the division of labour and the interrelationships involved in the earlier processes. In Burma, the British administration pointed with approval to the "rise" in the standard of living indicated by the rising imports of cotton goods and crockery; but actually this was also an index of changes in family life, of the idleness of the loom underneath the house where wives and daughters had traditionally woven rich silks for the family, and where husbands also sometimes did so, producing more beautifully patterned stuffs. The Tiv men felt that the marital relationship had been disrupted with the coming of manufactured cloth. The traditional picture of the wife was one in which she spun by the village fire at night, listening to the children's riddles, and to the myth-telling of the men, eventually making

[33] O. M. Green, 1950, pp. 76–77.
[34] Fong, *op. cit.,* pp. 2, 3, 56.
[35] O. H. Spate, 1941, pp. 75–90.

cloth which her husband could sell to make wealth for the family; cloth-making was a service from a wife to her husband. When manufactured cloth was introduced, the women demanded it of the men; the man had to leave home to make money to buy cloth for his wife, who had ceased to fit the traditional picture of a wife. In many parts of Africa the introduction of factory goods meant the rapid disappearance of local industries, with all that these involved in the way of family relationships and village life. In Northern Rhodesia, the smelting of iron declined, and pottery disappeared, with the introduction of the petrol tin. In the Union of South Africa, the products of local industries were sold to procure money for factory goods, which became increasingly important, and after the local industries themselves disappeared, there were no goods to sell to procure money, since cattle had a value beyond money, so that cash crops and wage-labour were the only answer, with an accompanying disruption in living-patterns.[36]

When men are forced to leave the village to earn wages, the economic inter-relationship is again affected. In Africa, in areas where men used to lop off the branches of large trees to burn as fertilizer for the garden, the young men are now absent and older men must take on this work, with the eventual result of deforestation and soil erosion, because the older men cannot climb the trees to cut off the branches, and so they cut down the trees at the root. Again, in many parts of Africa agriculture was an area of activity where there was division of labour between men and women, with the men clearing and preparing the land; women cannot make good gardens without the periodic assistance of their men, who are now absent for long periods working for wages at the industrial centre.[37]

The effect of the migration of the men on family and village life depends on whether there was a pattern for living without the men before the coming of industrialization. In Northern Burma, for example, there had apparently been a pattern for temporary migration to South Burma, among those in need of money; and it was this pattern that was followed when wage-earning became more important. Few Burmese went to the cities to work in factories or other urban wage occupations. In Greece, there was a centuries-old pattern, either of emigration of the man until he could take a wife or his family to the new country or until he could come back with the needed money; or of the man's going "on the sea." Many islands were accustomed to sending their men on the sea, as sponge-fishermen, or to man vessels. "My father used to come back every year to propagate another child," said the son of such a man. Where family ties are strongly structured, the family can build life which will take such absences without disruption, where the wife can turn to a brother or an uncle or her father, some man who has not left the community. And a Greek wife will do the work of a man when fortitude demands it. Sharing of work, rather than division of labour, is important in the Greek peasant family. In China, also, the family learned to follow its course in the absence of the male head. For the

36 Hailey, *op. cit.*, pp. 1408, 1420.
37 *Ibid.*, p. 885.

young Chinese man it has been traditional to enlist in the army or to enter a government office; the village was used to being without him.[38]

In India, too, the pattern in many sections has been for the man to go to the industrial centre without the family. Usually he did not go far, so that he could return after a few months to do the man's share in the cultivation of the ancestral lands. The men's lives were centred in the village, even though they did work temporarily in the cities—in the same way that in the traditional pattern of living, a man might have a store in the market centre and still have his life centred in the village where he had his home, his cows, and his fields.[39]

In Africa, on the other hand, there had been no precedent for the long absences of the men when industrialization came, with its demand and lure for men. Division of labour had been basic to family life and agricultural work, so that these were disturbed. The loss of production was not balanced by the wages the men earned, since these usually were spent to support the man while away, or to buy a few gifts to bring back, so the standard of living deteriorated.[40] Without the men, the home lost its place as an educational unit, and there was no way of passing on the values of the society to the growing boy.[41] With the dislocation in family life, the displacement of authority, came demoralization. Young girls, unwilling to stay in villages without men, followed the men to the cities, where they often became prostitutes.

Some idea of the sheer depletion of the villages can be gained from the figures on migration. "In 1933, it was estimated that 62 per cent of the ablebodied male population of the Mikuyu and Kiambu, 74 per cent of the Nandi, 43 per cent of the Lumbwa . . . left the reserves as labourers."[42] In China, in the mid-thirties, 50 per cent of the families in southern Shantung, western Hupeh, and northern Anhwei had been affected by internal migration, usually by having some member leave.[43]

The effect of the migration, as we have seen, differs according to whether or not the centre is at a great distance. If it is distant, the men may stay away several years at a time. In China, in the twenties, it was found that the largest percentage of the men migrants stayed away three years. In Africa, the men who work as labourers on plantations may go only for the day, or at any rate, are usually able to return after brief absences.

In some cases the whole family migrated. "Ordinarily, the migrating family, that is, the migrating immediate family, makes the most successful adjustment, but this is only true where, because of the system of relations previously in operation or the progressive changes which have taken place which have led to such a system, the immediate family is not too integrally knit to a larger struc-

---

38 Shih Kuo-Heng, 1944, p. 43.
39 Kelman, *op. cit.,* pp. 91–94; Marian W. Smith, 1946, p. 577.
40 Hailey, *op. cit.,* pp. 704–5.
41 Edwin H. Smith, 1934, pp. 333–34.
42 Aaronovitch, *op. cit.,* p. 203.
43 Hu Nai-tsiu, 1938, p. 256.

ture which provided for its members a major proportion of its emotional satisfaction."[44] The Greek migrating family manages to keep its emotional balance
through keeping in close touch with the rest of the relationship unit, or, as in
the United States, through reproducing the village relationships in the Greek
community of a large city. In Brazil, where migration of rural families was
common, migration itself was not a disturbing factor.

Where the tie with a social unit larger than the immediate family has been
strong, however, and when the people had a strong bond with the land, the
migration of the family makes for disruption. This is particularly true of Africa,
where moral law often loses its validity when the tie with the land is broken.[45]
It is true of the Tiv, where even elders strong in magical potency were uneasy
when travelling away from the land of their unit; and among the Nuer, who feel
that leaving their own soil will bring them illness unless they drink a dilution
of their soil in water, mixed with increasing amounts of soil from the land of
their new habitat.

What will happen upon migration depends on cultural structuring and values.
In the United States, different groups of immigrants present a differing picture
of strength and health; some groups, coming in families, quickly present a picture of disorientation, while others—whether in families or individually—present
a picture of inner stability and orientation. It appears, for example, that some
groups have the ability to maintain a construct of the unit they have left behind,
and to recreate it. According to Laura Thompson, when workers from the
Philippines, mainly Catholics, first went to Hawaii, they were mostly men who
went alone; but when one of them got married, a large number of men stood
as godfathers to the first baby, and a kinship unit was thus immediately created
out of a large number of unrelated men.

The extent to which urbanization of the family affects family relationships
again depends on what has been there to begin with. In Greece, the pattern of
interdependence often remains the same. Whereas formerly all the sons worked
in the common fields and added to the family income, now all the sons work
for wages which they bring to the family, keeping only a very small sum for
cigarette money. However, this pattern is reported to be undergoing change, and,
in many other cultures, wages for the sons have been a wedge, introducing
increasing atomization. Sons stop working for the economic welfare of the
family unit, and in turn cease being dependent on the father. Eventually, grown
children cease to be an insurance against old age, so old age brings indigence; or
else the parents must save toward it, or the state must take care of it. This
change of events, encouraged by changes in legislation and in land-tenure introduced by British administrators, took place in Burma in recent years. In the
United States, internal migration has increasingly meant loneliness for the old
people or unbearable displacement in their old age. An indirect effect of wages
and migration has been the rise of a younger generation in opposition to an older

---

44 Eliot D. Chapple, personal communication.
45 *The Industrialization of the African, op. cit.,* pp. 3–4.

generation. This is reported of the Tiv, of Spanish Americans in New Mexico and in Peru, and from other areas.

SOLUTIONS IN PROCESS

The waste in human welfare which came into being as a by-product of industrialization has caused much concern among governments, social scientists, and foundations. There appears to be general agreement that decentralization of industry, bringing work to the village or to its vicinity within the framework of known associations and associational ties, will make for less disruption and, at the same time, will bring the increase in income needed for raising the standard of living.

Village industries can provide the funds for raising the standard of living, and can fill the gap created when handicrafts give way to manufactured goods. They can also, in part, be the answer to the mechanization of agriculture, which often releases time for which there is no provision. As it is, in many villages in India, China, and the Philippines, the farmers are actually partly unemployed. In the Chinese villages it is estimated that the farmers and farm labourers are unemployed for periods of six to eight months a year.[46]

The introduction of village industries is not, however, without difficulties. In India it is found that the villagers often do not want to be organized into new co-operative units, or any created units. Demonstration of the advantages of the new products is often not effective, since the demonstration party does not stay long enough in the village to make a lasting impression on people who need a long time to assimilate new ideas.[47] In China, in 1935, village industry in the district of Kiangying was working havoc in family life. Before it was introduced, the women had spent much of their time helping the men in the fields and had raised silkworms; they had done their spinning and weaving only during their free time. When home knitting with a hand-machine was introduced, women knitted late into the night by kerosene lamps, and, since they had to spend so much of their time caring for old people and young children, they had no time even to eat their meals with the family, but ate at their work. In times of crop failure, when the home industry was the only means of subsistence, the loom had to be busy all the time if there was only one loom in the house. This meant that members of the family had to work at it in shifts 24 hours a day. This was an economic solution, but one that failed on the social level.[48] In southern Hopei, also in the 1930's, it was found that commercialization had brought a shift in power and authority in the village; not the farmers and producers, but the owners and administrators, were the ruling groups. "The centre of political power of the village has been definitely shifted from the elders and old gentry to the

46 Shriman Narayan Agarwal, 1949, p. 184; Chen Han-seng, 1947, p. 62; Erich H. Jacoby, 1949, p. 189.
47 T. Bheemacharya, 1949, pp. 12–13.
48 Lo-chun, *op. cit.,* pp. 239–40.

business firms wherein reside the trinity of usurers, landlords, merchants. Commercialization, unaccompanied by a healthy system of production, is thus shown to be a deteriorating factor in Chinese rural economy, although it at first brings a transitory period of prosperity."[49]

There have been difficulties and destruction; but through a study of the local situation, through an understanding of and respect for the existing framework, such difficulties are being solved. China's co-operatives have become increasingly successful in their social effects. The recently formulated programme proposes to carry over into industrialization the traditional co-operative relationships of guild and family; it aims at industrializing the already present village units.[50] In India, careful teaching by people who have an understanding of the need for a long period of instruction achieved the introduction of the idea of village industry. In one village, even the latrine was incorporated into the home-industry scheme, so that many homes now have two latrines, one in use while the contents of the other are being composted for sale as fertilizer. In Mexico and Ecuador, some home industries have fitted into existing, valued, and enjoyed patterns, with happy results.[51]

Additional References

Bendix, R. "Industrialization, Management, and Ideological Appeals," *Work and Authority in Industry,* chap. 1. New York: John Wiley & Sons, Inc., 1956.

Benjamin, Roger W., and Kautsky, John H. "Communism and Economic Development," *The American Political Science Review,* Vol. 62, No. 1 (March, 1968), pp. 110–24.

Cauthorn, Robert C. "Programming for Entrepreneurship Among American Indians," *Arizona Review,* May, 1968, pp. 11–15.

Dupree, Louis, "Kabul Gets a Supermarket—The Birth and Growth of an Afghan Enterprise," American Universities Field Staff Reports Service, South Asia Series, Vol. 10, No. 2 (February, 1966).

Fillol, T. R. *Social Factors in Economic Development, The Argentine Case.* Cambridge, Mass.: The M.I.T. Press, 1961.

Hagen, Everett E. *The Economics of Development.* Homewood, Ill.: Richard D. Irwin, Inc., 1968.

Hyman, Stanley. *Management and World Development.* London: Pitman, 1967.

Kerr *et al. Industrialism and Industrial Man.* New York: Oxford University Press, 1964.

Khalof, Samir. "Family Firms and Industrial Development," *Development Digest,* National Planning Association, Vol. 5, No. 1 (April, 1967), pp. 60–69.

McClelland, David C. "Achievement Motivation Can Be Developed," *Harvard Business Review,* Vol. 43, No. 6 (November–December, 1965).

———. *The Achieving Society.* Princeton, N.J.: D. Van Nostrand Co., Inc., 1961.

McKenzie, Cameron. "Incompetent Foreign Managers," *Business Horizons,* Spring, 1966.

---

49 Chi Ping, 1938, pp. 166–67.
50 *Training Rural Leaders,* 1949, pp. 19–27. (*See* United Nations, FAO.)
51 John Collier, Jr. and Anibal Buitron, 1949, p. 196; Nathan L. Whetten, 1948, pp. 445–47.

Ravenholt, Albert. "Shipbuilder for the Islands–The Role of a New Entrepreneur in a Developing Economy," *American Universities Field Staff Reports Service, Southeast Asia Series,* Vol. 12, No. 3 (April, 1964).

————. "Scissors from Tabaco–Filipino Rural Blacksmiths Start an Industry," *American Universities Field Staff Reports Service, Southeast Asia Series,* Vol. 12, No. 8 (October, 1964).

Schumpeter, Joseph A. *Capitalism, Socialism and Democracy.* New York: Harper Torchbook, 1962 (originally published 1942).

"The Technology Elite Approach to the Development Process," *Economic Development and Cultural Change,* April, 1966.

Yasuzo, Harie, "The Transformation of the National Economy," *The Developing Economies,* Vol. 3, No. 4 (December, 1965), p. 404.

chapter six
Origins of Managers

In Chapters Four and Five, we have been concerned with the historical and cultural background of management and economic development. In this chapter, we are interested in who managers are and where they come from under differing cultural and social conditions. From what social classes do they emerge?

Selection: "The Industrializing Elites," Clark Kerr, John T. Dunlop, Frederick Harbison, and Charles A. Myers

In this selection from their well-known *Harvard Business Review* article, "Industrialism and World Society," the four eminent authors review the different social groups that have played dominant roles in past industrial development.

Selection: "Social Class Background of Managers in Various Countries," David McClelland

Whereas the preceding article was historical in its perspective, this reading from *The Achieving Society* compares the socioeconomic backgrounds of current managers in several countries.

Selection: "Business and Class in Europe," David Granick

The sources and careers of managers in France and Germany are examined in this reading from *Tne European Executive.*

Selection: "The Dilemma of an Elite Group: The Industrialist in Latin America," John D. Harbron

The complex interrelations between social structure and business management in Latin America are discussed.

selection 13
The Industrializing Elites*

Clark Kerr, John T. Dunlop, Frederick Harbison, and Charles A. Myers

Most of the nations of the world are on the march toward industrialism. They aspire to higher living standards. They yearn to throw off economic backwardness, illiteracy, and disease. The economically underdeveloped countries are dedicated to a rapid reduction of the inequalities that have been growing in the past century between the few rich Western nations and the poor countries which comprise the mass of humanity. They know they face desperate tasks, and they must run twice as hard to narrow the large gap since the other, more advanced countries continue to make spectacular gains. Their leaders preach dedication and hard work. They are committed to an industrial future, and they have high expectations. They are launched on a long course that they realize is certain to change their communities into new societies.

In the 1850's the world had essentially one model of successful industrialization: that led by middle-class capitalists in Western Europe and the United States. Today the newly industrializing countries have a wide variety of prescriptions, a range of political and economic forms, and a growing body of industrializing experience from which to choose. The experimentation with methods of achieving the industrial society continues to grow, as the recent history in India, Yugoslavia, China, Brazil, and Egypt illustrates. This diversity of experience not only enriches the policy-making process within countries and international agencies, but it also affords a growing body of material well suited to the comparative study of the industrialization process and of the interrelations of workers, managers, and governments.

PIONEERING MINORITIES

Industrialization is always introduced by a minority group. It cannot come into full bloom overnight, except perhaps in small societies with unusual natural resources which attract external capital, like Kuwait, Arabia; but even there an initiating human agent is requisite. Usually industrialization starts in a restricted

---

*From "Industrialism and World Society," *Harvard Business Review,* Vol. 39, No. 1, January–February, 1961, pp. 114-22. © 1961 by the President and Fellows of Harvard College; all rights reserved.

geographical area or sector of a society, as a small subculture initiated by a subordinated group, which then spreads into new areas and new sectors until it is the dominating system of production affecting almost all the relations of men within the society.

The subordinated group initiating the industrialization process is, of course, a product of the particular culture existing in the preindustrial society. The range of issues which confront this industrializing elite is similarly shaped by both the cultural and economic constraints. As individuals, members of the industrializing elites do make choices, but these choices are affected by their values and by the fact that the culture and the economic environment have thrown them up as leaders.

At this juncture in world history there are five types of elite that customarily and variously take the leadership of the industrialization process:

1. A dynastic elite.
2. The middle class.
3. The revolutionary intellectuals.
4. The colonial administrators.
5. The nationalist leaders.

Each of these elite groups may have associated with it, or indeed may be composed of, several elements—political leaders, industrial managers, military officers, religious figures, top civil servants, and leaders of labor organizations, among others. Accordingly, when we speak of a certain type of elite, we refer more to the character of its central orientation than to the specific individuals who constitute it at any moment of time.

Each group has a strategy by which it seeks to order the surrounding society in a consistent and compatible fashion. An internal conflict between the old culture and the new culture, with its dominant theme set by the industrializing elite, is inevitably fought on many fronts—the economic, political, religious, and intellectual. And an external conflict, between alternative ideologies of industrialism, tends to be fought on all fronts at once. Each industrial system becomes a "way of life," no matter what its specific form, and a "way of life" demands internal acceptance and external protection if it is to function successfully in the long run.

THE ELITES

To understand the different forms and paces of industrialization and their varying impact on labor and management, we need first to take a closer look at the five types of elite. What are their distinguishing attitudes and characteristics? How do they typically work—and with what results?

Dynasts and Paternalists

The members of the dynastic elite are originally drawn from the landed or commercial aristocracy in most cases, since agriculture and commerce are usually the pre-existing forms of production.

Less often they are drawn from the military caste (as the Samurai were in Japan), a religious hierarchy, the government bureaucracy, or tribal chieftains.

This elite group is held together by a common allegiance to the established order. New recruits may be added from time to time from other strata of society and embraced into the aristocracy, but the emphasis is on a closed system based on family and on class. Its orientation is predominantly toward tradition and the preservation of tradition.

The "realists" within this elite acknowledge the rise of the industrial system and its eventual dominance. They seek to identify the essentials of the past and to preserve them in the face of the new form of production. Indeed, they will make whatever compromises are necessary to permit industrialization to proceed under their guidance.

By contrast, the "traditionalists" in the group may denounce and seek to defend against the new industrial system.

Only if the "realists" are dominant, strong, competent, and patriotic is a dynastic elite likely to master the industrialization process, as in Japan and Germany. When they get control of the industrialization process, their approach is quite distinctive:

The emphasis is on personal rule, involving perpetuation of the family which is "born to rule" and of the class within which alliances are made and from which managerial recruits are usually obtained.

The system rests on tradition but ultimately on the use of power.

Law and order and firm administration are part of the essence of the system, and this leads often to cartels and to a mixture of "private" and "public" affairs in the conduct of economic life.

The political system is paternalistic and so also is the economic system. The worker is to be cared for, and in return he is expected to be loyal. He is dependent on the employer for his welfare and his leadership.

The idea of tension between the employer and the worker is abhorred; and "harmony" is devoutly sought.

Rule making is held, as far as possible, solely in the hands of management; prerogatives of management are sacred.

The social and economic systems alike have a clearly stratified hierarchy of superiors and subordinates and a reciprocal series of duties and obligations.

Industrial progress will be no faster than necessary to meet the pressures placed on the elite; and the strong preference is for a smooth passage from the preindustrial to the industrial society. Industrialism is not fostered for its own sake but for the survival of the society it is replacing. Fitful and violent change is anathema; change too must be ordered. However, such a system, if under enough external pressure, can make rapid economic progress. The two elements which will change least readily are the two most central to the system—the dynastic elite and the paternal community.

For comparisons between the different management concepts of the dynastic and the other elites, see part a of Exhibit 1. The varying influences of the elites on worker organizations are shown in part b of Exhibit 1.

EXHIBIT 1

Outline of Elite Characteristics and Effects

a. management and the industrializing elites

Characteristic	Dynastic	Industrializing Elites			Nationalist Leaders
		Middle-Class	Revolutionary Intellectuals	Colonial Administrators	
Access to management	Access based upon the family with professionals subordinated to the authority of the family.	Access to management on basis of initiative and competence—early development of professional management.	At first, access on basis of political affiliations, later, on the basis of professional standards.	Top positions reserved for nationals of the home country.	Varying accessibility with emphasis on political and on professional qualifications.
Character of managerial authority over workers	Paternalistic concern for the "dependent" worker.	Constitutional or occasionally democratic.	Dictatorial and authoritarian, later becoming constitutional to a limited degree.	Dictatorial or paternalistic.	Varying systems of authority, depending on nature of managerial class.
Basis for managerial authority	Concept that certain families are "called" to manage. Personal rather than functional organization.	Authority of managers based on functions they perform.	Managers as servants of party and state.	Superiority of nationals of the home country.	Managerial resources regarded as necessary instruments for industrial development.
The education and development of managerial resources	Education of a small, elitist minority.	Education of the masses, and functional education in technology and management.	High priority to functional education at all levels.	Very limited educational development of the nationals of the colony.	Education of the masses, and priority given to higher education.

EXHIBIT 1
Outline of Elite Characteristics and Effects
b. worker organizations and the elites

Characteristic	Industrializing Elites				
	Dynastic	Middle-Class	Revolutionary Intellectuals	Colonial Administrators	Nationalist Leaders
View toward workers	Personally dependent on managers in time of need.	Independent workers.	Class of dependent workers.	Dependent on foreigners.	Partners in the new nation.
Functions of workers' organizations	Social functions at plant level; little constraint on management. Pressure for minimum industry conditions by legislation. Political activity challanges the elite.	Regulates management at the local and industry levels. Independent political activity accepted. Does not challenge the elite.	Instrument of party to educate, lead workers, and to stimulate production. No political activity except through the party.	Largely a part of the independence and nationalist movement.	Confronts the conflicting objectives of economic development and protection of workers.
Competition among workers' organizations	Limited rivalry at the plant level and over the distribution of functions between the local and industry levels. No exclusive representation.	Exclusive representation and keen competition. Some rivalry between the plant and industry levels over allocation of functions.	No rivalry or competition allowed.	Divided by ideological, regional, tactical, and personal leadership factions.	Tendency for consolidation among organizations recognized as loyal by nationalistic elite. Advantage over those not so recognized.

EXHIBIT 1
Outline of Elite Characteristics and Effects
b. worker organizations and the elites (continued)

Characteristic	Dynastic	Middle-Class	Industrializing Elites	Colonial Administrators	Nationalist Leaders
			Revolutionary Intellectuals		
Structure of workers' organizations	Relatively large number of industrial unions. Centralized confederation often limited by rival confederations. Unions perform narrow range of functions.	A variety of structural forms. Confederations not so centralized. Organizations perform a wide range of functions.	A few industrial unions. A centralized confederation. Organizations perform a narrow range of functions.	A wide variety of structures. Organizations not well developed, often personal.	Tendency toward industrial unions with one confederation acceptable to elite.
Sources of funds	Meager resources from irregular dues payments and indirect government allowances. Financial success is not highly regarded by workers' organizations.	Substantial resources secured by regular dues. The regulatory functions require administrative organizations and also large budgets.	Substantial resources secured by assessment of all workers; financial resources present no problems with support of regime.	Meager funds frequently raised outside workers' organizations.	Funds often secured indirectly from government in addition to meager dues. The officers receive other salaries.
Sources of leadership	Intellectuals and those ideologically oriented toward political activity. The leaders' income position is often insecure.	The ranks through lower levels of workers' organizations. They have an established career.	Reliable party leaders with experience in workers' organizations. They have an established career.	Nationalist or independence leaders. Intellectuals with a personal following.	National leaders and intellectuals except where confined to manual workers.

EXHIBIT 1

Outline of Elite Characteristics and Effects

b. worker organizations and the elites (continued)

| Characteristic | Dynastic | Middle-Class | Industrializing Elites | | |
			Revolutionary Intellectuals	Colonial Administrators	Nationalist Leaders
Ideology	Class-conscious and revolutionary except for a minority.	Reformist.	Preserve the true revolution.	Independence.	Nationalism.

Middle Class and Open Market

The human agents here are members of a new class, rising, as in England, in opposition to the elite but able to live in coexistence with it. They are most likely to be drawn from commercial or artisan groups already in being, often composed of religious or national minorities. Such groups, never entirely integrated into the old elite, are sensitive to the gains to be had from the new means of production. They do not advance on the wings of a rigid ideology; rather they tend to be pragmatic. They favor a structure of economic and political rules which best permits them to pursue their gains. This brings them into conflict with the old order, but they seek to impose their will piecemeal, and their assault is carried out through concentration on specific issues rather than as an explicit social revolution. In their conflict with the old order, the new group may find allies among the intellectuals wanting more freedom and also among the workers wanting more opportunity, particularly for political participation.

The middle-class ideology is economically individualistic and politically egalitarian. In practice, the rigor of this doctrine is softened by the social and religious beliefs embodied in the culture, but the emphasis is on progress and on the individual. Instead of the old and the community, there is the new and the self. Upward mobility in society is fairly directly related to knowledge of opportunities and capacity to make use of them. Family background and wealth are important not for themselves, but only insofar as they tend to affect the range of opportunities open to men. No one is born to rule, but some are destined to manage; and management relies more on policies and rules than it does on personal preference.

The system is based heavily on consent, and the appeal in politics and in economics is to self-advantage. Every manager is, in part, a politician adjusting, within the rules of the game but with some rapidity, to the pressures of individuals, groups, and institutions; mobility and self-interest are at the center of the social process, in practice and in theory.

The "good society" is an indistinct and shifting shadow. It is more a series of means than an end; and the means are reason, self-interest, and a relatively broad toleration of dissent. Relative emphasis is placed on many centers of decision-making power and on a system of checks and balances. The checks and balances in political life involve the separation of church and state and of the legislative, judicial, and administrative authorities. In economic life, economic units are typically separated into discrete and competitive entities. Rule making, in society as a whole, may be more or less equally shared—by management, by organizations of workers, and by the state—in a pluralistic type of arrangement.

Revolutionary Intellectuals

A new class of intellectuals and associated activists may take over the industrializing process and society in its entirety and sweep away, as fast as it can, the old elites and the old culture. From the beginning it intends to eliminate the former leadership groups and the pre-existing cultural arrangements, and to replace them with a new ruling class and a brand new culture. And the new wine shall be in totally new bottles, the principal new bottle being the centralized state. The contrast with the middle-class elite is as sharp as the difference in the industrialization approaches of, for instance, Canada and Communist China.

These intellectuals are self-identified for the task of leadership by their acceptance and espousal of a theory of history. This theory of history specifies for them the place to act, the time to act, and the means to act. Acceptance of this theory of history sets them off from other persons. They are, they contend, the bearers of the virtually inevitable historical process; the possessors of an ideology which they think will make it possible for them to create the future.

Once the new class has attained full power to control society in a centralized fashion, then the original revolutionary intellectuals within it give way increasingly to high-level political administrators and bureaucrats as the leaders of the system. It is still the same new class that controls the new society, but over time the upcoming bureaucrats may run it rather differently than the original revolutionaries. In fact, the revolutionary intellectuals and the bureaucrats to whom they give over power may be almost the antithesis of each other; emphasis on constant change gives way to greater conservatism; debate over basic policy yields place to reinterpretation of received doctrine. (We see something of this happening today in the U.S.S.R.)

This transition is of great importance in the evaluation of the system. But, with both the old intellectuals and the bureaucrats, instead of the self, there is the ideology, the party, and the state. Once the influence of the original, or old, revolutionary intellectuals is gone, the centralized state remains.

The "good society" as seen by the proponents of this system is quite determinant. Above all, the new technology must be served. The world conflict is seen in large part as a test of which system can make the best use of the new technology. This means forced-draft industrialization and the construction of a culture which is consistent with the new technology and its fullest utilization; thus education, labor organization, art, and literature must all be geared to the system of production in a single-minded fashion. The centralized state is the only mechanism which can fully conquer the old and create the new culture and undertake the forced-draft industrialization.

The society, of necessity, is relatively monolithic. There can be no real separation of economic, political, and religious institutions:

Rule making, generally and in industrial relations specifically, is inherently in the hands of the dominant class—the managers of this historical process who have their plans.

The worker is again dependent on the manager, and the manager in turn is dependent on the state, both economically and politically.

The worker's highest attribute is a sense of duty. "The productivity of labor, in the final analysis, is the most important, the main tool for the victory of the new order." (This quotation from Lenin appears on the front of a collective agreement in the Soviet steel industry.) The worker is a "citizen" with many duties and few rights. Overt conflict between the managers and the workers is suppressed.

This society is considered "good" by its proponents because they believe it follows the logic of industrialization to the fullest and thus has the greatest survival value.

Colonial Administrators

The colonial elite has been a major instrument for the introduction of industrialization in many areas of the world—supplying capital, techniques, and leadership. The colonial administrator, however, is an alien "alien"; he not only represents a new system of production but also an external society. Consequently he must carry the weight of two justifications—the justification of the new system and also of his personal intrusion into the indigenous culture. Thus his role as prime mover can be an unusually difficult one.

The other aspect of the externality of the colonial approach is the essential service to the home country rather than to the indigenous population. The home country may be served by a supply of raw materials, a market for finished products, a source of profits, an outlet for "younger sons" or surplus population, or an extension of an ideology and of political and military suzerainty. An alien elite and an alien purpose are the twin features of all colonialism.

The colonialism with the greatest survival possibilities is "total colonialism" because this ceases, once it is effective, to be colonialism. It becomes the system of the country itself under its own indigenous leaders. All colonialism, in the end, is either overthrown by the natives (as in our own Revolutionary War) or ceases to be colonialism by becoming the "native" system or a component part of it.

But whatever variation in the form of colonialism there may be, colonial administrators have in common with each other service to the home country or to an ideology above all. Also, in a colonial situation, the power of the government and of the management of enterprises is likely to be rather great in order to handle an indigenous labor force; the worker is likely to be viewed as being in a dependent or at least semi-dependent status, for the management represents a superior culture. Conflict between labor and management, subject to exacerbation by nationalist sentiments, is likely to be severely controlled or suppressed. And labor organizations, when they exist, are likely to be oriented toward nationalist goals.

Nationalist Leaders

The agent of industrialization may also be the nationalist leader, though the mantle of nationalism may be worn by many different types of persons. There is no single social base for nationalism and no single outlook on the nature of the industrial system. Historically important as a mechanism of transition, the nationalist leader may point his society in any one of several directions. Nationalism is more a sentiment than a system of thought. Some other element must enter here before the choice can be made, and this other element usually is the social orientation of the nationalist leaders. Beyond the fact of nationalism is the great question of who rides to power on its magic carpet.

Still, nationalism does predispose a society in certain directions:

> A nationalist revolt or campaign against colonialism usually raises a leader or small group of leaders to the forefront; men who are the symbols of the new independence and who carry with them the aspirations of the populace; men who are, at least at first, national heroes. Their personal influence is great and, given the instructured situation at the start of a period of great national development, they can guide or form a society within broad limits in accordance with their will. Some of the newer nations in the Middle East and in South Asia are examples.
>
> Instead of classes of people there tends to be a mass with great expectations for sudden improvement but with little appreciation of how that improvement will come about; a mass subject to ecstasy and to despair. The goals are extravagant and the means ignored. The attitude of this mass is open to sudden and erratic change, and thus the total situation is an unstable one.
>
> Emphasis on state-directed effort is likely. There may be no theory in advance as to how to proceed, but there must be a practice and this practice will involve the state. This tends to lead to the planned economy, to state or state-sponsored investment, to state-controlled labor organizations, to workers dependent on the state for economic benefits and political direction, to state guidance of the new industrialists, to state appeals for hard work and saving, and to a call for unity.
>
> The nationalist state requires a civil service in a crucial location within society, and the quality and the source of this civil service is a strategic factor in the development of the society. The worker is likely to be viewed as a "patriot" serving a national purpose, and labor-management conflict is likely to be controlled or suppressed.

The "nationalist society" is a plaything of history. Its recent past is of especial significance. If the nationalist leaders arise out of a violent rejection of a hereditary dynastic elite or of settler colonialism (e.g., Algeria), the emphasis is particularly likely to be a negative one stressing hates and fears. But if the transition is a more peaceful one, as, for example, a transition out of segmental colonialism (e.g., India), elements of the old system are more likely to be retained, and attention to be turned to positive developments.

If the nationalist approach is to be successful, it must attain a sense of national unity and substantial forward momentum. The tests are how soon the nation can be moved from the negative to the positive phase, and then how much effort can be pulled out of the nation and how sustained that effort will be.

EVOLUTIONARY TRENDS

The actual industrializing elites are seldom, if ever, pure or ideal types. At this stage in history, in the middle of the twentieth century, we can still identify many countries which adhere to one or another of these types, though relatively few of them illustrate the particular type in all its purity. Each type, however, seems to have its own natural tendencies for evolution. Consequently, there exist more or less parallel evolutions for countries equally patterned after a certain type. An awareness of these tendencies will be useful when, in a later section, we look at the probable future of industrialization around the world.

Decline of the Dynasts

Where the dynastic elite governs ineffectually, as it frequently has done in modern times, the country shifts either to a nationalist or a revolutionary intellectual leadership. If the elite governs effectively, it is also subject to changes. As industrialization proceeds, the hereditary elite expands and recruits new members from lower strata in its society, particularly by the process of selection through the mechanisms of higher education. It becomes less of a class apart. Also, industrialization requires a great deal of mobility in the labor force, from one occupational level to another, from one area to another, and from one enterprise to another. This tends to break down the paternal plant community as does the growth of social services provided by other institutions than the enterprise. Class lines are softened. The society moves more toward the middle-class ideal.

Adjustable Middle Class

The middle-class system is the most stable of our several types, partly because this class is also the mediating one in society and makes its adjustments a little at a time rather than in dramatic bursts. In fact, the middle class, once in full control of the industrialization process, has never in history lost its authority for internal reasons. This does not mean, however, that the middle-class system does not itself change significantly:

The size of enterprise becomes larger.

A separation takes place between ownership and management.

Workers add to their power through their own large-scale organizations. The state takes over new duties, providing social security, regulating competition and industrial conflict, redistributing the wealth, assuring a minimum level of economic activity and employment, entering the internal life of private organizations to guarantee equality of treatment and opportunities for participation, and becoming the biggest single employer.

The market loses some of its influence; decisions are supplied by rules and by group actions as well as by atomistic interchanges in the marketplace.

The worker becomes more closely tied to his particular employment through seniority rules and security benefits.

Individual self-advancement gives way increasingly to efforts at group advancement.

The middle class becomes less and less a definable leadership elite as many elements in society come to share urban middle-class status. The middle class still rules but less obviously so; and the markets are still major instruments for making decisions, but they are no longer so open.

Diluted Intellectuals

The revolutionary intellectuals are committed to the view that the great climactic change through which they seized power is the last great change in social relation. The "classless society" is the ultimate goal; and, according to Marx, the only other substantial change in prospect is the "withering away of the state." Thus far it has not withered, and it is highly unlikely it ever will. But other changes can and do take place.

The most persistent drive is probably in the direction of sharing power. The military makes its demands. The scientists and the new managers make theirs. Even the workers, as they get more skill and responsibility, and thus power, can make demands of their own. These groups may come to have their own areas within which they can govern; and while they may not share authority over society, they may be able to bring greater influence to bear on those who do. Universal education, which is an imperative of successful industrialization, may even open up an eventual possibility of sharing political power widely throughout the society.

The requirement of efficiency itself may force some fractionalization of power. As more enterprises come into being, and particularly as they become involved in the production and distribution of a myriad of consumer goods and in the provision of an increasing range of personal service, central control becomes less possible. The more successful the process of industrialization, the more reliance has to be placed on localized decisions and on markets, instead of on centralized decisions and plans; and markets bring the middle-class approach in their wake.

Also, the new generations of leaders become more secure, more professional, more bureaucratically interested in standard performance than in all-out effort, further removed from the old ideological considerations and the traditions of the revolution. The masses come to crave more of the product of their own labor. The drive for more consumers' goods and better housing changes the society, too.

The revolutionary intellectuals appeal particularly to the "transitionals" in the very early stages of industrialization. They promise an end to the old ruling elite or colonial power, to the old tribal or feudal culture, to economic and educational backwardness. They have little to offer to the members of a developed middle-class society. They may have some continuing appeal to the workers in a class society under a dynastic elite, but if this elite is successful in managing industrialization and moves over time toward the middle-class approach, the appeal lessens. In the nationalists, they meet competitors who offer the same things and who can hold the allegiance of the "transitionals" if they are reasonably successful in delivering what they promise.

The revolutionary intellectuals do have programs for the handling of the problems of transition—for instance, rapid commitment of a labor force, the fast build-up of an educational system, quick encouragement of labor discipline and productivity, enlargement of the gap between current consumption and current production for the sake of investment, development of an export surplus from the agricultural segment to feed the cities, and suppression of industrial conflict. However, they have much less in the way of programs for an advanced industrial society. Because of the rigidity of their ideology, they are inept in handling diversified production, in responding to the insistent calls for fractionalized power, and in giving the freedom for inquiry which goes along with highly developed educational and research institutions.

Fate of All Colonies

The colonial system is the most transient of the ideal-type elites. Both settler colonialism and segmental colonialism give way to nationalism or, in extreme cases, to the rule of the revolutionary intellectuals (although settler colonialism succumbs more reluctantly). And if total colonialism is successful, in that event it ceases to be colonialism by becoming the system of the country itself. No advance industrializing society has ever yet been run by aliens.

Experimental Nationalists

Nationalism, too, has its inherent tendencies. It relies heavily on the state, but not as rigidly as do the revolutionary intellectuals. Consequently, private enterprise and markets have not only a chance to survive but also the opportunity to take over larger areas of the economy as they become capable of doing so. Nationalism often conduces to one-party rule or domination, but again this is not based on ideology; as consensus develops in the society and as education spreads, a greater distribution of political power can occur.

The nationalist leaders, having many of the same goals as the revolutionary intellectuals, are, however, not bound by an all-pervading ideology. They are opportunists, experimenters. This has both its disadvantages and its advantages. The lack of an effective ideology leads to much stumbling and uncertainty in the early stages; but it helps avoid confining rigidities in the later stages of industrialization.

Generally, nationalism, if successful, will tend toward a modified version of the middle-class approach, modified by heavier emphasis on the state. But if unsuccessful, only the revolutionary intellectuals can readily attain leadership.

selection 14

Social Class Background of Managers in Various Countries*

David C. McClelland

Warner and Abegglen (1955), Lipset and Bendix (1959), and others have intensively pursued the question of what types of social background American business leaders have been drawn from. They have been largely interested in determining whether the proportions drawn from different sources have changed throughout the history of the United States. The question is important for economic development because it deals with the sources of managerial talent at different stages or levels in development. The U.S. studies show in general that 50-80 per cent of the business elite has come from a middle to upper status background in a fairly stable proportion over the last 150 years (Lipset and Bendix, 1959, pp. 134-135). The variation in proportions depends on how the social class categories are defined. Since the percentage of fathers enjoying such high status was smaller several generations ago than today (see Warner and Abegglen, pp. 40, 45), this means in effect that business leaders were drawn from a smaller élite group then than now. Warner and Abegglen (1955, p. 68), also note that the proportion of business leaders who were sons of laborers increased from 7 per cent in 1900 to 15 per cent in 1950, despite the fact that the percentage of such people in the total population remained fairly constant. There is evidence that as the United States has developed, business leaders have been drawn more widely from a less élite group.

What about the countries we have studied? Are the business leaders in the less developed countries drawn disproportionately from more upper class groups than in the more developed countries? Table 1 summarizes what data we were able to collect on the point. As far as the most underdeveloped country is concerned, Turkey, the expectation is borne out. A very high proportion of the business leaders in the private sector (54 per cent) come from the tiny segment of the Turkish population enjoying the highest occupational status (class 6). The government middle managers from the Istanbul region are drawn more democratically and predominantly from the much more common class 4 background as in other countries. To look at the other extreme for a moment,

---

*From *The Achieving Society*, Courtesy of D. Van Nostrand Company, Inc., 1961, pp. 276–80.

TABLE 1
Social Class Background of Managers in Turkey, Mexico, Italy, U.S. and Poland

Social Class	Turkey		Mexico	Italy		U.S.	Poland
	Private	Public	private	Public	Private	private	
	N = 39	N = 24	N = 69	N = 49	N = 61	N = 158	N = 25
	%	%	%	%	%	%	%
1-3. Lower	0	4	12	2	8	22	40
4. Lower middle	18	54	30	53	49	26	56
5. Middle	28	25	39	22	26	32	4
6. Upper middle and upper	54	17	19	22	16	20	0

Unclassifiable cases not included (e.g., military or government service backgrounds) or inadequate information.
(1) Unskilled, (2) semiskilled and (3) skilled laborers, foremen, public service workers, and tenant farmers.
(4) Clerical or sales occupations, small farm owners, small business.
(5) Minor professional (e.g., high-school teachers, medical technicians) medium business, and large farms with paid help.
(6) Major professionals, executives, and owners.

business executives in the United States, the most developed country, seem to be drawn in fairly equal proportions from all class groups. Our sample from the Advanced Management Program at the Harvard Business School is possibly somewhat less élite than the business leaders studied by others, but it is more comparable to our foreign businessmen. Even so, the percentages do not differ by much from those obtained by other investigators. In the Warner and Abegglen sample 19 per cent of the business leaders come from a blue-collar background (including foremen) vs. 22 per cent for our sample, and 26 per cent were from a class 6 background (professionals, owners of large businesses, major executives) vs. 20 per cent here. Bendix and Lipset report a stable percentage of such men coming from "manual" backgrounds of around 12 per cent (1959, p. 134) which is precisely what our percentage would be if we subtracted the 10 per cent of the group whose fathers were foremen.

The other two non-Communist and less developed countries, Mexico and Italy, are like Turkey in having a smaller percentage of men from blue collar backgrounds than in the United States. They are unlike Turkey, however, in drawing businessmen largely from the middle and lower middle classes. Thus there is support in these data for the commonly held view that outside the United States "access to managerial positions is rigidly restricted" (Harbison and

Burgess, quoted in Fayerweather, 1959, p. 100) but not in the extreme form in which the proposition is sometimes stated. The rigidity of restriction is much greater in Turkey than in Italy or Mexico. In fact, it is tempting to see a trend in these data, as the italicized figures show, for increasing proportions of business leaders to be drawn from lower and lower status groups as the country develops more. Going from less to more developed countries the largest percentages of business executives in the private sector are drawn from class 6 for Turkey, class 5 for Mexico, and class 4 for Italy. Then in the most developed country, the United States, significantly more (though not the largest number) are drawn from class 3 and below. However, the trend is no more than suggested by the data because comparable social class identifications in different countries are very hard to make and, furthermore, it is not certain that the managerial groups are exactly comparable.

Poland stands alone among the countries in that a very high proportion of the managers report a working-class background. Probably they exaggerate some-what since many such men would probably hesitate to admit an upperclass background in a Communist country. But the same bias should in fact be operating somewhat against the employment of such men as managers so that Polish managers may very well be drawn in greater proportions from the lower classes just as the data show. That is, Communist ideology may succeed to some extent in doing what it sets out to do—namely to create a "workers' " state which draws less on men of bourgeois origin. Granick reports (1960, p. 55) similarly that 55 per cent of a group of Russian factory department superintendents (comparable to our middle management groups) stated that they came from blue-collar families (our classes 1-3).

The interesting question is whether this or any other method of recruiting business managers is most likely to draw more efficiently on the supply of entrepreneurial talent (high n Achievement) in a country. Figure 1 has been drawn up in an attempt to shed some light on the problem. Interestingly enough, it shows that the Poles have not gained anything in n Achievement of their managers by recruiting them more from the lower classes because these men have lower n Achievement. The same thing is true of the Turks but in reverse. They recruit managers more heavily from the upper classes but these men also have lower n Achievement. The trends for the private and public Turkish middle managers are identical and have here been combined to give a more stable result. To put it in another way, the correlation between n Achievement and higher social status is positive ($r = .34$) in Poland and negative ($r = -.23$) in Turkey, the difference between the two correlations being significant ($t = 2.15$, $p < .05$). The findings agree fairly well with those for Italy which also show a peak in the n Achievement of managers from a "middle status" background, though it is at a different point (class 5) than in the contrast between Poland and Turkey (class 4).

While the findings are not conclusive, they suggest that the best place to recruit business managers is from the middle classes because they are more apt

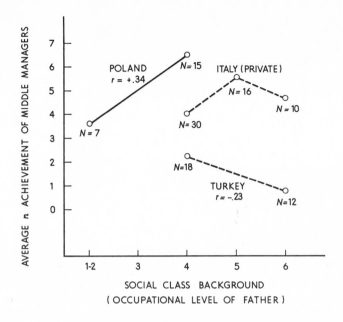

FIGURE 1
Average *n* Achievement Levels of Middle-Level Managers in Poland, Turkey and Italy
as a Function of Class Background

to have higher *n* Achievement from that background than if they come from a lower or an upper class background. If we add our tentative generalization for Table 1 to this one, it follows that countries at very low levels of development, like Turkey, are apt to recruit *n* Achievement talent inefficiently because managers are drawn in such large proportions from the upper class. In a sense they have to create a larger middle class before they can draw such talent from it. So a vicious circle is involved: development is necessary to create a larger pool of middle-class entrepreneurial talent which makes development possible. The Communist technique of recruiting more heavily from the working classes does not seem to be more efficient, to judge by the Polish data, although Communist ideology may have played a part in raising over-all *n* Achievement levels in Russia and here among the Poles.

selection 15

Business and Class in Europe*

David Granick

In 1945, a Communist was named by the coalition government of de Gaulle to one of the highest industrial posts open to governmental appointment. He held this position for two years, and was widely recognized as an administrator of vibrant personality and of great capacities. Before the war, he had been a simple worker in a large private firm.

One of the top managers of this firm was asked in the late 1950's what chances of promotion were open to this man within the company in which he had formerly worked. The manager's answer was clear and to the point: In the prewar period, his possibilities of promotion were absolutely nil. If he were to come back to the firm today, he might conceivably move up to the foreman level. But this would be his ceiling.

Undoubtedly, this limit was partly set by the fact that he was a Communist. But it was established primarily—and this was the point of the story as it was told to me—by his status as a manual worker, with the level of education and background that this implies in France.

If we are to understand traditional Continental management, it is this importance of class which we must grasp first and foremost.

In this connection, it was a revelation to me to discuss the Algerian question during the summer of 1960. It is a complicated matter and bitterly painful to Frenchmen; small wonder that French opinions should have differed sharply and be frequently offered in conversation. But what was striking was that once one left the world of the professional intellectual, and turned to the world of industry, opinions varied almost completely according to class.

Within the world of the trade unions, both the Communist and Socialist unions—although they automatically rejected cooperation with one another in virtually all economic areas—had the same policy as to Algeria: give the Algerians self-determination, and independence if they want it. The Catholic union had the same policy. Its officials differed from the others only in their boasts that they were not only more militant in pursuing this goal, but that they had also been first in the field.

One naïve but blatantly honest young Catholic official explained to me that her union always refuses to engage in politics. Some people, she went on, draw the conclusion from this that the union should not take a position as to Algeria; but they are completely wrong. The union's stand regarding Algeria does not mean an engagement in politics; rather, it is "a fight for justice."

Another official, whom I had been advised to interview as a local representative of clerical conservatism within the union, explained under my questioning the practical significance of the fact that the union was motivated by the Christian ideal. One of his three examples of this significance was the union's policy regarding Algeria: for, he pointed out, it stemmed from the basic Christian belief in liberty.

Here, then, was unanimity as to the Algerian issue among the three mutually hostile trade unions. From all accounts, this singular agreement reflected a similar unanimity existing among manual workers themselves.

When I talked to managers—and I discussed the matter with some twenty from different industries and from varying regions of France—there was absolute unanimity in the opposite direction. Algeria must remain French! Opinions differed as to the degree of self-determination possible and the proper tactics to employ, but there was no disagreement on the issue of independence—now or ever.

Could one imagine such a split among class lines in the United States? Mind, the Algerian question is not an economic issue in the same sense as the amount of unemployment which the country could properly bear without undertaking inflationary measures. It is not a trade union issue such as was the Taft-Hartley Act and its perennially proposed amendments. On a question which seems to be one of nationalism and "glory," the split in views was strictly according to class.

Here is a society basically different from our own. We cannot hope to understand European business unless we view it within the framework of its traditional social relations.

Of the countries studied, only Germany has seen traditional relations swept away in the holocaust of two wars. Or, at least, it is this image which some very knowledgeable Germans have of their country.

GERMANY: A BUSINESS SOCIETY

Before the First World War, German business had utterly failed to establish its prestige within the upper classes. The tale is told of an incident in which the Kaiser offered to a leading businessman, Werner von Siemens, the title of Kommerzienrat in acknowledgment of his business contributions. Von Siemens expressed his gratitude for the offer, but explained that he had already been honored by His Imperial Highness, who had given him a commission as *Reserveleutnant* in an army regiment, and by the Junker aristocracy which had socially accepted him. The business title would be unbecoming for a man who had received these other honors.

Between the wars, business became much more prestigious. But strong traditional rival groups remained: both the military and the Junker landowners. Then a third was added: the Nazi leaders themselves.

The Allied victory of 1945 swept aside these three dominant rivals. Temporarily, it also overwhelmed the business aristocracy—but this was the one group of the three which recovered. By the 1950's, for the first time in German history, the traditional preindustrial upper classes had lost their importance. Business society itself appeared to have become far more open, more subject to the invasion of the *nouveaux riches* and of outside recruits to management.

Germany had become a business society—with only the government hierarchy as a serious rival for either power or prestige.[1] Moreover, business itself had become more "open" to outsiders, more capable of absorbing them into its ranks, than ever before. One man, who in 1960 headed an organization of well over fifty thousand employees, boasts of being a farm boy without university education, and argues that even in the United States he would never have had the opportunities to rise which were his in postwar Germany. Whether or not his was in fact such a rags-to-riches story, it is a strange boast for a Continental. A French or Belgian topflight businessman would not proudly lay claim to such origin (even if it were true)—and would certainly never flaunt the fact that he had followed a route other than the traditional one of higher education.

FRANCE AND BELGIUM: CLASS AND EDUCATION

France and Belgium are countries in which the class lines are tightly drawn.

There is the line which separates the bourgeoisie[2] and white-collar officials of government and industry from the mass of manual workers, farmers, shopkeepers, and minor white-collar employees such as clerks, draftsmen, and even foremen.

If we look at class distinctions from the viewpoint of the upper classes, we find a merging of all the lower groups of workers, petty businessmen, lesser employees, and working farmers. The line is usually drawn at the level of the *cadres,* a term which has no parallel in America or Britain and only a loose parallel in Germany. The *cadres* are the higher employees—whether managerial or professional—and are included with the bourgeoisie. The definition of *cadre* is sufficiently restricted so that, in the larger firms, they comprise only some 1 to 3 per cent of the total labor force. The truly interesting feature about them is that virtually all those who will ever become *cadres* are given this status almost

---

[1] A German reader of this manuscript points out that the clergy, the academic community and the established professions also have considerable prestige.

[2] I trust that the reader will not bridle at the word "bourgeoisie" because of the Marxist flavor which it has absorbed in American usage. The American term "middle class" is utterly inappropriate; the French and Belgians use this expression *(la classe moyenne)* to describe petty shopkeepers and employees, and in conversation it seems often to carry a rather derogatory meaning.

immediately as they leave school and begin work. This is a rank of "higher employee" which a man enters due to education or family connections—or from which he is permanently barred.

What does this chasm between social classes mean in terms of living standards? Of breadth or narrowness of life?

During 1960, I renewed in southern France acquaintance with a peasant family I had known immediately after the war. Theirs was a typical story of farmers on bad soil the world over: the old folks left on the farm, the children gone off to the cities.

One daughter now worked in the post office, despite the problem of care for her preschool-age child. Joshing with her, I asked, "Have you had a fine marriage, Marie?" "But, no," she answered, astonished at my question. "Mine is a worker's marriage!" The very word "fine" *(beau mariage)* had a class connotation for her; it was a word for "the others."

A second daughter had the nearest thing to a "fine marriage" for which a peasant girl could realistically hope. Her husband was a worker's son who had gone to a teachers' college and was now himself a teacher in a junior high school. He had entered a field which is the traditional success-occupation for a French working-class or farm boy. It was a giant step up into the middle class.

Life was good to this young couple. The girl did not work, but could stay home and take care of her baby. They owned a car. During the two-month summer vacation—instead of the three-week one enjoyed by most French workers and employees—the husband felt no compulsion to take a temporary job in order to make ends meet. Nor was he a "moonlighter," as an American teacher in his place would often be. But the narrowness of his horizon, seeing that he was the very epitome of working-class success!

His school was one hundred miles from his home town, and in a region which he and his wife despised. The people were different, with none of the easy back-and-forth visiting of neighbors customary in his own region. Even the climate was different. It was a city barren of interest to the couple, yet one which they now thought of as their lifetime home.

Why not transfer? I asked. In particular, why not ask for a post in Paris—the mecca of the French bourgeoisie? To this, the teacher had no real answer. Yes, he was certain that he could get such a post; the French teaching shortage is as great as the American. But he would lose seniority—since this counted separately in each department of France! As his seniority was merely that of a few years, and his tenure of post would be secure as soon as he was appointed, this seemed to me to be a weak argument. In the end, under attack, his position boiled down to the fact that the very concept of leaving the South—happy or unhappy there—was inconceivable.

He had attained the lifelong security of a civil service post. His family was lifted above the poverty line of the working class—despite their cold-water flat. This economic catapulting was displayed in their ability to restrict themselves to one child—thus bearing the costs of child-rearing while foregoing a family allow-ance; to make do without a second income earned by the wife; and to have the ultimate working-class luxury of a car. What more could they reasonably desire?

As the teacher and I talked on, warmed by the *tutoyer* relation between my-self and his wife whom I had known as a young adolescent, I told him of what I was doing. I talked of my driving around France and of my interviews with French businessmen, professors, etc. He listened politely for a few moments, and then dismissed the description with a shrug and a remark to his wife that all this was a "different world." This shrug was not simply a response to the obvious fact that such activity was different from what he or those people he knew were likely to do. Such was likewise true of non-working-class Frenchmen I had met. Rather, it was because this was the sort of activity which to him fitted into that ultraluxury world of the "bourgeoisie," a world which to him was beyond fantasy.

One meets the same perspective of "two worlds" in the almost complete ab-sence of working-class sons in the *lycées,* the French academic secondary schools. Although manual workers constitute 45 per cent of the French non-agricultural male working population, their sons comprised a bare 5 per cent of the Paris *lycee* students in 1950. The disproportion is even greater when we go one step higher, and ask about the social backgrounds of youths in the post-diploma state secondary school courses. These latter classes are required as a prelude to the almost purely intellectual, competitive exams for the *grandes ecóles,* graduation from which goes so much farther than does a university degree in making possible a "fine" career."

In one French secondary school in 1960, presumably a reasonably typical one, the sons of manual workers, farmers, and employees—all lumped together—comprised only 13 per cent of the total student body in the post-diploma courses. (These groups total 72 per cent of the French working force.) Sons of independent businessmen, company directors, free professionals in independent practice, and government civil servants made up the remaining 87 per cent of the students here.

How account for the abstention of the blue-collar class from even the ordi-nary program of the academic high schools, since this is almost the sole route to major advancement for their children? This is a question I put to a number of trade unionists from both the Catholic and Communist unions. The first answer generally received from the union officials was that the schools are too costly. But when we consider that no tuition is charged, and that the cost to the parents is solely continued maintenance at home and the purchase of books, this argu-ment is hard to accept. All the more so today when French workers have begun buying cars and other hard goods on a substantial scale.

Pushing the question, I had the impression that the economic reason was usually presented by these trade unionists as a hastily constructed answer to what seemed to them a very foolish question. It was foolish because, in essence, everyone knew that the *lycées* were for "the others." These schools lay well outside the horizon of reasonable alternatives for most working-class children. They were part of the province of that other world, that of the bourgeoisie.

Contrast this life with that of the bourgeoisie. For such a comparison, let us take the lower and middle levels of those genuine *cadres* who are old enough to be well launched on their careers.

Talking with one group of middle management, assembled from Paris and from various French provinces, I told them about some of the results of a study I had made of Soviet managers. I had given this type of talk previously to similar management people, both in the United States and in Britain, and I was accustomed to certain types of comments. Most managerial reactions had dealt with the fundamental similarity of the management problem regardless of the social system. But what struck these French managers instead was the peculiar deprivation enforced upon the Soviet manager.

They did not refer to the pressure under which the Soviet manager operates. Nor were they particularly concerned with the political aspects of his job, with the problems of divided authority, or with his standard of living. What bothered them, instead, was the fact that he was deprived of the fundamental right of investing in company stocks. He had no operational way to build an inheritance of income-producing property for his children. Nor, although this was not brought out explicitly, was he himself the heir to such property. In short, he was not a "bourgeois."

What bothered them about the position of the Soviet manager—and what was difficult for them to accept as true—was precisely that lack of a family income-producing property which is almost equally absent among American middle management. If I had given the American instance of stock ownership being widespread among this group but producing an unimportant share of their income, I believe that it would have been totally unbelievable to them.

Speaking in Lorraine to a group of some twenty-five department heads in a steel mill, I raised the question of the position of their wives. None of the wives of these steel men worked, and each of them had a full-time maid. (The assistant manager of the plant considered it quite normal that his wife employed two full-time maids.) This was a pattern which I found to be fairly typical in the provinces, although the labor shortage in and around Paris makes servants much more difficult to obtain there. Even in the provinces, it is a way of life which is under strain, and women complain of the difficulties of finding help; but fifteen years of full employment have not yet broken the mold.

Since we were an all-male group, I dared to ask my Lorraine hosts what their wives find to do once the children are grown. For they are not club women, nor ladies bountiful in community affairs. An occupation must be found within the family; yet houses are generally small. In fact, apartments predominate even in this small town, so there is no large house and garden for which to plan.

My question was greeted with amusement, and the first answer was that they "pretend to work hard." Enlarging upon this response and becoming serious, they told me that sewing is a proper occupation for these wives. But above all, cooking; for "cooking is an art," and not to be entrusted to the servant by a wife who has time for it. No wonder the properly renowned French cuisine, and the two-hour lunch period allowing the husband to return home to patronize the arts!

The contrast of way of life seems to me much greater between the French bourgeois woman and the French working-class woman than it is between the men. The 8:30 A.M. to 7:30 P.M. office day seems common enough for businessmen and managers. They give the impression of being an enormously hardworking group, and this has been confirmed to me by Americans sent out for a time into branch firms located in France. Small cause for surprise that many French managers complain bitterly of the one-and-a-half to two-hour lunch period which pushes their work far back into the evening.

The working-class or shopkeeper woman, often working full time while simultaneously running her home without modern American household equipment, leads a tough life indeed. For her, France and Belgium comprise a man's world. But one wonders whether it is not these countries, rather than the United States, which are the woman's paradise for those whose husbands earn good incomes. Certainly, in a household of European friends of mine who had tried living in America, it was the wife rather than the husband who waxed most enthusiastic about their return.

A small-town Flemish banker of sixty discussed with me the problem of children in an older-generation bourgeois family, whether in Belgium or in France. Since he had married off both sons and daughters, he spoke from considerable practical experience.

Connections are a crucial matter for a son's career, and it is the father's duty, he said, to try to assure them. This obligation had been largely responsible for his leaving the small town where he was his own man, and transferring in a lesser executive capacity to a larger branch of the same bank.

One of the banker's sons was a doctor, and the move to the larger town was sufficiently successful that the son, when he finished his medical studies, was taken on as an assistant by a doctor in this town. The banker was convinced that without his own newly established connections this post could not have been attained. The son would have had to go to work in the hospital of his university, where he would not only have been paid little but would also have learned less than as a private doctor's assistant. Whether or not the banker was right in thinking of a hospital start as a poor one from the point of view in training—an hypothesis which strikes me as most unsound—certainly he was representative of the men of his generation in assuming that connections are an essential part of a father's responsibility.

Marriage of the children is a complicated matter. It is most usually founded upon a dowry which will have been carefully discussed beforehand by the families concerned. Partly the dowry will consist of furniture—enough so that the couple may enjoy so far as is possible, the housing standard to which they had been accustomed. In addition, the dowry will consist of property.

This can be an expensive business for the bride's family. Yet this dowry supplies only one of the basic equipments of the young couple: that of the traditional property which they in turn will pass on to the next generation. It does not provide for the further social necessity: that the couple's income be sufficient for a proper bourgeois style of life.

Since it is unlikely that the boy's earned income plus the property income from the dowry will furnish this minimum, the boy's family will seek to provide either a regular allowance to the couple throughout the early years of marriage or it will deed over property to be consumed in living expenses during these years. In any case, making good the husband's income deficiency is his parents' share of the marriage.

To an American, all this was most intriguing. It seemed curious that the normal social obligations of a young professional or manager should be well beyond the financial possibilities of one who does not come from a home which can provide the standard bourgeois supplement to his salary. The young man whose education is appropriate for business or professional success, but whose family fortune is nil, is virtually forced to marry properly if he is to have the wherewithal for a career.

Perhaps this distinction between the bourgeoisie and other classes in France and Belgium seems overdrawn. Yet we cannot stop here, but must have the further cut subdividing the bourgeoisie itself. This is the dividing line of education.

Within French industry, a higher-educational degree is virtually a requirement for any *cadre* post. Such a degree requires a minimum of three years of study beyond the *lycée,* graduation from which is often considered equivalent to the completion of two years of college work in America. A French survey of the metalworking industry showed that 85 per cent of management above the foreman level possessed a higher degree. In ferrous metallurgy, the proportion is still greater among *cadres* on the plant level.

But one higher degree counts very differently from another. In industry, the university degree—even the Doctor of Law—is treated with scorn. For a career, it is essential to have attended a *grande école* (great school).

The term *grande école* is used ambiguously in France. Often it is employed loosely to include virtually all of the schools of engineering (the prince of subjects for French industry, and one not taught at any university) plus some of the non-technical schools. At other times, it is used in a more restrictive sense to include only the peak engineering schools—Polytechnique, the School of Mines, and Centrale—and the two non-engineering schools which also partially service business: Sciences Politiques (the traditional administrative school) and Hautes Etudes Commerciales in Paris (the major commercial school, called H.E.C.). In its most rigid usage, only the top three engineering schools belong. The term will be used in the intermediate grade of restrictiveness—although normally with reference only to the engineering schools—throughout this book.

A questionnaire filled out in 1952 by directors of engineering schools of various types shows the varying educational emphases. This survey was carried out by Francois Jacquin and was reported on in his book *Les Cadres de l'Industrie et du Commerce en France.*

Polytechnique is the grandest of the *grandes écoles.* Symbolically, it is called "X" even by the Polytechniciens themselves. The student here spends three quarters of his time in scientific studies, and only after graduation may he receive technological training in an "applied school." At Centrale, the outer edge of the *grandes écoles,* a bare one quarter of the student's time is spent on science, 40 per cent on technology, and almost one third in laboratory and shop application. The Arts and Crafts *(Arts et Métiers)* student uses 40 per cent of his time in laboratory and shop work; and the student at the engineering schools still lower in prestige ranking, each of which specializes in a particular industry, devotes some 60 per cent of his time to this practical work. Although the graduate of these schools receives the same title of "diploma-engineer," they have clearly gone through radically differing types of educational processes.

The result of these differences, as well as of the major role of formal education in determining careers in French industry, is reflected in a major study of twenty-three thousand *cadres* at all levels in the various metalworking industries. (Union des Industries Metallurgiques et Minières, *Ingénieurs et Cadres Supérieurs,* 1956.) Five hundred firms, almost all of which had over one hundred employees, answered the questionnaire of their trade association.

Of the graduates of Polytechnique working in the metalworking industries, 46 per cent were in upper management at the plant or headquarters level. (Eleven per cent of all *cadres,* regardless of education, were included in this category of upper management.) Only 31 per cent of Centrale alumni were at this level, while the remaining *cadres* from this school spread out widely in the various technical sectors—giving a wide berth solely to the dead-end functions of design, testing, and research. The Arts and Crafts men were heavily in production, 50 per cent of them working there at some point below the top directing level. Although a goodly portion of the graduates of the specialized engineering schools were also in production, one third of them were occupied in design, testing, and research.

The above distinction between alumni of different types of engineering schools seems particularly marked when one remembers that large numbers of family and regional firms, which find it difficult either to gain admission for their scions to the *grandes écoles* or to recruit their graduates, are included in the sample.

In the large French firms, the line between the graduates of the *grandes écoles* and of the whole host of minor engineering schools is fairly rigid, although not completely so. The first group is at least offered the possibilities of "command";

the second is condemned to middle management. This is a distinction which also contains other consequences.

One firm I visited was a prototype of this situation although, I will admit, a somewhat exaggerated example. The *cadres* below the level of plant director and assistant director came from the minor engineering schools, and a few out of the science departments of the universities. Mostly these were men who had entered this industry and even this particular firm on leaving school, and were making their entire career within it. In fact, the career would normally be in one plant.

Men who mostly came from other regions of France, they were condemned to remain in this unattractive one-industry district until they retired. It was expected that the vast majority would then depart—and return to the family property and home in their "own" region.

These were true bourgeois, but fated from their very entrance into industry to a mediocre career. Just as the workers in the firm could rise no higher than foreman, so these lower *cadres* could rise no higher than the department-chief level.

The directors of the firm were a different breed. Men of the *grandes écoles,* the present heads were all completely new to the industry. The top man had come from another firm, technically unrelated to this one but in the same financial group. His main-plant director had come from the railroads, a nationalized service. The third man, handling production, was from the Navy. All had arrived in this firm within the last two years—and none had ever had any previous experience in the industry in which he was now operating.

Moreover, these upper *cadres* were most unlikely to remain long in this provincial firm. All saw their careers—at least if they were successful—as taking them to Paris. They expected rotation within the broader financial group of which their firm was a part. If this did not work out, then there were other groups in France. They were the men of the "fine careers," of mobility between regions, between firms, and between industries. Under them were the flunky engineers, whose future was that of routine. The barrier between these groups was almost as impassable as that between worker and engineer: a man fell to one side of the fence or the other depending on whether or not he had gone to a *grande école.*

There are no over-all statistics as to the backgrounds of the active presidents of major firms. But material from my interviews concerning fifteen of them reinforced the general picture painted by French managers.

Of the fifteen presidents, eight were graduates of Polytechnique. All the remaining seven were alumni of some other institute of higher education. Moreover, six of these seven were from firms which might be considered special cases. Three were in foreign-controlled firms, two were in nationalized companies, and the sixth was the head of one of the greatest French industrial families. Only one non-Polytechnicien was the president of a "normal" private French company.

Genuine top management is very small in these large firms, and we are safest in treating it as consisting only of the president and of the one or more director-generals in those companies where this office is separate from that of president. Taking the two groups together, we find that 61 per cent of these men came from the two grandest of the *grandes écoles* (Polytechnique and Écoles des Mines). Of the sample of thirty-one, only two had solely a non-scientific education, and one of these two had earlier served in the top civil service. (Two more had a legal training in addition to a science degree.) The sharpest contrast with the situation in the United States, Britain, or Germany is the fact that only one of the thirty-one had failed to complete a higher education program.

When we move down to the level of plant director, the pattern of education widens slightly. Of six plant directors for whom I have information, only two were Polytechniciens; but a third was from Centrale—the least of the three major engineering schools. Only one of the six had no higher education.

Leaving the great French firms with their headquarters in Paris, and turning instead to the predominantly family firms of the provinces and to the smaller firms of Paris, the profile changes radically. Here the *grandes écoles* play a much smaller role for a variety of reasons. These firms are much less attractive to graduates of these schools; family considerations predominate, and none of the family members may have been intellectually capable of winning admission to a *grande école;* sales and connections are local, and thus the need for governmental connections and the old school tie does not have the same importance as in the great firms.

In four such firms which are middling to large, two of the presidents had received a university degree in law (much value for family members in the provinces), one was from the minor engineering school Arts and Crafts, and only a single president was from Centrale. If our sample were wider, we would also have found a fair proportion who were graduates of local commercial schools or were even totally devoid of higher education. These last groups consist virtually entirely of heirs to the business or of men who themselves founded the company.

Men with a non-science higher education occupy a highly specialized position in French industry. Only within the smaller firms and in the provinces do they have any genuine possibility of moving into top management. It is true that in the larger firms they play a major role in the sales, finance, administrative, and personnel functions. Frequently enough, they become vice-presidents (directeurs) in charge of one of these functions. But, as we shall see in later chapters, these vice-presidential positions are not really part of French top management. Rather they are the end of a career line, representing the upper level of middle management. It is production management alone which lies in the main stream.

This fact makes French statistics misleading. The large-scale survey of the metalworking industry mentioned above indicates that 12 per cent of upper-management posts were held by men with a non-science higher education. But, aside from the family firms and very special cases, we can assert with confidence that these men held posts which represented in power, prestige, and even income far less than would the same position in an American, British, or German concern.

In the major Paris-based companies, I collected data on twenty-one vice-presidents in charge of sales, finance, administration, and personnel. Eight of the twenty-one had a legal or commercial degree as compared to ten with an engineering or science diploma.[3] In these posts, legal or commercial education are virtually as prominent as engineering. But it is worth looking closely at the men with these backgrounds. Of the eight, three are alumni of the traditional *grande école* of administration *(Sciences Politiques)* and two more of the *grande école* of commerce (H.E.C. of Paris).

Another way to regard upper management in French industry is to lump together all the presidents, vice-presidents, and plant directors in my survey of major firms. Of the total of sixty men, graduates from *grandes écoles* of top prestige were:

Engineering (Polytechnique and Mines) 31
Administrative (Sciences Politiques) 4

Together, they comprised 55 per cent of this group of upper management. In order to provide a frame of reference for this figure, we should note that graduates of these three schools total a mere 14 per cent of the total *cadres* (management above foreman level) in the metalworking industries.

In Belgium, the education distinction between engineer-technicians and university engineers is quite similar to that existing in France between graduates of run-of-the-mill engineering schools and of the *grandes écoles.* The promotional barrier is also the same.

Two thirds of all Belgium's *cadres* have a higher education of some form, at least equal to the American level in the poorer colleges. Despite the far greater spread of higher education through the population of the United States than through that of Belgium, management above the foreman level could not make a similar claim. Moreover, the Belgian proportion is rising just as is the American. Ever increasingly, a Belgian youth of good family who wishes to go into sales, accounting, or administration will first complete a non-engineering higher education.

If we consider only the top managers (director-generals), then the proportion with higher education rises to about three quarters of the total. But the really major difference from the picture for total *cadre* is that university alumni—graduates of the Belgian high-prestige educational system in both the technical and non-technical fields—comprise almost 70 per cent of top managers as compared to only 41 per cent for all *cadres* taken together. It is the graduates of the low-prestige higher-engineering institutions who are cut back from 18 per cent to 3 per cent. Top management bifurcates sharply; its members either have a high-prestige university education or they have no higher education whatsoever. Doubtless, the last group are almost all to be found in the medium-sized family firms.

---

[3] A nineteenth vice-president had graduated from a military academy.

The director-general of a medium-large Belgian company, located in a slum district which must have been unattractive to those engineering graduates with a real choice of workplace, defended the existence of the career separation between university engineers and engineer-technicians. In his own firm, he personally enforced it on the grounds that the engineer-technicians did not have a "general education"—including Greek and Latin. Nor was this, in his eyes, simply an issue of social background; some of the engineer-technicians came from "good families." Rather, it was a distinction made solely according to educational routes taken when the boys were eighteen—or often six years earlier at the time they made their secondary school choices.

In a small French town, a director from Polytechnique confessed that it was difficult to find company with which to associate. He sought it in other *grande école* men of the area, or among professionals such as a doctor with whom we dined. Nevertheless, although living in a small town in an area where he was a stranger, it would never have occurred to him to socialize with any of the department heads in his own firm. Nor would he have thought of the middle-class businessmen of the area as fit associates.

In another region, the top man of a local firm described himself as having friends from all levels of society—a result of his having lived in the town all his life. He had no social problems. On the other hand, his plant director—an "X," by the way—encountered considerable difficulties. This was because he was an outsider, having resided in that town for a bare ten years, and so was restricted in social acquaintance to people at his own level.

The distinction is not one of business vs. the arts, the law, etc. Rather it is a distinction between the men of "culture"—whether in private business, the civil service, medicine, or the law—and "the others." In Franch business and civil service, the cultured man—almost by definition is from a *grande école;* in the liberal professions, a rather select group of university graduates are admitted to the circle. In Belgium, where government service is given a low social ranking, the definition is still more restricted. Even men at the level of undersecretary of a ministry do not seem to fit into the definition of "cultured"; at least, they are not considered proper people to invite to parties given by businessmen and professionals.

One would expect that the class differences I have just sketched are an expression of differences in money incomes. With this in mind, I compiled data wherever possible from individual firms as to the earnings of their workers and of their managers at different levels. On collating these figures, I expected that they would provide the financial underpinning for my strong impression that class differences in standard of living are considerably greater in France and Belgium than they are in the United States. But they showed nothing of the sort.

Taking the annual earnings of an average worker in full employment as equal to 1, I found other incomes from salaries and bonuses to bear the following ratios:

	France	Belgium	United States
Foreman.	1½–2	2½–3	2–3
Beginning engineer		1½	1½
Lower *cadre*.	4	2	2–3
Head of a big department or the manager of a plant	4	5–6	4–5
Cadre immediately below the level of vice-president of a big company	4–6½	6½	6
Vice-president of a company			
Medium-sized firm	6–9	4½–6½	5–8
Very large firm	7–20	6½–13	13–21

All of these figures are crude, and small differences between the countries are not particularly meaningful. What the table does seem to show is that the French and Belgian firms for which I have data display much the same income pattern as do American companies. German firms are also similar. Only British companies differ—and there the income differentials are much smaller. The pattern of inequality as one mounts the hierarchy is no greater in the Old World than in the New.

Not only does this conclusion conflict with my observation of living standards, but it is also contrary to the observations of a number of French and Belgian businessmen with whom I discussed this matter. They commented unfavorably on the relatively low income differentials which they had observed in the United States.

Part of the explanation, perhaps, lies in national differences in taxation. Both French and Belgian businessmen have traditionally shown a successful hostility to the notion of paying taxes, and much of business activity is geared to the vital negative function of tax evasion. But there does not seem to be any well-developed avoidance of taxes on salaries or bonuses. The expense account, in fact, is a technique of avoidance considerably less evolved in these countries than in the United States. Thus tax differences would not seem to account for any large part of the discrepancy between national variations in relative living standards and national similarities in earned-income ratios.

More promising as an explanation is the difference in price structure between Western Europe and the United States. The price spread between low- and high-cost goods—whether they are housing, shoes, or restaurant meals—is less in Europe. Thus, since businessmen are purchasers of the more expensive types of goods, the European top executive is favored relatively to the American.

It seems to me, however, that the main part of the explanation lies elsewhere. This "elsewhere" is found precisely in the class nature of French and Belgian management; namely, the fact that it is bourgeois. Property ownership rather than management function is the crucial variable.

Perhaps it is the importance of property ownership that helps upgrade the standing of the non-business members of the bourgeoisie in relation to business managers. It is true that the successful business executive has a substantially higher earned income than the French civil servant, the university professor, or even the doctor. But all these latter, when one considers the role of property income in supporting their standard of living, can also maintain a proper bourgeois style.

The shopkeepers of Brugge, a famous tourist spot for the Belgians as well as for foreigners, were the victims in 1960 of this dependence on property income. With the collapse of stock prices of the Belgian companies in the Congo, Belgian tourist spending was sharply restricted. As the holdings of these shares were widespread, so too were the losses and resultant cutbacks.

The bourgeois marriage takes its due place in this context. It is an important means for the transmission of property, and for the maintenance of living standards above the salary level.

Speaking of the Polytechniciens, one French professor warned me that I would be misled if I took too seriously the fact that some of them come from outside the bourgeoisie—and are instead from the "middle classes." Look at their wives, he urged. The student at "X" is at the very center of Parisian society, and cannot help but meet the daughters of the Paris bourgeoisie while he is a student. Moreover, since he is a marked man due to his very admission to "X," he is one of the prime marriage catches of the season. If he then goes into the civil service after graduation, even when he himself has no great fortune, he can provide the family prestige while his wife supplies the funds.

During the nineteenth century, this phenomenon was officially recognized in one of the French official texts. Here it was admitted that the high civil servant is poorly paid, but it was pointed out that his compensation was the major perquisite of being able to make a "fine marriage." The Inspector of Finance could marry the banker's daughter.

Note that this type of marriage is not often the means by which a working-class or farm youth rises from his class. Rather it is normally the means of support for the bourgeois boy, who adds to his own property the dowry of his wife. With their combined property backing, he can live a "cultured" life quite out of proportion to his salary. Nor need this be an artificial "arranged" marriage; today, one hears of this only in old-fashioned areas such as the textile principalities of northern France. It is the natural joining of young people, coming from a similar background, and thrown together in the routine course of social life. But it serves its purpose just as well: that of providing a solid financial base from which the man can strike out into non-remunerative but high-prestige fields.

selection 16

The Dilemma of an Elite Group:
The Industrialist in Latin America*

John D. Harbron

The basic challenge facing the industrialist and the executive—indeed the entire managerial class in Latin America—is whether they now have the power—and the time—to change society within the existing, inadequate political and economic systems of the continent.

More than any other group in the class hierarchy of Latin America, the modern industrialist, both foreign-born and domestic, has become the principal vehicle through which the vast changes must take place which the continent demands. The modern industrialist's technology is in conflict with old methods, even old-fashioned leaders, especially the *latifundistas* who mismanage agrarian empires or ancient family companies and whose political influence to impede change outweighs their managerial talents. But is this technology enough to fill the gap? Or will the extremists by encouraging undisciplined university students, the chronically landless, the illiterate, sweep away the process of slow change in place of swift, revolutionary change and with chaos of an enduring nature?

In many subtle ways, the confrontation between the two systems, slower-moving middle-of-the-road social democracy (as practiced in Mexico, Venezuela, Uruguay or Costa Rica) and right or leftwing dictatorship (as it is practiced in Paraguay or Cuba), is now the experience of a different class factor in Latin American society. This is, broadly speaking, the growing middle classes of the continent and more especially the upper echelon within it—the industrialists and the progressive managerial elite.

In those republics firmly committed to slow social change the executive in private enterprise or government is replacing the self-seeking politician, the intellectual with humanitarian passions, but who cannot plan, and the rapacious militarist.

While the Latin American military is still inclined to maintain its historic "protector" role as the Brazilian Army did with traditional poise in the coup which overthrew former President João Goulart, in many other Latin countries, its leaders have traded gaudy uniforms for uninspiring mufti to become part of

*From *Inter-American Economic Affairs,* Vol. XIX, No. 2 (Autumn 1965), pp. 43–62.

the new, civilian industrial elite. Such militarists are now motivated by the sound principles of management science rather than by the less permanent one of narrow self-preservation in a hemisphere intensely restless for the arrival of the new order.[1]

In some Latin American nations treading slowly up the path from permanent dictatorship, must the new managerial elite continue to work, to plan, against the prospect that weak and centralist political systems, democratic in spirit, but committed to barrel politicians and sectional interests will succumb again to another Castro or another Trujillo? The answer to this question must, unfortunately, be yes. This is the lot of the modern, international executive in the emerging world, including the Americas.

Moreover, in old and traditionalist societies (and most Latin American national entities, typically Perú's, are among the world's oldest, surviving social structures), the modern executive is a newcomer. The system he is pledged to alter by slow change is deeply entrenched, a living, if not a vibrant remnant of the earliest European cultures in the hemisphere.

In many instances, the modern manager as the most aggressive element in Latin America's uneasy middle classes (as opposed to the *latifundista),* does not have a long background of either control or influence over property and government, as have say, Western European industrial elites. In many countries, for example, Argentina and Perú, he is, to a large degree, the product of post-1945 industrial expansion, usually an executive of an efficiently run American or European subsidiary corporation. In these firms, he is often a salaried executive, unable to cope, unless through company channels, with the *latifundista* who resists change or with interfering politicians who grease cranking government machinery only for selfish, short-term purposes.

Thus the recommendations of an economist in the private sector about, say, tariff reductions, can easily be side-tracked by politicians or redundant family-managed concerns who have direct pipelines to governments or local trade associations whose membership could be adversely affected by realistic planning.

The contemporary American and European industrialist has had the benefit of a century of conflict between the ideas and methods of the old order and the new, all within the era of the industrial revolution. These have affected all strata of American and European society. The Latin American industrialist on the other hand, must make progress a lot sooner, but in national societies still largely motivated by agrarian interests and in political structures little changed in their ideology from the centuries prior to the industrial revolution. Above all, he must get results even sooner in time than his earlier American and European counter-

---

[1] On the recent presidential crisis in Brazil see Juan de Onis, "Brazil's Changing Order," *The New York Times,* July 20, 1964; and Jordan M. Young, "Some Permanent Political Characteristics of Contemporary Brazil," *Journal of Inter-American Studies,* Vol. VI, No. 3 (July, 1964), pp. 287–301.

On the new role of the Latin American military see the author's "When the Military Are Managers," *Executive,* Vol. 5, No. 5 (May, 1963), pp. 48–51.

parts in countries which want to leap into the full benefits of the industrial age without wanting to experience its growing pains.

Even if such violent social changes are somehow delayed in Latin America, as the spread of Castro-style Marxism now seems to be, or are cast permanently aside as they have been in Mexico's institutionalized social democracy, the Latin American executive must ask himself another question. Has his small segment of the still growing Latin American middle class, generated enough strength to permeate millions of restless and often illiterate peoples with philosophies of life requiring a sophisticated and diversified economic system?

In all the Latin American republics (except Cuba and Mexico), the historic pattern of *latifundismo* is still strong. As the most powerful, surviving anachronism of the colonial period, it pays heed neither to modern "management methods" of the industrialists seeking change, nor to the statist concepts of the non-Communist left. *Latifundismo* is continent-wide and loath to change or give place. *Latifundismo* means the closed society. Modern management brings the open society. Both are in sharp contrast and in some places in sharp conflict. *Latifundismo's* historic pattern is most excessive perhaps in Perú. A single plantation in the rich Peruvian lowlands is one third the size of the island of Cuba, surely the largest *hacienda* in South America.[2] Lima's *la llamada* (the one hundred wealthiest families) live in an Indian nation where the indigenous races cling to living conditions of the Middle Ages while *la llamada* clings to an era of concentrated wealth and position which ended in Europe in 1914.

The confrontation therefore, is not only between systems, but between their institutions and their representatives. The *latifundista,* the eldest type of "manager" in the hemisphere will trigger social upheaval as long as he exists. The modern manager, what the Mexicans in their advanced nation call the *técnicos,* will trigger social change. Latin America's best hope for positive leadership and hence for economic and social stability, is through the progressive industrial elite. This is the growing directional element in Latin American public life from which springs the creative, imaginative domestic manager of public and private enterprise.

THE LESSON OF CUBA

The inevitable watershed in assessing all political, economic and social events in Latin America at the mid-point of this century is the fact of the Cuban Revolution—why it happened, what are its chances for widening success or failure?

Much of the blame for the wide social inequalities in pre-Castro Cuba has been laid at the feet of Cuban and foreign private enterprise and of an exceedingly efficient, but socially blind managerial elite which is now in complete and probably permanent exile from its homeland. At the same time, critics of the

---

[2] Samuel Shapiro, *Invisible Latin America* (Boston: Beacon Press, 1963), p. 43.

Cuban urban middle class have gone on to say that since 1959, Latin America's industrialists, like Louis XVI, "have learned nothing and forgotten nothing" from the mistakes made in Cuba.

This second assessment is not only inaccurate, but it is inapplicable in the widest sense in those larger Latin republics, chiefly Mexico, Brazil, Argentina and Chile where the managerial class has developed with strong influences from national patterns of political and economic growth alien to and unknown in Cuba before 1958. The most prominent exception, as we shall see, has been the growth and place in Mexican society of a business class which a revolution created rather than destroyed.

Nevertheless, there were important factors relative to the business methods and community attitudes of Cuban and American private enterprise in pre-Castro Cuba which have not been forgotten elsewhere in the Americas by the industrial elite. Undoubtedly in many places they have been the inspiration for some enlightened social aid programs by some of the continent's wealthiest industrialists and largest foreign subsidiary companies. As a result, a comment often heard in Latin America these days is, "after Castro, there are still plenty of millionaires, but few oligarchs."

In the lush years before Castro, Cuban and U.S.-owned firms throughout Cuba returned some of the largest profits . . . still on record for locally and foreign-owned enterprises in Latin America. Many Cuban subsidiaries of U.S. companies did better before 1958 than subsidiaries of the same parent corporations have since been able to do elsewhere in the hemisphere. The big sugar corporations whose output dominated Cuban exports were owned by Cuban millionaires like the Lobo family or by U.S. companies such as Cuban Atlantic and Cuban-American. Sugar firms like these made an average net profit of 23% a year between 1953 and 1957. In 1957 overall earnings on the $849 millions of direct U.S. investment in Cuba was 8.6% of which $48 millions or 5.6% was remitted to the U.S.A.[3] The Cuban business elite of the republic's prosperous big cities, Havana, Santiago, Camaguey expatriated so much capital that a nation with pressing social and educational needs never adequately met since independence at the turn of the century, had actually become a capital exporting nation. The foreign and Cuban corporation's sole responsibility before 1958 was first and foremost to make a profit and only occasionally to assist the decrepit social system in which it functioned.

Outwardly the Cuba of 1958 was the leading example of how to do business in Latin America, make a large profit and develop a skilled technical class to keep entities efficient. In 1957 about 160,000 Cubans were employed by American firms. If their benefiting families and relations were included, this accounted for about 700,000 in a population of 7.5 millions or nearly the total number now in exile. This industrial class concentrated in Havana, was highly "Americanized,"

---

[3] Footnote in David K. Eiterman, "American Portfolio Investor Discounting of Political and Social Risks in Cuban Securities," *Quarterly Review of Economics and Business.*

a result of advanced education and technical training in the best American colleges and of the comfortable living which employment with U.S. subsidiaries gave them. Today, as exiles, some of them are still the best cost accountants, marketing and sales experts, labor lawyers in Latin America and are in demand in Carácas, Mexico City, Puerto Rico and elsewhere.

At the same time, the mounting internal factors of decay, frustration, restlessness which dominated and corrupted Cuban public life, were ignored by the Cuban executive, or in some cases when he paid through the nose for government short-cuts, they were directly of his making. The wealth generated by this capable, self-centered type of Cuban was, to say the least, unevenly distributed throughout the economy. A million Cubans, one of every seven in the nation in 1958 went to bed hungry, badly-housed in a country which by the standards of even harder-hit republics to the south had the highest literacy rate in Latin America. Little attention was paid by the leaders of Cuban industry to the complex relationships which the rise of a Cuban *nouveau riche* had created since 1945 among those thousands of Cubans who remained outside of the money economy they augmented.

The Cuban upper class practiced tax evasion and *latifundismo* on a lavish scale. According to the Agricultural Census of Cuba for 1946, one third of all the crop land was owned by 900 corporations—many foreign-owned. Some of these estates covered 500,000 acres. The whole of the famous Isle of Pines, now seat of Castro's largest prison, was owned by no more than four Cuban landlords.

As a result not even the best intentions of the few concerned Cuban political and business leaders could stop the storm and save Cuba's executive class from extinction, nor their wealth from confiscation, nor the destruction of their pleasant way-of-life by a Communist state which has all the signs of permanency.

Castro's Communist take-over of Cuban industry has thoroughly scared but not discouraged a generation of Latin American industrialists. Like executives under acute external pressures anywhere, they are learning to adapt, to change their ways and to do it quickly. The Cuban Revolution has taught the Latin American executive who wants to survive that corporate responsibility in a country eager for change with enlarged ideas of state control over business, is now as important as pure profit-making. The lingering sophistication of Harvard-type courses on "the corporation's role in the community" have become down-to-earth realities for American foreign enterprise, not only in Latin America, but throughout the under-developed world.

WHAT KIND OF INDUSTRIALIST?

The most successful industrial elites in Latin America are those which have thrived under stable political and social conditions of a non-dictatorial nature and where they are products of such stability. Several of these have developed since the war. What do some typical Latin American industrialists and company managers look like? How do they function as a part of their national society and what if any, are the distinguishing features between executives in different republics of the hemisphere?

Two features predominate. The first is that the "industrialist", or the "executive", or the *dirigente* as he is styled in Venezuela, is not necessarily functioning as such primarily in the private sector. In both Mexico and Venezuela he is more likely to be employed by the public sector in large, efficient and often profit-making companies owned and operated by the state. This is because the percentages of state-involvement in all kinds of industry from steel mills to theatre chains in these two countries is very high. This pattern is most advanced in Mexico where 82.2% of the top 30 enterprises are state-owned. Yet Mexican private capital invested in 14 of the 30 largest private firms holds 100% ownership of eight firms and majority control of three of six joint ventures.[4]

In some of the largest state-owned corporations in Latin America, such as Mexico's PEMEX, Petróleos Mexicanos, the government-run oil, gas and petrochemical combine, there is an advanced middle management of engineering, labor relations, production specialists all applying the techniques of private enterprise.[5]

Second, Latin America is politically composed of 20 distinct national entities, most of the larger ones containing obvious racial and social distinctions. The Mexican as opposed to the Chilean or Brazilian industrialist, shares some of these different characteristics. Indeed the difference between management in Mexico and Chile, two countries I propose to investigate, are much easier to define than, say, the differences between Canadian and American executives. This is true even though all four national groups widely employ American methods of operating a company and language similarities exist, Spanish with the Mexican and Chilean, English with the American and Canadian. Scholarly analyses of Latin American management concentrate primarily on Mexico, Brazil, Colombia, Chile, Venezuela. These are mainly American in origin. It does occur to a Canadian observer that some parallels based on racial and class origins seem to exist between Chilean and Canadian management.

MEXICO: MANAGEMENT IN A REVOLUTIONARY SOCIETY

For many reasons, chiefly related to a more stable, if not always compatible political system, the industrialist in Mexico is permitted to follow a smoother road and to develop individual managerial traits, as well as corporate ones, in a way not yet possible in other Latin American republics.

This is because contemporary Mexico is the political product of a long, institutionalized, but once violent and distinctly anti-managerial revolution, in

---

[4] Frank Brandenburg, *The Development of Latin American Private Enterprise* (Washington, D.C.: National Planning Association, 1964), 135 pp. See pp. 61–62 and chart on page 63.

[5] See the author's "Pemex at Twenty Five," *Fortune,* August, 1963, pp. 88–89, written after a two-week, nation-wide survey of Pemex installations and management, March, 1963.

which the relationships between the public and private sectors are worked out at each stage in a basically tranquil, if not always pragmatic manner. The executive in government as well as the entrepreneurs in private enterprise work within the most advanced economic and political structure in the hemisphere. The Mexican managerial elite has advanced far, thanks to and in spite of the long, revolutionary process.

On the one hand, there is the small band of still recognizable pre-revolutionary industrial families who survived the confiscatory period and whose wealth is diversified throughout private enterprise, largely as a result of the material needs of the middle class consumer whom the revolution produced.

There are those purely professional managers and executives who function either as self-made entrepreneurs or as appointed presidents of private and public Mexican companies. They are as distinctively a product of the revolutionary process as the middle class they serve and from which they have arisen. These fortunate men, distributed through such Mexican public and private corporations and foreign-owned subsidiaries as Cervecería Cuauthémoc, the Garza Sada-G empire, Sears Roebuck de México, Celanese Mexicana, PEMEX, Teléfonos de México, Anderson-Clayton, are graduates of Mexico's largest universities and technical institutes and are the upper echelon of white collar elite which flourishes in strength and confidence in Mexico's major industrial centres.

Public companies employ a sizable portion of them to manage concerns involved with textiles, steel, theatre chains, warehousing, airlines and railroads, utilities, chemical plants and state banks. Private enterprise techniques employed widely in the country's big public sector, are a sign of managerial maturity to an extent unparalleled as yet in any other emerging nation either in Latin America or elsewhere. At the same time, Mexico's continuous one-party political regime which has produced a succession of peacefully-elected civilian presidents since 1940, has helped to produce the only large indigenous industrial elite to emerge so far in modern Latin America.

Combined with the country's political leaders in Congress and in the *presidencia* the Mexican executive makes up an even wider elite of about 100,000 professional Mexicans in a nation of nearly 40 millions who control the destinies of a "guided democracy" by *ad hoc* decision-making and economic planning. They are all ideologically products of Mexico's socialist revolution, whether as self-made millionaires or as the senior bureaucrats of government and the top hierarchy of Mexico's public administration.

At the same time, the main point to remember is that Mexican management (including Mexicans in senior positions in foreign subsidiaries and joint ventures) are now "revolutionary" only in the sense of their loyalty to its nationalistic inspirations and to the system it has created, and not to any new form of violent change. The Chilean pattern of executive development in which landed families, mainly of European stock, changed functions from that of landowning oligarchs to liberally minded leaders of industry never existed in Mexico. The senior executive of Sears Roebuck de México, a foreign-owned chain store concern or of Nacional Financiera, S.A., the government industrial development bank, is distinctively Mexican in this sense.

In another sense, the development of purpose other than profit-making, he is radically different from the pre-Castro Cuban oligarch. "Not all Mexican entrepreneurs are exclusively or even primarily interested in pecuniary motives," says a U.S. scholar, "adventure, power, social justice, social prestige, nationalism, patriotism, achievement and social responsibility are added motives."[6]

With his indigenous strength, product of a social system of an advanced nature for Latin America, the Mexican executive is the farthest in time and development from the other struggling industrial elites in the rest of the hemisphere. Like them, however, he is an unmistakable product of urban change, growth and diversification. Beyond him as in every other Latin American republic, lies the still demanding and still unfulfilled agrarian reform program of his nation, where his type of management talent is desperately needed but where, as yet, it has been neglected—and dangerously so.

CHILE: HOW LONG FOR THE "ARISTOCRATIC" INDUSTRIALIST?

Chile, that slim nation, built and developed by a blend of European races, with a delicately-poised democratic ideology, has produced a management elite, different in many respects from its counterpart in Mexico. The names of German, French, Italian, Irish, Jewish as well as distinguished Spanish families proliferate among Chilean executives. Indeed with the exception of nearby Argentina, where a similar pattern exists, this multi-racial quality is the outward and visible distinguishing mark of the Chilean industrialist. The inner, less visible one, is that of a liberally minded aristocracy of landowners and mild-mannered oligarchs moving of their own slow accord into the contemporary world of modern management methods and persuaded to do both by their country's needs and by the early dissemination of basically U.S. managerial techniques among them.

The arrival of visiting seminars organized by the American Management Association in 1956 and of U.S. management experts in Chilean universities, sparked the beginning of an American-oriented and inspired class of Chilean industrialists and managers, most of whom were already well-established in Chilean public and private enterprise. The slim victory of President Arturo Alessandri in 1958 over strong leftwing elements, linked together political stability and managerial science, because a lenient, pragmatic federal administration borrowed the best managers from industry to speed up the state's industrial diversification programs.

The Chilean executive became further "modernized" through the foundation of smoothly-running but small management institutes. There are at least five of these, the most important being ICARE (Instituto Chileno de Administración Racional de Empresas). The Chilean Institute for the Rational Administration of

[6] Frank Brandenburg, "The Case of Mexico: A Contribution to the Theory of Entrepreneurship and Economic Development," *Inter-American Economic Affairs*, Washington, Vol. 16, No. 3 (Winter, 1962), p. 21.

the Enterprise. ICARE was born as a result of a meeting between Chilean and U.S. management training experts associated with the Council of International Progress in Management in New York in the mid-1950's.

The brink at which Chilean management stands is similar but not parallel to the one facing Venezuelan management, the anticipated success of extremist leftwingers with an avowed determination to nationalize the total economy. In Chile, if it comes, it will come incredibly enough through the ballot box. In Venezuela, the only way it will come, will be through violent overthrow of an elected democracy.

One of the great advantages shared by Chilean management in so quickly founding a modern executive element from an upper class born to old-fashioned privilege, is the basically legalistic nature of Chilean society where change and alteration have come through agreement and bargaining, both vital factors in scientific management methods. This in turn has made the Chilean industrialist basically a non-political person in the Latin American sense of the word (but rather more like the Canadian executive whose politics a few years ago were taken more or less to be Liberal because so many of them had served a long-lived Liberal Government in war time and peacetime advisory capacities). [7] Because of this non-political nature and because of his ability to adapt professionally without political bias, the Chilean executive is in much demand throughout the Americas.

Chilean government experts from CORFO, the 26 year-old Chilean Development Corporation founded in 1939 to diversify Chilean industry, advised the Venezuelan Government when the Guayana Development Corporation was formed in Carácas in 1960 to open up the vast, underdeveloped Orinoco provinces of Venezuela. Chilean corporation lawyers serve throughout the hemisphere as consultants on the tangle of labor law which plagues new and old industries in Latin America.

In spite of all these factors, the question still begging an answer is whether the Chilean executive and industrialist, in spite of their changing role, have penetrated or influenced Chilean society deeply enough to be considered a legitimate liberalizing factor by the substantial "have-not" groups in Chile. If not, they will still look to demagogues and extreme socialist answers to end their poverty.

BRAZIL: SUCCESS AND FAILURE IN BRAZILIAN MANAGEMENT

The Brazilian executive appears to be more intimately committed to his cultural heritage than his compatriots in Hispanic America. In many Spanish-

---

[7] See the author's "Growing Manager Class in Chile," *Executive,* May, 1964, pp. 68–72. The Chilean periodical press recently carried public comment by some of the country's leading industrialists about their lack of political persuasion or political interest. In *El Mercúrio,* Santiago de Chile, January 10, 1964, appears an unusually frank interview with Luis Marty D., a former assistant finance minister, now director of several private companies and president of ICARE, in which he frankly admits to "political illiteracy." See "Presidente de ICARE, 'Soy Analfabeto Político'."

speaking Latin American republics the management methods of the open North American business society are in conflict with violent social revolutions or are the prey of harsh decrees of greedy militarists.

In Brazil, they are often swallowed up by the languid, compromising "wait-and-see" attitude tactics of an ancient Portuguese civilization, part African and part Arabic. As a result in Brazil, the management philosophy of the Anglo-Saxon American and the value system of the Portuguese Brazilian-American, are more inclined to blend than to conflict.

Lingering, deep-set paternalism not only dies slowly in Brazilian industry; but in some instances it finds new and inefficient leases on life when the attitude of *patrão* to worker, developed in an agrarian society, are carried over to the modern company's production line. This benevolence and failure to impose sound management principles, are most noticeable in Brazil's ailing public sector where the lack of them have made a shambles of most of Brazil's public companies. Competition to meet the restless needs of a literally exploding urban consumer class, compels private enterprise to become efficient and has forced many companies to acquire, rather quickly, North American management practices.

The main impetus for change, is, of course, the United States-owned subsidiary which in most Brazilian manufacturing industries plays a dominant role and often has secured a lion's share of the domestic market. About 600 United States' subsidiaries, with a book value of nearly $2 billions, form the backbone of modern private enterprise in Brazil. Along with them, hundreds of smaller and often less capable Brazilian-owned enterprises and a handful of giant Brazilian family company-empires—Chateaubriand, Klabin, Matarazzo—feed a growing and assured market.

The successes of the private sector (as opposed to the almost consistent failures of the public one) are undoubtedly aided and abetted by the oligopolic nature of Brazilian private enterprise. The Chateaubriand press holdings, still in disarray, once included 31 newspapers, 12 TV stations, 22 radio stations, 4 magazines, several coffee plantations and related non-publishing concerns to make up a huge family empire of 59 companies, once owned virtually by one man.

The electronics industry, the newest pace-setter and entirely in private hands, includes about 80 firms. But the big five, SEMP, 100% Brazilian-controlled and the Brazilian subsidiaries of General Electric, Standard Electric, Philco and Phillips, dominate the industry. Brazilian Traction, Light & Power Co., a Canadian-owned giant utility, is the largest foreign-owned company in Brazil. In terms of book value, two of its Brazilian subsidiaries, São Paulo Light and Rio Light are the fifth and seventh largest companies in Brazil.

Foreign-owned, but curiously enough, not Brazilian-owned oligopolies, have been open to constant attack from nationalistic and leftwing politicians and have, as a result, experienced piecemeal and arbitrary "takeovers" of their operations in remote provinces of Brazil. This has been especially true for foreign-owned utility companies. The strange prospect of native Brazilian industrialists make allegiances with socialist politicians to legalize nationalization procedures against their powerful, foreign-owned competitors, is not uncommon in Brazil.

The most tawdry example of public mismanagement is PETROBRAS (Petroleos Brasileiros), the Brazilian Government's hard-pressed petroleum monopoly. Not far behind was Panair do Brasil, one of Latin America's oldest airlines and founded in 1929 which was terminated in late February by President H. Castelo Branco with the write-off of the airlines $66.7 million deficit. No Latin American public petroleum corporation, with the outstanding exception of Mexico's giant and impressive PEMEX, (Petroleos Mexicanos) on which PETROBRAS is supposed to be modeled and Chile's smaller ENAP, have efficient management or operations. In spite of substantial earnings (PETROBRAS grossed about $345 millions in 1962), PETROBRAS' management have squandered human and financial resources on courses of action taken for purely and simply political, not professional reasons.

PETROBRAS is an unqualified mess. Since 1953, only one petroleum engineer has been its president. Two recent former presidents were political cronies of former President João Goulart. The first, Francisco Mangabeira, was the son of Goulart's Justice Minister. The second, Field Marshal Osvino Alvês, a Goulart crony, was an extreme leftist, better-known by his detractors as "the people's general." An earlier PETROBRAS' director during the Janio Quadros administration held the single qualification of having captained the presidential excursion boat! Only one president in recent times, General Albino Silva, tried to stem its internal corruption, reduce the bloated working force and cut the stranglehold of leftwing labor leaders. He was forced out of office.

As indicated earlier, the patriarchal element in contemporary Brazilian management has survived with greater influence and more strength than within most management elites in Spanish-speaking Latin America.

Under it, the Brazilian *fazendeiro,* assumed a father-like responsibility and direction over his tenants and their families. But there were not the hard lines of class distinction between worker and *patron* which existed in the harsher Spanish-American rural societies. "The Brazilian worker identifies himself not with the physical property to which he was attached," says a U.S. observer, "but with the personality of the patriarchal owner to whom he was a ward. This cultural characteristic of a sense of attachment of the employee to the *patrão* is carried over from the plantation to the production line. [8]

Both the U.S. executive in Brazil who comes neither from an elite ruling class in America, nor from an agrarian background, and the Brazilian immigrant manager, *arrivista,* usually a European from an urban industrial center, have found these values difficult to accept and hard to displace. American and European plant programs emphasize productivity techniques, such as merit ratings, wage systems. These take time to penetrate and to have effect in Brazil. For many native Brazilian industrialists, a laborer is a fixed asset, whose output can be easily increased only by hiring more of them.

In contemporary Brazil, the impact of an efficient, purposeful, culturally blind and largely immigrant industrialist class, is alien to old-fashioned family

---

[8] Gileno de Carli, *O processo histórico da usina em Pernambuco,* Rio de Janeiro, 1942.

managers who want to run an inherited family factory employing the familiar worker–manager relationship of the rural *fazendeiro*. Mixed feelings of shock and isolation springing at them from past and present experience, make change a slow and complicated process.

In Brazil's colonial and imperial periods, the old ruling class had strongly sensed their removal and their physical distance from the great intellectual world centers. The Portuguese language, went the old saying was, "the tomb of thought." In contemporary terms, it is perhaps hard for them to see it as a logical vehicle for the new technology.

Thus, alienation and withdrawal as experienced by many Brazilian executives—historic elements in Portuguese societies—play a more complex role in retarding rational management methods in Brazil than have so-called "Spanish pride" and conservatism in the Spanish-speaking republics of the Americas.

Those Brazilian managers who remain uncertain about their role and function in the new Brazil seek refuge and some prestige from *jeitinhos,* "finding little solutions," but purposely avoid trying the big problems which they know would bring them into contact with solutions outside their experience.

All these cultural conflicts create elements of frustration, delay and compromise in business relationships which perplex the forward-looking, often impatient foreign executive in Brazil. In spite of it all, he remains optimistic about the prospects for wide acceptance and use of modern business methods in the potentially most dynamic Latin American national society.

VENEZUELA: WHAT ROLE FOR THE MANAGEMENT MIX?

Venezuela's short-run experience with democratic government, begun in 1959, has permitted an executive class in both private enterprise and the public sector to develop and flourish as never before. The major source of managerial training, management principles, will continue to be the large, foreign-owned extractive and manufacturing industries which dominate the country's economy.

As a result, Venezuela's pressing need for trained managerial talent is making Carácas, the capital city, a hub of international management with individuals drawn from the huge foreign subsidiaries which still dominate industry and from the rest of Latin America. Executive talent from Mexico, Chile and from the exiled Cuban communities in Florida and throughout the Caribbean converge on Carácas and the growing industrial towns throughout the republic.

Such firms as Creole Petroleum Corporation, with its very advanced management programs (both for its own requirements and Venezuela-owned private enterprise) or Chrysler de Venezuela which concentrates on middle management, such as dealer operations, are developing an executive strata at a considerably faster rate than among many other foreign subsidiaries throughout the Americas.

Yet Venezuela's major crisis for the future—apart from the political one of restraining pro-Castro and right-wing extremists from turning Venezuela into a barracks again—will be a supply of adequate managers to widen secondary manufacturing in the private sector and open up the interior for the public one. The management mix of public and private managers is not hard to define. The country's own native-developed pool of well-trained executives are still concentrated within local Venezuelan-owned industrial consortiums, raised by both the Sosa Rodríquez and Mendoza corporate groups and which are solely committed to private enterprise.

In a country where 70% of secondary manufacturing outlets are dominated or owned by the state, and where government's Guayana Development Corporation, the largest industrial development agency in South America, is in full swing, the dearth of managerial ability is already serious. It is obvious in both the classic sense and in the local context.

In the classic sense, it means having enough trained managers to raise economic goals through efficient production of state and privately-owned corporation to meet the pressing needs of Venezuelan consumers. The paradox of Venezuela's under-population compared to Brazil's which is ten times as large, is that Venezuela cannot wait as long as Brazil to complete industrialization programs. First, Venezuela's still weak evolutionary democracy cannot endure either the political or economic shocks which Brazil, because of her size, has been able to survive.

After the overthrow of the extremist Goulart regime in Brazil on April 1st, 1964, Venezuela, along with Chile, remains the greatest potential bridgehead for another Castro-style revolution if present economic growth programs for social democracy fail or falter seriously. Venezuela's small 8 million population must be among the first, not the last of South America's larger republics to benefit from the creative and productive skills of a trained and capable management elite.

In the short term, the intense shortage of these skills under the present urgent circumstances, has already made Venezuela one of the leading international "marketplaces" for the best managerial skills. The Cuban exiled businessman and industrialist, for example, is in great demand in Venezuela where he already dominates the radio and TV industry and is prominent in food processing and packaging firms.

Private enterprise expansion is also enhanced by the Venezuelan concept of building related industries and new communities in areas where urban development is retarded. In these so-called "industrial clusters," Venezuelan-owned plants manufacturing hundreds of consumer products, are often protected by 100% tariffs against foreign imports. These in turn form the basis for the exciting *urbanizaciones,* the Venezuelan version of the "company town" which with its managerial class to run local industry, is only coming into its own in this growing republic. In this sense, Venezuela's need for managerial talent, especially at "middle management" levels, is not unlike that of Canada's during her boom years of the early 1950's when expanding resource industries urgently needed technical manpower to operate new industrial operations.

CONCLUSION

Finally, the old way of doing things in Latin America, in spite of the current pressures for change, clings fast, reflected in the greed, inefficiency and cynicism of the old landowning classes. The new social revolutions move quickly, destroying these colonial vestiges and attitudes, bringing chaos and unfulfilled promises instead.

Between extremism and lethargy stands the industrialist and the managerial elite. Professionally, they are unable to apply the methods of either of the above extreme alternatives. *Latifundismo* and the open market are diametrically in opposition. Except in Mexico, no social revolution in the Americas has made its peace with private enterprise.

Thus the managerial elite rely on the patience and the success of both responsible leaders of the evolutionary democracies and on the slow maturing of changing social structures to give time to train the new generations of industrial leaders who can create the balanced Latin American economies of the future.

Additional References

Clements, R. V. *Managers: A Study of Their Careers in Industry*. London: G. Allen and Unwin, Ltd., 1958.

Editors of *Fortune* magazine. *Businessmen Around the Globe*. Englewood Cliffs, N.J.: Prentice-Hall, Inc., 1967.

Hanna, Willard A. "The Kulai Oil Palm Scheme–Landless Workers Become Prosperous Planters" (Malaysia), American Universities Field Staff Reports Service, Southeast Asia Series, Vol. 13, No. 1 (January, 1965).

Harbison, F., and Myers, C. "Management As a Class," *Management In the Industrial World,* Chap. 4, pp. 68–86. New York: McGraw-Hill Book Co., Inc., 1961.

"Identifying and Developing Managers: World Wide Shortages and Remedies," *Quarterly International Survey of Business Opinion and Experience,* June, 1965.

Kerr, C. *et al. Industrialism and Industrial Man*. New York: Oxford University Press, 1964.

Miller, W. (ed.). *Men in Business*. Cambridge, Mass.: Harvard University Press, 1952.

Newcomer, Mabel. *The Big Business Executive: Factors That Made Him*. New York: Columbia University Press, 1955.

Randall, Laura. "Class, Race and Economic Policy," *The Journal of Development Studies,* Vol. 2, No. 4 (July, 1966).

Ravenholt, Albert. "J. V. Garcia Homecrafts–Philippine Woodenware and Weaving Make a New Millionaire," American Universities Field Staff Reports Service, Southeast Asia Series, Vol. 12, No. 14 (December, 1964).

————. "New Engines in Old Trucks–A Master Mechanic Turns Businessman" (Philippines), American Universities Field Staff Reports Service, Southeast Asia Series, Vol. 15, No. 11 (December, 1967).

U.S. Industry: Under New Management, Scientific American study, 1966.

Warner, W. Lloyd, and Abegglen, James. *Big Business Leaders in America*. New York: Harper & Bros., 1955.

chapter seven

Education and Management

Modern industry rests on educated people. Basic skills in reading, writing, and arithmetic have become essential for even semiskilled work, and increased education is an important factor among management around the world. The character of this education influences the style, pace, and effectiveness of management. Selected readings examine these developments.

Selection: "Industrialization and Fundamental Education in Developing Nations," Margaret Mead

A selection from a United Nations study reports on the development of broad education in industrializing nations.

Selection: "Higher Education and the Level of Economic Development," Frederick Harbison and Charles A. Myers

A critical factor in individual and collective business success is education, as the preceding selection indicates. Basic grounding in primary skills for the general working population is essential to begin industrializing. Secondary school technical training and university experience facilitate the process and provide managers. In this reading, the well-known economists survey advanced educational facilities available in countries in different stages of economic growth.

Selection: "Heroes, Homework, and Industrial Growth," William F. Whyte and Robert R. Braun

In a Chapter Five reading by David McClelland, we saw the critical role of achievement motivation in management and economic development. The authors suggest that in many countries schools often actively discourage the traits most important to entrepreneurial success.

247

Selection: "The Renaissance of Foreign Business Schools,"
Alan B. Coleman and Dan Throop Smith

Many of the readings on managerial philosophy and practice have pointed to the distinction between the "art" and "science" components of management—with the latter component holding attraction mainly for the United States until recently. Consequently, management education largely has been restricted to the United States. The authors of this selection from the *M.B.A.* suggest that other nations are changing their views on the possibility and desirability of education in management.

Selection: "Europe's Business Schools: A Good Start, But . . . ,"
John Hutchison

A sympathetic Columbia University professor finds much that is good in continental business education—much more that bears correction.

selection 17

Industrialization and Fundamental Education in Developing Nations*

Margaret Mead

Until recently, the need for literacy was considered one of the most pressing in under-developed countries. But the concept has now been broadened, and literacy is regarded as the tool of education in all areas of life. As long as the function of education was to maintain and pass on to the new generation the traditions of a culture, its skills, knowledge, and principles of inter-personal conduct, its religious tenets and values, there was no need for literacy, nor for education provided and stimulated by outsiders. Parents and other relatives educated the child in his cultural heritage by giving him increasing participation in the work involved in making a living, in community work and ceremonials,[1] as well as by giving him specific instruction. In some societies this training was supplemented by attendance at community schools for boys or for girls at special periods of their lives, often at adolescence, for the teaching of the special

---

*From *Cultural Patterns and Technical Change* (New York: New American Library, 1955), pp. 252–62.

[1] Richard C. Thurnwald, 1935, pp. 236–38.

knowledge needed to enter adult status. In either case, the function of education was the inculcation of the established tradition.

With the impact of civilization, and particularly because of contact with Western culture, the function of education has necessarily changed. The need now is to move away to new knowledge and skills, to a new place in a new social order; education is now not for the maintenance of the old, but for change. Whether these cultures have sought Western contact or not, whether they want to change or not, the fact is that they have felt the effects of Western contact, and must now be taught how to cope with these effects. The roads built to outlying villages have brought money wages to the people for building them, trade goods on which to spend them, and often the destruction of native industries with which these goods competed, thus taking away the livelihood of the craftsmen. A desire for trade has become an incentive for cash crops, introducing an imbalance in the agricultural process which has often robbed the land of its fertility and even of its soil, and in the diet, bringing malnutrition. A lack of understanding of the principles of money and credit has led to indebtedness and loss of lands. Along the new roads new diseases travelled, while the medical aid to combat and prevent them lagged far behind. Sometimes, as in Indonesia and the Philippines, when civilization brought its sanitation, its laws, and at times its religion, this has meant a large increase in the population, on land inadequate to support it by using traditional agricultural methods.

Education is needed in all these areas to cope with and repair the destruction already introduced; and beyond this, to make it possible for the peoples, if they choose, to take their place in the community of nations, and to take advantage of the progress of science and technology in improving their standard of living.

If the new education is to fill the place of the old, it has to cover all areas of living. Native education included all growing-up: it gave instruction in interpersonal relationships, soil conservation, and ways of making a living.[2] The task of fundamental education is to cover the whole of living. In addition, it is to teach not only new ways, but the need and the incentive for new ways. For the control of water-borne disease, for example, we must teach villagers not only how to boil their water or dig wells and install pumps; we also have to teach them how to recognize the need for this, to stop accepting all water as "water-and-therefore-good"; to recognize that *some* impurity in the water makes it bad and dangerous to health.[3] It is not enough to offer a change or an improvement; it is necessary to teach a dissatisfaction with the picture of health which includes some trachoma,[4] some infant diarrhoea, some infant death, as a matter of course.[5] It is not enough to introduce co-operatives or techniques involving co-operation; it is necessary also to teach the people to recognize as valid the created group, and to organize in terms of future benefits rather than according to established community patterns.

---

[2] Robert Redfield, 1943, pp. 642–45.
[3] Edmund de S. Brunner and others, 1945, pp. 98–99.
[4] *Ibid.*, pp. 94–95.
[5] Florence Kluckhohn, 1941.

For many years schooling was not only ineffective, but also disruptive, because it was applied only to the young. Roles were reversed in the home, so that the children became the teachers of the parents, creating confusion in relationships, and resentment on the part of the displaced leaders. A "younger" generation in conflict with an "older" generation was created where there had been no such categories. In some societies, where the structuring of authority was felt strongly, the responsibility placed on the young to teach the old created insupportable conflict for them. Children, taught in school not to spit on the floor, to take baths regularly, to be inoculated against epidemics, lived in homes which taught the opposite. [6] With the new conception of education as covering all areas of living came the recognition of society as the unit to be educated. In China, the mass-education programme initiated by James Yen was directed at adult groups as well as children, and covered simplified reading and writing as well as public health, agriculture, and similar areas. [7]

In the United States, and increasingly in other countries, it has been the function of the Extension Service of the Department of Agriculture to educate in areas of life other than literacy. In many countries now fundamental education is carried on by teams including social workers, graduate nurses, agricultural assistant, home-economists, hygienic experts. [8]

In past years, as Margaret Mead says, education of dependent peoples was for the purpose of their successful exploitation by more advanced economies. [9] It is now recognized that the dependent and under-developed peoples will have to be given education in literacy so that they can participate in the larger world-community. They have to be given the grasp of the framework of the economy of the civilized countries, an understanding of money and credit and the ideas of pure number involved therein, and some grasp of the implications of living by contract rather than according to established relationships. [10]

A number of factors must be taken into account in introducing literacy. The main one is the conceptual framework and the structuring of knowledge and relationships within the society. For example, when American teachers had their Samoan pupils skip a grade at school, parents were ashamed, since precocity is decried in Samoa. [11] When American teachers tried to spur Hopi and Navaho children through introducing competition, or to encourage by singling out for praise, they failed in the first case and caused intense misery in the second, since to stand out is painful and brings insecurity. The dichotomies and dualisms employed by some cultures are meaningless in others, and to present dualism as oppositive is confusing in many Pacific cultures where dualism is complementary, enclosing a whole. Concepts of success and failure are in the pattern of Western

[6] *Fundamental Education*, 1947, pp. 84–85.

[7] *Ibid.*, p. 82; Pearl S. Buck, 1945.

[8] Elisabeth S. Enochs, 1943, pp. 20–24; *Fundamental Education, op. cit.*, pp. 40–43; D. Spencer Hatch, 1944, p. 57; Ofelia Hooper, 1943, p. 252; Helen A. Kitchen, 1950, p. 5.

[9] Margaret Mead, 1946, p. 346.

[10] *Ibid.*, pp. 347–49.

[11] *Ibid.*, p. 349.

education; but in certain parts of the Orient, a "failed" A.B. is a classificatory statement of achievement.[12]

In addition, there are many questions of procedure. Should we teach literacy in the vernacular or in some world-language? To what extent should we develop principles and standards of literacy which we apply on an either-this-or-nothing basis? That is, do we believe that some literacy is better than none? Who is to make the decision as to curricular needs, and upon what principle? How much school attendance constitutes literacy? Who is included? children? adults? men? women? What body of literature do we use for people whose tradition has been entirely oral? Do we introduce our own classics, as a mission school did on the African Gold Coast, which proudly announced that every year its students performed a Greek play with all the odes in the original?[13]

In French Africa the policy at first was one of assimilation, based on ideas of equality of all men "before the law and before the future." At this time the school was transplanted from France, with all its syllabuses and legislation; the native languages were discarded and forbidden.[14] More recently, the policy has been to educate an *élite* group inspired with French ideals of civilization, who can then occupy administrative positions; and, in separate schools, to educate the masses, mainly in areas of living. French is the medium of instruction in both types of school.[15]

In the Union of South Africa the colour bar, whether legislatively operative or not, means that there is no correspondence between attainment and reward.[16] It has been suggested, therefore, that because the great bulk of Africans are to be unskilled labourers, they should be educated realistically.[17] But this is not acceptable to the non-Europeans who want book-learning and want to be taught in English. The non-Europeans are not compelled to go to school, but they want to. Education represents to them the open sesame of progress. Their hunger for education is not met, however, as poor provision is made for their schooling.[18]

In many areas the introduction of a school system interferes with the established pattern of life. The Ngone of Nyasaland complain that their herds are in poor condition, since the boys who were the traditional herders now go to school.[19] In Basutoland and Bechuanaland there are twice as many girls as boys in school, as boys stay with the herds.[20] In some areas the level of health is too low to make school attendance easy; where there is little energy, as in many villages in India, the children are needed to do their share of the work.[21] In rural Mexico the children are said to have little energy because of inadequate

[12] *Ibid.,* p. 350.
[13] William Malcom Hailey, 1938, p. 1245.
[14] *Fundamental Education, op. cit.,* pp. 48–49; Hailey, *op. cit.,* p. 1219.
[15] Haily, *op. cit.,* p. 1282.
[16] *Fundamental Education, op. cit.,* p. 73.
[17] *Ibid.,* pp. 78–79.
[18] *Ibid.,* pp. 70–71, 76; Hailey, *op. cit.,* p. 1223.
[19] Margaret Read, 1938, p. 35.
[20] Hailey, *op. cit.,* p. 1255.
[21] *Fundamental Education, op. cit.,* p. 102.

diet; and they have to do hard work at home. Yet school often includes exhausting competitive games and gymnastics.[22] Turkey, faced with the necessity of establishing schools in its 40,000 villages, adapted school work to the seasonal occupation of its villagers, "and class work, apart from the time devoted to practical training, has been reduced to 18 hours weekly."[23] Under the rural reconstruction scheme for the Menouf District of Egypt it was agreed to introduce schools working on a "full day system by which the pupils spend the first half of the day learning theoretical studies and the second half in practical training."[24]

To make schools a successful medium for literacy, the people have to be educated in the meaning of literacy; their co-operation must be enlisted, and incentives must be found or created. In many cultures there is no understanding of the need for continued attendance. Children will stay home for the slightest indisposition, or to keep a sick brother company, or because of a visitor or some family undertaking.[25] In Guatemala the one-crop economy does not require literacy, neither does the Church emphasize the need to read the Bible; the people do not see why they should become literate.[26] In the villages of India the co-operation of the older women—the mother-in-law and the grandmother—must be enlisted before the girls can attend school. And incentives must be created, strong enough to counteract the loss of a son who cannot now help in the fields, and will later feel above such work and will probably take a job in an urban centre. If the school can promise enough literacy to enable the son to read needed literature aloud to his illiterate father, and keep accounts, continuing his share in the familial system of interrelationships, a father might find enough incentive to encourage his son's attendance, because in this way the education would be for the family's welfare; it would not lead to separation, individual ends, atomization.[27] In Lebanon a visiting emigrant endowed his village with a school without first educating the villagers in the value of literacy; in three years, the school was in disuse.[28]

School attendance is not enough for literacy; and literacy itself is a means to education. It is also necessary, therefore, to introduce high-speed printing-presses for inexpensive reading matter, and to see to it that it reaches the people. It is reported from a number of areas that illiteracy increases with increasing age, because of forgetting.[29]

In some cultures, literacy seems to be an end in itself, because of past tradition, when it was the prerogative of an *élite* group. Higher education in areas

[22] Alfredo Ramos Espinosa, 1942, p. 9

[23] "Education in the New Turkey," 1950, p. 4; *Facts on Turkey,* 1950, pp. 14–15.

[24] Rural Reconstruction Scheme at Menouf District, Egypt.

[25] Thurnwald, *op. cit.,* p. 239.

[26] *Fundamental Education, op. cit.,* p. 32.

[27] *Ibid.,* pp. 99–101.

[28] Brunner, *op. cit.,* p. 97.

[29] Frank Smothers and W. H. McNeill and E. D. McNeill, 1948, p. 117; Emilio Vásquez, 1943, p. 177.

involving manual labour is rendered useless by such attitudes. Agricultural schools in Burma and Latin America have not yet had sufficient effect in the agrarian picture because the graduates will not live with the peasants, will not soil their hands. After they study veterinary science or agronomy, they are ready to teach these subjects or work in laboratories, but not to set up demonstrations in rural areas or cultivate a demonstration plot.[30] In Panama teachers refused to help with sanitation problems; in the Netherlands Indies and Burma nurses refused to do rural work, since it involved manual work which in the urban hospitals was performed by menials.[31] In China higher education tended to create a group of unemployed, since it was beneath these people to accept any non-academic position.[32] Specific cultural attitudes may make for difficulties in the specific area of instruction. In Afghanistan anatomy has to be taught from charts and prepared specimens, as the religion does not permit human dissection or autopsy studies.[33] Where the native population had been assigned inferior status, higher education could not afterward be applied.

Fundamental education in living deals with a number of issues common to all areas. For example, co-operation in terms of new groupings and new ends is necessary to the introduction of new measures in land conservation and improvement, in agricultural mechanization, in production and marketing. For hygienic measures, co-operative participation is necessary before latrines will be built and used, since these are for the protection of others; it is needed for the application of general immunization, for quarantine measures on the local, national, and international levels, and for general hygienic precautions, as in food-preparation or garbage-disposal. The absence of such co-operative concepts is mentioned as an obstacle to industrialization.[34]

Experience has taught us that change can best be introduced not through centralized planning, but after a study of local needs. In China the mass-education programme was carried out by intellectuals who lived in the villages and learned the needs of the people.[35] When this principle is not followed, the education programme fails, or even works harm. In many Latin American demonstration farms, for example, ways of keeping records on the basis of tractors and combines are shown to farmers who use only a foot-plough,[36] and agronomists trained according to principles developed on the national level present to the cultivator material which is inapplicable on the local level.[37] In Indo-China, efforts at practical education in agriculture failed because they taught the value of fertilizer to people for whom it was too expensive to buy,

---

[30] Charles P. Loomis, 1950, p. 125.

[31] Hooper, *op. cit.,* p. 251; John Lee Hydrick, 1937, p. 49; Gordon S. Seagrave, 1943, pp. 44–45.

[32] *Fundamental Education, op. cit.,* pp. 85–86.

[33] J. C. Cutler, 1950, pp. 690–91.

[34] T. Bheemacharya, 1949, pp. 12–15.

[35] Buck, *op. cit.,* pp. 3–7.

[36] Loomis, *op. cit.,* p. 124.

[37] *Ibid.,* p. 125.

at a time when they had to pay interest at the rate of about 80 per cent for three months if they were to finance the purchase of fertilizer by borrowing.[38] Actual harm was done when cultivators in Burma were persuaded to weed their rubber plantations, and found that this reduced the sap; and when they were persuaded to do deep ploughing in the rice-fields and thus broke the pan that held the water.[39] Again harm was done when young Turkish farmers were persuaded, also according to generalized principles, to remove from their wheat-fields the stones which had retained the moisture.[40] When Spanish Americans in New Mexico were requested by the health authorities to dig wells through 15 feet of solid rock so as to avoid the contaminated water of the ditches, without the accompanying education needed in this particular culture, the well-water was soon found to be contaminated.[41]

Excellent results, on the other hand, are reported in cases where the programme of education was based on local needs. In the village of El-Manayel in Egypt the building of a schoolhouse, carried out on the basis of discussions with the villagers, according to specific local needs, meant village co-operation in the filling in of an unhealthy pond for the school site, the levelling of the village streets to get material for filling in the pond, and as an indirect result, better communication.[42]

When the specific needs of a locality or culture are discovered, it is often still necessary to teach the people to recognize them, and the desirability of improvement. Fellahin in a Middle East village had to be taught to see that trachoma was not part of the picture of health; their attitude was that trachoma was part of a normal life, that it had always been with them; and even blindness was something to take for granted, since it was "from Allah."[43] In most areas people cannot be motivated to adopt new ways on the basis of logical evidence of better results or of charts or scientific arguments. Most people fear experimentation, or fear excursions into the unknown, since only the tried is known and safe; as when, for example, Chinese farmers refused to hatch the high-quality poultry eggs they had been given in exchange for their own inferior kind.[44] Everywhere, however, demonstration techniques carefully carried out have been found to be effective; in the Middle East they are indispensable, and have worked even when religious tenets threatened the effectiveness of the programme.[45] Demonstration has been effective in India, Africa, Greece. Films of the entire process are sometimes effective, but only when they are taken against a local background.[46] Lambert showed New Guinea groups graphic

---

[38] Erich H. Jacoby, 1949, pp. 152–53.
[39] J. S. Furnivall, 1948, p. 327.
[40] Nuri Eren, 1946, pp. 282–83.
[41] Loomis, *op. cit.*, pp. 126–27.
[42] Mohamed M. Shalaby, personal communication, on introducing change into the rural Egyptian village of El-Manayel, 1939–44.
[43] Brunner, *op. cit.*, pp. 94–95.
[44] *Ibid.*, pp. 57–58.
[45] Shalaby, personal communication, *op. cit.* See also Marie Puhr, 1950.
[46] L. A. Notcutt and G. C. Latham, 1937, pp. 31–34, 52, 81; Loomis, *op. cit.*, p. 124.

representations of the progress of hookworm through the intestinal tract, with good results. In the Middle East, however, where "slowly-slowly" is a maxim, movies are not entirely effective, as they move too fast for people who have to mull over things.[47]

Sometimes the traditional is so highly valued that no change is accepted as improvement. Workers find it difficult to motivate people in Latin America in terms of future benefits or an improved standard of living; and extra cash income through wages or cash crops is not used to raise the standard of living because this standard is not valued. In some regions of Africa, to ask the people to reduce their herds of cattle for the sake of their own better nutrition, or to exchange them for better breeds, or to sell some for cash to improve their own living conditions, is like asking a mother to exchange her beloved child for a fairer or more robust one, or for two strange children.

Sometimes people resist new ways because the old have the sanction of the valued past or of religion. In such cases the worker often introduces change by using this sanction in support of it. When artificial insemination was introduced in Greece under the auspices of the Near East Foundation in 1945, the bulls were first blessed by high church dignitaries in the customary religious inaugurative ritual of "making sacred"; and women were persuaded to give their children the milk forbidden during Lent when Greek bishops themselves drank milk at this time. In Saudi Arabia the radio and telephone were made acceptable by first having verses of the Koran spoken over them.[48] In Lebanon the installation of a village pump which was needed to get uncontaminated water found sanction in quotations from the Koran to the effect that "cleanliness was required from every faithful Moslem";[49] and the Koran was likewise used to provide sanction for co-operation and land improvement.[50] When Kemal Ataturk made his sweeping changes in Turkey, he went about the village talking with the people and showing them that he himself practised these things; for example, before he forbade the wearing of the fez, he visited the villages wearing a hat.[51] In the Middle East the glorious past is also used as a sanction, and conversely, an enemy's tradition is applied as an adverse sanction. Kemal, for example, told the Turks that the fez was the distinguishing head-gear of the Greeks. A Greek manual addressed to mothers urges that they suckle their own babies like the Homeric heroines, and that they stop swaddling them, as in doing so they are following the barbarous custom of the ancient Romans.

In many societies impersonality is abhorrent, or, at any rate, ineffective. Workers have found that programmes have a far greater chance of successful acceptance if they are personally introduced by people who show real concern. The expert may be held in high esteem; but the change will be accepted because

---

[47] Brunner, *op. cit.*, p. 94; Shalaby, personal communication, *op. cit.*
[48] Carl C. Taylor and others, 1949, p. 19; Richard S. Sanger, 1947, p. 181.
[49] Brunner, *op. cit.*, p. 99.
[50] Afif I. Tannous, 1950, p. 269.
[51] Selma Ekrem, 1947, pp. 54–55.

of him, and not for its inherent merit; it will derive its validity through him, and the motivation for carrying it out will be rooted in loyalty to him: "I shall try it for your sake" is common phrasing in this situation. In the Netherlands Indies change was more readily accepted when the expert was physically and structurally on a level with the people, sitting as they did.[52] In Turkey and Lebanon, the expert comes in as a villager, cultivating his own land, building his own home, and teaching; his daily life affords a demonstration.[53] In China the forestry-planting expert who refused to go out to teach tree-planting in the rain lost out; and the professor who took his shoes off to work in the rice-seeding plot won.[54] The exact medium of communication may vary. There are groups where discussion has been the medium for reaching unanimous agreement.[55] In other cases, an oration may be more effective. Discussion may be merely a medium of entertainment and of the sharpening of wits. Questioning by the expert may be acceptable in some areas, and may be regarded with suspicion as prying in others. Or the questioning may itself be distrusted as a sign of ignorance by people who believe that the expert acts through divine revelation.[56] The words used by the expert have an emotional effect apart from their other content. An agricultural expert writing for specialists can speak without harm of the Scandinavian variety of cultured milk as "a thick, slimy product," and the Greek variety—that of his own culture—as "a custard-like curd of fine smooth, firm texture."[57] But in an educational situation, such linguistic discrimination may defeat one's ends.

The channel of communication also varies with the culture. In the United States the housewife has been the channel for nutritional education. In Latin American countries the co-operation of the community priest helps to accomplish a project of education in only a fraction of the time otherwise needed, and with more effectiveness.[58] Experience in fundamental education in a number of countries points to the importance of working through local leadership,[59] both for the acceptance of the project and for ensuring its continuing success. In Costa Rica the peasants look to both lay and church dignitaries for direction; but these must be their own dignitaries, with whom they are in an established *patrón* relationship.[60]

These are factors common to the introduction of change in most areas. There are specific factors to be considered in particular areas. Land reform, for example, has not always had the anticipated results because the people, as in Turkey in the nineteenth century, and in Mexico, had not been educated to proprietorship.[61] The attempt to teach isolation of the sick fails because it

[52] Hydrick, *op. cit.*, pp. 18–19.
[53] Eren, *op. cit.*, pp. 284–85; Kitchen, *op. cit.*, p. 34.
[54] Brunner, *op. cit.*, pp. 54–55.
[55] Ruth Benedict, 1943, pp. 103–5; Redfield, *op. cit.*, pp. 642–45.
[56] Alexander H. Leighton and Dorothea C. Leighton, 1944, p. 58.
[57] D. A. Soulides, 1949, pp. 10–11.
[58] Brunner, *op. cit.*, pp. 123–24.
[59] Taylor, *op. cit.*, pp. 15–19.
[60] Loomis, *op. cit.*, p. 91.
[61] Omer C. Stewart, 1950, p. 27; Nathan L. Whetten, 1948, p. 566.

cannot be presented in the name of either the individual or the family. Where the family is not a collection of individuals but a unit in its own right, what is good for one is automatically good for the family; and since it is good for the sick to have loving companionship, this cannot be bad for the family.

Finally, it has been proved by experience that the vernacular is the most effective and the most emotionally satisfying medium of instruction. In this way literacy is not merely associated with the foreign, but becomes an instrument in familiar life. Learning to read and write can be experienced within the security of the known, and the hurdle of a new medium need not be surmounted. And in educating in areas of living, the use of the vernacular provides the greatest facilitation, as it can express immediately the meanings and specific concepts of the culture. What is true of the vernacular is true of all aspects of living. Working through the known patterns and the existing social groupings has proved to be the most effective procedure in fundamental education.

selection 18

Higher Education and the Level of Economic Development*

Frederick Harbison and Charles A. Myers

THE UNDERDEVELOPED COUNTRIES (LEVEL I)

In our typology, the Level I [see Table 1 for levels] or underdeveloped countries are those whose economic and social progress is dependent upon the continued employment of foreign high-level manpower in a wide variety of core positions in major public and private institutions. The stage of development of their indigenous human resources is insufficient to permit these countries to move forward on their own. They are or shortly will be sovereign nations, and they all seek to enhance their international standing and prestige in the community of modern nations. They are traditional societies, but for the most part their ruling elites recognize that rapid economic and social progress is a political imperative of modern times. Thus, most of these Level I countries are on the move, and some have been growing rapidly in recent years. Without exception, however, they all need external aid as a spur for progress, and they all are face-to-face with the problems of how to retain or recruit foreigners for key positions, how to use them to train their local nationals, and how to dispense with them

* From *Education, Manpower, and Economic Growth* by F. Harbison and C. A. Myers. Copyright © 1964 by McGraw-Hill, Inc. Used by permission of McGraw-Hill Book Company.

TABLE 1

Countries Grouped by Levels of Human Resource Development
According to Composite Index *

Index	Per Capita GNP $ per Year		Index	Per Capita GNP $ per Year	
		Level I, Underdeveloped			*Level III, Semiadvanced*
0.3	NA	Niger	33.0	262	Mexico
0.75	55	Ethiopia	35.1	96	Thailand
1.2	60	Nyasaland	35.2	73	India
1.55	50	Somalia	35.5	431	Cuba
1.9	50	Afghanistan	39.6	293	Spain
1.9	170	Saudi Arabia	40.0	395	South Africa
2.2	61	Tanganyika	40.1	142	Egypt
2.6	NA	Ivory Coast	40.8	224	Portugal
2.95	150	Northern Rhodesia	47.3	357	Costa Rica
3.55	92	Congo	47.7	648	Venezuela
4.1	100	Liberia	48.5	161	Greece
4.75	87	Kenya	51.2	340	Chile
4.95	78	Nigeria	53.9	379	Hungary
5.3	105	Haiti	53.9	490	Taiwan
5.45	NA	Senegal	55.0	144	South Korea
5.45	64	Uganda	56.8	516	Italy
7.55	60	Sudan	60.3	265	Yugoslavia
			66.5	475	Poland
			68.9	680	Czechoslovakia
			69.8	478	Uruguay
			73.8	1,130	Norway
		Level II, Partially Developed			*Level IV, Advanced*
10.7	189	Guatemala	77.1	1,057	Denmark
10.7	131	Indonesia	79.2	1,380	Sweden
10.85	60	Libya	82.0	490	Argentina
14.2	57	Burma	84.9	726	Israel
14.5	239	Dominican Republic	85.8	927	West Germany
14.8	99	Bolivia	88.7	794	Finland
15.25	173	Tunisia	92.9	600	U.S.S.R.
17.3	108	Iran	101.6	1,947	Canada
19.5	73	China (Mainland)	107.8	943	France
20.9	293	Brazil	111.4	306	Japan
22.6	263	Colombia	121.6	1,189	United Kingdom
22.7	114	Paraguay	123.6	1,196	Belgium
23.15	172	Ghana	133.7	836	Netherlands
23.65	356	Malaya	137.7	1,316	Australia
24.3	362	Lebanon	147.3	1,310	New Zealand
24.4	189	Ecuador	261.3	2,577	United States
25.2	70	Pakistan			
26.8	316	Jamaica			
27.2	220	Turkey			
30.2	179	Peru			
31.2	156	Iraq			

*Composite index of human resource development is the arithmetic total of (1) enrollment at second level (high school) of education as a percentage of the age group 15 to 19, adjusted for length of schooling, and (2) enrollment at the third level of education as a percentage of the age group, multiplied by a weight of 5.

as soon as their services are no longer needed. In the formulation of any strategy of human resource development, therefore, the issue of the utilization of foreigners or "expatriates" is of paramount significance.

Typically, the Level I country is an agrarian society. The vast majority of its population is rural or nomadic. And most of the rural population is engaged in subsistence activities, contributing only marginally to the market economy. Those engaged in production of cash crops such as tea, coffee, cotton, fruits, or vegetables are a small minority. The so-called modern sector of the economy consists of the central government and its regional and local branches, a few large plantations, trading establishments in the cities and the larger villages, and some industries such as cigarette manufacturing, bottling of beverages, food processing, or an occasional textile mill.

Third-Level (Higher) Education

Higher education, of course, is available for only a tiny fraction of the population. . . . Some of the Level I countries such as Senegal, Liberia, Kenya, Uganda, Tanganyika, and Sudan have their own universities or higher technical colleges, but they also send students abroad for higher education. Others, having no higher-level institutions, send all their students abroad or to neighboring countries. In all of the underdeveloped countries, the number of persons with higher education and the number able to qualify for it are pitifully small. For example, Nyasaland with a population of nearly 3 million people had in 1962 only 46 Africans with university degrees, and another 48 who were enrolled in higher degree courses, all outside the country. In Niger, with a population of 2.5 million, there were about 140 students studying at higher institutions in nine different foreign countries.

The typical underdeveloped country faces a real dilemma in higher education. It is almost certainly cheaper to send students abroad for higher education, and the quality and range of foreign education greatly exceeds that which can be provided locally. But there are obvious drawbacks. The students are removed from the local environment for a long period, and often face serious problems of readjustment when they return after having been educated in a foreign environment. Some students may never return if they are attracted to better positions abroad. Many leaders of the underdeveloped countries feel that it is politically unwise to rely completely upon foreign institutions for the education of persons who are to fill the senior ranks of the country's future high-level manpower. And finally, a university is a highly important symbol of national prestige as well as a monument of local culture. The African countries in particular emphasize that a major purpose of local universities is to stress African studies and national needs, along with other subjects which are considered to be important in the international community of scholarship.[1] For these reasons, most

[1] See for example *The Development of Higher Education in Africa: Conclusions and Recommendations of the Conference on the Development of Higher Education in Africa* (Tananarive, September 3–12, 1962, UN/Ed. 62D.20/A, UNESCO, Paris), p. 21.

of the underdeveloped countries think that it is imperative to establish their own universities despite the tremendous expense involved, and many of their political leaders are determined to seek external aid and assistance to build them.

Where local institutions exist, the teaching staff of necessity is largely composed of foreigners. And here the expenses involved in salaries, housing, provisions for home leave, and other emoluments of faculty members are very high. Another factor resulting in excessively high costs is the small number of students who are qualified and who are willing to attend the local institution if given the alternative choice of studying abroad. For this reason, some of the universities which have lavish buildings and expensive faculties have enrollments far below the optimum capacity of their facilities, thus raising the costs per student even higher. . . .

Incentives and the Allocation of High-Level Manpower

Because all skills are so critically scarce, the educated local national is in a commanding position. Upon graduation from a university, he can "start at the top." Quite naturally, he prefers an administrative job in the city to a field assignment in some remote rural area. In nearly all countries, the educated classes prefer "not to get their hands dirty.' In the underdeveloped countries this tendency is magnified because educated persons are usually in a strategic position to control their assignment to jobs.

The distribution of high-level manpower, therefore, is far from desirable. It is concentrated in the cities, whereas the most critical needs, such as agricultural extension and community development, are often in the rural areas. And its occupational composition, moreover, is usually ill-suited to the country's needs. For example, engineers are in very short supply, but engineering technicians are even more scarce. The result is that engineers must perform work beneath their skills simply because there is little or no supporting technical personnel. Doctors are in short supply also, but there is even more critical need for medical technicians and nurses. And the doctors, in many cases, may be more interested in the lucrative practice for foreigners resident in the country than in the development of a public health service. Also there is a preference for administrative jobs over technical jobs because the former are thought to carry more prestige and authority than the latter. And finally, the contact with and lure of the advanced countries and the international agencies causes many of the more ambitious elements to look outside their country for even better opportunities.

In all the newly independent countries the costs of government, secondary and higher education, and top management in private enterprises are fantastically high in terms of GNP and the general levels of income of the people. As Arthur Lewis has said in referring to African countries: [2]

---

[2] W. Arthur Lewis, "Economic Problems of Development." Reprinted by permission of Dodd, Mead & Co., Inc., from *Restless Nations: A Study of World Tensions and Development,* by the Council on World Tensions, Inc., New York, 1962, pp. 68–85. Copyright © 1962 by the Council on World Tensions, Inc.

In Africa, salaries in the upper echelons are actually higher than in Europe, in terms not only of percentages but of absolute money. This is because Africa recruits its upper echelons in Europe and has to pay higher emoluments (not to speak of passages and leave) than Europe in order to attract. This goes pretty far down the scale. It applies not only to University graduates, but also, because secondary education is so poorly developed, to mechanics, nurses, bookkeepers, secretaries, and similar intermediate grades. In consequence, almost any operation costs more in Africa than it does in Europe.

Thus, the high salary structure (inherited from colonial times and perhaps even increased subsequently to independence in order to attract the new foreigners who may be needed to start new activities) is a handicap to development, particularly if local nationals receive the same pay as the foreigners they replace. And as Lewis has suggested, it is also one of the causes of wage inflation, since the luxury cars and spacious dwellings of the new elites are a perpetual incitement to the masses.

Another serious problem in these countries which insist on rapid localization of the government services is the "leapfrog dilemma." Because of the strong pressure, particularly from the "backbenchers" in political parties, local nationals with very little education and experience may be pushed into senior positions for which they are not well qualified, simply because well-trained people are not available. But they nevertheless acquire tenure in these positions. In time, other local nationals with superior qualifications emerge from the schools and universities but are forced to accept the inferior positions. This may result in a tragic waste of precious talent, low morale, and undermining of the efficiency of the employing organization.

THE PARTIALLY DEVELOPED COUNTRIES (LEVEL II)

The "partially developed" countries which fall into our Level II category might also be called "relatively advanced" underdeveloped countries. Quantitatively, they have traveled a great distance in human resource development. . . . The average Level II country has a secondary enrollment ratio 4½ times that of Level I; the third-level enrollment ratio is 11 times higher; the primary enrollment ratio is nearly 2 times higher; and the average value of the composite index is 7 times higher than that of the Level I countries. Although our measures of stock of high-level human resources are much less reliable for countries at these two levels, they indicate that there are 2 times as many teachers (per 10,000 population) in Level II as in Level I and 6 times as many physicians and dentists.

Indeed, there is a somewhat greater relative quantitative difference between Level I and Level II countries than there is between those in Level II and those in Level IV. For example, the average secondary enrollment ratio of the advanced countries in Level IV is only 5 times that in Level II: the higher education ratio is about 7 times more; the primary enrollment ratio is somewhat less than 2 times higher; and the value of the composite index is more than 5 times that of Level II. There are twice as many teachers in Level IV as compared to Level II and 5 times as many physicians and dentists.

These partially developed countries, for the most part, are still dependent upon the more advanced countries for critically needed scientific and engineering manpower. But they are able to produce the greater part of their own nontechnical high-level manpower, such as teachers, managers, and supervisors, with some assistance from advanced countries. Although the Level II countries may have started the uphill climb on the road to economic and political maturity, they are not as yet "over the hump." They are still unable to develop enough strategic high-level manpower (particularly engineers, scientists, and highly qualified teachers) to progress on the road to industrialization completely under their own power.

As in the case of Level I countries, there are wide differences among countries in the Level II category. Those in the lower part of the range, such as Guatemala, Indonesia, Libya, Burma, and Eastern and Western Nigeria, still have many of the characteristics of Level I countries. And those in the upper part of the range, such as Turkey and Peru, are approaching a state of near self-sufficiency in high-level manpower that is characteristic of the semiadvanced countries in Level III.

Third-Level (Higher) Education

The partially developed countries are perhaps relatively more advanced in higher education than in either primary or secondary. All the Level II countries have their own universities, higher technical institutions, and higher teacher-training colleges. In most cases, there is ample opportunity for well-qualified graduates of secondary schools to attend higher educational institutions either within the country or abroad. In contrast to some of the Level III countries such as India and Egypt, the universities normally are not yet overcrowded, because they are shielded to some extent by the secondary school bottleneck, which holds back the pressure of students for entrance.

The major problems in higher education are the following: (1) overemphasis on faculties of humanities, law, arts, and medicine and underemphasis on sciences and engineering; (2) low quality of education resulting from poorly qualified part-time teachers, inadequate libraries, and poorly equipped laboratories; (3) underdevelopment of intermediate technical and subprofessional education; (4) poor university organization and stultifying instruction; and (5) in some cases the dispersion or "Balkanization" of higher education among too many institutions and separate faculties. This is the general pattern for Level II countries, but there are significant exceptions, as we shall point out.

High enrollments in law, humanities, and art reflect in part the orientation of students towards white-collar employment and perhaps to a lesser extent reflect the cultural traditions of the countries. For example, an unpublished manpower report of the Federal Government of Nigeria observed that in 1962 each of four new universities was opening faculties of law, despite the fact that there are 1,213 Nigerian lawyers, half of whom are underemployed.

A major reason for expansion of law, arts, and humanities faculties, however, is the fact that places for students in these fields are the cheapest to provide.

As a general rule, nearly all teachers are part-time, classes are generally very large, and standards are very low. The cost of education per enrolled student in these fields is probably between one-fourth and one-sixth of that in medicine, the natural or biological sciences, and engineering. In most of the partially developing countries, therefore, the law, arts, and humanities faculties provide cheap and poor education for large numbers of students, and thus satisfy in part the demand for numbers of places in the universities.

The reverse is true of medicine. The training of doctors is very expensive, standards must be reasonably high, more competent teachers are employed, and classes are not as large. Normally, the best students seek places in the medical faculties, largely because doctors enjoy high status and have comparatively high incomes in the partially developed countries. But the number of places for students in the medical faculties is limited, so many must enter other faculties as a second choice.

The costs and the standards in the faculties of engineering and basic sciences, like medicine, are relatively high. But in the partially developed countries, careers in these fields are still somewhat uncertain, so frequently there may be unfilled places in the engineering and scientific faculties.[3] One may point out, of course, that these countries need more scientists and engineers for their future development, but as long as nontechnical, white-collar positions are readily available for university graduates at pay scales equal to or higher than those for scientists and engineers, students will naturally select the cheapest and easiest route to a degree, and this means enrollment in arts, literature, law, and more recently commerce. Thus the required expansion of scientific and engineering faculties is not likely to take place until the relative pay and employment opportunities for scientists and engineers are significantly greater than for nontechnical personnel.

It is generally true that university professors, particularly in the humanities, arts, law, and commerce devote very little of their time to teaching and research. Because of low salaries in the universities and great demand for educated manpower in the society, most university professors have several jobs. In some countries, they are felicitously called "taxi" professors because they spend their lives traveling from university classrooms to government offices or commercial establishments. The poorly equipped laboratories and libraries give them little incentive for research. Thus, although the university position provides status and prestige, it is for many faculty members little more than a means of "moonlighting." The situation of course is likely to continue as long as the universities are unable to offer salaries and research opportunities which would encourage greater commitment by faculty members. The simple truth is that the funds available to universities are sufficient only to provide cheap education. And if the countries in question must build and maintain a higher education system at

---

[3] In the Western Region of Nigeria, for example, the new University of Ife had an enrollment capacity of fifty for courses in agriculture. It offered admission to sixty-eight students, but the actual enrollment was only thirteen by the beginning of the year in October, 1962. Likewise, it had an enrollment capacity of eighty in its Faculty of Science, but only forty-one students of a total one-hundred-nine who were offered admission actually enrolled. (From an unpublished report by the Federal Government of Nigeria.)

bargain-basement prices, the part-time employment of well-qualified persons, even if they are taxi professors, is certainly justifiable.

Even the most superficial manpower assessments in the partially developed countries reveal that in terms of numbers the need for technicians and sub-professional personnel are far greater than for university graduates. In Iran, for example, there are seven times as many doctors as professional nurses.[4] Engineers often outnumber technicians by as much as three to one, although the desirable ratio may well be one to three. But as most people who have visited these countries have discovered, there is a dearth of post-secondary intermediate training institutions for almost all kinds of technicians and sub-professionals. In Colombia, for example, there were in 1962 only 1,150 students in subprofessional higher schools as compared with 23,000 students in the universities. The reasons are rather obvious. The intermediate institutions do not command the prestige of universities, and thus attract neither competent teachers nor good students. The pay and status of subprofessional personnel in these countries is beneath that of university graduates, and the universities usually have places for most secondary school graduates who wish to apply. If a secondary school leaver can follow the university route to a position of high-status and pay, he is reluctant to train to be a mere technician or agricultural assistant, particularly when the top command posts of government and industry may be reserved for university graduates. And finally, the institutions which are established to offer subprofessional-level work are likely to neglect their purpose in order to undertake higher work for professional qualifications and thereby attempt to transform themselves into full-fledged universities. Deploring this situation, the Ashby Commission complained: "The Nigerian technical institutes will undoubtedly be exposed to this temptation, but we say emphatically that it must be resisted. There must never be any doubt that the proper function of these important institutions is to train technicians. . . . Nothing must be allowed to deflect them from their purpose."[5]

It is our feeling, however, that the proliferation of subprofessional training institutions is a wasteful expenditure, unless and until fundamental changes are made in the pay scales, emoluments, and prospects for advancements of the subprofessional and technician groups. As the Ashby Commission again noted with respect to agricultural education, "We are in a dilemma, . . . because the chief weakness in the present system is not the agricultural schools but the reluctance of students to go into them."[6] Thus, to a large extent, it is the nature of incentives in the operation of the labor market, rather than the short-sightedness of educators, which explains the underdevelopment of intermediate higher education in most of the Level II countries.

---

[4] George B. Baldwin, "Iran's Experience with Manpower Planning" in F. Harbison and C. A. Myers, *Manpower and Education* (New York: McGraw-Hill Book Co., Inc., 1965), pp. 140–72.

[5] *Report of the Commission on Post-school Certificate and Higher Education in Nigeria* (Lagos: Federal Ministry of Education, 1960), p. 19.

[6] *Ibid.,* p. 21.

Poor administration and stultifying methods of instruction are characteristic of most of the universities in the partially developed countries. The following description of the University of Teheran is a good example: [7]

Teheran is organized on the lines of the 19th Century French universities: separate, large autonomous faculties covering each major subject-area; a notable absence of unifying administrative services giving leadership and coordination to the University; didactic instruction by lecture methods that emphasize rote learning; all-or-nothing testing through a single examination at the end of the year; few contacts between faculty and students; little reading beyond lecture notes, and a pattern of part-time service from faculty members who tend to regard their posts as bases from which to engage in outside employment that often gets the lion's share of their attention.

It is understandable that under such conditions the dropout rates are high, the morale of students is low, and student demonstrations and strikes are frequent.

The tendency to have too many universities and too many faculties is also a serious problem in some countries. For reasons of prestige, each region or province of a country may want its own university. Then each university tends to duplicate the faculties of the others. In poor countries, such diversification is wasteful and tends to raise costs and to lower standards of higher education in general. In Colombia, for example, it has been suggested that the elimination of half of the 138 faculties in twenty-five institutions would have a negligible effect upon the output of professional manpower, and by putting only a part of the resources these faculties consume into those which would remain, the output actually might be improved both quantitatively and qualitatively at a substantially lower unit cost. [8]

There are important exceptions, however, to these broad generalizations. China, for example, has geared its higher education to science and engineering and has downgraded work in law, humanities, and the arts. It has expanded greatly its professional faculties at the university level and increased even more rapidly the subprofessional institutions which provide training in a very wide variety of specialized fields. As described by one study: [9]

Chinese higher education today can truly be called an industrial education—a far cry from the classical and moralistic education of traditional China. What was once the land of philosophers and artists has been transformed into a huge throbbing plant of bustling technocrats. Eager engineers, active scientists, and busy industrial workers become the mark of the New China, while dreamy classical scholars in flowing robes have long since passed into the oblivion of history.

China, in fact, is the third largest producer of engineers in the world (after the U.S.S.R. and the U.S.A. in that order), with an annual output rate of 75 per cent of that of the United States! An even more remarkable fact is that 90 per cent of China's 250,000 scientists and engineers have been trained since the Communist

---

[7] George B. Baldwin, *op. cit.*

[8] Duncan Ballantine, "Education and Manpower Planning in Colombia" (essay in a forthcoming volume to be edited by the authors).

[9] Immanuel C. Y. Hsu, "The Impact of Industrialization on Higher Education in Communist China" (essay in a forthcoming volume to be edited by the authors).

take-over in 1949.[10] Yet, even with this tremendous leap forward, China apparently still has critical shortages of technical personnel at both the professional and semiprofessional levels, and the emphasis on quantity has apparently lowered the quality of higher education except in a few centers which are reserved for those with the greatest capacity to be outstanding scientists.[11]

In Ghana, Eastern and Western Nigeria, and Jamaica the universities have very high standards, full-time professors (many of them expatriate), and rather good laboratories and libraries. In these countries standards of entrance, courses, syllabi, and examinations have been developed jointly with the University of London, and more recently with universities in other countries. The number of students is small, and practically all are residents devoting full time to their studies. But this high-quality, low-volume residential university system is very costly. Indeed, in some cases it exceeds the cost of sending students abroad for higher education.

And finally, in those countries where the prevailing standards of higher education are low, there are some universities which are centers of excellence and innovators of educational reform. Institutions such as, for example, the National University of Engineering in Peru and the University of the Valley in Colombia have mostly full-time faculties, reasonably good libraries and facilities, and instructional programs which compare favorably with those in the advanced countries. And even in some of the large national universities which in general are noted for their poor standards, there are some individual faculties which are successfully raising the quality of education and adapting it to the country's needs for more well-educated manpower.

To conclude this sketchy analysis of higher education, we might say that in general the Level II countries have emphasized quantity at the expense of quality, and have underemphasized science and engineering and particularly technical training at the subprofessional level. But there are important exceptions to such generalizations. China has if anything overemphasized technical education; Nigeria, Ghana, and Jamaica have stressed high quality; and in nearly all of the other countries there are a few institutions and a small number of faculties which, seeing clearly the need for basic reforms, are making heroic efforts to bring them about. And finally, it is important to remember that all of the Level II countries send a substantial proportion of their eligible students abroad for higher education. Quite understandably, some of these sooner or later seek employment outside of the countries which send them. But those who do return and remain greatly enrich the quality of the local high-level manpower. . . .

Incentives and the Allocation of High-Level Manpower

In most of the Level II countries, the high-prestige occupations are not usually those most critically needed for development. Landlords, lawyers, governmental

---

[10] *Ibid.*

[11] For a comprehensive and penetrating analysis of professional manpower and higher education in China, see Leo A. Orleans, *Professional Manpower and Education in Communist China* (Washington, D.C.: National Science Foundation, U.S. Government Printing Office, 1960).

officials, owners of large family enterprises, and often military leaders enjoy both high status and political power. They are the elites. And access to their ranks is likely to depend largely upon political and family connections rather than demonstrated competence or high intellectual ability. The status of professional engineers and scientists is usually inferior, since in most cases they are employed and perhaps also managed by these elites. And in some countries, a so-called "humanitarian tradition" may strengthen the tendency to downgrade agronomists, physicists, chemists, and engineers. The status of technicians, agricultural assistants, nurses, school teachers, and other subprofessional groups is even lower, for in most cases they have little or no opportunity ever to rise even into the professional ranks. Professional managers in private enterprises, as distinguished from owners or family managers, are not very high either on the status ladder. The compensation of such professional and subprofessional personnel, as expressed in opportunities to receive emoluments and extra income if not in actual salary levels, tends to reflect these status differentials.

Doctors, however, generally enjoy both high status and unusually high incomes, and this explains why the best students try to enter the medical faculties and why university expansion in this area is usually much greater than in the sciences and engineering. And in many cases, the medical profession is a well-traveled route to high political office as well. The partially developed countries, therefore, do not need to take additional measures to persuade young men to become doctors.

A social structure of this kind obviously is an obstacle to growth along modern lines; and it must be drastically changed if the newly articulated goals of the partially developed countries are to be achieved. In China, of course, the required changes have been made in a completely ruthless and arbitrary manner. There, the scientist, the engineer, the technician, and the factory worker are glorified, and other "intellectuals" who are not members of Communist ruling elites are roundly castigated.

It should not be necessary, however, to resort to totalitarian methods to bring about the required changes in the social structure. Most of the advanced countries, and many of the semiadvanced also have been able to raise the status of the critically needed occupations without destroying free choice and individual liberty. And indeed, the very pressure of expanding industries and emerging development plans is beginning to force these changes already in many of the Level II countries. In the modern world, scientists, engineers, and even technicians, because of their scarcity and the mounting needs for their services, are increasingly able to command higher status and pay. And it is certainly in the interests of the partially developed countries that they be encouraged to do so. . . .

THE SEMIADVANCED COUNTRIES (LEVEL III)

In terms of human resource development, the average semiadvanced country in Level III has traveled about half the distance between the partially developed and the advanced countries. Its secondary school enrollment ratio is more than 2 times that of Level II; its third-level enrollment ratio is 3 times higher; its primary enrollment is 50 per cent higher; and the value of its composite index is 2½ times higher. There are over a third more teachers, nearly 3 times more physicians and dentists, and 8 times more engineers and scientists than in Level II.

On the other hand, the average secondary school enrollment ratio for Level III countries is less than half of that in Level IV; the higher education enrollment ratio is two-fifths, the primary enrollment ratio is four-fifths, and the composite index is two-fifths that of Level IV. The average Level III country has two-thirds as many teachers, half as many physicians and dentists, and nearly three-fifths as many engineers and scientists as has the average Level IV country.

The semiadvanced country can produce practically all of the high-level manpower that it needs (with the possible exception of scientific and technical personnel), and it may even export some to less developed countries. Although shortages of scientists and engineers persist, there are enough to permit the country successfully to import and adapt modern technology without substantial external help. Only occasional technical assistance is required for its industrial development. In short, the average Level III country is "over the hump" in human resource development. It is on the road to becoming an advanced country, and it can travel that road largely under its own power. Whether it does or not will depend upon its strategy of human resource development.

The quantity and quality of high-level manpower in the Level III countries, of course, are still far below those in the advanced countries. The semiadvanced country is a follower rather than an originator of scientific, engineering, and organizational innovations. Although it has a broad base of primary education, with generally well-developed secondary schools and some good institutions of higher education, it has not been able to develop the research manpower and research institutes which are characteristic of the advanced countries. And its manpower-building institutions, though capable of supplying critical minimum needs, are often improperly oriented to meet the challenges posed by rapid modernization. In some cases, too many people are being trained in fields for which the prospective demand does not match the supply.

As in each of the other categories, there is great variation among the countries at the lower and upper ends of the range. For example, Thailand, India, and probably Mexico are barely self-sufficient in high-level manpower resources, but Uruguay, Czechoslovakia, and particularly Norway are scarcely distinguishable from advanced countries. . . .

Third-Level (Higher) Education

Probably more than any other single factor, the system of higher education brings Level III countries into the "semiadvanced" group rather than in a lower level of human resource development. There are distinguished universities in such countries as Mexico, India, Egypt, Chile, Italy, Yugoslavia, Poland, Czechoslovakia, Uruguay, and Norway. But within the group, the quality of higher education is uneven. Student enrollment ratios by fields of concentration give some indication of balance or imbalance relative to the high-level manpower requirements of economic and political modernization.

For example, 51.5 per cent of the students in higher education in Uruguay were enrolled in humanities, fine arts, and law, or almost ten times as many as in scientific and technical faculties. In the Communist countries, of course, the proportions are almost exactly reversed; Czechoslovakia had 46 per cent in scientific and technical faculties and only 6.4 per cent in humanities, arts, and law. Norway is a good example of a more balanced country: about 40 per cent enrolled in each group. The imbalance in India has already been mentioned: 27 per cent in scientific and technical fields and 58 per cent in humanities, arts, and law. Even more unbalanced enrollments are found in Spain and Costa Rica, while Egypt, Portugal, and Greece, among others, appear to have developed a better balance between fields.

The high concentration of the Communist countries in higher education for science and technology is, of course, a reflection of the educational philosophy and goals of the Soviet Union. . . . Nevertheless, there have been indications of dissatisfaction within at least one of these countries about such excessive concentration. Since part-time or full-time employment in industry is often combined with secondary technical and higher technical education in the Communist educational system, fundamental and theoretical training in science and mathematics may be neglected at the secondary level. The result is that some students cannot master university-level science and engineering studies. In Czechoslovakia, for example, there has been considerable discussion in the press about the problem, and one publication reported that "the average drop-out rate at the technical colleges is 65–70 percent and 60 to 70 percent at the other universities.[12] The lack of secondary school training in the humanities was also said to handicap subsequent performance at the universities.

On the other hand, the difficulty in countries with a high proportion enrolled in fields not closely related to economic growth is clear. They have not sufficiently modernized their traditional systems of higher education, which were designed to train an elite group either for colonial government administration (as in India) or for government of fairly static dynastic societies (as in some Latin American countries and Spain and Portugal). Admittedly, many of these countries have more recently expanded their university systems to accommodate the vastly increased numbers of students clamoring for places. But too often they have also lowered their admission standards, crowded their classrooms and inadequate laboratories, resorted to part-time and underpaid professors, and continued the traditional teaching methods which involve large lectures and rote memory of facts regurgitated in subsequent examinations. This is undoubtedly an overdrawn

---

[12] Reported in *The New York Times,* January 14, 1962, p. 6. In Poland, however, the complaint seems to be that university science is devoted too much to purely theoretical inquiries, and not enough to applied science and the training of competent technicians and engineers. *The New York Times* (Western edition) December 18, 1962, p. 7.

characterization, more applicable to Level II countries than to those in Level III; but the quality of higher education in Level III is still far below the average in Level IV.

The experience of Indian colleges and universities is almost a prototype of these problems. So a brief review of historical developments may be helpful. Higher education was a major force in attuning Indians (and other South Asians) to the values of the West under colonial rule. The British developed a top-heavy educational system in India, emphasizing higher education for a few rather than primary schools, and modeling Indian universities after English universities by emphasizing humanities and liberal arts rather than science and technology (of which there was precious little in England at the time anyway). "This philosophy fitted in well with the growing need in the late nineteenth century for English-speaking Indians and Ceylonese who could step into low-ranking administrative posts in government and business."[13] It must be added, however, that the British also opened their own universities and the British Civil Service in India to the brightest and ablest young Indians, with the result that the new Indian nation inherited perhaps the most competent government administrative service of any ex-colonial country. Thus, despite all its faults, the British-inspired university system did produce an important part of the high-level manpower subsequently required by India after independence in 1947. Earlier, the establishment in 1857 of universities at Calcutta, Madras, and Bombay also contributed importantly to India's subsequent political and economic development.

During the post-Independence period, there has been a phenomenal expansion. In 1947 there were nineteen Indian universities; in 1960–1961 there were forty-six, including an institute of medical sciences and an institute of technology. In addition, as "institutions of higher education," there were 1,316 affiliated colleges, eighty-three recognized graduate research institutions, and "581 institutions of higher education which were not affiliated to any university."[14] Presumably, among the latter were some ninety-seven engineering colleges.[15] The number of students enrolled in college and university courses in arts, science, and commerce during the Second Five-Year Plan period (1955–1956 through 1959–1960) increased nearly 50 per cent, from 634,000 to about 900,000, although the proportion of science students fell during this period.[16]

[13] Myron Weiner, "The Politics of South Asia," in Gabriel A. Almond and James S. Coleman, *The Politics of Developing Areas* (Princeton, N.J.: Princeton University Press, 1960), pp. 175–76.

[14] *A Review of Education in India, 1947–61*, First Year Book of Education (New Delhi: Ministry of Education, Government of India, 1961), p. 806.

[15] "Technical Education," in *A Draft Outline of the Third Five-Year Plan* (New Delhi: Planning Commission, Government of India, 1960), pp. 105–8.

[16] "One of the main tasks in the third plan will, therefore, be to expand the facilities for the teaching of science, the aim being to raise the proportion of science students to about 40 per cent. This is essential for meeting the increased demand in a number of different fields, science teachers for schools, students for engineering and other technical institutions, industries, etc. The proposed target can only be achieved if early efforts are made to provide increased facilities for laboratories and to obtain the personnel for teaching." "University Education," in *A Draft Outline of the Third Five-Year Plan*, p. 103.

The consequent overcrowding of Indian colleges and universities, the poor quality of much teaching, the low salaries for professors and lecturers, and the poor discipline of some students have been continuing causes for concern in the Indian press over the past decade, and have engaged the attention of the Government (through the University Grants Commission, the Ministry of Education, and the Ministry of Scientific and Cultural Affairs) as well as of university authorities.[17] While some improvements have been made, the difficulties are vast. Moreover, as secondary education expands, there is continuing clamor for places at universities, with the result that the University Grants Commission was considering the possibility of setting up twelve new universities during the Third Plan period.[18] At the same time, it recognized the need for "selective admissions" to discourage ill-prepared and immature students from seeking to continue their education in the colleges and universities when "some other form of training would be far less frustrating and more fruitful."

Unfortunately, the B.A. (even if failed) is thought to be the passport to job opportunities in India, although unemployment among poorly trained graduates is still very high. And the lack of student discipline continues.[19] Until there is more widespread recognition that college or university education is not a universal human right, and that some students should be educated in other fields by other means at India's stage of development, the difficulties will continue. Quite possibly, scientific and technical education at all levels has not received enough emphasis in the Third Plan,[20] and progress in higher education generally is further complicated by the debate over the use of "regional languages" at the college and university level as an alternative to English. . . .

In Latin American countries such as Mexico, Venezuela, Chile, and Uruguay, . . . the higher educational systems reflect Spanish as well as French university influences, with the intellectual environment "far more humanistic and artistic than scientific.[21] In the past, higher education has been restricted to an elite class; but pressures for expansion have been growing as the number of secondary school graduates has increased. Between 1940 and 1957, for example, enrollments in higher education in Chile increased 145 per cent. Yet only 1.2 per cent

---

[17] For further discussion of these difficulties, see S. N. Mukerji, *Education in India Today and Tomorrow* (Baroda, India: Acharya Book Depot, 1960), pp. 206–29.

[18] *Indian Express* (New Delhi), July 20, 1962, p. 7.

[19] "Students have demanded reduction in fees, free entry to cultural shows or tournaments, admission of undeserving students to the universities, the dismissal of some teachers, banning the publication of a report or book, the cancellation of action taken by invigilators for adoption of unfair means in examinations, etc. When the university authorities refuse to accept their demands, they start strikes and hunger strikes, stage processions and meetings, and indulge in defiance of law and physical violence which have ultimately led in some cases to police intervention and closure of the universities. This is a sad story and continues to repeat itself." Dr. K. L. Shrimali (later Union Minister of Education), quoted in *A Review of Education in India, 1947–61*, p. 814.

[20] This was the view of the Union Minister for Scientific Research and Cultural Affairs. *Hindu Weekly Review*, October 31, 1960, p. 11.

[21] George I. Blanksten, "The Politics of Latin America," in Almond and Coleman, *op. cit.,* p. 471.

of those who start primary schools enter the universities, and about 40 per cent of these fail to complete a degree.[22] Less than one-sixth were enrolled in scientific and technical fields. Even though Chile has some very good universities and technical institutes, the total number of engineers graduated annually increased only 132 per cent from 1940 to 1959. This was less than the total increase in all higher education enrollments. In some technical fields, such as agronomy, at least one student strike occurred in protest against outmoded teaching.

Similar student protests have taken place in other Latin American countries, and were not always politically inspired. Even in Italy, for example, architectural students at the University of Milan ended a twenty-one-day stay-in strike in March, 1963, after the faculty had accepted "their demands for harder class-work, stiffer examinations, lectures by successful practicing architects and a voice in arranging their college curriculum."[23]

Limitations on access to higher education, and the crowding and consequent poor quality of instruction, have led students in some Level III countries to go abroad for advanced training. This is certainly less true than of students in Level II or Level I countries, but it persists where the system of higher education is not yet adequate to meet the needs of a semiadvanced country. The OECD report on Greece, for example, comments: "A major indication of the need for rapid and balanced planning of university development in Greece is that a high, and growing proportion of Greek university students go abroad for their studies."[24]

This pressure for expansion of the system of higher education is also found in Level III countries at the upper end of the range. A report by the Norwegian Ministry of Education in March, 1961, recommended doubling the normal capacity of institutions of higher learning over the next decade, and pointed out that half of this expansion was necessary if students already enrolled were to complete their work under existing conditions of study.[25] In particular, the report recommended expanding enrollments at the Norwegian Institute of Technology, partly to accommodate some of the 1,200 Norwegian students studying engineering in other countries. (This is despite the fact that Norway has one of the highest stocks of engineers and scientists, per 10,000 population, in the world.) The situation was even more critical in Yugoslavia, despite doubling of enrollments in higher education in the five years preceding 1960–1961, with a larger increase in engineering than in other subjects. This rapid expansion has

---

[22] Rudolph C. Blitz, "Some Observations on the Chilean Educational System and Its Relation to Economic Growth" (paper for Conference on the Role of Education in the Early Stages of Economic Growth, University of Chicago, April, 1963), pp. 9–10. (Mimeographed.)

[23] *The New York Times* (Western edition), March 8, 1963, p. 8.

[24] *Country Reviews: Greece*, pp. 11–13. The number of Greek students studying abroad for all degrees was 31 per cent of the number in Greece in 1955, and by 1958–1959 it had risen to 33 per cent.

[25] *Country Reviews: Norway*, pp. 17–19.

strained existing facilities, and there has been a continued shortage of able teachers, especially in scientific and technical subjects. Resort has been made to part-time teachers; there are also many part-time students, some of whom are employed in industry and are taking university-level work after working hours, without requisite secondary education.[26]

The Yugoslav experience, oriented toward the requirements of national planning in a Communist society, is paralleled in part by developments in Poland since 1955. Up to that time, the emphasis was on training technicians for rapidly developing heavy industry, with a crash program in vocational training concentrated between 1950 and 1952. But a changing emphasis in Polish economic planning on consumers' goods, services, and research called for more emphasis on higher education to produce graduates "required to staff the expanding research institutes, the educational establishments and the growing facilities of the national health service."[27] There was also "a determined shift of emphasis in higher education from classical studies to technological ones. . . . It resulted from the need to provide new industries with qualified engineering and technically minded managerial personnel."

There may be some question about the quality of scientific and technical courses in higher education when there is a large proportion of students enrolled in these faculties. We have noted the overcrowding of laboratories and technical facilities in several countries, and there may be a consequent wastage or dropout of students beginning their education in these fields. Many fail to pass their examinations. A study in India in 1953 by the Planning Commission showed very high wastage rates during the first year in such fields as mechanical and electrical engineering, mining and metallurgical engineering, and civil engineering. The rates were slightly lower in the second year, and once they got beyond this hurdle they were fairly likely to finish their degrees or diplomas.

Finally, as a part of higher education in some of the Level III countries there is increasing emphasis on graduate training and research in science and technology. Furthermore, advanced scientific and technical research institutes have been established in some countries because there is need for research and development related to their industrial development. It is no longer so necessary for a less advanced country today to develop its own science and technology, but it is essential that it have trained scientists and engineers, with access to good research and development facilities to adapt scientific and technical discoveries and innovations from the advanced countries to their own economies and industries. These advanced research institutes are also one means of developing employed manpower.

---

[26] *Country Reviews: Yugoslavia,* pp. 12–13.

[27] *Report on the World Social Situation: Planning for Balanced Social and Economic Development in Poland* (New York: Department of Economic and Social Affairs, United Nations, December, 1960), p. 53. (Mimeographed.)

Incentives and Allocation of High-Level Manpower

In contrast to salary levels for village–agricultural program personnel, the salaries paid to high-talent manpower in science, engineering, and managerial positions in most of the Level III countries are sufficient to attract young people to train for these fields. The prestige of the technically trained men is high, and professional management is more highly regarded as a career than in less developed countries. Government administrative posts also carry high prestige and salaries, but they are no longer the sole high-status occupations. Indeed, government salaries may now be lower than in other professions requiring equivalent education and skills. We have already noted this tendency for agricultural extension and community development salary levels. It also exists in other government services as opposed to government administration.[28]

The shortage of teachers, particularly at the critical secondary and higher education levels, is a consequence in many countries of inadequate salary levels and other perquisites. For example, the average annual income per employed person in India in 1955–1956 was 700 rupees per year (about $34), while the average annual salary for primary school teachers in 1956–1957 was Rs. 694 and middle-school teachers Rs. 834. Secondary school teachers earned Rs. 1449, and most college and university professors two or three times more. But within the fields of higher education, professors in commerce faculties (already producing too many graduates) were paid average annual salaries of Rs. 4240 while engineering and technology professors received an average of Rs. 3960 annually.[29] These salaries, however, are quite inadequate to attract and hold enough competent teachers, especially in the science and engineering fields where alternative employment opportunities are available. Those who cannot move to other positions are forced to supplement their incomes by tutoring, writing, and selling lecture notes, etc.

The phenomenon of part-time teachers at the university level, meeting crowded classes during the morning or evening and holding down other jobs in government or in a profession, is a common one in Latin American countries. It has been estimated that in Mexico the proportion of such part-time professors in colleges and universities is as high as 70 per cent. Until the financing of higher education provides more adequate faculty salaries, the full-time teaching staffs

---

[28] For example, in Chile, several hundred trained nurses are said to have left for the United States "because there are not decently paid jobs for them at home," despite the need for improved medical services. "The reason it is difficult to squeeze an adequate salary for such purposes out of the government's budget is, in almost every case [in Latin America] that the budget is already overloaded with the cost of under-paying masses of underemployed officials who have obtained their jobs, in one way or another, through political patronage." A. Shonfield, *The Attack on World Poverty* (New York: Random House, Inc., 1960), p. 5.

[29] From data specially computed by the Perspective Planning Division of the Planning Commission, Government of India, August, 1962. We are indebted to Pitamber Pant, chief of this division, for preparing these data. It must be remembered that the annual salary for commerce faculty professors would average less than $74 a month!

found in higher education in most of the advanced countries will be slow in developing. . . .

THE ADVANCED COUNTRIES (LEVEL IV)

The typical country in the fourth level of human resource development is an advanced industrial economy. It is capable of making major scientific, techno- logical, and organizational discoveries and innovations. This is because it has a relatively large stock of high-level manpower, particularly scientists, engineers, and managerial and administrative personnel. It has made a heavy commitment to education, especially to higher education, and to human resource develop- ment generally. Since rapid changes in technology affect skills and occupations at all levels in the advanced industrial country, education and training tend to be geared to flexibility rather than to specialization.

. . . Here we find the industrial countries of Western Europe, the U.S.S.R., Japan, and the United States. Some contrasts with the data in other levels will show how far the advanced countries have progressed in the development of their human resources.

As measured by the composite index, the average Level IV country is 38 times higher than the average Level I (underdeveloped) country and 2.3 times higher than the average Level III (semiadvanced) country. The measures of stock of high-level human resources show the following comparisons: (1) in the num- ber of teachers (primary and secondary) per 10,000 population, Level IV is near- ly 5 times higher than Level I, and 50 per cent above Level III; the number of scientists and engineers per 10,000 population is 70 times higher in Level IV than in Level I, and 70 per cent higher than in Level III; (3) there are 70 times more physicians and dentists than in Level I and almost twice as many as in Level III. If quality differences were taken into account, these differences would have been considerably greater.

Measures of educational development show narrower differentials, but they are still substantial. For example, Level IV countries have over 3 times more students enrolled in first-level (primary) education (as a percentage of the age group 5 to 14) than do Level I countries, and about one-fifth more than Level III countries. The adjusted secondary school enrollment ratio is 22 times higher in Level IV than in Level I and more than twice as high as in Level III. The third-level (higher) education enrollment ratio in the advanced countries is 7 times greater than in the Level I countries, and over twice as high as in the Level III or semiadvanced countries. Even the percentages enrolled in scientific and technical faculties are higher and those enrolled in humanities, fine arts, and law smaller in the advanced countries than in the countries at lower levels of human resource development. Finally, the advanced countries spend over 1 per cent more of their national income on public education than do Level III coun- tries, and percentagewise this is nearly one-third more. . . .

Third-Level (Higher) Education

Higher education in the advanced countries is one of their distinguishing features. Quantitatively, enrollments as a percentage of the age group 20 to 24 averaged over twice as many as in the Level III countries, and ranged from 6.1 in West Germany to 32.2 in the United States. But this does not show that German higher education is the poorest among the advanced countries, or that the United States system is necessarily the best. So it is essential to go behind the data and ask, How have the systems of higher education in the advanced countries evolved? Are there patterns of development, and what significance do these have for the modernizing countries?

In their earlier years, the higher education systems of nearly all of the advanced countries were classical. Some, like those in Western Europe, antedated the industrial revolution and were primarily directed toward the education of an elite group: the clergy in Oxford and Cambridge as early as the Middle Ages and young English gentlemen beginning in the sixteenth century;[30] teachers and writers in the École Normale Supérieure in Paris; and philosophers and scholars in the German universities. The early colleges in the United States such as Harvard were at first primarily for the education of the clergy and the liberal professions. In short, higher education at the early stage had little science, practically no technology, and resisted any taint of "vocationalism."

Gradually, this united front gave way to a growing concern for science and industrial development in the countries of Western Europe, as well as in the United States. Perhaps the initiative did not come directly from industrial employers as much as it did from the students, who sometimes pressed for instruction in fields not offered in the traditional curricula. Whatever the reason, the first chair in science was established at Cambridge about 1764, and subsequently this university became a leader in scientific research and education in Great Britain. Earlier, the German universities were apparently the first to begin the serious study of science, and some German technical institutes were established before industrialization began in Germany.[31] Technical and engineering faculties were established at British universities, according to one account, because the British saw their lead in world history narrowed by Continental countries where

---

[30] Mark H. Curtis, *Oxford and Cambridge in Transition, 1558-1642* (London: Oxford University Press, 1959), p. 262.

[31] "It was from professorial chairs rather than associations of professionals that German scientific and engineering advances were made." W. H. G. Armytage, *A Social History of Engineering* (London: Faber and Faber, 1961), p. 188. Among the higher technical institutions established in Germany before her industrial revolution were the Academy of Mining in Freiburg in 1766, the School of Industrial Design at Chemnitz in 1796, and the Technical College of Dresden in 1828. W. H. Dawson, *The Evolution of Modern Germany* (New York: Charles Scribner's Sons, 1916), pp. 98-101. Dawson sums up the subsequent impact of this early start in the following words: ". . . when industry stood on the threshold of a new era, destined to prove more brilliant than any in the past, when the incalculable value of chemistry as a marketable science was beginning to be recognized, and electricity was proving its illimitable possibilities as an economic agent, Germany more than any other European country found itself fully equipped by education for entering upon a fierce competitive struggle, under entirely new conditions, for the economic mastery of the world" (p. 95).

technological education was more advanced.[32] The École Polytechnique was established in Paris in 1795, although its highly selective student group probably made only a limited impact on the total industrial development of France.

All of these changes extended higher education to students interested in science and technology, but they still reflected the elitist character of the educational systems of Western Europe at the time. For example, there were only 14,000 students enrolled in *all* German universities in 1870, 33,000 in 1900, and 45,000 in 1907.[33] The pre-World War I German university drew its students primarily from the upper strata of German society. In France, the situation was even more extreme; since their establishment the three grandes écoles have had highly restricted though brilliant student groups.[34]

Democratization of Higher Education

The German university system, with its stress on research, influenced the development of new universities in the United States such as Johns Hopkins, Cornell, Chicago, and others. But there was another development of equal or greater importance. Higher education was made available to more young people earlier in the United States than in Western Europe. This democratization was a distinctive feature of American higher education, and other countries have tended to follow this leadership. The recognition that ability to profit from higher education is not confined to certain classes in the society was an important lesson in the historical development of advanced societies, and they benefited from the additional high-level human resources which an expanding system of higher education provided.

There was an elitist character about higher education in the United States in the early years, but this changed dramatically with the passage of the Morrill Act of 1862, which encouraged the states to establish so-called "land-grant" colleges and universities. While there were a few state-supported colleges earlier, the Act was a turning point in higher educational development. In the words of one

---

[32] Sir Eric Ashby, *Technology and the Academies: An Essay on Universities and the Scientific Revolution* (London: Macmillan and Co., Ltd., 1958). Alfred Marshall also commented on the relationship between German scientific education and industrial development, although he rather deplored the narrowness of German university training: ". . . there are some reasons for doubting whether the average student at a German university is as well taught, or takes his studies as seriously as the average student at English universities. . . . But most of the vast number in German universities (some 65,000) get so far in touch with scientific studies that in after life they are inclined to take seriously any scientific issue that impinges on their business; and they then find some five thousand chemists ready to respond to invitations to earn their livelihood by special skill." *Industry and Trade* (London: Macmillan and Co., Ltd., 1919), p. 130.

[33] Fritz F. K. Ringer, "The German Universities and the Crisis of Learning, 1918–1932" (unpublished Ph.D. thesis presented to the Department of History, Harvard University, September, 1960), Table 1, p. 8.

[34] Only 458 students were reported as admitted in 1962. "The defect of all the grandes écoles is the defect of all French higher education: the number of graduates is far too small for the needs of a rising industrial nation. Only 3% of French students enter universities; only a handful of those reach the grandes ecoles; the bright children of workingmen and peasants rarely get through the sieve." *Time*, February 1, 1963, p. 69.

writer (on the occasion of the 100th anniversary of the Act), "Undoubtedly the scientific, technological and technical development of the past 100 years has been largely due to the emphasis on science and technology in American higher education which in turn stemmed largely from the land-grant college movement.[35] The Act provided grants of United States government lands to each state for the support of at least one college "where the leading object shall be, without excluding other scientific and classical studies . . . to teach such branches of learning as are related to agriculture and the mechanic arts . . . in order to promote the liberal and practical education of the industrial classes in the several pursuits and professions in life."

This revolutionary concept challenged the established university fields and was designed to broaden access to higher education to young people who heretofore had been denied it. There had been a few Mechanics Institutes in the 1820s in the larger cities; the University of Vermont began to offer civil engineering courses in 1829, and Rensselaer Polytechnic Institute awarded degrees in science and engineering in 1835.[36] Harvard and Yale established small engineering schools in 1847. With a few other exceptions, these were the only breaks with the traditional classical pattern until the Morrill Act of 1862.

It may be argued whether this Act was a response to the growing industrial revolution in America or whether there was an early recognition by Congress of the importance of providing industrial and agricultural leadership for subsequent development of the country. In any case, there was a close connection between the land-grant college movement and the emerging American industrial society. "The proliferation of railroads, canals, and roads and the development of the telegraph increased the need for technicians and technically trained managerial talent.[37]

By the 1850's the industrial potential of the United States was as apparent as its agrarian past, and there emerged a growing awareness that a new age required new training and new preparation. What were lacking, however, were any certain institutional foundations upon which to erect programs of agricultural and mechanical training as well as any deeply held respect for expertness. . . . Popular northern and western hostility to any kind of higher education had to be overcome. There was a deeply American ring to the insistence of the senator from Minnesota that "we want no fancy farmers; we want no fancy mechanics."[38]

While the land-grant colleges were slow in getting started and in being accepted, there is no doubt that by 1900 or 1910 most of them had made a substantial contribution to the improvement and modernization of American agriculture.

---

[35] Oliver C. Carmichael, "A Hundred Years of the Land-grant Movement," *Saturday Review*, April 21, 1962, p. 59. For an excellent historical discussion, see Allan Nevins, *The State Universities and Democracy* (Urbana: University of Illinois Press, 1962).

[36] G. Ross Henninger, *The Technical Institute in American Education* (New York: McGraw-Hill Book Co., Inc., 1959), p. 2.

[37] Richard Hofstadter and C. Dewitt Hardy, *The Development of the Scope of Higher Education in the United States* (New York: Columbia University Press, 1952), p. 27. See also Nevins, *op. cit.*, p. 60.

[38] From *The American College and University: A History*, by Frederick Rudolph. Reprinted by permission of Alfred A. Knopf, Inc., New York, 1962, pp. 248 and 250.

This occurred in part through the establishment of agricultural experiment stations attached to the colleges, and later agricultural extension programs to help farmers to apply new knowledge in practical ways.[39] Strong departments and colleges of engineering, particularly in newer fields like electrical, mechanical and chemical engineering, and metallurgy, developed in such institutions as Massachusetts Institute of Technology, Cornell University, Purdue University, and Pennsylvania State University. The first two were privately established, but received land-grant support.

Expansion of the land-grant colleges and universities was paralleled in the United States by the growth of other new institutions and the democratization of the older established universities. By 1962, 4.6 million students were enrolled in American colleges and universities for full-time or part-time work toward degrees. About 2.76 million of these were enrolled in public institutions, and 1.84 million in private colleges and universities. There were 2,040 universities, colleges, and junior colleges,[40] and in addition, there were nearly 150 technical institutes offering two-year programs beyond secondary school.[41] An outstanding example of a state system of public mass higher education (for tripled enrollments by 1975) is the California Master Plan of a three-tiered system of universities, state colleges, and two-year junior colleges.

While these developments were taking place in the United States, the British system of higher education also experienced dramatic changes. The "monopoly" of Oxford and Cambridge was broken by the establishment of London University in 1828. With all of its affiliated institutions, it became the largest British university. London inaugurated "external degrees" (for nonmembers) and "so provided a ladder for the next 12 modern universities to climb up to full university status."[42] The first of these were Manchester (1851), Wales (1872), Birmingham (1880), Liverpool (1881), Leeds (1874), and Sheffield (1879). These are the so-called "red brick" universities, and they were established in the major industrial centers, partly to bring higher education to those who could not gain admission to the older universities, and partly in response to the needs of a growing industrial society with many overseas commitments.

Simultaneously, technical institutes developed outside the university system in Great Britain. Their origins were in the Mechanics Institutes established between 1823 and 1850, although technical colleges and what came to be known

---

[39] The Morrill Act was supplemented in 1887 with the Hatch Act providing for agricultural experiment stations and in 1914 with the Smith-Lever Act for farm and home demonstration agents.

[40] "The Magnitude of the American Educational Establishment," *Saturday Review,* September 15, 1962, p. 55 (data based on latest available estimates from the U.S. Office of Education and the National Education Association).

[41] G. Ross Henninger, *op. cit.*

[42] "Universities," *The Observer* (Education Section), November 4, 1962, p. 12. See also George Louis Payne, *Britain's Scientific and Technological Manpower* (Stanford, Calif.: Stanford University Press, 1960), chap. v, "The Universities," pp. 151–91; and George E. Kneller, *Higher Learning in Britain* (Berkeley, Calif.: University of California Press, 1955), chap. iv.

as "polytechnics" did not develop until the period 1870–1905. "Whiskey money" (from excise taxes on liquor) was used to establish many of these during the Victorian era.[43] Subsequently, after the 1944 Education Act, there was a major expansion, including the establishment of a limited number of Colleges of Advanced Technology "in which there should be developed technological courses of a standard comparable with that of university degree courses." The importance of these technical colleges can be seen in the reported fact that 20 per cent of newly qualified scientists and 70 per cent of qualified engineers come up through nonuniversity channels in Great Britain.[44]

Despite these advances, there has been continuing concern with the state of higher education in Great Britain. For example, the Provost of King's College, Cambridge, said in 1963: "We have not yet begun to realize what vast numbers have got to be given higher education. We are still thinking in terms of an elite. We ought to think of at least 25 percent of our adolescents as fit to receive full-time training of some kind or other."[45] A special committee headed by Lord Robbins was appointed by the government in 1962 to make recommendations or improvements in the higher education system. The clamor for university admissions led the Labor party to propose in 1963 a plan for creating forty-five new universities—more than double the present number—within the next twenty years.[46]

Similar developments have occurred in other advanced countries. In France, for example, university enrollments (excluding the grandes écoles) have risen from about 139,000 in 1951–1952 to an estimated 241,000 in 1961–1962. According to one report, the relatively rapid growth in French secondary and higher education is explained by the demand for skilled and highly skilled manpower, and the changed attitude of parents toward financing further education.[47] The number of higher educational institutions in Japan increased steadily from around 1893, with the most rapid growth during 1913–1923 when Japanese industry was also expanding.[48] The educational reforms beginning in 1947 affected mainly the primary and secondary levels of education, although there were also some American-style changes in the university system. Admissions increased sixfold between 1947 and 1958 (although not as much as the applicants for admission) and by 1960 there were 245 Japanese universities with

---

[43] P. F. R. Venables, *British Technical Education* (London: Longmans, Green & Co., Ltd., 1959), p. 6. This summary of a longer study by Venables, and Payne *op. cit.,* chap. vi, "Non-university Channels to a Technical Education," have been drawn upon for this section.

[44] Payne, *op. cit.,* p. 193. By the end of 1957, 30,459 students were enrolled in its colleges of advanced technology, and this was one-fourth as many as in all British universities.

[45] Noel Annan, quoted in *The Times* (London), February 19, 1963, p. 12.

[46] *The Observer* (London), January 10, 1963, p. 1. Also, *The New York Times* (Western edition), March 8, 1963, p. 8.

[47] Raymond Poignant, "Establishing Educational Targets in France" (paper presented at Training Course for Human Resource Strategists, Frascati, Italy, September, 1962) (Paris: (Paris: OECD, 1962), pp. 10–12.

[48] After a visit to England in 1872 (four years after the Meiji restoration) a Japanese delegation recommended the establishment of an engineering college in Tokyo, which subsequently had a British principal and professor (Armytage, *op. cit.,* p. 233).

nearly 1.25 million students.[49] Nevertheless, the proportion of students enrolled in higher education was still below the average for advanced countries, and Japan was planning further expansion of its higher education system.

Finally, the Russian system of higher education has had a tremendous expansion, particularly since the war. As in Western Europe, the university system under the Czarist regimes was elitist; between 1755 (when the Imperial University of Moscow was established) and the end of the nineteenth century, only eight universities were established, in addition to some polytechnics or technical institutes. Under Communist rule there were twenty-nine universities by 1940–1941, thirty-three by 1950–1951, and forty by 1958–1959. The number of students enrolled during that period rose 280 per cent to 213,000, of whom 12,000 were part-time evening students and 78,000 part-time extension-correspondence students. A notable feature of the Soviet higher educational system is the relative increase in part-time and extension-correspondence programs since 1955.[50] In addition, there are some 656 "institutes" which offer professional degrees, as well as four-year higher Party Schools.

Much of the Soviet system of higher education is directed toward the production of the types of scientific, professional, and administrative personnel needed in the Soviet society. Of 346 known specialties offered in higher education as of January, 1959, 181 were in engineering and other industrial field specialties, 12 in agriculture and forestry, 41 in economics and jurisprudence, and 106 in education.[51] Altogether, 2,267,000 students were enrolled in all types of higher education in the U.S.S.R. in 1959, with the university enrollment as such representing less than 10 per cent of the total. Not only is Soviet higher education excessively specialized, but half of it is also part-time. Shortages of manpower and a belief in the value of work-study programs have led Soviet educational planners deliberately to hold down the number of *full-time* enrollments to around 1.1 million to 1.2 million since 1955. The resultant quality of education may have suffered.

Increasing Emphasis on Certain Professional Fields

The preceding review of higher education in advanced countries has also pointed to the growing importance of education for science and technology. This is a continuing need at all levels of human resource development, as we have seen; but once they reach the advanced group, countries are not spared the continuing effort to keep abreast of the demand for scientific and technical manpower.

---

[49] *Education in Japan: Graphic Presentation, 1961* (Tokyo: Ministry of Education, 1961), pp. 25, 50; and Walter Phillips, "The Educational System of Japan from 1872 to 1947," 1961. (Mimeographed.)

[50] Nicholas De Witt, *Education and Professional Employment in the USSR* (Washington, D.C.: National Science Foundation, 1961), p. 211 and Table IV–10, p. 232.

[51] *Ibid.,* Table IV–1, p. 227.

Some advanced countries do better than others in this respect. While the quality of Soviet education is deficient in other respects, the proportion of students enrolled in scientific and technical faculties is the highest of any advanced country: 45.3 per cent in 1959. Recent efforts of Great Britain and France to increase their enrollments in these fields are shown in their respective percentages: 33.5 and 32.1. Concern for lagging enrollments in Sweden, Japan, and the United States reflects the following lower percentage enrollments in science and technical faculties in 1959: 30.4, 22.1, and 22.7.

The United States percentage, while comparatively low, has increased substantially over the years, especially in relation to such traditional fields as law, and humanities and arts. . . . It is worth noting that, along with "education," the largest percentage increase has been in "business and commerce." Indeed the development of professional training in this field has been pioneered in the United States, with the establishment of the Wharton School of Commerce and Finance at the University of Pennsylvania and the Graduate School of Business Administration at Harvard University earlier in this century. Other western industrial nations and Japan have followed this pattern; the Soviets have not. Quite possibly the higher percentage enrollments in engineering and industrial fields in the U.S.S.R. include many who enter managerial positions in Soviet industrial enterprises. Industrial managers in Western Europe, the United States, Canada, and Japan are recruited from many university fields: law, liberal arts, and (especially in the United States) from schools of business administration. Professional training for management is a fairly recent development, but one which is increasingly important in an advanced industrial society.[52]

The difference in educational backgrounds of managers between the U.S.S.R. and other advanced countries points to a more fundamental difference in their systems of higher education. The Soviets gear their system almost exclusively to the production of specialized high-level manpower required for a highly industrialized society which is determined to make its voice heard throughout the world and to spread its ideology. Education and national purpose are inseparable. For example, in both technical and nontechnical curricula, students are required to take between 150 and 220 hours in "History of the Communist Party of the Soviet Union," 140 to 214 hours in "Political Economy" (presumably Marxian), and 100 to 140 hours in "Dialectical and Historical Materialism."

---

[52] Frederick Harbison and Charles A. Myers, *Management in the Industrial World* (New York: McGraw-Hill Book Co., Inc., 1959), especially chap. 5 and the country studies. Hofstadter observes: "Clearly the emergence of the business school as a flourishing center of specialized training came on the heels of the bureaucratization of American business, which was a well-established trend by 1900. In the entrepreneur's heyday of the mid-nineteenth century, when the characteristic form of business education was an apprenticeship in business, a collegiate business school would have been an incongruity" (Richard Hofstadter and C. DeWitt Hardy, *The Development of the Scope of Higher Education in the United States* [New York: Columbia University Press, 1952], pp. 90–91). For a view which holds that professional training for business has no place in a university, see Abraham Flexner, *Universities, American, English, German* (New York: Oxford University Press, 1930). "Modern business does not satisfy the criteria of a profession: it is shrewd, energetic, and clever, rather than intellectual in character; it aims—and under our present social organization—must aim—at its own advantage, rather than at noble purpose within itself" (p. 164).

Except for a foreign language, this is all the nontechnical work available in the technical curricula.[53]

In contrast, in the western countries and in postwar Japan, the individual and his own development count more heavily; he is not considered solely as an instrument in achieving a national purpose. The growth of his critical faculties, his ability to distinguish between conflicting doctrines, his appreciation of the arts and humanities—all these are objectives of higher education at the pinnacle of an educational system designed to enable individuals in a democratic society to develop and utilize their talents as they choose. Enrollment ratios reflect these choices. There is the further conviction in this type of educational philosophy that free men and women, broadly trained, may be more effective participants in an advanced industrial society than those educated more narrowly in specialized fields.[54] Apart from this general difference in educational philosophy, there is another significant qualitative factor in education for science and engineering. The "numbers game" of training more scientists and engineers than some other country neglects the quality of that training, especially graduate-level education. In the science and engineering of the space age, a bachelor's degree in science, mathematics, and engineering may prepare a young man or young woman for useful employment, but it will usually not contribute much to advanced work in these fields. Thus, postgraduate education of the ablest people is a more critical need in advanced countries than is education of more students at the undergraduate level. The physicists, chemists, biochemists, biophysicists, astronomers, mathematicians, and engineers required for advanced research and innovation are the really critical professions. No country today has enough people at the graduate levels in these fields in universities and advanced technical institutes.[55] . . .

Incentives and Allocation of High-Level Manpower

In the advanced countries, the prestige of the professions (including management) is generally high enough to induce young people to prepare for them

[53] M. A. Prokofiev, M. G. Chilikin, and S. I. Tulpanov, *Higher Education in the U.S.S.R.* (Educational Studies and Documents, No. 39) (Paris: UNESCO, 1961). Sample curricula are found on pages 26, 30, and 44 ff.

[54] See Harold Taylor, "Individualism and the Liberal Tradition," in Willis D. Weatherford (ed.), *The Goals of Higher Education* (Cambridge: Harvard University Press, 1960). "If the aim of education is to develop a creative intellect critical of society and its values, then Soviet higher education is an obvious failure. If its aim is to develop applied professional skills enabling the individual to perform specialized, functional tasks, then Soviet education is unquestionably a success, posing not only a temporary challenge, but a major threat in the long-run struggle between democracy and totalitarianism." De Witt, *op. cit.*, p. 548 (concluding paragraph). For a similar view, see Alexander G. Korol, *Soviet Education for Science and Technology,* published jointly by the Technology Press of Massachusetts Institute of Technology and John Wiley & Sons, Inc. (New York, 1957), chap. 12.

[55] An increase in graduate-level training in the United States, particularly for the doctorate, in science, mathematics, and engineering, has been recommended by a report of President Kennedy's Science Advisory Committee, *Meeting Manpower Needs in Science and Technology, Report No. 1: Graduate Training in Engineering, Mathematics, and Physical Sciences,* The White House, Washington, December 12, 1962.

through advanced education. Salaries are also generally better than in other fields, although there are variations among professions and among countries which may help to explain some of the particular shortages.

For example, teachers' salaries at the first and second levels in the United States have been low in relation to such occupations as truck driving, building crafts, etc., and municipalities are only recently waking up to the need to remedy this inequity. Market forces work slowly in this type of situation, as they do in public service. Salaries in government administration in most western countries are probably lower than in other professions (except teaching) for comparable educational attainment. However, the prestige and security associated with permanent civil service positions (especially in Western Europe) is sufficient to assure an adequate supply of competent people regardless of salary differentials.

Information on these matters in the Soviet Union is less accessible, but the available evidence suggests that the high salary differentials enjoyed by Soviet professionals for many years were reduced somewhat in 1957, possibly because the educational system had remedied some of the shortages.[56] Moreover, the prestige profile for occupations in the Soviet Union apparently is not significantly different from that in other advanced industrial societies. Despite the fact that factory managers, army officers, party secretaries, and farm chairmen are rated highest on "material position," the highest total ratings (including those on "desirability," "personal satisfaction," and "popular regard") are given to doctors, scientists, engineers, and factory managers in that order.[57]

These reflect the values which a society places on different occupations and consequently on the importance of training for them. One of the intangibles . . . is the influence of home environment on choice of occupation and on the amount of subsequent education which is sought. Perhaps the western advanced industrial nations, in which individual free choice is more important, differ from the Soviet Union in this respect, although family background and influences seem to have become more important in influencing occupational choice even in the U.S.S.R.

The allocation and utilization of high-level manpower are better in the advanced society than at earlier levels, but there is still considerable room for improvement in both processes. For example, the ratio of professionals to

---

[56] De Witt, *op. cit.*, pp. 540–42. "It is obvious that the often-expressed opinion that Soviet professional salaries are uniformly high and that they are several times higher than the average earnings of workers and employees appears totally unfounded. The salaries for primary school teachers are below the average wage. The salaries of secondary school teachers, ordinary medical doctors and agricultural professionals are barely on a par with the average wage. . . . the average wage of engineering and technical personnel is about 1.65 times that for production workers." Nevertheless, salaries for select professors in higher education and research, some directors of research institutes, and managers of large industrial enterprises are "extremely high" and are seven times the average wage in the U.S.S.R. (pp. 542–43). Except for industrial executives, this would not be true in western advanced countries.

[57] Based on interviews of former Soviet citizens by the Russian Research Center of Harvard University. P. H. Rossi and A. Inkeles, "Multi-dimensional Ratings of Occupations," *Sociometry*, Vol. 20, No. 3 (September, 1957), pp. 234–51.

subprofessionals or technicians in work groups is still far from optimal. A 1957–1958 survey in the United States revealed that the over-all ratio of technicians to engineers in ninety companies was about 0.8:1—far from the suggested ratio of 5 or more to 1. This may have resulted from a relative shortage of technicians, or from hoarding engineers and utilizing them on subprofessional work.

Some of the same factors may account for the relatively low ratio of professionals to semiprofessionals in engineering-industrial fields in the U.S.S.R. The number of professional graduates increased 17.4 times between 1927 and 1957, as compared to 24.6 times for subprofessionals. The officially sought 1:2 or 1:3 ratio of professionals to semiprofessionals was thus never met, and this was even more true of other fields.[58]

Effective utilization of professionals as well as other high-talent manpower is not simply a matter of ratios, however. Managerial skills in motivating people to high performance are extremely important; and these skills often reflect organizational structures in which employees are self-motivated rather than directed and controlled. A democratic-participative managerial philosophy, coupled with a more decentralized organization structure, has been carried further in many enterprises in advanced countries than in the less developed. Yet the gap between potential performance and actual performance is still pretty wide in many organizations and enterprises.[59]

Finally, lack of knowledge of alternative job opportunities and inadequate advice about career possibilities are weaknesses in the labor market as an allocator of manpower even in the advanced countries. For example, professional positions are filled as much by informal, word-of-mouth means as by referrals from public or private employment exchanges. Generally, public employment services have been less effective in professional than in blue-collar placements. Vocational guidance, particularly in the public schools in the United States, has not been as effective as its proponents have claimed. Counselors have not been well trained, they have been addicted to a pseudo science of matching traits of people and jobs, and they have not considered adequately the possibility that jobs in the future in an advanced industrial society may be vastly different than present employment patterns.[60]

Despite these weaknesses and the misallocation resulting from sticky salary differentials in certain occupations such as teaching, the market acts as a more effective allocator of manpower in the advanced countries than in the less developed. With some freedom to change jobs, this is even partially true in the

58 De Witt, *op. cit.*, p. 460.

59 For discussions of this point, see Douglas McGregor, *The Human Side of Enterprise* (New York: McGraw-Hill Book Co., Inc., 1960); Rensis Likert, *New Patterns of Management* (New York: McGraw-Hill Book Co., Inc., 1961); and Chris Argyris, *Personality and Organization* (New York: Harper & Row, Publishers, 1957).

60 Ruth Barry and Beverly Wolf, *Epitaph for Vocational Guidance* (New York: Bureau of Publications, Teachers College, Columbia University, 1962). See also "Vocational Guidance and Counseling," chap. ix in Henry David (ed.), *Education and Manpower* (New York: National Manpower Council, Columbia University Press, 1960).

controlled economy of the Soviet Union. However, apparently the statutory obligation of university graduates, educated at the state's expense, to take designated jobs for a certain number of years has neither been repealed nor modified.[61] Thus, some central direction still exists in the Soviet Union.

Swedish labor market policy is a good example of the way in which an advanced country has facilitated the operation of market forces in allocating manpower from labor surplus to labor shortage regions. Retraining allowances, payment of transportation expenses, and other measures are used. The Manpower Development and Training Act of 1962 in the United States is also designed to improve labor mobility and facilitate adjustments to job changes by financing in-school and on-the-job training programs for unemployed and displaced workers.[62] . . .

[61] Korol, *Soviet Education for Science and Technology*, p. 401. "Voluntary indenture" procedures were first introduced in the Soviet labor market before the war, and a compulsory labor decree was promulgated in October, 1940. Solomon M. Schwarz, *Labor in the Soviet Union* (New York: Frederick Praeger, Inc., 1952), pp. 91, 119.

[62] For further details, see *Manpower Report of the President and A Report on Manpower Requirements, Resources, Utilization, and Training*, transmitted to Congress, March, 1963, Washington, 1963.

selection 19

Heroes, Homework, and Industrial Growth*

William F. Whyte and Robert R. Braun

Industrial progress is all too often looked upon as simply the outcome of economic incentives. According to this way of thinking, where there are opportunities to make a profit, entrepreneurs will step in and form organizations to pursue that profit. Where attractive salaries are offered for executive positions, men will enter industry to compete for those salaries. Such an approach sees the role of government as essentially a passive one. Government should maintain law and order, avoid tinkering with the currency, and generally keep out of the way so that the entrepreneur can do his job.

This view is highly simplistic. As we look at developing countries around the world, we see that despite a felt need for their contributions, relatively few entrepreneurs and executives are coming to the fore. To be sure, political instability, anachronistic laws, and misguided governmental intervention often place serious obstacles in the way of entrepreneurship and business activity. But this cannot be the whole answer, for in spite of all obstacles, we find some successful entrepreneurs everywhere in the underdeveloped world. Yet the astonishing fact is that in most cases, these men are not native to the country but are

*From *Columbia Journal of World Business*, Vol. 1, No. 2 (Spring, 1966), pp. 51–57.

immigrants or sons of immigrants—and this is true even when the total number of first- or second-generation immigrants constitute only a small fraction of the population.

This finding points to the cultural basis of entrepreneurship. Apparently, in certain countries, as the individual becomes fully integrated into the culture of his nation, he learns *not* to see or *not* to value the possibilities of entrepreneurial success. Only those who come in from the outside with alien ideas, motivations, and values dedicate themselves to entrepreneurial activities.

If, in certain countries, the man who is well adjusted to his own culture is unlikely to contribute to industrial progress, then we need to examine the barriers a culture may impose.

Let us begin by trying to dispel some of the mystery that may surround the concept of culture. When the layman considers culture, he is inclined to think on the one hand of art, literature, and music, or, on the other hand, of strange and exotic religious beliefs and practices and colorful costumes. From the standpoint of the anthropologist, these are indeed parts of culture, yet they do not throw much light on our problem. In many underdeveloped countries of the world, we see men and women dressing very much like citizens of advanced industrial nations and professing the same religions found in these nations. Apparently, two peoples can dress alike and even go to the same churches and yet have drastically different attitudes, beliefs, and practices regarding matters relevant to industrial development.

In analyzing these differences we start with the proposition that a *culture pattern* consists of a set of *learned* behaviors and beliefs that are *widely shared* in a given society. The word *pattern* suggests that cultural items do not appear at random. A given item of behavior fits with other items of behavior and belief.

The words *widely shared* mean that, even though there cannot be universal adherence to a culture pattern among all the inhabitants of a given society, there are always central tendencies to be found. The discovery of these common characteristics is crucial to an understanding of the problems and possibilities of cultural change and economic development.

The term *learned* indicates that the culture pattern is not simply imposed upon man by natural or supernatural forces. In the course of growing up in his society, the individual learns how to act and think and feel. This has an important implication for cultural change; recognizing that the ways of culture in a given society today have been learned by those who have grown up in that society, it follows that if the coming generation can be subjected to different learning experiences, the pattern of culture in that society will also undergo changes.

Man learns what he does because he is *rewarded* for so doing and encounters *penalties* for not doing so. This is called reinforcement. Therefore, to understand the prevalence of a given type of behavior in a society, we must ask what rewards are received by individuals who produce this behavior.

This discussion of culture and learning is oversimplified, but one who follows this approach should be able to discern the main outlines of the pattern of a culture and grasp some of the first principles of the strategy of culture change.

Where should we look in order to discern this pattern? Man learns how to act, think, and feel throughout all of his life, but we state a scientific truth in common sense terms when we speak of the "formative years." Granting the possibilities of change in later life, man is most malleable in the years of childhood and adolescence. If those years have shaped him in a manner inappropriate to successful executive performance, a crash program of executive development will not make him over.

The child learns through his experiences in the family, among friends and associates, and in school. The limitations of space lead us to focus upon the last source. Family and friendship groups are not readily open to observation, and, even if we were to agree on possible changes in the pattern of these relations, it would be exceedingly difficult to get at the countless units.

The school is easily observed. There we can enter and see the culture pattern of tomorrow being shaped before our eyes. Changing a school system is not simple, but it is possible, and any change introduced may affect the learning of thousands of pupils.

Let us therefore focus our attention on the schoolroom, using actual examples to illustrate the way culture is learned and to diagnose some of the problems this may pose for industrialization. The cases are drawn for several developing countries whose cultural patterns appear to be quite similar. [1]

Case 1. A Nation's Heroes.   Theorizing that a nation's heroes serve as models of ideal behavior for its growing citizens, and would thus provide a clue to the society's values, sociologists have investigated who the national heroes are and how they are portrayed. One in particular began a survey of school history books and came to two general conclusions. In the first place, the outstanding heroes of that country were all military men. Men who had contributed to the economic development of their country were conspicuously absent. In the second place, these military men were not celebrated for achievements that required sustained and successful efforts to reach a long-range goal. They became heroes because of the gallantry of their words and actions in one short period of time—in some instances the event that produced the hero took only a few minutes or even a few seconds.

Of course, schoolbooks are not the only source for the presentation of heroes to the public. In this country there were several spectacularly successful industrial entrepreneurs who had contributed greatly to the economic progress of their countrymen. For over a year, the sociologist followed the leading newspapers and popular magazines of the country, looking for references to these individuals. In the magazines he found no feature stories about them: their humble beginnings, their early struggles, or their achievements. In the newspapers he found them mentioned occasionally, but only in brief impersonal

---

[1] For some of the cases presented here, the authors are indebted to Paul Doughty, David Andrews, John D. Herzog, and Gabriel Escobar. Others are drawn from the authors' own observations.

stories on the financial pages, presenting the dry details of their business dealings. No schoolboy would look for heroes there!

Later the sociologist wrote an article dealing with entrepreneurship, and described briefly the careers of three of these entrepreneurs. He thought he was presenting a flattering picture. When his local collaborator saw the draft prepared for publication in her own country, she urged that these personal stories be left out.

"Why?" he asked. "Do you think these men would object?"

"Not so much the men themselves, but it would be very embarrassing to their families to read about their humble beginnings."

"But I thought that this aspect of their personal histories was well known in your country."

"Of course it is, but it would be very humiliating to the families to be publicly reminded of it."

Apparently, in this country, members of the family try to bury the achievements of the entrepreneur even before he himself is buried. They seek to create the illusion that their family has always enjoyed social prominence.

The case of the heroes reveals that, in many developing countries, far from being regarded as heroes, industrial leaders are not even considered worthy of much respect. How is the growing generation to be attracted to positions of industrial leadership if the culture constantly emphasizes the superior values of other occupations? Furthermore, how are men going to be led to accept the difficult discipline of striving for long-range goals, when the culture models have achieved fame through dramatic but momentary actions? In other words, as psychologists would put it, how is the achievement motive to be developed, when the culture provides no popular models for it?

Case 2. The Three R's and Industrial Development.   An anthropologist was observing an arithmetic test in an elementary school grade. The teacher had put ten problems on the blackboard, each consisting of the addition of two two-digit numbers. Toward the middle of the period, one of the pupils raised her hand and said, "Teacher, problem nine is not fair. You have not given us that one before."

The teacher checked to see whether the pupil's statement was correct. Then she replied: "You are right. I have not given you problem nine before. Therefore you should all leave it out of your test."

In order to learn more about the way people in a town regarded their community, the anthropologist decided that he would offer a small prize for the best essay by high school boys on the most important recent public improvement in the area. He found he learned little from the essays themselves, but a great deal from the difficulties that stood in the way of carrying out the contest. In the first place, the teachers resisted the idea vigorously. The general complaint was: "The poor things will not be able to write anything. They have never had any experience in writing something on their own."

The contest was held, but it was hardly an exercise in independent thinking and expression. Most pupils seemed at a complete loss. Just two or three enterprising boys went out to collect information, and they were followed around by a number of pupils who copied what their more energetic fellow students told them. In other cases, it was the teachers themselves who took students to the local library or the municipal offices, pulled out records and pointed to passages saying, "This is what you want. Put this down."

In developing countries today, we hear much discussion about how the *content* of the school curriculum can be brought more in line with modern-day realities. While not denying the importance of content, we must emphasize that the way children are taught—the way they learn *how to learn*—strongly influences the way they will use their minds in their approach to the problems of later life.

NEEDED: GENERALIZATION NOT MEMORIZATION

The arithmetic test and the essay contest both demonstrate a teaching method emphasizing the memorization of material. Of course, memory is important in learning the multiplication table and certain formulae, but the pupil cannot learn to solve new problems by merely memorizing answers to problems the teacher gives him. Nor can we expect graduates of such a school system to express their own ideas orally or in writing, without great difficulty, when they get into an industrial organization.

An executive frequently faces problems that he has never encountered before, especially in a developing country. He must be able to diagnose complex situations and to identify the key questions whose answers will give him guidance for action. How can he develop such problem-solving ability if he attained his rewards in school simply through memorizing passages that were assigned to him?

Case 3. Submissive Children, Autocratic Teachers. An anthropologist noted that the children in the community seemed very submissive and lacking in initiative, especially in the school situation. In seeking an explanation, he observed the customary pattern of teacher–pupil relationships in several schools. He noted that pupils never raised their hands to volunteer information or to suggest an activity. It was always the teacher who controlled interaction.

Why was this? When a child was called on and gave a wrong answer, he received a severe reprimand from the teacher—and sometimes even a rap on the knuckles. On the other hand, when the correct answer was given, the teacher passed on to the next question without the slightest gesture or comment of encouragement. Another characteristic of the teacher–pupil relationship was revealed by the lack of class discussion. Everything that went on in the instruction process was entirely in response to the teacher's initiative.

In addition to maintaining tight, autocratic control, the teacher frequently informed her pupils how stupid she considered them. She gave the impression that pupils of their social and ethnic background could not really be expected to learn anything, but it was her duty to go through the motions of trying to pound knowledge into their thick heads.

Let us examine this school situation in terms of its effects upon the development of risk-taking capacity. We ordinarily think of risk-taking in relation to investment of capital in an enterprise, but there is also a risk inherent in every major decision an executive makes. Organizations need men who can size up the probabilities of success in alternative lines of action, weigh the penalties of failure, and decide to act, despite uncertainties, without undue strain and anxiety.

Decision making calls for a special combination of intellectual skills and personality characteristics that transcend the analytical skills needed for problem analysis. No doubt, there is some feature of the human personality that governs this risk-taking potential. Individuals are not born with this capacity for risk-taking, but their experiences in the family and school develop it—or stifle it.

To encourage risk-taking ability, we must create situations in which the man who takes risks is *sometimes* rewarded. If he is always rewarded, then there is no risk in the situation and he does not learn to take chances. On the other hand, if he is never rewarded, he does not take risks either. Why take a chance when there is nothing to be gained by it?

Furthermore, risk-taking ability depends to some extent upon the confidence the individual has in himself. He can hardly face the uncertainties involved in risk-taking unless he has learned to feel that he is a fairly competent person who is more likely to be right than wrong. A child does not develop this confidence if he grows up under a teacher who constantly tells him how stupid and incompetent he is.

Case 4. Authority and Peer Group Solidarity.   While the teacher's back was turned, a boy threw a wad of paper at another pupil. The teacher turned around and called out to the class, "Who did that?" Immediately, half a dozen of the pupils pointed at their guilty classmate and shouted, "José did it!"

The first time the visiting anthropologist observed such an instance, he was startled. He remembered that in his own country any teacher who asked for such information was always met by dead silence.

As the anthropologist further observed, this was not an isolated incident. It was the standard way in which classroom infractions were handled. If the teacher did not see the offense herself, she would always call out, "Who did it?" and there were usually many pupils prepared to give her the culprit's name. The only exceptions occurred when the pupils were so eager to give information that they shouted out the name of the guilty one even before the teacher had time to ask.

Apparently, divisive tendencies already existed in this culture, for otherwise the teacher would get no response when she called for information on disciplinary cases. Accentuating these cleavages, the teacher maintained control by dividing the classroom, every pupil against every other, competing for her favor.

EVERY MAN AN ISLAND

This kind of approach naturally leads individuals to feel that those on the same organizational level are rivals who cannot be trusted, and who will turn against them for any advantage that may be offered. However, an effective industrial organization requires both authority and some degree of peer group solidarity. A manager must learn to respond not only to his boss, but to develop cooperative relations with a number of people on the same rung of the organization, who are not related to him in terms of authority. He cannot give them orders nor can they command him; instead, the efficiency of the organization depends upon their learning how to work together. Men who have had no childhood experience in peer group solidarity are bound to have difficulties later in developing effective relations with others at the peer level.

These four examples illustrate that education is more than the imparting of knowledge. It also involves influencing the way people think, feel and act. This is not a new idea. In fact, it is everywhere assumed that the school's mission includes "character building." This feature, however, is often mistakenly considered to be separate from the intellectual learning process. Teachers tell children how they ought to feel and act. Yet behavioral science findings demonstrate that one of the *least* effective ways to change beliefs and behavior is to tell people "what is right." Research indicates that learning is a social process, so that the most effective change strategy involves combining intellectual and social experience.

It does no good to tell children they should aim to become entrepreneurs and work hard toward a long-range goal, if they find no models for such ambitions and values in their classroom experience. Nor will it help to tell them that cooperation is a good thing, if only individualism pays off in the classroom.

In the past, it was assumed that culture patterns were shaped by unknown and uncontrollable forces. Today, it is known that culture can be subject to the conscious control of men. Diagnosis of the current problems posed by the culture is the first step in a program of planned culture change. We have tried to show how an untrained person may approach such a diagnosis. Behavioral science research can proceed to define the problems more systematically and to test for possible lines of action.

Behavioral scientists are in fact turning in increasing numbers to the study of the cultural conditions for economic development in the nonindustrialized countries. Everett C. Hagan[2] has been examining some of the cultural barriers to industrialization in countries around the world. David G. McClelland[3] has been investigating the relationship between the achievement motive and the rate of economic progress. John J. Carroll[4] has presented a social and cultural analysis of the Filipino entrepreneur. Bernard Rosen[5] has shown there is less need for achievement among Brazilian children than U.S. children, and has related this

---

[2] *On the Theory of Social Change* (Homewood, Ill.: The Dorsey Press, Inc., 1962).

[3] *The Achieving Society* (Princeton, N.J.: D. Van Nostrand Co., Inc., 1961).

[4] *The Filipino Manufacturing Executive: Agent and Product of Change* (Ithaca, N.Y.: Cornell University Press, 1965).

[5] "Family Structure and Achievement Motivation," *American Sociological Review*, Vol. 27, No. 14 (October, 1962), pp. 612–24.

to the pattern of child rearing in the Brazilian family. Joseph A. Kahl[6] has been investigating the impact of industrialization upon the mentality of Brazilian and Mexican workers and executives. Alex Inkeles[7] is studying similar problems in surveys made in Pakistan, India, Israel, Nigeria, Argentina, and Chile.

In a survey of high school boys in Peru, Whyte[8] has not only demonstrated the unpopularity of careers in business and industry, but has also shown that the small proportion of boys inclined in this direction seem to be less motivated than other students to pursue their careers with a dedicated and enterprising spirit. Whyte and Lawrence K. Williams[9] have shown that the type of supervisory behavior most valued by Peruvian utility workers is quite different from the most highly valued pattern in the United States.

Although the list of research projects completed and now in progress could be substantially extended, we must acknowledge that behavioral scientists are still in the early stages of their exploration of this new problem area. At the same time, the urgency of the situation demands immediate action without waiting for all the relevant research findings to come in. Three such possible actions are offered here.

First, to increase achievement motivation among the rising generation, McClelland suggests that the schoolbooks read by children in the primary grades be examined for the prevalence of stories illustrating achievement motivation—stories of how the hero, through persistent efforts, overcame great obstacles and arrived at a distant goal. McClelland and his associates scored children's readers from thirty countries on the frequency of achievement themes and correlated their results with the rate of economic progress of each country over a subsequent period of approximately twenty-five years. With all the allowance for the complexity of the measurement problems, the relationship McClelland claimed between achievement themes and economic progress looks sufficiently promising to warrant investing money and talent in the revision of children's readers.

A NEW CROP OF HEROES

These revisions should be geared to the creation of new heroes, representing new qualities of mind and character. This does not imply throwing out the old heroes, for such a proposal would guarantee the indignant rejection of all ideas. Instead we urge that educators and writers of children's literature be encouraged

---

[6] *A Study of Career Values in Brazil and Mexico* (St. Louis, Mo.: Washington University, 1965) (mimeographed preliminary draft).

[7] Harvard Project on Socio-Cultural Aspects of Development. Surveys completed, analysis now in process.

[8] "Culture, Industrial Relations and Economic Development: The Case of Peru," *Industrial and Labor Relations Review,* Vol. 16, No. 4 (July 1963).

[9] "Supervisory Leadership: An International Comparison," paper presented at the 13th International Management Congress of the International Council for Scientific Management (CIOS), New York, 1963, pp. 481–88 of the proceedings, published by the Council for International Progress in Management (USA) Inc.

to reexamine the country's history to find men who might serve as models for the kinds of achievements and ambitions that need to be fostered. Perhaps in time such men could take their places in the schoolbooks beside the military heroes.

The same approach could be taken to children's fiction stories. Without downgrading physical courage and self-sacrifice, the writers might produce interesting stories around characters who are striving to overcome serious obstacles and reach long-range goals.

Second, if individuals are to have the capacity to solve problems they have not confronted before, their early education must provide them with the exciting experience of working out their own answers to problems. Instead of having to memorize a teacher's solutions, the teacher must learn to help children arrive at their own. Some countries are already actively experimenting with teaching methods designed to encourage problem-solving abilities.

Thirdly, if children are to learn to cooperate and to value cooperation, then they must be exposed to the experience of working and playing together—and find the experience rewarding. Furthermore, they must *not* be offered incentives that tend to turn one against another.[10]

These suggestions are obviously not solutions to the many problems faced by developing nations, but simply indicate the possibilities of achieving cultural change through the education system. Further action based on the information already acquired should go hand-in-hand with additional research by behavioral scientists. As men recognize the possibilities of *planning* culture change, leaders of industry and government can come together with educators and behavioral scientists to examine the cultural conditions for industrial growth. Together, they can even take the essential next step of creating the cultural conditions that will promote this growth.

---

[10] Paul E. Breer and Edwin Locke, authors of *Task Experience as a Source of Attitudes* (Homewood, Ill.: The Dorsey Press, Inc., 1965), have shown that it is possible to induce more favorable attitudes toward cooperation by involving experimental subjects in tasks that can be accomplished better cooperatively than alone. These changes have been induced without any mention of the idea of cooperation and without any material reward. Success in the task provided its own reinforcement for cooperation.

selection 20

The Renaissance of Foreign Business Schools*

Alan B. Coleman and Dan Throop Smith

Within the past few years, skillful management has come to be recognized as a major national asset. Effective operating combinations of capital, labor and natural resources do not come into being as a result of natural laws nor from a national economic plan. In both the industrial countries of Europe and the developing nations, belated appreciation of the role of management in marshalling and directing the other factors of production has led to a sense of urgency in establishing faculties of administration in existing universities or as new institutions. Those concerned with education sense that a school for management education is coming to be a symbol of economic achievement (aspiration), along with an international airline and a steel mill—and with considerably greater importance and justification.

As one might expect, there has been great diversity in the sponsorship, organization, manning and curricula of management schools abroad. No ideal pattern has become apparent and it is unlikely that one ever will be found. Just as the management of international business must adapt itself to cultural differences and existing circumstances, so must educators recognize that what is most appropriate, or indeed what is feasible, will vary with cultures and institutions.

A few conditions and policies do seem to be important if a new undertaking is to have a fair chance of success. Strong backing from a significant and responsible sector of the business community will greatly assist the faculty in developing a curriculum and teaching material appropriate to local conditions and increase the acceptability of graduates. The *Instituto de Estudios Superiores de la Empresa* (IESE) in Barcelona got off to a good start by offering its first program to senior management, thereby securing support for the institution in a variety of ways. The *Instituto Centroamericano de Administracion de Empresas* (INCAE) followed this example in Central America, as did the *Institut National de Productivité et de Gestion des Enterprises* in Tunisia.

The *Indian Institute of Management* (Ahmedabad) had an ingenious three-tier plan under which attendance in the early programs was limited to people from

* From *The MBA*, March, 1968, pp. 21–25.

companies which sent top, middle, and lower level management to overlapping programs of increasing duration. The purpose of the Ahmedabad approach was to prevent a single representative from a company from being isolated when he returned to it; a small group at different levels with mutual understanding in a company was considered more likely to produce an immediate impact. A somewhat different approach has been used in the *Universidad del Valle* in Colombia, where participation in an advanced management program is associated with subsequent faculty consultation with the firms which sent participants.

A successful first program with senior management in a new environment is a major challenge to any teaching group and is not likely to be successful without substantial preparation and some familiarity with the country. Too often, sponsors believe that an existing program could be imported intact and are impatient at the time and expense which is needed. But just as a good first program at a high level can save years in getting systematic management accepted and applied in a country, a failure or even a mediocre performance can set the process back by years.

Two other important factors are implicit in the foregoing comments. Only very able teachers can be expected to be successful in an advanced management program abroad. Though the level of sophistication of the participants may be less in terms of familiarity with management concepts, the scepticism about the value or even the possibility of education for management may be greater. A sensitivity to the doubts and needs of the participants is vital, and is not likely to be found in other than the most skillful teachers.

THE ELEMENTS OF SUCCESS

The use of local material in cases and teaching notes will greatly increase the acceptability of a program as well as its value. The difference in preparation and participation in discussion is notable. It is fair to say that an inferior local case can be more effective for teaching purposes than a superior imported case. A mixture of cases is, of course, inevitable for a good many years in any country starting management education, but an allocation of faculty time and effort to develop material within the country is usually well spent. The willingness of management to give the necessary information for cases usually comes as a pleasant surprise. Cooperation has often been outstanding, even in countries with traditions of extreme secrecy in business affairs. The pioneer work at the *Institut pour l'Etude des Méthodes de Direction de l'Entreprise* (IMEDE) has been helpful to other institutions on the European continent.

Faculties of management education, to be effective, must be primarily concerned with education for management and this means that they must be autonomous. Too often they are subordinated to faculties of law or economics, and even regarded as second-class members of the larger group. Membership in a university group is valuable to add status, at least in those countries where universities are themselves well regarded. But real and prompt autonomy within a university may not be possible, as we well know from early problems in management education in the United States.

New university faculties of business are in the process of formation at London and Manchester in response to the recommendations of the Frank Commission which carries sufficient weight to force acceptance of the idea of management education within a university. IESE has the advantage of status within the *Universidad de Navarra,* but a location in a different city which increases the chance for autonomy. In other places, the establishment of completely independent institutions has been regarded as wiser. In many developing countries, the traditional university structure and framework are resistant to change, including the creation of a full-time faculty and student body. Independence may also be necessary to avoid domination by political forces which too often stifle academic development in universities. The *Escuela de Administracion de Negocios* (ESAN) in Lima is among the institutions which started independently for these, among other reasons. Several other independent institutions are being established in Latin America. Hopefully, as the independent institutes develop their prestige and traditions, they will be welcomed into universities and thereby secure the advantage of being able to grant graduate degrees without loss of autonomy in setting standards and curricula. Their incorporation into universities may even improve the standards of the universities themselves.

The problems in establishing curricula for management education abroad are in many respects similar to those here, as is to be expected. At one extreme are those who are concerned with pedestrian vocational training; they would have a curriculum built around a multitude of bookkeeping and "commercial science" courses. At the other extreme are the theorists in various disciplines who find management an interesting area in which to build models or conduct field studies; they would have a curriculum concentrating on the disciplines with only minor attention to their applications in the actual conduct of affairs. The idea of a professional school for management, with emphasis on training for responsible decision-making rather than studies *about* management, has received much less academic acceptance abroad than it has in the United States, and even here acceptance is by no means universal.

The level of analysis appropriate to a particular environment is sometimes hard to determine. Intellectually, participants may have an excellent preparation in mathematics and can become intrigued, for example, with elaborate theories on cost of capital or refinements in comparison of rates of return on investments. The state of the art in the country may, however, make simple exercises in projecting requirements for working capital more useful. As a matter of intellectual interest, the participants in a program may be ready to follow a professor a long way in theory and even feel somewhat insulted if he insists on greater attention to simpler but more fundamental matters. A choice of the right balance is a further challenge to the judgment and skill of faculty members.

Unfortunately there exists in many parts of the world a belief that there is some secret formula of scientific management which the United States could export to be taught and learned abroad. Expectations are frequently very high that concentrated efforts in reading and note-taking will produce a skilled administrator. The realization that education for administration involves "only" practice in making systematic analyses, considering alternative courses of action and exercising judgment in selecting a least bad program with attention to its implications and implementation, may come as a shock to those who have expected to find revealed doctrines in management courses.

The tradition of authoritarian statements by faculty members in universities in many parts of the world reinforces the expectation that management education will consist of a series of principles and pronouncements which can be "learned." This same tradition adds to the difficulty of securing acceptance of the approach to professional training which has become familiar in this country. The remark of a visiting professor to the United States who left in disgust saying that it was inconceivable that any professor in his country would ever say that he did not know the answer to any question or problem, is an extreme example of an attitude which hampers professional education as we have developed it.

FACULTY: A STUMBLING BLOCK

The development of a faculty is a major problem, perhaps the major problem, in any educational institution. Too frequently there has been undue reliance on foreign faculty members who may be necessary in the early years but who should consider the speed with which they make themselves dispensable a principal measure of their success. A predominantly local faculty is perhaps slightly less important than predominantly local case material but it should be planned from the beginning.

Sometimes very able educators in existing disciplines become intrigued with administration as a profession and shift their efforts to it, as is often the case in this country. This occurs less frequently abroad, however, perhaps because management is much less recognized as a profession and an appropriate field for education with high intellectual content. For some years to come, faculties abroad will be considerably younger than those here. Some faculties abroad have been made up largely of men active in business. They are frequently brilliant teachers on individual subjects, but a part-time faculty inevitably does not have the time to develop a curriculum or even a full course systematically.

In many countries, the idea that graduates in engineering, science and the humanities could be eligible for and benefit from a program in management education is surprising and to many people unacceptable. Here again tradition is strong. It is at times amusing to find those who complain about the fact that engineers often become managers without knowing anything about management suspicious of proposals to admit engineers to programs for education for administration. The *Institut Europeen d'Administration des Affaires* (INSEAD) at Fontainebleau has been effective in securing and accepting graduates from varied faculties as students. The *Ecole des Hautes Etudes Commerciales* (H.E.C.) in Paris will presumably speed the process as it develops its graduate program.

Two final challenges in education abroad for management are to appeal to the elite of a country and to try to strike the right balance between stimulation of entrepreneurship and responsibility. The lack of adequate appeal of management education is familiar here; in some countries abroad it is much more pronounced. Even more striking in some places is the absence of any tradition of innovation and risk taking. At the other extreme one finds a preponderance of wheeling and dealing in economic activity. It is too much to expect an educational program to change attitudes and traditions quickly, but perceptive educators may find their greatest satisfaction in trying to foster the entrepreneurship and the responsibility which, when conspicuously absent, prevent the development of a fully productive system of enterprise.

selection 21

Europe's Business Schools: A Good Start, But....*

John G. Hutchinson

During a recent working visit to Europe I was continually asked how business education was conducted in "The States." Unsatisfied with preliminary explanations, my interlocutors usually subjected me to sharp and critical probing, much of which carried the clear implication that American business education was far and away inferior to that offered in European business schools and technical institutes. Fearful of bruising the American image abroad, I emulated George Bernard Shaw and avoided controversy by invariably stating, "My dear sir, you may be right."

In retrospect, it might have been more to the point to dispute the validity of comparisons of this type. Certainly it's neither sensible nor practical to expect European business education to emulate American concepts and techniques. Cultural, political and historical considerations in Europe are far too diverse to fit a mold constructed in the U.S. or anywhere else. It is, however, reasonable and prudent to hope that European educators may profit from the mistakes made by American business schools prior to and during their recent struggles to emerge from the mire of entrenched mediocrity—mistakes, I might add, that are still all too visible in some U.S. schools. Are our European friends so profiting? Perhaps. Yet, in some ways, they are clearly not; in fact, there are instances in which the worst errors of the American system are being reproduced.

*From *Columbia Journal of World Business*, Vol. 1, No. 4 (Fall, 1966), pp. 59–65.

To better understand the situation, it would be well to begin with a review of the major ingredients that most would agree are required to produce a superior business education in Europe, or for that matter in any country in the world. These key elements are the students, the faculties, the curricula and the quality of administrative leadership directing the education process.

THE STUDENT: HELP WANTED

The magazine *Business Week* recently estimated that half of the graduates of England's famed Eton school would go into business. No longer, it said, "are government, the church and the military the dominant careers." In France, Belgium, the Netherlands, Italy and Spain business is growing in size and importance and more and better people are needed to supply the needs created by this mushrooming expansion. Business education has not kept abreast of the demands of industry at either the college level or the secondary education level. Indeed, it has made relatively minor inroads at the secondary level and only a handful of college and university people elect business as an undergraduate major or as the subject for graduate study. Though this trickle may be increasing, it is still just a trickle—and one that could dry up at any time.

Because of its delicate nature, this flow of students contains elements of both promise and challenge. The promise is to offer good students the opportunity to develop the skills needed to hold positions of leadership in the European and world business communities. The challenge is to develop courses and instruction that will convince more and more European students that business offers meaningful and interesting career opportunities.

One problem facing European business education is that students currently enrolled have a mixed set of personal and academic credentials. Some hold Ph.D.'s; others, no degrees. They have technical educations and also training in the fine arts. Some have dubious educational qualifications but gain admission because their families have money and/or influence. In general, however, the bulk of the students possess an enviable grasp of the social graces and seem to have generous amounts of energy, drive and personal ambition.

Given a chance to work with a good set of course materials and stimulating faculty, there can be no doubt that European students can be as sharp and as successful as those found in the best schools in the western hemisphere. Unfortunately, curricula and faculty are not always the best and thus the number of promising young men enrolling in European business schools may fall below what is needed to exert a significant impact on the European business community.

One of the major student complaints about European business education is that the curriculum is deficient. Students say, with considerable justification, that courses are often not well thought out and not constructed to develop business leadership for the future. Moreover, they are either too theoretical or overly vocational. Furthermore, too few courses are concerned with the integration of ideas and the teaching of the techniques needed to handle complex problems.

HARVARD HERITAGE

These charges, though sometimes made in the heat of frustration, seem to have many elements of validity. When analytical methods are taught, they are oriented primarily toward theory, apparently on the grounds that anything that might be useful is not particularly academic. If not overly theoretical, courses tend to adhere dogmatically to a particular pedagogical pattern, typically the widely used Harvard case approach. Though the case method of instruction is effective in teaching certain subject matter, such as business policy, even its most ardent advocates concede that it offers little or no help in other areas, say, history or mathematics. Some institutions in Europe, however, seem to be afraid to break the pattern of case teaching and stick to techniques that may be unsuitable because they are fearful of departing from a pattern adopted by more mature universities.

Though new, many business schools in Europe already have full-blown curriculum rigidities and inflexible teaching methodologies. It seems that European business education may have to wage a determined fight against infant arteriosclerosis—the wholesale adoption by new institutions of ossified patterns inherited from prototypes that were conspicuously successful some decades ago. At least part of the blame for the rigidity in existing curricula apparently rests with the faculties and administrations. After all, curriculum revision doesn't happen by sheer chance; it takes time and effort from both teachers and administrators, and in many cases the impetus and drive seem to be either lacking or in short supply.

THE FACULTY: OUT TO LUNCH

For one thing, the faculty just isn't available a good deal of the time. Teachers are "out to lunch" when the students want them or need them. The "out to lunch" sign applies in both a literal and figurative sense.

Long lunch hours, up to three hours and more, and frequent coffee and wine breaks put even full-time faculty members out of reach of their offices for the bulk of the class day. There is little doubt that many European faculty members confuse time spent in or near their institutions with honest devotion to the job of educating students—but no amount of glib, or even profound, talk over the lunch table can make up for failure to be available when students need guidance and counsel. Long lunches are pleasant and relaxing, perhaps even restorative, but prolonged absences scarcely make for improved faculty–student relations.

The "out to lunch" label also applies in a figurative sense to most European business school faculties, since most of these faculties are made up of part-time instructors. The temporary nature of the instructional staff springs partially from the structure of the European university, since by custom the various European faculties are organized into relatively loose confederations of scholars rather than tightly organized schools.

Whatever its cause, part-time instruction has grave consequences. Most part timers have "other interests," and these interests may mean more to them than teaching. When a professor's main income stream is threatened, schools, students, preparation, etc., go by the boards. The pressures of business also prevent many part-time professors from remaining conversant with the latest research findings in their chosen fields. The resultant tendency is to rely on the familiar, and this contributes to curriculum rigidity. It is fallacious to argue that the use of part-time faculty members cross-fertilizes the curriculum with new ideas, new approaches and new pedagogical techniques. This happens all too rarely in practice. The first time a man teaches a course he learns the material. The second time around, he perfects it. After that, he is able to make changes and develop real improvements. Part-timers seldom stay around long enough to go through this entire cycle, and thus their pedagogical fertility is either questionable or extremely limited.

The part-time nature of the faculty is undoubtedly the greatest weakness of European business education and one of the chief reasons so many European business students seem more eager and more interested in the work than those who are paid to teach them. This problem is serious enough to cast a pall over the entire future of European business education.

Some of the same weaknesses found in European business faculties are also found among administrators. Though a handful of leaders are strong, these are the exceptions, and a general pattern of lassitude pervades all levels of the administrative hierarchy. Administrative procedures are antiquated and members of the directional staff often fail to understand what they are expected to do. Service to student and faculty, if given at all, may be offered grudgingly. Admissions may be handled by a part-time committee or director. Alumni relations are often virtually unknown. Placement of graduates is a hit-or-miss operation. Even when it is reasonably well organized, companies tend to dominate the placement relationship—sometimes to the extent of disrupting classes by insisting that interview schedules be set up for their convenience. But this is only symptomatic of a larger problem: in the relations between business and the schools, the business community is normally dominant and the administrative leadership distinctly passive.

Research is often misunderstood or ignored by the administration. The highest apparent degree of administrative achievement in some schools is to get a grant from some foundation or government—for whatever purposes anyone can dream up. Under these conditions, the administrative devices designed to support and strengthen the school's operation become nothing more than an almost pure example of C. N. Parkinson's fatal organizational disease, ingelititis—whose symptoms appear as administrative ineptitude.

Another problem stems from the fact that in the typical European business institute, the director is all powerful. Unlike the typical U.S. situation where the dean functions within educational policies set by the faculty and administrative policies established by the parent university, the director of the European educational unit acts as president, controller, dean of faculties and head of a school or department. This multiplicity of roles isn't necessarily undesirable, especially when leadership has high ideals, but when the top man is oriented to procedures rather than to concepts, the inordinate power he wields obviously threatens the quality of the education the school offers.

A DESCRIPTIVE PRESCRIPTION

There is nothing wrong with European business education that a good dose of timely effort, thinking and considered action can't cure, but this generality is true in almost any context, and thus specific solutions and suggestions may be in order. It is hoped that these comments will be construed as friendly criticisms from one who feels it important that European business schools achieve high levels of excellence in the least possible time. The need for such development is almost painfully obvious to those who understand the vital role which Europe must continue to play in world economic leadership. Since the description of the problems of European business education was presented under the headings of administration, faculty, curriculum and students, these proposals for change utilize the same general format.

The biggest need in administrative ranks is to locate and recruit individuals who have an understanding of what ingredients are needed to develop successful business managers. Leadership is important here as everywhere and more European business schools could profitably take a page from the books of similar American institutions when seeking key administrators. Many people now in top posts in U.S. business schools have impressive credentials in both academic life and business. The most successful of these leaders have done some teaching and understand its problems. They have also been in industry long enough to appreciate both its needs and its challenges. This combination of business and educational experience is not impossible to find in European countries if determined searches are made.

Whoever is selected to head the European business school must know his job thoroughly. The administrator should act in close collaboration with the existing faculty to insure proper selection of students, the development of a solid but flexible curriculum, the building of a strong, permanent teaching staff, and the cultivation of government and business relations in such a way that the school becomes renowned for its excellence. He must also make the contacts needed to support and maintain the physical plant and vital facilities, and must construct an administrative apparatus designed to expedite internal and external operations. Finally, he should try to develop the goals that will lead to the levels of academic excellence expected by both the student body and the business community. Since few directors of European business institutes are expected to perform all of the duties outlined above, serious gaps exist in administrative leadership. Until these gaps are plugged, European business education will be hard pressed to take its proper place in the ranks of world academic leadership. If the experience of the United States is any kind of signpost, the degree of expansion and development of business education in Europe will be directly related to the extent to which responsible officials are able to select experienced, dedicated and enlightened leadership.

Improving the faculty ranks high on the agenda of most pressing problems. It seems obvious that part-time faculty members will be needed in European business education until a cadre of permanent instructors is developed, but these people should nevertheless be selected carefully, and utilized only under certain conditions.

SHUCKING THE PART-TIME PSYCHOLOGY

Businessmen who are recruited part time would do well to accept the idea of a major commitment to teaching. Cancelling classes because of business pressures is obviously incompatible with such a commitment, as is the repeated failure to prepare adequately for lectures. The kind of part-timer the schools are looking for is not one who will regard the teaching assignment as an invitation to launch into a lengthy recital of personal experiences that are only tenuously related to the subject matter under discussion. If a businessman is tapped for a visiting professorship, it is reasonable to expect him to present topics that fit into an existing curriculum—not adjust the curriculum to satisfy a desire to present subject matter that is more congenial to him.

It is, moreover, a mistake not to ask the part-timer for help in student counseling, curriculum development, research projects and other activities important to the school's development. Too often visitors are treated as outsiders and do not really commit their full skill and talents. This is a great waste of available resources and it requires only a bit more forceful leadership on the part of the administration to use this latent asset to its fullest degree. American business schools also have characteristically failed to utilize such talents and have missed out on a rich lode of knowledge and experience. But at best, part-time instruction is a bridge between the present and a time when a permanent faculty will have been created.

Recruitment of faculty from industry should be done carefully. To be eligible for consideration a man would need the proper academic credentials, a desire to teach and a willingness to give up industry as his main career. One suggestion might be to look to large companies rather than to small firms, since there is always a temptation for small businessmen to get back into harness. Consultants are a risk for the same reason. They are often well qualified, but they are also the most likely to maintain their former contacts and thus offer less than full attention to the school's programs.

In any case, experience seems to indicate that not more than one-third of the faculty should be recruited from business practitioners. A higher percentage can bring an overbalance of mature recruits from industry at the expense of younger men from the various academic disciplines. Since their basic strength is usually found either in general management or in their areas of technical expertise, professors recruited from industry are most effective in teaching either "generalist" courses or advanced courses in their specialties. They seem to be least successful in teaching beginning courses in functional areas.

Recruiting men from other schools is one way to augment faculty rapidly. As a general rule, however, it is advisable to do this sparingly. Though men so acquired may come in with a commitment to full-time work and proven experience, the practice tends to develop power blocs within a faculty. Moreover, professors who succumb easily to enticements from other institutions may merely be bargaining for academic sinecures. Perhaps the best bet is to seek the assistant professor looking for promotion or the associate professor who wants to make a name for himself. Full professors are most effective in setting up advanced degree programs, establishing research or administrative institutes, or heading up key departments. It's also sensible to use the experience of these senior people to build curricula and to give the school academic stability and acceptability.

Students enrolled in advanced degree programs are also a potential source of permanent faculty, but some real problems exist here. One problem is to select the right students. Another is to obtain the support needed to maintain them while they undertake study leading to advanced degrees. This is sometimes done by tieing the student into a long-term contract, say, a two-year commitment to teach for each year's support. This approach is somewhat risky since it takes a long time for a man to complete his education, and he can always change his mind. It can yield good results, however, if financial resources are adequate.

Another possibility is to hire doctoral students enrolled in programs at other institutions. Doctoral students with an interest in the field of international business might be attracted to European business schools from the U.S. or the United Kingdom with an offer of a combined research-teaching position. Such people could help give a research program the requisitive visibility and good will, and there is always the possibility that they will remain on the faculty at the completion of their research. Even if they don't remain, these men can act as a liaison with the institution whose staff they eventually join. Research strength can be obtained in other ways, too. Individual research can be subsidized at another institution provided the recipient agrees to participate in a teaching and/or research program at the sponsoring European business school on completion of his research project.

All of these approaches are time consuming and costly, but they hold promise of attracting well-trained scholars into business teaching. It goes without saying, however, that favorable pay rates, the opportunity for research and the ability to reach good students must be available if these people are to remain on the job.

CURRICULUM: TEAR DOWN THE IVY

No one in the academic world would claim to have all the answers to curriculum problems, and one prime requisite is to retain an open mind. This point is especially important in the newly developing business school precisely because it is new and developing. If European business schools can remain adaptable in the face of changing conditions they will avoid some of the problems that have troubled, and still trouble, business education in the U.S.

American educators have tended to base a business curriculum on finance, accounting, economics, mathematical techniques, human behavior, marketing, production and various integrating courses such as managerial administration and business policy. In addition, they have developed useful courses in important background areas such as the intellectual and operational history of business and the process of group decision making. These basics are then supplemented by electives in the various fields of specialization. Though almost all of these course titles seem well suited to a European context, European business schools faced with scarce teaching resources must be aware of the perils of course proliferation. They should, however, be willing to add courses when required by changing situations.

Actually, there is very little wrong with the curriculum at the typical European business school that can't be cured by the establishment of a full-time faculty. Once able, permanent people come on the scene in adequate numbers they will take the steps needed to revise and redevelop the aims and goals of both individual courses and integrated degree programs. When these people tear the ivy down, the way will be clear to set up the kinds of instruction best suited to meet the needs of each institution.

Of all the problems found in European business education, the student problem is the least formidable. Students in Europe invariably are capable of doing more than their instructors demand of them. If they come from industry they are eager to learn and to establish a good record with their employers. If drawn from the college community, they are surprisingly mature and conscientious. Since many already have industrial experience they tend to know just what they want, and, given the proper direction, they work effectively and well. To quote a senior professor at a leading English school of business, "The students are, taken altogether, a rather pleasant and hardworking group of individuals."

One minor problem exists in student selection. Since selection may be performed quite casually, students with unequal degrees of preparation are often grouped together, and this tends to create a leveling effect on the entire program. The current practice of basing admission on personal evaluations and subjective standards administered by part-time admissions officers undermines attempts to achieve academic excellence. This problem can be corrected or alleviated by basing selection on such relatively objective criteria as grades and academic recommendations. Yet even with certain obvious deficiencies in admissions procedures, the quality of the student body is not a serious problem. There are enough good students presently on hand to more than occupy the resources available to train them.

What then is the current state of the art of business education in Europe? In one man's opinion, the situation is mixed, and the future, though not depressingly dismal, is nevertheless some cause for concern. In broad terms the following conditions exist:

1. Many administrators are unaware of the true nature of their calling and they may not possess the skills and training needed to perform their duties properly.

2. Faculties are generally of a part-time nature, and this lessens their academic effectiveness.

3. The typical curriculum tends to be either too theoretical or too committed to a particular type of pedagogical technique.

4. Students are generally well qualified but they could be selected more carefully.

It is an oversimplification to state that European business education is young and that time will correct many of its current difficulties. Similar institutions in the U.S. have in past years invited long-term hardship by adopting such a simplistic philosophy. Even a totally sympathetic viewer can see that certain positive steps must be taken before European business schools can assume their rightful place among the world's leaders. These steps must be taken soon: a dynamic and growing European economy needs the talent these schools can provide and deserves the best they have to offer.

Additional References

Corbett, E. N. "Some Problems of Management Education in Britain and a Proposed Solution," *Management International,* No. 6 (1965).

Cox, Robert W. "Education for Development," *International Organization* (World Peace Foundation), Vol. 22, No. 1 (Winter, 1968), pp. 310–31.

Developing Better Managers—An Eight Nation Study. Education Department—EGS, New York: National Industrial Conference Board, 1961.

Farmer, R., and Richman, B. "Environmental Constraints: Education," *Comparative Management and Economic Progress,* chap. 6, pp. 74–108. Homewood, Ill.: Richard D. Irwin, Inc., 1965.

Gordon, R. A., and Howell, J. E. *Higher Education for Business.* New York: Columbia University Press, 1959.

Harbison, Frederick. "The African University and Human Resource Development," *Journal of Modern African Studies,* Vol. 3, No. 1 (May, 1965).

Harbison, Frederick, and Myers, Charles. "The Development of Managerial Resources," *Management in the Industrial World,* chap. 5. New York: McGraw-Hill Book Co., Inc., 1959.

————. *Manpower and Education.* New York: McGraw-Hill Book Co., Inc., 1964.

"Higher Education for Managers," *Progress,* November 3, 1965.

"Identifying and Developing Managers: World Wide Shortages and Remedies," *Quarterly International Survey of Business Opinion and Experience,* June, 1965.

Lauterbach, A. "Management Education in Latin America: Attitudes and Tasks," *Management International Review,* Vol. 8 (February–March, 1968), pp. 147–57.

Layard, P. R. G., and Saigal, J. C. "Educational and Occupational Characteristics of Manpower: An International Comparison," *British Journal of Industrial Relations,* Vol. 4, No. 2 (July, 1966).

Marsh, John. "International Man and Management Development," *Advanced Management Journal,* January, 1968, p. 11.

Masson, T. M. *Management Education in Five European Countries.* London: Business Publications, Ltd., 1965.

Pierson, F., *et al. The Education of American Businessmen.* New York: Carnegie Foundation, 1959.

Rado, E. R. "Manpower, Education and Economic Growth," *Journal of Modern African Studies,* Vol. 4, No. 1 (May, 1966), pp. 83–93.

Ryoji, Itō. "Education as a Basic Factor in Japan's Economic Growth," *The Developing Economies,* Vol. 1, No. 1 (June, 1963), p. 37.

"Social Functions of Education," *International Social Science Journal* (UNESCO) special issue, Vol. 29, No. 3 (1967).

Wilson, A. T. M. "Some Sociological Aspects of Systematic Management Development," *Journal of Management Studies,* February, 1966.

chapter eight

Managerial Philosophies and Practices

In preceding chapters our selected readings have surveyed the relationship between culture and economic development with special concern for the role of the manager. In this chapter we shall examine a diversity of philosophies and practices of management—and how they are related to cultural factors.

Selection: "Social and Cultural Factors in Management Development," from the International Labour Review

In the introduction to a special issue on culture and management, the *Review* considers management and its development in different parts of the world.

Selection: "The Interplay of Culture and Management in a Guatemalan Textile Plant," Manning Nash

A specific case study dramatically illustrates the impact of culture on day-to-day leadership styles, communications, and training.

Selection: "Cultural Patterns in the Role of the Manager," Mason Haire, Edwin E. Ghiselli, and Lyman W. Porter

The authors of this selection made what is undoubtedly the largest effort so far to investigate the philosophies and attitudes of managers—3,500 managers in 14 countries. They relate their findings to cultural and economic factors. Their conclusions are interesting, and some are surprising.

Selection: "Contrasting Motives and Attitudes of Managers in More and Less Developed Countries," David C. McClelland

Several readings in Chapters Three, Four, and Five emphasized the importance of manager motivation in economic development. In this selection from his epic study, *The Achieving Society*, McClelland examines motives in countries in different stages of economic development—the United States, Italy, Turkey, and Poland.

Selection: "American vs. European Management Philosophy," Otto H. Nowotny.

With special attention to attitudes toward time, secrecy, and progress, in this *Harvard Business Review* article Nowotny graphically describes the differences—and growing similarities—between U.S. and continental managers.

Selection: "Group Management, European Style," F. Newton Parks

In the United States in recent years, there has been a trend toward top-level management by executive committee. The managing director of European operations for Booz, Allen & Hamilton, management consultants, discusses the longer tradition of collegial management on the continent.

Selection: "An Aspect of Management Philosophy in the United States and Latin America," Eugene C. McCann

The author examines the science and art components in management in the Northern and Southern continents. Science supposedly is dominant in the North, art in the South.

Selection: "Management Aims and Development Needs in Latin America," Albert Lauterbach

Professor Lauterbach surveys the historical experience, progress, and future of management in South America.

selection 22

Social and Cultural Factors in Management Development*

Editors, International Labour Review

The principal objective of an industrial enterprise is normally an economic one: the provision of goods or services to the community or some section of it in return for payment. This is true even where the undertaking is publicly owned and is primarily required to provide a public service which may not always be profitable. However, an enterprise is also a social organism composed of people, who are the products of the society in which they live. Managers in industry thus have social as well as economic and technical tasks to perform, since management, by definition, involves achieving specified ends through the medium of people.

Even in cases where both managers and the managed are the products of a society that has evolved its own body of management theory and methods over a long period of industrial growth the problem of maintaining the enterprise as an economic and social entity at peak efficiency is by no means a simple one.

But management theory and practice as they are known today have evolved largely within a restricted range of cultures and, as industrialisation spreads, it is becoming necessary to transfer them into cultural settings far different from those in which they originated. They may be introduced by a manager from one country going to manage a firm in another, or by people from a developing country coming to study and work in a more industrialised one and returning to take up management positions in their own country; or they may be transferred, as the I.L.O. and certain other bodies are trying to transfer them, through development and training programmes for managers in developing countries. In every case this involves the application of knowledge and practices evolved in one cultural and social environment in the circumstances of another.

Eleven years of experience on the part of the I.L.O. in over 50 countries have shown that, if management knowledge and practices are to be successfully applied in new conditions, then it is necessary to adapt them to suit those conditions and in some cases to assist local managers to evolve suitable new practices.

International Labour Review, Vol. 94, No. 2 (August, 1966), pp. 101–7.

This is especially true of areas of management that are directly concerned with people—less so with the purely technical areas. If managers in developing countries are going to learn and apply up-to-date management practices, they must be able to see the value of them in terms of their own needs and problems and the socio-economic context within which they are working. Such practices must be presented in ways that are acceptable in terms of the social and educational background of those who are to receive them. Unless these conditions are fulfilled, the transfer of knowledge is likely to be at most only partially successful.

THE KEY ROLE OF MANAGEMENT AND THE IMPORTANCE OF MANAGEMENT DEVELOPMENT

The last two decades have witnessed one of the greatest revolutions of this century: the revolution of rising expectations of people everywhere of a better standard of living. At the same time technological change (including automation) is proceeding apace in highly industrialised countries. In many developing countries industrialisation programmes, based on imported technology and know-how, are being carried out in large-scale units. These circumstances have brought to the fore the preponderant role of technology in society. It has been noted that technology greatly influences—and on occasion determines—social patterns. It disrupts established patterns and requires the development of new ones. Modern technology, in order to function efficiently, demands behaviour that is predominantly rational—i.e. logical behaviour as opposed to tradition-oriented behaviour—on the part of those directly connected with its operation, especially those at the place of work. In some cases it becomes so dominant that it is pursued as an end in itself instead of remaining a means in the service of man.[1]

Parallel to the revolution of rising expectations and the growing use of technology, a silent but pervasive management revolution has also taken place. Its features have been a continuing separation of management from ownership and a growing recognition of management as a profession that includes different specialisations. This has in turn influenced the criteria for the selection of managers and the approaches to managerial organisation. It is now being realised that effective management depends more on the co-ordination of human effort than on the control of operations; that it involves not only directing men and skills but also tapping knowledge and encouraging innovation; and that, though pecuniary reward is important, it is not sufficient in itself to motivate man to excel in his work or even to commit himself to a particular employment. Management is also discovering that changes in technique or organisation, even if they are for the common good by objective standards, will meet with resistance if not properly introduced. This is because those affected may have certain

---

[1]See I.L.O., *Report of the Director-General: Industrialisation and labour,* Report I (Part I) (Geneva: International Labour Conference, 50th sess., 1966).

sentiments, attitudes, customs, traditions or values that are incompatible with the proposed changes. It is increasingly appreciated that technical innovation affects the social fabric, and that in most cases social change is a prerequisite of technical innovation. This is in contrast with management practices at an earlier period when man was considered an exchangeable unit of labour, and when innovation, if not accepted, could be imposed and resistance in most cases subdued or oppressed—in spite of the tremendous social and material cost involved.

Many factors led to this evolution in management attitude. To cite but a few: the universal spread of ideas of social justice, industrial democracy, and the dignity of labour; the growth of trade unions and their challenge to unilateral management authority; increasing governmental intervention in labour–management relations; the elaboration and diffusion of new management concepts (scientific management, human relations); the shortage of labour; and the disruptive effects of rapid technological changes on social and cultural patterns—especially in developing countries. These disruptions, in turn, may retard industrialisation programmes which might otherwise be successful. As the Director-General of the I.L.O. has pointed out—

> Successful industrialisation . . . implies a social revolution. To set up industry and introduce new technology is not only a matter of acquiring capital and a knowledge of techniques. Modern industry calls into being its own kind of society. It requires attitudes towards work different from those of traditional rural communities; it functions at a different pace, and makes people organise their lives in a different way; it challenges old values, it creates new values. This social transformation which must accompany industrialisation affects, indeed, a man's whole view of the meaning and purpose of life and of his relations to his fellow man.[2]

During the first years of the I.L.O. productivity and management development programme the emphasis was on increasing productivity through industrial engineering techniques. Developing countries and the I.L.O. were soon to realise that this was not enough. The shortage of trained management was one of the strategically limiting factors to the realisation of industrialisation programmes aimed at increasing the national income.

The key role of managers and the importance of management development have been stressed in a recent I.L.O. report—

> No one class of people has more influence on the economic and social life of a nation . . . than its managers. . . . They have control over the utilisation of the major part of the nation's wealth, including most of its assets in foreign exchange. On their knowledge of their jobs and the efficiency with which they perform them depends the productivity of the material and human resources of the country. They are directly responsible for the large part of happiness and well-being of those, numbering from hundreds of thousands in some countries to many millions in others, who work under their direct control, and for that of millions who are affected by the result of their activities.[3]

---

[2] I.L.O., *The I.L.O. and Asia* (a public information pamphlet) (Geneva, 1962), p. 1.

[3] Idem, *The effectiveness of the I.L.O. management development and productivity projects* (Management Development Series No. 3) (Geneva, 1965) (offset), p. 73.

Small wonder then that such importance should be attached to management development, defined by the meeting of experts mentioned above as—

an activity directed towards the further development of the knowledge and skills of managerial personnel once they have passed the initial stage of training or have acquired experience through practice. It covers all functions of management and all levels of managerial personnel, up to and including top management. This latter group also includes any owner or employer who is engaged in managing his enterprise. It may be considered to include consulting and advising services designed to improve managerial performance.[4]

Yet the training of practising managers is comparatively new even in the most highly industrialised countries. The last years of the Second World War and the immediate post-war years saw a very rapid increase in the number of post-experience programmes for managers. Today, it is becoming widely accepted that management is a profession with its own body of academic knowledge and that a manager, like any other professional man, should continue to improve his professional knowledge during his working life. In 20 years there has been an almost complete change from the attitude, formerly prevalent everywhere, that it is impossible to train managers and that they must learn by experience.

THE ENTERPRISE: A SOCIAL SYSTEM

An enterprise does not exist in a vacuum. It is situated in a local, national and international context in which it finds its markets, and from which it draws its supplies and raw materials, its personnel and most of its ideas and knowledge. An enterprise and those who work in it operate within a culture or a plurality of cultures. While there are many similarities between different cultures, each has its own set of traits or elements in relation to knowledge, beliefs, and artefacts. These traits provide the individual with an image of what the world is like and with standards concerning what should be done or avoided and in which circumstances, and assist him in controlling the environment in which he lives.

When two or more cultures coexist in the same society, people who belong to one of them cannot be said to be intrinsically more backward or less intelligent than those who belong to the others. A man cannot be expected to learn anything but what is available to him within the framework of the cumulative knowledge and experience of his culture. To the extent that certain segments of the population may be denied the opportunity of learning or developing new skills, their aspirations and wants will be limited and they will consequently lack initiative. Culture is not a collection of unrelated or separate traits. On the contrary, these are "so interwoven that disturbance of one element has effects on many others."[5]

A cultural trait is not good or bad *per se,* but only as viewed within a cultural setting. For instance, what is considered loyalty in one society may be called

---

[4] Point 9 of the conclusions adopted by the meeting of experts.

[5] J. M. Juran, *Managerial breakthrough* (New York: McGraw-Hill Book Co., Inc., 1964), p. 143.

nepotism in another. Because of this "culture relativity" diverse traits, even if they do not seem at first glance to favour new techniques, should first be examined and their positive aspects retained instead of being completely disregarded. Such an approach to cultural traits may result in altering the techniques to fit existing conditions, or in modifying some of the conditions to suit the new technique, or in evolving the most appropriate combination for the situation.

It should be no cause for surprise that people employed in an enterprise largely persist in—or at least do not completely discard—the social patterns of behaviour they have learned in the culture in which they were brought up; to the extent that these patterns are compatible with those required in the operation of the industrial enterprise, they are able to further its objectives. Otherwise structural changes must take place both in the culture, if it is to survive, and in the enterprise, if it is to grow and prosper. Since cultural traits are learned they can also be unlearned and replaced by new elements—provided that requisite conditions for learning and adaptation are created and that new traits can be integrated into the existing culture without threatening its very existence. Failing this, there will be strong resistance, resulting either in external acceptance of, without internal commitment to, the new patterns, or in open conflict. Accordingly, in order to institute the indispensable minimum of rationality among the members of an enterprise—in terms of objectives, procedures, work regulations and the allocation of authority and responsibilities—its managers must attempt to understand the culture or cultures in which it operates or from which it draws its members. This will help them to decide what techniques are to be introduced or modified, how they should be promoted, and the proper timing for their implementation.

If the enterprise is fortunate enough to operate in a culture favourable to industrialisation, many existing ideas, beliefs and values will prove to be an asset to management in the form of hard work, internal discipline, innovation, initiative, personal ambition and achievement.

On the other hand, certain traditions and social institutions are incompatible with industrial employment and have a negative effect on the enterprise and on management as a system of authority.

For example, in rural societies, where kinship usually provides the basis for social security, the focus is not on the individual himself but on the family, usually in its extended form. An increase in pay for a worker often means an additional family member to support (who may come from the village to the city). In such circumstances it is understandable that there is little incentive for additional financial gain through promotion or hard work. Blind or excessive loyalty to one's relations or friends may lead to recruitment and promotions based only on social ties without regard to achievement, which endangers efficiency. But, on the other hand, it may enable management to adopt a paternalistic attitude as a method of minimising the disruptive consequences of industrialisation, limiting dismissals and instituting life-employment patterns.

Limitations on occupational mobility, because of restrictions on social mobility, exist in varying degrees in many cultures, sometimes overtly and in most cases in subtle forms. The more conservative and rigid the society in its observance of social stratification patterns, the more difficult it is for management to operate efficiently. Not only does this increase the cost of day-to-day operations; it may also restrict management's freedom of recruitment, especially of qualified managers, at least at the early stages of operation.

Enlightened management can modify these norms gradually; but even if it succeeds in doing so, while the community adheres to the older ways of doing things both management and employee may still have to live and work in two different cultures.

INTRODUCING CHANGE

The underlying theme here is that culture is learned from infancy onwards and that cultural traits are interwoven in a composite whole. While an enterprise is a society in its own right, it is also part of the larger society and wider culture in which it operates.

Introducing new techniques or methods of work in an enterprise is not like replacing parts of a mechanical structure or adding parts to it. It more closely resembles grafting a part of a living organism upon another; unless the new part is accepted, not only will it be rejected but also there is a danger that both organisms may decay. Changes in any society—and an enterprise is one—challenge existing knowledge and beliefs, disturb relationships among individuals and groups and impinge on the motives and values of the individual.

Not very long ago an enterprise may have had the power to impose changes down the line and crush resistance. This authoritarian attitude is now successfully opposed in most cases and management has learnt to rely on other methods of introducing change effectively. In this regard the value of prior consultation with the staff affected by the change is increasingly appreciated.

A body of knowledge now exists on the principles and methods of social change.[6] Changes in an enterprise may be recommended by an outside consultant either from the same culture or from another society, as in the case of international technical co-operation. In the latter situation the work to be done is a joint effort. Knowledgeable persons of the enterprise or of the country concerned should guide the foreign expert to learn about the local culture so that whatever advice he gives will meet local needs. Together they must overcome cultural barriers where they exist, and evolve methods most suitable to the prevailing conditions. Similarly, managers who have been trained abroad should appreciate the positive and negative influences of the existing culture on their work.

---

[6] Wilbert E. Moore, *Social change* (Englewood Cliffs, N.J.: Prentice-Hall, Inc., 1963).

This broad outlook is becoming increasingly important because of the conflict between the desire to achieve rapid industrialisation and that to keep the resultant social stress to a minimum; in the resolution of this conflict the study in depth of the experiences of different cultures will play a useful part.

selection 23

The Interplay of Culture and Management in a Guatemalan Textile Plant*

Manning Nash

INDUSTRIALIZATION: AN INQUIRY INTO IMPACTS

This is the story of the people of Cantel, an Indian community in the western highlands of Guatemala. It is the description and analysis of a people who have successfully moved from a simple farming technology not much removed from that of their pre-Columbian ancestors, to operating in their midst Central America's largest textile mill.

The adaptation of this Indian community to factory work, cash wages, and to wider ties with the modern industrial world is a precipitate of history. Accommodations between the Indian culture and the factory came through the process of trial and error over more than three generations, without blueprint, without planning agency, and nearly without notice. Today, in the highlands of Guatemala, a people still speaking Quiché, the women yet in costume, the world view of spirits and saints largely intact, have learned how to coexist with a factory regime. Cantel, of course, has changed since the coming of the factory. But the changes, as will be noted later, have been of the kind which permit the people to keep their social integrity and their cultural distinctiveness.

The study of Cantel serves two chief purposes. First, it tells of the way this particular community evolved mechanisms enabling it to adjust to a new mode of production with relatively little cultural loss or social disorganization. Second, Cantel's experience sheds light on the process of industrialization itself, sharpening our insight into social and cultural change, and clarifying our interpretation

*From *Machine Age Maya: The Industrialization of a Guatemalan Community* (Menasha, Wisc.: American Anthropological Association, Memoirs No. 87, 1958), reprinted in Charles R. Walker, *Modern Technology and Civilization* (New York: McGraw-Hill Book Co., Inc., 1962), pp. 357–65.

of cause and effect. . . . These twin theoretical or scientific goals conduce to the practical end at which all science, social included, eventually aims: the conscious and knowledgeable intervention of man in his own affairs.

THE PLACE AND THE PEOPLE

Cantel is one of a series of Indian municipios in the western highlands of Guatemala. Like many other Indian communities, it is a distinctive social entity. Its physical boundaries are clearly marked. Its inhabitants wear a distinctive costume, and they speak a local variety of Quiché. The customs of its population vary in small but infinite ways from neighboring municipios. Cantel's radical difference from other municipios is the presence within its boundaries of Central America's largest cotton textile mill and the employment in that plant of about a fourth of its economically active population.

THE FACTORY: ITS INTRODUCTION, HISTORY, AND RELATION TO THE COMMUNITY

In 1876 the Spanish firm of Sanchez y Hijos brought a cotton textile mill into the municipio of Cantel. The mill was set up along the banks of the Samalá River, because its flow gave enough power to run a turbine, which in turn powered the spinning machines and other machines in the factory. The Cantelenses resented the factory. Stories of the fears then current are recited today with a note of mockery. In 1884 this resentment turned to an attempt to oust the factory. In response to this threat, soldiers of the national army were stationed around the factory and in the town center of Cantel. The presence of troops curbed overt antagonism but the first workers in the factory were not from Cantel, and Cantelenses did not come to the factory in any numbers until about 1890.

Prior to 1880 the factory employed about 25 persons. Since the turn of the century the work force has fluctuated between 800 and 1,000 persons. Although my data are not full for the period prior to 1945, it is clear that absenteeism, worker discontent, and a fairly extensive turnover were chronic features of the factory until the third or fourth decade of this century. The factory management gradually began to add services and make concessions to the workers which reduced the attrition in the labor force and apparently helped stabilize it. The factory began building houses in 1910, increasing the numbers available to workers until 1945. The main streets of the factory settlement, the public buildings, and many of the factory-owned workers' houses were equipped with electricity in the early 1930's. A clinic was established, and twenty years ago a factory school was opened. Land was loaned to workers without charge. Random interviews with many workers indicate that long, continuous periods of employment are now the rule.

This earlier state of coercion, of bringing in foreigners, of recruiting marginal Cantelenses to work, of low wages and long hours, might be considered a deterrent to the present accommodation of the factory and the community and to the commitment of a Cantel labor force. But just the opposite has in fact obtained. What could easily have been a heritage of suspicion and fear has been converted by the Cantelenses, through comparison with the currently better and freer circumstances, into a base line from which to judge present advantage. The first responses of a people to cultural intrusion do not necessarily have the same positive or negative aspect after a time-seasoned judgement.

Relation to the Community

In the period since 1906, but chiefly since the 1930's, the factory and community have gradually worked out an accommodation. Through mutual concessions, the basis has been laid for a smooth integration of the factory into the community, and of community personnel into the factory. The modifications which permit the factory to go about its business of production and the community to continue its institutions were discovered in the process of living side by side, rather than planned.

Factory work schedules take into account the traditional holidays of the community, as well as the traditional obligations of community members. Periods of fiesta, like the town fair and Easter Week, are not factory work periods. These long holidays are covered by Saturday afternoon overtime, not a usual period of factory operation. Neither production nor wages are reduced as a consequence of holidays. The four-hour period between shifts allows the factory worker with a small plot of land to attend to his agricultural duties without taking time off. It also permits women to do some of their household chores or to nurse small infants. If a man's turn comes up in one of the civil or religious offices the factory gives him time off, ranging from an afternoon to a two-year leave, without his suffering loss of job or tenure.

When it is asked why Cantelenses came to the factory, the first answer is poverty. A real difference in income between factory and farm workers, coupled with the gap between ideal standard and the actual level of living, may be considered the propellant for seeking factory employment. Many of the factory workers were women and young men who, outside of the factory would earn no income. For these classes of workers the factory represents a complete economic advantage, not merely a relative one in terms of alternate income possibilities.

The factory wage has certain other characteristics which make it appealing when contrasted with farming income. It has regularity and continuity. Agricultural return, both for hired hands and proprietors, has peaks and troughs corresponding to the harvesting, planting, and marketing cycle.

The regularity and continuity of factory income are valued because Cantelenses like to be able to say that they are free of debt, independent and able to buy what they need when they need it. In addition to the pull of wages, the factory offers social services. Housing is provided in 125 rent-free houses. The social importance of having or owning a house cannot be overestimated in Cantel.

The factory also maintains its own school, clinic, and doctor. The school has a six-hour day in contrast to the four-hour day of the national school; this longer school day is considered advantageous for the absorption of knowledge. Medical facilities provided by the factory include a clinic where simple remedies are dispensed and medical advice and prescriptions are given.

To some 30 to 40 per cent of its workers, the factory loans up to two cuerdas of land. This loan of factory land may yield an increment to cash income as well as giving some of the landless a sense of ownership of soil, a strong value in this peasant community.

Factory work allows a man to become eligible for the Guatemalan system of social security, a kind of accident and health insurance rather than an old-age or retirement plan. There is no health service for the nonfactory workers in Cantel.

Such are the economic dimensions of the factory's attractiveness: a clear and significant income differential, social and medical services, and the possibility of house or land provided by the factory. They have pull in a context of rural poverty and inadequate land resources.

Adapting to a New Occupational Role

Between recruitment, which is accomplished by the factors enumerated, and commitment, which is personal involvement in the industrial work cycle, lies adjustment or adaptation to a new occupational role. The Canteleno in the factory finds himself working under conditions for which there are no homologies in his society or life experience. He often comes to the factory illiterate (for the past four or five years only "literates" have been hired), without previous experience with machinery of any kind—neither the gadgets of the housewife nor the motors and tools of Western men. The incoming worker is accustomed to small groups where work is carried out by men doing a variety of things rather than by division of labor which requires coordination and teamwork in adjusting to a machine tempo. He is accustomed to work without direction or supervision. He works with relatives or acquaintances, not strangers, choosing with whom he shall share effort. If he is tired or ill he need not go to his field, but the factory has a fixed hour for reporting and a fixed period of continual effort. In agricultural work, performances are judged by the farmer himself against a physical harvest; in the factory, output is measured by impersonal standards of so many inches of cloth, and there is no product which is the worker's own. This discontinuity between the occupational roles of farm and factory worker sets the problem of the individual's accommodation to factory work.

The factory work is now accepted as part of the natural landscape; the railroad that once whizzed by the Pueblo, the bulldozers that came to make the new national highway that is to pass below Cantel, the newly installed water system, and other such changes have their momentary upset in communal life and then are quickly taken as the "natural" part of the environment over which Cantelenses have no control. This can be put another way; as personalities, the run of Cantelenses have a streak of resignation to fate, be it of the natural world or of the larger social world, and when they see that a thing is inevitable they work out some kind of adjustment to it.

One final kind of personal trait strikes one about the Cantelenses. They are personally well disciplined and regular in habit. The clock is perfectly suited to the way they like to run their lives. An orderly, undeviating daily routine, seasonally adjusted, is an ideal nearly approached by Cantelenses. And this accords with the general lack of flamboyance or "style" in almost any aspect of personal life. There are no specialized skills in love-making, in cooking, in drawing embroidery designs, in songs, or in dances. Personal creative ability means a break with traditions, and the Cantelenses would be suspicious of it and perhaps would not even understand it. They have no desires or psychic energies to give to the creation of experience or beauty which passes ordinary and common occurrence.

Learning New Work Habits

New workers in the factory are trained by other Cantelenses, in a manner similar to learning situations in the home and throughout childhood. A man or woman is hired as an assistant on some machine, say a weaving or spinning machine. For five or six weeks the newly hired worker performs menial tasks such as bringing material to the machine or taking finished goods off of it, but most of the time is spent in observing the operations of the person running the machine. I have spent hours watching a new employee learning a job. In one case a girl was learning to tend a loom. She would take her place at the side of the loom operator in the morning, bringing the cones of dyed cotton. Standing by the machine she watched the operator go through the motions of running the loom. She neither asked questions nor was given advice. When the machine snagged or stopped, she would look carefully to see what the operator did to get it back into motion. When a table cloth was woven, she removed it from the loom. This constituted her daily routine for nearly six weeks, and at the end of this time she announced that she was ready to run a loom. Her foreman told me that at no time during her learning and apprentice period had she touched a machine or practiced operating. When she said she was ready, the machine she had been observing for six weeks was turned over to her and she operated it, not quite as rapidly as the girl who had just left it, but with skill and assurance. What went on in the "training" period? The apprentice was applying the way of learning she has been taught in Cantel. She observes and internally rehearses the set of operations until she feels able to perform. She will not try her hand until she feels confident, for to fumble and make mistakes is a cause for *vergüenza*–public shame. She does not ask questions because that would annoy the person teaching her, and they might also think she is stupid. After sufficient observation the apprentice arrives at the point where she feels that she can carry on the necessary physical operations. I have observed this method of learning among the home weavers with their young apprentices, among the young boys who learn to drive cars, and even in the case of a man who was learning to sing but never sang a note until after a five or six hour session of just listening. In this way the recruit is inducted into his new job and its new skills easily and according to customary training patterns.

This method of learning no doubt has severe limitations and may not function when the learning is symbolic or of purely mental operations, but it works in teaching the simple tasks of running cotton textile machines. Management reports six weeks as about the upper limit of anyone learning to run a loom or a spinning machine. I am told that operating the more complex jacquard requires more learning time, and the factory looks for the *listos,* the bright ones, among its working forces to train as operators. But for the other operations the illiterate farmer or housewife, a stranger to machinery, is converted into a reasonably proficient factory hand in six weeks.

The learning process is slightly modified when a Canteleno learns to be a caporal, machine shop worker, or assistant in the electrical shop. Here the technical staff gives verbal instruction and explains the principles and operations of the machine or instrument. The technical staff complains that Cantelenses do not practice and often make serious and costly mistakes when they think they can operate one of the more complex machines. In the more skilled jobs, the complaint is that Cantelenses are often "indifferent and unenthusiastic" when they learn. This complaint of the foreign technical staff is a recognition of the Cantelenses' desire to appear calm and dignified, even when a neophyte may be eager to learn new skills.

These qualities of reserve, patience, and caution often make the Cantelenses seem, to Western eyes, slow-witted or dullards. But this is not so; they learn quickly if the conditions are right as in the factory, and many are keen observers of their fellow men. It is only the necessity of exercising personal controls to appear reserved, calm, and prudent in public behavior which gives the social life of Cantel its characteristic tone of an unruffled, even tenor, of a placid, emotion-free existence.

Factory training, where results are rapidly achieved, contrasts with the training situation in the school. Teachers say it is difficult to get performance, and Cantelenses say that too much school work or thinking makes the head *caliente,* hot, and leads to minor illness.

Tempo and Routine of Work

The tempo of the machines requires constant attention and care, but such application does not appear to be a major factor in the adjustment to industrial work. The Canteleno will not take more machines to tend nor run one faster than he comfortably can, despite the incentive of piece work. Compared to North American mill hands, the factory managers report that the Cantel worker is slower and runs fewer machines. Whether this is due to the worker or to the age of the machine and its disposition in relation to the task, I do not know. But the pace of the machines does not appear man-killing, and the Cantelenses say it is not. The unaccustomed posture of standing all day or using the same set of muscles all day is not considered much of a strain. The minor changes in body work rhythm and in constant application required by the machine are taken to easily by the Cantelenses, and I could not elicit one complaint about factory work on that score. From watching Cantelenses run machines, it appears that changes in motor habits and working strains do not require much psychological reorientation or occasion physiological crises. For the majority the shift in work pattern is not a jolt, but at most only a little ripple which in a year or so is not even easily recalled, and questioning about the problem usually brings blank stares or long pauses while memory is ransacked for "difficulties" in adapting body tempo to machine tempo. Those who did not adjust to the tempo have left the factory, and of the ones with whom I have talked, none who are now engaged in economic activity left because of the difficulty or strangeness of the work. Only one man, whose bare feet on the wet concrete floor of the dyeing room bothered him, complained to me that he found factory work more unpleasant than farm work.

Supervision and Discipline

Working in coordination or under orders does not appear to make factory work less desirable. Work at the machines is coordinated by a caporal in charge of a line of machines. He is a Canteleno. He and the worker he directs understand each other. The caporal never raises his voice when giving directions, and rarely tells a man what to do. Only occasionally does he call out *"apúrate,"* or hurry up, when someone slows down at his machine. If the worker is on piece work, he is more likely to call out to the caporal to adjust the machine if it is stalled or slowed. The caporal's authority is limited by his sense of how it should be exercised; that is, he does not order but rather suggests what is to be done. Workers seldom complain that they have been mistreated or that a caporal is unreasonable in his demands.

Before the organization of the union, the supervision and discipline routine was less to the taste and custom of Cantel. The foreign engineer, not bound by conventional understandings as to the proper exercise of authority, was wont to circulate about the room and slap laggards across the head. The factory owners on their periodic visits did the same. Physical force and abusive language were used by the factory owner and the technical staff to get things done in the way they wanted them done. The workers always objected to this treatment, since being publicly reprimanded is scandalous and shameful, and being struck as a means of correction puts one in the category of a child. I cannot judge how great a factor this discipline was in labor turnover prior to the union; it was not given as a reason in any of the cases of which I have record. However, the union frowned on physical punishment of any sort. The British engineer struck a worker who had ruined an expensive machine, and the union brought a complaint against him; he was asked to make a public apology to the worker in the presence of the manager. This affirmed the principle, operative since the late 1940's, that discipline was the job of the caporal. Caporals could use any means except insult and corporal punishment.

There is little status difference and no sentimental differential between the caporal and the worker in his line. Both are workers, distinct from the clerical staff and the managerial interests. In exercising his authority, which stems from the imperatives of keeping the machines operating and coordinating work so that the flow of materials does not occasion lags between operations, the caporal takes his orders from the technical staff and passes them on to the line worker according to the impersonal needs of the job. But the way in which he gives orders is in terms of Cantel notions about how men are to be treated when they work for each other. The caporal is a worker who gets slightly more pay; he is not of, and not necessarily for, the management. Outside the factory walls the foreman's prestige is no greater than that of the mill hand. Inside the mill, the caporal does not flaunt his authority nor give many or unnecessary instructions and commands, and neither his dress nor his language marks him off from the machine hand.

Strict observance of the cultural definitions of authority and its legitimate exercise by the caporal gives supervision and discipline the same tone as the organization of simpler work groups in the agricultural tasks. The virtual status coincidence of caporal and line worker insulates the management from the workers, and keeps the owners in the dark as to why one set of machines turns out only so much when they think it should be producing more. The pace on a line of machines is set by the more experienced workers, and the others, including the caporal, take it as the given pace.

If the relationship between caporal and worker serves to isolate management from worker, it paradoxically encourages the paternalistic relationship between worker and employer, so common in Latin enterprises. Since the caporal is not an intermediary, the worker expresses his grievances directly to the patron—the owner or white-collar employee. Prior to unionization, and even afterward, the smallest grievances were carried directly to the patron. In our conception of him as policy maker or entrepreneur he would never concern himself with settlement of such picayune affairs, but he personally collected information and handled the problem in a face-to-face way. This mode of dealing with complaint and allegation is paralleled in community life by the *alcalde's* personal and prompt dispatch of civil grievances. . . .

selection 24
Cultural Patterns in
the Role of the Manager*

Mason Haire, Edwin E. Ghiselli, and Lyman W. Porter

We have a good many impressionistic reports of national managerial stereotypes, ranging from scholarly summaries through journalistic descriptions to tourist-anthropological anecdotes. Hardly a traveller finishes a whirlwind tour or a scholar a three-day conference at Salzburg or Copenhagen but what he is ready—even eager—to describe the way European managers think. Useful though these insights have been, we also need strictly comparable data—responses to the same questions asked of samples of managers in a number of countries. That was the task of this study: to find an empirical answer to the question of similarities and differences in managers' attitudes. In these days of rapid change in international trade patterns and increased proximity of countries, it is not necessary to emphasize the importance of a further understanding of managers' viewpoints, and if they exist, of national differences in such viewpoints. As a first approach, a questionnaire, asking identical questions, was administered to a sample of managers in each of a number of countries.

Carefully collected objective data offer advantages, although they are less immediately satisfying than global intuitive impressions. But something must be sacrificed for rigor. In asking identical questions in all countries, one is limited to the questions that apply to all countries. It is difficult to frame a question about pricing, wage-setting, or accounting practices that will apply equally well in the United States, Spain, and Denmark. One is forced back, for questions that are relevant to all, to fundamental issues that are common to all, rather than techniques and practices. For this reason, and also because of the investigators' professional interests, the present study focused on three phases of management thinking: (1) views on leadership and how one gets work done well and efficiently, (2) the way in which the role and practices of the manager are seen by managers themselves, and (3) the satisfactions a manager wants and gets from his job.

* From *Industrial Relations—A Journal of Economy and Society,* Vol. 2, No. 2 (February 1963), pp. 95–117. The findings in this article have been elaborated in the same author's *Managerial Thinking—An International Study* (John Wiley & Sons, Inc., 1966).

Before we go on to deal with results, a word must be said about two big problems in this kind of research. Sampling is one of them. The other is omnipresent in cross-cultural research. The thinking of managers is part of the culture itself. The instrument that asks them to express their thinking is, thus, both a part of the culture and the way we study the culture. Each of these points presents real difficulties for a cross-culture study of management.

About 3,500 responses were collected from managers in 14 countries. We aimed at a minimum of about 200 from each country, and, in general, we roughly fulfilled the goal. The sample for each country is not strictly representative of the total management population of each country. However, the samples are representative of rather large groups. Care was taken to sample different kinds of industries, geographical areas, levels of management, and the like. It seems unlikely that the discerned differences among managers in different countries are ascribable to sampling error. With all its limitations, the present sample is probably an adequate first approximation. To have been deterred by the difficulties of sampling would have meant accepting the counsel of despair. These data will add to the growing body of demographic descriptions of management which will eventually lead us to an ideal description.

Another real difficulty arises in translating a questionnaire of this type. Each item must be translated so it is not only literally correct but also carries the same impression. The first translations were made here by a translator native to the country involved. They were then independently translated back to English, as a check, by a second native. Finally, they were checked in the countries for which they were intended by social scientists and businessmen. The process is arduous and tedious and seems to have been fairly successful.

Incidentally, a good deal comes out of the job of translating itself. For example, *leader* does not translate well except in Scandinavian languages. Even before *Duce* and *Fuehrer* became loaded with special connotations, the word fit poorly in continental European languages. The word "manager" with its roots in the Latin *manus,* hand, means one handles, but in the Romance languages its use is virtually restricted to the rider's management of a horse—a connotation of simple guidance and unilateral control that would probably be unacceptable in industry. Many managerial terms are so specifically American in origin that they have been adopted unchanged in various languages. Finally, many psychological concepts—such as the need for esteem—are so closely tied to what esteem means in the culture that it is difficult to separate the thing measured from the means of measurement. These problems all restrict the things that could be asked about and occasionally involved undesirable circumlocutions.

The present report is a preliminary one in two senses. In the first place, it deals with only 11 countries out of the 14 studied and only about 2,800 managers out of the final total. In the second place, it reports the first analyses of the data. Because the full analysis of the data will not be completed for some time, however, it seemed worthwhile to prepare this preliminary report.

In general, the results will be reported in three parts: the section of the questionnaire devoted to leadership first, cognitive patterns and the cultural role of the manager second, and, finally, satisfactions of managers.

LEADERSHIP

The first section of the questionnaire consisted of eight statements to which managers were invited to respond by checking a point on a five-point scale from "agree strongly" to "disagree strongly." The items were chosen on the basis of a logical pattern and an attempt was made to cover a fair portion of the gamut of managerial attitudes on leadership. The description of attitudes of this sort as running from "democratic to autocratic forms of leadership" is too hackneyed and overloaded with meaning to be of great value, but this description is similar to many. To put it in the frame of international studies of management, the ends of the scale resemble the points Harbison and Myers describe as "dictatorial or authoritarian" on the one hand and "democratic or participative" on the other. The significance of the scale will become clearer as the results are indicated.

There are two ways one can look at these data: in terms of the substantive meaning of the items and the responses, and in terms of the way the countries group together. Taking up the first point, the eight items concerned with leadership were grouped into four logical categories. These categories were designed to represent concepts in the developing human-relations idea of a manager as a manager of people. They are as follows:

A. The belief in the individual's innate capacity for initiative and leadership.
B. The belief in sharing information and objects.
C. The belief in participative management.
D. The belief in internal control (essentially self-control of the individual flowing from the job and from understanding and commitment) rather than external control (punishment, reward, promotion).

In logical terms, the first category seems to be an absolutely essential first step to the other three. The basic reason for adopting shared objects, participation, and internal control is the contention that individuals have a capacity for initiative and leadership that is untapped by a formal unilateral command form of organization. The logical precedence of category A and its character as a building block for the others makes the results particularly striking. The outstanding first finding is that there is universally more acceptance of what might be called higher order concepts of management than there is of the basic conviction that the individual has initiative and leadership capacity. By "higher order" concepts, we mean those identified in categories B, C, and D. These *(a)* logically follow after category A, and *(b)* deal with management *practices*. No matter how we group the data, this finding stands out. In each country, in each group of countries, in all the countries taken together, the responses to the first category are different from any of the other categories or from all three taken together. The difference is large and compelling.

What can this mean? Presumably, unless one believes in untapped capacity for leadership in subordinates, a classical unilateral directive management is best. Here we find a lack of basic confidence in others and at the same time a leaning toward participative group-centered management. It is at least possible that this result is the effect of the partial digestion of 15 years of exhortation by the group-oriented consultants and professors of management. These ideas—at the level of management practices—have become common currency among management groups and in executive development programs and training courses. The data suggest that the ideas dealing with management practice have been persuasive, while the basic conviction about the nature of people remains unchanged. To the extent that this is true, and to the extent that the attitudes expressed in category A do indeed underlie sophisticated management practices, this is an unfortunate state of affairs. It is a little like building the techniques and practices of a Jeffersonian democracy on a basic belief in the divine right of kings.

This finding illustrates a sampling problem in all such studies. It is possible that those who are inclined to cooperate are also those who have been impressed by modern (human-relations?) management concepts. To the extent that this is true, it probably accentuates the commitment to the higher-order management practices represented in categories B, C, and D. However, even though this response-bias may exist, the fact remains that a large body of managers in each country—and presumably the most advanced—hold the views which have been described.

Among these last three categories of belief there is less difference in level of response. Attitudes of managers in all the countries cluster near the same value on all three scales. The belief in participation is perhaps a little weaker than in sharing information and internal control, but the difference is small in comparison with the gap between category A and all the others.

One can look at the data and be impressed by the relatively narrow range of differences among all 11 countries. They all cluster low on category A and roughly together on B, C, and D. Before considering the differences, the similarity is important to notice. In these areas of attitude there are not large, insuperable differences in beliefs about leadership among the countries. We are accustomed to some large differences in prevailing myths about these countries: the icy-eyed Prussian, the fiery, aloof Don, the equalitarianism of the shopkeeper of France and England, Sweden's Middle Way, and the like. At least in their expressed conviction, however, these cleavages do not appear sharply. Managers' views on how to manage people are somewhat similar.

Turning to the differences among countries, we ask: Are there groups of countries? How do they cluster? One way to seek an answer is to observe the way countries shift positions from one part of the chart to another. For example, England and the U.S. seem to shift as a pair. On each of the four scales they tend to be positioned—with respect to all the others—in much the same way. They usually are fairly close in scores, although that may be less useful as a sign of grouping than their tendency to move together relative to all the others. Japan does not fit neatly with any group of countries. It moves by itself. On the four scales, it moves with England and U.S. twice, with European countries once, and by itself once. It probably must stand alone on the basis of these data. The four continental European countries with a strong Latin background—France, Spain, Belgium, and Italy—move together rather tightly and can probably be usefully distinguished from the Northern European—Scandinavian group of Norway, Sweden, Denmark, and Germany. This gives us four clusters of countries: the Anglo-Saxon pair, Japan, Continental (Latin) Europe, and Northern (Teutonic) Europe.

The difference between the U.S. and all others is largest in category A. U.S. managers express the belief that all men are created equal more strongly than any of the others. Presumably managers think that they themselves have the capacity for leadership and initiative; U.S. managers feel, more than others, that the average person has the same capacities also. On the other categories the U.S. does not stand out from the group in the same way. Our textbooks and lectures may have exported a new concept of management which rests on a concept of man that is less accepted abroad.

Are the clusters ethnic or industrial? The answer seems to be largely ethnic. Norway and Sweden, industrially rather different, are very close together on the basis of these data. Denmark, though somewhat more agricultural than Sweden, tends to move closely with its Scandinavian neighbor. Germany, similar industrially to France, is close to the continental countries whenever the three Scandinavian countries are, but when it differs, it tends to swing with its Teutonic neighbors. France, Spain, Belgium, and Italy, a diverse package as far as industrialization is concerned, tend to swing together. England and the United States stand together, and Japan stands alone.

As far as the logical relationship among the categories is concerned, one might reason as follows. First comes the belief that most people have (untapped) capacities for initiative and leadership. If this idea is accepted, the manager might share information and objectives with them. Subsequently, and to a somewhat less extent, subordinates might be invited to participate in decisions. Finally, and to a still lesser extent, measures of self-control might be increasingly decentralized. Thus, the logical order of categories might follow their listing here, with a progressive embodiment in management practice of the basic belief in the individual. We have already pointed out that this relationship does not prevail, since attitudinal support for higher-order concepts of management (categories B, C, D) far outstrips the basic belief in the individual. How does the order work out, considering only the three categories of management practices? Is the logical pattern followed? Not often. Managers in England and the U.S. show more tendency to favor sharing information than eliciting participation or encouraging internal control. This at least approaches the logical model. In other clusters of countries the situation tends to be reversed. The commitment of internalized control tends to be greater than the willingness to share information or invite participation.

What can this mean? On the surface it appears impossible. How can an individual find direction and evaluation of himself in the work process if information and objectives are not shared? If we accept his self-direction, why stop short of participative management? In general, why is the psychological pattern different from the logical? It is perhaps easier to understand the variation in attitudes toward sharing information and objectives if we think in cultural terms and in terms of corporate tradition. In England and the U.S. there is a tradition of knowing and debating national issues and of full and frank disclosure of corporate financial data that differs from the rest of the countries taken as a whole. One can see why managers tend to share more in the Anglo-Saxon countries.

With respect to the categories on participation, the three major clusters of countries are substantially the same. Japan favors participation somewhat more. No clue is immediately available to explain this deviation. This leaves only the fourth category. Managers in countries other than the U.S. and England tend to believe more strongly that one finds reward and direction in the work. For the most part, managers in the other countries also believe in this more strongly than they do in either participation or sharing information. It may well be that this belief in work-centered reward and direction arises from the craft and guild tradition, perhaps stronger elsewhere than in the Anglo-Saxon countries. In any case, two things seem clear: first, the patterns of management beliefs about leadership do not follow any simple logical pattern, and second, the pattern is more or less explicable in terms of cultural traditions in the countries. Management beliefs seem shaped more by such traditions than by degree or kind of industrialization.

How do these data compare with the findings of other major comparative studies of management, for example, that of Harbison and Myers? Without being contentious, let us lift a group of relevant statements from their section on Comparisons among Countries.

1. In general, France and Italy have been characterized by a large number of small enterprises, looked on by the family as a source of personal security and conducted in an atmosphere of widespread absence of trust.

2. The British social system, although much more flexible than it was fifty years ago, still carries over a strong feeling of the virtue of "aristocratic" values and gives a high mark to the "right" background in a man. In this respect it may be less egalitarian than that of the Swedes, although in Sweden the business elite is still drawn predominantly from a small group.

3. Japan, among the advanced industrial countries, appears to have retained many of the precapitalistic features of an earlier period and has managed to harness many supposedly "feudal" values to the service of its economic development.

4. The German social system has also had a strong authoritarian element, but this has been modified to some extent by the early development of organizations outside of the dominant classes and the need, in a political democracy, for the elite groups to make concessions of various sorts in order to maintain their power.

These views are not exactly mirrored in our data. The absence of trust in Italy is perhaps apparent in the comparative reluctance to share information and allow participation, but France ranks considerably higher on both of these scales. Our data suggest that English managers are slightly less egalitarian than those in

Sweden in terms of sharing information and looking for internal control among subordinates. However, in England there is a greater degree of commitment to the basic capacities of man and to participation. The Japanese fit in fairly well with the U.S. and England on everything but participation; here they are more democratic. Finally, the German authoritarianism appears, but is almost exactly matched in Denmark, and fits the same general pattern of the non-Anglo-Saxon countries. The data presented here provide a more differentiated picture, and this perhaps accounts for some of the variations in findings.

Harbison and Myers go on to say:

5. The process of industrialization tends, other things being equal, to limit managerial authority, both as a consequence of its direct effects on the industrial system and of its indirect effects on society as a whole. Directly, the increasing complexity and interdependence of many tasks make it necessary to elicit the cooperation of subordinates; the much larger size of establishments makes it necessary to increase the number of people in key managerial posts and makes it much more difficult to recruit them entirely from a narrow group, such as the family. Indirectly, the broadening of educational opportunities, the assumption of welfare responsibilities by governments or independent institutions, and the growth of rival organizations (such as labor unions), place checks on the power of management and prompt it to seek accommodation rather than arbitrary power.

6. In none of the less developed industrial countries except Israel did we find "constitutional" management of the type prevalent in Sweden, England, or the United States.

7. Authoritarian and paternalistic practices are also common in France and Italy, despite the presence of labor movements. Centralization of control is characteristic in the French firm, as it is in the Italian or the Indian firm, for example. Despite the advanced stage of industrialization, the same pattern of authoritarian and paternalistic management seems to prevail in Japan—largely because of the social structure which, in prewar Japan at least, emphasized the unquestioning loyalty of subordinates to their superiors, as in the Japanese family.

As has been suggested, the shift from unilateral command to a more participative management does not so neatly follow stages of industrialization in our data. One might roughly identify England, Sweden, Germany, and the U.S. as the most highly industrialized of our group. Perhaps France, Belgium, and Japan would fall in a second group, and Italy, Spain, Norway, and Denmark would be classified as countries still in stages of growing industrialization. Our data on managerial control do not follow such a classification of industrialization (or any other simple one). As has been suggested, we seem forced to turn to cultural traditions to understand managerial beliefs about power and authority.

The argument based on the stage of industrialization has been prevalent for a long time, and this is perhaps true because most of the relevant studies have been done by scholars with a background in economics. The kinds of questions we ask here are determined partly by our base in other social sciences. It is, therefore, not surprising that we find other-than-economic indicators useful in distinguishing the clusters of countries.

Years ago psychologists began to argue with economists about the "economic man" concept as a tool for explaining the motivation of the individual at work. In some senses, the "stage of industrialization" argument is a more sophisticated and more complex form of the same phenomenon. One tries to see, for example, management's view of authority as a function of the level of technological and economic development. The attitude is treated as a dependent variable flowing from independent variables arising from the nature of the business activity. Another possibility—not entirely an exclusive alternative, but partly an enlarging complement—is the view that management's attitude about control is part of a broad web of values and beliefs determined by and part of a stream of cultural traditions outside the business—assumptions about man, political organization, human rights, and the like. The form of the organization, then, determined partly independently of the business, is imposed on a particular level of industrialization, which, in turn, is determined partly independently of the broad noneconomic cultural tradition.

When we view, for example, beliefs about control as part of a philosophy of management, it is not so surprising that we need to consider both economic and cultural traditions. We must have room for both the Protestant Ethic and scientific management in our causal texture. The appeal to "the conscience of the King" influences management's (and the public's) view of control as does the Industrial Revolution. Among our clusters there is a strong cleavage between the generally Roman Catholic countries and the Protestant North. It is not surprising that there are broad determinants of managerial philosophies, values, and the concept of man.

Are the Common Market countries similar on the basis of these data? No more so than the cultural-geographical grouping would indicate. It is possible that they were more different four years ago and will be more similar four years from now, but today they look like separate nations with common cultural streams, rather than a United States of Europe. One is tempted to ask, "Is England one of the leading Scandinavian countries?" Its isolation from the continent, its leadership in the Outer Seven, and the Anglo-Scandinavian political philosophy suggest the possibility. The answer here is "No." England moves with the U.S. and fairly independently of Scandinavia, which tends to move with Germany.

Japan's role in these clusters is interesting. While she stands somewhat alone in this particular family of nations, the difference is not as great as one might expect in a country so recently changed from an absolute monarchy, a cartellized and controlled economy, and a somewhat feudal concentration of capital. Where Japan stands out from the others it is almost uniformly in the direction of a more liberal position. It is perhaps well to remember that the scores represent agreement with statements of belief. There is no way at present to show how closely practice follows expression.

COGNITIVE PATTERNS IN THE ROLE OF THE MANAGER

Another part of the questionnaire attempted to get at the managers' perceptions of the role and practices of the manager. A variety of things depend on these views—what the manager feels is appropriate and inappropriate behavior in his role as manager, what kinds of values will be seen by one considering management as a career, the degree to which he can wholeheartedly invest himself in the role, and the like. In short, such views reflect the whole cultural assessment of the function of managing. To approach this problem, the more experimental and more projective semantic differential technique was used.

The semantic differential method aims, essentially, at discovering and defining a kind of cognitive map. With a group of concepts, it is possible to say how far each is from every other and in what direction. The meaning of the concepts and their psychological dynamics can be inferred from their positions in this kind of constructed mental space. Quantitatively, this is accomplished by asking respondents to rate each concept on a series of scales which remain the same across all concepts. In this case two groups of concepts were used, one dealing with management functions, and one with the superior–subordinate relationship in the culture. For functions, the concepts *to decide, to direct, to persuade, to cooperate,* and *to create* were used, as well as the more negative *to cheat, to reprimand,* and *to make a mistake.* An ordering of these into a cognitive pattern gives us some idea of a nation's view of what a manager does. In addition, hierarchical relationships were compared in three major social institutions: the army, the church, and business.

The detailed statistical analysis of the semantic differential is long and complex and will be reported more fully elsewhere. Preliminary results of this analysis are not as illuminating as in the case of the other two methods, but a brief mention is worthwhile because it illustrates further the kind of clustering of countries that occurs. For this brief presentation, four concepts and three scales have been selected. The concepts are *to direct, to persuade, to cooperate,* and *to reprimand.*

Taking all the concepts together, *to cooperate* is thought to be the most important. *To direct* is a close second, *to persuade* is next, and finally *to reprimand* is the least important (of these four) in the manager's repertory. The same order holds, roughly, for goodness. Cooperation and direction are very, very good, persuasion somewhat less so, and reprimanding the least of all. Difficulty, however, is another story. Directing is the hardest thing to do. Persuading is next hardest. Reprimanding is easier, but cooperating is slightly easier still.

Turning to the way the countries group together, we see essentially the same clusters we saw before. Spain, France, Belgium, and Italy tend to move together in a tight group. (In one case—which will be discussed later—Spain deviates markedly.) England and the U.S. behave alike, again fairly closely linked. In general, Germany and the three Scandinavian countries vary in a similar pattern. Japan, in these data, could be fitted into the (Latin) continental group of countries.

Spain stands out from all others on the function of reprimanding. It is more important in Spain, it is better, and, somewhat surprisingly, it is more difficult. Spain's isolation on this dimension is heightened by another outstanding feature of these data: there is remarkably close correspondence among managers in all the countries in their perception of these functions. While an occasional country stands out—e.g., Denmark finding direction unusually easy, or Germany finding persuasion relatively unimportant, and not very good—still, in general, they shift together. From cooperating to reprimanding, for instance, they tend to move down on all three scales in a bunch.

The broad implications of these data appear less clearly than in either of the other two sections of the study at this stage of statistical analysis. It is necessary to wait until the analysis is completed to give a good picture of cognitive mapping in these areas. Meanwhile, two points stand out in the preliminary clustering. Firstly, there is remarkable agreement among countries in their perceptions of these functions. They are not scattered widely, but tend to bunch together, indicating a strong common thread in the way people view these things regardless of country. Secondly, within this relatively homogeneous set of responses, clusters of countries are still distinguishable. Such variation as there is tends to preserve small tight subgroups. They are substantially the same ethnic or cultural clusters that appeared in the preceding section.

MOTIVATION AND SATISFACTIONS

The third section of the study was concerned with the types of satisfactions managers want from their jobs and with the degree to which they feel these different needs are actually being satisfied through their jobs. To obtain information on these points, five types of psychological needs were studied. These needs can be considered as arranged in order from the basic or most prepotent need for security through social, esteem, and autonomy needs to the least prepotent need for self-actualization. This order of needs on the basis of priority or prepotency stems from the theoretical thinking of a number of psychologists and has been used on a wide scale in recent psychological studies of motivation, especially in relation to work. Thus, the results obtained in this study for these different types of needs can be related back to an underlying theoretical foundation.

Before proceeding with a discussion of findings, it is useful to describe briefly the five types of needs. *Security needs* were not defined for the respondent, but were interpreted in a general way as one's feeling of safety and assurance in a particular managerial position. *Social needs* referred to the desire to develop close friendships and the opportunity to give help to other people; thus both ingoing (from others to the person) and outgoing (from the person to others) aspects of needs for social satisfaction were covered in the questionnaire. *Esteem needs* covered both self-esteem and esteem received from other people. *Autonomy needs* referred to the authority connected with the manager's position and the opportunity for independent thought and action. Finally, *self-actualization needs* tapped feelings of self-fulfillment, worthwhile accomplishment, and personal growth.

The specific questions in each of these five need areas asked managers to make three responses: (1) How important is this to me? (2) How much (of the need satisfaction) is there *now* in my position? and (3) How much (of the need satisfaction) should there be in my position? The answers to the first question were used to determine the importance attached to particular needs, that is, what the manager wants to get from his position. To determine degree of fulfillment or satisfaction, or what he feels he *is* getting from his position, the difference between responses to Question 3 and Question 2 was computed for each item for each respondent. Thus, the larger the difference between "should be" and "is now," the greater was the indicated *dis*satisfaction.

Importance of Needs

The most striking finding concerning managerial feelings about the importance of different needs is the relative similarity of thinking from country to country with regard to a particular need. That is, for example, those types of needs which are considered most important in one country tend also to be regarded as most important in other countries. Likewise, those needs considered least important in a particular country are usually also thought to be least important by managers in other countries.

Which needs *were* regarded as the most important? In every country, without exception, needs for self-actualization were deemed most important. French, Japanese, and U.S. managers felt most strongly about these needs, but the differences from country to country were very slight. In other words, not only did self-actualization needs consistently rank above other needs, but they were also given quite consistent ratings of importance by the various groups of managers. This means that, at least at the level of response, managers put primary emphasis on opportunities for growth, for realizing their potential, and for worthwhile accomplishment. The unanimity of this reaction across countries demands attention.

Needs for autonomy were generally regarded as second in importance, although for certain countries they were third rather than second. Managers in Sweden, Germany, and Japan felt slightly more strongly about these needs than managers in the other countries, while Norwegian and Danish managers attached slightly less-than-average importance to autonomy needs. Again, however, as was the case in needs for self-actualization, the differences among the countries in the ratings of importance assigned to these needs were small.

Third in importance among the five types of needs was the need for security. In contrast to the results for self-actualization and autonomy, however, the countries were more widely spread in the average importance they attached to this need. Managers in Spain and Germany, especially, regarded it as more important than did those in other countries, while French and American managers gave it less importance than those elsewhere. Its relative ranking among the five types of needs ranged from second to fourth in importance.

Social needs ended up in fourth place in importance for most of the countries, although they ranked third for the United States and Japan and fifth for Germany and Italy. German managers gave this need an especially low value, not only in relation to other needs but also in relation to managers in other countries. The social needs were similar to security needs in producing some degree of spread among countries.

Finally, needs for esteem were regarded as least important in all of the countries except Italy, where they were regarded as next in importance after self-actualization, and Germany, where they were rated fourth rather than fifth in importance. Needs for esteem thus were like security and social needs in producing some variation in ratings among countries. The Italian managers gave them a much higher rating than did managers in any other country; on the other hand, Danish managers gave them a particularly low rating.

As pointed out earlier, the most impressive finding in connection with the importance attached to different needs was the relative similarity in the way quite different countries and cultures felt about them. A Spanish manager is not very different from a German manager or each from an English or Japanese manager in the ratings they give to the importance of each need. This similarity, of course, is not complete. Especially for security, social, and esteem needs there was some degree of variation from country to country. But even for these the variation usually was not great except for an isolated case or two. And, for autonomy and self-actualization the similarity was very close. One should note especially that the similarities were greatest for the two needs, self-actualization and autonomy, which were regarded as most important. This suggests that managers feel most strongly about the needs that bring the closest agreement in the value assigned to them. Esteem and social needs produced the least agreement among countries and were thought of as least important.

The over-all similarity among managers in different countries in their evaluations of the importance of needs may indicate that what people want from their jobs is relatively unaffected by the cultural environment in which they operate. At least this seems to be true of managers. Whether it is also true of other groups of employees cannot be determined, of course, from our data. Managers, and perhaps all people, seem to be alike in terms of what they regard as important needs to fulfill in their work situations.

The Satisfaction of Needs

The findings for need fulfillment or satisfaction are in contrast with those previously reported for the importance attached to various needs. Although managers tend to be alike from country to country in what they *want* from their jobs, they tend to be quite different in what they *think they are getting* from their jobs. Both the absolute ratings of satisfaction for a particular need vary from country to country, and so also do the relative rankings of one or another need in comparison to all other needs. That is, the mean satisfaction for a given need, say esteem, may be high for country A and low for country B, but also country A may regard this need as the most satisfied of the five needs, whereas country B regards it as about third in satisfaction.

Because the absolute and relative satisfaction of most of the five needs varies considerably from one country to another, it is not possible to give any meaningful over-all ranking of the needs in terms of the degree to which they are satisfied. The greatest similarity among countries is with regard to satisfaction of the need for self-actualization. In all countries except Japan, it is considered as the *least* satisfied of all of the five needs. (The results for Japan show a peculiar pattern similar to no other country in that all needs, self-actualization included, are regarded as equally satisfied.) Although the need for self-actualization produces the greatest dissatisfaction in almost all countries, the dissatisfaction is greatest in Italy, Spain, France, and the U.S. On the other hand, managers in Japan, especially, and in the Scandinavian countries, to some extent, are not as dissatisfied on self-actualization as most of the other countries.

Needs for autonomy are seen as the second greatest producers of lack of need fulfillment in most of the countries. Managers in Spain, France, and Italy indicate somewhat greater dissatisfaction in this area than do those in other countries, while Scandinavian and Japanese managers again indicate slightly less-than-average dissatisfaction.

Needs for esteem rank as the third most unsatisfied needs in some countries, the fourth in others, and the fifth or least dissatisfied in still others. Social and security needs show an even wider variation, ranking in each case from second most dissatisfied in some countries to the most satisfied need in other countries.

Just as in the two major preceding sections of this paper, probably the most meaningful analyses of the data for perceived satisfaction or fulfillment can be made if the various countries are grouped by patterns or profiles of satisfactions for the five types of needs rather than if each need is considered separately. If this grouping is carried out, four fairly clear groups of countries emerge. First are the four countries of mid-southern continental Europe: Spain, Italy, France, and Belgium. The second group includes Germany and the three Scandinavian countries. The third cluster includes the two English-speaking countries, England and the United States. Japan stands by itself, its pattern being completely different from that of the United States or any European country.

The mid-southern continental European group of countries has one outstanding feature in its pattern of satisfactions, and that is the fact that considering all needs taken together, managers from these countries are more *dis*satisfied than those from any other countries or groups of countries. For four of the five need areas, self-actualization, autonomy, esteem, and social, the managers from these four countries indicate more dissatisfaction than each of the other groups of countries. Only in the security area is dissatisfaction in three of these countries exceeded, and that only slightly, by Germany. Thus, even in the security need area average dissatisfaction in this group of countries is comparatively high. The nation with the most dissatisfied managers by far within this first grouping of mid-southern continental European countries is Spain. Following in order are Italy, France, and Belgium. This group of four countries feels most dissatisfied with self-actualization needs, as do all of the other groups except Japan. Next in order of dissatisfaction for this group are autonomy and social needs. The fact that social needs are almost tied for second in terms of relative dissatisfaction (among the five needs) for this group is noteworthy, for this is a higher relative dissatisfaction for these needs than is the case with any of the other three groups of countries. Security and esteem needs are placed fourth and fifth in dissatisfaction by managers from these four countries.

Germany, in this section of the study, could in some ways be grouped with the preceding four countries of mid-southern continental Europe and in other ways with the group of three Scandinavian countries. Germany is somewhat similar to its four more southern European partners in having a relatively high over-all level of dissatisfaction, and is, in fact, closely related to Belgium in this respect. However, in the profile pattern of ranking of the five needs in terms of dissatisfaction Germany seems more similar to its neighbors to the north. Like the Scandinavian countries, it tends to feel relatively well satisfied in esteem and social need areas and relatively less well satisfied on security needs. Security needs for German managers, in fact, are as unsatisfied as autonomy needs.

Scandinavian managers are clearly "satisfied" managers, at least in terms of their own perceptions of their situations. They are most satisfied of any of the groups of countries on autonomy and, particularly, esteem needs. For the other three need areas—self-actualization, social, and security—they are the most satisfied among the continental European countries. Considering all five needs, the Scandinavian managers are definitely more satisfied than managers from the most southern European countries, Spain and Italy. The Scandinavian managers, like the German managers, feel that security needs are no better satisfied in their jobs than autonomy needs. Thus, among the five types of needs, dissatisfaction in the need for security ranks relatively higher for the Scandinavian countries than for the U.S., England, and the mid-southern continental countries.

The two English-speaking countries have a somewhat different pattern of satisfactions from any of the European countries. For the most prepotent needs, security and social needs, the U.S. and English managers are more satisfied than those in any other cluster of countries (including Japan). For esteem and autonomy needs, the English-speaking managers are more satisfied than German managers and those in most other continental European countries, but less satisfied than the Scandinavian managers. For self-actualization needs the managers from America and England again report more fulfillment—though not very much more—than the four mid-southern continental countries, but less fulfillment than German or Scandinavian managers. The pattern of satisfactions for the two English-speaking countries might be summarized best by noting that the satisfactions decrease exactly in the order in which the five needs are theorized to decrease in priority or prepotency. That is, the managers from these countries report the greatest satisfaction for the most prepotent need of security, less satisfaction for esteem and autonomy, and finally the least satisfaction for the least prepotent need, self-actualization.

Japan presents a picture of the "inscrutable East" as far as its pattern of satisfactions is concerned. Quite unlike that of any other country, the Japanese pattern shows an equal degree of satisfaction among the five types of needs. Japanese managers feel just as satisfied (or dissatisfied) about self-actualization needs as they do about esteem, security, or any other types of needs. This uniformity of response from one type of need to another was not approached in any other country, is therefore a truly unique response pattern, and is the reason that Japan has been grouped in a category of countries by itself. In terms of amount of satisfaction indicated by the Japanese managers compared to the amount shown by managers from other countries, the Japanese are considerably more satisfied than any other group of countries on needs for self-actualization. On needs for autonomy they are about equal with the Scandinavian countries in having the most satisfaction. For esteem, social, and security needs, Japan is about average in expressed satisfaction. Over-all, then, Japanese managers report generally high need fulfillment.

The findings with regard to the patterns of satisfactions among different groups of countries are relatively easy to describe. However, when one moves from description to interpretation, the task becomes more difficult. For example, there is the very clear-cut finding that managers in the northern European countries, especially the Scandinavian countries, are more satisfied than those in the southern European countries, especially Spain and Italy. (There is, in fact, almost a perfect correlation between the over-all degree of satisfaction and the median latitude of European countries.) Does this mean that geography or climate somehow influences how much satisfaction managers think they are deriving from their jobs? Can latitude determine attitude? This seems unlikely. Degree of industrialization is somewhat correlated with the north-south geographical axis in Europe, yet it would be difficult to say that this variable is necessarily highly correlated with the satisfaction findings. The lowest group in satisfaction includes, for instance, France and Belgium, highly industrialized, and Spain and Italy. The high group includes the three Scandinavian countries, very different from one another in degree of industrialization.

The answer seems to lie more in social-cultural factors, especially in terms of the role of the manager in occupational status hierarchies and the role of business in the day-to-day affairs of each country. Business organizations are probably more highly respected institutions in the Scandinavian countries and England, and managers who reach middle or top management levels can derive greater feelings of security, social, and esteem satisfactions. Explanations of greater satisfactions in the areas of autonomy and self-actualization, though, do not fit even this theory very well. Perhaps the reason these two needs are so much better satisfied in the northern Teutonic countries lies in the way in which business firms are organized. Middle and top managers in these countries may be given more freedom and more authority to make decisions unhampered by other parts of their organizations or by governmental regulations. This greater autonomy could in turn lead to increased opportunities for self-development and self-fulfillment, that is, to increased self-actualization satisfaction.

One interesting aspect of the findings on satisfaction was the fact that the theoretical classification of the five types of needs according to their priority or prepotency exactly fit the pattern of results for the United States and England, but not for any other group of countries.

It has often been suggested that basic needs—such as for security—are a necessary first step to others. As they are satisfied, and as the assurance grows that they will continue to be satisfied, the others become possible. A hierarchical necessity has been imputed to this ordering of needs. In these data, it appears only in the Anglo-American countries. This suggests, perhaps, that the theoretical formulation is especially relevant to the cultural conditions existing in these two English-speaking countries. It also may suggest that industrial and business firms in these two countries have succeeded in satisfying basic needs first and are currently in a position where employees, at least managerial employees, are directing their efforts increasingly to each higher step on the scale of need prepotency. In other countries than these two, past conditions in business organizations may not have led to such a systematic, step-by-step fulfillment of needs from the most basic to the least basic. In essence, then, this part of the findings for need satisfaction indicates either that the theory of prepotency of needs is particularly well adapted to organizational behavior in the U.S. and England, or that industrial firms in these countries have created conditions that fit the theory.

It is important to relate the findings for perceived satisfaction of needs to the results reported earlier in this section concerning managers' perceptions of the importance of needs. Needs which are considered most important by managers, regardless of country, tend to be those needs which are least satisfied in virtually all of the countries studied. This finding should suggest that it is particularly necessary for those who have ultimate responsibility for running a firm to pay special attention to incentives in these areas if they are concerned with managerial motivations. In the event of marked deficits in need satisfaction of the kind reported here, incentives probably must be geared to the deficiencies that are experienced. Where the sense of lack of satisfaction is more uniform, policy regarding incentives would presumably be based on the reported importance of various needs.

There is a fairly uniform agreement from country to country about which needs are regarded as most important and which are least important. But, when the question turns to "how well satisfied are these various needs?" the findings differ considerably from country to country.

The discrepancy between importance and satisfaction of needs raises a crucial question. These data indicate remarkable similarity in estimates of importance and wide variations in degree of satisfaction. This fact seems to go immediately to the question of whether managerial motives of the kind we have been discussing are general characteristics of people or products of the situation. The homogeneity of importance across a variety of cultures suggests strongly that the needs arise from the nature of people. Their satisfaction varies with situations. There is little evidence here to suggest that the basic motivational equipment with which the manager approaches his job varies from country to country. What does vary is what he finds there.

SUMMARY

This is a preliminary report of data. More exhaustive analysis will appear later. Meanwhile, some general findings emerge.

1. One cannot help but be struck by the consistent groupings of countries through all three parts of the study. Not only is the grouping consistent, but it tends to follow ethnic lines rather than level of industrialization.

2. The pattern of uniformity and diversity in the data is also striking. It seems possible to identify variables which are enduring and relatively culture-free characteristics of people and other variables which are more situationally determined. This is outstanding in the uniformity of importance of needs and the great difference in their satisfaction. It also appears in the uniform swings on attitudes toward leadership while preserving national differences and in the similar grouping on the semantic differential.

3. Managers in all the countries studied could profitably examine these data. They might ask themselves if this is the way they see it, if this is the way they want it, and what the differences may mean to their countries' economies.

selection 25

Contrasting Motives and Attitudes of Managers in More and Less Developed Countries*

David C. McClelland

Much has been written (see Fayerweather, 1959, 1960; Harbison and Myers, 1959) on how the American business executive differs from his foreign counterpart. The assumption is usually also explicitly or implicitly made that the American's attitudes are by and large representative of the best management practices because he is from the country which has been most successful in the economic

---

*From *The Achieving Society,* Courtesy of D. Van Nostrand Company, Inc., 1961, pp. 287–92.

sphere. We are in a position to see how his attitudes compare with those of managers abroad and we can to some extent escape the charge of ethnocentrism by arranging countries in order of their level of economic development to discover if the U.S. attitudes are shared most by the next most developed area (Northern Italy), somewhat less by the next developed (Southern Italy), and least by the most underdeveloped country (Turkey). Poland should perhaps be considered in a separate category because good management practices in a Communist-managed economy might conceivably be different.

Table 1 brings together the motivation scores and the attitude items that

TABLE 1
Average Motive Scores and Agreement with Various Attitude Items among Managers in the U.S., Italy, Turkey, and Poland
(scale = 1 to 7)

Attitude Items	U.S. N = 102	Italy (North) N = 41	Italy (South) N = 27	Turkey N = 17-42	Poland N = 31
Mean age	44.8	26.6	29.1	33.5	35.9
Achieved status					
Merit more important than seniority in giving promotions .	6.67*	6.07	5.74	5.41	4.58
Qualified workers should be promoted to managerial jobs	6.90	5.85	6.19	4.71	4.74
Pay scale not determined by education	5.21	4.78	3.74	3.51	3.06
Average for Business Items	*6.26*	*5.57*	*5.22*	*4.54*	*4.13*
A man with money can learn good manners without proper upbringing	5.52	2.68	3.15	3.93	2.06
Planning, optimism					
Plans work out	6.69	5.63	4.52	5.76	4.35
"Market morality"					
Can trust strangers in business . .	6.70	5.41	5.07	6.12	5.97
"Profit" motive					
Corporation not exclusively for profit.	3.97†	1.71	2.56	2.26	3.33
Mean *n* Achievement score ‡	8.90†	4.12	4.26	1.12	6.58
Mean *n* Affiliation score ‡	4.25†	5.15	5.70	5.31	2.16
Mean *n* Power score ‡	7.01†	6.61	5.59	5.93	5.48

Note: The U.S. sample consists of senior executives in the Advanced Management Program at the Harvard Business School (except as noted in note † below.

*Standard deviations for these distributions vary normally between 1.7 and 2.1 so that usually differences between means of the order of magnitude of .7 to 1.0 and 1.2 and up are significant at the .05 and .01 levels respectively.

†Middle managers from various companies in the Harvard Business School and the M.I.T. Sloane Fellow Program. Mean age = 34, $N = 38$ for item 50, $N = 67$ for motivation scores.

‡ Standard deviations for the distributions of motivation scores vary around 4.00 ± 1.5 so that differences between the means for different countries of the order of 1.2 to 1.5 and 2.0 are significant at the .05 and .01 levels respectively.

showed significant trends for the managers from the five areas. To consider the motivational differences first, the decline in *n* Achievement scores from the U.S., to Italy, to Turkey, has already been commented on. It agrees with the level of development of those countries, while the high level of *n* Achievement among the Polish managers suggests that some force, probably patriotism or Communism or both, has been at work to raise it. As for *n* Affiliation, the U.S. executives are lower (combined $p < .05$) than their foreign counterparts (again except for Poland). The finding nicely confirms observations of Fayerweather and others that foreign executives in countries like Mexico and Italy often seem more concerned with adjusting relationships among people than with solving a problem more efficiently, whatever the cost in personal relationships. For example, Fayerweather reports how an American executive working for a U.S. subsidiary in Mexico tried to get his Mexican purchasing agent to do something about the poor quality of some of the parts supplied and the erratic way in which they were delivered. Both problems were costing the company money because the production manager insisted on keeping a high inventory of parts against a rainy day. The difficulty did not seem great to the American: it was a simple matter of getting tough with the supplier, or finding another one. To the Mexican, however, it was more complicated because he was more interested in the personal relationships involved. He wanted to please the American and understood the efficiency problem, but he also felt that the American did not understand how loyal and helpful the supplier had been in a pinch in the past and how much the production manager just wanted a high inventory to feel better (Fayerweather, 1959, pp. 1–3). The data in Table 1 clearly explain the source of these contrasting attitudes, if we compare Italian (in place of Mexican) managers with American ones. Among the latter, concern for achievement is almost double the concern for affiliation whereas among the Italians, the concern for affiliation is significantly higher than the concern for achievement.

~ Again to quote Fayerweather (1959, p. 73): "In Mexico, very few people are actively opposed to being on time, following plans, or obeying any of the other rules of industrial discipline. When they do not obey them, it is because some conflicting avenue of action appeared and they felt it was more important." One of the main conflicting avenues of action in Mexico he feels is "the maintenance of personal alliances." If we translate the latter into *n* Affiliation and Mexico into Italy, our results strongly support this view. . . . In both Mexico and Italy *n* Affiliation is higher than *n* Achievement; there is some evidence that these needs tend to be complementary. In a random sample of 119 cases out of the 760 men tested in all four countries, *n* Achievement score correlates negatively with *n* Affiliation score ($r = -.32, p < .01$). Similarly . . . there is a significant negative correlation between the two variables in the children's stories in 1950. . . . People who are concerned about interpersonal relationships tend generally to be less concerned about achievement and vice versa.

But we must be wary of overgeneralizing about managers in different foreign countries. While it is true the Turkish managers also show a much greater concern with affiliation than with achievement (although the Turkish children's stories do not), the Polish managers are even less concerned with affiliation than the Americans. Probably the situation will be different in each country and Fayerweather's attempt to treat foreign executives as having a similar personality configuration represents a useful, but demonstrably limited oversimplification. The low *n* Affiliation of the Polish executives reminds one of descriptions of the severity of Communist production quotas to which interpersonal considerations may have to be sacrificed (Granick, 1960). People with low *n* Affiliation and high *n* Achievement might survive better under such pressure. . . .

The American executives are significantly higher in the need for power, the desire to control the actions of others, than the executives in any other place except Northern Italy, the next most developed region economically speaking. Perhaps here we find a reflection of the popular image of the business tycoon who is interested in building an empire and above all beating the competition. Compare W. H. Whyte's description of his training as a salesman for the Vick Chemical Company in 1940:

> "Fella," he [the supervisor] told me, "you will never sell anything until you learn one simple thing. The man on the other side of the counter is the *enemy*." It was a gladiators' school we were in. Selling may be no less competitive now but in the Vick program, strife was honored far more openly than to-day's climate would permit. Combat was the ideal—combat with the dealer, combat with the "chiselling competitors," combat with each other. (Whyte, 1956, p. 117).

The word "combat" as an image nicely combines the concern for achievement and power characteristic of American businessmen, according to our results. Sutton *et al.* point out (1956, p. 98) that the American business creed "resists in various ways any image of the business executive as an authoritarian figure of high status" because of the democratic value atmosphere in the United States. In fact it probably masks the power drive in the concept of competition which suggests the image of achievement which is less suspect. Whether *n* Power is an essential ingredient in managerial success, as we have argued *n* Achievement is, or an accidental feature of the private enterprise system cannot be settled with the information available. The first view is favored by the fact that managers from the next most successful region economically, Northern Italy, may also have a higher *n* Power ($p < .20$) than executives from less economically successful regions; the second is favored by the lack of evidence that managers are higher in *n* Power than professionals and by the evidence presented below that *n* Power is more apt to go with managerial responsibility in the private than the public sector.

To look at various attitude differences in Table 1, it is clear that belief in rewarding a man directly for what he has accomplished in business (achieved status) is closely associated with the stage of economic development of the region from which the managers are drawn. The average belief in reward solely for performance in business decreases sharply from left to right across the table as level of economic development of the region or country decreases. To take an extreme case, American executives believe to nearly the fullest possible extent that deserving workers should be promoted; Italian managers share the belief almost as fully, especially from the industrialized North. But among the Turks and Poles there is considerable doubt about whether workers should be promoted, because if they are, "it would destroy the respect for authority which the workers must have toward management." Similarly the U.S. managers reject seniority, education, and family upbringing as determinants of a man's standing more firmly than the Italians, who reject them more than the Turks who reject them more than the Poles. The results strongly suggest that belief among managers in a man's right to make his way in the world is at least a strong accompaniment or result of economic development, even if we could not find evidence . . . that it helped speed up economic growth.

The traditional optimism of Americans is also apparent. They strongly believe in making plans because they usually work out while managers abroad are less optimistic, perhaps because in fact their plans don't work out as often. There is something of a vicious circle in scepticism about planning: if you have doubts about its worthwhileness because others don't plan and wreck your plans, then *you* may not plan and may wreck theirs. On the other hand an irrational or unjustified faith in the future may justify itself by creating confidence all around.

The item labeled "market morality" is particularly interesting in view of the importance we assigned to this factor for economic growth. . . . It reads in full: "In business you can only really trust friends and relatives." The Americans disagree almost completely with this sentiment, or (as it is rephrased in Table 1) they believe that you can trust strangers significantly more than do managers in any of the other countries. . . . Fair dealings in the market with impersonal, unrelated "others" (i.e. strangers) is one of the necessities of advanced economic organization. If on the other hand, prices, contracts, supplies, etc. are a function of a multiplicity of particularistic relationships with friends, enemies or *compadres*—in a word, of personal alliances—then economic efficiency is bound to suffer. It is interesting to note that this factor, like *n* Achievement, differentiates the more from the less rapidly developing countries, not only in stories for children but in the attitudes of business executives.

Finally the Americans are less convinced than foreign executives that corporations are *exclusively* for profit. What do they think corporations are for, if not just for making profit? Possibly they are giving some implicit recognition to our point that corporations also satisfy achievement strivings or to a commonly held notion that they have a public service function. Actually the issue should be somewhat complicated for the ideal-type entrepreneur if our psychological analysis of his state of mind is correct. In the pure case, he should be primarily interested in achievement, not money—and not in selfish achievement at that. For if he is interested only in money or personal gain, he is likely to gamble, break the rules of the game or generally act like the competitive individualist that Fayerweather (1959) contends spends his time avoiding, competing with, and outmaneuvering others and thereby creating considerable inefficiency in a firm. If he idealistically expresses no interest in profit, he loses the main measuring stick by which he judges whether the organization is operating efficiently or not. This point is frequently misunderstood both by friends and foes of the private enterprise system. Both imply that profit is important as an *end,* or as an incentive, when actually its major importance is as a criterion or value in terms of which the efficiency of business operations can be judged. The conflict is unconsciously reflected by Fayerweather when he writes:

"Business leaders are generally inclined to accept many responsibilities, both as good citizens and as part of the job of assuring conditions which will be profitable over the long term. But that is not the same as viewing their enterprises as public instruments. Unfortunately, many well-meaning people do harm to their causes by forgetting the profit element and pushing business to act as though contributions to public objectives were its primary concern. . . . [The businessman's] first duty to the public is to keep his business strong" (Fayerweather, 1960, p. ix).

Fayerweather seems to be saying, somewhat paradoxically (just as our American executives say in Table 1), that business is for profit, but not exclusively. That is, if businesses are pushed to place other values (i.e. public service) above the profit motive, then they become weak, by inference because they have lost the yardstick that creates efficiency, not because they have lost an incentive system. Despite this emphasis on the importance of profit, he too mentions the businessman's "duty to the public" and the importance of over-all business conditions. Thus there are implicit sanctions invoked against the man who acts exclusively for his own profit to the disregard of all others. The conflict is just as we would expect it to be based on in theoretical analysis of the meaning of profit or money reward to students with high *n* Achievement. . . . It is and should be not exclusively an end in itself but the *measure of achievement.*

selection 26

American vs. European Management Philosophy*

Otto H. Nowotny

Most top executives develop and practice their *own* management philosophy. Obviously, then, there is nothing so clear-cut as a single managerial style which is uniformly adhered to by all American or all European business leaders. Yet underlying the behavior and attitudes of these two different groups of executives

*From *Harvard Business Review,* March-April, 1964, pp. 101–8. © 1964 by the President and Fellows of Harvard College; all rights reserved.

are certain general characteristics or common denominators which can be identified.

In this article I will attempt to deal in a systematic manner with some of the major aspects of American and European management philosophies, hoping to show where and why these philosophies differ and what we can learn from these differences.

Naturally, I am conscious of the controversial nature of attempts to generalize on such a vast subject, and I partly share the apprehensions of those who believe that all generalizations are false. Thus, what will be said in this article should be taken as a finger pointing in the direction of truth rather than the truth itself.

FACTS & VALUES

Oscar Wilde's well-known saying, "a cynic is a man who knows the price of everything and the value of nothing," is a poet's reminder that we tend to view everything in life in quantifiable "fact" and/or nonquantifiable "value" terms. We have done so since the beginnings of human history, and it is improbable that this dual way of looking at things will ever be replaced by a purely factual approach which eliminates all value judgments. Therefore, top executives—like all other people—will continue to base their decisions on so-called objective facts, on the one hand, and subjective values, commonly referred to as management or business philosophy, on the other.

The relative importance of "facts" to "values" in top-level decision making will naturally vary with each particular business situation. However, it is significant that top managers often make decisions because they value certain ways of action—in spite of the price they must pay. Yet rarely, if ever, will they do something they do *not* value just because the cost is low. Mere common sense, therefore, indicates that value judgments will usually have priority over purely factual considerations in making vital business decisions.

This seemingly trite conclusion is interesting, however, because it contradicts the popular and, I fear, growing belief that increasing complexity in business—necessitating a large staff of specialists and expensive data-processing equipment—will make top managers proportionately more dependent on "facts" for their decision making. It is, of course, highly probable that the vast amount of available information will tempt many business leaders to use "facts" as an escape from the freedom (and burden) of choosing the proper "values." But if business is to be led with creative imagination instead of being merely administered bureaucratically, *more* rather than less management philosophy will be required in the future.

Because scientific progress will force middle managers to spend more time in keeping up with the many technical developments in their areas of responsibility, top managers, to counterbalance this increasing specialization, will have to concentrate more on the fundamentals of management philosophy if they do not want to descend, gradually but surely, to the level of mere coordinators. To express it differently: "doing" will require more "knowing" by middle managers, and more "maturity" by top executives. And there is hardly a better way for top managers to become more mature than to try to understand and, if necessary, to assimilate the values and beliefs of others which are different from their own.

Let us, therefore, investigate the essential differences between European and American outlooks first and then analyze some of the differences in management philosophy.

PAST VS. FUTURE

The most striking difference between the outlooks of Europeans and Americans lies in their orientation toward time. It is as if they were standing back to back, with the European inclined to look at the past and present and the American seeing the present and future.

The European's attachment to the past accounts for his respect for such characteristics as wisdom, stability, convention, necessity, quality, and diversity. The American's more futuristic outlook leads him to respect vitality, mobility, informality, abundance, quantity, and organization. But unless Europeans abandon some of their excessive attachment to the past and Americans their more or less profound disregard for it, little change can be expected. I certainly do not share the optimism of businessmen who believe that what is best in the American and European management philosophies will automatically find its way from one continent to the other by a kind of effortless "osmosis." A brief analogy may clarify my point:

> If we connect two steel tanks, one containing high-pressure cold air and the other low-pressure hot air, we will inevitably end up with a tepid and rather pressureless mixture in both vessels, unless the lack of pressure in one and the lack of heat in the other are compensated for by supplying the required energy from the outside. In other words, an effort has to be made if the specifically high energy levels of each tank are to be maintained after having been connected to one another.

In management philosphy, as well, an *effort* has to be made, unless we want to run the risk of having the typically American and European qualities simply meet at the level of the lowest common denominator.

WISDOM VS. VITALITY

There is hardly a better way to illustrate the meanings of vitality and wisdom, and to show how differently these two qualities are valued in America and Europe, than by briefly comparing some of the typical traits of a man who is in his twenties with those of a man who is in his sixties:

> The *young* man, impatient to apply his overflowing energy (and wasting a lot of it in the process), is mainly interested in the "here and now," the practical side of life. His preoccupations are essentially short range, and he frequently ignores the side effects that his actions are likely to produce in the future. There is always a halo of naiveté around him, which his youth does not allow him to get rid of. His most positive characteristic, conditioning all his

others, is certainly vitality. But this greater urge for expansion, distinguishing the vital from the nonvital person, when combined with his youthful experience of life, keeps him swinging dangerously from one extreme to another and makes him correspondingly superficial.

The *older* man, whose vital energies have calmed down considerably since the heydays of his youth, has developed a certain amount of moderation. To him one can apply the words of the dean of a California law school, who, in defending his school's policy of hiring only professors aged 65 and above, said: "Most bad habits are out of their system. If they weren't, they'd be dead by now." Life has taught the older man to be skeptical and to prefer slow, organic growth to rapid change. He thinks a little more about the long-range effects of his actions and, appreciating the contemplative side of life, has lost some of his former gregariousness. His most positive characteristic can be called wisdom, although this quality may also make him less mobile and less enterprising.

Though neither continent can claim to have a monopoly on vitality or wisdom, it is reasonably true to say that American management philosophy is, in general, more vital than wise, while Europe's is more wise than vital. Here is an example:

One of the most rigorous belt-tightening operations by a major corporation was undertaken by Chrysler Corp. in 1961. It fired 7,000 of 36,000 white collar employees, from secretaries to high-ranking executives. The action helped lower Chrysler's break-even point to 725,000 cars and trucks from a million units. President Lynn A. Townsend says the cutback didn't impair efficiency.[1]

Obviously, some very superfluous things must have been allowed to happen in the past, or else the company could not have cut its white-collar work force by 20% without a loss of efficiency. Vitality (the urge to expand), not moderated by wisdom, had resulted in an extremely uneconomic situation which only equally extreme countermeasures could correct. But—and this again is a proof of vitality—the necessary measures were taken.

Slow Growth

In Europe the moderating influence of wisdom (that is, top management's preference for slow, organic growth) has admittedly prevented many production and clerical jobs from being mechanized a long time ago. But at the middle-management level and, even more, at the top-management level, in comparison with America, *under*staffing rather than *over*staffing seems to be the rule. Important decisions are still made by single individuals or at least by a much smaller group of top executives than in the United States.

With most of the strategic decisions concentrated at the top, there is also a pronounced tendency not to communicate the reasoning behind these decisions to those at lower management levels. Obviously, European top executives try to save a part of the time American executives spend on communications, though they do so somewhat at the expense of middle-management "learning." This fact, indeed, is reflected by the smaller percentage of key positions in European business held by executives aged 40 or less. The theory that a good wine requires

---

[1] "White Collar Cutback," *The Wall Street Journal,* January 3, 1963, p. 19.

many years of aging in a dark, coolish cellar has been extended to the business executive and seems to have become an integral part of European management philosophy. To complete the analogy, it must be added that no one pretending to know about wines and being responsible for their quality would think much of changing promising bottles from one wine cellar to another.

This particular way of thinking, I believe, explains the relatively small interest European top executives still show for training their potential managers in American or American-style business schools. In addition, they are convinced, though they will rarely admit it in public, that only the more technical aspects, and not the *essence* or the *style* of executive leadership, can be learned there. They would certainly agree with a comment recently made in *The Wall Street Journal* that "the individual manager's style will probably be decisive in the end, in terms of executive success, failure or mediocrity. *Style* is the secret plus or minus."[2] Or, as the French scientist and writer Georges-Louis de Buffon has put it even more briefly: *"Le style est l'homme même."*

As a result of this attitude, climbing up the corporate ladder in Europe takes the aspiring executive, generally speaking, more time than in North America. But once he reaches the top, the risk of his coming down again is also much smaller. Anyone who would go to the trouble of counting the number of executives who have been displaced from the top of their pyramid would probably find this percentage to be considerably higher in America than in Europe.

Combining the Advantages

Many examples, of course, could be cited to reveal how wisdom and vitality are given different weights in the American and European management philosophies. But they would all lead us to the same conclusion: to optimize our business performance it is necessary to combine the advantages of both characteristics. How can this be done?

In Europe large reserves of vital energy could certainly be released by dropping some of the most outdated conventions. For example, those that require most decisions to be made at the top rather than at the lowest possible level in the organization, or those that hold an executive responsible to his superior but do not require the superior to bother about *actively* developing his subordinate's capacities. Many of these conventions need close questioning so that the weight given presently to different values can be redistributed more logically.

In American business an increase in wisdom could probably be achieved if top executives would try to keep in mind wisdom's most basic definition—"Avoiding the unnecessary." Or as the Chinese philosopher Chuang Tzu put it nearly 25 centuries ago: "If one wants to act sanely, one must do but the inevitable. To stick to the inevitable is the way of the wise." Pointing in exactly the same direction, but of more recent origin, are the famous three laws of Parkinson:

---

[2] July 24, 1963, p. 12.

An official wants to multiply subordinates, not rivals.
Officials make work for each other.
Expansion means complexity, and complexity decay.[3]

All three of these laws are nothing else than a warning to top management to do only that which is absolutely necessary and to avoid "futile busy-ness." To put a conscious break between *stimulus* and *reaction*—as Napoleon is said to have done when he once decided to leave his mail unopened for a certain time, only to find that at the end of it most of the letters had taken care of themselves and so did not have to be answered—is one of the particular privileges and duties top management must make more liberal use of.

For wisdom requires deliberation, and deliberation requires time. The late Speaker of the House Sam Rayburn is reported to have said that one of the greatest statements ever made by anybody was: *"Just a minute."* He was pointing out the catalytic effect of time in the legislative process. The same is important in the judicial process and in life in general.

But are not most of us too much under the spell of the speed and short-cut psychology of our time to grasp the full meaning of this simple statement?

STABILITY VS. MOBILITY

After what has already been said, it is certainly not surprising to find stability and mobility two other typical opposing characteristics of our respective management philosophies.

Accordingly, intercompany job changes in the higher echelons are much less frequent in Europe than in America. In part this is a matter of language and geographical barriers; but it is also the result of Europeans being more skeptical about human nature than Americans. They prefer to let several years of observation pass before giving high-level responsibility to a new member of management, who, by the time he gets it, is of course no longer new. Switching companies at a frequency customary in America would normally lead to an intolerable loss of time in the career of a European executive.

Similarly, changing jobs within companies in the sense of job rotation has never been as fully accepted by big business in Europe as it has been in America. This is due partly to the fact that specialization on lower- and middle-management levels has not been pushed as far ahead as in America; thus, job rotation seems less urgent. It is also due partly to top management's belief that rotating people through various jobs is costly and can lead to situations where a great number of employees have had experience in a lot of areas but lack solid competence in any one. With all strategic and many tactical decisions still being made at or at least close to the top, there is also less need for vision on the lower levels. There is, however, more demand for highly competent "spade-work"

---

[3] C. Northcote Parkinson, *Parkinson's Law* (Boston: Houghton Mifflin Co., 1957), p. 4; and C. Northcote Parkinson, *Inlaws and Outlaws* (Boston: Houghton Mifflin Co., 1962), p. 233.

on which European top management can solidly build its decisions without having to resort to double- and triple-checking through extensive committee work. Committees are, therefore, far less important in the European than they are in the American management process.

Another illustration of stability and mobility can be found in the area of job titles. Business on the European continent uses, in general, a very limited number of official titles—much as the military forces do in employing a relatively small number of different ranks. Thus, knowing a European executive's title and the size of the company he works for makes it fairly easy to estimate his responsibility as well as his earnings. The latter are rarely, if ever, spoken of openly, contrary to the practice in America where knowing the earnings of an executive is often the only way to measure his responsibility—the number of titles being so great as to make quick orientation a rather hopeless affair.

"If the deserving employee is hungry for a title, the good manager gives him one, even if it turns out to be but Third Assistant to the Head of Sub-Assembly Department No. 3," is a typical bit of reasoning by the American manager which would find little acceptance in Europe. European top executives believe that the widespread use of custom-tailored titles to compensate for a lack of job satisfaction is a short-range expedient which merely starts a vicious circle, forcing top management to dole out ever more status symbols and leading ultimately to the highly sophisticated and eventually costly kind of human relations being practiced by large corporations in America. Indeed, by comparison, human relations in European business still have a kind of rustic simplicity.

CONVENTION VS. INFORMALITY

Although an open-door policy and a first-name basis are both widely accepted practices in American business, they are but two exterior signs of how American management philosophy has given preference to informality. This is, of course, contrary to human relations practices in Europe, where numerous conventions are still strictly adhered to. But the roots of our different convictions go much deeper, and it seems as if in the eternal dilemma of all executives—having to exercise authority and trying to be liked—European top management has constantly preferred to put more weight on the former and American top management more on the latter quality.

Thus, American managers seem to feel that human relations in Europe have an authoritarian and paternalistic flavor, and consider the social distance between individuals a remnant from feudal times. Europeans, in turn, believe Americans to be guilty of promoting excessive egalitarianism and status stripping which in their eyes is not only naive and unrealistic, but must inevitably destroy management effectiveness in the long run.[4] The results of these different attitudes are interesting.

---

[4] See, for example, Abraham Zaleznik, "The Human Dilemmas of Leadership," *Harvard Business Review,* July–August, 1963, p. 51. (For a contrary point of view see Robert N. McMurry, "The Case for Benevolent Autocracy," *Harvard Business Review,* January–February, 1958, p. 82.—*The Editors.*)

Whereas human relations in European business lack the outer nonchalance and friendliness found in America, they do not seem to share the inner tensions which are often apparent on the other side of the Atlantic. American tensions stem, it seems, largely from trying to adhere to the overly idealistic point of view that one must like everybody or, if that cannot be done, at least pretend to do so. Though the former is impossible except for those approaching sainthood, the latter—because of the pretense involved—creates all kinds of nervous tensions, feelings of guilt and frustration, which any ordinary person can easily detect.

But between the extremes of bullying or loving people there is ample room for the less spectacular but more effective way of simply *respecting* them. It will always depend on the maturity of the individual top executive how good a balance he can finally strike between convention and informality. However, no progress will be possible unless top executives give up the idea that only the American or the European brand of human relations is correct, and will admit that both have severely suffered from inbreeding the same ideas for many decades. Success will come only to the extent top executives learn to live with open minds.

NECESSITY VS. ABUNDANCE

The relative lack of natural resources in Europe and their abundance in America has not been without profound impact on the management philosophies of our two continents. Thus, the tendency toward thrift and the desire to avoid waste are only too evident in the thinking of European executives, to whom the concept of planned obsolescence still seems to be as foreign as ever.

Nowhere can this important aspect of managerial philosophy be observed any better than in the various types of automobiles produced in Europe and America. The differences in horsepower, in body design and finish, in fuel consumption, and in size, for example, all serve to illustrate the same point: Europe has been, and still is, subject to the law of necessity and cannot afford to conduct its business with American generosity and disregard for seemingly less important details. Cars such as a Volkswagen, a Citroen, or a Mercedes are the definite reflection of an entirely different management philosophy than are a Chevrolet, a Ford, or a Cadillac.

United States military strategy, to use another example, has also been based on the country's abundance of resources. This is evidenced by the American way of fighting World War II, namely, to concentrate large masses of troops and to act fast. This is, of course, the logical military application of Newton's Law: Force = Mass X Acceleration. But Europe, not having the same resources (mass), had to build its strategy mainly on flexibility (acceleration) and surprise. It was Churchill who said that "the good-luck charm of success in war is surprise," thus stating the typically European approach. Surprise and particularly its cause, secrecy, are therefore, a natural part of European management philosophy.

American executives and financial analysts often complain about the rudimentary information given by European companies in their balance sheets and profit and loss statements. But the smaller amount of information published is in strict accordance with local government rules. And if no voluntary supplements are handed out to the general public, it is only partly to seek additional protection from foreign competition behind the smoke screen of secrecy. It is also caused by the general conviction that the more information a company releases, the more explanations it has to give. The tendency toward thrift and the desire to avoid what is not really necessary are, therefore, two important reasons why European business seems to be playing its cards close to its chest.

QUALITY VS. QUANTITY

With economic necessity being such an important factor in European management philosophy, business in Europe has always found it necessary to stress quality much more than quantity. How else—to cite one extreme example—could a small country like Switzerland, with hardly any natural resources, have become a prosperous nation than by simply doing a few things better than anybody else would do them? "Quality, not quantity" is, therefore, the outstanding characteristic of European management philosophy and explains many facets of the way European executives think.

A very typical facet is the fairly general tendency of Europeans to *think before trying.* As a leading European businessman once said: "We are not in the habit of increasing through wastefulness the chance of a random hit."

And so, the technique of "brainstorming," which has been given much publicity in America, has never really been accepted in Europe. Preference has always been given to high-quality, individual thinking rather than to group thinking, which explains, as already mentioned, why the managements of European companies seem to be relatively understaffed in comparison with American firms. The following quotation reflects this difference:

> Europeans have learned by tradition to get along with less personnel, especially less university-trained personnel. I have been told that, after the war, United States and British industrialists could not understand how so important a drug as the antimalarial quinacrine could have been developed by researchers operating in three small rooms, since in the United States several hundred scientists were employed to test all possible variations of the basic formula and, in the end, came up with the same compound.[5]

Another technique which has never made much impression in Europe is "speed reading." Although the quantity of reading matter has increased as much for the European as it has for the American executive, the former has in general refused the *speed* solution, believing that it necessarily leads to an accent on quantity (at the expense of quality). He has relied more on *selectivity* to solve his reading problem.

He has also applied this same principle in his community and public activities, which seem to be but an infinite fraction of what many American executives

---

[5] Paul de Haen, "European Pharmaceutical Research," *Drug & Cosmetic Industry,* January, 1961, p. 44.

have accepted. The reasoning behind this consistent refusal to get too involved outside the immediate sphere of work is the European conviction that each individual should, above all, concentrate on his job, because nobody aiming at top performance can afford to dissipate his energies. Top performance in any field requires a multiple effort in comparison with merely average performance. . . . In general, any artist, sportsman, professional or businessman must expend several times as much energy if he is looking for exceptional rather than only normal standards of performance. I am assuming here, as does the European, that outside activities inhibit on-the-job performance, a fact which many Americans vigorously would deny. Thus, by preferring quality to quantity (sometimes without any regard to economic realities, to the extent of worshipping quality as an end in itself), European management is forced necessarily to favor selectivity and a concentration of efforts.

But by saying *yes* to quantity, one cannot say *no* to standardization, because these two characteristics of managerial philosophy are linked like Siamese twins. Quantity per se is certainly not bad. On the contrary, it has considerable social benefits, such as the increase in the standard of living resulting from mass production. But there are always the attendant dangers of excessive standardization trailing in its wake and of overorganization stifling individual initiative.

DIVERSITY VS. ORGANIZATION

Overorganization, the European believes, is a particularly threatening consequence. The ideal of all our national economies and individual businesses is, of course, to arrive at a proper balance between organized, controlled activity and that which offers an incentive for a freer use of individual initiative. The European achieves order through definite status levels in his organization, but he does not try to organize man's every effort as do many American firms.

No doubt, there can be too little organization, that is, too much diversity. And in many instances European business performance could be improved if there were more of it. But top executives must be aware of the fact that aiming at good organization is like trying to keep a small ball balanced on top of a big one. Good organization is always—although we do not seem to be conscious of it—in a state of unstable equilibrium, needing slight but constant corrective action from the top. . . . The goal is to strike a proper balance between European and American attitudes toward organization, with resulting higher performance.

Reaching this happy compromise is not easy and requires more wisdom than seems to be generally available. Here are the reasons:

The more vital energy we have, the more we want to *do* and the more we, therefore, favor organization, because organizing means *doing* things. There is a natural trend toward organization which is extremely difficult to resist, because organizational measures are not only easily set down on paper and made communicable (and "file-able!"), but also leave one with the exhilarating feeling that something has been done with apparently immediate results. Sometimes the result is much like that where an inoffensively weak virus is transferred from patient to patient and in the process becomes more virulent. So also can overorganization reach a dangerous stage.

Those who propose organizational measures to stimulate individual incentive are actually in a fairly weak logical position because the best incentive-building measure they often end up advocating is not to take any measures at all. This attitude lies at the root of one of our valuable educational tools, the case method, and is the basis of our free enterprise democracy. All three start out from the same principle—that individual incentive is best developed by the individual himself, with a minimum of order imposed from the outside.

CONCLUSION

The basic characteristics of American and European management philosophies are so strikingly complementary that a combination of what is best in both must lead to an improvement in the conduct of our Euro-American free enterprise economies. Of course, the crucial question is how to bring about this desirable change.

Surely no success whatsoever is to be expected of large-scale attempts to have top executives hold special international meetings in order to discuss some of the important topics of managerial philosophy. With "publicity" hanging over their heads like a sword of Damocles, few top executives, if any, would take the risk of seeing their statements misinterpreted. They would speak only in the most cautious terms—so cautious, indeed, that the essence of their statements would seldom be more than an agglomeration of euphemistic platitudes.

Although the written word is a wonderful medium for conveying "facts" to a larger public, we forget too easily that, in discussing "values," *oral* communication within a small group of individuals is by far the most preferable and practically the only way to avoid either banality or confusion.

Thus, the present trend in politics toward more personal and secret diplomacy might well portend the direction in which top executives will have to move if they want to make a synthesis of what is best in American and European management philosophies.

selection 27

Group Management, European Style*

F. Newton Parks

Various forms of group management have received increasing attention in recent years, not only in the literature but in the board rooms of American and European business. In the United States, beleaguered chief executives, overburdened by the sheer magnitude of their management work load, have responded

---

* From *Business Horizons,* Indiana University, Fall, 1966, pp. 83–90.

by spawning an increasing number of "multiple management" arrangements—some frankly experimental, others with substantial success records.

Research indicates that U.S. companies moving in the direction of executive teamwork tend to follow one of two courses: (1) a partnership team may evolve sharing the managerial duties of the chief executive, or (2) operating groups may be established where a number of executives work closely as a team, largely because their responsibilities form a natural work grouping.[1] Whether plural management was instituted through an evolutionary process, personal camaraderie, or corporate policy, American management rarely, if ever, abandons the basic principle of one final authority.

A more sharply defined version of multiple management, commonly called "collegial management" or "management by colleague," has long been practiced in Europe, where multiple management in its various forms and permutations has had a long legal and traditional history. (In the United States, this concept has a relatively brief and selective history of application.) Some European companies have undertaken programs recently to eliminate some of the weaknesses of collegial management while retaining its inherent strengths. Since these strengths and limitations are generally applicable to multiple management wherever it is found, American executives should be aware of the implications of European experience, not only to better understand the rationale behind the evolutionary trend now under way, but to assess its effect on management theory and practices in this country.

What is collegial management? It is, in general terms, the collective responsibility of a top management group for the conduct of the affairs of the enterprise. The basic objective is to maintain a division and balance of power among management members. Similarly, it is aimed at either preventing or restricting monocratic authority in the management of an enterprise (or any social or political entity). As Weber points out, the Roman consuls and praetors practiced an early form of collegial management. The roots in Germany are found in the councils of the Prussian states.[2]

The system is currently most common in Germany and Holland. In the German publicly held company, this top management group is known as the Vorstand, and in Holland as the Directie. The system is also found in Austria and Switzerland, and in France where recent legislation permits general management responsibility by a committee of two or more members.

The collegial system was set forth in the corporate charters at the time of the public formation of many present-day corporations. The emergence of the labor colleague in the German Vorstands in the Ruhr iron and steel industry, however, dates back only to the British occupation after World War II. In fact, the British Labor party in power at that time is credited (or blamed) for the strong position of labor in Ruhr management.

---

[1] Booz, Allen & Hamilton, "Executive Teamwork" (unpublished study, Chicago, 1965).

[2] Max Weber, *The Theory of Social and Economic Organization* (London: Free Press of Glencoe, 1964), pp. 392–403.

Collegial management in corporate affairs is also, to some extent, an evolutionary development in the growth of European family enterprises. The death of the founding entrepreneur frequently left the mantle of management in the hands of several branches of a family. Collegial management assured the equal protection and voice of all surviving family interests.

STRUCTURE

The Colleagues

Collegial management is composed essentially of the top management of the enterprise. Normally, it is made up of three or more management members, known as directors in Holland and in Germany. These "inside" boards vary in size as shown in the following random sample of Dutch and German companies:

Number of Board Members°	17 Dutch Companies†	33 German Companies
2	1	1
3	4	5
4	7	2
5	5	7
6		7
7		3
8		2
9		4
10		2

°Inside boards are composed of management executives.

†The Dutch sample does not include Unilever NV (twenty-three members) or Philips (eleven members), which, although seated in Holland, are more international in character than the companies tabulated above. Of the Philips board members, however, four are recognized as a senior group. In addition to the members noted above, there may or may not be deputy board members.

These directors usually represent different functional elements in the enterprise—technical, sales, finance, or personnel; seldom are they nonfunctional. They rarely have responsibility for a geographic area, nor do they take responsibility for management of a product division. In American terms, the German financial director is equivalent to a vice-president–Finance, except that he also has the collective responsibility for the general management of the business. In corporate affairs, the advocates of collegial management claim that it is the best management process to permit the various functional directors to express themselves on matters of general policy. In this regard, the system recognizes that individual members of management in Europe are educated and trained along rather sharply defined lines—technical, financial, or commercial—and that no functional executive emerging at the top has the required breadth of view to direct the entire enterprise. Accordingly, the colleagues bring the best thinking from each functional area of the business to bear in developing and executing the general policy.

The Chairman

The Vorstand or Directie may or may not have a chairman. In Germany, the chairman is called the Vorsitzer, and in Holland, usually the president. In the sample of companies noted above, four of the Dutch companies and five of the German companies had no chairman.

The role of the Vorsitzer or president varies. He may be a functional member of the Vorstand and also carry the Vorsitzer title. He thus may be what is known as the *primus inter pares* (first among equals), but still have no greater general management responsibility relative to his colleagues. Thus, regardless of the presence of a Vorsitzer, each Vorstand member still shares the collective responsibility for the direction of the business and is, in effect, even responsible for what takes place within the functional duties of another member. In some instances, the Vorsitzer has no functional responsibility, but is essentially a coordinator of the others; in still other instances, he is a recognized general manager or chief executive. At times, he is merely the voice of the Vorstand; he is then known as the Sprecher. The role may or may not be spelled out in the bylaws of the corporation. In certain instances, the chief executive role, or Vorsitzer responsibility, may fall to one of the colleagues because of the personal strength of the individual involved.

Management Structure

The Vorstand or Directie usually has a Secretariat, that is, in effect, a corporate staff. Its composition varies from company to company but usually consists of legal and secretarial functions, public relations, statistics, organization, and economics. The activities of these service or planning functions are a collective responsibility of the board—not of any one individual on the board (see chart). Similarly, the results of their work, such as the analysis of an acquisition prospect, often are submitted as a report to the board as a group.

The directors may also have deputy directors or vice-directors who are the administrators of those departments in which the directors have functional responsibility. In some companies, these deputies make up a subordinate coordinating committee. This substructure may also extend to plants or divisions. Two or three managers at the plant level may have the collective responsibility for the operation. These managers will normally represent the sales, technical, and financial sectors of the business. They manage the specific plant as a committee but look to their respective functional heads in the Vorstand for leadership.

TYPICAL COLLEGIAL MANAGEMENT STRUCTURE

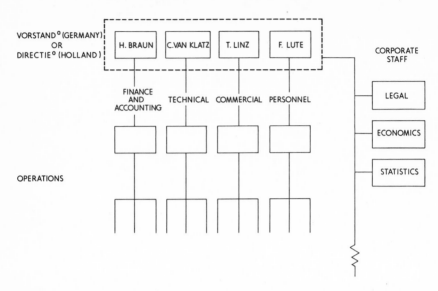

° May or may not have a coordinating chairman.

Legal Aspects

By law, Vorstand members in Germany cannot also be members of the "outside" board, the Aufsichtsrat. The Aufsichtsrat has the legal responsibility to appoint and dismiss Vorstand members and to accept or reject the results of the year's work as expressed by the annual balance sheet, P&L, and use of funds, including dividend payments. The number and specific duties of the Vorstand are seldom spelled out very specifically in a corporate charter, but are usually established by the outside board that also determines whether there is to be a Vorsitzer.

In Germany, the Aufsichtsrat represents both labor and ownership. One-third of the members are appointed by labor, except in the coal and steel companies of the Ruhr where labor is equally represented (except for the chairman). Frequently, the outside chairman is a banker. One prominent German banker was, at one time, the chairman or a member of more than twenty boards. The legal limit has since been reduced by a recent change in corporate law to twelve memberships per individual. Another significant change in this law is the limitation on the power of the Vorsitzer: he no longer can overrule the majority vote of other Vorstand members.

In Holland, labor has no representation on either the inside or the outside board (Raad van commissarissen), although there are union and governmental pressures in this direction at the moment. Legislation is under consideration that would place a labor member on the outside board. Under the proposed law, the board would control such policy decisions as mergers, acquisitions, labor force reduction, and manufacturing methods.

DECISION-MAKING PROCESS

It is difficult to define precisely the management decision-making process in collegial management. It varies from company to company, depending on the particular form of collegial management and the personal characteristics of the individual Vorstand members. Nevertheless, there are certain decision making characteristics of collegial management. Decisions often seem to evolve after extensive give-and-take discussion; thus, they develop more by indirection than direction. They come slowly, are influenced by considerable "input" from the various management sectors, and are finally arrived at, more or less, by mutual agreement.

Although the individual Vorstand member may not necessarily have strong decision-making powers, he does have strong negative powers—that is, a veto will definitely slow up or even stop a decision. This is particularly true in regard to the labor colleague in the Ruhr iron and steel industry. For example, his veto in a company labor force reduction program will, in effect, stop the program. The management process requires that his colleagues convince him that the required force reduction is for the over-all good of his constituents, the labor unions. This may well be possible in times of full employment, but is a formidable task in difficult times. Needless to say, the labor colleague himself is in an extremely ambivalent position as a Vorstand member since he represents, in theory at least, both management and labor. In view of his dual role, it is not unusual for his colleagues to work around him and behind the scenes on certain policy matters.

The collegial system also encourages certain Vorstand members to pool their strengths to force through a program for their mutual interests. Conversely, they may collectively block a program of a colleague that works against their individual interests. Collegial management, like any management process, is influenced by self-interest, with the obvious long-term limitations that result. Staff work is also strongly influenced by the system. For instance, in one major Swiss company, one of the staff groups has responsibility for facility expansion. Although this staff has a functional reporting relationship to the technical director, its reports are submitted to the Vorstand as a group for their review and decision.

STRENGTHS AND LIMITATIONS

Strengths

Since each colleague has a certain veto power on matters of corporate policy, any individual authority that tends to be autocratic is automatically limited by the collegial system. In Germany, where the memory of Hitler lingers, this balancing of power is a real concern. Moreover, as mentioned previously, the collegial system assures that each functional area of the business has a full voice in corporate affairs. At the same time, each colleague is more or less forced to become informed about the functional areas of the others, since they share the over-all responsibilities; with time, this broadens all the colleagues in their approach to problems. The system creates a policy-making group that is removed from the day-to-day, short-term problems of the business. It therefore encourages long-range thinking and objective appraisal of developments affecting the business.

By its very nature, the system calls for management teamwork and, strangely enough, breeds democratic management at the top to a greater extent than in America—known for its teamwork in business. The system also prevents precipitous management action on basic policy matters; careful and often painstaking deliberations take place before decisions are made.

From a personnel point of view—when the personalities mesh—there is a good spirit and camaraderie among the colleagues. They recognize their interdependence and responsibility and carry out their management task with élan.

Limitations

The requirement for unanimity, or near unanimity, of agreement *slows down decisions.* This is particularly true where there is no Vorsitzer or where the Vorsitzer is weak—either personally or because of his limited powers. In the framework of the intensifying European competitive situation, the laborious decision-making process is an obvious limitation in the collegial system.

Paralleling the management slowdown process is the *heavy demand on executive time.* The system tends to get directors enmeshed in each others' functional affairs, even though they may only bring limited judgment to bear on the specific problems. Vorstand meetings frequently result in long and involved discussions of relatively minor matters that should be resolved within a single department. As mentioned previously, the system exposes all members to a broad perspective. Yet, on the other hand, the respective efforts of individual directors tend to be thinly scattered.

Decisions are necessarily watered down since compromise is so often required in an attempt to arrive at a solution agreeable to everyone. Thus, some of the "hard" decisions are not readily made—high cost plants are not closed down, labor is not released, incompetence is not eliminated, and "sick" products are permitted to linger on.

Conversely, although the collegial system acts as a brake on certain basic decisions, it may also encourage imprudent programs through *logrolling.* For example, a labor director and a marketing director might give reciprocal support to a wage increase and an expanded sales program, neither of which may stand on its own merits.

The collegial system is adversely affected by the *diffusion of responsibility* within the group. Although the cause of sales force ineffectiveness may eventually be pinpointed as poor performance on the part of the sales director, he can always point to poor delivery or poor quality as a reason for lagging sales. It is difficult to reconcile these divergent factors with a collective general management. This diffusion of responsibility is particularly apparent in large multiproduct, multiplant companies, especially since there may also be a local group management at the plant level reporting to a different functional superior back at headquarters. The local responsibility for profit performance is obscure indeed.

The collegial system is slow in gringing policy and program into focus because the *power to force management action is limited.* In fact, the management process simply stops at times. In one instance, a marketing director in a consumer goods company did not believe in sales forecasting. He refused to make a judgment on an annual sales projection by amount, product, or market. Thus, the factory had no basis for planning production levels or ordering materials. Finance had no basis for projecting fund requirements or cash flow. Inventory control, labor needs, and capital requirements were impossible to manage because the collegial system had no directing force that could insist on a forecasting policy.

Since no one, in effect, "bangs heads together," *differences of management opinion tend to smolder* and be perpetuated among Vorstand colleagues. Situations develop that range from outright rudeness among colleagues to cold wars. While these attitudes are by no means restricted to general managements in the collegial system, they seem to linger on longer before being resolved by eventual resignation or removal of one or more members by the outside board.

Collegial management encourages group action. Conversely, it *tends to discourage strong, individual entrepreneurial instincts.* As previously mentioned, most of today's public companies evolved from a family group that had a strong founder as a leader and risk-taker. The collegial system restrains this type of executive; it obscures the individual and can convert him to the more "comfortable" member of a group. If the group has collective initiative and a venturesome spirit, all is well. On the other hand, if it is protective and overly conservative, the business is stifled.

The collegial system frequently *falls apart at the lower echelons.* This is due to the strong vertical control of directors within their respective functional areas. It is generally agreed in Germany and Holland that the walls between departments are quite high. Communications go up and down—seldom sideways. Obvious problems of coordination develop: products are designed that don't have sales appeal; costs are collected and analyzed by accountants without a clear understanding of the needs of the operating departments for control information; and, at the same time, departmental cliques and secretive practices may develop. All in all, there can be a serious absence of teamwork at the working level.

FUTURE OF COLLEGIAL MANAGEMENT

Many collegial managements are doing considerable soul-searching in an effort to retain the inherent strengths of the system while removing the apparent weaknesses. In recent years, the German electrical giant AEG has undergone a reorganization that breaks down the traditional vertical domination of directors into the functional areas of the business. Product line profit responsibility is being delegated to individual Vorstand members. This product responsibility, as well as functional responsibility, is being increasingly recognized at the Vorstand level in a number of companies. The basic issue is: how can the collective Vorstand delegate product responsibility to one of its members without, at the same time, abdicating its over-all responsibility for the well-being of the business? There is also the issue of a Vorstand product executive having executive authority in a particular division while being a member of the Vorstand that oversees this authority. Of course, the same situation exists in the United States in respect to any management member of the board.

Moreover, the role of the Vorsitzer as a chief executive is being more strongly emphasized. One major steel producer has recently relieved the Vorsitzer of his technical responsibility to allow full attention to general management affairs. He was replaced by a new technical director. On the other hand, although the need for a strong Vorsitzer is recognized, there remains the restraint on his authority as demonstrated by the recent change in German corporate law mentioned above. It is noteworthy that a major German company recently removed its young and vigorous chief executive, one reason being that he was overpoweringly autocratic.

As a general rule, German and Dutch companies have recognized some of the ambiguities of the collegial system and are becoming more organization conscious. They are spelling out, in some detail, the duties of Vorstand members and the duties and relationships of the subordinate levels.

Another improvement finds the decision-making process at the Vorstand level being speeded up by greater delegation of authority to the lower levels. This is being made possible through better management control programs and cost systems that permit delegation with the loss of control. The German steel industry now has the industrywide introduction of standard costing under study. This delegation also permits certain Vorstands to redirect their attention to the broader policy aspects of their business—mergers, diversification, international business, the reassignment of products to plants, and other aspects of corporate planning.

The importance of more formalized corporate planning is increasingly recognized by collegial managers. A major German paper manufacturer has recently established corporate planning as a function reporting directly to the Vorsitzer. One Dutch company has appointed a corporate planner reporting to the "coordinating" managing director. He, in turn, coordinates and brings into focus economic, financial, marketing, and technical plans that are generated by staff planners responsible to their respective Vorstand members. Formalized planning procedures, policy, and structure are finding more acceptance in the collegial process. In fact, "management by plan" is the only way that the Vorstand can delegate product responsibility to one of its fellow members and hold him accountable on an organized basis for results.

Without a doubt, the collegial system will continue as the accepted management system in parts of northern Europe. However, it appears to be moving more and more toward committee management as practiced in the United States, with a recognized chief executive officer who shapes and coordinates the ultimate policy.

One cannot predict the ultimate form of what appears to be a gradual evolution of collegial management. Increasing levels of competition and growing product diversification in Europe will undoubtedly create continuing pressures for speeding up the decision-making process. This has already led to examples of increasing delegation of product line profit responsibility, not only to establish "profit centers," but to expedite and encourage new product development. The growing use of computers in Europe increases the capability for improved planning and implementation of management information and control systems. Since information without authority to act is a pyrrhic victory indeed, pressure for delegation of authority will continue to come from this source.

The continuing growth of international trade and the need to respond quickly to competitive situations is another pressure for delegated authority. The manager on the scene with knowledge of local conditions can be counted on to apply this pressure, particularly where he has been given profit responsibility. Moreover, although collegial management has tended to stifle entrepreneurial types in the past, the climate of increasing competition is spawning a new breed of risk-takers. As these individuals rise in their organizations, they will tend to press for additional change in the collegial management concept.

American managers will do well to watch this metamorphosis—not only to assess its implications on the future of U.S. organization theory, but to weigh its effect on doing business with Europeans as well as competing with them in the marketplace.

selection 28

An Aspect of Management Philosophy in the United States and Latin America*

Eugene C. McCann

The question of whether management is more philosophy, art, science or some combination is frequently regarded as little more than useless academic debate. The position taken, however, has considerable bearing for research, education and practice in the field. The implications and consequences of that starting position can be profound in approaching management in diverse cultural settings. In these days of aroused interest in Latin American exchanges involving programs of business and public administration, one of the relatively neglected points is the contrast between North Americans and Latin Americans in appraising *scientific* components in management.

MANAGEMENT: ART AND/OR SCIENCE

If management contains no guides, laws, principles, or any of the other elements of a science, then it must be an art. If it is truly an art, then everything which has ever been written about management is of little or no use. All those who profess to teach management are either *estupidos* or frauds. Whether art can be codified and taught is not a settled matter. Art is skillful performance which comes from within a person and which can be learned only through practice and experience. Expression of an art is an individual matter. What can be taught, however, is science—truths, principles, laws. This aspect of a management philosophy, therefore, must satisfy the question of whether management is an art, a science, or a combination.

For the most part, U.S. business practitioners and business academicians agree that management is partly a science and partly an art. Businessmen and scholars have not always held this position. For instance, in the United States, before about 1880, management was considered solely an art.

A "manager" was born or was made so in the hot crucible of experience. He thus relied upon intuitive guidance when faced with a decision. . . . So in a sense he learned nothing

*From *Journal of the Academy of Management*, Vol. 7, No. 2 (June, 1964), pp. 149–52.

from previous generations and could pass nothing on to succeeding generations as far as managerial skills were concerned.[1]

Frederick W. Taylor, Henri Fayol, Henry Gantt, Frank and Lillian Gilbreth and others, however, were not convinced. They felt that somewhere in management there is logic, that management embodies basic principles and relationships which can be set down, codified, and communicated. The search for management principles carried on since the turn of the century has uncovered many. Admittedly, certain areas of management, for the moment, must remain in the realm of art. Nevertheless, modern U.S. businessmen and others who are concerned with group coordination believe that management does contain a science.

Management generally is considered an art in Latin America. Several indications tend to support this statement. Only rarely does one encounter a book or an article which deals with management in Latin America from a Latin American viewpoint. Furthermore, only rarely is management taught in Latin American colleges and universities. The major emphasis is on the liberal arts.

Another indication which lends support to the notion that management is considered an art in Latin America is the sparing use of scientific method in Latin American business operations. Since Frederick Taylor popularized the use of scientific method as an aid to managerial decision making, it has become basic to U.S. management philosophy. Though the scientific method has been stated many times in many ways, Ralph C. Davis explains it probably as well as any. "The term 'scientific method' may refer to any orderly method that seeks to apply the logic of effective thinking to the solution of some type of problem."[2]

In our culture, the utilization of this approach is widespread and not limited to business management. Scientific method meshes nicely with cultural attitudes that encourage an analytical approach to all types of decision-making activities. As a result, scientific method is the most used of any of the "tools" of U.S. management.

The lack of utilization of such a concept undoubtedly hampers Latin American decision-makers. Why they make little or no use of it warrants discussion.

CAUSES FOR IGNORING SCIENTIFIC METHOD

The effective utilization of scientific method requires patient, careful, orderly thinking and the ability to see reality objectively. The Latin American, however, tends to be impatient, impulsive, emotional, and to disregard objectivity.[3]

Basing action on emotion is accepted, expected, and desired among Latin Americans because giving immediate expression to one's feelings is accepted,

---

[1] Michael J. Jucius and William E. Schlender, *Elements of Managerial Action* (Homewood, Ill.: Richard D. Irwin, Inc., 1960), p. 20.

[2] Ralph Currier Davis, *Industrial Organization and Management* (3d ed.; New York: Harper & Bros., 1957), p. 61.

[3] Harry Stark, *Modern Latin America* (Coral Gables, Fla.: University of Miami Press, 1957), p. 70.

expected and desired. Latin Americans are men of passion. In writing about the Spanish influence on Latin America and specifically on using emotion and intuition as the basis for determining action, William Schurz noted: "So he may not do things according to reason or logic or cold calculation, for his mind is not orderly or systematic, but according to the light of intuition and the urge of strong feeling. He may even do something for no good reason at all, but only by the prompting of caprice."[4]

Latin Americans are not so interested in results as are Anglo-Americans.[5] Action is important to a Latin American but not from a results standpoint. The utility of results is relatively unimportant. Since he is a man of passion, action becomes more important than results because it allows the free expression of inner feelings. This is the important element—spontaneous expression. In fact, passion opposes logic. Logical action requires that expression be subordinated to the will; logical action reflects a deliberate speed and a predetermined direction. Passion reflects spontaneity of action at whatever speed and direction the emotion of the moment generates.[6]

DECISION MAKING—LATIN AMERICAN STYLE

The Latin American relies heavily upon intuition, the passion of the intellect, to point out the solutions to problems. Thought proceeds in a series of direct revelations or perceptions of "truths" concerning the object being contemplated. These perceptions are independent of any demonstrated reasoning process and, therefore, neither verifiable nor repeatable. The tendency is toward action which appears improvised (and often is). This characteristic frequently leads Latin Americans to act without planning, at least without conscious planning. Salvador de Madariaga touches this notion using the Spanish as examples:

> Intuition also excludes any possibility of establishing a method beforehand. And in fact, method is far from being a typical feature of Spanish thought. A method, we have said, is a road for the mind. It is difficult to imagine how a road towards knowledge could be traced by people who find themselves in knowledge before they set foot on the road. . . . Spanish thought has a method of its own which is certainly not the road-schedule. . . .[7]

While emotion, as a basis for action, may often lead to unsound decisions, improvisations, and ineffective results, attempts have been made to justify it—to explain logically the use of emotion as a basis for action. Those who attempt to justify it argue that man has been a reasoning being for, at most, a few thousand years. Before that, man survived by following his instincts and impulses. "The Latin could therefore advance good support for the assertion that those

---

[4] William Lytle Schurz, *This New World* (New York: E. P. Dutton & Co., Inc., 1954), p. 82.

[5] John Fayerweather, *The Executive Overseas* (Syracuse, N.Y.: Syracuse University Press, 1959), p. 63.

[6] Salvador de Madariaga, *Englishmen, Frenchmen, Spaniards* (London: Oxford University Press, 1931), p. 42.

[7] *Ibid.*, p. 78.

impulses that have survived the great sieve of evolution must be those best suited to man's survival and continued development."[8]

The proponents of this theory claim that the urgings of man's heart might spring from the sifted and stored up wisdom of all that man has learned throughout time. By comparison, recorded knowledge must appear rather insignificant. As one philosopher put it:

> It is not wisdom to be only wise
> And on the inward vision close the eyes
> But it is wisdom to believe the heart.[9]

In discussing thought in the man of passion, de Madariaga explains that he contemplates and waits in apparent passivity for the object of the contemplation to reveal itself. "He lets the continuous stream of life pass through him, until chance, a happy coincidence, a secret sympathy, will suddenly illumine it with a new light."[10] The Latin American is apathetic about circumstances until such time as a flash of perception or intuition moves him. Until he experiences inspiration, and because cold logic and results-oriented action have little appeal, he tends to do things in the manner which involves the least risk and effort. If he faces a situation requiring action about which he has no intense feelings, the manner which involves the least risk and effort is to conform to some existing pattern. "If he follows the rules there will be no complaints, he will not have to make a mental effort, and the situation will be taken care of."[11] But how did this characteristic become ingrained in the psychological make-up of the Latin American?

THE OLD WORLD'S BEQUEST

The great emphasis on science and utilization of scientific method resulted from the scientific revolution which swept Europe in the 1500's. This revolution was, in large measure, a result of the Renaissance and the Reformation. Before this time, Europeans patterned their lives and thoughts according to the dogma prescribed by authorities. These authorities were Church officials, political officials (frequently the same), or monarchs. For hundreds of years, people were told what to do and how to think about practically every aspect of their lives. They were accustomed to authoritarian leadership, expected it, and, perhaps, even demanded it. The Renaissance and the Reformation represented change. Man was expected to think independently and to reach his own conclusions about worldly and religious matters.

The Renaissance eventually spread into Spain, but the Spanish scholars directed their efforts not to revolt but to attempts at purification and maintenance

---

[8] Stark, *op. cit.,* p. 63.

[9] From a poem, "O World, Thou Choosest Not," by George Santayana and quoted in Stark, *op. cit.,* p. 63.

[10] Madariaga, *op. cit.,* p. 74.

[11] Fayerweather, *op. cit.,* p. 64.

of the Church. The Reformation, however, never reached Spain. Thus, the attitude of independent, analytical thinking was not emphasized and never became an important part of the approach to decision making and problem solution. This characteristic became part of the New World's legacy.

SUMMARY

The aspect of management philosophy considered in this article has been North American versus Latin American inclusion of scientific thinking in approaching management.

In the U.S., management is considered to contain scientific components. In Latin America, management generally is considered solely an art. The very heart of the U.S. approach to business management, scientific method, is ignored and denied in Latin America because of cultural and personality characteristics which lead persons to rely on intuition as a basis for decision making.

Because Latin Americans are not strongly results-oriented, management by objectives is not so common in Latin America as it is in the United States. Rather, Latin Americans regard action not in terms of how it aids in achieving desired goals, but as an end in itself.

These characteristics—regarding management as an art, viewing action as an expression of inner feelings rather than a calculated means to an end and ignoring scientific method as a decision-making tool—pose challenges that must be recognized in working out useful exchanges among Americans interested in better management.

selection 29

Management Aims and Development Needs in Latin America*

Albert Lauterbach

INTRODUCTION

Exploration of the attitudes and motives of managers is an indispensable complement to economic, financial, or administrative investigations of business activities. Without introducing psychological evidence into the study of such

*From *Business History Review*, Vol. 39 (1963), pp. 557–72, 577–88.

activities, the regularity, permanence, or "normality" of specific kinds of managerial decisions may be seriously misjudged. In order to decide to what extent behavior patterns from the past that are summarized in statistical series can be expected to continue in the future, it is essential to explore the driving forces of economic actions including unconscious or "irrational" factors, personality influences, group standards, historical heritage, and cultural values of the population in which the management concerned is rooted.

The present paper is focused on the views of managers in a newly developing area, in this case Latin America, concerning development conditions in their respective countries and their own role in the development process. Specifically, we shall discuss the expressed principal aims of management; managerial satisfactions and discontents; perceptions of competition, market limitations, and inflation effects; and interpretations of the development stage achieved and the measures still needed.

It was not, of course, assumed that the views encountered would be necessarily realistic or well-balanced. But the mere fact that certain views are held constitutes an important factor in the development trends of the areas under discussion. Studies of managerial attitudes in specific parts of the world may also contribute something to our more general understanding of what actually is to be interpreted as "development" in contrast to "growth" or "change," of what makes development happen, of what takes place concretely in the course of development, and of the interaction of economic, political, psychological, and sociocultural factors in such a process. This includes the extent to which the mentality of emerging managerial groups is colored by demonstration effects; the condensation of contemporary economic development into a much shorter space of time than was required in the now developed countries; the impact of recent international advances in technology and organization; and the economic aspects of new images of national assertion and independence.

It is intended, at the same time, to allow duly for the extent to which Latin American managers function on the basis of distinctive attitudinal or, for that matter, institutional characteristics in comparison with their colleagues in other parts of the world. It is not, in other words, necessarily assumed that management is (or should be) basically alike regardless of whether a manager runs a steel corporation in Pittsburgh or a coffee plantation in Guatemala. Neither is it assumed that generalizations about "Latin American" managers are necessarily more valid than other generalizations about Latin America.

It is especially important not to equalize similarities in office arrangements, organization charts, and official terminology with actual identity of managerial attitudes or behavior in highly developed and in underdeveloped countries or areas. Despite superficial resemblance a Latin American manager, in his actual role within the company and in his relations with employees, customers, suppliers, competitors, bankers, landowners, politicians, and government officials may follow faithfully, if often unconsciously, the feudal legacy of his society, the Indian, Spanish, or Portuguese outlook on life, and other influences that are absent or weak in North America and Western Europe.

In particular, three factors characterize management in a large part of Latin America:

First, business and management are still intertwined with family relationships and politics. Even when the form of a *sociedad anónima* is used, a controlling part of the shares typically remains in the hands of a large or small family group, perhaps with the participation of some close friends of the family. The professional hired executive is still confined to a few areas such as Mexico City, Buenos Aires, and São Paulo, and is even there a fairly new and limited phenomenon. In many more cases managers are selected on the basis of family links, personal recommendations, and financial participation in the enterprise. [1] They constantly use political pull in order to get things done or to secure special favors for their companies. They may also put in a short period of service as a cabinet minister or public administrator without being too fussy about continuing their private business interests at the same time. Money made through the political medium may go into new or old enterprises and the successful *político* may become a prosperous businessman, or vice versa. [2] There is, however, a newly emerging desire for executive training in many areas.

Second, there is still far-reaching absence of specialization in any one industry or field of business. The same person, family group, or executive office may administer a variety of enterprises which may range from textile mills or sugar plantations to mines and banks. [3] People with money, credit, or training tend to look for some promising business opportunity in general, rather than to apply specialized experience to new ventures in a given field. This pattern can in part be explained by the fact that many groupings of enterprises had their roots in agricultural holdings which, under a suitable stimulus or market threat, were expanded into processing, commerce, banking, and eventually non-related industrial activities. The traditional scarcity of cleancut industrial opportunities in most of Latin America has been accompanied by constant urge to invest *somehow* the inflationary gains. Finally, the ownership of industries and banks comes to confer prestige upon an originally agrarian family, though later on with the progress of industrialization the pattern is reversed and the acquisition of landholdings becomes a prestige factor for the urban businessman.

Third, despite frequent imitation of their *confrères* from more developed

---

[1] "In the Latin American culture, business is a part of the total scheme of things: It is part of the family, of the *compadre* relation, of friendships, and of the Church. Business is done among friends in a leisurely and understanding way. Material success is at the bottom of the scale. First of all comes the protection of the family, the *compadres,* the friends." Frank Tannenbaum, *Ten Keys to Latin America* (New York, 1963), p. 129.

[2] Compare the typology of managerial elites, including patrimonial, political, and professional management, as presented by F. Harbison and Ch. A. Myers, *Management in the Industrial World* (New York, 1959), chap. 4. Also Fritz Redlich, "Business Leadership: Diverse Origins and Variant Forms," *Economic Development and Cultural Change,* Vol. 6 (April, 1958).

[3] See United Nations, *Management of Industrial Enterprises in Underdeveloped Countries* (New York, 1958), pp. 4 ff. Also Professor Cochran's findings on factors in Puerto Rican business: Thomas C. Cochran, *The Puerto Rican Businessman: A Study in Cultural Change* (Philadelphia, 1959), chap. 4.

countries, either through individual behavior or through technical training methods taken over from them, Latin American businessmen as a group remain largely different in their basic mentality concerning the conduct of enterprises, national development needs, and life values in general. The economic legacy of feudalism, slavery, neglect of production by the colonial masters, military power aspirations ever since the wars of independence, volatile political parties, and economic dependence on one or two products of the soil is still there. It has, however, been markedly weakening in some countries, such as Mexico since Cárdenas, and is rapidly being modified in the industrialized areas of several nations. This study, therefore, is concerned with a transitional phase of Latin American societies and with the corresponding processes of changing mentality in one important social group.

The present investigation utilizes data obtained from 1959 to 1963 through interviews with a cross-section of business managers in Chile, Colombia, Peru, Argentina, Uruguay, Brazil, Venezuela, Mexico, Guatemala, and El Salvador. A few interviews were also held in Bolivia and Paraguay. In one country, Chile, a detailed study was carried out in 1959 and 1960,[4] followed up by some re-interviews in 1963. The total number of interviews with managers of private enterprises was 306, to which need to be added 19 managers of public enterprises and 78 non-managerial experts in the field of this study, such as economists, government officials, and productivity experts. The sample included managers in industrial enterprises, especially textiles, clothing, and footwear, metal products, electrical goods, chemicals, ceramics, foodstuffs and tobacco, as well as non-industrial enterprises in the fields of banking and insurance, commerce, transportation, construction, mining, and commercial agriculture.

For the reasons mentioned earlier, classification of a businessman or manager according to industry is often impossible in Latin America, and some of the interviewees had background or connections in more than one field. A conscious and mostly successful effort was made to include top business leaders or representatives of leading business families without whom any managerial sample in certain countries would have been quite incomplete. Chiefly, large and medium-sized firms were represented, but in a few cases it seemed desirable to include also some owner-managers of very small units with less than 25 employees. The term "manager" refers in this study to the heads or leading executives of enterprises regardless of whether they hold an ownership interest in them or not. The prevailing pattern in Latin America, however, is strong ownership participation of the manager or his family in the firm he manages. Some, but by

---

[4] Albert Lauterbach, *Managerial Attitudes in Chile.* Instituto de Economía,Universidad de Chile, Santiago, 1961. Also "Managerial Attitudes and Economic Development," *Kyklos,* 1961/2 and, "Actitudes Empresariales y el Desarrollo Económico," *Revista de Economia Latinoamericana,* Caracas, Venezuela, June, 1961. Compare the author's book, *Man, Motives, and Money* (2d ed., Ithaca, N.Y., 1959), chaps. 1 and 2. The earlier phase of the study was aided by the Fulbright Administration and the Social Science Research Council. The latter phase was carried out under a Brookings Research Professorship. The author is, of course, solely responsible for the content of this paper. His book *Enterprise in Latin America* (Ithaca, 1966) is in press.

no means all, of the managers interviewed would also fit into a classification as entrepreneurs, either in the Schumpeterian sense or in that of an independent source of authority, but there is no particular reason in this paper to enter into the perennial terminological debate on this point.[5]

All the interviews were carried out by the author of this paper. The questionnaire, which was administered in a flexible way, consisted of two main parts. The first was focused on the interviewee's own experience and that of the company, while the second was aimed at his views regarding the economic development of the nation. The response was mostly very cooperative and the interview was often interpreted as a rare opportunity to discuss things with a detached observer. Given the importance of the foreign-born element in Latin American business, the sample included a number of foreign-born persons with real roots in their adopted country. In addition, numerous publications and statements of trade associations and individual companies in the various countries were consulted.

The hypotheses from which the investigation started were the following:

(1) The aims of the managers in these countries are only partly financial, more so for their enterprises than for themselves, and partly directed at expansion of the firm or at the expression of creative or social needs.

(2) Managerial satisfactions are rooted more strongly in personal factors such as the challenge of the job itself than in financial rewards; discontents are focused on competition, labor, or government interference.

(3) Inflation is not viewed as an unmixed evil to the same extent that it is in more developed countries, and is often associated with economic development.

(4) The development stage achieved is generally viewed as unsatisfactory and a combination of private and public action is considered necessary.

These hypotheses were largely, but not entirely, confirmed. In a number of cases the answers were even more varied or contradictory than had been assumed.

AIMS OF MANAGEMENT

After initial queries about the main activity, age, and ownership structure of the enterprise and the interviewee's function in it, the following question was asked, "How would you describe the principal aim that guides the management of this enterprise?"

Responses to this question were extremely varied. Generally surprise at being asked this kind of question was greatest in the least developed areas, especially in smaller firms. The respondent either had not thought about such matters at all or had taken it for granted that the aim of management was to keep the

---

[5] Compare Bert F. Hoselitz, "Entrepreneurship and Economic Growth," in *Sociological Aspects of Economic Growth* (Glencoe, 1960). Bendix' interesting discussion, based on the industrial history of England, the U.S., and Russia, of a "change from entrepreneurial to managerial ideologies" seems to have very limited applications to Latin America thus far. Reinhard Bendix, *Work and Authority in Industry* (New York, 1956), esp. chaps. 1 and 4.

company going gainfully and nothing but that. An occasional, somewhat related answer referred to intended superiority over all the other competitors.

In more developed areas many responses showed that more elaborate thinking had been done on the subject. In these cases the answer was often in the nature of "to obtain profit, of course, but this is not all." A Mexican industrialist (#17,) for example, commented:

My purpose is to work, to create new industry and, through it, a higher standard of living. Not just money. If a business is well planned, profit will come anyway. If I wanted nothing but money I'd just be a moneylender and charge crazy interest rates.

Similarly, an industrial manager in Venezuela (#132) said:

Money is not the chief aim. Both my brother and I had plenty of it before we started this concern. Our aim is a good, strong industrial group which is basically adapted to the economy of the country and is not a parasite but makes a contribution. For this reason we don't go into land purchases, for instance.

Some answers were presented in such terms as "to provide quality products at low cost," "To provide employment and income for some of the people in this community," or, less frequently, "to make a contribution to the industrial development of the country." A Mexican banker and promoter (#28) said that he aims at industrial diversification, only promotes industries that are in the long-run national interest, and does not consider unnecessary consumer industries or amusements no matter how profitable, even though the financial success of a company is "revealing."

Another Mexican banker (#35) answered the entire question largely in terms of national needs:

There are several goals to be considered. First, to make savings more popular and with it, investment. The number of savers is still small; we want to increase it constantly. Second, agrarian financing for a growing number of small land-owners. But there are problems in it because their education level is precarious and they know nothing of credit or techniques and need protection against cheating. Third, industrialization, and a crusade for greater and more diversified exports.

Progress or expansion of the company was mentioned frequently as the principal aim of management. This also came out with even greater frequency in response to a later question about investment intentions. However, explicit association of such expansion with national development needs was infrequent. On the other hand, high income for stockholders or managers was rarely mentioned spontaneously, though it was probably taken for granted by many. Some managers whose companies had established medical, housing, or welfare facilities for their workers answered in corresponding terms. An industrial manager in Mexico (#39) claimed that his company had very special characteristics:

It is the *social* aspect of industrial relations that matters most here. We have long been supplying food, transport, housing, schools, and stores to our workers and they share the gains of the company.

In general, the principal aim was expressed in the form not of long-range but of immediate objectives. An approximation to long-range considerations was offered by a Venezuelan businessman who answered: "Defending the private-enterprise system by making it meaningful." A public-enterprise manager in Mexico (#6) felt that private enterprise had gone through an adventurer-entrepreneur phase but that more permanent aims prevailed now. The manager of a producers' cooperative in Mexico (#24) described its permanent aim as lowering the operational costs in distribution and to have the members save the difference. This was thought of as a service both to the members and to the public, and he emphasized that the cooperative had no profit aim even though it *could* make profit. Broad social goals of the enterprise such as jobs and stability were also listed by a number of managers in long-range terms.

For my private convenience, I would not live here, the political situation being what it is. But I am fulfilling a duty. My partners feel the same way. Without us, things would turn even worse. (Industrial manager, Venezuela, European-born, #121.)

A substantial number of answers were given in technical terms, especially by executives with such background as engineering or architecture. These answers included increasing the quality or variety of the product, acquiring the latest kind of machinery, improving the plant organization, and so forth.

In explaining why money, while necessary, was not the primary objective of management, an executive in Mexico, for example, said that his father had never worked for money's sake as he had more already than he could ever spend. A more definite connection was revealed by others between the level of education and the range of thinking about management aims. Those managers who had experienced little education had rarely thought ahead sufficiently to be able to answer the question under discussion in a meaningful way, and sometimes were bewildered by it. Especially did this apply to those in charge of smaller companies. Business was seen by many of them as pretty much taking care of itself; why strain one's brain about the future, with the only possible exception of external disturbances such as a runaway inflation or social radicalism?

At the other extreme there was a small number of highly educated, sophisticated, and socially responsible managers who tried to convert their fellow businessmen to their own views. An example is offered by the following statement:[6]

In the first place one must understand perfectly that the function of the executive is not to supply to the capitalist a rather high yield, and that the index of his success is not measured exactly by the rising curve of the economic indices of the enterprise. The executive has a goal and a cause. His goal is to get ahead of himself as a result of integration of his own personality . . . The real asset of the enterprise is the human element. This is precisely the cause for which the executive works: human betterment and social justice; human betterment to be achieved through economic effort, work designed to raise the standard of living through greater productivity, effort for systematic organization of economic resources in order to achieve the last aim of prosperity, abundance for everybody.

The executive, in order to perform, must love. He cannot limit himself to the sharing of benefits without knowing how to share the joy of life and work. To love is to give, to give of oneself, and wealth does not consist in what one has got but in what one gives. Wealth is not to be found in capital but in service.

---

[6] Ivan Lansberg Henríquez, President of Asociación Venezolana de Ejecutivos, interview in EL NACIONAL, Caracas, December 18, 1962, and paper on Management: An Idea in Action," mimeo., February, 1963.

Only a small minority related their own activity or that of their firm clearly to development trends or needs of the country. In fact, the greater were the objective development needs of an area the fewer business managers there seemed to think in these terms. The prevailing attitude might best be summed up by saying that the majority of the managers interviewed had a vague feeling that there was, or should be, more to the conduct of an enterprise than merely to keep it profitable, but that any definite aims or tasks in long-range terms of a contribution to the economic and social advancement of the country remained confined to a sophisticated minority.[7]

By way of an appendix to this section, there follows a rather illuminating statement made by a managerial executive of an important public enterprise in Mexico regarding the current development stages of business groups with the corresponding management aims:

In this country there are three groups of businessmen, with different attitudes:

The *first* faces no risk regarding the demand for his product. He normally can plan his investment regardless, for example in the production of beer and bottles. His opinions on development have effective channels to express themselves politically. The development of these companies is tuned to national development and they can wait, even absorb losses or else pass them on to the State. This applies chiefly to business in the large centers.

The *second* group is that of the *beginning* entrepreneurs and it is quite different. For them things don't work well yet. They use promoters from the outside, have little resources themselves. They expect immediate profit especially from new products such as appliances, in the interest of capital formation, but they also need bank credit or other help. They suffer frequent losses. Much depends for them on government contracts. This group is very promising but has had no time yet to think in terms of economic development. The Common Market, for instance, is vivid in the minds of the first but not the second group. This latter group needs fiscal protection and counseling.

Third comes the forgotten man. He interprets industry as improvement of handicrafts. Especially is this true in the provinces. He works for the local market and is interested in *local* development, has no economic viewpoint. He is fearful of foreign competition. The State can destroy him, too. He thinks more of survival than of profit or investment. This group is very numerous, if you think of tailors or silversmiths, for instance, but it is not important insofar as its total investment is concerned. From it, however, come the best entrepreneurs! Just look at the shoe industry. They depend heavily on protectionism, though. But this group is very promising because Mexico must develop according to the European not the North American pattern.

The difference in geographic conditions is extremely important in this country. Monterrey, for instance, is developed. Economic development is largely a regional problem. Some parts of the country are still Spanish colonies, in a sense.

MANAGERIAL SATISFACTIONS AND DISCONTENTS

In comparison with the expressed principal aims of managerial activity, what are the chief satisfactions of managers in a newly developing economy, and what are the main sources of discontent? This was the subject of the following questions:

---

[7] Compare Daniel R. Fusfeld, "Heterogony of Entrepreneurial Goals," *Explorations in Entrepreneurial History,* Vol. 9 (October, 1956).

(a) "What are the chief satisfactions which you find in your activity as manager?"

(b) "Are there any discontents?"

On the whole, Latin American managers were found to be very eager to talk about such questions even though they were of a more personal nature than the entire rest of the questionnaire. It was clear that many interviewees had thought before about related issues or, at least, felt that they should have thought about them, from their own point of view, and that the interview offered a welcome stimulus to do so.

Theoretically, it would have been conceivable that the predominant answer to the first part of the question would be "money" or "high income." Actually, the response was far more complex. Leaving aside some who were taken by surprise by the question and were too puzzled to give a coherent answer, only a small minority mentioned money or income first. However, a good many took financial rewards for granted in some way or, at least, included them among their standards of satisfaction.

Many more commented that the high income resulting from their managerial or business activity was pleasant, desirable, or reassuring, but that it constituted a mere starting point or precondition for satisfactions of more important kinds:

Profit is not decisive. Personal factors are more important—to *do* something with life. We began to produce with national resources and now we use 95 per cent domestic materials. We had confidence in our government and in the consumer needs of our people as economic factors in development. We have achieved the leading position in our field and want to help the mechanization and automation of industry here. *Otherwise* we have no "aim." (Industrial manager, Mexico, # 59.)

I am a man who is *inquieto* and impassioned for his country. I am financially well off, but am not interested in money. I believe in Mexico, have very many friends, and enjoy my life. (Lawyer and businessman, Mexico, # 25.)

I am a man with drive—I hail from Catalonia. I like to build up something new. I suffer from lack of people I can trust, and of investors, but I always have some new projects going. (Industrial manager, Guatemala, #75.)

Several commented that money was not an important yardstick because they or their families had more already than they could ever spend for personal purposes. Family traditions and roots in the kind of enterprise which they headed were felt to be the decisive factor of satisfaction in a number of cases.

Growth of the company and the earning of profits required to finance such growth were mentioned repeatedly as the mainstay of managerial satisfaction. It will be shown, however, that this was usually only one aspect of satisfactions derived from meeting a challenge, doing the job itself, or fulfilling the desire to "create," to build up a large enterprise, to promote, to acquire modern facilities, to offer new products to the consumer, or—less frequently—to make a contribution to the industrial development of the country or to high employment and standard of living. Creativity and social utility emerged in various ways as an important driving force and, when fulfilled, a major source of satisfaction.

As a boy I was a shift boss in a gold and silver mine. It was a soulless occupation. On this job here, I handle a noble product which serves humanity. As a boy I wanted to be a captain of industry. I did not quite get there, but I am making a certain amount of money without hurting anyone. I have everybody as friend. I am a spiritualist by religion; I believe in general laws of the universe. My religion says, 'You should not be materialistic.' I want to be liked, then I'll be better off financially, too.' (Manager, industrial company, Mexico, # 22.)

Financial and personal success is very important to me, but I must also feel that I am making a civic contribution. But the majority of businessmen do not think this way, are lacking in social sense. (President of an employers' group, Mexico, # 30.)

Among the managers of public enterprises there were repeated expressions of a related satisfaction that came from working directly for the welfare of the country, a satisfaction which was felt to make up for possible factors of a less favorable nature such as lower pay in certain categories.

Personally, I prefer public management. Many people think that public management is badly administered; I want to prove the opposite. Our incentives are just as good as those of private enterprise. The government has a complementary part in making up for many deficiencies of private enterprise. It is more difficult to manage a public enterprise, but it can be done and then has a chain reaction in creating good-will. We try, though, to avoid political interference at any price. (Manager, public enterprise, Mexico, # 62.)

Closely related to creativity needs was a desire for independence, which was clearly manifested by owner-managers but also led to the widespread claim on the part of hired managers that *they* run the show and derive much satisfaction from this decisive role. In some cases this claim was at odds with evidence from other sources regarding the actual distribution of power within the company, but this did not impair the strength of the aspiration to be independent and, thereby, truly creative.

I like independence, freedom of action. I like the problems, too. When there are none, I'll retire! (Industrialist, Mexico, # 14.)

I like to be busy and creative, to put together the financial, industrial, and human elements. Once an enterprise is going, I turn over the management to others and dispose of details. (Industrialist, Mexico, # 17.)

Construction constantly transforms everybody, it is always different, one always plans new things. (Manager, construction firm, Mexico, # 31.)

To have conquered successfully a past challenge rooted in the newness of the enterprise or any other kind of difficulties, or to keep conquering emerging challenges continuously, was listed frequently in various forms as a factor of satisfaction.

To carry through the program, to carry out a constructive activity, to apply foreign experiences to Mexico insofar as applicable, to hold the product prices down through savings to the producers; to carry out an idea. (Manager, producers' cooperative, Mexico, # 24.)

Some but not all of the challenges listed specifically were implicit in the nature of an insufficiently developed economy; for example, in lack of education among the workers or in shortage of transportation facilities, difficulties which, it was felt, the management of the company had successfully struggled against. In other cases a related source of managerial satisfaction was expressed in terms of doing the job itself; for example, the constant stimulation and interest that are implicit in supervising people, selling goods and talking to customers.

It is a difficult job with many adverse moments during recessions, in particular. During prosperity it is pleasant work which makes a contribution to the national economy. I am an economist and *as such* find bank work very interesting. I am the *pater confessor* for many people and get insights into the human psyche. (Bank manager, Venezuela, #112.)

Cotton is like a beautiful woman who gets more interesting every day. The problems never repeat themselves. (Manager, commercial company, Mexico, #3.)

An industrial manager in Mexico (#20) said that he personally feels the strain of work and prefers loafing, but that he feels an obligation to live up to the moral compulsion to make an effort in the interest of the growth of the company.

Relations with associates and other people concerned were mentioned frequently as a factor of managerial satisfaction, though they were listed in other cases as a cause of discontent. "Associates" meant sometimes the executive staff, at other times the workers and employees in general; in a good many cases it referred to close relations among members of one family who were all active in the enterprise, usually on the managerial level. A financial manager in Venezuela (#105) said:

I feel satisfied when I see a contented and happy personnel here. Also when I can fulfill my "mission" and ambition to grow. These two things go together. I feel dissatisfied when we have failed to give good service according to my own judgment.

The European-born manager of a financial enterprise in Chile (re-interview, 1963, #142) said that his dealings with the Board of Directors are most satisfactory because they are men of "European culture," though not necessarily Europeans. The manager of a construction firm in Mexico (#21) spoke of the satisfaction coming from:

the living together of a group of people, the sense of obligation among them, their conviction about what they all are doing, once the physical necessities have been satisfied.

Another one said:

My satisfaction is "nationalist." I want to see this big enterprise managed entirely by Mexicans, and also to know that the foreign investment in it is good for Mexico. I don't like, though, to have to be apologetic about this foreign ownership. (Industrial manager, Mexico, #64.)

Incidentally, the same man said later in the interview:

I am for unrestricted foreign investment including oil. The American and British companies were stupid to hand oil over to Cárdenas. They should have offered him candies, not resistance.

Paternalist feelings toward the personnel were found to be fairly frequent, especially in the least developed areas.

My brothers and I were the first in this industry. Our objectives are not only economic but social and the latter are much more important. For me the enterprise is a family. Everybody including the workers is equally interested in it. More employment and welfare for everyone in the company, with continuing training and better wages, gives us satisfaction. (Industrial manager, El Salvador, #94.)

In all probability the workers in many cases did not actually hold the feelings of affection toward the managers which the latter assumed to exist, but such possible discrepancies did not seem to interfere with the managerial satisfactions felt or rationalizations.[8]

As for *discontents,* some interviewees said that they could not think of any at all (an industrial manager in Venezuela, #132, said, "Nothing. I do only what I like to do") but many more had some to register. To begin with, the same factors that were listed as satisfying when fulfilled became sources of discontent when frustrated. This was true of growth ambitions, profit yields, wishes of independence, creative urges, challenges encountered, expectations regarding the nature of the job, and desires for friendly, mutually understanding relations with the personnel and other people. In particular, it was pointed out in some cases that the family roots of an enterprise may not only limit its financial scope but may lead to problems in family relations. One interviewee (Mexico, #63) listed as main discontent, "to have to *work,* and the number of things I have to do." A small businessman in Chile (#141A) stated:

We are independent, but my wife and I have to work from 8:00 a.m. to 8:00 p.m. and *then* to prepare work for the next day. I fall into my bed, read a little, then sleep. On Sunday I often sleep, too. We see nothing of the beauties of Chile. Our world is the apartment and the shop.

In a more general way, the performance of labor was a fairly frequent source of complaints. This was true primarily of the educational level and training of the workers and, in a lesser degree, of the effect of labor unions when they are guided by adverse political or ideological influences. The prevailing attitude of managers in these cases was that the worker in the country concerned is intelligent and learns fast but that unions or agitators prevent him from doing his best. Fear of radical influences or outright communism was a not infrequent, but by no means, universal, source of discontent.

Complaints about government and politics, on the other hand, were extremely frequent, even though the typical complexion of such complaints varied considerably from one country to another. Corruption on many or all levels of government, inefficiency, red tape and paperwork, the prevalence of political pull, legal complexities or uncertainties, competition from state enterprises, and instability or indecision in public life were cited time and again, though a few interviewees added that business often *asks* for specific kinds of state intervention. An industrial manager in El Salvador (#94) also complained about lack of understanding on the part of many capitalists who still have an agrarian mentality and think a factory is like a coffee plantation.

In summary, company profit as the basis of high individual incomes offered by no means an adequate explanation of managerial satisfactions or discontents. More indirectly, as the basis of company growth, it came somewhat closer to the explanation of such feelings. Even so, however, a variety of additional factors

---

[8] Compare José Medina Echavarría, *Consideraciones Sociológicas Sobre el Desarrollo Económico de América Latina,* United Nations Economic and Social Council—UNESCO, Santiago, 1962 (mimeo.), pp. 32ff., section on "Paternalism, Anxiety, and Impersonal Organization."

such as the desire for independence and creativity, the conquest of a challenge, the nature of the managerial job as such, relations with associates and others, and political and governmental influences must be taken into account in order to understand the managerial attitudes in question. To this must be added the perception of competition, market limitations, and inflation effects, which will be discussed in the following section.

COMPETITION, MARKET LIMITATIONS, AND INFLATION EFFECTS

Certain attitudes toward competition and market limitations were revealed by many interviewees in response to the question about managerial satisfactions and discontents, especially the latter, but also emerged from answers to various other questions. The attitudes toward competition which were encountered were more ambivalent than attitudes regarding most other issues raised in the interviews. The abstract principle of competition was usually approved heartily, especially where the influence of North American business ideology is strong such as in Venezuela. There were a few instances of company managers saying that they welcomed "constructive" competitors or that they needed "normal" competition in order to be kept on their toes.

Such responses, however, were overshadowed by mistrustful interpretation of competition as a bothersome source of discontent, usually leading to the conclusion that "excessive" competition, at least, should be restrained either by private or by public action.[9] This especially applied to fears of superior foreign competition, and to the frequent belief that competition in general was an expensive luxury for an underdeveloped country.

A financial manager in Venezuela (#105) claimed that:

the Latin American can only compete when he is furious. He interprets competition as personal aggression. This is why there is so little business competition here!

On the other hand, very many interviewees commented that competition did not bother them in practice, either because of monopolistic advantages or understandings they enjoyed or because of the readiness of markets in a rapidly growing population to absorb practically all the products offered no matter from how many sources they came. A Mexican banker (#35) claimed, "We are all friends and there is no foul play."

Strangely enough, belief in a pre-established growing market for consumers' goods, at least, was often coupled within the same business population (and

---

[9] An Argentinian management expert comments: "We all know from experience what inefficiency is caused by the obstructionism of the businessman toward the release of certain data because he is afraid of competition, and what disastrous results come from bureaucratic carelessness which mistrusts the statements of businessmen and in many cases acts as judge with insufficient knowledge of situations or under selfish pressure from rival groups— groups which, because of their respective backgrounds, are only capable of seeing immediate effects without being interested in the implications of any measure which they demand in the firm belief that it is just." Juan Llamazares, *Empresas Modernas: Ensayos Sobre Dirección Organización* (Buenos Aires, 1955), p. 16.

sometimes the same individuals) with an equally firm belief in the existence of intrinsic limitations to the size of markets as a result of smallness of the country or the ignorance and poverty of the rank and file. Such reservations were frequent especially in response to a question asked about any recent progress in productivity. The smallness of the national market was perceived by many as a kind of law of nature against which nothing could be done. Productivity (often confounded with high production) was considered pointless in such a situation. "Why should I make more goods than I do if there are no more buyers around than I have now?" [10] Competition abroad was usually not even considered insofar as manufactured goods were concerned. In other words, the prevailing attitude assumed that the minority who constituted an effective market was eager to buy almost anything that was offered, and that this minority would keep increasing in absolute terms with the constant growth of the population, but that the rest of the people, especially in the countries with a large Indian population, might as well not exist insofar as the national consumers' market was concerned. . . .

DEVELOPMENT STAGE ACHIEVED AND MEASURES NEEDED

The questions, "Do you think this country in general is well on its way to full economic development or not?" and "What do you think is needed most badly in order to stimulate economic development?" were more definitely designed to bring out the business managers' thinking on national development problems. A considerable variety of answers were received not only according to the developmental stage of the country and region concerned but also according to the age group, managerial background, education, and personality of the respondent. There was much uncertainty and confusion on the part of the smaller, older, less educated, and more isolated businessmen who had not really thought before in these terms or in those of the national economy in general.

An understandable response of many was that development of their respective country was on its way but that it still had a long way to go or was not fast enough in relation to the legacy from the past or the recent population pressure. Similarly some others classified the present stage as the mere beginning of development, the main reason given being that the common people get little out of it as yet. A sizable group, especially in countries like Guatemala and Peru but including several others, even some with sizable industries, felt in effect that their country was still distinctly underdeveloped, though this word was not especially popular because of its possible non-economic connotations.

Compared with other countries, this one is still underdeveloped since nearly all of its income depends on agriculture. There has been some industrialization but not on the basis of its own raw materials. We have chiefly assembly industries. Moreover, income per head is very

---

[10] "The owner seeks essentially to make a living rather than maximize profits." "Use of Accounting as an Aid to Management in Underdeveloped Countries," George Ronson, *Industrialization and Productivity,* Bulletin #1, United Nations, 1958, p. 60.

low, there is complete lack of education among the Indians and 60 per cent of the people produce practically nothing. They need to be educated not only in reading and writing but in producing. A total transformation of the culture is required. There is no definite plan for economic growth; private enterprise has tried to grow as best it could but lags behind population growth. The trouble with this country is that it is too rich by nature, so that few people do any real work. We need diversification of agriculture and of the entire economy, but without *economía dirigida*. (Agricultural manager, Guatemala, #84.)

Everywhere, even including Argentina, managerial thinking emphasized the substantial development needs of the country. This was stressed not only in the North American sense of never standing still but in the sense of an urgent and decisive need to amplify industrial facilities, raise agricultural productivity, and secure modern housing, education, and health facilities for the general population. In Chile, re-interviews in 1963 showed wide dissatisfaction with the pace of development during the intervening period, with the possible exception of roads and housing.

On the other hand, an industrial manager in Mexico (#20) claimed that "Mexico is the least stupid of the Latin American countries and is growing much faster than the others, with a minimum of planning." Some others thought that Mexico was not an underdeveloped country any longer or that it was definitely heading for full development. But a number of interviewees felt that Mexico was still deeply underdeveloped and that much of the industrial growth consisted of unhealthy, expensive hothouse industries.

Sometimes development was related to business fluctuations:

Comparatively, this country is the one-eyed in the realm of the blind. In absolute terms, we had a fictitious boom after the war, then a slump which brought us back to our senses, and now development is far more solid. Enterprises plan better now, the good ones survived and are growing. (Industrialist, Venezuela, #111A.)

Qualified statements concerning the current stage of economic development were frequent; for example, in commenting that in some respects it was well on its way while in others it was not, or in regarding "underdeveloped" a misleading term altogether. A Mexican banker and promoter (#28), for instance, defined underdevelopment as imbalance among the sectors of the economy insofar as the relative demand originating in them is concerned. Agriculture, education, housing, and in some cases communications or water and power supply were seen as laggards behind a relatively advanced condition of industry, mining, and commercial construction. "Infrastructure" had clearly become one of the most popular and perhaps most misused words in economic conversations in Latin America.

What *is* the borderline of "development?" Generally this country still requires enormous activities for development. It needs new investments in line with the population increase, better education, infrastructure, aid to the neglected regions. All the sectors are interdependent and a coordinated plan is needed including both agriculture and industry, capital goods and mechanization, employment, housing, and so forth. (Manager, financial company, Mexico, #54.)

Venezuela today is like a teen-ager who can already use his father's shoes but not yet his pants. There has been *uncoordinated* growth, for historical reasons. Independence cost more lives here than anywhere else in Latin America. There followed a sequence of personal regimes of various dictators, and each time the proposition and the intellectuals wound up in jail or in exile. Gómez and his successors brought haphazard industries, with far reaching lack of managerial and intellectual organization. These are the roots of our present stage. (Industrial manager, Venezuela, #137.)

Regional differences in the economic development within the country were often pointed out. Such feelings are understandably strong in Brazil, not only in the poverty-stricken Northeast but in the more developed South. However, a northeastern interviewee felt that there really are *three* Northeasts, and that compared with Pernambuco or Bahia his own state of Ceará represents the forgotten area. Thinking of São Paulo in all the parts visited of the Northeast was frequently found to be in terms of a foreign, wealthy, perhaps imperialist nation.

I am so involved in this company that I study little about Brazil in general. But all the Presidents have been southerners and political considerations have dominated the economic policy of the nation. The North has practically been abandoned, especially Bahia. And in local decisions concerning roads, for instance, political yardsticks also prevail. The State Government mostly knows what is right but does not do it. Too many things are done as favors to friends, even when economically useless. (Industrial manager, Bahia, Northeast Brazil, #156.)

The "country of the future" phrase is still an excuse. Brazil as a whole is well on its way to maturity, despite its people, but the Northeast still depends on politics. Either it solves its problem by providing jobs in unorthodox ways or it will blow up. The Northeast is like a country of its own, but the sugar kings don't see the times and the needs. This area is not so much underdeveloped as undertreated. It could be another São Paulo. (Industrial manager, Northeast Brazil, European-born, #167.)

"Exports" mean in the Northeast not only sales to the United States or Great Britain but to the Brazilian states of Guanabara or Minas Gerais as well. Even in the much smaller Chile, for that matter, managerial thinking in such areas as Osorno and Puerto Montt was found to be focused in a large degree on regional, rather than national, underdevelopment.

Political preconditions of, or obstacles to, fuller economic development were often cited in response to the question mentioned. It was said, for example, that the country concerned *could* be well on its way to full development if it were not for the vagaries of politics, governmental indecision, red tape, encroachment upon private enterprise, or corruption and theft of national funds. Others said in a somewhat similar vein that development would be in full swing if it were not for communist or radical propaganda, unrest, or violence.

However, affirmative aspects of governmental development activities, such as public financing of private enterprise, were also mentioned frequently. In Mexico, pride about the Revolution and the reconstruction of economic and social thinking it had brought about was mixed with misgivings about a political and agrarian degeneration of the Revolution in recent years. Statements about the interdependence and the necessity of parallel development of agriculture and industry were also frequent in Mexico.[11]

As for the role of private business itself in the economic development of the

---

[11] Compare Raymond Vernon, *The Dilemma of Mexico's Development* (Cambridge, Mass., 1963), esp. chap. 6.

nation concerned, any positive perception of this role as a dynamic factor was confined to a distinct minority of the interviewees and in some areas to a few persons only.

Many businessmen are not especially satisfied with economic development thus far. Now they must really work in order to survive in the market! So they complain, even though they are not enemies of the development idea. (Bank manager, Mexico, # 2.)

In most of the areas visited the business manager who thought of himself or his firm in general terms of Schumpeterian entrepreneurship or a pioneering role in economic development had remained a rare bird. Economic development was something that seemed to happen independently of business decisions, though simultaneously with them, and it was something for which "they"—the government, the development planners, perhaps the foreign aid agencies—were responsible, not "we" in the sense of business managers as individuals or as a group. Such restraint could reflect the institutional and social changes of the last few decades[12] and it might be healthy insofar as it had prevented excessive dreams of social leadership on the part of the business groups, such as existed in some other parts of the world; but it had also remained an impediment to specific perception of the need for active participation in the national development process on the part of every major group of society. Even in São Paulo, probably the most advanced area of industrialization in Latin America, a United Nations study came to the following conclusion: [13]

It can be ventured to state that the major part of industrialists hold a false idea of the economic development process in which they are involved and to which they contribute in practice. In reality, the social conditions of the formation of an industrial bourgeoisie in São Paulo have had the effect that many industrialists do not notice that they are the principal beneficiaries of the development of a domestic market and that they derive advantages from the processes that promote it even when such processes may present different and negative aspects to other social groups.

An exception to such perceptual limitations was supplied by an industrial

---

[12] "Latin America no longer lives in the era of the Schumpeterian innovator, nor can economic development be left to the impulses of the entrepreneur, the public official, or the empirical politician. If growth is to be speeded up, it must also be recognized quite consciously that the educational system and the prevailing forms of social organization— labor unions, producers' groupings, public administration proper, and others—must create managerial or executive elements which are professionally trained, both in the private and in the public sectors, in order to assume the responsibilities and to take the decisions which are necessary for economic progress." Victor L. Urquidi, *Viabilidad Económica de América Latina* (Mexico, 1962), p. 85.

[13] Naciones Unidas, Comision Economica para America Latina, *El Empresario Industrial en America Latina*. Part 2 (Brazil), p. 66. Mimeo., Santiago, Chile, 1963. (Other parts of this interview study deal with Argentina, Chile, and Colombia.) Compare the following statement from Eugenio Heiremans D., President of the Sociedad de Fomento Fabril in Chile, "In formulating national development plans, private enterprise can adopt no other attitude than to cooperate diligently in the preliminary study and implementation of such plans." Inter-American Development Bank, *Private Enterprise and Latin American Development* (Washington, 1962), p. 6. Also Chandulal N. Vakil, "Business Leadership in Underdeveloped Countries," United Nations, *Industrialization and Productivity*, Bulletin ≉ 2, 1959. For a discussion of some related motivational and behavioral characteristics of entrepreneurs and managers in less developed countries, David C. McClelland, *The Achieving Society* (Princeton, 1961), chaps. 6 and 7.

manager with academic background in Chile (re-interview, 1963, #147) who commented that the real problem was how to make the private sector parallel public investment.

The Government does not understand this problem and concentrates on public finance. Private business must organize itself, too, in order to understand the Government's problem and to take an active part in the development program through appropriate investments in the private sector.

Another kind of exception was provided, up to a point, by a four-day meeting of most of the leading Venezuelan businessmen on the social responsibilities of private enterprise, held in Maracay in February 1963. [14] Even on this occasion, however, emphasis was placed mainly on the contribution of private enterprise to education, low-cost housing, and health facilities for workers, rather than on active private cooperation in national development planning. Some speakers felt that the first social responsibility of private enterprise consisted in producing, thus achieving profit. An earlier, much-discussed document from business sources on economic development, known as *Carta Económica de Mérida* (Federación Venezolana de Cámaras y Asociaciones de Comercio y Producción, Caracas, 1962) had confined itself mainly to pointing out the necessity of a definite development policy.

What were the greatest needs of the various countries assumed to be at this juncture in order to create stronger general stimuli to economic development? A great variety of responses to this question were received even within each area. The most frequent answers can be grouped as follows:

(a) *Good Government.* It was interesting to find the answer to an economic question presented with such frequency in *political* terms, especially as this occurred all over Latin America. The specific content of this kind of answer ranged all the way from emotional charges of radicalism or corruption in the government to the detached discussion of cumbersome import licenses or tax procedures, to incompetence of public administrators despite well-meaning intentions, or to the inner workings of the political party in power, but the basic approach was similar in each case. [15] The number one stimulus to fuller economic development was always considered to be "confidence" based on a better political system with greater stability and more clearly defined goals.

What we need most urgently is a political system that would resolve the socialist, statist, and fascist tendencies in our economic development including pressure-group influences from cotton or meat producers, for instance. We need a third position. Mexico is not a capitalist country because there is no private initiative, just protectionism. On the other hand, the socialist tendencies here are not Marxist. The real danger is fascism a la Spain.

---

[14] See various mimeographed materials of the Asociación Venezolana de Ejecutivos, Caracas, 1963, including a summary by Ivan Lansberg Henríquez under the title *Una Nueva Actitud* (A New Attitude). Reprinted in *La Responsabilidad Empresarial en el Desarrollo Social de Venezuela* (Caracas, 1963).

[15] Professor Hirschman points to the possible energizing function of the dissatisfaction both of entrepreneurs and policy-makers with past governmental policies. Albert O. Hirschman, *Journeys Toward Progress: Studies of Economic Policy-Making in Latin America* (New York, 1963), pp. 244 ff.

Mexico needs to define its development in a way which is neither socialist nor fascist. "Revolution" is quite insufficient, and Rostow's "stages" don't help us much either. Thus far all the development planning has been in government hands, private enterprise has not contributed to it though it should. They should say what *they* will contribute to development! But the employers' groups have no positive plan and no research departments. (Manager, public enterprise, Mexico, #62.)

We are still in the underdeveloped category and shall be for many years. There is no continuity in government with regard to economic development. They only speak of it in an abstract way, don't know what to emphasize and what to do. (Industrial manager, El Salvador, #94.)

(b) *Education.*   In this case, too, the answer to the economic question asked was at first glance, at least, non-economic. Here again, education was seen as the fundamental need in the interest of economic development by numerous managers all the way from the Rio Grande to the Tierra del Fuego.

Economic development must be rooted in cultural development. High incomes without education do not result in proper use of the increased resources. We need extensive rural education, not only the three "R's" but hygiene, better living, better land use, production techniques. The land is fertile here, but people eat watery fruits with little nutritive value. They produce them on much land and keep eating them, even though vegetables would be much better for them. Cooperatives for production and distribution are also needed. (Manager, industrial and agricultural enterprise, El Salvador, #103.)

There were some responses to the contrary, to be sure. Some scepticism or fear of dangerous thoughts was voiced toward the education of *indígenas*, rural laborers, or urban slum dwellers. Some qualifications were also made concerning the kind of education most badly needed; for example, priority for technical instruction or for secondary schools. But such occasional reservations were far outweighed by the stress which a number of business managers put on education in general and, with it, on the rise of a new generation as the most important precondition for effective economic development. "Education is an investment with an extremely high yield, economically and otherwise." (Industrialist, Venezuela, #111A.)

(c) *Agrarian Reform.*   Great regional, as well as substantive, differences were encountered in this respect. To begin with, spontaneous mention by business managers of reforms or changes badly required in the agrarian structure or policy of their country was very frequent in some areas, such as Mexico, and infrequent in others such as Chile, especially during the original interviews there in 1959–60. Even more important, the kind of measures required was interpreted in very different ways. In Northeast Brazil much "hydraulic thinking" was still encountered. Of those who mentioned the need for agrarian changes there (many did not) some thought mainly of building reservoirs and pipelines in order to reduce the irregularity of water supply in the *sertão* or dry hinterland. In Mexico, which had started its agrarian revolution over half a century ago, business managers criticized chiefly slowness, inefficiency, credit abuses, or political favoritism in the *ejido* system. Many recommended a transition to full peasant ownership of the land and an end to new, illegal concentration of land in the hands of politicians.

In both of the areas mentioned and in various others there was frequent emphasis on the need for efficient size of farms, rural mechanization and credit, utilization of unused land, prevention of erosion, water supply, education, and cooperative organization. The most widespread agreement, including areas where agrarian changes were not mentioned spontaneously as urgent need by the majority, consisted in emphasis on including the rural masses into the national market of which they are not yet part today. This was often mentioned as an essential condition of industrialization as well.

Rural education and housing are decisive; without them there can be no real consumption. The agrarian problem is very complex. My family has suffered from the reforms, but I think they are in order if they lead to higher consumption and individual property rights, not just to political influence in agriculture. (Industrial manager, Mexico, #55.)

(d) *Industrialization.* Interestingly, only a minority of interviewees, even those in manufacturing, spontaneously mentioned industrialization as the most urgent aspect of economic development. The apparent reason has been indicated already. With the exception of some of the major industrial concentrations already in existence, such as São Paulo or Buenos Aires, some aspect of the "infrastructure"—be it education, roads, sanitation, or some other need—or else the creation of a larger consumer market out of the poverty-stricken, ignorant *rural* masses was considered by many managers interviewed an indispensable setting for a substantial industrial development, which would also absorb rural manpower. Given such a setting, indeed, the belief in developmental emphasis on extensive industries was quite widespread both among manufacturers and among other businessmen. This also applied to more general views on the need for diversification of the respective national production.

The importance of small and medium-sized industrial plants in rural areas, even when the production costs of such plants are somewhat higher than those of larger units, was pointed out repeatedly. So was the need for ample and cheap supply of credit and capital for industrial purposes, but there were some warnings against excessive mechanization which a poor country with small markets could not afford.

Industrial orientation toward foreign markets, on the other hand, appeared to be rare at the time of the interviews. Few were the industrial managers in Latin America, even in Brazil, who were thinking seriously about the prospects of a successful competition abroad, even in other parts of Latin America. This hesitation restricted considerably managerial thinking about the possibilities of a Latin American Common Market, with the notable exception of the more limited Central American Common Market which had entered distinctly into the consideration of many managers interviewed in Guatemala and El Salvador. One of them commented:

This is a moment of *incipient* industrial development, of transformation away from an agricultural economy. Agriculture will always remain essential here, but in a more mechanized form and this applies to coffee, too. Only the efficient agricultural enterprises will survive, and agriculture will be reduced to an economically feasible extent. The bulk of the working force will go into industry, though the latter must remain somewhat limited here. (Manager of industrial and agricultural enterprise, El Salvador, #103.)

(e) *Monetary Stability.* This need was mentioned by many interviewees in Chile and Brazil, but even in these countries with their long history of monetary instability some other need appeared to a number of interviewees more urgent. In other areas, such as Argentina, the question of monetary stabilization was seen by many primarily as one aspect of the more general problem of political stability. But in Venezuela, where political conditions were very much on the mind of nearly every interviewee, spontaneous mention of monetary stability as principal requirement was rare, though one commercial manager (#106) was emphatic in claiming that there was a *hidden* inflation which was of no benefit to commerce as demand was inelastic. In Mexico monetary instability was usually referred to only as a thing of the pre-1954 past. In other words, vivid recollection of monetary instability and the emphasis on monetary stabilization as the chief requirement of development policy did not appear to have survived, longer than for a few years, the actual conspicuous conditions of unstable money.

It is interesting to note that foreign aid and investment were very rarely mentioned as the principal requirement for successful development even though the overwhelming majority of interviewees in most countries thought of both as a continuing need of their economies in a *complementary* sense. In every country the questions about the stage of economic development and the measures needed were answered almost invariably in terms of some kind of domestic requirement. Only in those cases where the interviewee was under the erroneous impression that the interviewer was connected with aid-granting agencies abroad was a casual or joking hint made that the country needed a lot of dollars. There was no evidence anywhere, least of all in the large countries, of real or basic reliance on foreign development aid. This would seem to be at odds with widespread preconceptions in the United States including the Congress, according to which nearly everybody in Latin America either thinks or claims that he depends on U.S. funds for future development.

In summary, the prevailing managerial thinking encountered perceived the economic stage of the country in question as incipient development, with regional differentiation and frequent qualifications including some of a political nature. There was very little perception of private entrepreneurship as the real spark in economic development. Among the greatest needs in developing the country concerned, good government, education, agrarian changes, industrialization, and monetary stability were mentioned most frequently, while foreign aid and investment were mostly considered a complementary but not a decisive need.

CONCLUSION

In their thinking on management aims and development needs, business managers in Latin America as a group were found to bear at this point largely a resemblance on the semantic level to their colleagues in the United States, Great Britain, or Western Germany. To be sure, there was a small minority of managers in several countries who had been trained in North America or Western Europe and tried hard to apply managerial techniques from these areas to their local environment. But even in these cases the nature of the cultural and historical heritage, consumer markets, personnel relations, and political influences required far reaching adjustment of managerial techniques derived from more advanced economies, and very many businessmen and companies in Latin America had remained almost untouched by them even when similar terminology was used. At the same time, lack of realism in the perception of managerial functions and of the general environment was widespread.

The aims of many business managers were ill-defined, especially in the long run, and were often unrelated to national development needs. Their satisfactions and discontents were influenced by various factors that were far less important in more advanced economies, such as family status and tradition, although some other strivings such as creativity seemed to characterize many managers in almost any stage of national economic development. Paternalism, while still strong, seemed slowly on its way out.

Prevailing concepts of competition looked very different from the theory of North American management though somewhat less remote from its practice. The perception of insuperable market limitations was still vivid though it was modified by the expectation of fast population growth and possibly of rural progress. Inflation, at least within certain limits that looked rather permissive compared with the standards of businessmen from more advanced economies, often was not considered an unmitigated evil but an inevitable concomitant of economic development. Governmental measures designed to encourage the development of the country concerned including its private sector were overwhelmingly regarded as essential, though the emphasis varied from infrastructure in general to sound administration, education, agrarian changes, stimuli to industrialization, or monetary stabilization in the external sense. Foreign development aid and investment were thought of as complementary, rather than fundamental, factors.

Under these conditions it would not be very promising to expect in Latin American countries an early imitation of North American or Western European management attitudes, or even identical tendencies later on as industrial development proceeds. The employment of office techniques and some basic concepts of accounting, cost calculation, inventory control, and social legislation can be expected to utilize increasingly the experiences available from North America and Western Europe. But the attitudinal patterns of Latin American business managers and their corresponding behavior toward consumers, employees, and public institutions are likely to remain strongly influenced by the cultural and historical heritage of each country and region. It is at least doubtful to what extent future economic development in that part of the world, with the strong impact of conscious development planning by organized society along with international demonstration effects, will follow the patterns of Western entrepreneurship from the last two centuries.

Additional References

Bain, Joe S. *International Differences in Industrial Structure—Eight Nations in the 1950's.* New Haven, Conn.: Yale University Press, 1966.

Bendix, R. *Work and Authority in Industry.* New York: John Wiley & Sons, Inc., 1956. Harper Torchbook, 1963.

Blass, Walter P. "Economic Planning, European Style," *Harvard Business Review,* September-October, 1963.

Fox, Alan. "Managerial Ideology and Labour Relations," *British Journal of Industrial Relations,* Vol. 4, No. 3 (November, 1966).

Giesbrecht, Martin Gerhard. "Entrepreneurship vs. Modern Management: A Co-Aim for Business" (Taiwan), *Business Topics,* Michigan State University, Vol. 16, No. 1 (Winter, 1968), pp. 23-31.

Granick, D. *The European Executive.* New York: Doubleday-Anchor Books, 1962.

Grosset, Serge. *Managers: American and European Styles.* Belmont, Calif.: Wadsworth Publishing Co., Inc., 1968.

Haire, M.; Ghiselli, E.E.; and Porter, L. W. *Managerial Thinking, An International Study.* New York: John Wiley & Sons, Inc., 1966.

Harbison, F., and Myers, C. "Management as a System of Authority," *Management in the Industrial World,* chap. 3, pp. 40-67. New York: McGraw-Hill Book Co., Inc., 1959.

Havens, Eugene A., and Potter, Harry R. "Organizational and Societal Variables in Conflict Resolution; An International Comparison," *Human Organization,* Vol. 26, No. 3 (Fall, 1967), pp. 126-31.

Hays, S. "International Comparisons of Output per Man and Standards of Living," *Progress—The Unilever Quarterly,* Vol. 51, No. 290 (April, 1966), pp. 245-49.

Lewis R., and Stewart, R. *The Managers.* New York: New American Library, Mentor Book, 1961.

"Management Concepts and Practices European Style," *Business Horizons,* Winter, 1964, pp. 25-36.

Negandhi, Anant R. "Advanced Management Know-how in Underdeveloped Countries," *California Management Review,* Vol. 10, No. 3 (Spring, 1968), pp. 53-60.

Summers, Clyde W. "Labor Relations in the Common Market," *Harvard Business Review,* Vol. 43 (March-April, 1965), pp. 148-60.

"Technological Competition: Europe vs. the U.S.," *Harvard Business Review,* July-August, 1966.

chapter nine

Examples of Management in Specific Countries

Most of the selected readings in the preceding chapters were comparative in scope; they considered an aspect of management in abstract or in a number of countries. The authors of the following readings confine themselves to single countries. Most discuss the broad historical and contemporary philosophy, practices, origins, and so on, of management in that nation. These readings vary widely in their format and intent; not all are organized similarly nor do they consider all the cultural and economic factors discussed in Chapters Four through Eight. Nonetheless, enough is given to allow one to make many comparisons—from the gentlemen amateur managers in the United Kingdom to the engineers running business in Soviet Russia.

Selection: "The Socio-cultural Setting of Management in the United Kingdom," Rosemary Stewart

Many writers on British management point to the heavy hand of tradition. An oft-expressed fear is that present philosophy and practice will not be able to meet the present economic challenge. This selection discusses the impact of British culture and tradition on contemporary management.

Selection: "I was a Soviet Manager," Gregory Ryapolov

With its emphasis on heavy industry and technical specialists as managers, Russia has been very successful in developing economically. This reading indicates some of the problems (including human costs) and methods (including a surprising use of money) of Soviet management.

393

Selection: "Japanese Management—The Cultural Background," William Brown

Japan is a fascinating amalgam of East and West, and nowhere is the mixture more interesting than in business management, where the Japanese successfully compete with the most advanced nations. This reading by a long-term American resident of Japan considers management and managers in the most industrialized country of Asia.

Selection: "Social and Cultural Factors in Management Development in India" Kamla K. Chowdhry

Much less industrialized than Japan, India is also attempting to fuse Eastern culture and Western industry. The results still are not foreseeable, but this reading examines the process.

Selection: "The Manager in the Polish Enterprise: A Study of Accommodation under Conditions of Role Conflict," Solomon J. Rawin

In this systematic analysis, the author pinpoints the problems for the manager in a culture that is rich in religion, individualism, and privacy, but one that is trying to develop under a hybrid public enterprise system.

Selection: Capitalists and Managers in Communist China," Barry M. Richman

Little has been written on management in Communist China. In contrast to Japan, which has industrialized by emulating the West, contemporary China has borrowed from the Soviet Union. But there are many differences between the two Communist states. The chairman of the International Business Program at U.C.L.A., and an extensive traveler in Russia and China, discusses management in the most populous country on earth.

Selection: "The Egyptian Executive: A Study in Conflict," Harold Q. Langenderfer

Using the U.A.R. as an example, Professor Langenderfer describes institutional and personal barriers growing out of the economic and cultural conditions (particularly in underdeveloped nations) that limit a manager's effectiveness and inhibit economic development.

Selection: "Business Management in French Canada," Gaston Pelletier

Much closer to home, this selection describes the great difference between managers and management in French Canada and its neighbor to the South. Note that the differences are probably due more to differences in cultural values than to different levels of economic development.

selection 30

The Socio-Cultural Setting of Management in the United Kingdom*

Rosemary Stewart

Research into the social and cultural factors in management development in the United Kingdom is not a simple exercise, especially if the findings are to be limited to a short paper. This is due not only to the complexity of the subject but also to the fact that industrialisation there has been in process since the early days of the Industrial Revolution.

SOCIAL FACTORS

Impact of Beliefs and Attitudes

Three of the areas in which beliefs and attitudes in the society will help to form the environment within which management must work are: first, the extent to which society's values are similar to business values; second, and related to this, the attitudes to industrial employment; and third, the attitudes to work. There are, of course, many other attitudes that affect the role of management, but these can best be discussed in terms of institutions such as government, education and family. In a long-industrialised country like Britain we shall also have to look at the way in which industry has developed if we are to try to understand the historical legacies of this development.

Relationship between Society's and Industry's Values. To what extent are the values of British society congruent with those of business? It is clear that they do not correspond as closely as those of United States society. There is not the same conviction in the United Kingdom as there is across the Atlantic of industry's creative value to society. This can be explained in part by the comparative lack of efforts to professionalise management, but the main explanations must be sought in the attitudes to industrial employment, in the attitudes to possessions and in the extent to which in Britain one's income determines one's social standing.

Industry relies on acquisitiveness to make increased production possible— other things, such as the income to buy the goods with, are of course essential—

---

* From *International Labour Review,* Vol. 94, No. 2 (August, 1966), pp. 108-31.

but the desire to buy goods and services, and ever more of them, is a prime condition for industrial success. The manager must strive to create a fashion-conscious society: "not that nasty old car, not that unfashionable old dress" is the attitude that he wants. In this he has not been very successful in Britain, where an affection for old possessions is still often stronger than the attractions of the new or the dictates of fashion.

Many British managers believe that the workers are interested only in money, yet one of the conclusions of the Anglo-American Productivity Teams[1] was that British workers, and particularly British wives, were not sufficiently acquisitive. This is much less true now than it was when the teams wrote their reports in the early 1950s. This change may be due partly to better housing, which has made people more houseproud and more interested in spending money on improving their homes and gardens. It may also be due to the break-up of some of the close family and neighbourly groups when young couples were rehoused in new towns or in different areas. The greater optimism engendered by full employment has probably also encouraged people to acquire (on hire-purchase) goods that their parents in times of economic insecurity did not aspire to.

Improving one's standard of living is one aspect of acquisitiveness; having as visibly good a standard of living as one's neighbour is another. A society dominated by business values would have both attitudes. One's social standing would tend to be equated with one's economic standing. This has not been true in Britain, where in the middle and upper classes who one's father was counted more than how much money one had. In the upper classes who one's great-great-grandfather was counted still more. Sufficient worldly goods could help to compensate for one's parents, but it was only compensation. The working classes developed group solidarity as a defence against their employers and against insecurity; hence whether one was a good mate was more important than what one earned. Indeed, high earnings might be frowned on as being at the expense of one's mates. In all classes one's social status was not primarily determined by one's property or income. This is still true today.

Attitudes to Industrial Employment.   Traditionally business has not been the occupation of a gentleman. The eldest son inherited the estate, the younger sons went into the armed services or the Church. Middle-class sons went into the professions, the civil service or the family business; many emigrated overseas. There was little opportunity in business for those who had no special entrée through family connections. Few, anyway, wanted to adopt a way of life, and mix with a type of associate, so different from those of the professions.

Really successful businessmen moved up the social scale by marrying their daughters to men with birth but not money. They could also become public figures, not because of what they did in business but because of what they did outside it. Until very recently a businessman who wanted to get a title had to

---

[1] These were teams of managers, technicians and trade unionists from different industries who were sent from Britain, shortly after the last war, to study United States practices in the same industry as their own.

work hard for public causes, devoting less and less time to business and more and more to public service. Now this is changing; success in business, particularly success as an exporter, is being recognised as meriting public honour as much as distinction in other occupations.

Business is becoming a respectable choice of occupation for young men from any walk of life; finance always was. This is fortunate, for business needs—and for a long time has needed—a fairer share of the country's intelligence. The joke "It is easy to succeed in business, you only have to compete with other business-men" is losing its relevance. But not every business has become respectable employment for the middle and upper classes. A gentleman still should not engage in certain types of trade: he should not, for instance, sell second-hand cars—which is one reason why public school boys[2] are in great demand by car dealers. To be able to hold up one's head with one's friends who have been called to the bar or have entered the civil service, one should work for a large well-known company. Such companies have a lot to offer the ambitious young graduate: money, more money than he can earn in most other occupations; untaxed perquisites; a chance to see the world; and, if he is successful, more power than in most other occupations. Today many arts graduates who have no definite profession want to go into vaguely cultural jobs but they settle for business when they are unsuccessful, giving "money" as their main reason for doing so.

Attitudes to Work. We have discussed two areas in which attitudes help to determine the environment within which management works. The third area is attitudes to work. Why do people work? There are many possible answers: because they must to stay alive—a more pressing reason in a harsh climate than in a fertile tropical one; because they want to raise their standard of living; because they would be bored if they did not; because they would lose social prestige; because they feel that it is morally wrong not to do so; or because they enjoy it, whether the enjoyment comes from the exercise of skill of brain or hand, from the overcoming of problems or from the companionship. Most people, at least in the temperate zones, work for a number of these reasons. The explanation of the relative strength of the different reasons can be found in the society's history, as well as in the local climate and natural resources. It can be argued that as long as people work it does not matter to the manager why they do so, but he will find it easier to understand their behaviour if he understands their work motivation. In the United Kingdom, as in some other countries, managers tend to over-estimate the monetary satisfaction of work for their workers, and to under-estimate the importance of social satisfactions. Managers should also understand why people may prefer leisure to a better standard of living—something that many managers in the Western world, imbued with notions about the advantages of material goods and the moral value of work, find difficult to do.

In Britain, as periods of unemployment have shown, a man's sense of worth

---

2 "Public schools" are the more successful of the independent schools. The best of them have high social prestige.

in the working classes, and increasingly in the middle classes, derives in large part from his work. Hence unemployment and, to a lesser extent, retirement can rob a man of part of his feeling of self-respect. Now, with full employment, unemployment is less of a threat than retirement. Hence the concern of some humanistic managements to educate their employees, and especially their managers, for retirement so as to help them to learn how to live without work.

Social Stratification in Industry and the Role of the Family

The part played by family businesses in the United Kingdom has been declining for some time. The greater capital needed by modern technology, the increase in the size of companies, the decline in the size of families, and the growth of taxation and death duties have all made family businesses more difficult, particularly the successful business that could expand if it had the capital. Far fewer of the large companies are still privately owned, though in 1951 of the 102 companies with a capital of over £3 million, 24 had 50 per cent. or more of their shares owned by the 20 largest holders. This compared with 40 of the 82 companies in the same size bracket in 1936.[3]

In small companies, and some of the medium-sized ones, the top posts may still be earmarked for members of the family, provided that the family feel that this will not endanger the prosperity of the company. An ensured succession for the top post can make for more peaceful relations among its senior managers, who will not be in competition with each other for the top job. There are still companies where the staff watch and talk with pride of the new generation being trained for the top jobs and, when such a company is sold, many employees may feel a personal sense of loss. Even if the acquiring company is more generous it will be thought that, compared with the family, management is less interested in the individual employee.

In large companies today, particularly those in manufacturing industry, and in many of the medium-sized ones too, the only link with the original family or families is likely to be the company's name. All posts will be open to the talents; but how open will depend upon the company's tradition and the views of the present top managers. They will be less open in the City[4] than elsewhere, and most open in the newer scientific industries. In some companies the network of public school and family is still the surest way to the top. A study in 1958 showed that about one-third of the top posts in finance were held by former pupils of one public school (Eton).[5] Another study of the background of more than a thousand company directors showed that at least half had been to a public school.[6]

---

[3] P. Sargant Florence in a paper to the British Sociological Association, 30 October, 1956.

[4] The City of London is the traditional centre of finance and trading.

[5] T. Lupton and Shirley Wilson, "The social background and connections of 'top decision makers'" (The Bank Rate Tribunal evidence: a symposium), in *The Manchester School of Economic and Social Studies,* Vol. 27, No. 1 (January, 1959).

[6] G. H. Copeman, *Leaders of British industry: a study of the careers of more than a thousand public company directors* (London: Gee, 1955). This study also analysed the background of 2,850 middle and junior managers.

A study of the background of 455 top managers who came from 51 of the largest manufacturing companies in the United Kingdom analysed which factors appeared to have been most helpful or most unhelpful to their prospects of promotion.[7] The most helpful were an arts degree from Oxford or Cambridge and attendance at a major public school. It was better to have non-technical than technical qualifications and advantageous to have been a trainee. The greatest disadvantages were to have been a foreman and to have been only to an elementary school. Those top managers who came up from the shop floor were likely to have avoided the normal straight line system of promotion through the foreman's job; many went into the drawing office instead. This study of top managers was made in 1955, in the larger companies, where, we have argued, there is most chance of promotion by ability rather than by social background. A repeat study today might show more emphasis on technical qualifications and perhaps less on the public schools, though the latter is doubtful.

The popularity of a public school background is due partly to the habit of like recruiting like. The men who do the recruiting of young men, especially of graduates, are often themselves from a public school and feel that they know better what they are recruiting when they take a public school boy. They will also know the masters and be able to judge the worth of a reference. The public school is also valued by some top managers because it seeks to train its students for leadership, and is more likely to produce young men with an assured air and with a belief in their inherited (or acquired) right to lead. This can give them an advantage over the less assured products of grammar and secondary schools. In some companies, however, the public school boy may be at a disadvantage. If the managers have mostly worked their way up from the bottom they may be suspicious of a young man who speaks English with a different accent and who has had a softer life.[8] Will he, they wonder, be able to control men, will he be accepted by them? Will he know what work means?

Clements in a study of 670 managers examined them at all levels, so that one would expect to find here a wider variety of backgrounds than amongst top managers where, as the Acton Society showed, a privileged educational background considerably increased the chance of promotion.[9] He distinguished six basic career patterns. These can be indicative only, as no representative figures exist. Only 4 per cent. of his managers started as "crown princes" by going into the family business. Ten per cent. started as management trainees in a company where they were not "crown princes." The third group, accounting for 20 per cent., entered industry with professional qualifications and usually were promoted up a specialist ladder. The fourth group, with 12 per cent. of the managers,

---

[7] Acton Society Trust, *Management succession* (London, 1956).

[8] The way one speaks is still one of the most reliable indices of social background in Britain today, though persons with a good ear may learn to suppress their local accents if they go to Oxford or Cambridge. The importance of how one speaks is declining as more people with the "wrong" kinds of accent are climbing the educational ladder, but possession of the right accent is still valuable if one wants to be recruited for certain types of jobs such as selling.

[9] R. V. Clements, *Managers: a study of their careers in industry* (London: Allen and Unwin, 1958).

consisted of other types of entrants who did not start at the bottom, including those whose parents paid for their apprenticeship. Just over half the managers were in the fifth and sixth categories, the later school leavers who usually started as clerks and the early school leavers who would usually begin as manual workers.

These three studies of managers and directors showed that something like one-third of British managers in the mid-1950s had succeeded with no special advantages other than their own abilities. The proportion was a little less for the top posts and more than one-third for all management posts.

The greatest disadvantage to promotion in industry has not been mentioned here so far: it is to be a woman. Industrial management is still almost exclusively a man's world.[10] The only area in which more than the very occasional woman is to be found is personnel management, and even there men usually hold the top posts. Financial management is, if that is possible, even more masculine. In retail trade a number of women managers are found, but then it can be argued that in buying goods for other women their sex may be an advantage. If a woman has managerial ambitions her best chance of success is in the civil service, where some women can be found at all levels, including the highest.

Tradition does not in general determine the age of promotion to different posts in industry, though it may do so in particular companies. Opportunities for young men to climb quickly will depend more upon the rate of expansion of the company, and upon how recently it was founded, than upon ideas as to what is a suitable age for holding particular jobs. The existence of a compulsory retirement age, usually 65 but sometimes 60, also affects the number of posts for younger men. Directors often stay till 70 and sometimes much longer. In the Acton Society's study of 455 top managers 12 per cent. were under 40.[11] The average age was 50, but in younger and smaller companies it is probably less. Promotion by seniority plays little part at the management level, though in a few industries it is important in the manual grades.

Authority Concepts

Research into leadership, particularly that carried out by the Bureau of Business Research, Ohio State University, has shown that there are many different kinds of successful leaders and that a man who is a good leader in one situation may not be a good leader in another. What kind of leader is most suitable in a particular situation depends in part upon the type of authority that is acceptable. There has been a substantial change in the nature of management authority, and in the ways in which it is exercised, in the course of Britain's industrial history. The general trend is away from the more authoritarian type. A variety of reasons are responsible for this: the more democratic nature of society as a whole; the

---

[10] Very few women study to be engineers or accountants. Those who do, have difficulty in being accepted in a man's world.

[11] *Management succession, op. cit.,* p. 7.

higher level of education; the growth of trade unions and full employment. In very few companies, however, could the leadership be described as democratic though it is now true to say that management can manage successfully only with the goodwill of labour.

The management of the older kind of industries is usually more autocratic as regards all levels of employees than that of the newer scientific industries. One explanation is given by Burns and Stalker, who distinguished two extreme types of organisation in their study of a rayon mill and firms in the electronics industry: one, the mechanistic and authoritarian; and two, the organic, in which there are more consultation and exchange of information than commands.[12] They argue that the first type is suitable to stable conditions and the second to those of rapid change, where men at the top are often not in a position to know what is the best thing to do. Most organisations fall between these two extremes. This kind of analysis, which is based on studies of organisation and leadership patterns in different types of companies, suggests that problems of the kind that management has to deal with are more important in determining the nature of authority than is tradition. To what extent is this true in countries in which a stronger authoritarian tradition of leadership has survived?

The ways in which management exercises its authority have changed, but they have changed more at some levels than at others. Management of the shop floor has usually remained more autocratic than has management of staff. The management of managers, and those seen as potential managers, is often much more democratic. One factor making for democratic management is the wide distribution of the information necessary for decision-making, but the growth of information technology may change this. In the rapidly changing scientific industries the fact that the youngest graduate may be more up-to-date in his scientific knowledge than the managing director is likely to affect the authority relationship. Sometimes, however, managers may be more subservient to their superiors than are manual workers, because they have more to gain or lose from their superior's good opinion. If they are ambitious for promotion they will be particularly keen to please him, and if he is an autocratic type they may think it wise to adapt themselves accordingly. Managers who have been in a company a long time, and who have no qualifications with a market value, will often be more dependent upon the company, and upon the good opinion of their superiors, than a manual worker in an area of full employment.

Management authority in the United Kingdom is very much restricted by government regulations, particularly in defining conditions of employment and in the location of new factories. The only other important source of limitations to management authority is the trade unions. The managements of some industries and some companies are much more restricted than others. In many companies there is 100 per cent. trade unionism; in some there is none. In some companies the unions ensure that it is almost impossible for management to

---

[12] Tom Burns and G. M. Stalker, *The management of innovation* (London: Tavistock, 1961).

dismiss a worker—this can, or should, do much to make management take more care over its selection procedure.

In general the nature of management authority in public enterprise is not much different from that in large public companies. Earlier the British labour movement was keen to secure worker participation in the direction and control of industry, but by the time of the post-war nationalisation measures there had been a change of view to the belief that the trade unions should not be too closely involved in the management of the enterprise, for fear that this would destroy their independence. Instead the trade unions were to exercise their influence through negotiation and compulsory joint consultation. The nationalised industries have elaborate joint consultative machinery, which in the nationalisation Acts was empowered to concern itself with safety, health, welfare, and "the discussion of other matters of mutual interest including efficiency . . . ." A few public companies have gone further in the scope of joint consultation than any of the nationalised industries.

EDUCATION

Educational Emphasis

English education in the last hundred years has been characterised by a distinction between classical, for those who did not need useful education, and scientific. The latter was divided between pure and applied science. Pure science had, and still has, more social prestige than applied science. Classics are declining, but the popularity of other arts subjects, such as history, remains high. The choice of subjects by a child in his teens has a strong influence on his later choice of occupation, because of the high degree of specialisation from the age of 16 onwards which is one of the distinguishing features of English education. Hence, compared with some other industrialised countries, relatively few of Britain's young men and almost none of her young women study scientific subjects that are of direct use to industry.

Employers' Attitudes to Education

The attitude of employers to the education of their employees at all levels influences management development. The kind of qualifications and experience they want in their managers is, of course, a key factor in management development. But the educational level of other employees is also relevant, both because some of them may become the managers of the future and because the level of knowledge and skill amongst employees will affect the nature of the managers' jobs. If their staff are well educated and have the necessary technical, scientific or commercial knowledge and experience, managers will be better able to delegate responsibility.

Top management's conception of the kind of employees it wants will determine the level of education it demands in its recruits for different kinds of jobs, the encouragement it gives (or does not give) to them to further their education, and the training provision it makes for them. The extent to which employers demand educational qualifications will affect both the provision that is made and the extent to which people take advantage of it. If employers are really keen on education they will take the initiative in trying to reduce or eliminate financial barriers to its provision and to its utilisation.

British employers in the past have not been much interested in the education of their employees. In part this was because many of them were self-made men who felt that the best way to learn was in the hard school of experience. They saw further education either as unnecessary, even harmful, or at best as something that an ambitious employee should make the effort to acquire for himself. Any help was, and sometimes still is, seen as molly-coddling. In part the lack of interest in the education of their workers stemmed from a fear that education might give them ideas above their station and make them unwilling to do manual work.

Manufacturing employers might be expected to support technical instruction, even if they were not in favour of other types of training. Yet Cotgrove, in his survey of the evidence at public inquiries into scientific education from 1867 onwards, reports that "Apathy and even hostility were the most general attitudes of this section of the community."[13] The apathy probably stemmed from Britain's early industrial start, which made manufacturers feel that with their history of success there was no need to change. The hostility was to something that might lead to disruptive changes, but there was also the fear that trade secrets might be passed on if workers from different factories came together at classes. One of the reasons given at public inquiries for the indifference to science and to technical instruction was that few of the managers or owners were technically or scientifically qualified. This contrasted with the position in Germany, where the manufacturers in scientific industries, such as the chemical industry, were highly trained men who were sympathetic to research. Their training was made possible by the more developed state-assisted education, and by the fact that scientific studies received more attention than in Britain.

Cotgrove concluded that the extension of technical education that took place in the latter part of the nineteenth century was—

the outcome of efforts to elevate the working classes, rather than any concern with the contribution of education to industrial proficiency. It was the child of educationists, philanthropy, and the demands of students, and received little blessing or guidance from the manufacturing and business community.[14]

Britain was behind its competitors in the number of scientifically trained managers. It was also behind in other fields of education. In 1899 the Sub-

---

[13] Stephen F. Cotgrove, *Technical education and social change* (London: Allen and Unwin, 1958), p. 23.
[14] *Ibid.*, p. 65.

Committee on Commercial Education of the London County Council Technical Education Board reported that—

In conducting our investigations upon the subject of commercial education, we have been greatly impressed with the feeling that the matter is one of supreme national importance. The great increase of foreign competition which has been felt by those engaged in almost every branch of commerce and manufacture has aroused a widespread feeling of alarm in the community. It is becoming more and more clear that among the principal causes which are threatening us with a grave diminution of international trade must be placed the better education enjoyed by many of our competitors. [15]

Criticisms of employers' lack of interest in technical education continued after the First World Warr. The Balfour Committee of 1927, which considered the effect of technical education on industrial efficiency, and the Malcolm Committee on Education and Industry in 1928 both concluded that industry in general was not interested in the technical education of its recruits. The Malcolm Committee said that there was a theoretical recognition by trade and industry of the importance of technical education, but indifference in practice. [16] It found that even those firms that did take a practical interest in part-time technical and commercial education were concerned mainly with part-time evening instruction, not with instruction during working hours. [17]

The growth of state education made employers more interested in the educational attainments of their office staff. In the inter-war period School Certificate [18] became the entry requirement for many clerical jobs. Since the Second World War many employers have specified the number of passes they expect in the examination at the O level or the A level [19] for recruitment to certain types of jobs. The more forward-looking employers aim to recruit from each level of school leavers, using the recruit's educational level as a measure of his suitability.

One of the lessons that can be drawn from British industrial history is the need for management to be concerned about the education of its employees, both that received at school before joining the company and the opportunities for further education. Management needs to try to estimate its needs for different types of skill and education and to do what it can to ensure that there is an adequate supply. The lack of interest in scientific training shown by manufacturers is one of the reasons why the provision of people with such training has for many years lagged behind that of Britain's competitors.

Availability of Educational and Training Facilities

Before the Second World War the demand for and supply of technically and scientifically trained personnel was roughly in balance. During and since the war

---

[15] London County Council, Technical Education Board, United Kingdom, *Report of the Sub-Committee on Commercial Education* (1899), p. ii, quoted in Cotgrove, *op. cit.*, p. 20.

[16] Board of Education, United Kingdom, *Report of the Committee on Education and Industry* (Malcolm Committee), Part II (London: H. M. Stationery Office, 1928), p. 42.

[17] *Ibid.*, p. 62.

[18] Awarded to successful candidates in the ordinary school-leaving examination.

[19] The junior and senior school-leaving examinations.

the demand has exceeded the supply. There has been considerable public anxiety about the small proportion of young people going to university compared with some of the other industrialised countries, notably the United States and the U.S.S.R., and more specially about the shortage of scientifically trained people. There has recently been a public inquiry into the higher educational needs of Great Britain. The report (the Robbins Report of 1963), which was accepted by the Government, advocated increasing the proportion of young people taking degree courses from 216,000 full-time students in all higher education in 1962–63 to 560,000 in 1980. This increase is to be achieved by the expansion of existing universities, by making some of the colleges of advanced technology into universities, and by founding more new universities. Eight new universities have been started in the last few years.

POLITICAL FACTORS

Degree of Political Stability

The only political uncertainties in Great Britain that affect management are doubts as to how long one of the two major parties will be in office. Elections have to be held every five years, but may be held more frequently; the party in power can usually choose the date of the election at any time within the five-year period. Before the general election of 1966 there were doubts about how long the Labour Government could stay in power with such a tiny majority. These doubts were of most significance to the steel industry, which did not know whether the Labour Government would be able, or even really wanted, to implement its nationalisation plans.

Extent of Government Interference

Government regulations and actions affect nearly all aspects of management in industry and commerce. Most important is the control that government attempts to exercise over the economy of the country. The main reason, since the war, for government intervention has been to protect the balance of payments. The maintenance of full employment has been of much less concern, because unemployment has not risen above 3 per cent. and has generally been under 2 per cent., though in certain areas, particularly Northern Ireland and parts of Scotland, it has been much higher than the national average. This uneven distribution of unemployment has posed both social and political problems for the government in power.

Both of the major political parties are currently committed to trying to achieve a better distribution of employment. This policy is implemented through restrictions, negotiation and incentives. There are restrictions on the expansion of factory and office buildings in some of the big cities. The Labour Government has introduced a ban on new office buildings in London. A company in a crowded area that wishes to put up a new factory must negotiate with the Government for planning permission. The Government tries to persuade it to go either to one of the development areas—that is, a designated area of relatively high unemployment where the Government is trying to encourage industrial expansion—or (for a suitable type of industry) to a new town. The final site will be the result of negotiation, as the company can always refuse to build if it does not like the sites that are suggested. The Government also offers incentives for companies to go to the development areas.

One of the methods to try to reduce congestion in the main cities has been the establishment of new towns to take the population overflow. A number of companies have successfully shifted a factory with many of its staff to such a new town. These moves pose considerable problems for personnel management. One of the obstacles to moving, particularly if the new location is far away from London, has been the opposition of managers, or their wives, to transplanting themselves. Attempts to persuade companies to transfer their headquarters from London have had little success, as managers want to remain close to the centre of activity. But a large-scale relocation of office staff, if not of certain key departments, seems increasingly possible because of improved methods of processing and communicating information.

There is a long history in Britain of government regulations affecting employment, which limit management's freedom to employ people as it likes. The early Factory Acts, which date from 1802, limited the hours of work for women and children. These have been continually added to until there is now comprehensive legislation, covering terms and conditions of employment, which has recently been extended to include compensation for redundancy. One difference between the United Kingdom and some other Western European countries is that more of the cost of social security is financed by taxation and less by employers' contributions.

Since the Second World War both political parties have sought, rather unsuccessfully, to limit inflation by exhorting management and workers to restrict increases in pay and in dividends to the percentage increase in the national income. In the nationalised industries the Government has, in the past, disallowed some proposed wage and salary awards as being too far above that level. Currently the Government can refer prospective price increases and wage claims to the National Board for Prices and Incomes. The Board can give its views but has no power to enforce them.

One of the distinguishing features of the relations in Britain between government on the one hand and industry and the trade unions on the other is the network of permanent consultative committees, both bipartite and tripartite. Close consultation between government departments and employers' associations under the T.U.C.[20] takes place whichever party is in power. In addition, large companies would consult government departments on some major policy issues.

---

[20] Trades Union Congress, the central trade union body.

Role of Political Parties

Traditionally the difference between the Labour and the Conservative Parties is that the former favours greater government intervention, a more equal distribution of income and capital, and the nationalisation of the means of production and exchange. There is now much less difference between their attitudes to industry and commerce. The Labour Party has lost most of its enthusiasm for fresh nationalisation, the main exception being the possible renationalisation of the steel industry. The Conservative Party has become much more committed to government intervention in the economy. The parties still draw part of their support from different sections of the community. The Conservatives are supported financially by big business and the upper classes and Labour by the trade unions, but both attract voters from the middle and working classes, though in different proportions.

The most striking political change in recent years from the point of view of management development is that both political parties are now committed to trying to improve industrial efficiency. Their commitment has come from the need to protect Britain's balance of payments and to improve Britain's competitive efficiency in international markets. The Conservatives abolished resale price maintenance[21] in 1964 in the hope of encouraging greater competition and limiting inflation. They also introduced the Industrial Training Act in 1964, which gave the Minister of Labour power to set up industrial training boards to promote training in different industries, financed by a levy on employers. Grants are made to firms from these levies, according to a performance rating of the quantity and quality of the training, and taking account of the level of skill needed in that section of the industry.

The Labour Party took the first steps in 1958–49 to investigate monopolies and restrictive practices: measures of control, however, are still much less rigorous than in the United States. The Labour Party has threatened nationalisation of inefficient industries, and has also suggested that it might set up a publicly owned company in an inefficient industry to be an example of good management practice. There are no immediate signs that either of these ideas will be put into practice, though one of the arguments for steel nationalisation is that the existence of too many small units prevents low-cost production. The Labour Government has recruited a few very successful young managers for its new Department of Economic Affairs and is setting up national economic development councils in different industries to try to improve productivity. Each is chaired by a leading businessman.

Both parties are committed to trying to force, prod or persuade British managers to become more efficient. The deficiencies that, in their different ways, they are trying to overcome, were pointed out shortly after the war by the Anglo-American Productivity Teams, whose general view was that, in comparison

---

[21] A system by which manufacturers fix the prices at which their products are sold by retailers and consumers.

with United States management, British managers were less cost-conscious and less interested in improving productivity.

MANAGEMENT-WORKER RELATIONS

The attitudes of trade unions must be seen in their historical context. The nature of the industries on which Britain's industrialisation was built affected the attitudes of those who owned and managed them. They were primarily non-scientific industries, with a low level of capital per employee. Management's attitudes to workers varied with the nature of the technology of the industry. In the main, management in the older industries tended to try to make a good profit from a stable output; hence, in such labour-intensive industries, they sought to keep wage costs as low as possible. In the newer, capital-intensive industries, management has been more interested in trying to get labour's co-operation so as to make the fullest use of its expensive plant.

Since the failure of the general strike in the late 1920s government, management and trade unions have usually sought to limit or avoid industrial conflict and to reach agreement through negotiation. A distinguishing feature of British industrial relations is that these negotiations take place at the national level on an industrial basis. This national bargaining has grown from the development of employers' organisations, the centralising tendencies of the trade unions, and the government's encouragement, which has sought to avert strikes. As a result basic wages and the main conditions of employment are generally dealt with centrally for different industries.

Today management ideology in the United Kingdom tends to stress partnership in an enterprise and endeavours to get the workers to identify themselves with it. But British workers have long memories—memories that have been seared by unemployment and by the lesson of history that a worker's defence against management lies in group solidarity. These memories are strongest in the older industries such as heavy engineering, coal and the docks. They are memories that persisted after nationalisation.

There is in much of British industry a legacy of restrictive practices, which the workers built up in the past to protect themselves and their mates from unemployment. Many of these were designed to spread a limited amount of work among different people by strict rules as to who should do what kind of job, or by restricting the intake to the occupation by specifying the ratio of apprentices to skilled men. Other restrictive practices developed from craft jealousies embodied in struggles between different unions. These practices continue even in times of very high employment. For some categories, such as dockworkers, they restrict the introduction, or the efficient use, of labour-saving machinery. Attempts to get trade unions to abandon restrictive practices as part of a wages bargain have met with very limited success. There are, however, a few striking exceptions, of which the most notable is the Fawley agreements by which Esso, the United States oil company, succeeded in negotiating substantial changes in practice.[22]

One of the institutional features of post-war British industry has been the persistence of overtime, which has averaged from three to five hours a week for male manual workers. The extra money has become part of the income expectations of the worker and the practice has often resulted in underemployment during the normal working day. A few firms have succeeded in reaching an agreement—Fawley is again an example—that finances the rise in basic rates by increased labour productivity during the standard working week.

SOCIAL AND CULTURAL CHALLENGES TO MANAGEMENT

Modernisation of Attitudes

The attempt to improve productivity through the modernisation of the attitudes of both managers and workers in many industries and companies is by far the greatest current challenge to British management. Some managements have not adjusted themselves to the demands of a technological age, or to the efforts necessary to meet foreign competition. In some companies there lingers the idea, a carry-over from the days of British industrial supremacy, that British goods are automatically the best. The attitudes of many workers are still conditioned by the experience of the depression in the 1930s.

The Fawley productivity agreements underlined the need for managers who wished to get workers to abandon practices that restrict efficiency to take a more active role in labour relations; to initiate rather than merely to respond. They showed, too, what could be achieved through the collective bargaining of productivity agreements.

The need for a modernisation of attitudes is not confined to trade unions. The greater need, because of its greater potential effect, is for a change in management attitudes. One of the striking characteristics of British industry is the size of the gulf between the most efficient and the least efficient companies, even in the same industry. There is also a great gulf between the efficiency of different industries. Numerous attempts, of which the Labour Government's national economic development councils for specific industries is the latest example, have been made to get the more progressive and efficient managers to arouse the others.

The Immobility of Managers

One of the obstacles to a change in management attitudes is the lack of mobility within management. Each company, often each department, is a self-

---

[22] Described in Allan Flanders, *The Fawley productivity agreements* (London: Faber and Faber, 1964).

contained unit in which a man frequently spends his whole career. In consequence he is exposed to a limited range of management attitudes and ideas. He is likely to become an organisation man, in a sense different from that described by Whyte;[23] a man who has become so immersed in the way of thinking of his department and his company that he is unlikely to be able to think outside this pattern of beliefs, attitudes and presuppositions.

The three studies of the backgrounds of managers and directors which were quoted earlier showed that those who are successful in British industry have spent most of their working life in the same company. Forty-four per cent. of the managers studied by the Acton Society spent all their working life in the same company and a further 33 per cent. came to their present company before they were 30.[24] Forty-one per cent. of the directors studied by Copeman had remained in the same company and a further 31 per cent. had made only one change.[25] A time of rapid industrial change makes variety of experience and exposure to different approaches to management of special value. If the typical career pattern does not normally provide much opportunity for these, then either the pattern should be changed or management training must try to compensate for these limitations.

Policies for Industrial Mobility

Technological change brings with it the need for industrial mobility. Management needs to be conscious of the social consequences of such mobility and to consider what policies should be adopted to make it easier. Since the Second World War there have been a number of much-publicised cases of redundancy following automation or the closing down of surplus aircraft works. Few companies have formulated a policy for dealing with redundancy in advance of need, nor have the unions shown much interest in prompting them to do so. Redundancy has generally been dealt with as it arose—usually at the urging of the trade unions, on the basis of last in first out, and with compensation payments for different lengths of service, sometimes starting with one week and going up to six months. Minimum payments were fixed in the Redundancy Payments Act, 1965, which provides for compensation related to length of service. The more progressive managements try to prevent or restrict redundancy by prior planning of major changes, including restricting recruitment. The Government operates a few training centres for retraining displaced workers, and some companies have adopted their own retraining schemes.

Many managements seek to encourage a feeling of loyalty and a sense of belonging amongst their employees, some of whom may have been working in the

---

23 William H. Whyte, *The Organization Man* (New York: Simon and Schuster, Inc., 1956), 429 pp.

24 *Management succession, op. cit.,* p. 33.

25 Copeman, *op. cit.,* p. 107.

firm for 20 years or more. A sense of belonging and of identification with a particular industry and company is not consistent with easy industrial mobility. Men who throughout their working lives have been proud to work for the railways take it hard when society tells them that fewer railways are needed in the modern world. This poses a moral, as well as a practical, problem for management. To what extent, if at all, should management seek to encourage a sense of belonging when the needs of industrial change may make a mockery of such identification?

Industrial mobility, particularly that which involves geographical mobility, creates wider social problems, as it often separates parents and grown-up children, and tends to break up long-established neighbourhood groups. The British people do not seem to have adapted themselves to a casual friendliness such as characterises United States society, which makes moving to a new community easier.

Changes in the Composition of the Working Population

Since the Second World War there have been marked changes in the composition of the British population, due to younger marriages, a decline in the number of single women, a higher birth rate and an increasing proportion of elderly people. These changes, combined with virtually full employment, have meant that companies such as banks, which formerly would not employ married women, have had to change their policies. Some companies have introduced special shifts to suit married women with families, but few, if any, provide crèches for their employees' young children.

Currently there are two main sources of manpower that are underemployed: one is the educated married woman with children; the other is elderly people who did not want to retire at the set retirement age and who are still capable of doing useful, if not full-time, work. If present conditions of nearly full employment continue, management will need to try to be more flexible in its employment policies.

Preparation for Retirement

The greater proportion of elderly people and the more widespread application of a fixed retirement age have left many more people than formerly with from 10 to 20 years of life expectancy after they have retired. A few of the more progressive British companies have recently been talking about preparation for retirement, and are running preretirement courses for their employees. Retirement, as mentioned earlier, causes particular problems in a society where a man's sense of worth derives in large measure from his work. The problem is often greatest at the management level, where involvement in the job is highest.

The Effects of Education on Promotion Policies

Traditionally management has stressed the opportunities open to an ambitious young man—young women were, and are, not expected to have ambitions other than marriage. These opportunities were, as pointed out, much better for those who had been to a public school, but in many companies they existed for all. This is becoming progressively less true as, with greater educational opportunity, more and more companies model their career patterns according to educational achievement. Management should consider how exclusively it should do this, and in what ways, if at all, it should try to help those with lower educational qualifications who show ability. It should also consider how honest it is nowadays to stress the opportunities for industrial advancement for all entrants.

MANAGEMENT APPROACHES TO SOCIAL PROBLEMS

Historically the British workers' view of management was not improved by the fact that the large majority of British employers remained indifferent to the social problems of the community and of the society at large. Only a small minority of managers concerned themselves with the welfare of their employees and adopted a policy of benevolent paternalism. A few built model communities for their employees. Most of the remainder were concerned solely with the employment of "hands." The improvement of social conditions, both inside the factory and in the community, was due to the efforts of philanthropists, including a small number of businessmen, and of the workers themselves, through their trade unions and friendly societies and later through political pressure.

During the Second World War the government promoted a widespread extension of welfare policies and of personnel management in an attempt to ease the workers' adjustment to the industrial and geographical mobility made necessary by the war effort. Since the war, personnel management has continued to develop in the more progressive companies. Most companies now offer fringe benefits in the form of a subsidised canteen and sports facilities. The number providing retirement pensions, which supplement the state pension, sick pay and medical facilities, is increasing. Many employ a welfare officer whom employees can consult when they are in trouble in their home life. Otherwise social problems and social welfare are seen as the province of the government. Recently, companies have been most likely to be concerned about social problems if they are planning to move their factory or to start a new factory in a virgin area. Then management is likely to feel that the social problems of the move, or the founding of a new factory, should be primarily its concern rather than that of the local authorities.

British managers are not expected, by their superiors or by anyone else, to be active in the community or visibly good citizens, as some United States companies expect their managers to be. They do have to refrain from being visibly bad citizens. It is left to the individual to decide whether he would prefer to lead a purely private life or to become active in the community. A managing director may decide that it is good public relations to be seen supporting community or national activities, but the choice is his, and many do not so choose.

SOCIAL AND CULTURAL FACTORS IN MANAGEMENT DEVELOPMENT

British industry has been slow to take an interest in management development. Some of the historical background to this has already been sketched— the early history of industrial leadership in non-scientific industries, which encouraged complacency; and the lack of interest that employers, through the years, have shown in their employees' education. Another reason may be the tradition of amateurism, which has a long history in British society. Traditionally the English gentleman took neither his work nor his sport too seriously; he was expected to be good at them, but the ideal was a well-rounded man, and that precluded specialisation. The tradition of the English gentleman is dying as education becomes increasingly specialised and the leisured class disappear, but there still lingers the belief that it is better to learn by doing; that it is better to pick things up than to have a formal course of training.

Changes in Recruitment Policies

The post-war extension of educational opportunities for all able children, which includes both free education at university and a grant to cover living expenses, has necessitated a change in employers' recruitment policies. Before the Second World War many firms recruited no one from the universities. Many also recruited no one from public or grammar schools. They took all, or practically all, their recruits from the earliest school leavers, plus a few with School Certificate for some of the office jobs. This was the pattern in many of the engineering companies, where men learnt by experience and obtained engineering qualifications by studying at night school, usually at their own expense. The lack of educational opportunities for the poorer classes, who even if they won a place in a grammar school might not be able to afford the loss of potential earnings to the family, meant that companies with this type of recruitment would still get a number of able people.

In the last 15 years more and more of the large companies, and some of the medium-sized ones, have realised that, if they want to get their share of the country's intelligence, they must change their recruitment policies. They must now recruit from all the different educational levels. They must also seek actively to attract the better educated, rather than wait passively for people to come and ask for employment. Now, many large companies have one or more managers whose job it is to try to attract the right kind of graduates and school leavers. They seek to do this by establishing good relations with the local schools, with selected public and grammar schools, and with selected universities. At the latter the appointment board's secretaries will be assiduously cultivated and graduate managers will be encouraged to keep in touch with their old professors.

Some companies joined the chase for graduates only reluctantly and belatedly; some still have not done so. These companies think that graduates have been spoilt by being at university, do not have a practical approach, expect too much, and are hard to fit into the organisation. The existing staff often resent the introduction of graduates, who come in part of the way up the ladder and who seem to be a threat to their own future. The likelihood of resentment is greatest in companies in an industry such as steel, that is changing from a technology based on experience to one increasingly based on science. The development of a Diploma in Technology, on a sandwich basis (alternating academic study with work in a company), has been designated to overcome some of these objections.

The change in educational opportunities and the consequent change in recruitment policies have important social implications. Many of the larger companies now produce recruitment booklets that describe the ladders of promotion for young people entering from different educational levels. The bottom rung of each ladder is the entry point from a particular level of schooling or from university and the ladder is the expected career pattern for those who do reasonably well. The extent to which it is now possible to step from one ladder to another depends in part upon the importance of technical or professional qualifications and in part upon the provision the company makes for those of unusual ability on the lower ladders to acquire the necessary qualifications before it is too late. There is likely to be an increasing tendency for management to think of recruitment and promotion as consisting of a number of self-contained hierarchies. This potential rigidity of career patterns is likely to be intensified when more of the top managers are university graduates. Since like tends to recruit like, those who have successfully passed through all the educational hoops will find it difficult to believe that potential managers may still be found amongst those who have not been to university.

What Kind of Manager?

What kind of person do British companies seek as their managers? There is no one answer. Many different kinds of people are successful managers, as one would expect, since there is a great variety of management jobs. People sought as managers are now expected to have a different type of mental outlook from that which they were expected to have in the past. There is now less scope for the entrepreneurial type. One of the most important changes in the recruitment of managers and potential managers for large companies is the widespread emphasis on "acceptability" to colleagues. Management is much more of a team affair than it was—a team that works through discussion with other managers. It is the man who can get his ideas accepted by others, and who is willing to co-operate in implementing other people's ideas, who is wanted, rather than the individualist who seeks to drive ahead against all opposition. Management education is therefore preoccupied with teaching managers how to communicate rather than how to initiate.

The Growing Interest in Management Training

The history of management training in the United Kingdom can be summed up as—pre-war: no talk and no action, with the exception of a small number of management trainee schemes in large companies; 1945–55: a lot of talk and some action; 1955 up to the present: an increasing amount of action culminating in a flood of activity. In the ten years after the war the main steps towards the development of management training were the following: the establishment of the British Institute of Management and the inauguration of its Diploma in Management Studies; the establishment of the Administrative Staff College with its three-month courses for those on the brink of promotion to top management; and the start of a few short residential courses.

In 1954–55 the writer examined what 51 of the largest manufacturing companies in the country were doing to provide for their future managers. The answer was that a third of them were doing nothing systematic; another third were doing something, though it might be as little as running a one-week course for foremen; only the remaining third had a systematic approach to the recruitment, selection, training and promotion of their managers. Yet these were the largest companies, which had most need to think about their future management requirements. Since then the number of companies running courses for their managers, often in their own residential training centre, has grown steadily, and so has the use of outside courses. A management training scheme is now one of the marks of a progressive company.

It is in the last two or three years that the most striking change has taken place in the acceptance of management training. Only a few years ago management education was not considered a respectable activity for most British universities. Now there is a queue of universities anxious to be included amongst those that are to have a business school. The main credit for this change seems to be due to pressure groups of leading managers who raised the money to finance management training at universities. The idea of one or more British "Harvard Business Schools" suddenly had strong management appeal. Two business schools, one associated with Manchester University and the other with London University (through the Imperial College of Science and Technology and the London School of Economics and Political Science), are just starting.

What accounts for this sudden and belated enthusiasm for management education? There are probably many reasons for it, but the most important may be the fact that more and more expanding companies have been finding that the limits to a firm's expansion, in the words of a director of one of them, "will largely be set by its managerial resources."[26] Industrial development means more managers, not merely because of the growth in the numbers employed in industry but also because the proportion of managers increases. Another reason for the recent burst of activity in management training is the emergency of an effective pressure group of leading managers. Yet another reason was the growing

---

[26] *Progress,* the Unilever quarterly (London), Vol. 50, No. 279 (Spring, 1964), p. 28.

awareness that a company cannot afford to let its competitors acquire a dispro-
portionate share of a scarce resource—trained manpower. Indeed one of the major
reasons may be the impact of changes in education on industrial recruitment,
which caused many companies to develop a definite recruitment policy for the
first time. This led the more thoughtful managers to develop policies for manpower planning, for selection, for training, and for promotion as well. Those that
did not found that some of the graduates they sought to attract wanted to know
about the company's career structure and what would be done to train them for
management.

The current enthusiasm for management training in the United Kingdom is
primarily for training in quantitative techniques, in decision-making and in the
economic framework of business. It is likely that little attention will be given to
the social and cultural factors in management, though in some schools there may
be training in the social organisation of a factory. Since one of the main needs in
Britain today is for a modernisation of the attitudes of management and workers, this seems unfortunate. The attitude of those who are trained at the business
schools will probably be very different from that of most managers in British
industry today. They will have a more scientific approach to management, but
they will not necessarily have more understanding of why other managers and
workers think and behave as they do.

selection 31

*I Was a Soviet Manager**

Gregory Ryapolov

The Soviet press is carrying on a lively polemic on how best to manage the
economy of the U.S.S.R. The discussion ranges from questions of the most
theoretical nature to those of the most practical. A great deal has also been
written in the American press on the changes taking place or proposed in Soviet
industrial management. Many U.S. economists and writers have tried to provide
a detailed and honest analysis of the essence of these changes.

While not pretending to be a trained economist or an expert on theory, I can
offer some practical information on the role played by the key men in Soviet
industrial production—i.e., the factory manager (called a "director") and his
chief assistants—and on the existing management practices in industry. I can
presume to attempt an explanation of this subject because, until a few years ago,
I was a Soviet factory manager. At present I reside in the United States. Since

---

* From *Harvard Business Review,* January–February, 1966, pp. 117-25.

coming to this country I have naturally kept close watch on developments in the Soviet Union.

It is not easy to be completely objective in these matters. Therefore, I will try to avoid all hearsay and relate only what I have witnessed, thought, or experienced personally, to avoid making subjective judgments as far as possible. I must make it clear in advance that I have the utmost admiration for the accomplishments of Soviet managers. The observations which follow regarding their predicament are in no way intended to minimize the progress they have made or their potential for the future. What is most remarkable is that they have been able to accomplish so much despite so many handicaps. There are lessons here for businessmen in economies everywhere.

STATUS & TRAINING

The salary and benefits of a Soviet plant director are very low when compared to those of an American. However, if one compares the status of a Soviet director with that of an ordinary Soviet citizen, then it has considerable advantages. For example, the plant director and the chief engineer (second in command in a Soviet factory) are afforded comfortable apartments or houses at company expense. They are given automobiles for official and personal use. They are also given preference in obtaining vacations in rest homes and sanatoriums at the expense of their enterprise. They get 24 days' leave a year, as against the regular two-week vacations for other employees. Directors of large and important plants are entitled to even longer personal leave.

Directors of factories have other special privileges. Many plants, particularly the large ones, have special executive dining rooms. The director of the Elektrosila plant in Leningrad, for instance, has a private dining room, bedroom, and reception room. Some managers have personal rest rooms and let their secretaries keep the keys.

Management personnel in the U.S.S.R. see themselves as belonging to a special economic category, almost resembling a military rank in the army. As is known, a very sharp division of society into classes exists in the Soviet Union. Class affiliation is determined by the material, administrative, and Party position of the people concerned. It is characteristic of the upper classes to be contemptuous of the lower. The greater the class difference between two individuals, the greater the gulf between them in mutual relationships. For example, when a director's wife has a new baby, he invites only the people of his own rank to the celebration, and never an ordinary worker or an engineer.

'Mutual Protection'

In Soviet society people are very distrustful of each other and are suspicious of any manifestation of friendship. Each man has too great a responsibility to the regime, which controls almost everything, to risk being open and honest with people. Everyone is afraid of the Party or police informer.

To counterbalance this risk, a special antidote, "collective responsibility" or, as it is sometimes called, "mutual protection," has been developed. The essence of this antidote in the case of managers is as follows:

Each director of an enterprise, big or small, considers the selection of reliable assistants as his primary task. The attitude is: "All for one and one for all." The people know they must sink or swim together. This is why the plant director always supports his subordinates. If they get in trouble, he bails them out. His subordinates in turn give their wholehearted loyalty and support to him. In many instances, when the plant director is transferred to another plant, he takes his loyal assistants with him to ensure a continuation of this secure relationship.

I have many times been involved in such a relationship. When there was a crisis, especially an investigation of the plant for one reason or another, I knew I could count on my subordinates to back me up as I had done for my chiefs. We always had our stories straight, and had the necessary papers to prove whatever we wanted to. If we were accused of falsifying the gross output or some other plan, or of pirating workers from other enterprises, or of procuring raw materials illegally, I could always count on every member of my team to deny it. I have heard of instances where one member of a group—out of fear, or in the hope of reward—would turn traitor, and then all the other members would be done for; but such cases are rare.

Promotion & Advancement

Under the present system, before a person becomes a director, he undergoes a long period of technical training at a factory; he starts as a line engineer and ends as chief plant engineer. Unfortunately, there are no special schools for the training of management personnel in the U.S.S.R. There are no business schools such as those in the United States. A plant manager thus spends the major part of his life working in factories. As a result, he is dedicated to production and loves it. He loves it for its own sake, not for the material rewards.

Prior to World War II, only loyal members of the Communist Party, devoid of any technical training, were appointed plant directors. This situation was radically altered in 1950, and the changes then made have continued in effect to the present. Currently, only an engineer with a great deal of practical experience can become a plant manager.

A similar change took place in the management of Party organizations in factories; only engineers can now become secretaries of plant Party committees and of district Party committees in industrial districts. Similarly, in agricultural districts, only trained agronomists can be Party secretaries in *kolkhozi* (collective farms) or *sovkhozi* (state farms), or be district Party secretaries. The same practice prevails in *oblast* (comparable to a county) and republic Party organizations. Engineers, agronomists, and other specialists with higher education have even made their appearance in the Central Committee of the Communist Party of the Soviet Union and its Presidium.

When a young engineer is graduated from a higher technical school (called an "institute"), he can follow one of three possible courses:

1. He can enter the academic field, which would mean remaining at the institute for graduate school. This is generally considered the most desirable course. It is open, however, only to young people with high Party patronage. The eventual goal in this case would be to become a professor.

2. He can become part of the bureaucratic apparatus, which would mean working as a functionary in some ministry or *sovnarkhoz* (regional economic council, now being abolished), or in some other administrative organization. This course is open to students with less important or less powerful political connections than those who receive institute appointments.

3. He can join a production shop or some other department at a factory. This course is the most readily accessible to the majority of young specialists, and it is the only one open to young engineers who have no political connections. Of course, to young engineers who love production for its own sake, this is the most desirable course, but it would be spurned by the sons of high Party officials.

PRECARIOUS POSITION

During the period of Stalin's dictatorship the term "manager" was a derisive one. Professional Communist leaders contemptuously referred to their Party colleagues who were directors as "managers" and gave the term a derogatory connotation. They did this because often these managers deviated from the general Party political line in defense of production and economic interests. In fact, to this day directors are swamped with bureaucratic administration to such an extent that they would have no time for politics even if they wanted to.

Plant directors are the most apolitical class in the Soviet intelligentsia. I was not the only director who had not read the *History of the Communist Party of the Soviet Union* beyond the fourth chapter! Many is the time I have seen a director, in giving a speech or report to the plant Party committee or some similar group, stumble and stutter in trying to remember the appropriate phrases of praise to the Party, to its great leader or leaders, and to its policies. I myself would sometimes have to stop and think how I should begin and end even the simplest report.

The great majority of directors are not enthusiastic supporters of the goals of the Communist society. They do, however, support the idea of socialism, i.e., public ownership of industry. I would not say that they all wholeheartedly believe in it, but they do not actively oppose it. None of them desire the restoration of capitalism. But they are not dogmatists and are not against adopting rational ideas, whether capitalist or not.

Soviet managers dare criticize the present system only within certain permissible limits. They see, probably more than do other elements of Soviet society, the disparities between economic rationality and Party policies, and within the limits of what is practical and possible they try to sabotage these policies. From the standpoint of Party morality, Soviet managers are amoral. They do not represent a politically stable class. The higher Party organs distrust them. Their activities are controlled by frequent checks by Party, state, economic, and police organizations.

Caught in the Middle

The plant director is not his own boss. He is caught in a vise between the Party and the state organs and bureaucrats, on the one hand, and the plant workers and employees, on the other. The former pressure, threaten, and punish, while the latter are sullen and passive. A "good" director is not the one who concerns himself with the needs of his workers; he is the one who faithfully serves the Party. The Party bureaucrats cannot harm the director if he dutifully and carefully implements the tasks set forth by the Party and the state organs. But a catastrophe ensues for the director when he fails to carry out the Party's directives. Then the Party tries to set the workers and employees against him, and, under the guise of worker criticism, it will ruin him completely.

This almost happened to me once; I was saved by sheer luck. Here is what happened:

Before I was named director of the AEG Union plant (producing generators, switchgear, and electrical components) in Vienna, the Party had decided to make a Communist show-place of the factory. The previous director had been forced to hire as many Austrian Party members as possible for the factory. When I took over, almost 90% of the workers and employees were Communists. (The other 10% were primarily engineers and other technical and highly skilled workers. Communists could be found to fill only a few of these positions.) Although some of the Party members were good workers, many were lazy and incompetent. Some, in fact, were just bums. Consequently the factory operated very badly. Plans were not fulfilled—not even on paper; the reject rate was very high; labor discipline was terrible; and productivity was low.

The situation got steadily worse, and I decided on desperate measures. One morning—it was in early March 1953—I dismissed the head of the cadre section, and with him some 200 of his workers, almost all of whom were Communists. The Party secretary immediately got on the phone to the ministry in Moscow. That afternoon he called a meeting of all workers in the plant. I half expected to be dismissed on the spot, or worse. But just as the meeting was about to get underway, we received word from Moscow of the death of Comrade Stalin. In the resulting confusion, my firing of this group was overlooked, and apparently forgotten.

Defensive Tactics

A great deal of responsibility is imposed on the Soviet director. He must continually defend his actions before the Party management and government officials. The scope of his responsibility is so great that he is constantly subject to political or criminal action. In order to be always prepared to defend himself, he issues a tremendous number of written orders and directives. It is completely immaterial that no one carries them out. What is important is that they can be used for defense in case of a plant investigation. The director carries out directives from above only if they are received in a written form. He does not acknowledge any oral or telephone instructions from his superiors. To give an example:

An official in the ministry called me up one day and told me to invest over a million rubles in the purchase of some new machine tools, which we badly needed for the plant I was managing. I told him no, not unless I got a written order. He ranted and raved, said there was not time, was no need for it in this case, and so on, but I refused to give in.

I told him: "An order may not be armor, but it can protect me just the same." I never received the order, and I still do not know why he refused to write it out.

MANAGERS VS. PLANNERS

The greatest evil lies in the system of planning, accounting, and control. Approximately 2,000 different planning and accounting forms, containing more than 3,000 indicators, are used in large electrical engineering plants such as the Elektrosila plant in Leningrad. It is not hard to imagine the size of the work force required to carry out this nonproductive task. I have heard from directors of large machine-building plants that about 2,500 different plan-reporting forms are in use in that industry. The forms cover 3,000 indexes, and each form is filled out from 2,000 to 3,000 times a year. Up to a billion numerical entries have to be made annually. These facts were recently repeated by a plant director writing in *Izvestia*. [1]

Production plans are issued to the plants without due consideration of real capabilities. Plan fulfillment of the preceding year serves as the chief criterion. If the plant has overfulfilled the plan by 10%, the next year's plan will be increased by 5% to 8%. If the plan has been underfulfilled by 10%, the next year's plan will be reduced by 5% to 8%. This is what is called "scientific" socialist planning.

In most cases, production plans are drawn up on the basis of national requirements, without serious reference to a particular plant's capabilities. In the course of the year, the previously approved plans are changed and supplemented hundreds of times. These directives are issued by various planning authorities and very often contradict one another.

As a rule, there is a complete lack of coordination between the plans for output and those for raw material and technical supply. The plants continually experience a shortage of materials. Material quotas for plants are planned on a quarterly basis but are issued monthly (I am writing about the electrical engineering industry). A particularly difficult situation exists in the case of very critical items, such as copper insulating materials, rolled and calibrated steel products, ball and roller bearings, and insulating varnishes and paints. It is impossible to secure delivery of these materials on time.

The Invaluable Tolkhachi

In order to obtain hard-to-get materials, the plants hire representatives who live permanently near the supply bases. By the end of each month these representatives, through superhuman efforts, scrape up the necessary materials. These are shipped by plane, train, trucks, and sometimes even in briefcases. These plant representatives are known as *tolkhachi* (expediters). They are officially carried

---

[1] N. Yakubow, "Put Simple Principles into Economic Management," December 20, 1964, p. 2.

on the plant's rolls as engineers and economists, but they do not work in the factory. They belong to an illegal class, a special category of swindlers engendered by the Soviet economic system. Their job is to deliver the raw materials to the plant on schedule. To achieve this, they resort to all kinds of illegal machinations. I think that in America they would all end up in jail.

It seems to me that many in the West have an erroneous conception of the role of *tolkhachi.* They perform an absolutely vital function, even if it is illegal. The fact is that material supply is extremely poorly organized. The plants are given monthly allocations of certain materials with a list of bases where they may be obtained. In reality, however, there will be no materials or very few materials at the bases listed—except for those who arrive first or who bribe the base chief. Consequently, in order to push their orders through ahead of turn and get the needed materials, plants must have their *tolkhachi* permanently stationed near the bases.

It is impossible for a factory to obtain any material or equipment on time without these representatives. Sometimes the materials are available at the base, but there are no transportation facilities. The *tolkhach* on the scene must then find transport vehicles, such as trucks or railroad cars, and load and ship the materials to his plant. To do this, he must again bribe the officials in charge of the vehicles. The following experience is illustrative:

> When I was working as chief engineer in the Svobodinskaya Electrical Machine Building Plant, located in Kursk, we ordered five trucks from the Stalin Works in Moscow. This plant replied that it could deliver the trucks, but since the plan for production of truck bodies had not been fulfilled, it would have to ship the trucks without them. What were we to do? We could not use the trucks without bodies, but if we did not accept the order, we would receive no more trucks that year.
>
> We called in the plant *tolkhach* and asked him what to do. He said to just leave it to him; he'd find a way. He went out and bought two tons of apples and some geese from the *kolkhozniki* (members of farm collectives), loaded them on a factory truck, and brought them to the Stalin plant in Moscow. The following week we received the five trucks—complete with bodies.

Master of Deception

This distressing situation is permanent, and because the plants cannot operate on schedule, the plans are either underfulfilled or falsified. The principal cause lies in the fact that *Gosplan* (State Planning Commission) generally plans for more materials and equipment than are actually available. As a result, everyone is engaged in tearing the others apart, outbidding each other, and reselling materials as one would a ticket to a concert by the pianist Horowitz.

As a rule, enterprises do not work on a regular schedule. Procedures with which I became familiar are typical almost everywhere. In the first 10 days of the average month, most of our workers would do nothing or continue to work illegally on the last month's plan. The second 10 days would be used to produce 10%–15% of the current month's plan. In the last 10 days of the month, 70%–80% of the production plan would be fulfilled. Part of our piecework force at that time would work more than 12 hours a day without overtime pay, since it had not earned anything in the preceding 20 days. The last 10 days at the plant would resemble a mad rush. In this confusion neither I nor my assistants could pay more than scant attention to quality. We knew that rejects could be included in satisfactory output. People deceived each other just to meet the plan and get the payments for plan fulfillment and overfulfillment from the ministries.

Of course I did not like this. Who did? But the controlling administrations and ministries put my plant in a position where we were compelled to resort to deception. Let me cite two typical examples:

1. A plant supplying parts to my factory was in the process of drafting a material and technical supply plan. In order to obtain the materials it had to draw up raw-material norms for each part. It was probably manufacturing more than a million parts. The materials were issued only in accordance with the fixed norms. But the normal reject ratio was 10% to 15%. Where, the director of this plant asked, could he obtain the missing 10% of the materials? To secure them he instructed his engineers to draw up inflated raw-material input norms. This made the whole plan a fraud.

There has been no change in this situation, despite much criticism of it in the U.S.S.R. I know the situation is exactly the same today as when I experienced it.

2. Plans are drawn up annually by the planning authorities for specifying the projected increase in labor productivity and reduction in cost of production. I learned to expect that, on the average, an annual plan would call for:

a) A 10% decrease in the input of raw materials and semifinished products.
b) A 20% to 25% cut in time-norms (rates) for pieceworkers.
c) A 15% to 20% increase in the output norm.

I could regularly fulfill and overfulfill such a plan on paper, but not in reality. If plants like mine had actually implemented these plans, then in a few years products would have had to be manufactured out of thin air and labor productivity would have had to rise to fantastic proportions.

Art of Falsification

The punishment for nonfulfillment of a plan is very harsh. Plan falsification under the Soviet system is technically simple and always possible because it is done within an extremely limited and trustworthy circle of people. The participants generally include the director, chief engineer, chief bookkeeper, and production shop chiefs.

Falsification of plans is not an unusual or rare occurrence in Soviet practice. A preponderant number of plants engage in it. In most cases, the lower echelons of the administrations and ministries are aware of it but keep silent. Their functionaries, too, must account to the higher organs if plans are not fulfilled, and stand to lose their bonuses and promotions in the event of failure.

Generally, plan falsification is discovered only because a director is careless or because he commits some offense in front of his chiefs. There is a saying among Soviet managers, called the Directors' Seventh Commandment: "We must respect our superiors because they are more clever and more noble than we." When falsification is suspected, or a higher official or officials want to "do in" a certain manager, inspectors are sent to the plant with instructions to uncover evidences of plan falsification. Sometimes they succeed and sometimes not. Everything depends on the director's assistants.

As an example, I cite a typical case from personal experience:

> This event occurred in Budapest, Hungary, at the Magyar-Siemens electrical engineering plant, where I was the general director. The plant received a new American Chrysler automobile. A former Chekist named Dekonozov, who was a Soviet official in Budapest, demanded that I relinquish the car to him. I refused because the car belonged to the plant and could only be confiscated on orders from Moscow.
>
> This refusal offended Dekonozov, and he appointed a commission to investigate the plant. A check did not disclose any plan falsification. But he knew very well that such was not the case; plan falsification *must* exist in a plant. Therefore, he sent a special economic commission from Moscow for a second check. It consisted of experienced "diehards" who were old hands at similar investigations in the Soviet Union. But they did not know the Hungarians. As a result, they too could not find anything.
>
> Now I can admit without fear that the plan was falsified—and to a considerable degree. The Hungarians are a remarkable people; there are almost no traitors among them. They always helped me, but they hated the Soviet Union.
>
> Later, fate freed me from Dekonozov. He was shot along with Beria. But, as a memento, he left me a "strict reprimand with a warning."

Quality Breakdowns

Actually, no plant I managed or knew about had or could have any technically sound or scientifically calculated norms for pieceworkers. Instead, we used the so-called empirical-statistical norms. The cost of inputs was kept within the planned limits by reducing product quality (e.g., less prime coating, polishing of parts). Durable and costly materials were replaced by cheaper and sometimes worthless substitutes. Sometimes this common practice took on an "all-union" character, with official blessing:

> A few years after the end of the Second World War, the Elektrosila factory in Leningrad, in an attempt to economize on silver in the production of magnetic starters, "invented" a cheaper alloy for use in electrical contacts. Eletrosila was praised highly for this accomplishment, and on orders from above all factories in the U.S.S.R. producing electrical apparatus which used similar components were required to copy this innovation. As a result, in a short time starters and other kinds of electrical gear throughout the whole country began to break down. Even after the cause became clear, the order was not rescinded for several months.

Such economizing is particularly severe in the case of consumer durables, and in large part it accounts for the almost unbelievably poor quality of these goods. Complaints about the breakdown of washing machines, refrigerators, TV sets, and the like appear regularly in the Soviet press. Farm machinery is another area of production which suffers greatly from this practice.

POLITICS BEFORE ECONOMICS

Bureaucrats from the higher administrative organizations and the Party always seek to convert the director and the chief engineer into mechanical robots for carrying out their unrealistic plans by crudely threatening them with a stick.

The administrative bureaucrats rarely visit the plants. When they do, it is not for the purpose of obtaining information or rendering assistance but, rather, for enforcing authority, preparing charges, or imposing penalties.

The Party and its various control organs place politics before economics. Managers hold to the opposite view, that economics and technology are more important and that politics must serve to advance them. They see what economic setbacks are caused by Communist dogma. Consequently, they try to soften and reduce the damage by doing everything they can think of to thwart the politicians, but it is not easy to do.

Credit & Blame

During my years in Soviet industry, the majority of us in management tried to show concern for our workers and employees. We requested overtime pay, increased wages, and improvement of the workers' living conditions. We also opposed the use of economic pressure on the workers, such as raising piecework norms. But the ever-watchful eye of the Party very carefully scrutinized all such actions that we directors took. The Party could not permit one of us to become popular with our employees. And when it did permit small material gains, then it announced that it was the Party—not the director—who was showing concern for his people.

All that was good was attributed to the Party, and all that was bad, to the director. For example, if the workers' wages were low and they were not provided with living quarters, if the dining rooms were dirty and the food was bad, if the rest rooms and shower rooms were filthy—all that was the fault of the director. I remember experiences like the following:

One director for whom I worked became concerned about the excessive number of accidents on two of his production lines—a common situation in Soviet industry, where safety measures are all but overlooked. On his own initiative he installed new lights and provided guard rails and other protective equipment. The Party secretary promptly gave orders to the members of the Party committee to spread the word among the workers that the Party had thought of this and, in its concern for the welfare of the workers, had demanded that the director take measures to protect them. Naturally the director did not dare deny this.

As long as a plant's operations are progressing well, the Party supports the director. It praises and rewards him. But it always stresses that he is the Party's pupil and its loyal son. However, as soon as the plans cease to be fulfilled and there is no hope of immediate fulfillment, the Party shoves the entire blame onto the director. It asserts that all this happened because he lost touch with the Party and became a poor Communist.

Promotion & Incentives

The Party exercises a great deal of control—some would say total control—over the plant director, and he fears that. The Party actually arranges the appointment of the directors and chief engineers. This is done as follows. Each ministry and (formerly) *sovnarkhoz* has two personnel divisions, one for regular personnel and one for management personnel. The regular personnel division lists all the line engineers, and the management personnel division lists all the managerial personnel—that is, chief engineers, directors, and other top enterprise officials. The chief of the ministry selects the candidate for one of these positions jointly with the personnel division. And only after the approval of the Party's Central Committee can he confirm him in the role of director or chief engineer.

The entire roster of industrial managerial personnel in the Soviet Union is listed in a special roster of the Party's Central Committee. In all the administrative and operational functions, the directors and chief engineers are directly subordinate to the administration chief or to the ministry.

Monetary bonuses for plan fulfillment are also granted by the administration chief or the minister. There are, however, a great number of reasons for denying the bonuses. One need only miss one item in the plan or fail to carry out some order—and this can happen all too easily. The plant director and the chief engineer live in the midst of constant conflict among the administration or ministry, the plant Party apparatus, the trade union, and the workers—all with their own interests and demands. For example, the plant Party committee always demands from the plant director a monthly and a quarterly accounting of plant operations, as a check on him. In any dispute, the trade union always sides with the administration against the workers, which causes tension. The union helps to lower workers' wages when the planners so decree and compels them to work better and faster.

It is true that all directors and chief engineers (but not lower level management and personnel) are Party members. Moreover, they are now closer to officials in the lower Party organs in the factories, inasmuch as the majority of the latter now possess a higher education. They can speak the same language and be frank with them. Nevertheless, the directors greatly fear and distrust the Party itself. Because of this, they applaud every error made by high-ranking Party leaders. There is no doubt that they rejoiced at Khrushchev's downfall because it temporarily weakened the punitive powers of the Party.

The Soviet director is greatly overloaded with work. He works a 12-hour day. He envies the professor because the professor enjoys more serene work and has regular hours and a higher salary. And the professor is merely under Party supervision, not Party control. He does not have to worry about the future. If he should get thrown out of a teaching job, some other work will be waiting for him, and he will always remain a professor.

PROGRESS AHEAD?

What about "Libermanism" and the new economic reforms announced late in 1965 by Premier Alexei N. Kosygin?

Many people in the West interpret Libermanism incorrectly. It is true that in the beginning—in September 1962—Ye. Liberman proposed to upgrade considerably the role of profit in the Soviet economy. Profit was to become the prime mover of the economy and a major stimulus in the growth of labor productivity. Economic process was to develop from the bottom, not from the top. These proposals were evaluated in the West as "creeping toward capitalism," which in fact they were. However, because these proposals affected the basic principles of the Communist doctrine and thus threatened the role and rule of the Party, Liberman was censured.

When Liberman spoke again, it was in terms more acceptable to the Party. This time he proposed the upgrading of the role of profit, not for the purpose of promoting capitalism, but merely as an aid in evaluating and encouraging performance and only for the purpose of achieving profitable operations. "Profit in our country is not a social goal and the prime mover of the economy," he said; or again, "Although profit is not the purpose of production, it can be used as a guide in evaluating the efficiency of enterprise operations." Recently he has been trying to reduce the role of profit in the Soviet economy to a purely functional status, as one of the numerous indicators of enterprise performance. In fact, this is what the role of profit currently amounts to.

Under the present socialist system, net profit alone cannot become the main indicator of enterprise efficiency. In the first place, the amount of profit in a Soviet enterprise does not depend directly on the organization, since industry must be guided by the so-called wholesale prices, which are administered and bear no relation to enterprise efficiency. Besides, with the use of profit as the main indicator, other planning gradients, such as product assortment and quality, would get out of control, and there would be many problems with the turnover tax (a sales tax at the wholesale level).

The Crucial Weakness

In the critical analysis of management practices taking place in the Soviet press, the planning system has come under the strongest attack. It is precisely this system that breeds bureaucratic methods of management and retards economic development. The critics claim that the planning system has outgrown itself. I am certain they are right.

The economy of the country has become so complex that central planning and coordination of all economic operations is becoming impossible. Currently, approximately 10 million persons seem to be engaged in various stages of planning. How can the directors of industrial enterprises exercise their skills and initiative under such a system? It is practically impossible. The newly promulgated "Statute on Socialist State Productive Enterprise" eases the problem somewhat, giving the factory director more discretion in the allocation of working capital, distribution of wages, and hiring and firing. But this "factory charter," as it is popularly called, contains only token gestures.

It is hard to believe that the Party will abandon centralized planning. The system of Party dictatorship has been propagated for decades, and it cannot change instantly. Moreover, the strength of the Party and its dictatorship lies in the fact that it controls all sectors of the Soviet economy.

The original Liberman proposal may help somewhat on the consumer front. But total adoption of his methods of industrial management will depend on the evolution of the socialist order itself. In this respect I am not optimistic. Many of the proposals advocated so far by Party critics of the present system suggest even greater pressure on the workers, and even greater control over the fruits of their labor. The proposals advocating an increase in the number of economic indicators clearly testify to that.

In the final analysis, the whole Soviet economic controversy seems to have been reduced to the problem of expanding and improving the present system of indicators and criteria for evaluating "enterprise efficiency." Of course, many Soviet economists realize that the fault does not lie in the administrative system alone but in the nature of the economic order itself. Thus far, however, everyone has been "going around in circles" and hoping for the best, with the discussion centering principally on criticism of procedural details.

The Party is aware that its numerous reorganizations of industry have failed to achieve the desired results. But it has not yet come to grips with the agonizing question: Is it really possible to employ generally accepted methods of good economic management within the confines of the Soviet socialist economy?

selection 32

*Japanese Management—The Cultural Background**

William Brown

Since the end of the Pacific War the "modernization" of Japanese ways of life has emerged as a national goal. One expression of this ideal can be found in the efforts to rationalize the management practices of large and small businesses. During recent months, under the stimulation of the "technical revolution" taking place in production methods and the increasing integration of Japan into the international economy, the problem of rationalization has become a major concern of both government and industry. Journalists have been particularly

*From *Monumenta Nipponica—Studies in Japanese Culture*, Vol. 21, No. 1-2,. pp. 47-60, Sophia University, Tokyo. The author is an instructor at Sophia University.

vigorous in their castigation of the "feudalistic" and "premodern" characteristics of personnel administration. Words like "familism" and "paternalism"
have become epithets stigmatizing those elements in Japanese human relations
sanctioned by traditional management practices. It is widely assumed that these
traditional patterns of work-relationships constitute an intolerable obstacle to
the rationalization of the economy and a serious impediment to economic
growth.

In reaction to this attitude some students of the situation have taken a more
"realistic" approach and advocated a compromise between the ideal of rationalization and the more intractable elements of Japanese society rooted in a long
tradition.

In this paper I would like to present an aspect of the situation from a position
somewhere between these two points of view. I do not wish to deny that there
are some features of present management practices which indeed present obstacles to the goals of economic growth and international competition which
Japan has necessarily set herself. Nor on the other hand do I reject the view that
some features cannot be changed but must be accepted and put up with. I rather
prefer to center my attention on those elements of Japanese social relations
which actually have proved quite "rational" in the past and promise to do so in
the future.

In the course of consideration I will take up those features of Japanese managerial practices which have been most severely criticised and I will investigate
the two systems alleged as their causes, the promotion system and the lifetime
employment system. Then I shall present some features which seem to have
been overlooked in the criticism of Japanese management. The paper concludes
with a sketch of what I believe to be important cultural and ethical roots of the
Japanese approach to work.

LENGTH OF SERVICE

Foreign students of Japanese management have frequently observed that the
age of executives in Japanese companies appears much higher than that of, say,
executives in American companies. Few men ever become executives before the
age of fifty. In a survey of 235 companies in 1958 it was found that the average
age of 3,277 executives was 57.2 years old. A little more than 10% were below
the age of fifty, while about one third were above the age of sixty.[1] It was also
found that the ages differ quite clearly according to the rank held.

It appears that the ages of those occupying these positions vary little from
company to company. In other words, promotions take place at regular intervals, the basic qualification for promotion being the length of time spent in the

---

[1] Cf. Keizai Dōyūkai 1958 Survey Report, "The Structure and Function of Top Management of Large Enterprises in Japan," reproduced in Noda Kazuo, *Big Business Executives
in Japan* (Tokyo: Diamond Press, 1960), pp. 317, 320–21. The Committee for Economic
Development has just finished a five year survey on management practices in Japan. Most
of the figures in this paper are taken from reports on this survey.

service of the company. Seniority is also the basic unit for determining wages. Thus a man on the day he enters a company can predict with fair accuracy his wage and position in that company at any given year in the future.

This so-called "escalator system" of promotion has for some time been under attack by those who urge a more rationalistic promotion system. The proponents of change, by now far in the majority, argue that the efficient operation of a company depends to a large extent on the discovery, reward, and promotion of ability to get work done. Since 1958 many attempts have been made to change this system by introducing various methods of job-evaluation and skill-evaluation. These attempts have met with many obstacles. In a survey published in 1963 it was found that 87% of the 484 companies surveyed were still employing the length-of-service and age standard; 20% of the companies interviewed were employing a job-rank system, while 65% were trying an ability-rating system.[2] Nevertheless, the companies using combinations of these systems paid 68% of the total salaries for length-of-service considerations and only 21% for job-ability.[3] Even where the job-skill system is employed, there is no clear distinction in evaluation between skill and length-of-service,[4] and in the job-evaluation system 29% of the companies have deliberately included length-of-service considerations in their evaluation categories.[5]

It seems clear that so far attempts to modify the length-of-service system, accepted by both employers and employees, have met with only modest success. Indeed there seems to be a kind of moral pressure upon employers to see that men who entered the company together are advanced to positions of equal importance more or less at the same time.[6] Nevertheless, it must be admitted that there are other minor factors which establish slight, but decisive differences in rank and prospects of further advancement among members of a group which entered the company together.[7]

LIFE EMPLOYMENT

Lifetime commitment of the employee to his company is a phenomenon nearly universal (92%), and the larger the company the more firmly is it entrenched.[8] Only about one quarter of the companies questioned in 1963 were

---

[2] Keizai Dōyūkai Survey, "Management Decision Process in Japan (IV): Changes in the Labor Market and Enterprise Behavior" (Tokyo: Tokyo Center for Economic Research, 1963), p. 88. Hereafter referred to as Doyukai IV.

[3] *Ibid.*, p. 89.

[4] *Ibid.*, p. 230.

[5] *Ibid.*, pp. 92, 231.

[6] Cf. Ono Toyoaki "Nōryoku-shugi jidai no ningen kanri" ("The Management of People in the Age of Talentism") *Bessatsu chuo koron: keiei mondai*, Spring, 1964, pp. 34–35. Also Ishikawa Hiroyoshi and Ujigawa Makoto, *Nihon no white collar* (Japan's White Collar) (Tokyo: Japan Productivity Center, 1961), pp. 90–92.

[7] Kamata Isao, "Chūkan sarariman no shōshin to shōkyū" ("Advancement and Pay Raises of the Middle Level Salaryman"), *Bessatsu chuo koron: keiei mondai*, Spring, 1964, p. 74–85.

[8] *Dōyūkai* IV, p. 22.

inclined to do much about it.[9] Opinion as to whether this system was likely to change very easily was evenly divided.[10] Those who believed that the life-employment system was likely to change expected that it would give way under modernization of management practices or the attempts to cope with the technical revolution. Most of the companies which took, shall we say, a more pessimistic view felt that the "familistic mentality" of the Japanese, upon which this system is thought to be based, is not likely to change.[11] The *defects* of this system were considered to be the inability to lay off superannuated or unnecessary labor, the "preservation of the length-of-service system," the fostering and spread of that prudential attitude which prompts workers to seek their own security first and the tendency toward indifferentism. But this system is believed to have its good points too: more than half the companies questioned (53%) thought that the life-employment system produces a sense of security among the employees. Nearly as many companies (47%) said that the system provides a "basis for nourishing the spirit of a cooperative body *(kyōdōtai teki seishin)* in the enterprise."[12]

This lack of mobility in the work force is strikingly reflected in the top levels of management. It is quite rare for the board of directors to contain many directors who entered as directors from another company. According to a survey of 159 companies made in 1956 by Ono Toyoaki, only 6.5% of the executives came from outside the company.[13] Another survey of 235 companies made in 1958 by the *Dōyūkai* found that of 2,428 executives, 324 (11.8%) were from other companies.[14] Sometimes an executive of a bank or high ranking government official who has been looking after the interests of a company may be invited to join that company on the executive level *(yokosuberiyaku)*. Professor Noda Kazuo estimates that as many as 10% of Japanese executives in industrial enterprises get their jobs in this way.[15] In another survey by the *Dōyūkai*, only 5.7% of the companies reported that they had representatives of major stockholders on their board, and even fewer (2.3%) reported representatives from their financial agencies.[16]

The life-employment system and the seniority system are intimately related and appear to be two expressions of the typical social structure of a Japanese company. We will examine the nature of this social structure in more detail later, but here I would like to call attention to the closely knit relations among employers and employees. Such close relations would naturally be expected where the members of an organization realize that they will be together for the

---

[9] *Ibid.*, p. 29.
[10] *Ibid.*, p. 31.
[11] *Ibid.*, p. 23.
[12] *Ibid.*, p. 25.
[13] *Ibid.*
[14] *Ibid.*, pp. 170–74.
[15] *Ibid.*, pp. 170–74.
[16] "Wagakuni kigyō ni okero keiei ishi kettai no jittai" ("The Actual Condition of Management Decision Processes in Japanese Enterprises"), *Keizai dōyūkai*, Tokyo, 1960, pp. 26–28. Hereafter referred to as *Dōyūkai* I.

rest of their working lives. They also expect that promotions, instead of separating them, will keep them close together. The relation with superiors is also usually quite close. The superiors in a company feel obligated to call their subjects together frequently for an informal talk and they make it a point to be present at company outings and other forms of recreation.[17]

AUTHORITY AND RESPONSIBILITY

Foreign observers are invariably amazed at the lack of a clear definition of authority and responsibility, not only for the various sections of a company but also for the members of middle and top management.

Many of the usual means for marking out areas of authority are slow to catch on. The organization chart is by no means universal. According to the 1960 *Dōyūkai* survey, 26.2% of the companies questioned did not have one. Small companies would conceivably have less use for an organization chart than large ones, but even among the biggest companies (capital of over 20 billion yen), 12.2% had none.[18] The existence of a set of rules delineating an official's authority is far less common. In the same survey, 66.3% of the companies replied that they had no such rules for the chief of the general affairs division *(sōmu buchō)* or for the chief of the accounting division *(keiri buchō).*[19] In a survey made by the Japan Productivity Center in 1959, 36 out of 54 companies replied that they had no stipulations for areas of authority connected with various jobs.[20]

Not only is there a lack of clarity in areas of authority. Frequently the nature of the job itself is not clear. We saw above that Japanese companies have not been very successful in introducing job-rank and job-qualification systems. Even of the companies actually using some form of job-rank system, only 48.5% make the job analysis necessary for this system.[21] The list of difficulties these companies encountered in introducing the job-rank system is enlightening: "the difficulty in standardizing job content," "lack of agreement on the social evaluation of equal work," "individual differences in workers' efficiency," "lack of job-consciousness among employees."[22] This last item is not without significance. It has been noted more than once that when a Japanese is asked what his job is, instead of saying what he does, he is likely to reply that he is a member of such and such a company.[23]

So far we have considered the theoretical disadvantages of the length-of-service system, the life-employment system, and the lack of clear areas of responsibility and authority. Now let us consider those factors which tend to offset these disadvantages.

---

[17] *Dōyūkai* IV, pp. 233–35.
[18] *Dōyūkai* I, p. 42.
[19] *Ibid.*
[20] Cited in Noda, *Jūyaku,* p. 372.
[21] *Dōyūkai* IV, pp. 91, 230.
[22] *Ibid.,* pp. 92, 231.
[23] Ōno Tsutomu, *Bijinesu man (Business Man)* (Tokyo: San'ichi shobō, 1964), p. 42.

TALENT

The usual objections to the systems described above are that they tend to impede the discovery and development of talent and that the incompetent are allowed to reach positions of high authority. In reality, however, the incompetent rarely reach such important positions and the larger enterprises are assured of a generous supply of really able persons.

The supply of talent *(nōryoku)*, as we might surmise, is taken care of by a careful selection of candidates in the beginning. Large firms usually call upon a certain few famous and highly rated universities to present candidates for the company entrance exam.[24] These candidates first must present a record of their experience, their academic record, information about their family, and the names of those whom they know in the company who are willing to sponsor them. Then they are informed whether they may be admitted to the exam. Perhaps one tenth of these may pass the exam and thus be admitted to the firm for life.[25]

But the selection by the company is only the final stage in a long process. In reality, the educational system, and with it the greater part of the population, is mobilized toward the one purpose of providing industry and government with the cream of Japanese talent. Few other nations in the world can show a comparable example of such perfect rationalization. A separate study of the history and social psychology of the Japanese notion of "success" *(risshin shusse)* would be required to explain the intensity of the competition for these routes to the company entrance examinations.[26] The way lies through a rigorous series of elimination contests in the form of entrance examinations into the best high schools, the best middle schools, the best grammar schools, and even the best kindergartens.[27]

A priori then we can expect that Japan's business elite should be an elite in the true sense of the word. Recent research has provided a posteriori proof of this fact. Although 7% of the population between the ages of 50 to 69 obtained higher education, 71% of the industrial elite had the equivalent of a college education or above. We realize what a high percentage this is if we compare this figure with two other countries of high industrial and educational levels. According to M. Newcomer, as of 1950, 62% of the American business elite had obtained a college education or above, while in England, according to G. H. Copeman, only 36% of the business elite had an equivalent education. Mannari and Abegglen estimate that within another generation the figure will reach 100%.[28]

---

[24]Cf. Noda, *Jūyaku,* pp. 160–65.

[25] Personality, ideology, health, and academic achievements are listed among the most highly desirable qualities. Cf. *Dōyūkai* IV, p. 42.

[26] For an interesting study of *risshin shusse* cf. Kamishima Jirō, *Kindai Nihon no seishin kōzō* *(The Spiritual Structure of Modern Japan)* (Tokyo: Iwanami shoten, 1961), pp. 269–90.

[27]This phenomenon, popularly known as *shiken jigoku* (examination hell), is described by Ezra Vogel, *Japan's New Middle Class* (Berkeley: University of California Press, 1963), pp. 40–67.

[28] H. Mannari and J. Abegglen, "Nihon no sangyō shidōsha to gakureki" ("The Educational Background of Japan's Industrial Leaders"), *Bessatsu chuo koron: keiei mondai,* Winter, 1963, pp. 190–97.

The fact that more than seventy percent of the Japanese business elite have had a college education tells only half the story of just how select this elite is. It was mentioned above that large companies ask only certain universities to present candidates for their entrance exams. These are the institutions which have a long tradition, superior educational facilities, and by far the best students. There are today more than 250 colleges and universities (compared with 45 before World War II), but less than a dozen of these have supplied Japanese industry with more than two thirds of its executives.[29]

Seen in this light, the traditional Japanese promotion system is not the enemy to talent that it is alleged to be. The initial recruitment of extremely capable and industrious young men every year solves the problem at the outset. Given the general range of human intelligence, it might be safely presumed that the variation of ability in this group is not great enough to warrant the employment of a promotion system based mainly on this one discriminatory factor. After all, the white collar employee in Japan gained his job in competition with literally millions of other Japanese. Presupposing then that the company is staffed by a group of highly intelligent young men, it would appear more reasonable to promote them according to the *experience* which they have been intelligently accumulating.

RETIREMENT

Let us now turn our attention to another factor operating in the selection of talented managers. This is the mandatory retirement age system *(teinen seido)*. In spite of the seniority system, obviously not everyone is made a president nor even a director. Most employees are retired first at the age of fifty-five.[30] Only those who have attained the title of director by the age of fifty can feel assured that they will be allowed to stay on after the mandatory retirement age, and even then it is not certain. The decisive factor in a man's career is whether he can reach the position of division head in the home office; accordingly, more care is exercised in choosing men for this post than for others.[31]

DECISION-MAKING

Even granting, then, that the length-of-service system and life-employment systems are not such obstacles to the promotion of talent as is often supposed, there remains another and more serious objection to the organization of the Japanese company. This is, as noted above, the lack of clarity in defining authority, responsibility, and the rarity of delegation of authority.

---

[29] In 1959 the Japan Productivity Center in a survey of 900 executives found that of these, 32% were graduates of Tokyo University, 10% from Hitotsubashi University, 8% from Kyoto University, and 7% and 4% from the private universities, Keio and Waseda, respectively. Survey reproduced in Noda, *Juyaku*, pp. 345–81.

[30] An idea of how low the Japanese retirement age is can be gained by comparing it with that of other countries: France, 60; England, 65; America, 65; West Germany, 65; Switzerland, 65; Norway, 70; Canada, 70. Cf. Ishikawa and Ujigawa, *White Collar*, p. 185.

[31] *Dōyūkai*, IV, pp. 67, 224–26.

The evidence seems to indicate that the real authority of a company rests in the hands of a few, for example, the Regular Affairs Committee *(jōmukai),* or more frequently only one, the president or board chairman.[32] The decisions are made by these few and this authority is rarely if ever delegated to subordinates on the division and section level.[33]

A closer examination of the way this planning and decision process is actually carried out will show us many things about the locus, function, and conception of authority in Japan. If we take up one of the papers *(ringisho)* that are constantly crossing an executive's desk we find that it has received fourteen, sixteen, or more seal impressions. These seals are a record of the journey of this paper from section to section, division to division, from subordinate to officials to the president. This circulation of papers is the life of the decision-making process in the Japanese company. What are the characteristics of this system? Professor Noda describes them for us:

1. *The drafting of a plan by middle management:* certainly when the initiator is below the middle management level, and even when the initiator is a member of the highest managerial level, the drafting of the plan is always carried out in the name of an organizational unit of middle management (the section, for example) or its administrator.

2. *A careful horizontal consideration:* before the *ringisho* is submitted to higher officials, it is sent around to related organizational units of the same rank where it is confirmed, perhaps after additions or corrections. Sometimes, before the plan is drawn up in a formal *ringisho* the related organizational units of the same rank are called together for previous discussion.

3. *A careful vertical consideration:* the submitted *ringisho* does not receive the independent authorization of a particular individual; it receives the authorization of several people in succession along the order of occupational rank.

4. *The formality of affixing the seal:* regarding the above-mentioned confirmation or authorization, since it is carried out by the affixing of the responsible person's seal, it is feared that the confirmation or approval of the contents of a *ringisho* may fall into a mere formalism.

5. *The lack of clarity in authority and responsibility:* the nature of the act of confirmation or approval is very vague in its relation to the enactment and effects of the items in the *ringisho.* In other words, this is a skillful device for obscuring both the locus of authority for carrying out the plan and the locus of responsibility for its effects.[34]

Almost every company has some form of this system. About 94% of the two hundred companies surveyed in 1961 were employing this system, and of these only 19% were thinking of doing away with it.[35] To abolish the system, or even

---

[32] The board of Directors, the organ established by law for the direction of Japanese companies, has, for various reasons, during the past several years become more or less a mere formality, its function being taken over by regular affairs committees. Cf. *Top management no soshiki to kinō: wagakuni kigyō ni okero keiei ishi to jittai,* II, *Keizai dōyūkai,* Tokyo, 1961, pp. 18-26, 73-77. Hereafter *Dōyūkai* II. Cf. also Sakaguchi Akira, *Keieisha (Managers)* (Tokyo: Kawade shobō shinsha, 1964), pp. 79-82.

[33] Cf. *Dōyūkai* I, pp. 18-24.

[34] Noda *Jūyaku,* pp. 115-17. (All translations are the author's unless otherwise stated.)

[35] *Dōyūkai* II, pp. 50, 57. Even by 1964, of 397 companies again questioned about this system 92% said they employed the system and 5% said they did not. *Wagakuni kigyō ni okeru keiei ishi kettei no jittai* (V): *keiei rinen to kigyō katsudo (The Actual Condition of Management Decision Processes in Japanese Enterprises: Management Ideology and Enterprise Behavior)* (Tokyo: Tokyo Center for Economic Research, 1964), pp. 116-17. Hereafter referred to as *Dōyūkai* V.

to make changes in it usually requires major changes in other organs of management in the company. This is an indication of how deeply interlaced this system is in the network of the company.[36] Although few firms think they can get along without it, almost all are trying to perfect this system, either by clarifying what matters are to be treated in this way, or by simplifying the routes of the *ringisho.*[37] In an attempt to focus responsibility for the origins of plans, 52% of the firms have rules determining who is authorized to draw up a *ringisho.*[38]

Theoretically, if a matter to be decided is within the competence of a subordinate, there should be no need to resort to the *ringi* system. Nevertheless, in those companies which have rules defining this authority (65%), in nearly half the cases a *ringisho* is sent around anyway, sometimes as a mere notification, but more usually in order to get the superior's approval.[39]

It is widely assumed that authority is concentrated in the person of the president. This phenomenon is probably explained by the fact that the final approval of proposals is given by the president. Professor Noda, however, makes the rather unexpected assertion that the Japanese company is in effect managed by subordinates. In fact, he goes so far as to claim that, because of the *ringi* system, "Japanese management is middle management":

> The essence of the *ringi* system lies in the fact that the middle management level conceives, plans, and can actually carry out almost all of the affairs which pertain to administration. It certainly appears that, insofar as approval of superiors is required, authority is formally located on the upper level. Supposing, however, that the superior merely goes through the formality of placing his stamp upon the *ringisho,* which has been submitted to him after obtaining the confirmation of each organizational unit concerned, it can be said that, in effect, authority *has been delegated to the middle-management level.*[40]

Noda goes on to develop this opinion convincingly, but his whole thesis rests on the supposition that the superior gives his approval automatically and as a mere formality. This is an assumption that should definitely be proved. Why must we suppose that the superiors do not take their job as seriously as their subordinates? (It would be interesting to know how frequently plans are turned down by superiors.)

I feel that professor Yoshino Yotarō of Stanford University comes closer to the actual state of affairs: *"Ringi* management is said to be a centralization of authority and so it is—formally; but in actual fact one has the strong impression that it neither centralizes authority nor decentralizes it, but rather disperses it throughout the enterprise."[41]

The difficulty in grasping the locus of authority really comes from attempting to discover what corresponds to the western concept of authority in a non-western social organization. The *ringi* system shows the course of the decision-

---

[36] *Dōyūkai* II, p. 52.
[37] *Ibid.,* pp. 56–57.
[38] Usually the division head or section chief, *ibid.,* p. 53.
[39] *Ibid.,* p. 55.
[40] Noda, *Juyaku,* p. 117. Emphasis added.
[41] "Soto kara mita Nihonteki keiei" ("Japanese-style Management as Seen from Outside"), *Bessatsu Chūō Kōron: keiei mondai,* Summer, 1964, p. 98.

making process, but does not establish it. Ideas and plans are worked up, developed, and polished in informal discussions among men who have been working in close association for years. The *ringi* system appears essentially to be a means of knitting together as many people as possible into the vital activity of the company. All are given an opportunity to make their contribution and most do so. The *ringisho,* with all its seals affixed, is the concrete manifestation of a unity of wills, a unanimous consent. The same phenomenon can be observed in committee meetings. More often than not they are an organ for the explicitation and "celebration" of a unanimous consent previously existing in a general and implicit state. The real decision-making process is frequently carried on in an area subliminal to the formal apparatus of organizations and is catalyzed by the harmonious spirit of what is known as the *kyōdōtai.*

THE ENTERPRISE AS KYŌDŌTAI

In the preceding description of Japanese management processes I have confined the discussion to the "phenomenology" of the situation, without entering into the cultural causes. In the following pages I would like to present in outline an area of the cultural background of Japanese management which I think merits further study.

If we suppose the fundamental economic unit of contemporary Japan to be the large company, it might be instructive to compare it with the fundamental economic unit of pre-Meiji Japan, the village *kyōdōtai.* [42]

The theme of mountains and water is perhaps the most frequent and beloved in Japanese art and literature from ancient times. The Japanese terrain has until recent times defined not only their aesthetic life but their economic life as well. The agrarian culture of Japan began with the *Tayoi* Period and the introduction of wet-rice culture. As is well known, the cultivation of rice requires a constant and abundant supply of water which in Japan could only be insured by an elaborate system of irrigation. Since the numerous canals, dams, etc., which make up this system could not be built nor maintained by individuals, cooperative forms of labor were needed. The mountains surrounding the village supplied building materials, fuel, and fertilizer, but careful cooperation was required for the development and conservation of these resources. The village, through the cooperation of its members, was economically independent from other villages, just as it was physically separated from them by geographical conditions.

The ecology of Japan, then, indicates how the social and cultural patterns developed in dependence upon mountains and water. Old village records vividly illustrate the social and legal life of the village centered around these geographical features. [43] Watsuji Tetsurō in his famous work on the history of ethical thought in Japan, argues convincingly that the basic Japanese ethical attitudes had already

---

[42] This term is more easily described than translated. It refers primarily to cooperative and mutual assistance organizations, and is frequently translated simply, "community."

[43] Cf. Matsuyoshi Sadao, *Mura no kiroku (Village Records)* (Iwanami shoten, 1961.)

been established in the primitive village *kyōdōtai* life and that all the other social institutions which grew up throughout the nation's long history were characterized by these same ethical patterns.[44]

Professor Kamishima Jirō has made a very interesting study of the relationship between the social and psychological structure of the village and its influence on urban life in Japan. Let us consider his concepts of "primary village" and "secondary village" in reference to the problem we are now examining, the cultural roots of the modern large enterprise in Japan.

The Primary Village (dai ichi mura)

The socio-cultural principles of the way of life in the village of the Tokugawa period are enumerated by Kamishima:

1. "Mental Autarky": the economic independence of the outside and the internal interdependence produced a social, cultural, and psychological self-sufficiency, a group solidarity, and group consciousness. All the necessities of life could be supplied by the group. In short, economic autarky produced mental autarky.

2. Shintoism (not the state-sponsored religion, but that of the common people): the Shintoism of village life was focused on the *matsuri* or festival. The many annual festivals played an important part in village life. Their function was to supply the emotional unification necessary for smooth functioning of the *kyōdōtai*.

3. "Gerontology": in a self-sufficient and unchanging society, wisdom is equated with memory and experience. These qualities naturally grow with age. Thus older people are truly wiser and are the natural leaders. Such a situation is supported by the youth: all they need do is obey and wait to take their position of leadership when the time comes.

4. Familism: the extended family unified by the authority of the family head was the social unit of the village. Members were not necessarily blood relations.

5. Feudalism: families, being the basic social element of the village, were obliged to participate as units in the preparations and celebrations of the main village activity, the festival. Roles were assigned to each family, and it was by this that family status was determined. An individual's worth was determined by the standing of the family to which he belonged, and the family's standing was determined by the extent of its *participation* in the festival. With the decline of the family system personal status came also to be more closely identified with age, since age was the only immutable criterion for quality.

The Secondary Village (dai ni mura)

The rapid development of bureaucracy and industry consequent upon the Meiji Restoration demanded a swift mobilization of manpower. This was supplied by the rural areas (villages). No social organization can function without generally recognized and accepted social patterns of behavior. There was no time to form new ones; the required social patterns were supplied by the village.[45]

---

[44] *Nihon rinri shisōshi (The History of Japanese Ethical Thought), Watsuji Tetsurō senshū (Collected Works of Watsuji Tetsurō)* (Tokyo: Iwanami shoten, 1962), XII, XIII.

[45] It must be admitted that the extent to which peasants from the village were a constituent part of the new bureaucratic system is disputed. Former samurai and merchants were probably *leaders* in the development of these institutions, but the question is whether they also were responsible for the social patterns which appeared in these institutions.

The former villagers instinctively adapted the only patterns they knew to the situation in which they found themselves.[46]

The Enterprise as Secondary Village

Let us now apply the sociocultural principles described above to the modern Japanese company viewed in the light of a "secondary village."[47]

1. "Mental Autarky": the departmentalization and lack of communication between divisions in a firm can be partially explained by this notion.[48] The emotional bonds which exist in a typical Japanese company may have strong social and psychological roots in the parent social unit, the village.

2. Shintoism: Shintoism as an explicit religious belief and practice is no longer very vital in upper classes. Although there are no more religious festivals to lubricate the friction points and strengthen the emotional ties necessary for the smooth operation of the company *kyōdōtai*, the function of the festival is fulfilled by company outings, sports events, and after-work gatherings with office companions.

3. "Gerontology": the principle of seniority was established early in Japanese bureaucracy and has not been questioned until recently. Now the need for innovative talent and ability to appraise risk, not usually associated with older people, begin to threaten the length-of-service system. As was pointed out above, however, experience is still perhaps the most valuable discriminatory factor and is justly rewarded by promotions.

4 and 5. Familism and Feudalism: in the village a person's character or worth was determined by the status of the family to which he belonged. But under the impact of social changes just previous to and after the Meiji Restoration the large family system declined. In the large cities the small nuclear family was relatively insignificant as a social unit. It could no longer provide identity and status. Its place has been taken by the government ministries and later by the large private enterprises. So it is that a man's worth, his character, or his status is determined by the extent of his firm's participation in the economic life of the nation. More than perhaps salary, position, or any other single factor, the standing (size) of the firm indicates personal success *(shusse)*.

In brief, gerontology may be viewed in principle as the cultural origin of the length-of-service system. The close cooperative or *kyōdōtai* spirit may be explained in terms of mental autarky as the traditional approach to a work situation. Life employment may reflect mental autarky, familism, and feudalism.

Kyōdōtai Ethics

The cultural sources of life employment and also the peculiar concepts of the superior–subordinate relationship, of authority and responsibility may ultimately be found in typical Japanese ethical attitudes. Robert Bellah in his book, *Tokugawa Religion,* attempts to find in Japanese ethico-religious attitudes at least a partial explanation of the country's economic development in recent

---

[46] Kamishima Jiro, *Kindai Nihon,* pp. 22–164.

[47] One must be careful to avoid the idea that a "modernized" or "rationalized" system is one which is free from the taint of rural sociocultural patterns. The continued popularity in America of the famous "Turner Thesis" is an indication that most Americans are proud of the role the rural past has played in their country's modernization.

[48] On the "vertical organization" of Japanese firms, cf. Ono Toyoaki, *"Nōryoku-shugi,"* pp. 103–12.

times. Presupposed is an animistic or pantheistic approach to nature. The basic religious drive is to union with this nature thus achieving union with the Absolute. The Japanese tends to regard the society of which he is a member as the expression for him of Nature. From this society or group he receives benefits, all that he has and values. He feels obliged to express his gratitude to this group by dedicating himself to its advancement. In this way, by complete self-forgetfulness, he manages to achieve a kind of mystical union with his group (Nature, the Absolute).[49]

Watsuji, in his intriguing analysis of early Japanese myths, considers the leader of the group as a kind of mediator, one representing the Absolute to the group and the group to the Absolute.[50]

Bellah and Watsuji show how the group-oriented ethics of Japan have a long history and go very deep. This ethic may ultimately explain the particularism of Japanese economic life as well as its dynamism, but as yet the surface of this aspect of Japanese culture has hardly been scratched.

CONCLUSION

It is precisely the group-orientation of the members, the cohesion, and the insistence on harmonious personal relations which, I submit, are the strength of Japanese organizations and the source of their efficiency. Such a type of organization gives an individual's particular talents and abilities a wide range of play. Furthermore one man's deficiencies are obscured because they are made up for by his companion's strong points. Finally, a sense of satisfaction is achieved through the awareness of a real contribution to and participation in the vital activity of the company.

In spite of the strong attraction exerted by imported management theories, the Japanese, persuaded perhaps by their own common sense rooted in a long tradition, have resisted the urge to parcel out a firm's myriad operations in neat little bundles of authority and responsibility. The Japanese approach to the work situation dictated by modern industry seems to me much more realistic than the habit of mind which insists on designating one individual as the responsible scapegoat for a plethora of details which he could not conceivably have contributed. In effect, responsibility is automatically distributed in proportion to the demands of the task, in degrees impossible to isolate and measure. According to foreign notions of work allotment, men are pegs which must be fitted into preexisting holes. Once a man's area of responsibility has been marked out it becomes his territory. As a result, any attempt by a fellow worker to make up for his inevitable shortcomings or oversights is tantamount to an invasion. Only recently have foreign efficiency experts come to realize how much heat is generated by these friction points. The Japanese work force, on the other hand, might be compared to a jig-saw puzzle. Compared with the polished pegs, the

---

[49] Robert Bellah, *Tokugawa Religion: The Values of Pre-Industrial Japan* (Glencoe: The Free Press, 1957).
[50] Watsuji Tetsurō, *Nihon rinri*, XII, pp. 55–95.

individuals seem very irregular, "irrational." But the pieces themselves, through their intimate knowledge of one another's peculiar shape and coloring, fit together neatly and a clear picture emerges. To the westerner, the lack of work rules, job analysis, lack of definition of responsibility, etc., are evidence of the oriental's lack of a sense of individualism. The Japanese approach to the work situation is not only an illustration of a certain degree of individualism but a means of preserving it and developing it. The executives of companies are instinctively aware of this native trait. On paper all authority appears to be in their hands, but as the operation of the *ringi* system shows, the trust and approbation of the subordinates' collective good sense and initiative is the most accurate delegation of authority possible.

Recently some voices have been raised in opposition to what has been called an infatuation with theories of management rationalization developed in the West. Professor Tsuchiya Takao is particularly vigorous in his attack upon this form of "worship of the West."[51] One cannot help feeling that there is indeed among some Japanese students of management a certain implicit trust in formulas which have proved successful in the West and a deep distrust of Japanese "feudal" traditions. It cannot be denied that in Japan there is a strong tendency to consider the science of management as another form of technology which can be imported just as it is. It is also possible to discern in this attitude what Professor Maruyama Masao has called "faith in theory," the tendency to hypostatize theories and to trust in the complete effectiveness of the perfect system. In the political sphere "faith in theory" appears in the emphasis on "structural reforms."[52] In the economic sphere we may see the same phenomenon in the emphasis on the rationalization of management as an ultimate goal.

On the other hand we can also perceive in some quarters a hidebound traditionalism, an insistence on the traditional way of doing things because it is traditional. This type of thinking is based on a misunderstanding of what tradition is. "Real traditions are not principles from which one can draw conclusions as to one's lines of conduct in new circumstances. They are ways of existence incorporated into a temperament, which determines a way of reacting more than they dictate a solution. A true tradition is constitutive, not constituted."[53]

The real test for the rationality of a system is not to be found in any one theory or any set of historical facts. It can be found only by considering results and comparing them with the goal to be achieved. The process of rationalization is nothing other than adapting means to ends. A productive system is to be judged by its efficiency, not in terms of some abstract formula.[54] If a formula

---

[51] Tsuchiya Takao, *Nihon keiei rinenshi (The History of Japanese Management Ideology)* (Tokyo: Nihon keizai shimbun, 1964), pp. 3–95.

[52] Maruyama Masao, *Nihon no shisō (Japanese Thought)* (Tokyo: Iwanami shoten, 1961).

[53] Yves Montcheuil, *For Men of Action* (London: Geoffrey Chapman, 1957), p. 152.

[54] It is not impossible that many of the real difficulties which harass Japanese management flow from an imperfect understanding of the built-in goals of industry as such. It must be remembered that technology and industry have grown up in a culture in which, due to philosophical and theological traditions, man is considered to be distinct from the natural world precisely because he is a creator and manager of it.

is after all required, it must be worked out by the Japanese themselves through their own experience of their encounter with the demands of reality. The questions they need ask themselves are simple: "What are we really trying to do, and are we really doing it?" Only in this way will this great nation, which has learned much from western experience, contribute the richness of its own experience to the West. Meanwhile, western observers would do well to take a harder look at the Japanese way of doing things in terms of results, remembering a saying dear to the pragmatic Anglo-saxon heart: "There is more than one way to skin a cat."

selection 33

Social and Cultural Factors in Management Development in India*

Kamla Kapur Chowdhry

In an introductory note to a publication on cultural patterns and technical change[1] the Director of the World Federation for Mental Health pointed out that—

Rapid changes in the industrial or social structure in any country are apt to lead to unforeseen disturbances even when such changes are initiated or supervised by nationals of that country. When men and women with technical skills set out to help in shaping new developments in a country or a culture other than their own, there are clearly many more possibilities of producing unfortunate consequences. Sometimes great harm can be done to the people of that country, especially through the creation of social psychological stresses and the disorganisation of family and community life.

This statement is particularly relevant to the management development programmes introduced by the more privileged to some of the less privileged countries of the world. To understand the social and cultural factors involved we need to consider three things—relevant aspects of the traditional structure in developing countries; the objectives and methods of management development programmes suitable to those countries; and the role of the instructor and the foreign expert, especially in terms of his perceptions, values and sensitivities in dealing with his assignment. These aspects will be discussed here with reference to experience in India.

---

*From *International Labour Review*, Vol. 94, No. 2 (August, 1966), pp. 132–47. Mr. Chowdhry is Director of Programmes, Indian Institute of Management, Ahmedabad.

[1] U.N.E.S.C.O., *Cultural patterns and technical change*, ed. Margaret Mead (Paris, 1953), p. 6.

HISTORICAL, SOCIAL AND CULTURAL FACTORS

I would like to discuss first the management practices that emerged from the historical background of industrialisation in India, and second the Indian family system and its influences on management practices. I will then attempt to identify some social and cultural factors, such as the role of ritualism, that need to be taken into account in relation to management development.

Historical Background

Managing Agency System.   Industrialisation in India was pioneered largely by the managing agency system. This came into being in the early stages of the development of modern factories and plantation industries as a result of the division between the financing sources, which were in England, and those managerial functions which necessarily had to be carried out in India. It was the custom in those days to raise money in London for enterprises to be started in India, and to appoint some trading office in India to run the factories as a managing agent of the company. Later, even when money was raised within India by Indian entrepreneurs, the system of managing agents continued. Almost all modern industries in India were established by managing agents, whose three primary functions were promoting, financing and managing. For the most part the agencies were either family units or small private companies dominated by members of one family. Usually members of the agency family occupied key positions in the companies managed.[2]

The growth of industry in India was characterised by the success of small businesses started with comparatively little capital, which was usually supplied by the managing agents themselves or borrowed from their own credit. The system on the whole worked with success. The typical organisation of a managing agency can be described as highly centralised and personal, with a rigid social structure.

Subsidiaries of Foreign Companies.   Another step in the industrialisation of India before independence was the establishment of British and European companies which set up their own manufacturing and selling facilities in India and generally sent out the top personnel from the home office. The management of the subsidiaries in many respects corresponded to the managing agency system. Authority was highly centralised, relations among the senior staff were informal, and the third-level managers (who were largely Indian) had very few chances of promotion, however much they might merit it. A few Indian executives were, indeed, promoted to the second level; but in such cases not only the possession of technical skill but also participation in the social and cultural life of the senior staff played a significant part.

---

[2] See K. Chowdhry and R. Tarneja, "India," in *Developing better managers: an eight-nation study* (New York: National Industrial Conference Board, 1961), pp. 89–90.

Public Enterprises. After India had become independent the Government sought to promote the rapid growth of industrialisation by establishing many key industries in the public sector. These included plants for fertilisers, antibiotics, transport, heavy engineering, communications, etc. These enterprises are quasi-autonomous bodies and are responsible to Parliament for their functioning.

The pattern of management in public enterprises also is similar in many ways to that of the managing agency or that of subsidiaries of foreign firms. Authority is centralised, and key positions are given to civil servants whose major experience has been in government rather than in industry.

The historical models of management practices provided by managing agency firms, as well as by subsidiaries of foreign companies and public enterprises, were those of centralised authority, with personal and informal relationships at the senior levels, and with key positions held by family members, persons from the "home country" or civil servants, as the case might be.

Family System

In order to understand the basis of industrial leadership and of interpersonal relationships (be they conflict or collaboration) it is useful to have some idea of the Indian family system, especially the concepts of authority and of the relationships among peers and between generations.

The most common form of the family system in India is the joint family. This means that members of more than one nuclear family live together. The head of the family is responsible for and has authority over its other members. The children are taught obedience to their elders. The degree of authority exercised and obedience demanded in the Indian family system seems excessive to Western observers, and many maintain that the authoritarian system in India is responsible for the lack of delegation in management and for the serious delays, inefficiencies and low morale in industry.

I would like to suggest that the functioning of authority in a joint family system is somewhat different from the Western concept. The head of the joint family is called the "karta," the "doer" on behalf of the family. It is a concept of trusteeship. There are many subtle constraints operating which prevent authority from taking the form of giving directions without consultation with senior members of the family. Discussing the functioning of authority in a joint family system, Mr. Prakash Tandon, Chairman of Hindustan Levers, had the following to say:

Contrary to popular belief, a joint family is not built around a central authority.... Like any cognate organisation, a joint family has an authority which directs its affairs but there are two peculiar features. First, the authority is diffused and, second, there is a good deal of consultativeness built into it.

The karta cannot order people about but has to consult. This he usually does by means of a council whenever a major problem arises. For instance, if it is a question of an external transaction like selling a house or acquiring land, or an internal transaction like sending one of the younger members of the family to a university and arranging for the payment of his fees, etc., he will call the younger men together and discuss the matter with them. He cannot just go ahead and decide without their agreement. . . . He is the chairman of the board, where he will take very few steps of any importance without consulting the board; likewise the board will meet quite frequently and informally.

When a problem cannot be solved by mutual agreement within the joint family some senior member of the autonomous group is usually approached— perhaps an old uncle.

Referring to the influence of the joint family system on the outlook of the community Mr. Tandon said—

I find from my personal experience that the traditions of the joint family system permeate into our working institutions and quite often the reactions of people, even managers, to situations of a certain kind are influenced by the norms of the joint family system.
. . . Indian managers like to be kept in touch and consulted more than their Western counterparts. I think this arises from the diffused authority in the joint family, where the young adults are consulted even though they have no powers and most of the decisions are taken by the seniors. Similarly, the younger Indian managers feel that they ought to be in on things and not kept out, whereas their Western counterpart will say that this has nothing to do with me and they have the right to decide because they have the authority.
. . . In the Western industrial culture delegation works better than it does in India because authority and responsibility are more clearly defined and not bedevilled by constant consultation merely to keep people happy.

Since children are brought up in large joint families and since there are many children in each family, they acquire considerable familiarity, practice, and skill in dealing with peer relationships. There is much criticism of each other at the peer level, but there is also a high degree of tolerance, which experience and circumstances have taught. For instance, a long gossip session usually ends up with some such statement as "This is his way of doing things," "It is up to him." The lack of competitiveness on the one hand and the strength of peer relationships on the other are distinctive factors in the Indian social system as compared with Western culture, and have great relevance to the style of leadership and of management practices in Indian business and industry.

The Indian family and social system, therefore, seems to provide sanctions for the exercise of authority—authority which guides rather than coerces; and for critical, tolerant and co-operative peer relationships. Perhaps this could be made clear by an example which is indicative of the quality of authority and peer relationships in the setting of an Indian company.

The chairman of a certain chemical firm in India had to appoint a new managing director. Both he and the outgoing managing director believed that the best choice would be Mr. Ram, the sales director. So he sent for Mr. Ram, and the ensuing conversation provided a good example of the authority relationship between chairman and sales director.
The chairman told Mr. Ram that he himself and the former managing director considered him the ideal person to become managing director. Mr. Ram, however, hesitated to accept, and gave two reasons—he felt inadequate for the position, and he was not in very good health. But he made it clear that if the chairman's considered judgment was that it would be good for the company to have him as its chief executive he would abide by the decision of the chairman. He would be willing to try, although he had no particular desire for better status or salary—indeed, he would not mind working under somebody who had been his subordinate. As he owed his career to the chairman he would not insist on refusing to move from his present job. The chairman thereupon summed up what the sales director had just

said, adding at the end: "But I am not going to make the decision for you; you have to decide for yourself."

The peer relationship was shown on the same occasion in a conversation between the sales director and the production director, who encouraged Mr. Ram to take the post of managing director, and assured him of full support. Lack of competitiveness was very evident here, for the production director knew that if his colleague refused he himself would be offered the post of managing director.

To many Western observers this seems an unusual set of attitudes and implies unusual relationships. Many would doubt if such a person as Mr. Ram ought to be persuaded to become chief executive—indeed, if he had it in him to do the work. In the firm, however, the whole affair was considered quite natural—that the sales director should hesitate and that a colleague who was also a rival should try to persuade him and should assure him of loyalty. As a matter of fact, Mr. Ram was appointed managing director and the firm is prospering.

Ritualism and Stress

Another aspect of social and cultural life which has significance is the role of ritualism. Ritualism has implications affecting ability to live under strain and stress, and to take decisions in conditions of uncertainty. In most cultures there are ceremonies and rituals for the important stages of growth and development: for pregnancy and birth, for adulthood, marriage and death. In the Indian scene, however, many more rituals exist—rituals which seem to impinge on the daily activities of life.

There are two important implications of ritual. First, it reduces anxiety, like other "given" ways of doing things provided by tradition and society. The term "precedent" used in the governmental or commercial bureaucracy serves the same purpose. Rituals and precedents help in the smooth functioning of a system or an organisation, and reduce anxiety and tension relating to new situations. Secondly, ritual prevents the development of the exercise of discretion and the power of decision-making in situations of uncertainty.

The introduction of industrialisation in developing countries entails many profound changes in the social and cultural life of people. The rituals that society had developed to deal with problems of growth and to cope with anxiety and tension are no longer appropriate in a technological age. One of the significant aspects of an industrial society is the rate of technological growth and change. For managers (and those related to them) it means living in an environment which is full of changes and uncertainty. This often leads to anxieties, stresses and strains, and problems of identity. In my opinion the increase in the number of management consultants, management development programmes and conferences shows that attempts are being made to find some institutionalised and ritualised methods of dealing with new knowledge and new stresses.

It is important for persons responsible for management development to be sensitive to the concept of authority and peer relationships as they function in Indian society, to the need for providing practice in decision-making, especially under conditions of uncertainty, and to the need for dealing with stresses and problems of identity.

REQUIREMENTS OF MANAGEMENT DEVELOPMENT PROGRAMMES IN INDIA

New technology requires new knowledge relating to production methods, new distribution and marketing methods, new concepts for organising and planning, new methods of information control and so on. A fund of factual knowledge of management subjects will be indispensable. Business managers and leaders also require an understanding of the social, economic and political environment in which business operates. They need, too, the capacity to discern and evaluate relevant facts in complex systems of inter-relationships, an ability to make choices among alternative methods, and a sense of security and identity so as to sustain the integrative forces in their society. Management development programmes must therefore provide not only new knowledge in management subjects but also a familiarity with management practices as related to a coherent social and cultural system.

In this connection it may be interesting to note how the East India Company encouraged its administrators to acquire familiarity with the social and cultural factors related to administrative and management practices. In the eighteenth century the company encouraged its administrators and officers in India to marry women of the country, set up homes, and raise families. One notice in a gazette from Fort St. George in Madras, for instance, states that the Company offers a bounty of £5 to all men who do this. The custom lasted for a century or so and it was quite usual for the officers of the Company to marry into upper-class Indian families. This sytem offered many advantages to the Company. It also offered security and stability to the administrator and made him feel less of a foreigner in the country. It permitted him to establish relationships with Indian society and to acquire in the process a deep understanding of the social and cultural factors of the country. Knowledge of local customs and languages, of what constitutes injury, insult, or challenge, will affect administrative practices. It can be acquired only through experience in a society, and can rarely be learnt from books.

In my opinion, therefore, management development programmes, especially in developing countries, must provide knowledge of management subjects; knowledge of management practices as related to a social and cultural system; practice in decision-making; opportunities for dealing with stress and problems of identity.

Knowledge of Management Subjects

Knowledge *per se* is free of social and cultural factors. Knowledge of management subjects that derives from the mathematical and behavioural sciences can be given without modification in any culture. The selection of what knowledge and how much of it should be in a programme will be determined largely by the level of the participants and the complexity of the knowledge they require in relation to their businesses. Western consultants often suggest that there is no point in including highly sophisticated quantitative methods or computer information systems if these are not relevant to the educational level or to the industrial base of the country. Although analytical knowledge of a higher order cannot be taught unless the preliminary steps have been learnt, it is wrong to gear the programmes to a level which would have been relevant in the industrialised countries a few decades ago. The developing countries are going in for the latest technology, and management knowledge must be related to it. Also in India, as in many developing countries, there is a very diverse technological base, from the bullock-cart to the supersonics level of technology. Sophisticated technology and related management practices act as a spearhead of development in the country.

Familiarity, Practice and Skill

There are many decisions in management which require familiarity with the complex inter-relationships existing in a culture—a familiarity which comes from an "intuitive" feel of things, and from having been born in a culture. A skilful carpenter who works with various kinds of woods, for example, has a great deal of familiarity with the properties of each. He knows what they will and will not do under certain conditions—at least sufficiently for his purpose of fashioning them into useful objects. He does not have, however, that kind of analytical knowledge about woods sought by the scientist.

Similarly a manager requires knowledge of the kind of phenomena he deals with. In any culture there are certain prescribed and customary ways of doing things. As a person grows up in his culture he learns to relate himself to the other persons around him: he learns the kind of behaviour expected of him and what he can expect from others. These norms are a part of the individual's way of life sanctioned by his society. They are the unstated assumptions, the most sacred and cherished beliefs on which behaviour is based. A manager cannot ignore them. Very often he shares these values with the people he is managing. A management expert who is dealing with a culture entirely different from his own must be sensitive to the "sacred" values and behaviour of a people before he can effectively examine these assumptions and relate them to business and management practices. Many of these assumptions are difficult to identify, and even more difficult to express in words. Although the behavioural sciences have made significant advances, knowledge about society, cultures and their relationship to management practices has not progressed much. That is why familiarity with, or the intuitive understanding of, the environment and the people is important. The role and functioning of authority, the nature of peer relationships, the use of competitive methods, ideas of responsibility, integrity, social values—

all these influence management practices in a given society. For national and international institutions dealing with management education or management development programmes it is very important that case research be done before teaching responsibilities are undertaken. Management subjects like administrative practices, business policy and marketing are especially culture-bound, and require to be understood in relation to the social and economic environment of the country. . . .

Dealing with Stress and Problems of Identity

In the newly independent and developing countries there is a great sense of emotional uprootedness. Their social, political and economic institutions are all being challenged by nationals and foreigners alike; there is a sense of urgency to achieve planned goals; a sense of impatience and sometimes disillusionment with the new goods of industrial society. All this means that persons in developing countries are faced in many ways with greater doubts, anxieties, stresses and strains. Tradition has as yet not sufficiently developed in industrialisation; there is not enough familiarity with new things and with new ways of life. The younger generation and the younger managers cannot fall back on the experience of the previous generation. If the experience and authority of the father have to be discarded, there are a hundred other things that must also be discarded with it, for at present no adequate substitutes exist. New institutions for spreading new knowledge and new institutionalised ways of dealing with new types of stresses become especially important in developing countries—at least in India.

When the learning and relearning is related to basic relationships—as it is in management development programmes—there are serious problems of identity. To quote Margaret Mead, it is as if "a man is in fact being asked to turn his back on the past, to discount previous accomplishments, to divest himself of earlier prides, to disidentify himself with old practices, old allies, and even old loves."[3] Management development and training is not merely a question of new knowledge and new attitudes. It involves a loosening or abandoning of old and cherished ways of doing things, and these changes can lead to emotional crises and to problems of identity.

In India management and management development are very much at the same stage as adolescence in the growth of the adult personality. At critical stages of development persons require a moratorium for experimenting with new attitudes, relationships and alliances. India is now going through such a stage.

Just as technological, social and cultural changes are inevitable in a society moving towards industrialisation, so are the accompanying conditions of stress. There are many different ways of handling stress; management development programmes are among the methods used by managements and executives. Some typical examples of executives who used management development programmes as a moratorium may be cited.

[3] *Cultural patterns and technical change, op. cit.*

Fry is 32 years old and is the president of a small electronics company. He joined his family business six years ago when his father died. He worked two years as vice-president and then became the president. Fry's mother is the chairman of the board of directors and the secretary and treasurer of the company. There is a general manager who has been with the company for many years. Between the chairman and the general manager Fry does not seem to have much of a role. As he said—"I feel like a paper president; I am neither made to feel useful nor wanted in the organisation."

In deciding to come to the programme Fry was trying to escape from the organisational and family conflict and the psychological isolation in the company and the sense of being unwanted. He had arrived at a stage where he felt the need for some critical decisions. Should he declare independence from his mother's interference and authority? Should he let the general manager go? And what would be the implications and consequences of his actions to the company, to himself and to his family relationships? Does he have enough confidence to leave the family business and seek employment elsewhere?

Missumi is 28 years old and is working in an international trading company as an assistant to the vice-president, international division. Missumi's father is the president of the company, and is also chairman and president of a number of other economic and commercial organisations in the country. During the interview Missumi mentioned that he was not sure that he wanted to work in his father's company. He said: "I am watched all the time by everyone and there is no recognition of my worth because I am considered my father's son. I have to be doubly careful and doubly good in everything I do. I feel as if I have been put on the railway track and am going along without any choice in the matter. . . . I have come to the programme to find out: who am I really?" [4]

In many family owned and managed firms, especially when they are small and medium sized, the senior positions are occupied by family members. The position in the management hierarchy depends to some extent on age and the position in the family hierarchy. The strengths and weaknesses of family relationships influence the working relationships in the firm.

In general, however, young executives in family businesses live in an atmosphere of conflict, torn between obligations to the family and to the family business, between the social pressures of family and community, the norms of the profession, and the demands of technological culture. Such conflicts are found among many young executives, especially in India, where 80 per cent. of businesses are family owned, and where family obligations play an important part. Young executives, therefore, especially in India, need a sanctioned moratorium for minimising stress and anxiety, for rejecting old roles and experimenting with new ones, and for exploring new relationships and new careers. . . .

THE ROLE OF THE EXPERT AND INSTRUCTOR

Margaret Mead, in discussing the role of the foreign expert in technical assistance, mentions "the question of the extent to which the special preoccupations and value systems of the members of international teams, drawn from Western cultures or educated in Western values, affect the work which such teams are able to do." [5] She also points out that—

---

[4] K. Chowdhry, "Management development programs: moratorium for executives," in *Human Organization* (New York: Society for Applied Anthropology, 1964), Vol. 23, No. 3, pp. 256–57.

[5] *Cultural patterns and technical change, op. cit.,* p. 19.

The objectivity which combines respect for the values of another culture, a determination to bring about change in ways which promote the mental health of the population, and a certain amount of detachment from the clash of old and new values going on within the culture, are invaluable assets which come from long experience in working with members of other cultures. Many of the members of technical assistance teams will not, however, have had that experience, that sum total of memories of felicitous suggestions and disastrous mis-steps, of plans that misfired and plans that succeeded inexplicably, which make up the delicate certainty of the experienced expert.[6]

These statements indicate to some extent how complicated and delicate a task is the introduction of change and of management development into old cultures rooted not only in the habits of the people but also in the relationships between generations, in the way the child is hushed, rewarded and punished, in the vocabulary of the people, and so on.

The role of an instructor in management development programmes in developing countries must be seen in three contexts: first, the changing social, economic and political conditions, and the accompanying doubts, stresses and strains; secondly, the limited existing knowledge of management subjects; and thirdly, the application of knowledge and practices developed in one culture to another. This has two implications.

The instructor or the expert in the field of management education, especially when working in a different culture, cannot play the traditional role of imparting wisdom or of knowing all the answers. He needs to discard the accustomed role of dominance, of being the licensee of knowledge. This is one of the most difficult things he has to do—to create a new role for himself for which there is no model. But it seems that, in management development programmes in developing countries, he must either create this new role, encompassing compassion, humility, and objectivity, or fail.

As we have seen, management education requires some knowledge that is objective and is based on research, but to a large extent it consists of clinical insights. This means that instructors dealing with management development must relinquish the kind of security that comes from employing more objective methods. Just as we want the participants to relinquish the security of old ways of thinking and doing things, so also we want the instructor to relinquish the security of old styles of teaching, based on authority of position and objective knowledge. The security and satisfaction derived from professional omnipotence are difficult to give up. The instructor must come to the class with no predetermined or ready-made solutions: he must follow the Socratic method of encouraging dialogues, of keeping an atmosphere of learning on both sides.

The foreign expert brings with him an intellectual selectivity which often blinds him to some of the relevant meanings of experience in a given culture, but he also brings an "uncorrupted" way of noticing things which escape the attention of those born into the culture. To observe feelings, relationships, or ways of doing things in what is to him a foreign culture, and to pick out significant meanings, an expert must have first learnt to recognise them in his own experience.

---

[6] *Ibid.*, p. 15.

Management development programmes often convey to the participants an impression of censure of their existing ways. In the process of examining old and new management practices, insufficient attention is paid to helping the individual to sort out his conflicts, clarify his crucial choices, and find a new identity in the new society that is being created.

I therefore suggest that every instructor and expert needs to acquire—

1. A respect for the dignity of the culture he works in.

2. A new role that is based not on authority of status but on objective knowledge.

3. A tolerance for the conflicts and uncertainties of the participants, and the strength to withstand his own conflicts, insecurity and uncertainty as they arise in the unfamiliar surroundings of a new culture.

4. An understanding of his own motives.

5. A sense of responsibility for the mental health and welfare of those he tries to change and develop.

If programmes of management development question some of the more crucial aspects of family, social and institutional relationships, it is equally important that those responsible for such programmes maintain a continuing relationship with the organisations they are trying to develop and change. Many young executives come to programmes to settle questions of responsibility and obligation, to clarify roles and relationships, and to seek knowledge. Once the participants have joined the programme the instructor cannot escape the responsibility of working through some of the problems and concerns they bring. Opportunities for further help should be provided if the participant or the organisation so desires. It would be quite wrong to leave the participants in an unresolved emotional state or one of conflict. An institutional relationship where the instructor has some kind of continuing commitment, rather than one just for the time span of the programme, is essential.

The instructor, and even more the foreign expert, are looked upon by the participant in the programme with a peculiar mixture of overesteem and mistrust. They react to this by an equally peculiar mixture of desperately wanting to live up to an image of themselves, and of anger against responsibility they did not seek and find difficult to meet. We all bestow this kind of an image on people in significant positions—superiors, doctors, leaders, and even adversaries. This transfer of an early "father image" to later individuals and events has been called "transference" by psychoanalysts, and the reaction to it "counter-transference." It is of great importance that the instructor and the expert realise what is happening, and do not permit themselves the luxury of playing "God" or the "autocratic," "benevolent" or "karta" father, for these very relationships are being tested in the learning situation. The instructor, especially in a foreign culture, will be confronted, sometimes above and sometimes well below the threshold of awareness, with the conflict between the desire for an emotional participation and acceptance and the rigour required to be vigilant about his own motives.

selection 34

The Manager in the Polish Enterprise: A Study of Accommodation under Conditions of Role Conflict*

Solomon John Rawin

The subject of this study is the manager in the state-owned factory in Poland. The state-owned sector represents only one-third of all industrial enterprises of the country, but its weight in the national economy is overwhelming; it accounts for 89 per cent of gross industrial output and employs 86 per cent of factory labour. Virtually all larger enterprises—those with one hundred employees or more—belong to this sector. This analysis is centred on these enterprises; the medium and large size factories that form the so-called "key industries," and are subject to direct central control. In this category the typical manager is in charge of a factory employing between two hundred and two thousand workers, which is engaged in one of the main industries of the country, such as heavy machinery, mining, textiles, and chemicals. The analysis presented in this article may not apply to the small category of managers—those in charge of some huge enterprises of exceptional national importance—who enjoy a semi-ministerial status.

THE ENTERPRISE AND THE CENTRAL CONTROL SYSTEM

Two main levels of organization may be distinguished within the industrial structure: the central control system and the enterprise. At the top of the central control system is the national Plan Commission and the ministerial Economic Committee. Over-all economic planning, with yearly and long-term production targets for each branch of industry, emanate from there. Production targets are channelled through respective ministries and "Industrial Associations" to individual enterprises. The task of the Industrial Associations is to provide each enterprise with detailed production plans and directives, to co-ordinate procurement of raw materials and equipment, as well as the distribution of products. The Industrial Association represents also the immediate level of control and supervision.

*From *British Journal of Industrial Relations,* March, 1965, pp. 1–16.

The enterprise's output, the assortment of goods to be produced, the input of labour and material, allocation of funds for wage expenditures and for investment, the programme for technological improvements and, in general, all essential elements of economic activity are prescribed by means of quantitative specifications known as "indicators." A set of indicators represents the production tasks, and provides also the standards for evaluating the performance of each enterprise. "Economic incentives"—monetary rewards for attainment of targets and penalties for underachievement—are attached to each indicator. Thus the total amount of pay-roll, and particularly the earnings of the managerial and administrative staff, depend on the degree of fulfilment of the plan.

Within the general framework of the economy the enterprise is regarded as a closed system. Indicators are allocated, and performance is evaluated for the enterprise as a whole; units below the enterprise level, production shops and technical and administrative departments, are considered as an integral part of the enterprise, and any allocation of tasks and distribution of rewards as an internal matter.

This special position of the enterprise is reflected in the formal status accorded to it. Though part and parcel of the state economy, the enterprise has a legal status of its own, somewhat similar to that of a corporate body in a capitalist society. It has the right to enter into business agreements with other legal persons, to acquire and dispose of property, and in financial matters it is considered as a separate entity with its own accountability.

The internal organization of the enterprise is built on the principle of the personal responsibility of the man in charge. At the top level, the general manager, an appointee of the ministry, is responsible, both in the administrative and the judicial sense, for all activities in the factory. Delegation of authority, even when officially provided for, does not reduce this personal responsibility.

A corollary of the principle of personal responsibility is the formal position of the manager as the sole source of authority in the factory. His orders are binding; neither the statutory powers of the workers in regard to self-government nor the inherent prerogatives of lower-level management have comparable authority. The hiring and dismissal of personnel (with the exception of a few high-level executives who derive their appointment from the Industrial Association) rests with the manager.

A characteristic feature of the organization of work is the pattern of integrated control on each level of command. Thus, for instance, the superintendent of a shop has under his control, besides the regular production personnel, a full staff of auxiliaries such as technologists, production analysts, repair men, etc. This system follows the principle of one-man responsibility, and tends to make each production unit a miniature replica of the factory organization.[1] In its

---

[1] Compare the following description of the Soviet factory organization: "The organization of the shop is like a microcosm of the firm itself, with the shop chief as the microcosmic director. He has a staff of assistants such as a shop chief engineer, a shop accountant, a shop mechanic (for maintenance work) and a shop planner." Joseph S. Berliner, *Factory and Manager in the USSR* (Cambridge: Harvard University Press, 1957), p. 15.

general outline the organization of a factory follows accurately the hierarchical patterns of the state bureaucracy. The position of the manager provides the only exception:

> The factory manager performs a dual function in the socialist industry. On the one hand, he is an official of the state administration in charge of the enterprise. . . . On the other hand, he performs economic tasks related to his role as head of the enterprise. . . . As an official of the administration he is limited by orders [of the central authorities]; in his activities as the head of an enterprise he is guided by economic considerations.[2]

THE ROLE CONFLICT SITUATION

This dual role of the manager is directly related to the concept of the enterprise as an integral part of state property and, at the same time, as an independent economic sub-system. The manager is placed within two sets of contingencies. As a functionary of the state he has his tasks circumscribed by his role within the industrial hierarchy; he is required to follow orders and regulations imposed within the framework of a unified economic structure. Above all, he is expected to treat his own enterprise merely as a component, one among many, of the national economy. At the same time, however, as the head of a self-contained entrepreneurial unit the manager finds himself facing business contingencies in some ways similar to those of the capitalist world. He has to compete with other enterprises for supplies of material, equipment, and manpower; in general, he is bound to direct all his efforts towards the maximization of gains, as defined in terms of plan indicators. The manager is expected to combine the role of an employee of the socialist state with the residual functions of an independent entrepreneur.[3]

These two concepts should complement one another and act as a mutual reinforcement. In practice they seldom coincide, and often conflict. This is due primarily to the inadequacy of the indicator system as a measure of performance. The problem raises some basic questions about the economic system, and is a major concern of economists and the political leadership.[4]

> Socialist enterprises, . . . in order to meet the needs of the society, have to fulfil their targets within the framework of the National Plan. However, the specific goals of an enterprise may, to a certain degree, conflict with national goals. This is particularly true with

---

[2] J. Kwejt, *Elementy teorii przedsiebiorstwa*, as quoted in Aleksander Matejko, *Socjologia zakladu pracy* (Warsaw: Wiedza Powszechna, 1961), p. 250.

[3] A reflection of the entrepreneurial role of the manager is the claim to the "right to risk" as a prerequisite of managerial effectiveness; see "Prawo do ryzyka," *Polityka*, No. 7 (17 February, 1962). During the Fourth *Plenum* of the Central Committee of the Party, Deputy Prime Minister Jaroszewicz spoke about "the need . . . to support those who risk, those who think about innovations and whose thought extends outside the circle of existing technical achievements." Matejko, *op. cit.*, p. 255.

[4] Cf. John Michael Montias, *Central Planning in Poland* (New Haven: Yale University Press, 1962), particularly chap. 6. For a general analysis of this problem under conditions of directed economy the reader may be referred to: Janos Kornai, *Overcentralization in Economic Administration* (London: Oxford University Press, 1959); A. Nove, "Economic Rationality and Soviet Growth," *Cahiers de l'Institut de Science Economique Appliquée*, No. 104, Série G (August, 1960), pp. 5–31; P. J. D. Wiles, *The Political Economy of Communism* (Oxford: Basil Blackwell, 1962).

regard to the system of evaluating performance, and in connection with remuneration of employees, especially of those within the managerial category.[5]

One of the sources of centralizing tendencies is the fact that many essential elements of the present system of planning and incentive bring the interests of the enterprise and its personnel into conflict with the interests of the national economy.[6]

This situation furnishes the setting for the role conflict in the managerial position. Some generalized patterns of managerial behaviour, pointing to the character and extent of this condition may be distinguished.

1. *Concealment of reserves.* Probably the role conflict most openly manifests itself during the process of planning and allocating production targets to individual enterprises. As an employee of the national economic organization, and in terms of his over-all commitments, the manager should aim at maximizing his enterprise's contribution to the national economy. But in his capacity as the head of an enterprise, he is interested in keeping his economic indicators at the lowest possible level. The lower the assigned targets, the more chance the enterprise has of attaining them. Because of this the manager tends to resort to "concealing the reserves": which in its most direct form means under-reporting the productive capacity and resources of his factory.

This condition leads to the paradoxical situation whereby the manager, despite his intimate knowledge of his enterprise's productive capacity, is virtually excluded from participation in economic planning. At best, he is assigned a peripheral role; his point of view is considered by his superiors as that of an outsider.

2. *Restriction of performance.* The pattern of concealing reserves, a practice essentially illegal but prevalent in all areas of economic activity, extends beyond simple under-reporting of available resources. In typical cases, plan analysts at the ministerial and Industrial Association level have only a superficial knowledge of the productive conditions in factories; they work on the general assumption of inherent capacity of the industry for continuous improvement of performance, and resort to a semi-automatic increase of a more or less fixed percentage, from one year to another. In this way, high performance in one year, due perhaps to exceptionally favourable and unrepeatable conditions, is penalized with unrealistically augmented tasks for the future. A prudent manager will therefore apply restrictions on performance in all entrepreneurial activities; he will maintain output at the level of, or just slightly above, the plan targets; he will use up all the allocated resources such as finances, manpower, with little consideration for savings. In general, he will aim at average, rather than above average results. The problem has been stated by one writer as follows:

What is the policy of an enterprise towards the Industrial Association . . . ? This policy is based on the precept: "Don't put yourself out!" This can be seen from the consistency with which plans are executed at 100 per cent or 100.1 per cent, though much higher levels could be achieved.

---

5 Bronislaw Minc, *Ekonomia polityczna socjalizmu* (Warsaw: Panstwowe Wydawnictwo Naukowe, 1961), p. 73.

6 W. Szyndler Glowacki, "Co hamuje demokratyzacje," *Zycie Gospodarcze*, No. 27 (8 July, 1962).

Enterprises are obliged to act this way in defence of their interests (or their bonuses), because an achievement of, say, 108 per cent would result in a 10 per cent increase in plans for next year. . . . This peculiar "manœuvring" leads to concealment of reserves. . . . There is no need to bring forward examples of this situation; everybody, from the plan analysts in the factory to the officials in the Ministry of Heavy Industry, is aware of this.[7]

One of the by-products of this behaviour is a kind of double book-keeping to which managers have to resort continually in order to maintain their control over the factory. "In order to know the true state of reserves at their disposal, managers, besides providing 'official' information for the use of the Industrial Association, collect data for their own use only."[8]

3. *Indicator substitution.* As criteria of performance, indicators form an interrelated system, but each indicator carries with it a separate reward–penalty factor. Thus, it is possible to offset under-achievement in one respect by over-achievement in another. This leaves the manager with ample room for manœuvring, by means of what might be described as indicator substitution. Depending on individual factory conditions, some indicators may be easier to achieve or may prove to be more rewarding than others, and managers are usually inclined to concentrate their efforts on these. In those instances too, economic rationality gives precedence to the requirements of plan fulfilment. For example, a manager may keep down the cost of manpower by stripping his maintenance department of the necessary labour if he finds that the rewards for fulfilling (or the penalty for not fulfilling) the manpower-cost target exceed the penalties for neglecting the equipment conservation rules. Or he may inflate the monetary value of gross output by using excessively costly material.[9] The most common form of indicator substitution is probably over-fulfilment of output targets at the cost of quality and assortment of produced goods.

The common characteristic of all these manipulations is that, while they help the enterprise to maintain a satisfactory level of performance, they tend to frustrate the central planning mechanism, and produce results not intended by the government and often detrimental to the economy. The practice of substitution, when regarded from the national economy point of view, turns incentives into disincentives; an enterprise may attain a high performance rating though its actual contribution may be mediocre or even negative.

The conflict between the interests of the enterprise and the interests of the wider community is part of the everyday reality of managerial activity. On the face of it, the Polish manager seems to be confronted by a situation not dissimilar to that of his capitalist counterpart. This similarity, however, is largely spurious. Under capitalism, the problem is generally openly recognized and sufficiently institutionalized to prevent, except under unusual conditions, any

---

[7] Jozef Rostek, "Zmierzch taktyki manewru?" *Zycie Gospodarcze,* No. 48 (1 December, 1963).

[8] Karol Szwarc, "Dyrektorzy o analizie," *Zycie Gospodarcze,* No. 17 (28 April, 1963).

[9] An employee of an automobile factory notes: "Only because of reasons outside our control we don't use gold for producing car bodies. . . . This would allow us to increase our output tremendously. Technological advancement that brings savings in material is not to the advantage of the enterprise." Antoni Gutowski, "Magia wskaznikow," *Polityka,* No. 39 (28 September, 1963).

serious conflict of norms. Maximization of profits is the avowed goal of the capitalistic enterprise, and the manager has no difficulty in pinpointing his commitments. The situation is different in a socialist society. Here, maximization of profits and the financial gains of individuals are regarded as secondary and incidental by-products of the main goal, which is the production of goods for society at large. The accepted concept of a manager of a state enterprise is that of a public servant committed to furthering that goal. And no manager who shares this general outlook can avoid a sense of transgression in his daily activities.

The incompatibilities in the managerial role bring the manager in direct conflict with the legal system of his own organization. Operating on a purely business basis, he is often faced with tasks for whose accomplishment the bureaucratic structure is able to make little provision. These tasks vary greatly: they may include such daily routines as cultivating friendly relations, through gifts, entertainment and personal favours, with suppliers of goods essential for maintaining the uninterrupted flow of production; they may involve shifting funds earmarked for less essential purposes, such as welfare projects or cultural activities, towards payments for unscheduled and unauthorized overtime work, indispensable for the fulfilment of plans. Even though these operations may appear justified in terms of the exigencies of production and form part of general practice, officially they remain unacknowledged and, at best, carry with them a tinge of illegality.[10]

This situation is exacerbated through the propensity of ministries and other authorities to issue minute directives and regulations, sometimes contradictory and often manifestly unsuited for implementation.

Under these conditions the manager's freedom of action means not much more than a choice between two sets of directives: some to abide by and others to ignore. Usually this involves a close evaluation of possible consequences, a keen perception of priorities, and an ability to shift policy according to the order of the day. Press articles, enunciations of Party leaders, and particularly resolutions of the *Plenum* of the Central Committee supply important clues as to the appropriate decision. Periodic "campaigns" aiming at some particular problem, for example over-employment in industry, the atrophy of workers' self-government, or the substandard quality of consumer goods, provide a guide that no manager can afford to ignore. He has to be able to adjust his policy

---

10 "The present system of procurement of raw materials is unsatisfactory, and it forces managers into illegal practices. I know instances when purchasing agents were provided by their managers with two sets of travel orders: one to cover the actual cost of the trip, and another to pay for a dinner with the warehouseman (of the supply firm). . . . A manager gave me the following explanation: 'Should I ever get caught I will be sent to prison. But two hundred zloty (i.e. the cost of the fictitious travel order) does not mean much, and if I don't issue two travel orders I shall have to close the factory for lack of material. . . . One day lost may result in failure of our production plans. . . . Thus I prefer the lesser evil, and I hope that nobody will find out about the cheating.' There are hundreds of managers in this situation, and all are criminals. They know about this, and they should be hauled into court. But then, who would run the factories in their place?" Janusz Zelezik, "Taniec zonglerow," *Polityka*, No. 4 (27 January, 1962).

at short notice, always keeping in mind the uncertainty of his legal situation.

The journal *Polityka,* initiating discussion on this subject, poses the following question:

Is it possible to work efficiently and, at the same time to abide by the variety of regulations, ordinances, orders, and verbal and written decisions, emanating from various ministries, from the Plan Commission, from the Industrial Associations, and from other sources? Where should the line between the praiseworthy dynamism and the personal initiative of management, on the one hand, and arbitrariness, on the other, be drawn? And where does arbitrariness end and crime commence? [11]

Outright arrests and prison terms for managers are at present much less of an occupational hazard than they were before 1956. Nevertheless, few managers are able to operate within the confines of legality. Routine inspections by central authorities always carry with them an element of uncertainty, and there is no way of telling how an irregularity, though seemingly insignificant, may be interpreted. "From the formal point of view, there is not one manager in Poland who could not be arrested for neglect of his duties according to the letter and intent [of the code]." [12]

PATTERNS OF ACCOMMODATION

The manager's reaction to this situation is to develop a system of defences that could provide him with reasonable security and at the same time allow some room for exercising his own judgement. Essentially, he sees it as a matter of dodging the ever-present legal and administrative pitfalls without being reduced to immobility through fear of a false step. Subtlety in manipulating rules and skill in manœuvring within the bureaucratic maze are essential.

There are two main rules which a successful dodger always keeps in mind. One rule is generally recognized under the pattern of *asekuranctwo:* roughly translated as "hedging." [13] The other rule calls for tight control over all lines of communication between the enterprise and the outside world.

The pattern of hedging involves minimum exposure in decision-making. Ideally, the manager-dodger would like to be covered against personal responsibility at all times, preferably by having all his decisions approved in advance by his superiors. However, this is not always possible. In daily factory practice there are many decisions to be taken *ad hoc,* with no time to seek the necessary endorsement. Other operations may be of doubtful legal validity or contrary to established rules, and the manager may prefer to keep his superiors in the dark.

The most obvious safeguard available to a manager bent on hedging is limiting his activities to routine action along established lines. Innovations in production,

---

11 J. Smietanski, "Obywatel dyrektor a dyrektor partyzant," *Polityka,* No. 1 (6 January, 1962).

12 W. Korzeniowski, "Kontrola ale jaka?" *Zycie Warszawy,* 7 November, 1962. Cf. "It seems a fair generalization that all Soviet managers are *ipso facto* criminals according to Soviet law." David Granick, *The Red Executive* (London: Macmillan, 1960), p. 43.

13 Compare the pattern of "strakhovka" in Soviet enterprises; Berliner, *op. cit.,* pp. 76–113.

technological or organizational changes and, in general, anything that is outside the approved scheme and calls for independent decision will be avoided. And whenever decision-making is unavoidable the manager will endeavour to share the responsibility with other members of the staff. Also, at least a formal endorsement of the "social factor" of the enterprise—the Party organization and the workers' self-government—will be sought. This does not reduce the formal responsibility of the manager, but provides the advantage of a united front against external assault and discourages snipers from within the enterprise.

From the latter point of view, intra-factory loyalty is a primary condition for the proper functioning of the managerial structure. In a situation where the enterprise cannot stand too close a scrutiny, the manager depends considerably on the good will of his staff. His ability to act effectively within the factory and to maintain his position *vis-à-vis* the central administration hinges on his control over the personnel and over all organized activities in the enterprise.

This control may be easily upset. Any complaint, no matter how trivial, an anonymous letter to the Central Committee or to the state prosecutor's office, or information leaked out to a newspaper reporter, may result in an investigation of unpredictable ramifications.

The structure of industry is conceived in terms of multiple lines of communication and control. The Party, with its factory organizations hierarchically linked with the centre of political power, provides the main framework, parallel to that of the general administration. The Trade Union councils, and to a certain degree the workers' councils, furnish secondary channels linking the enterprise with the central control system. Individual members of the factory staff, those in intermediary and higher managerial positions, have their access to central authorities institutionally provided. The manager, in order to secure his own control, has to neutralize these channels.

The most direct way to achieve this aim is for the manager to place men of his choice in all positions of significance. The pattern of recruitment to managerial and supervisory jobs in factories reflects this orientation. There exists a central system of allocating technical manpower through ministries and Industrial Associations; generally, however, it is regarded as of limited effectiveness. The prevalent pattern of filling vacancies is through private "connections" and recommendations. A technician reports on his experience of job hunting in the textile industry:

Only after I became unemployed did I realize the importance of connections and pull. For two months I kept applying for work. The Central Board and the Employment Office were not able to find anything . . . ; they suggested I should look for a job on my own, or accept manual work. I went to all larger enterprises . . . , I replied to various ads. in the press, but without any success. One day I went to an old school mate, a man in an important position, and told him about my plight. He telephoned to one of his friends and, indeed, within ten minutes I was on my way to negotiate for a job as a shop superintendent.[14]

---

[14] Salomea Kowalewska and Zdzislaw Kowalewski, "Inteligencja techniczna klasy robotniczej," in Jan Szczepanski (ed.), *Wyksztalcenie a pozycja spoleczna inteligencji,* Vol. 1 (Lodz: Panstwowe Wydawnictwo Naukowe, 1959), pp. 290–91.

The traditional inclination among bureaucrats to exchange personal favours finds ample reinforcement in the working of the managerial bureaucracy; it forms an important element in the manager's self-protection system. A member of a manager's staff brought in privately may be counted on to show more loyalty than one recruited through impersonal channels. The persistence of "clique" relationships (a term commonly applied to any group of workers with close informal ties), despite constant efforts of the hierarchy to break them up, may be explained by their functional character within the informal industrial organization.

Another element in the manager's system of defences calls for the establishment of a *modus vivendi* with the "social factor" of the enterprise: the Party organization and the workers' self-government.[15] These socio-political organizations form a quasi-independent structure within the organizational framework of the enterprise. Their formal position reflects the political contingencies and ideological commitments of the régime; they are endowed with broad prerogatives, largely overlapping the authority of management.[16] In fact, a serious attempt to implement the legal provisions concerning workers' self-government would inevitably provide an ever-present area of conflict and conceivably could render the organizational structure of the enterprise unworkable. Indeed, during the years 1956-7, when the newly emerged workers' councils tried to assert their rights within the administration, clashes between management on the one side and Party activists and labour leaders on the other were frequent and had a disorganizing effect upon the industry. Only the unequivocal assertion of managerial supremacy provided a workable solution.

The background for this solution was furnished through the process of coalescence between management and the factory Party organization. In a sense—through advancing Party members of labour origin to positions of management—this process had started early after the war. After 1956 it gained momentum

---

[15] The three organizations, the Party organization, the Trade Union factory council, and the workers' council, form together the "Conference of Workers' Self-Government." The structure of the system of self-government varies somewhat from factory to factory, and its terminology is not clearly defined. In everyday parlance the term "self-government" refers to the Conference as well as to the workers' council only.

For the history and role of self-government after 1956 see: Jiri Kolaja, *A Polish Factory* (Lexington: University of Kentucky Press, 1960); Janina Miedzinska, "Social Policy under Gomulka," *Soviet Survey,* No. 35 (January–March, 1961), pp. 39–45; Adolf Sturmthal, *Workers' Councils* (Cambridge, Mass.: Harvard University Press, 1964).

[16] According to the 1958 legislation, self-government has, apart from matters directly related to workers' welfare, the following responsibilities: "(1) to establish the basic lines of activities of the enterprise (evaluation and approval of plans, decisions regarding major investments from decentralized funds . . .); (2) to supervise the activities of the enterprise and of its administration (verification of financial reports, analysis and evaluation of operations, scrutiny of daily activities . . .); (3) to improve the economic performance of the enterprise . . . ; (4) to distribute the Enterprise Fund, to issue regulations regarding working conditions, to vote . . . operational plans, etc." Jozef Balcerek and Leszek Gilejko, "Rozwoj samorzadu robotniczego," in Bobrowski *et al., op. cit.,* p. 106.

The same legislation confirmed the status of the manager as the supreme authority within the enterprise. Provisions were made for appeal from managerial decisions to higher levels of control. However, "the self-government does not exercise its rights to appeal, despite frequent infringement of its prerogatives." *Ibid.,* p. 122.

and, with the virtual elimination of "advanced workers" from managerial jobs, acquired a different significance.

An understanding of this development is provided by Bauman in his report on Party organizations in industry.[17] His investigation took place during the years 1959–60, and covered 107 large factories, each with a Party organization of over 400 members. The study was focused on the occupational distribution of Party members and Party *aktyw.*

Foremen supplied the largest share of Party membership in proportion to their numbers among all employees; unskilled and skilled labour were the least represented. The data regarding the Party *aktyw*–the category comprising the leadership of the organization and all those who take part in activities besides routine meetings—were particularly significant. Here the participation of manual labour was negligible. In proportion to their numbers in the factory, engineers and technicians—the category which is most closely identified with management—provided 13.3 times as many activists as unskilled workers, and 5 times as many as skilled workers; foremen provided 24 times and 9 times as many, respectively. The share of the administrative and office staff was smaller than that of the two supervisory categories, but significantly higher than that of manual labour.

The over-representation of foremen, and to a certain degree also that of white-collar workers, may be explained by the practice of elevating Party members from manual jobs to lower supervisory and non-manual positions. However, the high proportion of the engineering category reflects the prominence of their position within the Party organization. All tasks of importance, particularly tasks which put the Party unit directly in touch with management and with higher authorities, were allocated to them:

Technicians with secondary and above secondary education . . . were charged mainly with tasks of propaganda and political agitation; internal organizational jobs were given to activists with incomplete university education; . . . work in mass organizations was usually carried out by young white-collar workers. . . . Older manual workers, with long standing in the factory and in the Party, were assigned to social activities outside the factory. Engineers with higher education were in charge of organization and control of production.[18]

The main factor in this development is undoubtedly the primacy of economic considerations in the general Party policy. The Party bureaucracy see their own tasks and the tasks of the organizations under their control in terms of economic achievements, chiefly through the furthering of industrial development. Inevitably this leads them to the adoption of the managerial perspective of industrial problems. The convergence of the Party line of activities and that of industrial management is unmistakable. With this, the trend to recruit the Party *aktyw*

---

[17] Zygmunt Bauman, "Czlonkowie Partii i aktyw partyjny w zakladzie produkcyjnym," *Kultura i Spoleczenstwo,* Vol. 6, No. 4 (October–December, 1962), pp. 55–69. An English version by the same author was published under the title "Social Structure of the Party Organization in Industrial Works," *Polish Sociological Bulletin,* No. 3–4, Warsaw (July–December, 1962), pp. 50–64. In some respects the English version differs from the original; throughout this article references will be made to the Polish paper.

[18] *Ibid.,* p. 67.

from the ranks of engineers and other managerial categories is understandable; they may be relied upon to concur with the Party policy to a much higher degree than any other category; and they are unique in their ability to provide expert knowledge in areas of major preoccupation of Party committees and rallies.

Factory management welcomes this attitude and encourages members of the staff to join the *aktyw*. The manager and all those in positions of responsibility see in the fusion of the Party organization and management a logical solution for the dichotomy of leadership. To them many activities of the Party *aktyw*, especially those concerning labour–management relations and production organization, appear as a normal extension of managerial functions. In this way the organization that originally was conceived as an instrument of central control and which formed a constant threat to the manager's freedom of action was turned into an effective support of managerial authority. Bauman describes the relations between the Party and the technical intelligentsia in the following manner:

According to all indications [engineers and technicians of the younger generation] represent the most Party-oriented and active category among industrial workers. . . . They introduced new values and attitudes into Party activities.
. . . .
This convergence is due to the dynamism of the Party policy. The Party and the technical intelligentsia found a common language in their struggle against irrationality in economic life, and in their drive towards sober and purposeful management. . . . The Party became the spokesman for goals which have their institutionalization in the social role of the Technological Man. . . . On the basis of our investigation it is possible to hypothesize that a fusion of the Party organization and of the technical intelligentsia of the factory takes place at present. This fusion adds weight to the engineer's outlook in matters concerning the enterprise. . . . It introduces essential changes in the traditional style of work of the Party factory organization, in the distribution of power relations within the organization, in its interests, its language, and its modes of operation.[19]

With Party activists occupying all key positions in the workers' self-government, the evolution of Party–management relations provides the pattern for all organized activities in the factory. The Trade Union factory organization ceased to be an independent factor early after the consolidation of political power during the 'forties. Its functions became purely administrative, mainly limited to welfare activities, and its influence among labour and within the factory organization remains negligible. Administratively, the factory council forms part of the state-controlled national Trade Union organization; in everyday activities, it follows the lead of the Party organization, and for practical purposes it is considered as part of the factory administration.

The position of the workers' council is in many respects similar. There is a statutory requirement that at least two-thirds of the members of workers' councils should be recruited from manual labour. But even in those factories where this requirement is adhered to, the effective leadership rests in the hands of non-manual employees, mostly Party members. According to a survey performed

---

[19] *Ibid.*, pp. 68–69.

on behalf of the Central Committee, a typical presidium of the council, consisting of between eleven and fourteen members, comprises two or three manual
workers only.[20] "The majority are non-manual employees, usually occupying
managerial positions such as heads of departments, shops, etc."[21] The pattern of
co-operation among members of the council "differs very little from the hierarchical relation existing within the formal organization of the enterprise."[22]

There is seldom any attempt to extend self-government outside the narrow
area of workers' welfare, cultural activities, or propaganda. In matters concerning production and administration self-government is limited to formal approval
of managerial decisions, a rubber-stamping procedure often taking place at semi-
private meetings between the manager and the selected leaders of the three
organizations. Public meetings of workers, a major source of embarrassment and
vexation to managers in the past, are rarely held and treated as a formality;
would-be critics and challengers to managerial authority have to be prepared to
face the concerted reaction of the amalgamated leadership.

Factory labour recognizes this situation and accepts that self-government is
merely an extension of the administration. There is a consensus among social
analysts, including Party writers, regarding the extent of alienation among
workers and the absence of identification with the system of self-government.[23]

The situation is not always under the manager's control, and some intra-
factory conflicts do extend outside the confines of the enterprise and are
referred to higher authorities. As a rule, these conflicts reflect interpersonal
friction among members of the staff and have little relevance to administrative
policy. It is probably safe to say that whenever a division between management
and the Party organization, or in the system of self-government, is brought into
the open, it serves as a cover for a personal struggle between warring cliques. One
of the main preoccupations of the manager seems to be mitigating internal
squabbles; keeping them within the confines of the enterprise and, above all,
dodging personal involvement.[24]

---

20 Balcerek and Gilejko, *op. cit.*, p. 108.

21 *Ibid.*, p. 109.

22 J. Balcerek, "Istota samorzadu robotniczego," in B. Biegeleisen-Zelazowski *et al., Jak
pracuje czlowiek* (Warsaw: Ksiazka i Wiedza, 1961), p. 512.

23 In a survey sponsored by the Economic Council, workers were asked the question:
"Whose interests, mainly, does the workers' self-government represent?" About 14 per cent
of respondents felt that the self-government represented the interests of labour, 44 per cent
felt that it represented the interests of management or of the enterprise, and 42 per cent
were undecided or failed to answer. Wladyslaw Doberski, "Swiatlocienie samorzadu robotniczego," *Zycie Gospodarcze,* No. 31 (30 July, 1961).
An analysis of self-government activities concludes: "The workers' self-government,
deprived of support of labour, gives in relatively easily to the pressure of management and,
in extreme cases, becomes an addition to management." J. Balcerek and L. Gilejko, "Kilka
problemow dzialalnosci samorzadu robotniczego," *Nowe Drogi,* Vol. 16, No. 3 (March,
1962), p. 26.

24 An engineer occupying a high position in industry claims: "No manager is able to
exercise his functions in full. He cannot make any decision on his own; he is limited by
contradictory orders and hampered by seemingly democratic institutions. Each enterprise
is full of intrigues, animosity and envy. People complain to the Industrial Association, to
the Ministry, or to the Central Committee of the Party, about the most trifling grievances,
often without any foundation. . . . Members of the self-government are busy with details,

CONCLUSION

These are the general conditions under which the process of accommodation within the industrial structure takes place. This accommodation may be seen primarily as a compromise between the traditional centralism of the Soviet-type command economy and the exigencies of industrial production. The formal structure calls for centralized direction and subjects the manager to day-by-day scrutiny by the multiple agencies of central control. Yet the manager is able to frustrate this control and, more often than not, to convert its agencies—the factory Party organization, the system of self-government, and his own staff— into instruments of his independence.

The remarkable thing about this process is that it takes place with the support of the Party hierarchy and with the acquiescence of the central control bureaucracy. In practice, though not in theory, managers are granted considerable latitude in the internal affairs of their factories; without this latitude the process of accommodation would hardly be possible. In that sense the compromise is a concession exacted by the decentralizing forces in industry; it reflects the tacit recognition of the inadequacy of the formal organization and the inconsistency of the enterprise's position within the economic structure. Probably more than anything else, the coalescence of the Party organization with factory management indicates this attitude.

The main effect of accommodation is to attenuate some of the weaknesses of managerial office and to provide the manager with a margin of freedom indispensable for carrying out his tasks. Only under these conditions is he able to attain a high level of performance and to meet the targets of the economic plan. On the other hand, some of the major dysfunctional aspects of the structure, notably the pattern of concealing reserves and the practice of indicator substitution, remain unabated. Also, the role conflict inherent in the manager's position and the marginal legality of his activities persist. The manager cannot escape the fact that his success in performance is the result of a chain of manœuvres and contrivances, often contrary to the sense of propriety and rationality; or that his authority depends on his ability to frustrate or pervert some of the avowed aims of the system. He is conscious of this situation, and usually he tends to relate it to structural conditions. He will justify his behaviour as the only available alternative to personal failure and to the frustration of his economic efforts. With apparent reason he will blame the industrial organization with its fallible indicator system and its over-centralization.

and they consider all problems from their personal point of view; they are interested mainly in bonuses and advancement." Z. Kowalewski, "Problemy identyfikacji z zawodem," in Biegeleisen-Zelazowski *et al., op. cit.*, p. 221.

Again, this evaluation may be contrasted with conditions in the Cegielski Works: "The remarkable thing about the Cegielski enterprise is the absence of informers. . . . A strong general manager is able to put an end to delatorious practices in the factory. . . . [In Cegielski] promotion is a matter of an orderly development, and not the result of 'strong elbows' or of whisperings in the office of the manager or the Party secretary." Jarecki, *op. cit.*

The general acceptance of the validity of these arguments, among the public at large, within the factory, and also within the central control system, provides an important element in the accommodation process. Its effects upon the relation between the manager and the central authorities were pointed out above. Within the enterprise, it helps to cement the intra-factory solidarity, and provides the background for labour–management relations. To a large degree these relations are circumscribed by the common dependence of labour and management on the central control system. Industrial conflicts do exist, but the sense of common dependence on an outside factor provides a mitigating element in everyday relations. The substance of disputes is directed outside the factory organization, and the manager, by placing himself in an intermediary position between labour and the central system, is able to maintain a tolerable day-to-day working arrangement with his men. In a sense, the notion of unity of interests against central authorities, as manifested, for example, in the pattern of restriction of performance, cuts across the intra-factory management–labour conflicts.

One may ask why, with the general recognition of inadequacy in the managerial position, the process of adjustment stops half-way and fails to provide a more radical solution. The answer seems to lie in the structural origin of the managerial dilemma and in the broad ramifications which any available solution would be liable to produce.

The obvious answer to the inconsistencies in the present system would be full acceptance of the autonomous character of the enterprise and the concomitant independence of management. Some attempts in that direction were made, but they were soon abandoned. They brought out some structural problems for which, under the conditions of the Polish economy with its arbitrariness of price structure and absence of reliable standards of performance, no solution appeared possible. Conceivably the extra-economic and secondary aspects of decentralization would produce problems of a different nature but of equal significance. For example, a meaningful autonomy would have to entail managerial independence of an order hardly compatible with the existing socio-political structure; considering the conditions of modern technology with its requirements for long-term planning and investment outlays, the manager's status would have to include extended tenure of office, immune from short-term considerations and from outside interference. This, in itself, would place the manager in an exceptional position, in some ways more akin to that of an entrepreneur of the capitalist system than to that of a servant of a socialist society. With managerial independence, the precarious balance in management–labour relations would be lost; the unifying factor of common dependence on the central system would disappear, and the focus of industrial disputes would shift to the factory. This could bring into the foreground the problem of the freedom of labour association: a matter at present kept uneasily dormant under the covers of the self-government propaganda.

As matters now stand, this discussion of the effects of decentralization may be regarded as a digression into the realm of conjecture, with little relevance to the actual situation. Its main purpose is to bring out the structural origin of the managerial dilemma and to place it within the general perspective. The accommodation process to date has introduced some measure of stability and provided the framework for a tolerable *modus operandi* within the industrial structure. And it is unlikely that, with the present economic and socio-political orientation, a more radical solution will be sought.

selection 35

Capitalists and Managers in Communist China*

Barry M. Richman

It was indeed disconcerting for me in Shanghai in May 1966 to be picked up by a native Chinese capitalist in a new Jaguar, taken to his large factory for a day of discussions, and later to his sumptuous home where he still lives as a wealthy industrialist does in a capitalistic nation. Mr. Wu, my Chinese capitalist acquaintance, not only lives like a capitalist but also looks like a capitalist, and at times still thinks and acts like a capitalist. Wu, who went to college in England, admits that he has not yet been completely remolded into a good Maoist Socialist man. However, he does not talk like a capitalist. In fact, he is verbally enthusiastic about the joys of communism and has much to say about the evils of capitalism.

Mr. Wu is one of the four native capitalists whom I met in Red China, a land where some 300,000 capitalists still receive interest on their investments, and where many of them still are serving as managers of their nationalized enterprises.

In spite of the "Great Proletarian Cultural Revolution"—which has become greatly intensified since I left China in June 1966—Wu and his fellow Red capitalists will probably continue to live and work in about the same way that they have in recent years. Perhaps they will continue in this way until they die. For these capitalists have served and are likely to continue to serve several useful purposes for the Red Chinese regime. The recent political purges, "Red Guard" actions, and other upheavals in Red China may even be fortifying the role of capitalists like Wu.

*From *Harvard Business Review,* January–February, 1967, pp. 57–71, 78.

Author's note: I would like to thank the University of California, Los Angeles; The Ford Foundation; the Massachusetts Institute of Technology; and the President of the University of Toronto for their cooperation in my research project on Red China.

It is through an odd combination of rational pragmatism and the implementation of the purest Communist ideology in the world that Red China has been making impressive—but erratic—economic progress since 1949. The nation has done better with regard to industrial development than the Soviet Union did during its first 18 years under communism. It has done substantially better than India has to date. However, the implementation of an extreme degree of pure ideology was one of the main reasons for China's temporary, but severe, economic crisis during the Great Leap Forward period of 1958-1961; and pure ideology could spell such a crisis again in the future.

The Chinese leaders seem to follow an oscillation theory of industrial and general economic management, with pure ideology implemented most intensively when economic conditions are relatively good and relaxed when the reverse is true. For the regime has seen from the Soviet experience that economic progress and affluence can lead to revisionism and softness with regard to pure Communist ideology. This situation may explain much about the current Chinese revolution; its growing fanatical emphasis on pure ideology at all levels of society follows several years of very substantial economic progress. Hence a type of vicious circle is in operation where economic progress results in great stress on pure ideology, which in turn leads to economic crisis, which in turn leads to a relaxation of pure ideology. How long this can or will go on is anyone's guess.

This article is based primarily on research conducted in China during the April–June period of 1966. With my Canadian citizenship and letters of introduction from a number of leading Canadian educators and businessmen, the Chinese were quite willing to issue me a visa, and this enabled me to undertake my firsthand study of industry and management. I visited 11 major cities and surveyed 38 enterprises (factories) in a wide range of industries as well as 3 of the country's largest retail department stores. In addition to interviewing and observing managers, workers, Communist Party cadres, and trade union officials at work, I also met many key personnel at various central, provincial, and municipal-level planning, industrial, and commercial organizations. Some leading officials at educational institutions also talked with me.

THE CAUTIOUS CAPITALISTS

While China's 300,000 capitalists represent a very small proportion of a total population of some 700,000,000 people, they are playing a significant role in that country's industry. After making a few general observations I shall return to the case of Wu.

Official Encouragement

Following the 1949 takeover, the Red regime differentiated between two types of capitalists—(a) "bureaucratic" and (b) "nationalistic." The former were very small in number and controlled large business monopolies. They also had considerable power in Chiang Kai-shek's corrupt government. The latter may or may not have had big businesses, but they did not strongly support the Chiang Kai-shek regime or play a significant role in politics. Most of the bureaucratic capitalists fled Red China; those who remained behind were usually killed or imprisoned.

As for the nationalistic capitalists, the Communist regime encouraged them to stay on and run their businesses. The regime also did much to persuade those who fled to return home and run their companies. These capitalists were assured good treatment, their old incomes, and even interest on their invested capital once their businesses were nationalized.

In the early 1950's a type of state capitalism emerged in the private sector, with the government and party gradually exerting more and more control. In 1956 legislation placed all private businesses under state ownership. Such businesses have since been referred to as *joint state and private* enterprises. About 30%–35% of all textile enterprises and numerous retail stores in Shanghai are of this type, while the figure for Peking and Tientsin is around 25%–30%. In Shanghai alone there are more than 90,000 capitalists.

Under the joint enterprise setup numerous capitalists were asked to stay on and manage their businesses, but they were to do so under party leadership and state direction; also, the state appointed a counterpart top manager. Today the capitalists are usually referred to as general managers, and the state appointees as directors. The capitalists receive, in most cases, not only the same salaries that they used to draw, but also 5% interest on the value of their invested capital as assessed by an appointed committee under state and party control.

The Wooing of Wu

Wu is quite representative of the Chinese capitalist class, although he is wealthier (but by no means the wealthiest) and more important than the average.

Before 1949 Wu and his family owned 30% of the Sung Sing Textile Corporation, which controlled nine textile mills in Shanghai. He was the major owner and top manager of Mill No. 9, which I visited. A man named Yung and his family were the major owners of the corporation, and there were a number of smaller owners.

In 1948 Wu and his family fled to Hong Kong, and his factory was run by one of his deputies. After the Communist takeover the factory was not confiscated, however, and Wu went back to Shanghai for a visit in late 1949. There he learned about the new regime's policy toward national capitalists and was encouraged to return and run his factory. Wu told me he was classified as a nationalistic capitalist because he fought bravely against the Japanese and was imprisoned by them, and also because his business suffered at the hands of the bureaucratic capitalists and foreign imperialists. In addition, he was always relatively fair and humane with his workers.

In 1950 Wu returned with his wife to Shanghai. In 1951 their four children joined them. Because of pressure, and seeing the writing on the wall, the board of directors of the Sung Sing Textile Corporation applied for joint ownership in 1954, even though the transition deadline was not until 1956. In 1955 the state appointed a party secretary, a director, and two vice directors to Wu's factory to manage it along with Wu and the eight minor owners who had stayed on in managerial positions.

The state and party appointees, and particularly the enterprise party committee, are in control at Wu's old factory, which currently employs 6,000 people. This is generally the case at all joint enterprises. Joint enterprises are managed pretty much like pure state enterprises. However, Wu and numerous other capitalists, because of their experience and skills, still play major roles in decision making and running their enterprises, although they are, of course, subject to the veto powers of state and party appointees and higher authorities.

Between Two Worlds

Even though Wu has been studying the works of Chairman Mao and undergoing ideological education and remolding since 1951, he still admits that he at times regresses and behaves as he used to when his company was privately owned. For example, he sometimes thinks in terms of maximizing profits at the expense of human welfare, or he wants to buy some components rather than make them in accordance with the current state policy of self-sufficiency at all levels of the economy. But fortunately, he points out, the enterprise party committee or the state-appointed director makes him see the errors in his thinking and potential behavior. In general, he seems to have more leeway in making technical decisions and in drawing up plans than in making decisions directly involving personnel matters.

Wu's investment in the corporation and factory was valued at 16 million yuan in 1955. (One yuan is equivalent to about 40 U.S. cents; hence the valuation was about $6.4 million.) This investment has given him annual interest payments of 80,000 yuan, or $32,000, a huge fortune in a country having a per capita income less than 3% of that of the United States. While his interest income is the largest of the incomes of the four capitalists whom I met personally, many get even greater fortunes. For example, Liu, also a textile tycoon, gets about $400,000 a year.[1] Another capitalist by the same name in the match business gets $320,000 annually.

Interest payments to capitalists were originally supposed to end in 1962, but at that time a three-year extension was announced. In 1966 the interest payments are still being made, and there are no indications that they are going to be stopped.

In addition to his interest, Wu draws a monthly salary of 380 yuan, and the other capitalists in this factory draw 220 to 375 yuan, compared to 100 to 110

---

[1] See C. Lynch, *China: One Fourth of the World* (Toronto: McLelland and Stewart, 1966), pp. 75–78.

yuan for the party secretary and the state-appointed director and vice directors. Liu, the textile tycoon just referred to, gets 750 yuan per month.

Wu is still allowed to keep the profits he earns from a Hong Kong business in which he is one of the owners. This is how he gets foreign exchange to buy imported goods. He lives in his original house in an old plush section of East Shanghai, and several of his pre-1949 servants still work for him. He spends some of his income on luxury goods, antiques, and art, although he has been "persuaded" to turn over some of his best antiques to the Shanghai museum. He admits that he cannot find ways to spend most of his money, so he banks it and earns 3.3% interest on it.

None of his four lovely children—two in college, two in high school—wants his wealth when he dies, since they say that they want to be good Socialists and perhaps get into the party someday. (His charming teenage daughter, who played "Granada" for me on her Steinway piano, is apparently not fully re-molded yet.) Two of Liu's children do already belong to the Communist Party. However, Wu and the other Chinese capitalists cannot become members of the party. Many of them are members of the Democratic Party, a party especially for capitalists. Wu is Vice Chairman of the Shanghai branch of this party. He is also an elected member of the National Peoples Congress—the highest level government body—and is on the Executive Committee of the Shanghai Federation of Industry and Commerce, another capitalist body. (Yung, the former General Manager of the Sung Sing Textile Corporation, is now Vice Mayor of Shanghai and Deputy Minister of the Textile Industry in Peking.)

There are indications in the press that under the current "Cultural Revolution" so-called "opposition parties" may be banned in China. This could include the capitalists' Democratic Party, although it has never really been an opposition party, but rather merely an advisory group. There are no indications that the National Federation of Industry and Commerce, a more influential capitalist organization with regard to the regime's policies and economic plans, will be liquidated.

Wu and many other Chinese capitalists are caught between two worlds, and I sympathize with them. On the one hand, I believe they feel that the present regime is much better for the country and for its people than the former highly inept one. Being patriotic, proud, and nationalistic, as most Chinese tend to be, they feel that they should contribute what they can to their country, regardless of who is in power. On the other hand, they are now mere cogs in a great machine, with very little real freedom, prestige, or power as compared to the past. In fact, they are, in a sense, freaks, put on display for the local population as well as for visiting foreigners such as myself.

Keeping Capitalism Alive

Why has the Red regime behaved as it has toward the national capitalists while the Soviet Union eliminated most of their business capitalists? There seem to be several reasons:

1. The capitalists' experience and skill in running industry and business was seen as, and has proved to be, highly beneficial in Red China. When the Communists took over, both the educational level of the population and native experience in running industries were substantially below those of the Soviet Union following its revolution. Industry, in general, has become much more complex in recent decades than it was in the 1920's and 1930's.

2. The Chinese also probably felt that numerous capitalists could be trusted because they were basically nationalistic. It is a fact that many of them did suffer at the hands of the old regime, the bureaucratic capitalists, and foreign interests. If given a fair chance, the Communist regime felt that they could even be remolded into hybrid Socialists. If such remolding proved to be effective, it would give them and their supporters even greater confidence in the possibility of a remolded, pure Communist "One World."

3. The Chinese also felt secure about their revolution in the early stages because Russia was around to give them protection. They were not greatly worried that their capitalists, through contacts in capitalist countries, would be able to spearhead an effective counter-revolution – something that the Soviets had been concerned about in the Bolshevist revolution.

4. By following the policies that they did, the Chinese regime also hoped to attract back many of the capitalists, professionals, and other talented people who had fled the country. In this respect, they have apparently been quite successful.

5. The regime felt there could be good general propaganda value in displaying an image of a humane and fair government that allowed capitalists to coexist with Communists.

6. An important reason pertained to the Maoist concepts of contradiction and class struggle. By having the capitalists live as they used to, the regime could keep various aspects of the past alive–for example, the relatively few "haves" living in splendor amongst masses of poverty-stricken "have nots." Today, as then, the Communist Chinese feel that contradictions or conflicts in society are good in that they keep people on their toes. By having the capitalists around, people can be kept "fighting" to wipe out all elements of bourgeois mentality and behavior. The capitalists give the regime a good–though largely impersonal–target for carrying out the class struggle and moving forward to the pure Maoist Communist society.

It is interesting to note that there are no reports in the press about capitalists of the type discussed in this article being abused by Red Guards in the current Red Chinese purge. The capitalists have relatively little real power in setting basic national policy and are, therefore, no real threat. The purge involves mainly Communist Party and important government officials whose ideology is at variance with that of Mao and his conservative supporters, and who are secure enough and powerful enough to vie for top leadership positions.

Looking ahead, it appears that the current generation of Chinese capitalists will probably continue as at present because they will continue to serve the aims of the regime.

CHINA VS. RUSSIA

There are some basic similarities between the Red Chinese and Soviet economies. For instance, the Chinese have copied much from the Soviets in their system of central planning, resource allocation, and industrial management. Also, the industrial enterprise in both China and Russia resembles in many respects a U.S. company producing almost entirely for one customer, such as the government or a large American mail-order company. Moreover, the types of inefficiencies at Chinese factories that arise because of errors in central planning and resource allocation are similar to those encountered in Russia. For example, a Wuhan paper factory that I visited has had an annual production capacity of 40,000 tons since 1957, but has been producing at the rate of only 25,000 tons. The director claims this is due to coordination problems at publishing plants.

There are, however, many significant differences between the Red Chinese and Soviet industrial systems; China's toleration of a capitalist class is by no means the only contrast. Let us examine several of these differences.

Noneconomic Objectives

The Chinese do not seem nearly as concerned as the Soviets about economic inefficiency at the factory level resulting from state planning and resource allocation problems. For the Chinese enterprise is not viewed as a purely economic unit where economic performance clearly takes priority. In fact, Chinese factories seem to pursue objectives pertaining to politics, education, and welfare as well as economic results. Moreover, in their overpopulated country, with very low wages, the regime is not very concerned about underemployment or disguised unemployment which lowers per capita productivity at various factories.

The Chinese factory is a place where much political indoctrination occurs both at the individual and at the group level, with the aim of developing the pure Communist man as conceived by Mao. It is a place where illiterate workers learn how to read and write, and where employees can and do improve their work skills and develop new ones through education and training. It is a place where housing, schools, recreational facilities, roads, shops, and offices are often constructed or remodeled by factory employees. It is also a place from which employees go out into the fields and help the peasants with their harvesting.

Hence, if supplies do not arrive according to the plan, Chinese factory workers generally do not remain idle or unproductive—at least, by the regime's standards. In factories I visited where this type of situation arose, workers undertook some education or training during the period of delay in order to improve their skills; or they studied and discussed Chairman Mao's work; or, as was the case at the Tientsin Shoe and Wuhan Diesel Engine factories, they undertook various construction and modernization activities; or they worked on developing new or improved processes and products.

This type of activity makes more sense than meets the eye in a country where illiteracy has been widespread, the level of industrial skill generally low, and factory housing and other welfare facilities sparse and inadequate. The benefits of political indoctrination seem more questionable, but even this activity seems to have a favorable motivating impact which is difficult for the capitalistic Western mind to grasp fully.

Flexibility in Planning

In spite of similar problems of economic inefficiency resulting from state planning and resource allocation in China and in Russia, the Chinese seem to have a much more flexible attitude toward planning. If supply failures arise, the production plans of Chinese factories are quite often adjusted by higher authorities.

The Soviet manager, striving to fulfill the key aggregate targets of his plan and thus earn his bonus—as well as praise—has much more difficulty in formally adjusting his operating plan. Responding to top-down pressure, the incentive system, and inflexibility in planning, he tends to resort to illegal procurement practices and, often, outright bribery; he may conceal productive capacity, hoard resources, sacrifice product quality, produce items not in accordance with his production plan, resist innovation, and/or even falsify results.[2] Such behavior patterns are apparently much less extensive and intensive in China, not only because of greater flexibility in planning, but also, as will be discussed later, because of the absence of a similar managerial incentive system and because of the emphasis on bottom-up rather than top-down pressures on factory managers.

Whereas the Soviets have a highly monolithic and fairly clear-cut system of planning, the Red Chinese have a system of planning and resource allocation that is flexible to the point of being sloppy. Most enterprises do go through the motions of getting some type of annual plan approved—through a down-up-down process of negotiations with higher authorities. However, while the key operating document for some plants is the annual plan, for many it is the quarterly, monthly, and in some cases the weekly plan. For example, the large Shanghai Machine Tool factory works primarily according to an annual plan which is revised quarterly; for the Peking Pharmaceutical factory the quarterly plan is the key one; for the Tientsin Shoe factory the monthly plan is the crucial document; and for the Hangchow Clothing factory the basis is monthly plans which are often revised weekly. Regardless of the time perspective of planning, formal revisions tend to be quite common.

With such flexibility in planning it is natural that many important decisions get overlooked and serious coordination problems arise. For example, in mid-1965 the Tientsin North Lake Instrument factory was ordered to begin production of two types of expensive scientific equipment. As of May 1966, the factory's 1966 plan was still not approved, and it was continuing to produce the two new types of equipment as fast as suppliers came up with the necessary components. By May the plant had produced 30 pieces of equipment, which accounted for about half of its total production. Yet the equipment was lying in the warehouse because no customers had yet been assigned. In fact, a sales price for the equipment had not yet been formally established.

Decentralized Authority

The reason that flexibility in planning does not get completely out of hand in China is that this country has a higher degree of decentralization of authority

---

[2] See, for example, Gregory Ryapolov, "I Was a Soviet Manager," *Harvard Business Review*, January–February, 1966, p. 117.

than does Russia. This means that administrators closer to the operating level have the authority to take more timely action in light of changing local conditions. This greater decentralization of authority is chiefly at the provincial and municipal levels rather than at the factory level.

The Chinese chain of command is essentially territorial, extending from the center down through provincial industrial departments, municipal industrial bureaus, and finally the factories. There is still a small proportion of important factories directly under the central branch of industry ministries. However, in recent years the government ministries have come to exert functional rather than direct line authority over most industrial enterprises. Most factories are now under the jurisdiction of municipal authorities.

Territorial decentralization has never worked very well in the Soviet Union because of tendencies toward economically irrational self-sufficiency—referred to as "localism" or "autarky"—and deep-rooted vested interests on the part of industrial administrators. On the other hand, the Chinese regime is trying to promote long-run regional self-sufficiency in the economic sense, and does not seem very concerned about the short-run inefficiency that results from this strategy. In addition, the existence of a vast number of small enterprises in China makes a high degree of central planning and control extremely difficult. Major deficiencies in the Chinese statistical and accounting system have the same effect.

But perhaps the major reason that decentralization works in China is effective party control. There are party committees at all levels of the economy that typically have the upper hand over industrial administrators—more so than in the Soviet Union. These party cadres tend to identify with national rather than local interests, and this does much to fight localistic tendencies and "undesirable" vested interests. To achieve a balance between national and legitimate local interests, the provincial governors and municipal mayors—whose positions are government, not party, jobs—are usually local persons, and key party officials in local areas are typically from other parts of the country. While the current purge may lead to the dismissal of some of these party cadres, it is not very likely that the basic structure itself will change.

Bureaucracy & Control

The Red Chinese leaders have always been anti-bureaucracy in attitude, since they feel that bureaucracy impedes the right interpretation of national and party policy because of vested interests, localism, and routinization. Yet a bureaucratic structure is needed to help design and implement economic plans. By giving the party cadres the upper hand, the regime feels, the proper interpretation of important policies is more likely to evolve.

Since local party cadres have been viewed as generally dependable, the regime has not established a cumbersome system of checks, controls, and super-controls similar to that in the Soviet Union. In fact, with the exception of the State Bank and direct higher authorities, the trend in China has been away from government controls over industrial enterprises and their managers. For example, the powerful Ministry of Supervision—a pervasive national control body established in 1954—was abolished in 1959.

A prominent official of the Chinese State Planning Commission whom I interviewed declared that in the 1950's Peking went too far in imitating the Soviet system of bureaucracy and control. He said that this proved highly ineffective and that China no longer has a cumbersome overstaffed bureaucracy and control system comprised of officials who tend to place vested- and self-interests above the interests of the country. He also pointed out that in China more stress is placed on education and on controlling individuals in key positions than on controlling the performance of the organization.

Role of "Experts"

In the Soviet Union the professional administrators and technicians who can be referred to as "experts," not the party cadres or "Reds," have long played the major role in industrial management. It is true that the party formulates basic national goals, policies, and programs; but the operation and implementation of programs are placed quite firmly in the hands of the experts.

In Red China the pattern has been different. Since 1949 the Chinese have oscillated back and forth between expert and Red control of their industrial enterprises. During Red China's First Five-Year Plan (1952–1957), the Soviet system of industrial management was implemented with the experts in charge, and great stress was placed on one-man authority. Under this system there was substantial economic progress. By 1957 the leaders felt that conditions were auspicious for the implementation of much purer ideology. This led to the disastrous Great Leap Forward of 1958–1961. At the enterprise level managerial authority and responsibility were placed under the collective leadership of the party committee, with the party gradually assuming full operational authority for designing and carrying out plans. At the same time there was substantial decentralization of authority, under party surveillance and control, at the provincial and municipal levels.

By 1961 a severe economic crisis had taken place, and the experts at the enterprise level were asked by the regime to help pull the country out of this crisis. Once again factory managers assumed considerable independent operational authority. During the next few years much industrial progress was made. Then in 1964 articles began to appear in leading journals and newspapers calling for purer ideology again in practice.

At the time of my visit to China in 1966, enterprise management was once more officially under the collective leadership of the party committee. However, in most factories the role of the party in management seemed to be mainly to give formal approval of the main targets of the enterprise plan and to define unclear priorities, major personnel matters, and welfare. There seemed to be a fairly reasonable balance between Reds and experts, with the latter making the types of technical and managerial decisions that they were best equipped to make. There were, however, some factories where incompetent party cadres seemed to run the show, and as a result there seemed to be considerable confusion and inefficiency in these places. If the current Great Proletarian Cultural Revolution continues, and leads to the management of factories by Reds *rather than* by experts, serious problems are once again likely to emerge.

The Reds are primarily interested in policies and ends rather than plans and means, which are the chief concerns of the experts. Plans involve economic and technical criteria and analysis, while policy in Chinese industry tends to be intimately linked with ideology as well as with the sometimes basically abstract goals of the regime. For example, "democratic centralism," which involves mass worker participation in the management of enterprises, is a policy which receives much attention by factory party cadres. They have considerable leeway in interpreting and implementing this policy, and if they are too fanatical, much inefficiency can result.

When choices involving priorities must be made with regard to the design or fulfillment of the enterprise plan, the party cadres often define these priorities in accordance with their interpretation of policy. At times they can and do go overboard in implementing a specific policy. For example, at several enterprises there seemed to be an irrational stress on "self-sufficiency," even where alternative sources of supply were available. Some factories were making all types of machines and components about which they knew relatively little. At others, so much time was spent on trying to "innovate" that many production bottlenecks resulted.

Money Incentives Deflated

While the Soviet regime has accepted monetary incentives and self-interest as key motivating forces for both managers and workers for decades, the Chinese regime takes a less sanguine view toward such rewards. During the 1952–1957 period, great stress was placed on monetary incentives for spurring productivity. Many workers were put on piece-rate schemes, and enterprise managers as well as party officials were paid bonuses primarily in relation to gross output results. This led to some complaints in the press and journals about undesirable managerial practices similar to those found in Russia.

During the Great Leap Forward of 1958–1961, the regime tried to wipe out self-interest—and hence monetary incentives—as a key motivating force. With the Reds in charge, it was felt that they could organize and motivate the work force to respond to nonmaterial stimuli. When the experts once again gained favor in 1961, worker as well as managerial incentives were also revived. However, profit rather than gross output became the key success indicator. Profit could be a reasonably meaningful measure of efficiency, it was felt, since enterprise managers were given greater independence over product decisions, marketing, and procurement, and more say in the pricing of their products. By 1964 some articles had begun to appear about the ideological conflict involved in stressing profit as the key success indicator and in emphasizing monetary incentives and personal gain. This was at a time when economic conditions were once again favorable and when China and Russia were engaged in an open, heated fued about proper ideology and revisionism.

I found during my visits to 38 Chinese factories that piece-rate incentives for workers had been completely abolished. However, at about 80% of the factories workers could still earn monthly or quarterly bonuses. And, interestingly enough, such bonuses were not based solely upon productivity; politics and helping co-workers were also key criteria.

Middle level managers, such as department heads and workshop directors, can still earn bonuses at about 80% of the factories surveyed. It is the middle managers who are usually the experts because of their formal education and training. (By contrast, the director of a factory is likely to be more Red than expert, and the vice directors are typically a mixture of Reds and experts.) For middle managers to earn bonuses, the fulfillment of certain enterprise targets is a required condition at only about 20% of the factories; they are more commonly evaluated for their "contributions" rather than on the basis of overall enterprise performance. Where enterprise targets have to be fulfilled for bonuses to be paid, in most cases profit is not the only success indicator. Quantity and value of production, sales, production costs, labor productivity, and/or quality are other key success indicators at various enterprises.

During the past few years, directors, vice directors, and party secretaries have not been eligible to receive bonuses at any enterprises. Can top-level enterprise managers (or middle managers, too, for that matter) be adequately motivated over time to perform efficiently without bonuses? I doubt it. At present there seems to be considerable dedication, zeal, patriotism, and other nonmaterial stimuli motivating many of them to do the best job they can. But these stimuli cannot do the job alone for long. Compounding the difficulty is the fact that salaries, powers, and living conditions of top managers are relatively low in relation to those of their subordinates. Let us turn now to the question of status, income, and living standards.

WHO'S WHO IN BUSINESS?

In a Soviet or an American industrial enterprise there are generally clues which enable an outsider to distinguish the top managers from the workers, and perhaps even the top managers from the lower-level managers. During my visits to Russian enterprises a few years ago, observable differences in the salary and wage scales, working and living conditions, dress, appearance, education, work patterns, and even interpersonal contacts typically gave me adequate clues to guess who was who. But in Chinese enterprises there are fewer clues than in probably any other country in the world.

In order for a Western mind to make sense out of some of the more surprising and strange things going on in Chinese factories, one must be aware of two pure Communistic ideological tenets which the regime takes seriously and has gone a long way in implementing: (1) the abolition of classes, class distinctions, and elites; and (2) the abolition of distinctions between mental and physical labor.

Incomes & Living Standards

In the Soviet Union upper-level industrial enterprise managers have long been paid substantially better than workers, generally live significantly better with favored housing and an allocated car, and have become a type of elite. In fact they are recognized as an integral part of the Soviet intelligentsia because of their special knowledge, skills, abilities, and/or education. Not so in Red China. The Chinese regime realizes that one sure way to breed class distinctions or elites is to pay managers substantially more than workers and provide them with substantially better living conditions. Hence when great stress is placed on pure ideology in practice, one can expect a narrowing of such gaps between managers and workers. There are indications that this is happening today. Thus:

At the 38 Chinese industrial enterprises I visited, the director alone is the top paid employee at only 3, while he shares the top pay slot with the party secretary, experts, and/or workers at 12 others.

At 2 of the enterprises, the party secretary alone gets top pay, and at 12 others he shares this slot with other personnel.

Vice directors, department heads, and engineers are the highest paid at 12 factories, and share this position at 7 others.

Workers are the highest paid employees at 8 factories – mostly fairly small ones – and share this slot at 2 others.

At some of the enterprises I was told that recently the directors and other key managerial and technical personnel had "voluntarily" asked for and received cuts in salary to put them more in line with the workers. This happened at the Wuhan Iron and Steel Corporation, Wuhan Heavy Machinery factory, and Loyang Tractor factory. The director of the Nanking Chemical Fertilizer factory claimed that he had refused a salary increase. At most factories the ratio between directors' incomes and the average factory pay was less than 2 to 1; the highest ratio I found was about 3 to 1.

Is there a significant relationship between managerial compensation and factory performance? I believe there is. For instance:

I would rate nearly all of the enterprises where workers or party secretaries are the highest paid employees as below average or poor in terms of effectiveness of management and operations. In such cases the directors probably qualify more as Reds than as experts.

On the other hand, I would rate as above average or relatively good most of the enterprises where the director is the highest paid or one of several top paid employees. Here the directors probably qualify as both experts and Reds.

In factories where engineers, technicians, or managers other than the director receive top salaries, some operations seem relatively well run while others are not.

At Chinese enterprises there also seem to be no really very substantial differences in the housing conditions of managers, technicians, Reds, or workers. At the Nanking Chemical Fertilizer, Wuhan Iron and Steel Corporation, and Peking Cotton Textile No. 3 enterprises I spent quite a bit of time inspecting the factory housing. Top managers, lower-level managers, engineers, technicians, party cadres, and workers are all integrated in the apartment houses, for which a nominal monthly rent—typically 1 to 4 yuan per room—related to income is paid. However, some of the better paid employees live in larger and better furnished flats, and this could be some type of incentive.

All personnel eat together in the same canteen during working hours. Even though the larger factories have cars (some of them old U.S. models), top managers, key experts, and party officials claim that they walk, ride bikes, or take the bus to work. I was told that cars are only for official use or emergencies, and are used by all personnel. One can tell usually very little from dress or personal appearances in Chinese enterprises. Most personnel at all levels generally wear the conventional blue suits with caps—even the women. (In fact, it is usually difficult to tell the women from the men!)

What Makes Wong Run?

In the absence of income and living standard differences, what does motivate the directors, party officials, and experts to perform well and to improve their performance at Chinese enterprises? Dedication, loyalty, identification with the country's goals and progress, a deep sense of commitment and purpose—all these must play significant roles, particularly for the Reds and possibly for many of the experts.

Individual power is quite limited, but there still does seem to be considerable status and prestige attached to being a key enterprise official; this could be a significant motivating force. For example, at larger enterprises there are as many as a dozen vice directors, and even at those enterprises having a few hundred employees or less, there are typically three or four vice directors. Why appoint so many if the title does not mean much? As for the Reds, they have a certain status since they are still a type of elite or class, although much different from the old Chinese elites or ruling classes. The title of engineer or even technician seems to be highly respected, even though such titleholders may from time to time be somewhat self-conscious about being part of the intelligentsia. When technicians are promoted from the ranks of the workers, they seem to be even more openly proud of their titles than in cases where they are technicians or engineers because of their formal education.

It seems to me that in the long run material gain and self-interest will have to play significant roles in motivating the Chinese experts, and perhaps even the Reds, unless the regime can actually mold a nation of pure Communist men. The Russians have tried that, failed, and seem to have given up the attempt. The Chinese are much more persistent, but centuries of world history and experience are clearly against them.

Workers in Management

Worker participation in management in Chinese factories takes the form of committees, meetings, suggestions, and elections. Some Chinese managers interviewed admitted that in the past—apparently during the Great Leap Forward period—workers spent too much on-the-job time in meetings, and now most of these meetings are held "voluntarily" after hours.

The major formal on-the-job meeting of workers is generally held monthly or quarterly to discuss the enterprise plan and performance. At most factories only a committee of worker representatives elected by the various sections, shops, and departments participate. The worker representative committees can and apparently do exert considerable influence at times, even to the point of reversing managerial decisions. For example, at the Canton Electrical Appliance factory some managers wanted to buy a new machine; the workers made them reverse the decision, and the factory rebuilt an old machine at a fraction of the cost. This, I was told, is in line with the state policies of self-sufficiency and innovation.

Much time is spent in after-work meetings (and I did unexpectedly drop in on some when I stayed late at various factories). The workers discuss how to improve performance and their own skills, and of course they talk much about politics and ideology. They also vote on who should get what size bonus, as well as on which members of their group should be elected to lead during the period. Even though management and the party committee formally approve the election results, the workers' recommendations are generally accepted. However, there is one type of worker election that seems to be a pretense, according to what I was told:

> The "election" of managers started quite recently. Such elections reportedly take place annually or every few years at about 40% of the factories surveyed. Several other plants are contemplating elections in the near future. (Most of the factories having elections are in Peking and Shanghai.) The workers supposedly elect the directors, vice directors, and group leaders (who are like front-line supervisors).
> The workers may play a major role in the selection of group leaders, but it is doubtful that they do so with regard to the other managers. The elections, not surprisingly, are under the direct leadership of the party. It seems that all successful candidates are elected with a 99% to 100% majority.

Apparently, the Chinese regime is not yet willing to have the workers play major management roles at their enterprises. If they did, chaos would surely result. It is significant that at the majority of factories I found no workers on the enterprise party committees, and at the other factories workers did not make up more than about 10% of the committee membership.

As for the factory trade union committee, it is supposed to play a major role in motivating and organizing worker participation, but here again the party clearly plays the dominant role. In fact, the trade union in Soviet enterprises, although not very strong, seems to be significantly more influential and important than in China.

Yet elections and worker participation in general do seem to have some favorable impacts at Chinese factories. They give the workers a sense of identification, loyalty, belonging, and commitment to their enterprises. They also keep managers on their toes, since they must at least listen to the workers; also, the latter can and do evaluate the managers and point out what they view as deficiencies in administrative performance. The workers still earn bonuses for favorable economic results, and if their bonuses are lost because of poor management, their voices are probably not silent. Perhaps more important to the regime is that worker participation results in a form of bottom-up control not only over economic performance, but also over the proper interpretation of state policy and ideologically correct behavior.

Managers in Manual Labor

During my first visit to a Chinese factory, Peking Wool, I thought it was a joke or strange aberration when, during lunch in the cafeteria, I was introduced to the director who was cooking dumplings in the kitchen. He was doing one of his two days a week of physical labor. I soon learned that all enterprise directors, vice directors, party secretaries, and trade union leaders spend from one to two days each week in physical labor. So when I later saw the director of the Tientsin Watch factory cleaning up a shop, and a vice director of Shanghai Steel No. 3 working on a machine, I was no longer shocked. In fact, managers, experts, and key Reds of organizations above the enterprise also come to plants each week to engage in physical labor. For example, when I was at the Shanghai Truck factory, there were three managers from the Shanghai Bureau of Transportation and Communication working in the shops.

It seems, however, that some of the better managers at fairly well-managed factories do not take physical labor very literally. For example, they spend their one or two days of manual labor each week working out technical or managerial problems through the physical process of writing.

Management participation in labor at Chinese factories appears to have some favorable effects. It seems to create a type of cohesive team spirit, and to enable managers to observe and keep in close touch with concrete operating conditions and problems in their enterprises. But where experts—in a country that has a critical shortage of experts—are forced to spend as much as two days each week in physical labor, may not the disadvantages outweigh the advantages, especially in terms of economic performance?

Informal Organization

In virtually any industrial enterprise with several or more employees, one finds both a formal and an informal organization. In its pure form the formal organization is a technical system with clear-cut hierarchical relationships, a clearly defined division of labor based on technology and specialization, and many routinized activities. An informal organization is built around personalities, natural human behavior patterns, and interpersonal relations independent of formal hierarchical positions.

In probably no other country does informal organization play such a pervasive and significant role in the functioning of enterprises as in Red China. In Chinese factories one commonly observes workers violating the formal chain of command and going directly to middle or top-level managers for advice or instructions; also, managers are often seen going directly to workers, and personnel from different shops and departments can be seen communicating and interacting directly with one another and undertaking joint decisions and tasks. Reds play the role of experts, experts play the role of Reds, workers train each other, managers train and help each other, and so forth. In numerous cases "leading workers" float around doing all types of jobs, from working on different machines and technical problems to innovating and giving advice and even orders. (In fact, on several occasions workers popped uninvited into my discussions with managers and made themselves at home.) In any random group of factory employees, it is indeed often difficult to tell who's who.

Such disregard for the division of labor, work specialization, and formal relationships can and often does lead to considerable confusion, unproductive time, and general inefficiency. However, this great stress on informal organization also makes more sense than meets the eye in a country that does not have nearly enough skilled people or experts to meet its minimum needs.

When relatively few employees are highly skilled, the pooling of know-how, the sharing of information, mutual aid, and cooperation may frequently lead to net gains in productivity and efficiency over time. In addition, such activities often seem to promote trust, cohesiveness, harmony, unity of purpose, and, perhaps, better information for decision making at all levels. However, if Chinese industry is to progress substantially, and hence become more complex, it appears that more stress must be placed on formal organization.

In appointing key enterprise personnel, the regime seems to be more concerned about how the key people will perform together *as a team* than about their individual capabilities. An attempt is made to design organizations, especially at the upper level, more around personalities than around individual abilities. This may explain in large part why there is apparently much less transferring of key people back and forth between enterprises than is the case in Russia.

MANAGERIAL KNOW-HOW

How sophisticated is the manager in Red Chinese industry? How does he compare in this respect with his counterpart in India, Russia, or the United States? What kinds of progress, if any, is he making?

Before trying to answer these questions, let me comment briefly on managerial authority and independence in Red China. By managerial authority I mean enterprise autonomy, since the organization is officially under the collective leadership of the enterprise party committee. The degree and extent of autonomy vary substantially at the factories I surveyed. Enterprises directly under government corporations generally have less authority than those under municipal, provincial, and especially central organizations. Some of the enterprises that seem to have a relatively low degree of authority and independence are the cotton and woolen mills and the Shanghai Pharmaceutical No. 3 factory. On the other hand, most of the small machinery and instrument plants and the large machine-tool factories have relatively great authority and independence.

Those Chinese enterprises with the least authority and independence may be compared to U.S. *factories* where the manager has a fairly low degree of autonomy. Even those enterprises with the greatest autonomy are roughly analogous to product *divisions* of U.S. corporations where management has a fairly low degree of autonomy. Organizations referred to as corporations, which operate under municipal bureaus—and in some cases central ministries—and control similar types of enterprises in an area, are generally more comparable to U.S. product divisions than to U.S. factories.

How Wong Learns

Thus far Red China has achieved substantial industrial progress, more because of managerial motivation and attitudes than because of managerial or technical know-how. In many respects the Chinese manager is like our commonly held view of an American manager. Both have what David McClelland calls a "high need for achievement."[3] Industrial managers who have a high achievement drive are inclined to desire and strive to accomplish fairly challenging—but realistic—enterprise plans and objectives. They are also likely to take calculated rational risks, to innovate, and to be quite favorably disposed toward change in the direction of greater progress. One difference between the Chinese and American managers is their attitudes toward individual responsibility, with the former being more concerned about group or collective responsibility and achievement.

Many Indian managers I have met seem to *know* more about managerial techniques than most of the Chinese managers do. The former often read the Western management literature, and many have even attended formal management education programs. Chinese managers, on the other hand, may read purely technical literature and undergo technical training, but are not generally exposed to much management literature or formal management training. However, perhaps because of a relatively low achievement drive, the Indian manager frequently does not apply much of his potential know-how effectively in practice. The Chinese manager is typically more pragmatic, inventive, flexible, action-oriented, and interested in improving performance and results. He learns much through trial and error and persistence.

---

[3] "Business Drive and National Achievement," *Harvard Business Review,* July–August, 1962, p. 103.

Chinese industry has also made significant progress because of the motivation, dedication, resourcefulness, hard work, and other attitudes of its labor force. Here greater credit must be given to the Reds than to the experts or managers. The Communist Party has organized and motivated workers on a national scale to identify with and strive for national economic progress and power. Hence enterprise management has much of its job of motivating personnel done at the outset. In fact there is a sharp dichotomy in responsibility. The Reds typically play the key role in personnel matters, overall direction, leadership, selection, and, to a lesser extent, training and appraisal; the managers and experts are primarily involved in planning, technical decision making, control, organizing activities, technical training, and some personnel appraisal work. In these latter areas Chinese managers do not in general seem to have as much know-how as Soviet industrial managers, and much less than their U.S. counterparts.

Gaps & Inefficiencies

At a majority of the Chinese enterprises surveyed there is an apparent lack of integrated, in-depth planning throughout the organization. A systems approach, which is essential to well-balanced and coordinated plans, is clearly lacking. In designing the plans, almost complete reliance is placed on historical labor and material input norms, historical inventory norms, and other relationships based on past performance. Practically no use is made of such tools as time and motion studies. At most enterprises there seems to be considerable difficulty in integrating technical and economic factors in decision making. Also, little use is made of contingent or alternate plans; if a plan breaks down because of supply failures, for example, a completely new plant must often be drafted.

Control systems found at many enterprises are also far from efficient. Apart from after-the-fact control and information feedback related to aggregate targets, managerial control seems to be weak, and much inefficiency and waste results. Perhaps the Chinese factory is not bureaucratic enough, since more formal reports, procedures, and policies would probably improve efficiency in most cases. Chinese managers do not seem to make much use of written reports for control or of written communications in general. In-process cost control or controls over material and labor usage are practically nonexistent at many factories. There is much stress placed on finished-product quality control—and this generally seems to be done quite well—but in-process quality control tends to be quite ineffective. Hence, many rejects are frequently sent back through the production process.

There appears to be a great deal of stress on preventive maintenance in order to preserve equipment. However, this type of work seems to be frequently carried out in an inefficient manner because there is no clear-cut division of labor. Maintenance and repair work are often done by production workers rather than by personnel from the repair and maintenance department. Even managers often get involved in this type of work.

Most of the Chinese managers clearly lack experience in organizing work efficiently. Poor organization is also due in part to the nature of the informal organization and the constraints placed on reorganizing departments and shops by higher authorities. Work flows suffer greatly in many cases because of the lack of specialization or efficient integration of activities. This ties in with poor planning and norm setting. At many plants there are large auxiliary work forces— in some cases they exceed the number of production workers—and this is due in large part to inefficient planning and organization of activities.

In general, Soviet industrial managers seem to have more know-how than the Chinese in the functional areas of production, procurement, finance, accounting, and research and development—although they often do not make effective use of this know-how because of the incentive system they work under. The Chinese manager, however, seems to have a greater flare for and interest in marketing. More attention is typically given to product planning, marketing research, product development and improvement, customer satisfaction, and even analysis of finished-inventory levels at Chinese industrial enterprises.

It would seem that without considerably more basic and more extensive managerial know-how, Chinese industry will undoubtedly run into serious trouble as it develops and grows more complex. It is not too difficult to achieve substantial industrial progress in an industrially backward country, even with poor management, so long as people have the basic drive, motivation, and resourcefulness to improve their economic performance and productivity. However, at a certain point along the development spectrum, managerial know-how becomes just as important as motivation and attitudes. If such motivation and attitudes lose some of their potency, managerial know-how will become more important that much sooner.

I believe the Chinese will have to face up to the problem of managerial know-how in the foreseeable future. If they do not, they certainly will not develop an efficient industrial system. Indeed, they probably will not even be able to maintain an effective one....

CONCLUSION

There appears to be an inherent conflict between the basic ideology and ultimate objectives that the Communist Chinese leaders are pursuing. They clearly want Red China to be a leading world political, military, and economic power, with their ideology dominating the universe. In order to achieve such international power and influence, the Chinese domestic economy, and industry in particular, must develop on a very substantial and impressive scale; the effectiveness of the industrial management system is crucial, since it is at the factory level that the economic progress, wealth, power, and influence of a nation are so largely determined. However, key aspects of the Red ideology are in basic conflict with effective and efficient industrial management, and hence with the attainment of Peking's ultimate national and international objectives.

It is true, as pointed out earlier in this article, that the Red Chinese have learned much from the Soviet Union's experiences and mistakes in industrial management. The Chinese are apparently following a more balanced and flexible approach to industrial development than the Soviets did. It is also true that various aspects of Maoist-Marxist ideology have had a favorable impact on productivity and industrial development to date. Yet at the same time the Chinese regime stubbornly tries to implement certain aspects of pure ideology which the Soviets long ago abandoned because the ideas were found to be unworkable from a managerial, technical, and economic point of view.

Take, for instance, the basic question of self-interest and monetary incentives as opposed to pure altruism and nonmaterial incentives. Centuries of world history and experience strongly indicate that the Chinese regime will not be able to eliminate self-interest and material gain as key motivating forces—for managers, technicians, or workers—and at the same time achieve sustained and impressive industrial development in the long run. If by some miracle the Reds do succeed, this would have a very great philosophical and cultural impact on the functioning of the world. But I am betting against such a miracle. I am also betting against the workability of a classless society with no noticeable distinctions between managers and workers, leaders and followers, experts and nonexperts, and mental and physical work.

There is also the crucial conflict between ideology and managerial, technical, and economic reality. If the Reds maintain the upper hand as Chinese industry develops and becomes more complex, this would surely lead to serious problems, including stagnation in the economy and probably even regression at a certain point. It may be possible to develop a large and adequate pool of managers and technicians who are both Red ideologists and experts, but this would take decades, and may prove extremely difficult.

A final key point worth restressing is that of managerial know-how. Thus far, party officials, industrial experts, and workers have had great motivation to improve, dedication, resourcefulness, willingness to work hard, and pragmatism—all admirable traits in much of the Chinese population. These qualities have played a substantially more important role in Red China's industrial progress than basic managerial know-how has. But if the country is to progress from an underdeveloped or developing economy to a relatively developed economy, managerial skill and ability of a much higher order are essential. For there is clearly vast room for improvement in the formal organization of work, in integrated planning based on deep analysis, in the design of effective managerial control systems, in systematic training and appraisal of personnel, in general coordination of activities, and in many other important aspects of sound management.

Substantial progress in managerial performance will require much more than ideology, zeal, dedication, or trial-and-error pragmatism. The Soviets have discovered this fact of life;[4] indeed, much of the developing world is discovering

---

[4] See my book, *Management Development and Education in the USSR* (East Lansing: Michigan State University Press, 1966).

it. But it remains to be seen if, how, or when the Red Chinese can come to grips with this fact. If they do not, they cannot achieve their ultimate international objectives of economic and political power; truly effective international military power, too, would seem to require a relatively strong and effective economy. On the other hand, if the Red Chinese do recognize management realities in order to develop first-rate political, economic, and military power, they will have to abandon the more important aspects of pure Maoist-Marxist ideology.

selection 36

The Egyptian Executive: A Study in Conflict*

Harold Q. Langenderfer

INTRODUCTION

Beginning in July, 1961, the government of the United Arab Republic (Egypt) issued a series of nationalization decrees which shifted the country from a private enterprise economy to essentially a socialist society. All industry of any substantial size or influence is now owned or controlled by the government. These decrees followed by approximately a decade the political revolution (July, 1952) which ousted the king (Farouk) and created a dictatorship under the eventual leadership of Gamal Abdel Nasser. The nationalization decrees reflected President Nasser's thinking that the desire for a better way of life for his people had to come through a conversion from an agricultural society to an industrial society. Furthermore, he wanted the industrialization of the economy to be carried out as rapidly as possible. He felt that this could best be accomplished through government control and central planning. The nationalization decrees allowed for some private ownership, in agriculture and in the retail and service trades; however, the total impact of the private sector is, and will be, far outweighed by the influence exerted by the public sector.

This radical shift in the economic environment has been supplemented by numerous other government actions, both mandatory and persuasive, which have affected nearly every aspect of the Egyptian people's way of life, including their opportunities for work, their preferences as to language, their mode of dress,

*From *Human Organization,* Vol. 24, Spring 1965, pp. 89–95.

their freedom to travel, the amount of income they can earn, and the nature of their schools. In essence, the political revolution of 1952 and the economic revolution initiated in 1962 have been accompanied by a cultural *evolution* which has or will affect the thoughts and actions of all Egyptians for a long time to come.

Like most developing countries, the U.A.R. desires economic development *now*. President Nasser would like to accomplish in years what it has taken other countries decades to do. It is not a question of *whether* economic development will take place; rather it is a question of *how rapidly* it will be accomplished. One cannot help but be impressed by the industrial strides that have already taken place in the U.A.R. Further progress seems assured. A significant question, however, is whether economic progress can take place as rapidly as President Nasser and his advisers would like. Are there not some important forces militating against *accelerated* economic development?

On the assumption that the management function plays a vital role in economic development, an attempt will be made to demonstrate that there are certain institutional and personal barriers growing out of the economic and cultural environment that limit a manager's effectiveness and act as a "drag" on economic development. Too little is known about economic development to state absolutely that the forces which retard the management function necessarily impede economic development. But the institutional and personal barriers to management effectiveness might be thought of as restricting tendencies which may well operate against *accelerated* development. This article will be concerned, then, with the type of restricting tendencies that impede the management function in its impact on the rapidity of economic development.

The task set forth here is not a simple one. To draw conclusions out of the complexity of a changing environment which has not yet "jelled" seems like an impossible task, even for the most experienced observer. If the observer is fundamentally a foreigner to the culture on which he is reporting, as this writer is, then the reader should be warned that the observations to follow must be subject to important qualifications, which may or may not outweigh the usual advantage of objectivity. The nature of these qualifications has been well expressed by another consultant who said:

> ... there is almost certainly a culture-shock element—which may edge the consultant away from full objectivity—a quicksand factor that may keep him so preoccupied with each step he takes that he loses correspondingly in perspective—a communications difficulty which may keep him in a kind of information smog—a time dimension differential which may focus his attention too much on the calendar and too little on the facts of life about him—and perhaps even an American middle class aggressiveness that may produce a partial eclipse of realism by impatience. The foreign consultant, in short, is not as a psychiatrist whose strength in virtually every aspect of his relationship stands in sharp contrast to his client's weakness. He is rather caught up in a comprehensive learning-adjustment experience, and his understanding of the total context within which he is functioning cannot but be affected by the change dynamics he is himself undergoing.[1]

---

[1] Unpublished remarks by a consultant on management development in the Middle East.

With these types of qualifications to put the reader on guard, let us proceed to examine the economic, political, and cultural environment within which the Egyptian business executive moves. This background will serve as a basis for understanding the problems and restricting tendencies which this environment creates for him.

RECENT BACKGROUND AND CURRENT ENVIRONMENT

Prior to the revolution of 1952, the head of the government of Egypt was King Farouk. In his youth, Farouk was greatly admired by the Egyptian people. Many thought he would make an excellent king who would institute much-needed reforms to help raise the standard of living of the people. For many reasons, however, he squandered the assets of the country to facilitate his life of luxury and dissipation. As a result of his actions, the country did not progress industrially, and the substantially agricultural economy tended to perpetuate a small, wealthy elite and a large mass of relatively poor people, with virtually no middle class. During Farouk's reign, the economic activity of the country was dominated to a great extent by foreigners who held most of the key jobs in industry. Egyptians were used primarily for manual labor and menial tasks.

The country was ripe for the 1952 revolution which placed Mohammed Naguib, and subsequently, Nasser, in power. During most of the first decade of its existence, the new government was so involved with such international problems as control of the Suez Canal, independence for the Sudan, and Arab union, that little progress was made on the domestic front. There were some land reforms, as well as the initiation of the Aswan Dam project and the development of a few basic industries. Although there was no evidence of a comprehensive plan for economic development during this first decade, it became apparent that several basic aims were to be the cornerstone on which the country's political and economic policies were to be based. These aims included: (1) the intention to remain neutral in the struggle between the Western and Eastern blocs of nations; (2) the desire to foster Arab unity to counteract the power of Israel; and (3) the determination to raise the standard of living of the masses through a vast industrialization program.

The nationalization decrees of 1961 marked the introduction of the plan to achieve the third aim—a higher standard of living—to be built on an industrialization base that would be owned or controlled by the government. Whatever the reasons were for seeking to achieve economic development by means of the social control of industry, this decision was the initiating force for a complete upheaval in the cultural and economic environment of the country. The nationalization decrees resulted in control by the government of approximately 80 percent of the economic resources of the country. This control was acquired in three ways: (1) in some cases the government supplied all of the capital and is the sole stockholder; (2) in other cases, private stockholders were required to exchange their stock for government bonds for all holdings over L.E. 10,000 (approximately, $23,000); and (3) in still other cases the assets of many wealthy citizens were confiscated.

The government further decreed that it was to be in control of any company in which it owned at least 25 percent of the stock. Recently (April, 1964), another decree declared that companies which previously had been only partially owned by the public sector would now be under full control and ownership.

Other government actions that were taking place about the same time as the original nationalization decrees served to insure continued control by President Nasser and his vice presidents. These actions included the sequestration of the properties of wealthy people considered to be political risks, the restriction on the international flow of Egyptian currency, the discouragement of Egyptian citizens from visiting foreign embassies or associating with foreigners except for business reasons, the censoring of mail, and restriction on news from abroad. All of these actions tended to invoke fear and uncertainty in the minds of the people, especially the management and professional classes. Whether all of these actions were necessary to solidify the new social order is a moot question; nevertheless, they were done. Their combined effect was sufficient to make most thoughtful Egyptians aware that they were living under a dictatorship in which many of their accustomed freedoms had been taken away. There was clearly a new order of priorities which required a new set of actions if a person was to maintain his "place in the sun" in the new society.

Now let us introduce the business executive to this new environment. There had been little opportunity for developing management skills since foreigners had dominated the industrial scene until a few years before the nationalization decrees. Furthermore, many of the leading private citizens of the country were not available to join the manager ranks because they were politically suspect. Add to this the fact that the nationalization laws had put government into business on such a scale that it required large numbers of politically acceptable businessmen to manage the enterprises in a manner consistent with the new social order. As might be expected, this new environment required a new breed of businessmen. They were drafted from the army and from government positions, and to a lesser extent from the supervisory ranks in other companies. They were selected to implement the new economic order which was being built on a base of hope, a vague notion of a new economic philosophy, and a limited reservoir of human talent and economic resources. A brief look at the nature of the *economic* environment created by the government and at the nature of the managers selected for the operating companies will contribute to a better understanding of the institutional and personal barriers being erected that tend to limit the rapidity of economic development, at least to the extent that managers are contributors to development.

The government organization structure for controlling business was built on a base of three fundamental precepts: (1) private enterprise is exploitative by nature; (2) the self-interest principle of private enterprise does not lead to the greatest good for the greatest number of people; and (3) government can achieve economic development through industrialization much more rapidly than can private enterprise because it can control the allocation of resources according to a rational plan.

Certain basic operating principles have grown out of these precepts. First, if a person is wealthy, he must have achieved his wealth by exploiting the masses and capitalizing on their ignorance. (The sequestration of properties in 1962 was done to rectify this wrongful exploitation of the past.) To avoid a similar opportunity in the future, profit is restricted to a fair return. There cannot be any exploitative profit. Secondly, since the objective of the government is to raise the standard of living of all of the people, everyone should contribute his best efforts without any personal motivation or rewards. Furthermore, control over the allocation of resources necessarily implies centralization of authority. An outgrowth of central control is the lack of individual company autonomy and a complementary policy that companies should cooperate rather than compete. Although competition is not eliminated, it is substantially reduced; although private enterprise has a role, it is restricted to small retail and service enterprises where there is little chance for exploitation. A final operating principle is that workers and employees[2] must have a share in the profits in addition to their wages and a voice in management in lieu of an opportunity to strike, which is forbidden.

These operating principles are reflected in the organization structure of business–government relationships within which the business executive must function.

The operating companies are controlled directly by public holding companies. Originally, one holding company controlled all government companies. As more companies were taken over under the nationalization decrees, two additional holding companies were formed. Together, the three holding companies controlled over 300 companies, with little if any pattern of classification. Within a few months, this pattern was changed to put control on an industry basis. At this writing, the operating companies are administered by 39 public holding companies classified by type of industry. Each holding company reports to one of several ministers who in turn serve as a cabinet of ministers to report to the Supreme Council of Public Organizations headed by President Nasser.

Each operating company is directed by a managing director who is also chairman of the Board of Directors. He was designated for the position by name in a decree issued several months (February, 1962) after the 1961 nationalization decrees. The delay was caused by the need for making a thorough study of the managers' professional qualifications and political acceptability. In the same decree naming the managing director, two other board members were *appointed* by position, typically the production manager and the financial manager. The managing director had some choice in selecting the two men who would serve on

---

[2] Employee and Worker are special terms used in Egypt to distinguish between white-collar workers and blue-collar workers. All supervisory personnel are considered to be members of the employee group, up to and including the managing director. All manual workers are classified as workers.

the board, but the designated names had to be submitted to the government first for a security clearance. The other two members of the five-man board of directors must come from the employee and worker ranks and are *elected* by their respective groups for one-year terms. The three appointed members serve indefinitely. The decision to exclude outside directors is consistent with the socialist philosophy of the government and at the same time represents a reaction against the abuses that occurred prior to nationalization when many boards were interlocking and were used as a device for supplementing the incomes of the members.

Workers do not have a right to strike, but they have several strong weapons in lieu of the strike privilege. In addition to being represented on the Board of Directors, they cannot be fired, and their interest is represented by a recently organized Arab Socialist Union. There is a Socialist Union Committee elected in each public sector company, and the main function of this committee is to look after the interests of the workers.

There is little information about the elected members of the operating companies' Boards of Directors, but much is known about the appointed members,[3] especially as to education, age, and social origins. They are well educated, generally with college degrees, and some with advanced degrees. There is an acute awareness of the amount of education each person has, and it is felt to be inappropriate to appoint supervisors who have less education than those supervised. The date of obtaining a degree determines seniority for positions if otherwise qualified. Since other functions in a business are considered to be an automatic consequence of production, engineers are considered to be the persons best qualified to manage companies. Accordingly, a large percentage of managers have an engineering education.

The average Egyptian manager is in his early forties. Older managers were excluded because they were considered to be too old to accept and adjust to the new economic order. The majority of managers come from managerial or professional families. Although Arab Socialism is especially sympathetic to the farmer and the worker, there are relatively few cases of management talent from these sources because of the lack of opportunity for higher education. Many managers have received their education abroad or have been on technical missions abroad. These opportunities for travel and the strategic location of Egypt, which permits frequent contacts with foreigners, contribute to the cosmopolitan flavor of the management group. They frequently speak several languages (usually Arabic, English, and French), are interested in world affairs, and are acutely conscious of the benefits of international trade. It is doubtful, however, whether this cosmopolitan outlook will continue. As more stress is put on the Arabic language in schools, as there becomes less need for technical training abroad, and as the spirit of nationalism increases, there probably will be a trend away from a cosmopolitan viewpoint. The impact of this trend remains to be seen.

---

[3] For a more detailed description of employee characteristics see Ralph Westfall, "Business Management under Nasser," *Business Horizons*, Summer, 1964, pp. 74–77.

THE BARRIERS TO EFFECTIVE MANAGEMENT

An analysis of the political, economic, and social environment suggests that there are several types of barriers to effective management that will make it difficult for the U.A.R. to carry out its industrialization objective as rapidly as it would like. These might be labeled institutional and personal barriers. Although they will be discussed in the order listed, they are clearly interrelated. They are a part of a complex set of forces impinging on economic development generally. (Although this paper is focusing attention on the barriers that impede the business executive's effectiveness, there are others which affect him only indirectly. These other barriers might be called external ones for the purposes of this paper, and they include the problem of population growth, scarcity of natural resources, and lack of sufficient trained personnel. Although space precludes a discussion of them here, they have a significant impact on development generally and are important among the factors influencing accelerated development.)

Institutional barriers might be defined as those created by the policy-makers which determine the climate within which management must operate. They are the outgrowth of several underlying assumptions as to how rapid industrialization can best be accomplished. These assumptions are: (1) that a socialist economy can achieve massive industrialization more rapidly than can a private enterprise economy; (2) that personal incentives are not necessary to motivate people; and (3) that government control and planning can make up for the lack of management talent.

These barriers include the following: (1) lack of guiding principles and clear objectives; (2) the bureaucratic nature of the government superstructure; and (3) the lack of criteria for evaluating performance.

National Objectives

The Army officers who were responsible for the revolution in 1952 *assumed* that the removal of King Farouk would correct the evils fostered under his regime. They were not immediately concerned with any long-range objectives as a basis for solving the country's problems. Their objectives were vague, if indeed they existed. There were no central guiding principles, and there appear to be none today. As one author puts it,

Arab Socialism has no Karl Marx; it is an emotional reaction to some of the injustices that existed in Egypt and that Nasser believes were caused by the private enterprise system. Because no central theory guides the organization of economy, decisions are made and rationalized ex post facto. Managers in such a system have no clear understanding of their responsibilities or authority, nor do their supervisors or subordinates. . . . , in the absence of any coordinating theory, the locus of decision making seems bound to change as people change. Solutions will always be reached on pragmatic grounds.[4]

---

[4] *Ibid.,* pp. 77–78.

There is much evidence for the lack of clear objectives. When the public holding companies were formed, no clear assignment of responsibility was made between them and the operating companies. There was, and is, considerable confusion as to which organization is responsible for which policies. The issues are typically resolved by the relative aggressiveness of the managing directors of the respective companies, and this frequently determines how much authority is and is not delegated.

An educated Egyptian's typical response to a question about the country's economic philosophy is that "we are taking the best ideas of the Western bloc and of the Eastern bloc to develop our concept of Arab Socialism." How these "best" concepts will be integrated and reconciled with their own culture is not clear.

A pragmatic approach to solving problems may be inherent in the Egyptian culture. There are strong indications that this is so. If such is the case, special efforts will have to be made to spell out the basic economic philosophy and delineate the objectives for entities in the organization structure if economic development is not to flounder on a hidden reef of submerged principles—unclear and unstated. The lack of a guiding principle not only hinders the policy-makers in developing coordinated plans, but it also results in disharmony among various institutional groups which dissipates their efforts in relation to national objectives. This chaotic situation appears to be a crucial deterrent to economic development and to the industrialization process. Clear national objectives may well be the most important single adhesive that encourages the people of a nation to a united effort and a strong nationalist feeling. But it seems clear that their absence is a significant barrier to management effectiveness in Egypt.

Bureaucracy

The development of management talent and skills has progressed much faster in the industrial than in the public administration sector. There has been a sad neglect of the application of modern management techniques in the administrative hierarchy, and this is a serious drag on the industrial sector generally. The bureaucratic nature of public administration is a product of a social and cultural framework built up over a long period of time. The machinery is ponderously slow and cumbersome. There is reluctance to delegate authority to subordinates. Authority is guarded jealously to maintain status. Delegation is not only not practiced; there is an unwillingness by subordinates to accept it. There is a too frequent sheltering under the umbrella of high authority.[5] For example, it takes several signatures and much time to get a check cashed. The man with authority spends too much time with routine decisions; Nasser, himself recently was approving all salaries above L.E. 27 (about $62). All decisions of the operating company's Board of Directors must be approved by the holding company

---

[5] States M. Mead, "Management in Developing Nations," *Proceedings, International Management Conference,* CIOS, Vol. 13, 1963, p. 428.

board regardless of their relative importance. Although this bureaucratic framework is much more prevalent in the public administration superstructure above the operating companies, the same characteristics, although to a lesser degree, can be found in the business sector. To the extent that former public administration officers are now company executives, they frequently view the company as a government department instead of a dynamic producing entity and apply many of the bureaucratic techniques in its operation.

No effective way has been found to help the bureaucrat understand the problems of the business executive. Although the National Institute of Management Development provides training in modern techniques, protocol and class consciousness prevent the managing directors of holding companies and ministers from participating in such programs. Such joint training of operating company and public administration management would not only increase the administrators' knowledge of business problems, but would contribute to two-way communication which is now clearly lacking. Under the present arrangement, businessmen take orders from government bureaucrats who follow set rules and have no concept of management problems.

The restricting tendency that bureaucracy imposes on economic development is an example of the fact that the sociological and cultural development of a society is not rapid enough to keep abreast of the shift to industrialization and therefore becomes a barrier to continued rapid economic progress. This may be a much more serious limiting factor than is realized by the policy-makers in underdeveloped countries.

Performance Appraisal

The Egyptian government operates on the philosophy that intelligent human beings do not need positive incentives to work effectively. There is therefore no appreciation of the need for performance appraisal as an incentive device. A person is expected to do his best for the general welfare of the country. Actions based on this motivation are supposed to result in the most good for himself. It is not clear that Egyptian businessmen really believe this, but the policy-makers act as if they do.

It is not possible to appraise performance without a clear understanding of what objectives are being sought. Managers' personal goals are expected to be compatible with enterprise goals, but the enterprise goals are not clearly stated. Thus appraisal is precluded because of the philosophical rejection of personal interest incentives, and because there are no clear objectives to serve as a standard.

A lack of effective standards limits the amount of desirable control that can be exercised over managers and is an effective limitation to positive motivation. Planning is ineffective because there is no incentive to carry it out. Financial planning is especially weak. There is a great need for competence in cost accounting and related controls. Yet this is not surprising in the light of the lack of controls for which planning is the base. The ultimate result is poor allocation of resources and costly mistakes.

In summary, the government's philosophy concerning incentives, the bureaucratic nature of the administrative superstructure, the inability to develop and effectively communicate a basic economic philosophy, and the lack of effective standards for performance appraisal are all interrelated institutional barriers to economic development. When these barriers are coupled with the personal ones that the management group must overcome, rapid industrialization is difficult indeed.

The personal barriers are those attitudes of managers that prevent them from performing effectively their role in accelerated economic development. The manager's ability to develop and utilize his skills is conditioned by his attitude toward the traditional society which resists change, by his understanding of the scope of his job, and by his reaction to the lack of positive personal incentives.

The Impact of the Traditional Society

Man feels at home with the old and the familiar. It is human nature to resist change. Anything new might affect a person's economic security or his sense of his usefulness to society. This reluctance to accept change means that a country's social environment cannot be changed very quickly. The social environment is made up of a sense of values, relationships between individuals and groups, and the habits, customs, and traditions that are the results of history.[6] There is an inevitable clash of interest between the traditional society and the new society that is a logical consequence of an industrial culture. Those persons in the management class need to acquire new attitudes and new values related to an industrial culture if they are to be effective managers. Yet they are connected with the traditional society through their contacts with the family, religious and other institutions and through their own normal resistance to change. The speed by which managers overcome these barriers may be one of the most crucial factors that governs the speed of economic development.

Perhaps the most significant barrier that the Egyptian people must overcome is their fatalistic outlook on life. The general attitude is, "if Allah wills it, then it will come to pass; if not, so be it!" This has many ramifications. It deters the desire to lead, destroys an appreciation of the need for planning, impedes the spirit of inquiry, perpetuates an unbalanced attention to the spirit of other-worldliness, and obstructs an appreciation of the value of time. In short, it must be replaced by a spirit of logical reasoning if the society is to develop managers who can contribute to economic development.

There are encouraging signs that the management class is shaking off some of their traditional thinking, but it is a slow process. The spirit of inquiry among Egyptian managers is especially lacking. There are no management journals published regularly in Egypt, and there appears to be little desire to import them

---

[6] For a fuller discussion of the social and philosophical problems of underdevelopment, see K. Sundaram, "Social and Human Problems in Introducing Technological Change," *Proceedings,* CIOS, Vol. 13, pp. 495–98; also Charat Ram, "Management Development in the Developing Economy," *Proceedings,* CIOS, Vol. 13, pp. 306–9.

from abroad. The spirit of inquiry is a basic ingredient of education for change; yet it seems to be sadly lacking in many segments of the society.

Two other traditional attitudes have handicapped development. One is the low status of manual work which fosters class consciousness and inhibits cooperation, communication, and opportunities for advancement. The other is the lack of trust outside of the family group. Trust provides the social cement necessary for an effectively functioning organization. A lack of it is inherent in Egyptian culture and is perpetuated by government policies which take away human freedoms and emphasize political acceptability rather than professional capability.

THE MANAGER'S CONCEPT OF HIS JOB AND HIS INCENTIVES

The typical Egyptian manager feels insecure and lacks confidence. These characteristics stem partly from relatively limited experience in managing, but they flow more basically from the philosophy of centralized planning and the government's attitude toward the management group. The government seems to suspect that managers by nature have different goals from those of the socialist regime. The managers recognize that this suspicious attitude exists, and it makes them feel insecure and on the defensive. The government is critical of this narrow viewpoint,[7] yet it little recognizes that its own attitudes foster it. This problem is reflected in managers' fear of delegating authority to subordinates and in their desire to diffuse responsibility through collective actions. By getting approval of all decisions from his Board of Directors and by having all company board decisions reviewed by the holding company board, the manager effectively distributes responsibility away from himself.

Even without the problem of unclear objectives and government suspicions of management's motives, the very nature of centralized decision-making tends to narrow the manager's outlook concerning his job since there are relatively few alternative courses of action to choose among at the enterprise level. Where management has little or no choice in its future actions, there is little need for planning. The unfortunate consequence is that while operating management is the logical source for generating ideas regarding alternative courses of action involving the enterprise, Egyptian managers do not have the incentive to do so since planning is executed at a higher level. Ideas only flow one way, from the planners down to the managers. The ultimate impact of this is the development of defensive mechanisms by managers and a narrower concept of their role.

The incentive system should be arranged so that people will be motivated to act in ways which are not only in their own best interests, but also in the best interests of their company and their country. This may not always be possible, but at least the system should not encourage the individual to act against the best interests of the country.

A fundamental problem exists in the U.A.R. regarding the relationship of

---

[7] Westfall, *op. cit.,* pp. 78–79.

control to motivation. Should enterprise management be controlled by taking decisions out of its hands? Should enterprise management be given more freedom of decision, with control exercised through incentives, budgets, cost systems, and clearly stated objectives? Whatever the reasons for the centralization of decisions in the U.A.R., it has not operated as effectively in practice as might be expected. A major reason seems to be that there is no appreciation of the factors that motivate people.

What incentives do managers have? Other than their salary and the prestige of their position, they have none. Financial incentives are allowed to workers in the form of a share in profits, but none are allowed to managers. Although managers used to get bonuses equivalent to as much as 50 percent of their annual salaries, their only compensation now is their salary which is set by the government. Fringe benefits are negligible. In effect, the incentive system is fundamentally negative: the manager either does a good job or he is demoted or retired. Furthermore, his general attitude is not improved by the government policy of favoritism toward labor. Prior to Nasser's socialism, management was concerned with its authority and preservation of its prerogatives. Under Arab Socialism, government officials and workers exert considerable influence on the manager. As mentioned earlier, workers not only share in the profits but also cannot be fired, and they have a representative on the Board of Directors and the Arab Socialist Union Committee of each company.

It is too early to tell what the impact will be of this policy of reducing the authority and prestige of the managers. If the policy-makers of the U.A.R. think that management can do an effective job in the face of no positive personal incentives and some questionable negative incentives, it will be necessary to develop an effective performance appraisal system to demonstrate that this policy is correct. Otherwise, the rapid industrialization objective can be thwarted because of an erroneous assumption as to what factors motivate managers effectively.

CONCLUSIONS

A basic assumption of this paper is that enterprise managers play a vital role in economic development. If there are significant barriers to effective management, then economic development cannot be accelerated to the extent that developing countries would like. With respect to the United Arab Republic, there appear to be institutional and personal barriers growing out of the business-government organization structure and the prevailing political and social environment that may have a serious impact on management's ability to serve an effective role in accelerating economic development.

The most important single barrier has been the government's inability to formulate, and to translate to managers and to the populace generally, any fundamental economic philosophy. Arab Socialism is not a clear idea; it does not have a central guiding philosophy; it is a reaction to some of the injustices of the past. Its very lack of clarity may be the most crucial barrier to economic development.

A second significant barrier is the impact that the social and cultural environment has on economic development. In Egypt, the revolution and the nationalization of industry have been two key events in the establishment of a new society. It will take time for this new society to mature. Whether rapid economic progress can be achieved in the face of a slowly changing cultural pattern is a moot question. There are many who say that progress must be accomplished in a balanced manner—that the adaptation of proven technologies to a different environment is a long and complicated process. If this is so, then the problems of economic development will be solved only after the cultural aspects of development are understood. Egypt has devoted little attention to this problem. The human factors in development have been shunted aside in favor of concern over technology and production. The personal attitudes of businessmen are considered to be relatively insignificant in the overall development picture. This lack of appreciation by the policy-makers of the role of human resources in economic development helps to explain the absence of an incentive system for managers, the lack of a performance appraisal system, the favoritism toward labor, and the suspicious attitude regarding the motives of managers.

A further dilemma for managers is the emphasis on the latest production technology. Their education and training frequently take place in the Western bloc of developed countries where they are exposed to a culture and economic system which is alien to the system in their own country. Yet they must work and live in an economy which has turned its back on private enterprise and has severely restricted their freedoms. They are expected to absorb any useful technical training, but it is assumed that they will not be influenced by the social, economic, and cultural patterns of the countries where they study.

When these kinds of barriers are combined with the others that have been discussed, it is clear why there are severe obstacles to significant contribution by management to accelerated economic development.

selection 37

Business Management in French Canada*

Gaston Pelletier

INTRODUCTION

Ever since French Canada has realized that a society requires an economic foundation to flourish, it has been concerned with its relative poverty as a group and its lack of control over the economic environment. This concern has been particularly pronounced since the beginning of the twentieth century. . . .

That social and political developments are compromised without a sound autochthonous economy is a theme that has been presented in many fashions over the years. In recent years the necessity and urgency for French Canada to develop a class of entrepreneurs and managers has been the major concern of influential academicians such as Edouard Montpetit, Esdras Minville, Richard Arès and François-Albert Angers. Others have tried to measure the presence, or absence, of French Canadians in the economic life of Québec. From Victor Barbeau[1] in 1936 to Jacques Melançon[2] in 1956 the common denominator of evaluations in this area is that very little was controlled, at any rate not more than 20% of private investments. Others have rationalized on the subject and have justified the situation on different grounds. Probably the best known rationalization on the subject, which had a profound influence at the time, is the concept of the spiritual vocation of the nation. Mgr. L. A. Paquet is a good representative of this school of thought; his ideas expressed at the beginning of this century might be summarized and simplified as follows: French Canada has a providential and spiritual mission to perform in America, it should not condescend to put its energies on material and economic matters; this other nations could do.[3] Michel Brunet on the other hand has suggested an historical justification. According to his theory the conquest has drained the country; its élite and its class of entrepreneurs having returned to France the nation would not have recovered from this drain after two centuries. For certain members of Cité Libre, among other, religion has presented a conception of life incompatible with the aspiration for material success and for terrestrial accomplishment; in

---

*From *The Business Quarterly—Canada's Management Journal,* Fall, 1966, pp. 56–62.

[1] Victor Barbeau, *La Mesure de notre taille* (Montréal: by the author, 1936).

[2] Jacques Melançon, "Retard de croissance de l'entreprise canadienne-française," *Actualité Economique,* Vol. 31 (Janvier–Mars, 1956), pp. 503–22.

[3] Mgr. L. A. Paquet, *Discours et Allocutions* (Québec: by the author, 1915).

other words, a Catholic ethics having an opposite stimulus than that proposed by Max Weber on Protestant ethics. These interpretations and others, have contributed to circumscribe the causes of persistent negative attitudes towards business accomplishments. However, two recent sociological theories are being applied to French Canada with growing acceptance and will be discussed later.

DOES FRENCH CANADIAN MANAGEMENT EXIST?

Managers Require Organizations

It is evident to most people that French Canada as a group is economically poor. A rapid examination of business enterprises of any size controlled by its members would soon confirm this situation. In 1956 Jacques Melançon estimated at only 1% of the total market value the value of such enterprises listed on the Montréal and Canadian Stock Exchanges.[4] While the number of companies has increased from 26 to approximately 40 since 1956, and a number of larger institutions are not listed, this type of approach gives a clear idea of the stage of evolution of business enterprises. Another indication of economic anemia is confirmed to a certain extent by the fact that the majority of French Canadians are employed by organizations which they have not built themselves. Large industrial and financial corporations having more than 50 years of existence do not number more than 10. Under these circumstances, management traditions which require the inter-action of managers and organizations, have a very limited influence on the present generation of managers. This generation has inherited a limited number of tools (i.e. managerial concepts, structures, philosophies), from their predecessors. For example, the largest organization, although not strictly speaking a business enterprise, in which a management thought is being shaped, is the Hydro-Québec with 12,000 regular employees and assets totalling $2.3 billion. This, through government action, was the first opportunity to go "big" twenty years ago. Another government initiative permitted the establishment of Société Générale de Financement which is polarizing leadership in the industrial sector (total assets under control $100 million). Corpex, Zodiac, Sogena are other groups created in recent years and active in the industrial areas; other groups occur such as Sogestion, Prêt & Revenu, Groupe Desjardins and Gelco which represent financial institutions assuming growing responsibilities. These rather new organizations are relatively modest by North American standards, but do represent a change of patent in the management structure of the last ten years. The Gelco Group would now have control over $1.3 billion in assets.[5] The Groupe Desjardins, which, in the opinion of the writer, is the most influential financial organization of all (1) by the number of people it implies, (2) its objectives, (3) the quality of management and (4) the assets under its control.

Managers for new enterprises originate from the more influential segment of

---

4 Melançon, *op. cit.*
5 *Financial Post,* October 23, 1965.

society at the present time. As an indirect consequence of industrialization, the middle class of French Canada—some 100,000 families—composed of professionals and executives has become wealthier and is found to be less and less traditional in its outlook towards managerial activities. Members of this class feel they will be succeeded by a young generation that will be more involved in large-scale enterprises.[6]

Sense of Achievement and Environment

The recent works of McClelland have presented additional information on the contribution of French Canada to business realizations.[7] McClelland has scientifically measured the achievement motivation of different ethnic groups in the United States and in other countries to demonstrate his theory. According to his theory the achievement motivation would receive its main influence from religious values, child-rearing practices and social class status, and would be largely responsible for economic growth of a group. His findings indicate that the French Canadian group in the United States scored one of the lowest in the groups measured—in terms of Achievement—and that French Canadians of Québec have a somewhat lower average Achievement score than for either the general Canadian readers or the Catholic readers for the English-speaking population. The contribution of McClelland is important here in that it scientifically measures and confirms recent and past observations about the sense of achievement of French Canadians, whatever the reasons justifying the situation. . . .

The Separatist Movement of Québec generally, and the Parti Pris group specifically, has attributed the lack of achievement to a so-called status of colonization that the French population would be enjoying.[8] Montréal psychiatrist, Pierre Lefebvre is a strong supporter of this theory which is an adaptation of the theories of American economist Hagen on colonialism. Essentially, the theory could be summarized as follows: (1) in a colonized group there exists a tendency to retire within oneself; the group doubts its possibilities of realization; (2) the group over evaluates the past by maintaining the structures prevailing before colonization and remains in a sort of immobility; (3) the people avoid reality and find their refuge in myths. . . . Generally speaking the Separatist Movement simplifies the problem and attributes the present anomalies in numerous areas, including that of business achievement, to a sole cause: the effects of the conquest on French Canadian psychism.

MANAGERIAL EDUCATION AND THOUGHT

It is generally accepted today that future generations of managers will be university educated and will require continuing management training through

---

6 Jacques Brazeau, "Québec's Emerging Middle Class," *Canadian Business,* March, 1963, pp. 30–40.

7 David C. McClelland, *The Achieving Society* (Princeton, N.J.: D. Van Nostrand Co., Inc., 1961).

8 "Portrait du colonisé québécois," *Revue Parti Pris* (Été, 1964).

executive development programs. To what extent French Canadian institutions have perceived these changes can be determined by what they are doing at present.

Schools of Commerce

The number of graduates from the three main schools of commerce (Laval, Hautes Etudes Commerciales and Sherbrooke) was 250 in 1965 and present enrolment totals 2,200. To what extent these institutions have given their graduates the desire and the instruments to become good managers can be determined to a certain degree by the field of activity chosen by their graduates. Over its 55 years of existence H.E.C. has produced more than 2,500 graduates; traditionally the accounting profession (public and private) has attracted a large proportion of its graduates. A very popular idea in the 1950's at H.E.C. was that the C.A. diploma was the surest way to success and that the C.A. was the best "spring-board" to enter industrial and financial organizations.

The writer has analysed the current field of activity of five graduating classes of H.E.C. (1960 to 1964); the results are summarized in the three following tables.

TABLE 1
Functions Currently Held by Graduates
(B. Sc. Com. and L. Sc. Com.) of
L'Ecole des Hautes Etudes Commerciales
Classes of 1960–1964*

Functions	Number	Percentage
Accounting	106	33
General management	46	15
Marketing and sales	40	13
Finance	31	10
Teaching	25	8
O.R. and systems	10	3
Economics	8	2
Personnel	4	1
Student	20	7
Others	27	8
Total	317	100

*Information for 3 tables derived from Annuaire général 1965, Association des diplomés de l'Ecole des H.E.C.

Accounting (public and private) attracts the largest proportion of graduates; general management refers mainly to management trainees; teaching includes graduates joining the staff of H.E.C. and, very recently, high schools; others include twenty-two for which no information was available. Accounting excluded, there are no significant fields of concentration.

Of the 317 graduates the occupational choices are known for 275 (excluding 25 students and 22 referred to earlier).

Graduates' preferences go to French Canadian organizations, although 36% are with Anglo-Canadian organizations (including American companies). An interesting aspect however is that only 56% of the graduates join business enterprises, although the eventual orientation of the young C.A.'s should increase this proportion. Another indication of current trends is given by the fact that out of the 153 working for business enterprises, 99 are employed by larger firms (i.e. more than 200 employees) of which 59 are Anglo-Canadian and 40 French Canadian. Only 4 graduates during this period have chosen to go in business on their own, which would tend to confirm that the generally accepted role of a school of commerce is not to prepare businessmen going on their own, but rather to prepare managers for organizations. . . .

TABLE 2
Organizations in Which Graduates
Are Currently Employed

Organization	Number	Percentage
French Canadian	156	57
Anglo-Canadian	99	36
Federal government	11	4
Québec government	9	3
Total	275	100

TABLE 3
Nature of Organizational Activities

Activities	Number	Percentage
Business enterprises	153	56
Chartered accounting firms	77	28
Educational institutions . . .	25	9
Governments	20	7
Total	275	100

MANAGEMENT IN PRACTICE

French Organizations

Originality and innovation in the practice of management has not shown any signs of vitality in French originated organizations. In recent years efforts have been made to recapture arrears in most domains including that of management. Exceptions are the Caisse Populaire and the co-operative movement as practiced in Québec which have attracted the attention of many countries and international organizations. Delegates and trainees from countries under development are continually coming to familiarize themselves with the organization. In some cases experts are sent to those countries requesting assistance through international agencies. It might be pointed out however, that the co-operative organization is more a socio-economic institution than a strict business organization.

Norman W. Taylor[9] noted that the French Canadian businessman was conservative, did not delegate, had little drive and was not innovation-minded. While others have proposed that these characteristics were generally those of the small and medium sized firms, larger firms the writer believes, have shown similar weaknesses in French Canada. This is particularly true of the banking industry where as a result of lack of planning and forward thinking, the two commercial banks are faced with serious competitive problems. Today these are quasi absent of the shopping centers. Because of difficult recruiting policies and absence of management development, their managers are generally incompetent and outdated. Businessmen find that their business relations with these two banks are difficult. Although management is very conscious of this situation and initiating changes, their effects will not show any material improvements for several years.

One traditional belief that vanished with the bankruptcy of Compagnie Nationale de Gestion Inc. in 1963, was that the quality of a businessman could be best measured by his ability to reorganize a company in difficulty or to revamp a declining enterprise. This learning-the-hard-way method has lost much of its popularity and the accent would now appear to be on innovation and creation.

Bilingual Management

An unusual feature of French Canadian managers is that a good percentage of them work in another language. To what extent this necessity has handicapped the quality of their work remains to be demonstrated. Jacques Brazeau has suggested that French Canadian managers are handicapped by their dependency on two languages and thus are without one with which they can express the whole range of their experiences.[10] Personnel communication and sentiments might also be involved. When a person is unable to express his thoughts with facility and the nuances which he would like to attain, he is devaluated in his own mind as a communicator.

In recent years the demand from English-speaking organizations for bilingual managers has increased dramatically for various reasons. This demand would appear to be in contrast with the traditional pattern where access to certain areas in larger corporations was said to be closed. On the other hand the reason advanced by representatives of these corporations was that there were no com-

9 Norman W. Taylor, "L'Industriel Canadien—français et son milieu," *Recherches sociographiques,* No. 11, p. 125.

10 Jacques Brazeau, "Language Differences and Occupational Experience," *The Canadian Journal of Economics and Political Science,* Vol. 24, No. 4 (November, 1958), pp. 532–40.

petent candidates. While the truth might be a composite of both arguments, a recent study made in the United States might put some light on such a delicate subject. Lewis B. Ward, in a recent study on selection policies, pointed out "the failure to find members of certain minority groups represented in the management ranks of companies in which top management clearly believes in the ideal of equal opportunity for all."[11] The conclusions of this study suggest that subtle barriers to management careers exist. The same problem might or might not exist in Canada; however some organizations have gone a long way in a new and positive direction to relieve the language difficulties. The impetus was given some ten years ago in professional services by a firm of chartered accountants and is attributed to the perspicacity of Mr. J. R. Wilson, a partner of Clarkson & Gordon & Co. The novelty consisted in the establishment of French lines of management from partners to staff. Probably for the first time French could be used in all phases of work in an English organization. The example has since been followed by a growing number of organizations such as business consulting, law firms, insurance companies. The advantage of this type of structure is obvious. A French market can be offered services without restrictions by the language of communication. The employee can work in a familiar environment and has access to the higher positions. Furthermore, it will permit access to large and sophisticated organizations to an increased number of French Canadians who normally prefer to work in their language. New attitudes are thus being developed which will permit practical solutions to the general problem of cultural environment of business firms.

EMERGENCE OF A MANAGERIAL CLASS

Traditional Beliefs and a New Spirit

The extent to which the young generation believes it is part of a strictly religious society is evidenced by the very concrete and action-oriented activities of the young generation, of which the Separatist Movement is but one facet. The avidity to do things, for example, is reflected in the popularity of investment clubs. The writer's own estimate is that there are approximately 400 such clubs in Québec having individual capital varying from $500 to $100,000. . . .

The socialistic touch of some of the new institutions is certainly in conflict with the traditional economic thought of Québec which accepted the intervention of the State on a suppletory basis only and was free enterprise minded. However, the participation of private capital in new ventures and the number of new private enterprises established recently is an indication that the State will not be called upon to solve all the problems. Rather, the mixed corporation formula, which has been used successfully in Europe, is now adapted here for larger investments such as the steel complex.

---

[11] Lewis B. Ward, "The Ethnics of Executive Selection," *Harvard Business Review,* March–April, 1965.

Educated Business Drive

A good foundation and the seriousness of recent developments lie in that the leading managers are well educated; they represent a change from the previous pattern in which businessmen originated from the less educated classes.[12] The management of major holding companies – Gelco, Corpex, Zodiac, Prêt et Revenu, Sogena, S.G.F. – are university graduates. In recent years schools of commerce have attracted students of a better quality and sons of successful businessmen.

The organization which synthesizes best the characteristics of growth and drive, and which has unusual resources in men and capital is the Groupe Desjardins. . . .

In 1965 Mr. Desjardins' Caisse has grown to be 1,300 in number with assets of more than $1.5 billion under the control of the group with membership of 1.7 million. Caisses are autonomous and without a federated body they would have limited possibilities—although some individual caisses might have more than $15 million in assets. In recent years a number of satellite institutions has been added to the original structure giving the group a complete financial network. . . . In addition to investments in affiliated companies the group holds 30% of the shares of Société Générale de Financement. According to a recent study 1/6 of the annual personal savings in Québec is deposited in Caisses populaires.[13] The group received its basic impulse from the co-operative doctrine and is still associated with modest people and the working class, and is generally perceived by the public as being more a social institution than a financial organization. Management is recruited mainly from graduates of social sciences and commerce of Laval University; recently however some Montréal financial organizations have seen their best men attracted by the dynamic image and financial strength of the group. In recent years another objective was added to the above. This last objective is oriented towards the expanding industrial sector of Québec's economy. A 30% participation in the creation of Société Générale de Financement was a first move in this direction; it is expected that the steel complex will be the occasion of a second contribution.

There are growing indications that a class of managers is now emerging in Québec. The fact that a larger number of businessmen, technocrats and entrepreneurs share similar values and ideas about opportunities, realizations and success, is in itself an indication. This action-oriented group having its own beliefs, its own clubs is a society in itself. For this group of persons challenges do exist.

---

12 Taylor, *op. cit.*, p. 125.

13 Ministère de l'Industrie et du Commerce, *Les Caisses Populaires au Québec, 1953–1962* (Québec: Imprimeur de la Reine, 1965), p. 41.

Additional References

AFRICA

General

"African Paradox—Tribalism Still Exerts Firm Grip on Loyalties, for Both Good and Ill." *Wall Street Journal*, December 1, 1967, p. 1.

Harbison, Frederick. "The African University and Human Resource Development," *Journal of Modern African Studies*, Vol. 3, No. 1 (May, 1965).

Housman, Warren H. *Managing Economic Development in Africa*. Cambridge, Mass.: The M.I.T. Press, 1963.

Meyer, Frank (ed.). *The African Nettle*. New York: The John Day Co., Inc., 1965.

Pearson, D. S. "African Advancement in Commerce and Industry," *Journal of Modern African Studies*, Vol. 3, No. 2 (August, 1965), pp. 231–47.

Prasad, S. Benjamin. "Some Managerial Aspects of the African Economic Problem," in *Management in International Perspective* (ed. Benjamin S. Prasad), pp. 160–70. New York: Appleton-Century-Crofts, 1966.

Rado, E. R. "Manpower, Education and Economic Growth," *Journal of Modern African Studies*, Vol. 4, No. 1 (May, 1966), pp. 83–93.

Rose, Alvin W. "Sociology and the Transitional African Societies," *The American Journal of Economics and Sociology*, April, 1966.

African Countries

Bayre, E. A. "Somalia and the U.S.—Part I, the Somali Predicament," American Universities Field Staff Reports Service, Northeast Africa Series, Vol. 14, No. 1 (April, 1967).

Beling, Willard A. *Modernization and African Labor: A Tunisian Case Study*. New York: Frederick A. Praeger, Inc., 1965.

Fowler, Alan E. "Personnel Management in a New Overseas Company—A Nigerian Case Study," *Personnel Management* (Journal of the Institute of Personnel Management) (UK), Vol. 48, No. 377 (September, 1966), pp. 132–37.

Gallagher, Charles F. "The Moroccan Economy in Perspective," American Universities Field Staff Reports Service, North Africa Series, Vol. 12, No. 1 (July, 1966).

———. "North African Problems and Prospects—Part II, Industrialization and Development," American Universities Field Staff Reports Service, North Africa Series, Vol. 10, No. 3 (March, 1964).

———. "A Note on the Maghrib—Morocco, Algeria, Tunisia, and Libya in 1967," American Universities Field Staff Reports Service, North Africa Series, Vol. 13, No. 6 (May, 1967).

"The Men Who Build Nigeria's Big Business," *Business Week*, September 18, 1965.

Peil, Margaret. "Factory Management and Workers in Accra (Ghana)," *The Economic Bulletin of Ghana*, Vol. 10 (1966), pp. 23–35.

Sokolski, Allen. *The Establishment of Manufacturing in Nigeria*. New York: Frederick A. Praeger, Inc., 1965.

ASIA

China

Funnell, Victor C. "Social Stratification" (in China), *Problems of Communism,* Vol. 17 (March–April, 1968), pp. 14–20.

Richman, Barry M. *Industrial Management in Communist China.* Los Angeles: Graduate School of Business Administration, University of California, 1967.

Wilson, Dick. "The Capitalists of Mao Tse Tung," *Management Today* (UK), May, 1968, p. 84.

India

Agarwala, Amar N. "The Government Business Relationship in India," *Business Topics* (Michigan State University), Vol. 16, No. 2 (Spring, 1968), pp. 15–28.

Jain, Sagar C. "The Man in the Gray Flannel Achkan," *Columbia Journal of World Business,* Fall, 1966.

Kennedy, Van D. "India: Tendermindedness vs. Tough Problems," *Industrial Relations,* October, 1965.

Lambert, Richard D. *Workers, Factories and Social Change in India.* Princeton, N.J.: Princeton University Press, 1963.

Myers, Charles A. *Labor Problems in the Industrialization of India.* Cambridge, Mass.: Harvard University Press, 1958.

———. "Recent Developments in Management Training," *Indian Journal of Public Administration,* Vol. 4, No. 2 (April–June, 1958), pp. 154–64.

Phatak, A. "Environmental Constraints and Managerial Problems in a Developing Economy— Case Study of India," *Management International Review,* Vol. 8 (February–March, 1968), pp. 137–46.

Sheth, N. R. "Society and Industrial Work in India: A Case Study," *Human Organization,* Vol. 26, No. 1–2 (Spring–Summer, 1967), pp. 77–89.

Shoji, Ito. "A Note on the 'Business Climate' in India, with Special Reference to the Naktukattai Chettiars," *The Developing Economies,* Vol. 55, No. 3 (September, 1966), p. 367.

Singer, Milton. "Religion and Social Change in India," *Economic Development and Cultural Change,* July, 1966.

Israel

Derber, Milton. "Worker Participation in Israeli Management," *Industrial Relations,* Vol. 3, No. 1 (October, 1963).

Radom, Matthew. "Military Officers and Business Leaders in Israel," *Columbia Journal of World Business,* Vol. 3, No. 2 (March–April, 1968), pp. 27–34.

Various issues of *Work* (General Federation of Labor in Israel).

Japan

Abegglen, James C. *The Japanese Factory.* Glencoe, Ill.: The Free Press, 1958.

Bennett, J., and Ishino, I. *Paternalism in the Japanese Economy.* Minneapolis: University of Minnesota Press, 1963.

de Mente, Boye. "The Japanese Executive and His Management Philosophy," *Worldwide P & I Planning* (U.S.), Vol. 2, No. 1 (January–February, 1968), pp. 42–51.

Honda, Masu-ichi. "Managing Personnel in Japanese Industry," *Personnel Journal* (U.S.), Vol. 47, No. 3 (1967), pp. 191–97.

Management, Supervision and Skill Development in Japan. Japan Productivity Center, 1961, pp. 1–20.

Miller, Stanley S. "Management by Omikoshi: Traditional Features of Modern Business in Japan," *Management International,* Vol. 1 (1963), pp. 59–69.

Noda, K., and Glazer, H. "Traditional Japanese Management Decisions-Making," *Management International Review,* Vol. 8 (February–March, 1968).

Norbeck, Edward. *Changing Japan.* New York: Holt, Rinehart & Winston, Inc., 1965.

Olson, Lawrence. "The Motono Co. Revisited," American Universities Field Staff Reports Service, Vol. 11, No. 3 (April, 1964).

Paus, Robert K. (ed.). *Business in Japan Workshop.* Tokyo: Sophia University Press, 1966.

Reischauer, Edwin O. *Japan—Past & Present.* 2d ed.; New York: Alfred A. Knopf, Inc., 1964.

———. *The U.S. and Japan.* 2d ed.; Boston: Harvard University, 1965.

Ryoji, Ito. "Education as a Basic Factor in Japan's Economic Growth," *The Developing Economies,* Vol. 1, No. 1 (January–June, 1963), p. 37.

Ways, Max. "Why Japan's Growth Is Different," *Fortune,* November, 1967, p. 127.

Other Asian Countries

Dupree, Louis. "A Note on Pakistan—The Political, Economic & Historical Background of a Muslim Nation," American Universities Field Staff Reports Service, South Asia Series, Vol. 7, No. 8 (May, 1963).

Hanna, Willard A. "A Note on Malaysia, Singapore & Brunei," American Universities Field Staff Reports Service, Southeast Asia Series, Vol. 14, No. 14 (June, 1966).

Insor, D. *Thailand: A Political, Social, and Economic Analysis.* New York: Frederick A. Praeger, Inc., 1963.

Jacobs, Norman. *The Sociology of Development—Iran as an Asian Case Study.* New York: Frederick A. Praeger, Inc., 1966.

Riza Shah Pahlevi. "Advancement of Management in Iran," *Advanced Management Journal,* July, 1965.

Stringer, Robert A., Jr. "Toward an Understanding of Human Behavior in Organizations," *The Philippine Review of Business and Economics,* Vol. 4, No. 1 (April, 1967), pp. 27–33.

EUROPE

General

Granick, David. *The European Executive.* New York: Doubleday & Co., Inc., 1964.

Czechoslovakia

Michal, Jan M. *Central Planning in Czechoslovakia.* Stanford, Calif.: Stanford University Press, 1960.

Prasad, A. "Prague Goes Pragmatic," *Columbia Journal of World Business,* Vol. 2, No. 2 (March–April, 1967).

Sestakova, Monika. "The Firm in the Czechoslovak Economy," *The Journal of Industrial Economics* (UK), Vol. 16, No. 1 (November, 1967).

Sokol, Miroslav, "High-Level Manpower Planning: An Analysis of Czechoslovak Experience," *International Labour Review,* Vol. 95, No. 1–2 (January–February, 1967).

Finland

Herzberg, F. "The Motivation to Work Among Finnish Supervisors," *Personnel Psychology,* Winter, 1965.

France

Bauchet, Pierre. *Economic Planning: The French Experience.* Trans. Daphne Woodward. New York: Frederick A. Praeger, Inc., 1964.

"Management Stirs Up a Storm in France," *International Management,* Vol. 22, No. 2 (February, 1967).

Ross, Arthur M. "Prosperity and Labor Relations in Western Europe: Italy and France," *Institute of Industrial Relations,* Reprint No. 195, University of California, 1963.

Germany

Fulmer, R. M., and Brunner, L. "An Analysis of U.S. & German Practice of Product Management," *Management International Review,* Vol. 8 (February–March, 1968), pp. 25–36.

Hahn, W. "Higher Education in West Germany: Reform Movements and Trends," *Comparative Education Review,* Vol. 7 (June, 1963), pp. 47–51.

Hartman, H. *Authority and Organization in German Management.* Princeton, N.J.: Princeton University Press, 1959.

Lewis, R., and Steward, R. *The Managers.* New York: New American Library, Mentor Books, 1961.

Marburg, Theodore F. "Government and Business in Germany: Public Policy toward Cartels," *Business History Review,* Vol. 38 (1964).

Worms, H. J. "How Does German Industry Plan," *European Business Review,* February, 1967, p. 20.

Greece

Coutsoumaris, George. *The Morthology of Greek Industry.* Athens: Center of Economic Research, 1963.

Hellenews. *Economy of Greece 1966.* Athens: C. H. Christou, 1967.

Italy

Dull. "Business Italian Style," *The Director,* June, 1965, pp. 484–87.

Guzzardi, Walter. "Boom Italian Style," *Fortune,* May, 1968, p. 136.

Hildebrand, George H. *Growth and Structure in the Economy of Modern Italy.* Cambridge, Mass.: Harvard University Press, 1965.

"Italian Industries Father Figures," *The Economist,* December 5, 1964.

Marzotto, Antonio. "Communists and Employers in Italian Industry," *European Business Review,* July, 1966, p. 37.

"The New Italian Manager," *Fortune,* December, 1962, p. 96.

Scimone. "No Managerial Miracles in Italy," *The Manager,* May, 1965, pp. 55–57.

Netherlands

Scott, James D., and Waterman, M. H. "Innovation in Dutch Middle Management Education," *Michigan Business Review,* Vol. 20, No. 3 (May, 1960), pp. 25–30.

Poland

Feiwel, George R. *The Economics of a Socialist Enterprise—A Case Study of the Polish Firm.* New York: Frederick A. Praeger, Inc., 1965.

Kolaja, Jiri Thomas. *A Polish Factory: A Case Study of Workers' Participation in Decision Making.* Lexington: University of Kentucky Press, 1960.

Rosner, Ian. "Management by the Workers in Poland," *International Labour Review,* Vol. 76, No. 3 (September, 1957), pp. 257–77.

Spain

"Awakening Land," *Time,* January 21, 1966.

"Spanish Temper Heats Up," *Business Week,* August 6, 1966.

Whitney, Fred. *Labor Policy and Practices in Spain—A Study of Employer-Employee Relations Under the Franco Regime.* New York: Frederick A. Praeger, Inc., 1965.

Sweden

Elson, Robert T. "The Wallenberg Dynasty," *Fortune,* Vol. 65, No. 5 (May, 1962), pp. 77–86.

Fleisher, F. *The New Sweden.* New York: David McKay Co., Inc., 1967.

"Sweden's Way," *Economist,* March 30, 1963, pp. 1235–64.

Waldenstrom, Erland. "Works Councils: The Need to be Involved," *Columbia Journal of World Business,* Vol. 3, No. 3 (May–June, 1968), pp. 59–66.

Turkey

"Turkey Rediscovers a Satisfying Blend," *The Columbia Journal of World Business,* Spring, 1966, pp. 65–71.

Eren, Mari. *Turkey Today and Tomorrow: An Experiment in Westernization.* New York: Frederick A. Praeger, Inc., 1963.

Yugoslavia

Kolaja, Jiri. *Worker's Councils: The Yugoslav Experience.* New York: Frederick A. Praeger, Inc., 1965.

Rusinow, D. I. "Laissez-Faire Socialism in Yugoslavia," American Universities Field Staff Reports Service, Southeast Europe Series, Vol. 14, No. 2 (September, 1967).

LATIN AMERICA

General

Alexander, Robert J. *Labor Relations in Argentina, Brazil, and Chile.* New York: McGraw-Hill Book Co., Inc., 1962.

Blum, A. A., and Form, W. H. *Industrial Relations and Social Change in Latin America.* Gainesville: University of Florida Press, 1965.

Brandenburg, F. *The Development of Latin American Private Enterprise.* Washington, D.C.: National Planning Association, 1964.

Ferguson, J. Halro. "Latin America—Image and Reality," *Progress—The Unilever Quarterly,* Vol. 51, No. 286 (4/1965–66), pp. 72–96.

Gomez, R. A. "Latin American Executive: Essence and Variations," *Journal of Inter-American Studies,* Vol. 3 (January, 1961), pp. 81–95.

Lauterbach, Albert. *Enterprise in Latin America, Business Attitudes in a Developing Economy.* Ithaca, N.Y.: Cornell University Press, 1966.

————. "Executive Training and Productivity: Managerial Views in Latin America," *Industrial and Labor Relations Review,* Vol. 17, No. 3 (1964), pp. 357–79.

————. "Government and Development: Managerial Attitudes in Latin America," *Journal of Inter-American Studies,* Vol. 7, No. 2 (1965), pp. 201–25.

Prasad, S. B. "Comment: Decision Making in Latin America Business," *Journal of the Academy of Management,* Vol. 8, No. 4 (1965), pp. 326–28.

Urguidi, Victor L. *The Challenge of Development in Latin America.* New York: Frederick A. Praeger, Inc., 1964.

Whyte, W. F., and Holmberg, A. R. "Human Problems of U.S. Enterprise in Latin America," *Human Organization,* Vol. 15, No. 3 (1956), pp. 1–40.

Argentina

Cochran, T. C. *Entrepreneurship in the Argentine Culture.* Philadelphia: University of Pennsylvania Press, 1962.

Fillol, Tomas R. *Social Factors in Economic Development—The Argentine Case*. Cambridge, Mass.: The M.I.T. Press, 1961.

Loughran, J. A. "Some Reflections on the Argentine Problem," *Inter-American Economic Affairs*, Vol. 18, No. 1 (1964), pp. 29–45.

Rowe, James W. "A Note on Argentina—Change, Stagnation, and Unrealized Promise," American Universities Field Staff Reports Service, East Coast South America Series, Vol. 11, No. 3 (June, 1964).

Brazil

Baer, W. *Industrialization and Economic Development in Brazil*. Homewood, Ill.: Richard D. Irwin, Inc., 1965.

Rosen, S. C. "Socialization and Achievement Motivation in Brazil," *American Sociological Review*, Vol. 27, No. 5 (1962), pp. 612–24.

Rowe, James W. "Brazilian Development and the 'Swinging' Back Country," American Universities Field Staff Reports Service, East Coast South America Series, Vol. 13, Nos. 3, 4 (1967).

————. "A Note on Brazil—Observations on the Brazilian Environment, People, History and Social Institutions," American Universities Field Staff Reports Service, East Coast South America Series, Vol. 13, No. 5 (August, 1967).

Walker, Gilmer E., Jr. *Industrial Management in Brazil: A Measure of Economic Potential*. Washington, D.C.: Industrial College of the Armed Forces, 1963.

Chile

Lauterbach, Albert. *Managerial Attitudes in Chile*. University of Chile, 1961.

Mamalakis, M., and Reynolds, C. W. *Essays on the Chilean Economy*. Homewood, Ill.: Richard D. Irwin, Inc., 1965.

Mexico

Brandenburg, F. "The Case of Mexico: A Contribution to the Theory of Entrepreneurship and Economic Development," *Inter-American Economic Affairs*, Vol. 16, No. 3 (1962), pp. 3–23.

Cline, Howard F. *Mexico, Revolution to Evolution, 1940–1960*. London: Oxford University Press, 1962.

Mosk, Sanford A. *Industrial Revolution in Mexico*. Berkeley: University of California Press, 1954.

Vernon, Raymond. *The Dilemma of Mexico's Development, The Roles of the Private and Public Sectors*. Cambridge, Mass.: Harvard University Press, 1963.

Vernon, Raymond (ed.). *Public Policy and Private Enterprise in Mexico*. Cambridge, Mass.: Harvard University Press, 1964.

Other Latin-American Countries

Patch, Richard W. "A Note on Bolivia and Peru," American Universities Field Staff Reports Service, West Coast South America Series, Vol. 12, No. 2 (June, 1965).

Reynolds, Lloyd, and Gregory, Peter. *Wages, Productivity and Industrialization in Puerto Rico*. Yale Economic Growth Center Series. Homewood, Ill.: Richard D. Irwin, Inc., 1965.

Whyte, W. F. *The Cultural Environment and Industrial Relations: The Case of Peru*. Ithaca: New York State School of Industrial and Labor Relations, 1962.

————. "Culture, Industrial Relations, and Economic Development: The Case of Peru," *Industrial and Labor Relations Review*, Vol. 16 (July, 1963), pp. 583–94.

Whyte, W. F., and Williams, L. K. *Supervisory Leadership: An International Comparison*. Ithaca: New York State School of Industrial and Labor Relations, 1963.

UNION OF SOVIET SOCIALIST REPUBLICS

Azrael, Jeremy R. "Bringing Up the Soviet Man: Dilemmas and Progress," *Problems of Communism* (U.S. Information Agency), Vol. 17 (May–June, 1968), pp. 23–31.

————. *Managerial Power and Soviet Politics.* Cambridge, Mass.: Harvard Russian Research Center Studies, 52, 1966.

Bendix, Reinhard. "Entrepreneurial Ideologies in Eighteenth and Nineteenth Century Russia," *Work and Authority in Industry,* chap. 3. New York: John Wiley & Sons, Inc., 1956.

Berlinger, Joseph S. *Factory and Management in the U.S.S.R.* Cambridge, Mass.: Harvard University Press, 1957.

Broderson, Arvid. *The Soviet Worker.* New York: Random House, Inc., 1966.

Bronson, David W. "Soviet Experience with Shortening the Work Week," *Industrial and Labor Relations Review,* Vol. 21, No. 3 (April, 1968), pp. 391–97.

Fedorenko, N. "The Reforms in Industry: Initial Results, Problems of Raising Efficiency," *Problems of Economics* (International Arts & Sciences Press), Vol. 10, No. 6 (October, 1967), pp. 12–23.

Granick, David. *The Red Executive.* New York: Doubleday & Co., Inc., 1961.

Herzberg, F. "A Case Study of Attitudes to Labor in the Soviet Union," *Personnel Psychology,* Fall, 1965.

Horwitz, Bertrand N. "Profit Responsibility in Soviet Enterprise," *Journal of Business* (University of Chicago), Vol. 41, No. 1 (January, 1968), pp. 47–55.

Liberman, E. G. "The Role of Profits in the Industrial Incentive System of the USSR," *International Labour Review,* Vol. 97, No. 1 (January, 1968), pp. 1–14.

Richman, Barry M. *Management Development and Education in the Soviet Union.* East Lansing: Michigan State University Press, 1967.

————. *Soviet Management: With Significant American Comparisons.* Englewood Cliffs, N.J.: Prentice-Hall, Inc., 1965.

Rostow, W. W. *The Dynamics of Soviet Society.* New York: W. W. Norton & Co., Inc., 1967.

Smith, H. R. "Robber Baron and Russian Manager: Curious Cognates," *Columbia Journal of World Business,* November–December, 1967, pp. 73–79.

Yadov, V. A. "The Soviet and American Worker: Job Attitudes," *Soviet Life,* January, 1965.

UNITED KINGDOM

Acton Society Trust. *Management Succession.* London: The Trust, 1956.

Adderley, John. "Organization and Methods Activities in the United Kingdom," *Systems & Procedures Journal,* Vol. 18, No. 6 (November–December, 1967), pp. 33–35.

Bendix, Reinhard. *Work and Authority in Industry.* New York: John Wiley & Sons, Inc., 1956.

Bonham-Carter, A. D. "UK Industry and the Universities: Are They in Step?" *Progress—The Unilever Quarterly,* Vol. 51, No. 290 (4, 1966), pp. 224–28.

Carson, David. "Problem Schools of Management," *Management Today,* August, 1967, pp. 71–73, 102–4.

Clements, R. V. *Managers, A Study of Their Careers in Industry.* London: George Allen and Unwin, Ltd., 1958.

A Companies Act 1970? PEP Planning, Vol. 33, No. 500 (October, 1967) (UK).

Copeman, Dr. G. H. *Leaders of British Industry.* London: Gee and Co., 1955.

Florence, P. Sargant. *The Logic of British and American Industry. A Realist Analysis of Economic Structure and Government.* London: Routledge & Kegan Paul, Ltd., 1961.

Guzzardi, Walter. "The Second Battle of Britain," *Fortune,* February, 1968, p. 108.

Ivens, Michael. "Behind the Organization Man," *20th Century* (Oxford University), Spring, 1965, pp. 15–25.

Lewis, R., and Stewart, R. *The Managers*. New York: New American Library, 1961.

McGivering, Ian C.; Matthews, D.; and Scott, W. *Management in Britain*. Liverpool: Liverpool University Press, 1960.

"The Missing Ingredient in British Business," *The Director* (England), September, 1965.

Morrison, J. Roger. "Britain's Quiet Managerial Revolution," *The McKinsey Quarterly*, Winter, 1968, pp. 2–9.

Sampson, A. *The Anatomy of Britain Today*. New York: Harper & Row, Publishers, 1965.

Shinn, John. "Britain: The Revolution that Nobody Sees," *International Management*, October, 1966.

Wider Business Objectives. PEP Planning, Vol. 32, No. 495 (May, 1966) (UK).

White, Sheffield. "The Underdeveloped British Businessman," *The Atlantic*, January, 1966, pp. 75–78.

Winsbury, Rex. "Industry's Education Gap," *Management Today* (UK), May, 1968, p. 110.

chapter ten

Convergence in Managerial Philosophy and Practice?

The title of this chapter is a question. Perhaps the answer depends on the level we consider. At the top of the firm and at the level of man–machine relationships, there does seem to be convergence. Governments are playing larger economic roles in capitalist countries, the market more in socialist countries. The hired managers of large autonomous firms are gaining more control everywhere. Similarly, the basic technology of the industrial age is very much the same in Oshkosh, Minsk, and Brazzaville. In the middle, however, where managers make decisions, communicate, and motivate, convergence may be less dramatic.

This chapter deals with forces of uniformity and of diversity. A common economic motivation is manifest in technology, education, and philosophy; diversity is found in time, natural resources, demography, and culture. The factors that foster uniformity appear to dominate at the macroeconomic and the microtechnical levels—the place of business in the nation and the use of modern technology in the plant. The forces of divergence (especially culture), however, assert stronger influences on the philosophy and practice of managers within the firm.

THE FORCES OF UNIFORMITY

Technology

Whether macro or micro, the most common argument for convergence is the imperative of industrialization itself. Technology, like the language of mathematics, is universal. By obeying laws of reason and science, men of varying cultural and ideological positions presumably can agree on the best machine design or most desirable production system. For the most part, this technology is Western. The hardware of Europe and America is spreading over the globe, so that the machine tended by the American worker may be more modern (although in some industries it is older), but it is not fundamentally different than that of the worker in India or Brazil where industrialization is just taking place. Demands for attention, response, and care exerted by the machine on the man are essentially the same. Farmer and Richman write:

> In the process of creating a modern industrial society, it is clear that in the scientific realm all nations are constrained by natural laws. Water freezes at the same temperature in Moscow as in New York or London, and atomic physicists follow the same methodology in science wherever they may be. There are certain chemical problems relating to steel production which are immutable for all firms, regardless of location or ownership, or even how they are managed. If one wishes to obtain some end product, he must usually follow rigorously the scientific laws relating to this production. Production basically is the transformation of input, including products of the land itself, into useable output; and technological constraints force firms everywhere to follow the same general production patterns. This in turn forces production managers to be somewhat similar regardless of other differences in firms. Such managers may use more or less labor than others, build bigger or smaller furnaces, use coal or electricity for fuel; but the logic of production sharply limits the range of choice in this sector of management.[1]

If there is only one best technology, and if a country wants to industrialize, the resulting arrangement of work affects occupations. Traditional manual and hand systems of power and manufacture are eliminated or reduced to marginal importance. Elaborated division of labor and graduated skill levels emerge. The unskilled hired hand, handyman, or millhand, all tend to become irrelevant—witness how difficult it is for unskilled minority groups to find jobs in U.S. cities—jobs they could usually obtain (if sporadically) years ago in rural America.[2] So the dumb, phlegmatic, oxlike Schmidt that Frederick W. Taylor made famous 50 years ago becomes the literate and fairly articulate Smith with skills that management needs, and for which substitutes are much harder to find.

As skill rises, power rises. Employees are given responsibility for more expensive equipment and more critical decisions. Since a manager now finds it much harder to supervise everyone, his subordinates' commitment to work conscientiously becomes more important. As David Mechanic has pointed out in "The Sources of Power of Lower Participants in Complex Organizations,"[3] the need for subordinate consent gives them influence. Power becomes less unilateral and management less autocratic.

The imperatives of the machine cannot be confined to the shop. Off the job, a man's position in society tends to change, and the social structure becomes more open. Choosing one's parents is still important, but it should become less so. What a man does becomes increasingly important over what a man is. Kerr, Dunlop, Harbison, and Myers maintain that this leads to convergence.

---

[1] Richard N. Farmer and Barry M. Richman, *Comparative Management and Economic Progress* (Homewood, Ill.: Richard D. Irwin, Inc., 1965), pp. 394–95.

[2] See Arthur M. Ross and Herbert Hill, *Employment, Race, and Poverty* (Harcourt, Brace & World, 1967).

[3] *Administrative Science Quarterly*, Vol. 7 (1962–1963), pp. 349–64.

The same technology calls for much the same occupational structure around the world—in steel, in textiles, in air transport. The occupational role of a man gives him a place in society that affects his behavior in many ways. Also, there comes to be a growing diversity of occupations and of levels of management, and no really clear-cut dividing lines are visible to all. The occupation takes the place of the class.[4]

In a Chapter Six selection from David McClelland, "Social Class Background of Managers in Various Countries," we did, indeed, see that industrialization tends to be associated with greater opportunity for the relatively modest born. The performance of the high achiever, rather than nepotism, becomes the determinant of success.

More sophisticated technology and greater educational requirements give workers more mobility. With skill there is additional freedom to move, as has occurred in the U.S.S.R. in the postwar era. When Ivan has a skill that the state needs, and for which a number of plant managers are willing to pay, it is not easy to limit his mobility without recourse to expensive and inefficient policing. Technology, therefore, will be a major force in making work more similar wherever industrialization occurs—fewer unskilled jobs, greater division of labor, less paternalistic or autocratic management, social level defined by occupation, and greater opportunities for sons to move higher up the occupational and social ladder.

Education

Industrialization must be served. And education becomes a servant. As we have seen, complex technology and sophisticated organization require training in a variety of specialties. Vast expansion of the educational system is required to support this industrialization, but equally people demand education as a right over and above any contribution it makes to economic growth..The way of life facilitated by industrialization calls for other specialists to attend to needs off the job. In short, an industrial society must educate its people, in order that workers are literate, so that they can understand instructions, follow directions, and keep records, and so that managers, engineers, and civil servants are trained to operate the new mixed public and private production system. Beyond that are the needs for doctors, lawyers, scientists, professors, and others.

The correlation of educational development and per capita income shown in the Harbison and Myers selected reading, "Higher Education and the Level of Economic Development," in Chapter Seven, suggests that higher income is associated with expanded education, although cause and effect are not entirely clear. The demand for education and educated people supplements and coincides with management's demand for capable people, regardless of their origins. One result is a leveling of economic and social disparities. The scarcity of skilled persons is gradually reduced, lessening their economic advantage; greater numbers of intel-

---

[4] Clark Kerr, John T. Dunlop, Frederick Harbison, and Charles A. Myers, "Industrialism and World Society," *Harvard Business Review,* January–February, 1961, p. 124.

ligent people are needed, so the advantages of the highly born are undermined.

In terms of socioeconomic and educational backgrounds, the gap between managers and workers may shrink with industrialization. Managers will remain substantially more educated than workers, but the workers' education will improve, and the relative gap between a high school and college education in an industrialized country is less than that between the "no education" of workers and the "some education" of managers in less-developed nations. Decreased social distance and greater education are apparently reflected in the findings of the managerial survey reported in the selected reading by Haire, Ghiselli, and Porter in Chapter Eight, "Cultural Patterns in the Role of the Manager": managers in various countries tend to share a fairly high opinion of the individual's capability for initiative and leadership. There is less agreement, however, with the desirability of sharing information and objectives, or with workers' participation in management.

Philosophy

Jet set is the term applied—part enviously, part critically—to the modern elite who fly between the capitals of modern life. But they may be a force for uniformity. As the elite of the economic world become a true elite—the best of people regardless of birth or advantage—they may become more alike in their pragmatism. Ideology tends to fade because of its irrelevancy for the problems faced. Man has a great ability to maintain belief in false ideology in the face of contradictory evidence, but Kerr, Dunlop, Harbison, and Myers suggest realism will replace it.

Thus the conflict of ideology is blunted and fades between societies. Consensus develops wherever industrialization is successful. The labor force becomes committed to and settled into industrial life. It accepts the pace of work, the web of rules, the surrounding structure. The sense of protest subsides. The business managers, left to their own devices, push less hard. Society provides more of the amenities of life. Men learn from experience how better to do things, and the rough edges are evened off. Industrialization is accepted. Finally, as the elites become less differentiated and the ideological controversies become more barren, the cultural patterns of the world intermingle and merge. These changes are in evidence although the majority of nations in the world have been in the active throes of industrialization only two generations or less.[5]

We have suggested that the aims of economic development—elimination of poverty, a better life, and so on—are more universally accepted than ever before. This commitment to economic development tends to undermine adherence to ideological principles, to the dismay of dogmatists both left and right, who with equal indignation cry that we are compromising our integrity (be it capitalist or socialist), compromising our principles (be they Marxian or Smithian), and flirting with the devil (be he solid red, or red, white, and blue striped)—all in the name of economic expediency. Echoing what many Eastern European economists elsewhere have believed but dared not say, a Communist official of the

---

[5] *Ibid.*, p. 124.

Czechoslovakian Institute of Management states,[6] "No one can touch the United States in industrial management." The institute presents an unabashedly American-influenced program of case studies, industrial games, marketing, sociology, psychology, research and development, and other Western techniques that until relatively recently were either unknown or unmentionable in the Communist world. Jaroslaw Jirasek, director of the program, says, "We are in a very bad position after those years when entrepreneurial decisions were made by centralized management. It is not easy to change men's minds," he maintains, "but if we cannot change men's minds we must change the men because one clever man cannot be replaced by a thousand idiots." The reason for these changes? Economics. Faced with serious economic problems, Czechoslovakia "has no choice but to change and in a very short time. Otherwise, we will not be able to keep in the front of the European Movement." [7] Farmer and Richman write:

Increasingly, there's a trend to use whatever seems to work empirically in a given country. It is unlikely that we shall see again in the West the kind of mass unemployment or depression of the 1930's, caused by the failure of leaders even to consider alternative courses of action, nor shall we see advanced communist countries suffer their equivalent of depression (actually the increased production of useless and unneeded output) because leaders must follow the Marxist Dogma. Economic convergence may be closer than we realize, if we search for it. [8]

We want efficiency. Hindering ideologies, beliefs, and dogmas must surrender to economic pragmatism. In obtaining this efficiency, we need knowledgeable men, rather than family members or political appointments, to make the important decisions. This implies managerial autonomy. In *The New Industrial State,* [9] John Kenneth Galbraith points out that the large-scale production that characterizes industrialization requires enormous capital accumulation and complex technology. This involves elaborate organization. Risk must be minimized in order to facilitate and safeguard the expenditure of time and money to set up the operation. Communist enterprise managers and corporate executives all want to minimize uncertainty; they want to control everything that can adversely affect their organizations. This means autonomy and control—autonomy from uncontrollable pressures, be they market or bureaucratic in origin, and as much control as possible over prices, supply, and demand.

To effectively manage this organization, executives must be free of interference from incompetent owners or ignorant politicians. Only professional managers and specialists have the knowledge necessary to run the modern complex enterprise. This thesis is elaborated further in Galbraith's selected reading in this chapter, but the point is that organizational decisions are increasingly centralized in professional management. For a socialist country, this implies

---

6 Quoted in Jonathan Randal, "Czech Executives Going to Classes," *New York Times,* January 27, 1967.

7 *Ibid.*

8 Farmer and Richman, *op. cit.,* p. 399.

9 (Boston: Houghton Mifflin Co., 1967).

decentralization from state decision making; for the capitalist nation, it means increased central control by human decision makers (usually corporate planners and executives) versus impersonal control of the market. In either system, the central government has responsibility for alleviating further sources of uncertainty stemming from economic cycles, and especially for insuring a high-level of total economic demand.

Observing these economic developments, a prophet may maintain that national societies will become more alike because nations will disappear. Why? Because they are irrelevant. In politics, we have heard these arguments for a long time: Communists, Nazis, United World Federalists, and super United Nations supporters, men as different as Karl Marx, Adolph Hitler, Wendell Willkie, and Pope John XXIII—all have argued that national governments and boundaries divide men, promote war, and compound the human tragedy. Always, however, economic interests, as well as military and political factors, presumably contradicted their arguments. Exploitation of markets, protection of industry, enrichment of the mother country, and insulation from foreign depressions or inflations, and indeed frequently protection of liberty, have all called for strong national boundaries. Recently, it is possible that the economic pressures have changed, or are starting to change. Adam Smith's old fear of corporations apparently is being realized. Modern business firms—capitalist or socialist—are transcending national boundaries. Governments only get in their way. Frank Tannenbaum, a veteran observer of international developments, writes:

> An industrialized world is held together by the large number of corporate bodies, and by their widening role. The corporation groups the nationals into a new loyalty—a functional identity across all borders. The day may well come when the majority of people in all nations will have their functional loyalties to one or more supra-national corporate bodies. They may well become conscious of basic commitments, values, and interests unrelated to the state or the nation. [10]

It was the dream of Marx and the early socialists that workers everywhere would perceive their common interests, throw out the anachronistic national states, and institute a communist society in which national boundaries would disappear. These dreams were consumed in the fires of World War I, when the workingmen of the Western world marched to battle in the names of their various fatherlands. They went willingly and even happily, if the accounts of the era can be believed. [11] It is ironic that now the more potent forces for internationalization are the business interests so hated by socialist reformers.

FORCES OF DIVERSITY

We have discussed the forces of uniformity in economic activities and management. They are potent. Does this mean inevitable similarity around the globe?

---

[10] Frank Tannenbaum, "The Survival of the Fittest," *Columbia Journal of World Business,* Vol. 3, No. 2 (March–April, 1968), p. 19.

[11] See Barbara W. Tuchman, *The Proud Tower* (New York: Macmillan Co., 1966).

Inevitable is a vague term. "Inevitably," quite likely, there will be convergence in managerial, economic—and even political—philosophy and practice. Nonetheless, the time is far off, for there are forces of diversity as well.

Time

Modern technology has been grafted onto societies at different times, when the societies were at different stages of economic development. Hence, in the selected reading, "Are Industrial Societies Becoming Alike?" Feldman and Moore suggest that when this technology is introduced into a culture it is not automatically accepted. Stresses are produced. These may be suppressed, but the tensions spring up elsewhere. Society may adapt to suit the technology, but unintended changes also occur in other areas. This cycle of stress, accommodation, and new stress may dampen out, but the process is undoubtedly slow. Thus, the introduction of modern technology and industrialization to Japan produced factories and machines very like Great Britain's. However, life within the plants has not been identical. The countries were different at the onset of development, so the stresses produced in the two countries were different: family-centered in Japan, class-centered in Great Britain. The unanticipated and uncontrolled propagation of this stress affects different aspects of each culture, producing new diversity at the same time that the forces of uniformity are being felt.

Basic Resources

Of course, the natural resources of countries differ, which places real limits on the direction of development. Technology may eventually diminish the importance of natural resource differences: atomic power can substitute for water power, plastics for wood, and so on. But these differences are real, and they cause industry and management to differ. For a long time to come, political boundaries will continue to hinder the free travel of goods and resources, thus limiting the elimination of natural resource differentials.

The special character of the basic resources and the central industries causes variations from one country to another. Plantation agriculture, crude oil production, heavy industry, light industry, and so on, each give a tone to their society. Some industries are more prone to industrial unrest than others; some are more likely to engage in paternalistic practices; some are occupationally more highly stratified; some are more subject to a system of norms; some have more large scale enterprises. Each industry has its own character—the waterfront, coal mining, banking—and these cast their reflections on the surrounding society. A small or newly industrialized economy is more likely to reflect the special character of one or a few industries than is a large or mature economy. Thus oil gives a special flavor to Iraq, much as textiles and coal mining once did to England.[12]

Demography

The density of population obviously varies and exercises a divergent influence.

---

[12] Kerr, Dunlop, Harbison, and Myers, *op. cit.,* p. 122.

A relatively empty country is likely to have a course of development different than a heavily populated one. As we pointed out in Chapter Three, the United States always had higher wages, and labor recruitment was more difficult than in Europe. Labor efficiency was more critical, and a significant increase in the standard of living was made easier. High valuation of the individual worker and the attention he deserves were more common, and so forth. Barriers to immigration and man's uncertain ability or willingness to control births suggest that these differences will not soon disappear.

Cultural Inertia

Existing institutions, ideologies, and practices have lives of their own. They are persistent in the face of change. Thus, bare bottoms are an issue in Tanganyika: the puritanistic president, Julius Nyerere, has ordered the Massai tribe to alter their mode of dress.[13] The haughty Massai, who have long considered themselves superior to their more advanced countrymen, are strongly resisting the government directive to cover up the one buttock that they proudly bare. The Massai's vanity will probably give way to the demands of a more sophisticated state, but it will not be an easy battle. Attitudes toward life and acceptable behavioral patterns are slow to change, even under the pressures of economic necessity. They will probably change only as little as necessary to adapt to the new technology of modern industrialization. Residual differences, especially in national character traits, will remain for a long time.

Uniqueness is really the basis of diversity. At any moment, every country is unique in its cultural factors, economic development, natural resources, and demographic characteristics. Some of these may be similar to other countries, but the net mix is unique. Values, beliefs, and habitual behavior patterns strongly resist change because of the security they supply, as we saw in Chapter Two.

Now let us put together our forces of uniformity and diversity, and summarize how they affect management.

THE FUTURE

We cannot analyze the impact of these forces on management as a whole. Because the factors of uniformity and diversity differently affect the various aspects of management, we need to distinguish among three relationships in management. These are the three levels or interfaces: (1) man and his job, (2) man and man (superior–subordinate, lateral and diagonal relations), and (3) organization and its environment. Exhibit 1 summarizes the elements.

Arithmetic does not help us. At present, there is no way of adding up the forces for uniformity and those for diversity in a single country to obtain a net

---

[13] *Newsweek*, March 4, 1968.

number that suggests the rate or direction of movement. It appears, however, that the arguments for convergence and divergence vary on the three interfaces. Thus, the case for convergence in the relationship between man and his work—especially man and the machine—is compelling. Technological and economic pressures are so clear and strong that work for the average man will tend to become more uniform. His equipment, his portion of the task, his training for the job, the expectation that he appear and be on the job not at his own but at the employer's volition—all will tend to be similar in the not very distant future.

EXHIBIT 1
Summary of Elements

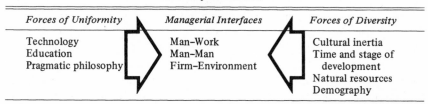

Forces of Uniformity	Managerial Interfaces	Forces of Diversity
Technology	Man–Work	Cultural inertia
Education	Man–Man	Time and stage of
Pragmatic philosophy	Firm–Environment	development
		Natural resources
		Demography

Similarly, the forces of convergence are strong on the relationship between the firm and its environment—customers, competitors, and government in particular. The growth of professional management administering the fairly autonomous firm is widespread in both capitalist and socialist countries, as we have pointed out. They must be relatively free from the interference of ignorant owners, politicians, and bureaucrats. Nonetheless, managers must be responsive to customers, or they will not produce needed goods—or, as the Russians have found, they will produce unwanted goods that will pile up in warehouses.

Recently, Premier Aleksei N. Kosygin called on Soviet industry to overcome the consumer goods gap between the U.S.S.R. and the United States. Invoking the example of "capitalist monopolies," he urged Soviet management to reduce delays in producing and marketing new consumer products. "In the capitalist countries," he said, "the monopolies are obliged to react quickly to the needs of the customers and produce modern types of products and search for new rational forms of organization of production and its control."[14] Just how U.S. firms are "obliged" is not entirely clear; if the market forces them to respond, then they must not be completely monopolistic. But the point is valid: some avenue of influence from customers to managers is essential, and is developing in the Communist states.

Less clear is convergence in the man to man, superior–subordinate, and peer relationships within the organization. We have described the possible trend toward strengthening the subordinate's importance and bargaining power through his increased knowledge and the more intricate technology he operates. This

---

[14] Quoted in Henry Kamm, "Soviet Exhorted on Consumer Gap," *New York Times*, February 19, 1968.

implies greater responsiveness by superiors to subordinates. Philip Slater and Warren Bennis have suggested that democracy is inevitable in economic organizations because of the two-way flow of influence arising out of technical sophistication and employees' skills; fear and power become less effective.[15]

Equality in decision making and harmony of interests, however, is not implicit in this evolution of influence processes. If these predictions have validity, conflict and bargaining between interest groups undoubtedly will characterize the more democratic business firms just as they exist in every democratic state. Hierarchical structure may change, but the general shape will remain. As I have discussed elsewhere,[16] differentiated positions in a hierarchy are probably essential because they reflect fundamental functions in the managerial process.

Superiors and subordinates will remain, but the basis of motivation may shift. With industrialization, government generated security, and improved living standards, management can no longer concentrate its appeal on low-level physical and security needs. Higher drives for competence, achievement, and autonomy become relevant. If the manager wants to tap the ability of skilled subordinates, he must gain their commitment. This means he must provide on-the-job opportunities to satisfy higher needs. At least among managers, the Haire, Ghiselli, and Porter study indicates the universality of higher-level drives for self-actualization in 14 nations and various cultures. As man gains freedom from slavery to basic needs, he will strive to satisfy higher motives.

Management must respond to this. Satisfied needs are irrelevant for motivation. To obtain commitment and effort, management must motivate by appealing to the next appropriate level of unsatisfied needs. If the hierarchy of needs is truly universal, management the world over will have to provide opportunities for participation, competence, and autonomy. From civil rights to education, from poor ghetto dwellers to affluent students—whether in Washington or Warsaw, the most profound social revolution in the world today is the struggle for democratic processes in decision making.

In addition, in the drive for efficiency there are pressures to impersonalize the managerial process, as we discussed in Chapter Two. Family membership, social class, religion, perhaps even color may tend to become irrelevant as management rationalizes its decision-making processes, and the organization changes from traditional to rational. Exhibit 2 summarizes this aspect of evolving management, and a selected reading from Chadwick Haberstroh elaborates on evolution of organizations.

In spite of these forces for uniformity in managerial philosophy and practice, however, the process will be slow. Thus, managerial leadership is affected by demographic conditions, whether or not there is an excess of labor. If there is, management is unlikely to be overly concerned about employees. Even more

---

[15] Philip E. Slater and Warren G. Bennis, "Democracy Is Inevitable," *Harvard Business Review,* March–April, 1964, pp. 51–59.

[16] David R. Hampton, Charles E. Summer, and Ross A. Webber, *Organizational Behavior and the Practice of Management* (Chicago: Scott, Foresman & Co., 1968). See chap. 4, "The Impact of Formal Organization: Structural Factors in Organizational Behavior."

important, the diversity of cultural values, beliefs, habits, and traditions exert profound influence on managerial relations. The patterns of respect, awe, contempt, deference, and so on are deep-seated. What is thought desirable or worthy in life will influence interpersonal relations—especially leadership style. The cultural factors discussed in this volume—attitudes toward authority, achievement, personal risk, and others—exercise more influence on the interpersonal aspects of management than on the man–technology or firm–environment interfaces. The forces of uniformity are less clear and imperative on the methods management uses to communicate, coordinate, and motivate. The sharp differences that exist in these processes within American companies, and among departments in the same companies, testify to the divergence in managerial philosophy and practice that we have, and may always have, within organizations. So, for a long time at the least, cultural factors will exert a strong and differentiating influence on managerial philosophy and practice—less so on technological and production decisions, less so on the relations of man and job, less so on the firm's relationship to its customers and society, but more on the methods of motivation, patterns of communication, and styles of leadership.

EXHIBIT 2
Modern versus Traditional Organization*

Factor	Modern	Traditional
Selection of key personnel	"Best" man selected using objective criteria.	Hereditary selection or from narrow social class.
Evaluation of key personnel	Continuous, quantifiable, based on as objective evidence as available.	None or irrational (based on religious, racial, caste, family, etc.).
Changes in evaluation of key personnel	Continuous search for improved techniques through improved planning-control-feedback loop systems.	None.
Criteria of evaluation through time	Expected continuous improvement and growth in abilities of key men.	No change expected.
Removal of key men	Resignations expected on failure. Transfers to less demanding positions common. Systematic effort to eliminate the less capable.	No legitimate removals. May occur through overthrow of organization.
Succession of key men upon retirements, deaths, etc.	Attempts to determine new "best" men.	Predetermined and known.

*From Richard N. Farmer, "The Revolutionary American Businessman." Reprinted from the *California Management Review,* Vol. 9, No. 4 (Summer, 1967), p. 82. Copyright 1967 by the Regents of the University of California.

SELECTED READINGS

Selection: "The Road to Similarity," Clark Kerr, John T. Dunlop, Frederick Harbison, and Charles A. Myers

The well-known academicians presented one of the classic arguments for convergence in this portion of their 1961 *Harvard Business Review* article, "Industrialism and World Society." They summarize the point:

> From Southeast Asia to Western Europe and from Chile to the Congo, the forces making for uniformity—especially uniformity in the all important relations between labor, management, and government—tend surely to become stronger than the forces perpetuating diversity. The imperatives of industrialization cause the controlling elites to overcome certain constraints and to achieve objectives *which are the same in all societies undergoing transformation.*

Selection: "Evolving Organizations," Chadwick J. Haberstroh

A sociologist examines the technical aspects of organizational structure essential to utilization of modern technology and managerial practices. The argument is that traditional organizations will change to reflect these aspects. Social arrangements extraneous to the task may retain their differences.

Selection: "The New Industrial State," John Kenneth Galbraith

The eminent economist, statesman, and political activist describes and analyzes the need for management—whether capitalist or socialist—to have autonomy to run their organizations. Freedom from owners or government is perceived as essential to allow application of sophisticated technology and management.

Selection: "Creeping Capitalism in the Soviet Union?" Harry Landreth

Professor Landreth takes issue with the convergence theme. Despite un-Marxian thinking in the U.S.S.R. and federal concentration in the United States, he asserts that the two economic systems are not converging.

Selection: "Are Industrial Societies Becoming Alike?" Arnold S. Feldman and Wilbert E. Moore

"Yes, but" . . . such is the theme of this selection. The authors survey the forces for uniformity, but point out the rich and varied sources of diversity at the national level.

selection 38

The Road to Similarity*

Clark Kerr, John T. Dunlop, Frederick Harbison, and Charles A. Myers

If we watch the way the world is industrializing day by day, we are likely to get a confusing and bewildering picture. There seems to be little consistency in the multitude of patterns followed by various nations, except that the under-developed ones are trying to catch up, and the developed ones are trying to stay ahead. Long-range predictions about the future of industrial man seem impossible.

But if we stand back from the day-to-day news picture and take a broader, more historical perspective, we find that there *is* a pattern to all the apparent chaos. From Southeast Asia to Western Europe and from Chile to the Congo, the forces making for uniformity—especially uniformity in the all-important relations between labor, management, and government—tend surely to become stronger than the forces perpetuating diversity. The imperatives of industrialization cause the controlling elites to overcome certain constraints and to achieve objectives *which are the same in all societies undergoing transformation.*

This conclusion is vastly different from traditional economic doctrines. Take, for example, the Marxist claim that capitalist development, unlike socialism, forces labor into a hostile role. Our study shows that, in truth, worker protest against management does *not* play a growing, intensifying role under capitalism, does *not* produce a basically different pattern of industrial relations from that produced by socialism. Worker protest may rise to a quick peak in the early stages of transformation, but then it characteristically declines.

Again, it appears that, whatever the society or ideology, the distinctions between managers come to be based more on the size and scope of their enterprises than on the ownership of the means of production; and that conflict between the different powers in society, while continuing to persist, becomes marked increasingly by bureaucratic skirmishes rather than by class war. Even ideological differences tend to fade as industrialization proceeds. The once vast discrepancies between capitalism and communism, or any other system, give way to more pragmatic considerations.

Thus, more and more the questions before the controlling groups become

*From "Industrialism and World Society," *Harvard Business Review,* January–February, 1961, pp. 113 and 122–26.

technical. How can this problem best be handled? How can the transition to industrialism best be made, given these conditions? Increasingly, the bosses all appear to wear gray flannel suits. They become aware of the similarity of many problems and of the similarity of some solutions. They become more attentive to the inherent nature and problems of industrialization and less attentive to the "great personalities" around whom historians so frequently weave their stories....

THE ROAD TO SIMILARITY

We have seen that the natural, historical tendency of each of the five types of elite is to change—sometimes completely. Will these changes keep on occurring in the future as in the past and, if so, in what direction? This brings us to some important—and unconventional—conclusions about the strength of pressures for uniformity.

It will help us to appreciate these forces all the more if we keep in mind that the sources of diversity are great, too, and are all the time working in the world, even if with not quite so much effect. Thus:

1. *The differing elites each want to organize the process of industrialization in a different fashion.* Once structured, the institutions and the ways of doing things tend to develop a life and a persistency of their own, provided the ruling elites are reasonably successful in handling industrialization and other problems of the nation. There are, after all, several possible ways of organizing an industrial society. Furthermore, the slogans, the heroes, the vested interests that collect around an ideology and a strategy for organizing society give any system considerable tenacity and are a great source of diversity in an industrializing world.

2. *The culture of a nation and the degree of its continual adherence to that culture also create world-wide diversity.* The family and the class carry on, particularly under the dynastic elite. Education often adapts quite slowly from its traditional forms, again particularly under the dynastic elite. But other national traits carry on as well. Take, for instance, the discipline and energy of the Germans, the individualism of the French, and the easy-going approach of the Indonesians.

3. *The stage of development makes for variation.* Early industrialization, regardless of the overall strategy, has its own special problems, its own special attitudes, its own special approaches. Mature industrialization, with its well-developed institutions and web of rules, its full complement of industries and services and trades, its settled labor force, its greater consensus, is a different phenomenon regardless of the organizing forces. Degree of development, of course, relates both to the date of the start and the rate of the change.

4. *The special character of the basic resources and the central industries causes variations from one country to another.* Plantation agriculture, crude oil production, heavy industry, light industry, and so on, each give a tone to their society. Some industries are more prone to industrial unrest than others; some are more likely to engage in paternalistic practices; some are occupationally more highly stratified; some are more subject to a system of norms; some have more large-scale enterprises. Each industry has its own character—the waterfront, coal mining, banking—and these cast their reflections on the surrounding society. A small or a newly industrialized economy is more likely to reflect the special character of one or a few industries than is a large and mature economy. Thus oil gives a special flavor to Iraq, much as textiles and coal mining once did to England.

5. *The demographic aspects of a nation impart to its industrialization continuing characteristics.* A relatively empty country, like Australia, has quite a different course of development than a heavily populated one, like India. Wages tend to be higher, recruitment more difficult, a significant increase in the standard of living more possible, a high evaluation of the worth of the individual worker and the attention he deserves more likely, and so forth.

But time moves along and, as it does, many a battle is joined between the forces perpetuating diversity and those promoting uniformity. Many of these battles are the impersonal clashes of old ways and new facts, and in any case they are fought under many banners and in a myriad of places. But the more we look at these battles collectively, in some kind of time and intercontinental perspective, the more impressed we become with the power of the forces for uniformity. What are the most striking ones?

History & Homogeneity

The passage of history itself is a force. Each industrializing nation moves farther from its introduction into the industrial world, from its pre-existing forms, from its original leadership. The early elites bring in new recruits from other strata. The elite group grows in size and becomes less identifiable, merging into each successively lower level in the new hierarchy. The second, third, and fourth generations of leaders and the led alike are different from the first.

The age of ideology fades. When man first entered the irreversible journey into industrialization, there were innumerable views about the best way to organize society. Some of them have largely disappeared from the scene: anarchism, syndicalism, communalism, cooperativism. Others of them have been blunted and revised from the original form, particularly capitalism and socialism. The age of utopias is past. An age of realism has taken its place—an age in which there is little expectation of either utter perfection or of complete doom. One of the results of the past century is the accumulation of experience about the realistic alternative.

Thus the conflict of ideologies is blunted and fades between societies. Consensus develops wherever industrialization is successful. The labor force becomes committed to and settled into industrial life. It accepts the pace of work, the web of rules, the surrounding structure. The sense of protest subsides. The business managers, left to their own devices, push less hard. Society provides more of the amenities of life. Men learn from experience how better to do things, and the rough edges are evened off. Industrialization is accepted.

Finally, as the elites become less differentiated and the ideological controversies become more barren, the cultural patterns of the world intermingle and merge. These changes are in evidence although the majority of nations in the world have been in the active throes of industrialization only two generations or less.

Technology & Society

Technology is also a unifying force. At one moment of time there may be several best economic combinations or social arrangements, but only one best technology. The technology can be up-to-date or antiquated, but there is no question which is which, and the modern is constantly replacing the ancient.

The same technology calls for much the same occupational structure around the world—in steel, in textiles, in air transport. The occupational role of a man gives him a place in society and affects his behavior in many ways. Also, there comes to be a growing diversity of occupations and of levels of management, and no really clear-cut dividing lines visible to all. The occupation takes the place of the class.

The technology is dynamic and it calls for change. Men change their locations and their occupations. A labor market must be created with substantial mobility within it. A fully paternalistic system at the plant level becomes less possible. Mobility calls at least for the semi-independent rather than the dependent worker.

The skill level rises. Men are given responsibility for more expensive equipment, more essential processes. Their consent becomes more important. The need for their consent gives them influence. It may even give them organized power, for there is a tendency to organize around the occupation. True, only scientists may be given this right at first, but the pressure will always exist to spread professional and occupational organization.

Push of Progress

The thrust of progress also serves the cause of uniformity. The industry mix, country by country, becomes more balanced and thus more like that elsewhere. There is insistent pressure to obtain a rough balance of supply and demand in the labor market.

The development of consumer-goods industries and service trades requires the creation of markets—in spite of the addiction to plans (the market mentality and planning mentality are quite different). The rising standard of living and increasing leisure create the capacity to read and travel and compare. They also encourage an aggressive materialism on the part of people. Progress brings the great metropolitan center and the city as the natural habitat of man. The city has been the home of variety and of freedom throughout the centuries.

Education & Equality

An industrial society must educate its people. There are at least two imperatives: (1) The vast bulk of population must be literate in order to receive instruction, follow directions, and keep records. (2) Managers, engineers, and civil servants must be trained to operate the new productive system. Beyond that are the needs for doctors, lawyers, scientists, and university professors. Education becomes a leading industry.

Out of education come several results. Education is intended to reduce the scarcity of skilled persons, and this after a time reduces the wage and salary differentials they receive. It also pulls people out of the least skilled and most disagreeable occupations and raises wage levels there. It conduces to a new equality which has nothing to do with ideology; in fact, it may come faster and more fully in a middle-class society than in a society under the revolutionary intellectuals who proclaim equality as a primary goal. This equality is at first economic, but it also affects class status and political outlook.

Out of education may also come a new call for freedom. This call will be most insistent at the highest levels in the educational pyramid, for knowledge knows no geographical boundaries; but it may spread down through many of the ranks of society. Education and personal independence have usually walked the road together. With an educated labor force, jobs tend to change or be changed. On the average, more responsibility adheres to them; they are made more interesting; and their incumbents are treated more individually and humanely.

Government & Business

The state, everywhere, becomes an important instrument in society. It becomes responsible for the general rate of growth, the level of economic activity, the distribution of power in society, the settlement of conflicts, and the prevention of economic or other sabotage of the economy by special interest groups. It may, of course, do much more. But at least it must set the many basic rules for the economy, *and it inevitably becomes a partner, if not the sole partner, in labor-management relations.*

At the same time, the productive enterprise, whether public or private, becomes a large-scale organization in many industries. It comes to be run by professional managers, recruited and trained through the educational system, separated from ownership and protected from power politics. These enterprise managers must be placed under the constraints of the market or planning budgets to assure their suitable performance, and the structuring of these pressures and controls is an essential task in society. The professional administrator has great power, but it is power subject to checks and balances in all developed industrial societies.

The managers are basically responsible for the web of rules in the plant and industry which relate them to the managed, although they share this responsibility with the state and organized workers. Basically, this web of rules must spell out the authority of the managers and how far they may go, for economic enterprise is always essentially authoritarian under the necessity of getting things done, and the limits to executive authority must be specified.

Compulsion of Comparisons

Man everywhere wants progress and participation. The two are substitutes for each other, and often progress will be accepted for a time in lieu of participation; but in the end industrial man wants both and will keep pressing for both. Progress means a higher standard of education, better health, more consumer goods and services; participation means choice of jobs, choice of consumer goods, a chance to influence the web of rules, and even an opportunity to influence those who guide society itself. These same pressures develop regardless of culture and ideology.

The pressures for progress and participation are enhanced by the world-wide character of industrialization, by international trade, by travel, and by the exchange of ideas. Generally the impact will be to bring greater uniformity in the nature of the societal product which people widely judge to be the best. People may not be willing to settle for much less in their own systems than the standards and performance of competing systems.

PLURALISTIC INDUSTRIALISM

Men attempt to peer ahead, to understand the structure of history, and to alter the process of history, if possible, in accord with their preferences. The future they appear to be choosing and pressing for is what might be called *pluralistic industrialism.* We use this term to refer to a society which is governed neither by one all-powerful elite (e.g., the monistic model) nor by the impersonal interaction of innumerable small groups with relatively equal power (e.g., the atomistic model in economic theory). The complexity of the fully developed industrial society requires, in the name of efficiency and initiative, a degree of decentralization of control, particularly in the consumer-goods and service-trades industries; but it also requires a large measure of central control by the state and conduct of many operations by large-scale organizations.

As the skill level rises and jobs become more responsible, any regime must be more interested in consent, in drawing forth relatively full cooperation. For the sake of real efficiency, this must be freely given. The discipline of the labor gang no longer suffices. With skill and responsibility goes the need for consent, and with consent goes influence and even authority. Occupational and professional groups, of necessity, achieve some prestige and authority as against both the central organs of society and the individual members of the occupation or profession.

Education brings in its wake a new economic equality and a new community of political outlook. This, in turn, along with many other developments, helps bring consensus to society. The harsh use of power by the state is no longer so necessary to hold society together at the seams. Education also opens the mind to curiosity and to inquiry, and the individual seeks more freedom to think and to act. It brings a demand for liberty, and can help create conditions in which liberty can safely be granted. It leads to comparisons among nations with respect to progress and participation.

Industrialism is so complex and subject to such contrary internal pressures that it never can assume a single, uniform, unchanging structure; but it *can* vary around a general central theme, and that theme is pluralism. While it will take generations before this theme will become universal in societies around the world, the direction of the movement already seems sufficiently clear.

Unwithering State

The state will be powerful. It will, at the minimum have the responsibility for:

The economic growth rate.
The over-all distribution of income among uses and among individuals.
The basic security of individuals (formerly the family was the basic security unit).
The stability of the system.
Providing the essential public services of education, transportation, recreational areas, cultural facilities, and the like, which will become more important as the standard of living rises, leisure increases, education improves, and men multiply in numbers.
Providing a favorable physical environment for urban man.

In addition, any pluralistic society is subject to three great potential internal problems, and the state is responsible for handling each:

1. *Conflict among the various power elements*—The state must set the rules of the game within which such conflict will occur, enforce these rules, and act as mediator. Conflicts between managers and the managed are the most noticeable, but by no means the only ones.

2. *Collusion*—The state must control collusion by producers against consumers, by any professional against its clients, and by labor and management against the public. Undue aggrandizement of sectional interests is always endemic if not epidemic in a pluralistic society; in fact, one of the arguments for monism and for atomism alike is the avoidance of such sectionalism.

3. *Organizational rules*—The state will come generally, under pluralistic industrialism, to set the rules relating members to their organizations—who may get in, who may stay in, what rights and obligations the members have, what the boundaries for the activities of the organization are, and so on. It will, almost of necessity, be against too much conflict among, or collusion between, or domination of the members by the subsidiary organizations in society.

All these responsibilities mean that the state will never "wither away"; that Marx was more utopian than the despised utopians themselves. The state will be the dominant organization in any industrial society. But it may itself be less than fully unitary. It may itself be subject to checks and balances, including the check of public acceptance of its current leadership and its policies.

Crucial Role for Business

The productive enterprise, whether private or public, will be in a dominant position under pluralistic industrialism. It will often be large, and it must always have substantial authority in order to produce efficiently. But there will be no "managerial revolution," as James Burnham suggested, with the manager reigning supreme over all of society.

The distinction between the private and public manager will decrease just as the distinction between the private and public enterprise will diminish; and the distinction among managers will be more according to the size, the product, and nature of their enterprises. The controlled market and the controlled budget will bring more nearly the same pressures on them. The private enterprise, however, will usually have more freedom of action than the public enterprise.

Battles in the Corridors

The occupational or professional association will range alongside the state and the enterprise as a locus of power in pluralistic industrialism; and there will be more occupations and particularly more professions seeking association. Group organizations around skill and position in the productive mechanism will be well-nigh universal. These organizations will affect output norms, comparative incomes, access to employment, and codes of ethics in nearly every occupational walk of life. Their containment within reasonable limits will be an all-enduring and all-pervading problem; and some of the groups will always seek to invade and infiltrate the government mechanisms which are intended to supervise them. Class warfare will be forgotten and in its place will be the bureaucratic contest of interest group against interest group. The battles will be in the corridors instead of the streets, and memos will flow instead of blood.

Uniting the state, the enterprise, and the association will be a great web of rules set by the efforts of all the elements, but particularly by the state. Persuasion and pressure and manipulation will take the place of the face-to-face combat of an earlier age. Executives in industry and government will pore over narrower, more technical issues than in earlier times when there was real disagreement over the nature of and the basic arrangements in industrial society.

Labor organizations will not be component parts of class movements urging programs of total reform, for the consensus of a pluralistic society will have settled over the scene. Nor may they be very heavily identified by industry, particularly with the increasing multiplication and fractionalization of industries; rather, they may tend to take more the craft or, perhaps better, the occupational form. With skills more diverse, at a generally higher level, and obtained more through formal education, and with geographical mobility greatly increased, professional-type interests should mean more to workers than industry or class ties.

The New Bohemianism

The individual will be in a mixed situation far removed either from that of the independent farmer organizing most aspects of his own life or from that of the Chinese peasant in the commune under total surveillance. In his working life he will be subject to great conformity imposed not only by the enterprise manager but also by the state and by his own occupational association. For most people, any true scope for the independent spirit on the job will be missing.

Outside his working life the individual may have more freedom under pluralistic industrialism than in most earlier forms of society. Politically he can be given some influence. Society has achieved consensus, and it is perhaps less necessary for Big Brother to exercise political control. In the "brave new world" genetic and chemical means need not be employed to avoid revolt, either. There will not be any rebellion anyway, except little bureaucratic blowups that can be handled piecemeal. An educated population will want political choice and can be given it. There will also be a reasonable amount of choice in the controlled labor market, subject to the natural confining limits of one's occupation, and in the controlled product market.

The great new freedom may come in the leisure-time life of individuals. Higher standards of living, more free time, and more education make this not only possible but almost inevitable. Leisure will be the happy hunting ground for the independent spirit. Along with the bureaucratic conservatism of economic and political life may well go a New Bohemianism in the other aspects of life—partly as a reaction to the confining nature of the productive side of society. There may well come a new search for individuality and a new meaning to liberty. The economic system may be highly ordered and the political system barred ideologically; but the social and recreational and cultural aspects of life should be quite diverse and quite changing.

CONCLUSION

Pluralistic industrialism will never reach a final equilibrium. The contest between the forces for uniformity and for diversity will give it life and movement and change. This is a contest which will never reach an ultimate solution. Manager and managed will struggle all up and down the line of hierarchies all around the world; quiet but often desperate little battles will be fought all over the social landscape.

The uniformity that draws on technology, and the diversity that draws on individuality; the authority that stems from the managers, and the rebellion, however muted, that stems from the managed—these are destined to be the everlasting threads of the future. They will continue in force when class war, and the contest over private versus public initiative, and the battle between monistic and atomistic ideologies, all have been left far behind in the sedimentary layers of history.

selection 39

Evolving Organizations*

Chadwick J. Haberstroh

THE ORGANIZATION IN A CHANGING SOCIETY

The foundations of this line of research were laid down a generation or two ago by the sociologists Weber, Tönnies, and Maine. The major themes of their work are (1) the contrast and conflict between a traditional, person-oriented type of social organization and a rationalized impersonal, task-oriented type, and (2) the transition in the course of the social and economic development of Western society from the former to the latter. Before dealing with the differences, it is well to analyze certain aspects of structure which seem to persist from relatively primitive organizations in traditional societies to the most complex of our modern bureaucracies.

The first of these is the relatively great importance of the organization head, whether he is king, chief, president, or chairman. He seems invariably to perform a major role in the definition of the organization's character. The second aspect is the principle of hierarchy, the maintenance of definite status levels among the participants in the organization implying degrees of worth. The third aspect is the attention to processes of making the lower echelons responsive and tractable in the service of the interests represented at the top. I do not wish to suggest that these are immutable principles of administration, but only that they are empirical regularities in the mainstream of organizational evolution as we have observed it to date. An important qualification, however, is the substantial weakening in degree of each of these features where the influence of authoritarian values has declined.

Now let us turn to the dimensions along which major changes have occurred and explore the implications of these changes for the arts of organization and management. First, the man at the top of the organization changes during this process from the master whose status is guaranteed by inheritance of title, land, or wealth, to the functionary whose qualification for office is his ability to achieve. His position is not given by custom or tradition, but rather by some form of examination. In the same way, the relationship between hierarchical levels changes from that of master–servant to that of supervision of one office

*From "Organization Structure: Social and Technical Elements," *Industrial Management Review,* Vol. 3 (1961), pp. 64–77.

by another. In modern organizations, authority rests in the office held and has a defined and limited jurisdiction over subordinate offices only, not the persons in them.

The second dimension is the change in emphasis from the personal rights and welfare of the individuals concerned to some impersonal task to which all are equally committed. In traditional society, the chief aim of an organization is the satisfaction of the personal desires of the master. In return, the servants are guaranteed certain rights and privileges. The tasks they work on, however, are given almost entirely by custom and tradition. In the newer organization, the personal welfare of the participants is secondary. The emphasis in the actual day-to-day functioning of the organization is on an impersonally determined task to which personal interests are either artificially related, as in the wage bargain, or only remotely connected, as in the interest we all have in a stable and productive economy. Thus, when authority is exercised, the decision takes into consideration primarily the implementation of task goals, rather than any personal preferences. Under the traditional system, the goodness or worth of an organization could be judged directly in terms of the welfare or preferences of the participants. In modern organization theory, we need to add the dimension of effectiveness in achieving the impersonal purpose to which the organization is committed.

There is another dimension that perhaps underlies both of those discussed above and extends more broadly to every aspect of organizational functioning. This third dimension for change is change itself: the degree and rapidity of innovation with which the organization must cope. In traditional society it was a rare generation that could not look forward to living essentially the same life as its immediate ancestors lived. In modern society, few people can slip quietly into grooves clearly defined and made smooth by their forebears. The patterns are swept away by outside forces, among which is an unceasing quest for increased technical efficiency. The quest for technical efficiency, in turn, is enforced by the existence of organized commitments to an impersonal task.

Even the most traditionally oriented societies of today, however, are not immune to change. Developments in North America and Europe spread to create crises in the most remote parts of South America, Africa and Asia. What is lacking in the more traditional societies is the capacity to cope with change, and that deficiency is mainly in the organizational forms they have developed and in the cultural values those forms reflect. One simple example of this which has developed in New Guinea is the "cargo cult." Natives have reacted to European encroachment by forming cults whose mission is to bring them the material advantages of the whites by supernatural means. They thus try to adapt to change within their standard technology and organizational form, but with no chance of success. However, even in the most advanced societies, the magnitude of present-day change is difficult to cope with. Our own managers may be making the same type of mistake less obviously.

As mentioned previously, the most important elements carried over from the traditional position of the master to that of the modern administrator are the central importance of his own role, his superordinate position in hierarchical relationships, and his need to control the actions of subordinates. More briefly stated, he inherits the power position of the former privileged classes. But whereas the power of the master was used for his own personal ends, the power of the administrator is used for the accomplishment of the impersonal task. One does not normally find a complete transition even in so-called "developed" societies. Incumbency in a high-level administrative position confers high social status and increased personal welfare, and when a high-level position is to be filled, an effort is made to find a person whose present social status is nearly equivalent. But the difference in emphasis is clear enough, and the trend may be expected to continue even in "developed" nations as ideological forces work themselves out.

The most important feature of administrators' power is their control over the affairs of the organization as a whole. The primary focus is in the choice of the organization's purposes, those actions that give the organization a unified, coherent character. This is mainly an aspect of the organization's relationship with the rest of society. It is in this phase of its existence that the organization has an impact on the affairs of its time.

The policy choices involved may have consequences for the internal equilibrium of the organization. In particular, certain of them may be crucial for its continued survival. The need to assure the survival and continued good health of the organization will be an important influence in administrative policy. The need is hard to separate from the personal desires of the officials for status, power, and remuneration. In a person-oriented cultural matrix, one would expect to find relatively more expression of the latter need and less concern for the organization as such or as a means for achievement of the impersonal purpose. The fulfillment of these internal needs may require adaptation, the act of seeking for a new equilibrium with a changing environment, even including major realignment of the impersonal purposes in the interest of preserving the organization. In his way, the social instrument may itself create forces that influence the ends for which it is used. The aims of organized power have thus become depersonalized, subject to contention and decision and accordingly greatly increasing the range of alternatives open to a society.

Among the impersonal ends of modern organizations we can find many that correspond to social ideals, as contrasted to material interests. A corporation may be dedicated to improving the welfare of its work force or to promoting a "free-enterprise" ideology as well as to profit-making. It could work toward all these ends and at the same time maintain a policy of nondiscrimination in employment between races, a valuable service to the ideal of racial equality. These possibilities arise because of the use of formal rules as a technique of administration. Once the practice of administration by rule is established, organization power can be mobilized around whatever ends are chosen by the administrators.

The techniques of holding power (or of administration, if one prefers) have changed as much as the objective of its use. The functionary does not rule by virtue of personal position or property, nor by force of personality. His central instrument of power is the creation and maintenance of the fictions of organizational authority and jurisdiction. In modern organization these are made the subject of conscious and rational planning, not inherited as in traditional social structures. There is a limitation, however, to the power position of the administrator. If he is not aware of the power position of others as well as his own, his organization will founder in opposition and conflict. The organization's purpose and its means of attainment must be so chosen that the different elements of the organization can unite in their realization. In addition, they must be so chosen that they will not run afoul of external and superior political or economic power.

The nature of organizational authority has been discussed extensively in the literature. It is generally agreed that authority owes its force not to the command of him who holds the authority but rather to the obedience of those who accept it. Thus we must seek the origins of authority in the feelings of legitimacy held by the subordinates.

This was a major starting point of Max Weber's analysis of social organization. Weber, however, devoted his efforts mainly to exploring the social consequences of variation in the culturally given source of authority, i.e., whether the people perceive legitimate authority to lie with the emergent leader, with the family, with clerical or secular organization, with traditional or legal government. His closest approach to discussing the origins of these perceptions of legitimacy is the concept of "charisma." This is the relation of dependence and subservience that is observed between the emergent leader and his followers. Weber hypothesized that this could be routinized by transference to the leader's family or to an organization founded by him. This process could begin or reinvigorate a traditional system of government such as patriarchialism or feudalism. The development of a legal, bureaucratic system of governance was more a new and flexible method of employing existing authority (that of religion, sovereignty or property) than of any new concept of its origin.

Although modern society has long been accustomed to the legal processes of delegation of authority and definition of jurisdiction, it is only recently that the question of the origins of the sense of legitimacy has come under scientific scrutiny. Although charismatic leaders seem always to have used doctrine to win and inspire their followers, a psychological theory of how the process of influence takes place is a recent development.

The result of this for organizations is that we have now not only the legal technique of manipulating the perceptions of legitimacy of those who are already convinced, but also a scientifically-based technology for doing the convincing, for creating the sense of legitimacy in the first place.

With this new technology available and commonly understood, the traditional sources of authority (sovereignty, religion, property) can no longer be taken for granted. The words "lobbying" and "subversion" are two of the most common words in our vocabulary for discussing government, and they do not connote obedience to or respect for the legitimacy of sovereign authority. The legitimacy bestowed by property ownership cannot realistically be taken as the basis of authority in the modern corporate business community, although it remains so legally.

As the tempo of economic, social, and political change increases, organizations will find it increasingly necessary to adapt not only their policy but also very fundamental aspects of their institutional structure in order to continue operating successfully. It remains to identify a few common aspects of organization structure and explore their social and technical functions before discussing some possible changes.

SOME STRUCTURAL ELEMENTS AND THEIR FUNCTIONS

The preceding section has, by exploring the natural origins of some basic aspects of organization, laid the foundation for the assumption that organization structure can be engineered to realize specific purposes. The question of whether a given element of structure serves social or technical purposes resolves into the question of the function of that element in the total picture. The technical elements are those that are functional to the execution of the work ostensibly being performed. Elements are social to the extent that their role is determined by the social *milieu*. A social element in a given organization may be tailored to the self interest of an individual person, family, or elite; or it may be an institutionalized element of the culture as a whole.

There is probably no better or more generally appreciated example of the difference between social and technical elements than the sociological distinction between ascription and achievement. In the context of organizations, these processes appear most clearly in the distribution of rewards and in the recruitment of members. Rewards and positions are given by ascription when they depend on the class or family background of the participant, and by achievement if they depend on performance. Ascription is a broad enough term to cover such extremes as nepotism in public service and the inheritance of a family business, as well as many in-between areas where the question of public approbation is less determinate. In our stereotype of traditional society, virtually all positions and rewards are determined by ascription. In modern society achievement is the dominant ethic for both recruitment and reward in organizations, although Mills advances the thesis that the really large payoffs are made and all organizational positions above a certain level are filled by ascription from a "power elite."

Almost anyone will accord the task-oriented organization, that recruits and rewards according to achievement, technical superiority over the person-centered organization that uses ascription. The evidence for this proposition, however, although sound enough, is global and impressionistic in nature. Although some environmentalists would blame it on the contiguity of coal, iron ore, and lime-stone deposits, the best evidence is the wide disparity in national income be-tween the underdeveloped, traditionally organized societies and the modern, rationally organized ones—and not the least important datum is the rapidity with which Russia was able to change from being one of the former to one of the latter through a purely organizational revision.

The evidence for the technical utility of more microscopic variations in orga-nizational structure is also mainly impressionistic because of the lack of a generally applicable standard of technical effectiveness. This does not mean that the evidence we have is useless, however, and I will attempt to employ it to evaluate certain important aspects of organizational structure. These are the use of hierarchy, the basis for specialization, the use of auxiliary labor as opposed to an autonomous work force, and the use of authority over property.

The use of a hierarchy of authority is almost universal in complex organiza-tions, and it plays a part in most of the management topics that are current in the literature. These topics include decentralization, participative management, and executive development. Not the least of them is the whole modern emphasis on management as a function, a kind of work. Much of the discussion of these topics has in one way or another focused on the dysfunctions of the hierarchical principle and ways of overcoming them in order to realize maximum organiza-tional effectiveness. For example, ideas of decentralization and delegation in-volve an expansion of executive resources by locating ultimate decisions at lower and more numerous points in the hierarchy. Participative management also attempts to enlist creative talent from lower ranks, but without entirely giving up jurisdiction by the upper layers. All of these techniques also lighten the psychological burden of authority by reducing the degree of domination of the upper levels over the lower. Executive development and other topics in the area of managerial functions refer directly to rationalizing the use of hierarchy in the service of the organization goals by exploring the contribution of managerial personnel to task achievement. Executive development concerns rational plan-ning for the continuing availability of competent managers at each hierarchical level. That this may be functional for the task is shown, for example, by Trow's work which demonstrates a relationship between conscious planning for execu-tive succession (whether of a family member or not) and later profitability of the organization. All of the developments mentioned weaken as well as modify the traditional principle of hierarchical authority, either by reducing hierarchic domination or by proposing objective tests of performance for candidates for these positions.

The idea of specialization has been touted at least since Adam Smith as enabling the kind of technical progress that leads to social wealth. This concept refers primarily to horizontal specialization as between different kinds of crafts-manship. A large part of organizational thought has been devoted to the inven-tion of effective bases of specialization, for example, place, time, persons, things, and processes. The notion of managerial functions opens up the question of vertical specialization, and the manager has been presented in turn as a planner, a coordinator, a specialist in interpersonal relations, a personnel recruiter, a communication link, and a blesser of proposals. The traditional specialties of the upper social classes, however, have been less varied and can be grouped rather easily under the categories of dominance, ownership, and leisure. These social factors are certainly not independent of organizational effectiveness, however. Dominance and control over resources are common and obvious ways of maintaining coordination, although they just as obviously are not always so used. Time to think has always been mistaken for leisure, although leisure is not always accompanied by thought.

Modern trends tend to make many of the managerial functions horizontal rather than vertical specialties. It is probably also true that this can be carried much further than it has been, and many writers have emphasized the use of hierarchy to conceal dysfunctional dominance, ownership, and leisure. The result of this line of thought is a presumption in favor of the flat organization, although it cannot be said to justify the complete abolition of hierarchical relationships.

Another interesting sidelight on specialization comes from one of Udy's results. In the portion of his sample where data were adequate, there was a definite scale relative to specialization. Virtually all organizations that had developed specialization of labor did so in the presence of a system of compensation of workers by managers. Beyond this, the presence of specialization in work was a uniform precondition for the payment of rewards according to achievement criteria. In turn, compensation, specialization, and reward by achievement all seemed to be necessary for the development of a basically contractual system of recruitment. This finding may be relevant to problems of economic development in societies where compensation and specialization are well developed, but where modern organizational techniques are compromised by absence of the institution of reward according to achievement. This tendency was evident in Presthus' study of the Turkish coal administration and in my unpublished studies of various Latin American work organizations. One might compare the Russian case, in that whereas the Czarists had developed systems of compensation and specialization, the Communists added material achievement as a dominant ethical consideration. Communism does not noticeably emphasize participation on a limited contractual basis, but some recent events (i.e. increased permissiveness toward mobility of labor) tend in this direction.

Pre-industrial work organizations tend to polarize into two classes: the traditional bureaucracy, permanently organized, with diffuse ends, recruited on the basis of prior membership in other social organizations, and with ascriptive rewards; and the rational, task-oriented organization, having specific limited material objectives, recruited on the basis of an equal chance of participation for all available persons, having an autonomous work force, and emphasizing achievement in the distribution of rewards. One of Udy's main conclusions is the paradox that economic and social development from primitive society tends to lead into traditional bureaucracies rather than into the rational, task-oriented organizations that can contribute to further substantial progress.

It is also interesting to note that the contractually recruited organizations in Udy's sample tend to be of the rational, task-oriented type, whereas an organization that differentiates its members into a permanent cadre plus an auxiliary, temporary work force tends to be a traditional bureaucracy. It is easy to spot the exploitative element in the use of an auxiliary work force, as for example in the distinction in many of our own industrial organizations between the permanent management cadre and the expendable hourly-paid work force. This idea is nicely illustrated in Presthus' study where there was a large auxiliary labor element employed at subsistence wages and under conditions only slightly removed from serfdom. This, of course, results in low productivity, and this is one ground for recommending employee security as a factor contributing to organizational effectiveness. More relevant in modern circumstances where security has been realized are the great gains in effectiveness experienced by some companies that have clasped their labor force more closely to them by such devices and profit-sharing and participative management.

One might similarly speculate about Udy's finding that traditional bureaucracies tend to rely on managerial or absentee proprietorship, whereas task-oriented organizations tend to show corporate proprietorship (i.e. participation in control over property by all members). This is also a primary distinction between the owner-controlled company in a capitalist economy and the giant corporation. In the corporation the machine belongs much more nearly to the worker than to his department chief, much more nearly to the department chief than to the plant manager, and much more nearly to the plant manager than to the company president. This is also, of course, one of the main distinctions between Communist ideology and that of the traditional or capitalist societies it has successfully replaced. It is not, however, a distinction between Communist society and modern Western society.

ORGANIZATIONAL CHANGE

The preceding discussion has suggested or confirmed some ideas as to what elements of organization structure can be appropriately modified in the interest of greater effectiveness in doing work. The pressures toward this kind of change in today's world are of a greater order than organizations have encountered in the past. Thus effective organization more and more requires that adaptation be one of the recognized functions of the permanent executive system.

Basically, many of the problems of adaptation that organizations have been encountering arise from the great reliance they have put on informal organization and intuitive judgment at the highest executive levels. Informal relations are necessarily personal, and they permit the introduction of social considerations that are extraneous to the task to a much greater extent than do procedures that must be stated and defended officially. Moreover, personal confidence and understanding can be built into a large organizational structure only over a long period of time. Changes in personnel disrupt the process and interfere with the informally developed ways of getting things done. Therefore such changes will be resisted in the name of task efficiency as well as presumed injustice to persons.

The result is a need for a system that relies less on informal and more on formal techniques at top levels, especially with respect to the assignment of personnel.

Many practices that have recently come into favor tend to have this effect. First among these is a conscious, planned approach to executive development so that people of appropriate training and proved competence may be available for assignment to key positions as needed. A second is the use of the task-force or project form of organization. This permits the assembly of personnel of a variety of appropriate specialized competences for assignment to the completion of a specific task or project in its entirety. Such groups can be created and broken up rapidly and without a sense of unfairness on the part of the individuals concerned.

Perhaps if we could remove many of the social implications of hierarchical positions, reassignment of key managerial personnel would be a useful device to create rapid and thorough change in larger organization components. If the development of a new and radically revised plan of operation were given to a competent task-force, then that team could be used to replace the previous management, which in turn would be freed for other activities and relieved of the impossible assignment of attempting to learn a new task while still fully occupied in executing an old one. Rotation of personnel in such situations could also be part of a systematic program of executive development.

Increased flexibility in assignment of personnel at the managerial level would also tend toward further professionalization of management. This emphasizes of course the functions of management rather than the hierarchical status. It would imply greater emphasis also on standardized training for managers; more standardized pay scales – and probably lower pay relative to other occupations; mobility, geographically and between organizations; and objective achievement as the basis for remuneration or promotion. At the same time, this tendency would deemphasize policies that rely on organizational loyalty, tenure, hierarchical promotion, and other paternalistic devices.

As with any possibility for action that is opened up by technological progress, organizational change raises questions of value and ideology. One never expects vested interest to approve of divestiture. Likewise, traditions can be defended for their own sake and not judged on the basis of their contribution to material ends. Nevertheless, almost everyone will agree that he should approach a question of choice with as much knowledge as possible. Questions of value can be obscured by sheer ignorance. It is hoped that this paper will contribute a little information to some of these value judgments.

selection 40

The New Industrial State*

John Kenneth Galbraith

In the past, leadership in business organization was identified with the entrepreneur—the individual who united ownership or control of capital with capacity for organizing the other factors of production and, in most contexts, with a further capacity for innovation.[1] With the rise of the modern corporation, the emergence of the organization required by modern technology and planning and divorce of the owner of the capital from control of the enterprise, the entrepreneur no longer exists as an individual person in the mature industrial enterprise.[2] Everyday discourse, except in the economics textbooks, recognizes this change. It replaces the entrepreneur, as the directing force of the enterprise, with management. This is a collective and imperfectly defined entity; in the large corporation it embraces chairman, president, those vice presidents with important staff or departmental responsibility, occupants of other major staff positions and, perhaps, division or department heads not included above. It includes, however, only a small proportion of those who, as participants, contribute information to group decisions. This latter group is very large; it extends from the most senior officials of the corporation to where it meets, at the outer perimeter, the white and blue collar workers whose function is to conform more or less mechanically to instruction or routine. It embraces all who bring specialized knowledge, talent or experience to group decision-making. This, not the management, is the guiding intelligence—the brain—of the enterprise. There is no name for all who participate in group decision-making or the organization which they form. I propose to call this organization the Technostructure. . . .

In the industrial enterprise, power rests with those who make decisions. In the mature enterprise, this power has passed, inevitably and irrevocably, from the individual to the group. That is because only the group has the information that decision requires. Though the constitution of the corporation places power

---

*From *The New Industrial State.* Copyright © 1967 by John Kenneth Galbraith. Reprinted by permission of the publisher, Houghton Mifflin Company.

[1] "To act with confidence beyond the range of familiar beacons and to overcome that resistance requires aptitudes that are present in only a small fraction of the population and [they] define the entrepreneurial type as well as the entrepreneurial function." Joseph A. Schumpeter, *Capitalism, Socialism and Democracy* (2d ed.; New York: Harper & Bros., 1947), p. 132.

[2] He is still, of course, to be found in smaller firms and in larger ones that have yet to reach full maturity of organization. . . .

in the hands of the owners, the imperatives of technology and planning remove it to the technostructure.

Since technology and planning are what accord power to the technostructure, the latter will have power wherever these are a feature of the productive process. Its power will not be peculiar to what, in the cadenzas of ideology, is called the free enterprise or capitalist system. If the intervention of private authority, in the form of owners, must be prevented in the private firm, so must the intervention of public authority in the public firm. Otherwise, it will be damaging as the intervention of Ford [Henry I] and Avery [Sewell Avery of Montgomery Ward] was damaging.

As a further consequence, puzzlement over capitalism without control by the capitalist will be matched by puzzlement over socialism without control by the society. A final consequence is a drastic revision of the prospects for socialism in the form, at least, in which most socialists think it worth having. Three cases of the technostructure under socialism throw light on these matters.

EVOLUTION OF SOCIALISM

Following World War II Great Britain committed herself to limited socialism under parliamentary auspices. The British, who have a superior instinct for administration, recognized the need for autonomy for the nationalized industries. A key issue, seemingly small but in fact decisive, was that of parliamentary questions. Were these allowed on the decisions of the technostructure, ministers would have to be informed of such decision in advance. Otherwise they would confess neglect of duty. But the decisions, or the important ones, which Parliament would be most likely to question would depend on complex and technical information. If the minister were to exercise informed judgment he would need the help of a staff. Responsibility would thus be removed from the firm to the ministry. The cost in time would also be high. Only if such parliamentary intervention were excluded could the firm, and therein the technostructure, act responsibly and promptly on decisions requiring specialized information. Coal, electricity, gas, transport, the airlines and other publicly owned industries have, in consequence, all been accorded such autonomy.

This autonomy is necessary both for small decisions and what appear to be large questions of policy. Whether to rely on atomic energy for power has the aspect of a question of policy. But the comparative advantages of atomic and molecular reactions for the generation of electricity are decided only by a variety of scientific, technical, economic and planning judgments. Only a committee, or more precisely a complex of committees, can combine the knowledge, training and experience that must be brought to bear. So also with the question of whether the North Atlantic should be flown by American or British aircraft. So, in only slightly less measure, the question of how wage scales are to be revised or the railways rationalized. Everywhere the group has the monopoly of competent knowledge. In consequence in Britain ". . . the public corporation has not up to the present been in any real sense accountable to Parliament whose function has been limited to fitful, fragmentary, and largely ineffective *ex post facto* criticism."[3]

For most socialists the purpose of socialism is the control of productive enterprises by the society. For democratic socialists this means the legislature. None, or not many, seek socialism so that power can be exercised by an autonomous authority. Yet this is where power must reside. And, to repeat, this is true not only of small decisions where delegation might be expected but of great ones where Parliament might reasonably be expected to have a voice. It does not matter that the capitalist, the ancient enemy of the socialist, himself suffers from the same exclusion. Most socialists set great store by traditional belief as distinct from reality. They do not see, or admit, that the capitalist is similarly excluded from power. Capitalism is still capitalism. But there is considerable distress over how little difference nationalization of an industry means. "If an intelligent observer from Mars or Venus could come and examine all large contemporary industrial concerns—public or private—as *working enterprises,* he would notice, I suspect, only their overwhelming sameness."[4] The technostructure in the cases of both public and private ownership assumes similar powers and uses the same group methods for arriving at decisions. That it looks very much alike is not surprising.

The late Aneurin Bevan reacted to the gravitational descent of power into the technostructure of the public enterprise by asking for much stronger parliamentary control. This, of course, would have collided with the vulnerability of the technostructure to outside interference. Control would then be at the expense of competence. This has occurred; I will examine some cases in a moment. A much larger number of socialists have come to feel that public corporations are, by their nature, "remote, irresponsible bodies, immune from public scrutiny or democratic control."[5] They have given up the fight for public ownership or accord it only lip service. Socialism has come to mean government by socialists who have learned that socialism, as anciently understood, is impractical.

In a number of new countries the effort to exercise social control, forsworn in the British experiment, has been tried. It has been, perhaps, the most uniformly dismal experiment of countries seeking economic development.

At Oxford, the London School of Economics and the Sorbonne, the British and French trained the elites of their erstwhile empires to a deep faith in socialism. To this was later added a practical case. Much of the capital for development in new countries comes from abroad as publicly organized aid. Or

---

[3] C. A. R. Crosland in *The Corporation in Modern Society,* ed. Edward S. Mason (Cambridge, Mass.: Harvard University Press, 1959), p. 268. Mr. Crosland is an economist, a senior figure in the British Labour Party and, at this writing, Minister of Education.

[4] A. M. F. Palmer, "On Public Accountability," *Socialist Commentary,* January, 1960, p. 13.

[5] Crosland, *op. cit.,* p. 268.

it is raised locally not from voluntary savings of individuals and corporations but from domestic taxation or other public sources.[6] It has seemed plausible that the state should invest publicly raised funds in publicly owned firms. And private entrepreneurs of requisite competence and responsibility have not always been abundant.

In India and Ceylon, as also in some of the African countries, public enterprises have not, as in Britain, been accorded autonomy. Here the socialist faith has been thought to require parliamentary control—the right to examine budgets and expenditures, review policies and, in particular, to question management through the responsible minister on any and all actions of the corporation. Here, as elsewhere, if the minister is to be questioned, he must have knowledge. He cannot plead that he is uninformed without admitting to being a nonentity—a condition, common enough in politics, that cannot however be confessed. Technical personnel are less experienced than in the older countries. Organization is less mature. These lead to error, and suggest to parliamentarians and civil servants the need for careful review of decisions by higher and presumably more competent authority.[7] Poverty makes nepotism and favoritism in letting contracts both more tempting and more culpable than in the rich country where jobs are plentiful and business is easier to come by.[8] This calls for further review. And rigid personnel and civil service rules, the established British answer to primitive administrative capacity, extend into the public firm and prevent the easy constitution and reconstitution of groups, with information relevant to changing problems. This, we have seen, is the essence of effective action by the technostructure.[9]

The effect of this denial of autonomy and the ability of the technostructure to accommodate itself to changing tasks has been visibly deficient operations. Delay occasioned by checking decisions has added its special dimensions of cost. In business operations a wrong decision can often be reversed at little cost when the error becomes evident. But the cost of a delayed decision—of the men and capital that stand idle awaiting the decision—cannot be retrieved.

As a further consequence of this interference, social control bears most strongly on the two decisions which are of the greatest popular interest—on the prices charged the public and the wages paid to workers. This has the effect of keeping prices lower and wages higher than the more autocratic technostructure

---

[6] Notably by buying resources away from private individuals and firms, and thus imposing a form of saving on the private sector of the economy by inflation.

[7] India, in particular, as a legacy of its colonial past has an illusion of official omnipotence which extends to highly technical decisions.

[8] "Employment policies are especially likely to be subject to external pressure; decisions on how many people are hired—or more important—fired and who they are, invite political intervention where employment is rife and highly particularistic loyalties persist." Elliot J. Berg, "Socialism and Economic Development in Tropical Africa," *The Quarterly Journal of Economics*, Vol. 78, No. 4 (November, 1964), p. 570.

[9] I have discussed these matters, in the context of India, in *Economic Development* (Boston: Houghton Mifflin Co., 1964), chap. 8. Also *Economic Planning in India: Five Comments* (Calcutta: Indian Statistical Institute, 1956), and with regard to Ceylon in *Papers by Visiting Economists* (Colombo: Planning Secretariat, 1959).

would permit. It eliminates net earnings and therewith this source of savings. The poor country, which most needs capital, is thus denied the source on which the rich countries most rely. In India and Ceylon nearly all publicly owned corporations operate at a loss.[10]

The experience with public enterprises, where autonomy is denied, thus accords fully—and tragically—with expectation.

When the case of democratic socialism began to emerge in the closing decades of the last century, the capitalist entrepreneur was still in authority. The firm was small enough and the state of technology simple enough so that he could wield substantial power of decision. The belief that his power could be exercised instead by a parliament or by a directly responsible agent was not an idle dream. Certainly a public body could supersede his power to set prices and wages and therewith his power to exploit the consumer and the wage-earner.

The misfortune of democratic socialism has been the misfortune of the capitalist. When the latter could no longer control, democratic socialism was no longer an alternative. The technical complexity and planning and associated scale of operations, that took power from the capitalist entrepreneur and lodged it with the technostructure, removed it also from the reach of social control.

In nearly all of the non-Communist world, socialism, meaning public ownership of industrial enterprises, is a spent slogan. Like promises to enforce the antitrust laws in the United States, it is no longer a political program but an overture to nostalgia. The choice being between success without social control and social control without success, democratic socialism no longer seems worth the struggle. There have been few more important consequences of the take-over by the technostructure.

It is possible that there is, in fact, more to the case for the autonomous public corporation than the modern socialist now sees. The problem of the technostructure, . . . is whether it can be accommodated to social goals or whether society will have to be accommodated instead to its needs. The nature of the legal ownership has an undoubted bearing on the amenability of the technostructure to social goals. . . .

If autonomy is necessary for the effective performance by the technostructure, it should be needed by the firm in the Soviet-type economies. The requirement begins with the need to combine the specialized information of different men. There is nothing about this requirement that is peculiar to any economic system or which can be dispensed with by any ideology.

---

[10] The exceptions in India in recent years have been Air India and the Hindustan Machine Tool Company, both of which have a substantial measure of autonomy and thus affirm the point, and the railroads which have an ancient tradition of substantial independence. It is interesting that governments, which are reluctant to grant autonomy to other enterprises, regularly accord it to their airline and often with very good results. It seems possible that public officials, who are among the important patrons, sense the unique dangers of denying autonomy in this industry.

The need for autonomy in the Soviet firm could, however, be somewhat less, for its functions are far fewer than those of an American enterprise of comparable size in a similar industry. That is because much planning that is done by the American or Western European firm is, in the Soviet-type economy, done by the state. The large American corporation sets its minimum prices, organizes the demand for its products, establishes or negotiates prices for its raw materials and components and takes steps to insure supply. It also establishes or negotiates rates for various categories of trained and specialized talent, as well as of labor, and here again takes steps to insure supply. In the U.S.S.R. these functions are all performed, well or less well, by the state planning apparatus.[11] Production and investment targets, which are established by the American firm for itself, are given to the Soviet firm, though with some flexibility in application, by the state. The firm is the basic planning unit in the Western economies. In the Soviet system it is still the state.

In consequence, the organization of the Soviet firm is far simpler than that of its American counterpart. There are no comparable sales, merchandising, dealer relations, product planning, procurement or like departments. Most of the top positions in the Soviet firm are held by engineers. This is in keeping with its much greater preoccupation with technical and managerial as distinct from planning functions.[12]

It would appear, nonetheless, that considerable and increasing store is set by the autonomy of this, by American standards, very simple organization. There are two[13] major sources of outside interference—the state planning apparatus and the Communist Party.[14] Soviet economic literature recurrently warns against bureaucratic interference by either with the operations of the firm. "The Russians have learnt by experience that you cannot have responsible and efficient action at the level of the firm with continuous intervention and instruction from numerous outside authorities. Conflicting instructions from outside give the manager innumerable excuses for failure, and waste and inefficiency may result from a serious attempt to run the firm from a distance. Every argument for delegation, decentralization, and devolution used in discussions about business administration in the West is echoed, although in a different jargon, in Russia. And the case for such devolution has been pressed with increasing emphasis as Russian industry has grown and become more complex."[15]

---

11 Although the public supply of materials and components is far from reliable, the firm is prohibited, under penalty of law, from hiring "expediters" or otherwise intervening in the procurement process.

12 "In the United States and other Western countries the problems of management include planning and innovation. . . . These decisions are taken in the U.S.S.R. above the level of the enterprise manager." Report of the IIE Seminar on Industrial Technology in the Soviet Union, March 24–25, 1960, Institute of International Education, New York.

13 A third, the trade union, is clearly of lesser importance. . . .

14 I draw here not only on the literature of Soviet planning but on fairly extensive first-hand observation in the spring of 1959 and very briefly in the summer of 1964. I am extensively grateful to Soviet economists and plant managers for help and hospitality.

15 Ely Devons, "The Enigma of the Russian Economic System," *The Listener*, Vol. 58, No. 1483, London (August 29, 1957).

Plant managers do not hesitate to stress to visitors both their need for autonomy and their past difficulties. On occasion they defend the need to ignore or violate orders from outside.[16] On the other side, managements, especially those of large firms, are frequently condemned for breaking off diplomatic relations with higher authority and behaving as "feudal lords" above the law. In the Soviet Union the most important medium of social comment, poetry apart, is the novel; one of the half-dozen most discussed works since World War II has been Dudintsev's defense of the small and independent inventor and his condemnation of the mindless bureaucracy of the great metal *combinat*.[17]

The position of the Party secretary is also predictably difficult. He enters the plant hierarchy horizontally as a member of the staff or working force and is subject to the external authority of the Party. If he participates as a member of the decision-making group, he naturally becomes responsible for the decisions. He is no longer an independent agent of the Party. If he does not participate, he no longer knows what is going on. If he is too good a source of information, "he may be raised in [Party] rank but . . . then he will not be able to find out what is going on in the plant. Nobody will have any confidence in him. . . ."[18] Professor Granick concludes that the relationship is "an uneasy compromise."[19] Given the imperatives of group decision and the need of the group to protect itself from outside intervention, this would seem to be the only possible result.

In sum, it seems likely that the Soviet resolution of the problem of authority in the industrial enterprise is not unlike that in the West—although no one can be precisely sure. Full social authority over the large enterprise is proclaimed. Like that of the stockholder and the Board of Directors in the United States, it is celebrated in all public ritual. The people and Party are paramount. But in practice large and increasing autonomy is accorded to the enterprise.

This is further suggested by the trend to decentralization, so-called, in the Soviet and other Eastern European countries. This has accorded greater authority over prices, individual wage rates, production targets, investment and other employment of earnings, to the firm. In the West, especially among professional ideologists and volunteer propagandists, this has been widely hailed as a step

---

[16] On this see David Granick's *The Red Executive* (New York: Doubleday & Co., Inc., 1960), pp. 162 *et seq.* And his earlier volume *Management of the Industrial Firm in the U.S.S.R.* (New York: Columbia University Press, 1954), especially pp. 127 *et seq.* The following reference to feudal lords is from page 128 of the latter.

[17] Vladimir Dudintsev, *Not by Bread Alone* (New York: E. P. Dutton & Co., Inc., 1957). The author's affections are in close harmony with the American who, in the tradition of Brandeis, argues for the genius of the small entrepreneur as against the stolid, unimaginative behavior of the great corporation. Both have more support from humane instinct than reality. Neither sees that modern technology makes essential the machinery for mobilizing specialized knowledge. Dudintsev's inventor, however attractive, could have made no useful contribution, as a lone individual, to getting the cosmonauts into space.

[18] Joseph S. Berliner, *Factory and Manager in the U.S.S.R.* (Cambridge, Mass.: Harvard University Press, 1957), p. 265. This study is based on information from individuals familiar with Soviet industrial life who have come to the West. This speaker was an engineer and a former high official of a large machine-building plant. The obsolescence rate of such observations must be kept in mind—along with the danger of attaching undue importance to any single view.

[19] Granick, *op. cit.*

toward control by the market. It isn't. There is no tendency for the large Soviet firm to become subordinate and subject to uncontrolled markets for its products, production needs or labor supply, and thus for its production decisions. Given the level of technology, the related commitment of time and capital and the effect of technology on the functioning of markets, this would no more be possible in the U.S.S.R. than in the United States.

Decentralization in the Soviet-type economies involves not a return to the market but a shift of some planning functions from the state to the firm. This reflects, in turn, the need of the technostructure of the Soviet firm to have more of the instruments for successful operation under its own authority. It thus contributes to its autonomy. There is no tendency for the Soviet and the Western systems to convergence by the return of the former to the market. Both have outgrown that. There is measurable convergence to the same form of planning. . . .

THE FUTURE OF THE INDUSTRIAL SYSTEM

In the latter part of the last century and the early decades of this, no subject was more discussed than the future of capitalism. Economists, men of unspecific wisdom, Chautauqua lecturers, editorial writers, knowledgeable ecclesiastics and socialists contributed their personal revelation. It was taken for granted that the economic system was in a state of development and in time would transform itself into something hopefully better but certainly different. Socialists drew strength from the belief that theirs was the plausible next stage in a natural process of change.

The future of the industrial system, by contrast, is not discussed. The prospect for agriculture is subject to debate—it is assumed to be in course of change. So are the chances for survival for the small entrepreneur or the private medical practitioner. But General Motors, General Electric and U.S. Steel are viewed as an ultimate achievement. One does not wonder where one is going if one is already there.

Yet to suppose that the industrial system is a terminal phenomenon is, *per se*, implausible. It is itself the product, in the last sixty years, of a vast and autonomous transformation. During this time the scale of the individual corporation has grown enormously. The entrepreneurial corporation has declined. The technostructure has developed, removed itself from control by the stockholders and acquired its own internal sources of capital. There has been a large change in its relations with the workers and a yet larger one in its relations with the state. It would be strange were such a manifestation of social dynamics to be now at an end. So to suggest is to deny one of the philosophical tenets of the system itself, one that is solemnly articulated on all occasions of business ritual—conventions, stockholders' meetings, board meetings, executive committee meetings, management development conferences, budget conferences, product review meetings, senior officer retreats and dealer relations workshops. It is that change is the law of economic life.

The future of the industrial system is not discussed partly because of the power it exercises over belief. It has succeeded, tacitly, in excluding the notion that it is a transitory, which would be to say that it is a somehow imperfect, phenomenon. More important, perhaps, to consider the future would be to fix attention on where it has already arrived. Among the least enchanting words in the business lexicon are planning, government control, state support and social-ism. To consider the likelihood of these in the future would be to bring home the appalling extent to which they are already a fact. And it would not be ignored that these grievous things have arrived, at a minimum with the acquies-cence and, at a maximum, on the demand, of the system itself.

Such reflection on the future would also emphasize the convergent tendencies of industrial societies, however different their popular or ideological billing; the convergence being to a roughly similar design for organization and planning. A word in review may be worthwhile. Convergence begins with modern large-scale production, with heavy requirements of capital, sophisticated technology and, as a prime consequence, elaborate organization. These require control of prices and, so far as possible, of what is bought at those prices. This is to say that planning must replace the market. In the Soviet-type economies, the control of prices is a function of the state. The management of demand (eased by the knowledge that their people will mostly want what Americans and Western Europeans already have) is partly by according preference to the alert and early-rising who are first to the store; partly, as in the case of houseroom, by direct allocation to the recipient; and partly, as in the case of automobiles, by making patience (as well as political position or need) a test of eligibility. With us this management is accomplished less formally by the corporations, their advertising agencies, salesmen, dealers and retailers. But these, obviously, are differences in method rather than purpose. Large-scale industrialism requires, in both cases, that the market and consumer sovereignty be extensively superseded.

Large-scale organization also requires autonomy. The intrusion of an external and uninformed will is damaging. In the non-Soviet systems this means excluding the capitalist from effective power. But the same imperative operates in the socialist economy. There the business firm seeks to minimize or exclude control by the bureaucracy. To gain autonomy for the enterprise is what, in substantial measure, the modern Communist theoretician calls reform. Nothing in our time is more interesting than that the erstwhile capitalist corporation and the erst-while Communist firm should, under the imperatives of organization, come together as oligarchies of their own members. Ideology is not the relevant force. Large and complex organizations can use diverse knowledge and talent and thus function effectively only if under their own authority. This, it must be stressed once more, is not autonomy that subordinates a firm to the market. It is auton-omy that allows the firm authority over its planning.

The industrial system has no inherent capacity for regulating total demand—for insuring a supply of purchasing power sufficient to acquire what it produces. So it relies on the state for this. At full employment there is no mechanism for holding prices and wages stable. This stabilization too is a function of the state. The Soviet-type systems also make a careful calculation of the income that is being provided in relation to the value of the goods available for purchase. Stabilization of wages and prices in general is, of course, a natural consequence of fixing individual prices and wage rates.

Finally, the industrial system must rely on the state for trained and educated manpower, now the decisive factor of production. So it also is under socialist industrialism. A decade ago, following the flight of the first Sputnik, there was great and fashionable concern in the United States for scientific and technical education. Many argued that the Soviet system, with its higher priority for state functions, among which education is prominent, had a natural advantage in this regard.

Thus convergence between the two ostensibly different industrial systems occurs at all fundamental points. This is an exceedingly fortunate thing. In time, and perhaps in less time than may be imagined, it will dispose of the notion of inevitable conflict based on irreconcilable difference. This will not be soon agreed. Marx did not foresee the convergence and he is accorded, with suitable interpretation, the remarkable, even supernatural, power of foreseeing all. Those who speak for the unbridgeable gulf that divides the free world from the Communist world and free enterprise from Communism are protected by an equally ecclesiastical faith that whatever the evolution of free enterprise may be, it cannot conceivably come to resemble socialism. But these positions can survive the evidence only for a time. Only the most committed ideologist or the most fervent propagandist can stand firm against the feeling that an increasing number of people regard him as obsolete. Vanity is a great force for intellectual modernization.

To recognize that industrial systems are convergent in their development will, one imagines, help toward agreement on the common dangers in the weapons competition, on ending it or shifting it to more benign areas. Perhaps nothing casts more light on the future of the industrial system than this, for it implies, in contrast with the present images, that it could have a future.

. . . It is part of the vanity of modern man that he can decide the character of his economic system. His area of decision is, in fact, exceedingly small. He could, conceivably, decide whether or not he wishes to have a high level of industrialization. Thereafter the imperatives of organization, technology and planning operate similarly, and we have seen to a broadly similar result, on all societies. Given the decision to have modern industry, much of what happens is inevitable and the same.

selection 41

Creeping Capitalism in the Soviet Union?*

Harry Landreth

Recent developments in the U.S.S.R. indicate that a profound and probably prolonged reexamination of economic theory and of the correct principles of economic planning is under way.

One immediate reaction by Western observers to these developments is that at last the socialist planners have seen the error of their ways and are turning from Karl Marx and toward Adam Smith. In particular, it is felt in the West that Russian economist E. G. Liberman's proposal to use profit as a firm's success indicator is a strong and clear sign that creeping capitalism is at work in the Soviet Union.

If this alleged tendency in the Soviet Union is coupled with the often-asserted trend of creeping socialism in the United States, one can easily deduce that the economic systems of the two major powers of the world will inevitably converge. Greater use of the market mechanism in the Soviet Union and of economic planning in the United States has led many Western observers to the conclusion that these economic systems will at some point in the future be difficult to differentiate.

I am convinced that these forecasts are in error. And in this article I shall argue that the Soviet Union and the United States are not converging in any fundamental way. My brief stands on two points:

1. The two systems have contrasting economic and political goals, and they will evolve different institutional structures to achieve those goals.

2. Recent developments in economic thinking and practice in the Soviet Union do not represent a movement toward a capitalistic system.

But before I elaborate on these points, I shall summarize the current reevaluation of long-cherished economic principles in the Soviet Union, particularly Liberman's proposals and the attack on the labor theory of value.

*From *Harvard Business Review,* September–October, 1967, pp. 133–40. ©1967 by the President and Fellows of Harvard College; all rights reserved.

Author's note: I wish to thank Professor Reo M. Christenson of Miami University for his helpful comments on and criticisms of this article, which is an adaptation of a paper delivered at the Spring 1967 meeting of the Ohio Association of Political Scientists and Economists.

A GOD THAT FAILED

An understanding of recent economic thinking in the U.S.S.R. is possible only against the historical background of Marxist ideology. It is not unusual for the American in the street, as well as the editors of some of our newspapers, to think that Karl Marx set forth in *Das Kapital,* in some detail, the economic principles that should govern the operation of a socialist system. This is incorrect. Marx was absorbed in studying capitalism, and his works contain almost no writings on the operation of a socialist economy.

After a successful revolution in Russia (an unlikely place, according to Marxian theory), the Russians turned to Marx's writings to find a blueprint for socialism. They found nothing to assist them in economic planning, although they did find a great deal of ideology that has continuously prevented rational thinking about economic questions.

The new direction which Soviet economic thinking has taken in the past few years can be characterized as a growing awareness that much of Marxian ideology is a positive *hindrance* to sound economic planning. Further self-examination by Soviet economists will certainly reveal that some of the economic ideas developed in Western Europe and the United States, and now taught as part of every college elementary economics course, must be comprehended before rational planning is possible.

The part of Marxian ideology that inhibits economic calculation is contained in the labor theory of value; the supply–demand theory of value accepted by Western economists is needed to make possible rational calculation in the Soviet Union. As the current debate among Soviet academicians indicates, however, it is easier to borrow technology than economic theory.

Marx Makes Planning Difficult

One part of the general body of knowledge called economics is value theory, an attempt to explain those forces that determine the *relative* values or prices of economic goods. It is known that any product or service that is scarce (or for which there is demand) has a price. Price relationships between goods or services can be thought of in barter terms (2 diet colas = 20 cigarettes) or in monetary units. Value theory is not an explanation of absolute price (why 20 cigarettes have a price of 30 cents) but rather a theory of relative prices, that is, the exchange *ratios* between commodities.

Relative prices of commodities, of course, play a crucial role in the process of producing, distributing, and consuming goods. To have efficient resource allocation, it is essential that the relative scarcity of goods and services be correctly revealed in their prices. This requires that prices reflect two aspects of economic reality: (a) the amount of resources used to produce commodities (the social costs of production), and (b) the gains expected from use or consumption of the goods (the role of demand). The failure of prices in the Soviet Union to reflect correctly the scarcity or demand value of goods has resulted in increased criticism of Soviet economic planning by some of the more liberal Soviet scholars.

2 Colas = 20 Cigarettes. Suppose that it takes two hours of labor to produce 20 cigarettes and one hour to produce a bottle of diet cola. If we ignore certain complications for the sake of clarity, the Marxian labor theory of value would hold that the relative price or value of these commodities is 2 colas = 20 cigarettes. In a planned economy prices could then be set so that commodities exchange at ratios reflecting their cost of production measured only by labor time. Objections can immediately be raised to such a system of pricing:

1. It ignores the role of demand and places exclusive emphasis on the cost, or supply, side of the market. Not allowing for demand in setting prices results in a number of difficulties in a planned economy. Two more obvious manifestations of inadequate attention to demand by Soviet planners are the shortages and resulting queues (prices set too low) and the excessive inventories of certain retail goods (prices set too high).

2. It does not include as a part of price the return to capital (interest) or the return to land (rent). In the above example, the commodity prices made no allowance for the amounts of capital and land used in the productive process. It is at this point that Marxian ideology has most severely damaged rational planning in the Soviet Union. Marx held that rent and interest were payments peculiar to a particular type of institutional structure (capitalism) and that labor was the only true productive factor of production. Since interest and rent are not payments for the use of productivity, Marxian ideology contends, they are not socially legitimate claims on the national product, but rather bourgeois notions that contaminate planning in a socialist society.

Failure to allow for interest and rent as factors in price has caused considerable difficulties in planning the Soviet economy. Part of the recent thinking of some Soviet economists has been a reaction to these difficulties and a recognition of the inadequacies of the Marxian labor theory of value.

I shall return to this controversy shortly, but first I want to discuss a closely related matter.

The "Radical" Liberman

It is probably unfortunate that the term "Libermanism" has become synonymous with the critical reexamination of economic thinking and planning now taking place in the Soviet Union. The recommendations of Liberman are important, but his proposals represent only part of a much broader and more important development.[1] Liberman's criticism of some current practices does not

---

[1] Some of the best expositions and summaries of Liberman's proposals are: A. Nove, "The Liberman Proposals," *Survey,* April, 1963, p. 112; Alfred Zauberman, "Liberman's Rules of the Game for Soviet Industry," *Slavic Review,* December, 1963, p. 734; and Marshall Goldman, "The Economy at the Crossroads," *Survey,* October, 1965, p. 125.

really reach the heart of the inadequacies in Soviet economic thinking; his suggestions for reform are mild compared to the necessary correctives.

Better Goods, New Technology.   Liberman's goals are to improve the quantity and quality of currently produced commodities and to encourage the firm to bring forth new products and new technology.

His basic proposal to achieve these goals is to reduce the number of targets assigned to the firm by central planners, thus giving it greater latitude in its decision-making ability. The major effect of his proposal would be to simplify the planning process and to decentralize, to some extent, decisions formerly made by central planners.

But after eliminating numerous targets, or directives, now handed down from higher levels, the firm would still be required to meet centrally planned targets for quantity of output, product assortment, and destination and date of delivery. So it is apparent that Liberman does not reject central planning.

One key element in Liberman's suggested reforms has caught the attention of Westerners. He has proposed that many of the present bonuses paid to firms be eliminated and that a firm's bonus depend solely on its profitability rate, which is defined as the ratio of a firm's total profit to its capital. A firm can augment its bonus by actions that increase the numerator of this ratio, for example, by increasing profit (the difference between revenue and cost). If a firm earned the same profit with a smaller amount of capital, then its bonus would be larger.

The use of incentive payments for plant managers is certainly nothing new in the Soviet Union. Superficially it appears that Liberman is suggesting that Soviet plant managers act like their capitalistic counterparts, and thus that their attempt at increasing the firm's profitability rate would result in better allocation of resources. An interesting aspect of Liberman's proposals, and one equally disturbing to Marxist ideology, is his suggestion that the quantity of capital used by the firm be inversely related to its bonus.

Insidious Criticism.   By defining the profitability rate as a ratio of profit to capital, Liberman has made a fundamental and insidious criticism of Marxian ideology. His method of calculating bonus payments implicitly accepts the principle that interest charges should be made to the firm for the use of capital, since the more capital it uses, the lower its bonus. Computation of the firm's bonus by this method would have the consequence of placing a price on the use of capital. From the point of view of the firm, the price of using more capital would be the reduction in its bonus.

This abbreviated discussion cannot pretend to do justice to Liberman's proposals; rather, it serves to place his ideas in the context of a much broader and more significant movement and to indicate the shortcomings and basic timidity of his criticisms.

Even if the government accepted Liberman's recommendations and everything worked as he hoped, the Soviet economy would still experience major difficulties in efficiently allocating resources. As long as prices in some sectors of the economy do not truly reflect the scarcity values of commodities, efficient resource allocation is impossible.

In short, only a fundamental attack on an important building block in the Marxian ideological structure will suffice. Such an attack on the labor theory of value has begun, and the ramifications of this development are of vital importance and interest.

Attack on Labor Theory of Value

The assault on this Marxian pillar has come about not as a broadly conceived thrust, but as a by-product of attempts to solve everyday problems in planning. The strength of ideology and the authoritarian nature of the Soviet system are evidenced by the time lag between the papers in 1939 by L. V. Kantorovich and V. V. Novozhilov,[2] which were the first to implicitly question the labor theory of value, and the fuller discussion of these issues that began with Khrushchev's sanction in the early 1960's.

"Shadow Prices."   In the late 1930's Kantorovich, a mathematician, was asked to help solve a scheduling problem in the plywood industry. Soviet mathematicians long before had developed certain techniques that had application in industry. Since the particular problem presented to Kantorovich was not adaptable to existing techniques, however, he developed a new method for its solution. Kantorovich thus became the originator of linear programming, a technique independently developed in the United States in 1947.

In the solution of a linear programming problem, certain so-called multipliers are derived. Although Kantorovich did not immediately perceive their importance and implications, his further investigations of the application and economic significance of linear programming made apparent their usefulness in economic planning. These multipliers are what economists term "shadow prices" and reflect the scarcity values of commodities.

It soon became clear to many Soviet economists that planners employing these shadow prices as indicators of value would achieve a much more efficient allocation of resources than planners using prices set by a planning board and derived from some mixture of ideology and expediency. Others were equally quick to see that the shadow prices generated by linear programming models implied that relative prices, rather than being just a function of labor time, depend also on the scarcity value of capital and land. Use of shadow prices was therefore an obvious and fundamental attack on the labor theory of value.

"Opportunity Costs."   The other pincer in this movement against orthodoxy also started as an attempt to solve limited practical problems of planning.

Suppose that a planning board must decide among several investment alter-

---

[2] Kantorovich's paper has been translated as "Mathematical Methods of Organizing and Planning Production," *Management Science,* July, 1960; Novozhilov's paper has been translated as "On Choosing Between Investment Projects," *International Economic Papers,* No. 6, 1956.

natives. Should it allocate funds (capital) to build a hydroelectric plant, a steel mill, or a machine tool plant? A labor theory of value that excludes interest from consideration does not help solve this everyday problem even in an economy institutionally organized like that of the U.S.S.R. This is only one example of a series of problems which can be rationally solved only by admitting the productivity and scarcity value of capital.

Problems such as these engaged the attention of the economist Novozhilov in the late 1930's and led him to write a series of papers. Novozhilov's solution to the problems of rational calculation is rather complicated in its details but is clear in its outline and main thrust. He proposed to measure value or price by what economists would term "opportunity costs" and thus allow not only for labor costs but also for capital and land costs. By expressing his concept of opportunity cost in units of labor, he gave the impression of remaining within the tent of orthodoxy.

Opening Pandora's Box

In the post-Stalinist period there has been a relatively free and open discussion of Kantorovich's and Novozhilov's proposals, and the pot has started to boil.[3] The orthodox traditionalists probably lost their case once discussion of the issues was permitted.

It is, of course, difficult to predict the outcome of this great debate. There are strong signs, however, that a more rational, pragmatic approach to pricing will prevail. In time, the ideology of Marx will give way. Moreover, further debate surely will disclose the weaknesses in the measures of value suggested by Kantorovich and Novozhilov. While their measures of value are a giant step beyond the Marxian labor theory of value, they are cost of production theories that stress the role of supply exclusively, ignoring the role of demand.

The ideological bias in the U.S.S.R. today requires acceptance of the theory of value developed by Ricardo in England in the early nineteenth century and further elaborated by Marx about the middle of that century. By 1900 economists in Western Europe and the United States had rejected the labor theory of value as well as cost of production theories of value (such as those of Kantorovich and Novozhilov). What we are witnessing today in the Soviet Union is the beginning of a great change in economic thinking. While it required some 50 to 80 years for this change to gain acceptance in the Western world, there is no reason to expect a similar time lapse in the U.S.S.R. Part of this improvement in economic thinking will take place without outside stimulus and part by borrowing from Western academicians.

It is reasonable to expect the Soviet Union to develop economic thinking as sophisticated as ours. Ideology can only delay these developments, not stop them.

---

[3] For a discussion of their contribution to current economic thinking in the U.S.S.R., see Robert W. Campbell, "Marx, Kantorovich, and Novozhilov: *Stoimost'* versus Reality," *Slavic Review*, October, 1961, p. 402.

CONVERGING ECONOMIES?

It is often asserted that there is a tendency toward a convergence of the economic structures of the two major powers of the East and West. How will the recent developments that I have outlined be interpreted in this context? It would seem that the answer to this question has been given:

> Liberman's proposals for greater use of profit as an incentive, for some decentralization in planning, and for increased use of the market mechanism have already been hailed as indications that the Soviets have seen the errors of socialism.
>
> The movement away from a Marxian labor theory of value toward a bourgeois supply-demand theory of value is acclaimed as another triumph for capitalism.

The belief in convergence is widely held, although different reasons for it are advanced. Those who expect it represent a wide spectrum of political ideology and professional training: Erich Fromm, Arnold J. Toynbee, Robert Heilbroner, and Jan Tinbergen, to name just four from a long list.[4]

I recognize that a clear and certain answer is impossible for such a difficult question as the future courses of economic systems. But, at the least, those who foresee convergence are hasty in their conclusions; stronger arguments exist for nonconvergence than for convergence.

Growth vs. Freedom

On close examination of the goals and the problems of the two economies, the convergence thesis does not stand up. For when two countries face radically different problems, they are not likely to evolve similar economic institutional structures.

A list of the goals of economic activity shows that the United States and the Soviet Union have common economic goals. It is in their relative importance or priority that differences exist. The primary economic goal of the Soviets is economic growth—a goal of the United States, but not one with as high priority. The primary economic goal of the United States is security—a low-ranked economic goal in the U.S.S.R.

Differing Political Goals. An examination of political goals reveals different patterns. An overriding political goal, or end, in the United States is individual freedom. A maximum amount of political and economic freedom is a goal of such high priority that others are often qualified in these terms—for example, security with maximum individual freedom, or full employment in an institutional framework which allows a maximum of individual freedom.

In the Soviet Union individual freedom is more a means and less an end. Greater freedom is permitted not so much as an end in itself but rather because it is used to promote other goals. In the economic sphere, for example, granting

---

[4] For such a list, see Lynn Turgeon, *The Contrasting Economies* (Boston: Allyn and Bacon, Inc., 1963), p. 4.

greater individual freedom has resulted in more efficient resource allocation and higher labor productivity.

In giving growth highest priority, the U.S.S.R. has had economic problems which the U.S. economy seldom encounters. The institutions that evolve in the U.S.S.R. to solve these problems are not likely to resemble those of the United States. In their planning for high rates of growth, the Soviets are consistently, in the words of one observer, "over-committing their economic resources."[5] This leads to the kinds of pressures and problems that the United States encountered during World War II. U.S. wartime arrangements for solving these problems bear great similarity to the usual nonwar planning procedures used in the Soviet Union.

The major U.S. economic problem appears quite the opposite, one of undercommitment. The post-World War II era, especially following the "prosperity" of the Korean war period, has been characterized by large amounts of unemployed capital and labor resources. While the United States characteristically produces fewer goods than it could, the Soviets seem always to be striving to produce more than possible. One does not solve the problems of overcommitment with the institutions of undercommitment.

Changing Ideologies.   Convergence of economic institutions is considered inevitable by some who hold that the priority of Soviet economic goals will more closely resemble those of the United States after the Soviets have achieved a higher level of per capita income. As economic goals converge, they say, so will economic institutional arrangements. The goals, beliefs, and ideology of any society are not rigidly fixed; one can expect a change in the priorities of economic life over a long period of time. On the other hand, ideology has a persistency that cannot be denied.

A good argument can be advanced that a relatively young and new ideology is much easier to change than an ideology which has had time to "harden." The Soviet focus on economic growth is a relatively new one, dating possibly from the industrialization debate of the 1920's and the first Five Year Plan in 1929. Those who argue for a convergence of economic goals foresee it as a process over a long period of time. I suggest a more plausible possibility: the longer the Soviet orientation toward growth exists, the more likely this fetish will persist.

It is possible to grant these points of mine and still see convergence. As the United States makes greater use of now well-known economic tools to control the level of economic activity, it becomes more like the U.S.S.R. It might be argued that one can solve the problems of undercommitment with the institutions of overcommitment.

This possibility certainly exists, but it is extremely doubtful that the United States would attempt to solve its problem of less than full employment with central planning of the Soviet type. One important reason why certain monetary and fiscal controls are used in the United States is that these devices do not

---

[5] *Ibid.*, p. 8.

impinge on individual freedom to the extent that central planning does. As long as maximum individual freedom remains a paramount political goal, our attempts to achieve greater economic stability are unlikely to result in institutional arrangements like those of the U.S.S.R.

Toward Market Socialism

A final case for convergence could be put in terms of the recent developments in economic thinking and practice in the Soviet Union. The argument can be made like this: while the economic problem of first priority in the Soviet Union—achieving a high growth rate—is not susceptible to solution by the institutional structure of U.S. capitalism, a problem of lower priority on the Soviet scale—rational resource allocation—is. The suggestions for the use of profits as an index of firm success, greater decentralization of planning, the displacement of Marxian value theory, and increased use of the market mechanism are all cited as examples of creeping capitalism.

It is an error to interpret these developments as movements toward capitalism.

Market Mechanism.   Prices may be used to allocate scarce resources through the market mechanism in either a capitalistic or socialistic system. A convergence of mechanisms or means to achieve different goals should not be confused with a convergence of economic systems.

For the Soviet economy, the market mechanism may be used in an increasing degree to achieve ends set by the central planning board. This is clearly different from the U.S. economy, where the very ends of the whole economic process emerge from the market system.

One of the crucial differences between the U.S. and Soviet economies is that the market performs two functions in the U.S. system but only one in a Soviet-type socialistic system. In the latter case the market is purely a device for achieving the planners' goals — there is almost a complete lack of consumer sovereignty. In the U.S. economy the market is a mechanism for achieving the goals as disclosed by the market itself. Here the market allocates resources through fluctuating prices toward those goods demanded by consumers, and not toward those goods deemed desirable by the State. For example, demand for more automobiles is manifested through the market; then they are supplied. The Soviets use the market mechanism in a very different way. If the planners should decide that increased automobile production was desirable, they would lower the price of automobiles and thus, through the market, expand purchase of them.

Allocating Resources.   The distribution of capital provides another contrast between the market mechanism as a device for allocating resources and as a procedure for determining the ends of the economic process.

In the U.S. economy a prime manner in which resources are allocated between industries is by differences in the rate of return on capital—the rate of interest. If the rate of return is greater in an industry supplying recreation materials than in one providing technical education beyond high school, for example, capital flows to the recreation industry.

The Soviets are willing to calculate rates of return in order to make more rational choices among certain investment alternatives (steel mills, aluminum facilities, oil refineries, and so forth). They do not, however, let the rate of return determine allocation of capital to those industries which in the minds of planners are not in keeping with their value judgments of the good society, or which are detrimental to the overriding goal of achieving high rates of growth. If the market were allowed to direct economic activity in the Soviet Union as it does in the United States, then the Soviets would produce more automobiles and housing than at present.

One basic question decided by every economic system concerns the division of each year's total product between capital and consumer goods. In the United States the market mechanism is a major factor in determining this division—gross investment is usually about 15% of total output.

Since slicing the economic pie in the Soviet Union is done by state planners, gross investment runs between 25% and 30% of total output there. They use the market mechanism and set high prices on consumer goods to discourage consumption expenditures; they will not permit a free market to allocate resources between the capital and consumer goods sectors.

Adapting Modern Theory.   All of this suggests that the Soviets are increasingly willing to use modern economic theory as a means to achieve the ends set by central planning. The essence of the differences between these systems lies in the role of private property and consumer sovereignty—in the manner in which the ends of economic activity are determined. Current economic thinking and practice in the Soviet Union does not indicate that private property or consumer sovereignty will play important roles in the economy.

Recent experience in the Soviet Union is not an example of creeping capitalism. Closer examination reveals the opposite—creeping socialism. The Soviet economic system has never been a very good institutional structure for rationally allocating economic goods. With the present reforms in theory and practice, the Soviet Union is beginning to develop a more efficient system which might be termed "market socialism."

It is interesting to note that these trends in the U.S.S.R. were suggested some 30 years ago. At that time some economists questioned the ability of a socialistic economic system to rationally allocate resources. Subsequent discussion led to the conclusion that market socialism could efficiently allocate resources by using a number of theoretical constructions developed to explain the operation of a capitalistic economy.[6] Although the Soviets are just now awakening to these possibilities, it would be a mistake to misinterpret what they are doing. Their actions, if successful, will result in a system closer to the textbook version of

---

[6] See the papers by F. M. Taylor and Oscar Lange in *On the Economic Theory of Socialism,* ed. Benjamin Lippincott (Minneapolis: University of Minnesota Press, 1938).

socialism. It is to be hoped that one outcome will be a more humanitarian socialism closer to utopian dreams.

SUMMARY

A significant number of Western writers of differing political persuasions and training hold that the economic systems of the Soviet Union and the United States are converging. Increased use of the market mechanism in the U.S.S.R. and increased planning in the United States have led to this conclusion.

I have made a case that the economic systems of the two leading world powers are not converging in any fundamental way. The economic priorities of the two systems differ, and these systems will evolve different institutional structures to achieve contrasting goals.

In the Soviet Union, the proposals of the economist Liberman, the movement away from a Marxian labor theory of value, and greater emphasis given to the market mechanism do not represent creeping capitalism, in my view. Instead, the U.S.S.R. is proceeding toward a more rational system of resource allocation that is better described by the term market socialism than by capitalism.

selection 42

Are Industrial Societies Becoming Alike?*

Arnold S. Feldman and Wilbert E. Moore

To many sociologists the answer to our titular question is so clearly affirmative that one might simply say "Yes," and let us proceed with suitable dispatch to the next question. In behalf of an affirmative reply, one could note the marked extension of merit-based educational opportunities in England, the increased incidence of marital choice based on romantic love in urban France, and the ubiquity of organization men in Soviet industry. But let us not be too hasty. We must also concede the durable qualities of one-party government in Russia, the alternation of multi-party instability and charismatic political unity in France, and the hardy survival of parliamentary government in England. No trends now in evidence would lead us to expect a convergence of political systems, unless one truly accepts the hopeful or dire prediction of eventual Communist victory for the entire world.

---

*From Alvin W. Gouldner and S. M. Miller (eds.), *Applied Sociology* (New York: Free Press of Glencoe, Inc., 1965), pp. 260–65.

Our answer, then, must be "Yes and No," and the clarification of the ambiguity may justify a continuation of the discussion. In what follows, brevity imposes on us a mode of presentation that is more taxonomic and dogmatic than would otherwise be tolerable in polite discourse.

Much of the support for the common structural characteristics of industrial societies derives, in fact, from analysis of the industrialization process, particularly in the contemporary context. These analytical studies typically ask, what are the social changes that can be expected to accompany and follow successful industrialization? Implicitly or explicitly, some salient structural features of industrial societies are identified as the terminus of a path of progress, and resistances, tensions, and strains in the transformation of the pre-industrial social order to an industrial one are then identified and appraised.

The degree of functional determinism, that is, the extent of the requiredness of elements in an industrial social structure, differs from one interpreter to another. Nonetheless, virtually no one rejects the notion that industrial societies share a core set of social structures that together provide a kind of extended operational definition of industrialism itself. This core would include the factory system of production, a stratification system based on a complex and extensive division of labor and hierarchy of skills, an extensive commercialization of goods and services and their transfer through the market, and an educational system capable of filling the various niches in the occupational and stratification system. If one goes much beyond this list, the degree of requiredness or variability becomes distinctly controversial.

Now we do not reject this mode of interpretation, and have ourselves recently indulged in it in our chapters in the volume on *Labor Commitment and Social Change in Developing Areas.* However, there are two major difficulties in extending this analysis to all elements and features of social systems, and to a prediction of a growing and enduring convergence among industrial societies.

Let us take first the industrialization process. From what has been said so far our titular question, taken literally and restrictively as concerned with *industrial* societies, could not be answered. Rather, one could say, all societies will become more alike as they become industrial, and at least with respect to core structures this is clearly true. But it does not follow that no variability of any consequence remains. The sources of that variability we can deal with at least taxonomically, although without full explication and illustration.

For convenience, let us distinguish three principal sources of variability, although these can and must be subdivided. The first is the character of the pre-industrial social structure and its influence on subsequent social states. The second is the route or trajectory of industrialization. The third is the structure of industrial societies, structure being used in a loose and extensive sense. The last of these gets close to the heart of our initial question, and in proper fashion of manufacturing suspense, we shall discuss it last.

One certainly need not enumerate here the ways in which historians, anthropologists, and sociologists have documented cultural diversity. The principal critical issue is one of relevance to economic development or industrialization. For the true functional determinist, the question of relevance does not arise. It is a matter of faith and conviction that everything is related to everything. And anthropologists and sociologists are generally most impressive when they trace out the connections between, say, a given change and a consequence in some seemingly remote aspect of culture or social action. Yet, surely the examples are a radically unrepresentative selection from among the myriads of variations and changes that are essentially inconsequential. What still remain to be codified are the necessary or highly probable routes and mechanisms of systemic articulation, and, conversely, the kinds of variability that barely escape the derogatory designation of "chance," if they escape it at all.

We are essentially forced back to a minimal position. Some elements of any pre-industrial culture or social system cannot accompany industrialization. These represent impediments or required changes. The inconsistent elements of pre-industrial systems do not simply disappear, lost without trace. Rather, if industrial development does continue, they become attenuated, partially suppressed, partially adapted to changes in the core structure. But by their persistence, they constitute a continuing source of tension, a focus of social problem solving, a challenge to scholars and administrators alike who want the system tidy. The solutions, we suggest, are always partial, and always have further consequences that in turn provide new points of tension. For example, an industrializing economy may face labor shortages, either absolute, or because of structural and motivational impediments to mobility. Any solution, ranging from coercive tactics to the offering of exceptional inducements, will have enduring consequences, and, to repeat, new solutions will provide their own new problems.

Now let us turn to the question of route or trajectory. The first point to be noted is that in some situations history itself prevents its own repetition, for its lessons and results become the basis of new social actions. The simplest illustration of this is the lack of necessity for a newly developing economy to repeat either the timing or sequence of technological change. More fundamentally, there now exist a number of advanced industrial economies, which, whatever the answer to our initial question, *still* provide alternative models of ideology, political control, and peripheral or noncore structural features. The available models permit a degree of choice to the developing area that earlier innovators did not have.

Here, however, we find an unexpected dividend for the believers in growing homogeneity. All industrial societies, and perforce all industrializing societies, exhibit a degree and extensity of deliberate and administered social change that is historically unmatched. The attempt to predict and control secondary and tertiary results—to reduce the number and salience of unanticipated consequences—will not, we believe, finally succeed in a perfectly manipulated system anywhere, and there is no reason to expect the failures or inhibiting costs to be uniform. So we have a second foretaste of our final answer.

Trajectories of industrialization do differ, not so widely as to make them randomly variable or incomparable, but enough to caution against singular generalization. In form, social change may vary in *sequence*–the order in which different components change, in *rate*–the relative rapidity of change in one or another systemic component, and in *timing*–a special attribute of rate calling attention to intervals among component changes, and especially the phenomena of leads and lags. In context, societal change will vary in *historical era,* as just discussed, in *relationship between a given society and others,* and rather importantly, in the *kind of economic regime* directing any program of change.

Although each of these variables might be discussed somewhat extensively, we shall concentrate here on questions of sequence. This has been an arena of somewhat inconsequential conflict among adherents of various determinisms or "key strategies," and between all of the single-factor proponents and those who argue for the simultaneous change in everything.

The initial difficulty in the search for the magic key is that not all doors have the same locks. Less figuratively, any pre-industrial society has a somewhat different array of resources and shortages, of facilitating and impeding elements in the social structure, of bottle-necks and overfull vats, of leads and lags. The second difficulty is that the sequence of change does involve allocation priorities, whether or not these are consciously made. Thus, in some sense all positions are equally right or equally wrong, since any sequence involves costs and will be disequilibrating.

Those who argue for simultaneity of change have a kind of correct premise and the wrong conclusion. It is true that anything short of simultaneity will adversely affect some institutions in that their energy and resource allocation will be lessened. It is also true that eventually the disparity between "leading" and "lagging" sectors can threaten seriously an industrialization program. Nevertheless, this is exactly the sequential route that societies undergoing industrialization will experience.

In other words, equivalence of change in major institutions is impossible, but failure to achieve it will introduce profound strains and tensions. This is intrinsic to industrialization. Thus the sequential order involves shifting rates and intensities of change. Modernization may begin in any one of various spheres of a society–the work place, the market, political structure, or others. It will proceed by various leads and lags, but no single sphere will predominate throughout. (Technology, for example, will often be substantially behind a change in goals or their priority.) The sequence will reflect shifting leads, since continued advances in any one sphere will require some approximation to equivalence in other spheres.

Questions of rate and timing essentially provide multipliers or divisors for the basic question of sequence. Sequence, as a matter of fact, is more often characterized by differential rates of change than by a singular dynamic element and a residue of static ones.

Industrialization, then, does have a partially specifiable and common destination, but reaches that destination from different starting points and follows different routes or trajectories. Neither pre-industrial societies nor the modes of social transformation are randomly or uniquely variable. We do not have to abandon ourselves to the exaggerated particularity of history or descriptive ethnography. But restraints imposed by systemic characteristics, by a kind of functional determinism, are less precise and less predictive than seekers of simplicity would wish.

Now this finally brings us to the question of the increasing similarity of industrial societies. Here our basic theoretical position, with readily manifest empirical grounding, has far-reaching interpretive consequences. Stated baldly, the crucial fact is that there is no stable and enduring terminus to the industrialization process. In general, the rate of change increases at an accelerating rate. This casts in doubt, to put it mildly, all the conventional notions that the similarities of all industrial societies, and all industrializing ones, will become virtually complete, if, like mystical Marxists or millennialist Christians, we are content to wait.

Let us recapitulate the persistent sources of difference. Societies start a process of industrialization from different antecedent conditions. Part of those conditions will constitute problems or barriers, a typology of which can be constructed. But the problems are never finally solved, for even victory carries with it its own train of peculiar consequences. Societies undertake economic development with a high quotient of deliberate change, including the kind of problem solving required to overcome impediments. Deliberate change, however, can scarcely be complete and completely controlled, if for no other reason than the lack of infinite resources for knowing, predicting, and controlling everything. Among the unanticipated changes will be some that are continuously consequential, although others may constitute rather random or chance variability or "noise."

Persistence and its consequences and deliberate change and its consequences constitute the first two orders of variability in industrial societies. They lead to a third, which is a very familiar one when restated. It is the lack of close, organic, functional integration in social systems. The tracing out of relationships, in terms of a sort of scale of requiredness, limited ranges of viable variability, and wider degrees of random or only historically explainable variation, is still an unfinished and worthwhile investigative enterprise. But it must be faced with an open mind, and not from a partisan position of functional determinism.

The final source of variability, however, is of crucial relevance for any attempt at functional interpretation. This is the essential and inherent instability of the core elements and their first-order associated variables. Industrialism generally increases the comparability among societies and their principal structural elements, but does not necessarily increase their operating similarity. The problems may be typologically standard but the solutions somewhat more variable, if for no other reason than the differences in starting points and trajectories. It was not accidental that the examples of persistent dissimilarity noted at the beginning of this paper were political. The political order, almost by operational definition, is the residuary legatee of unsolved social problems. Because a viable polity is essentially a tension-management system, and tensions are not the same or likely to become the same, there is no reason to expect greater and greater convergence of the tensions of industrial societies, or their ideological rationalization, or the political and other modes of partial containment. Surely most of the changes in industrial societies, and certainly the major ones by any crude scale, are disequilibrating rather than equilibrating.

We have not retreated to the womb of relativistic particularity, for both structural and dynamic generalization is possible. But we do think the leverage provided us by comparative statics is rather less than had been hoped, because the place to stand turns out to be moving at high speed and is very shaky in transit. It is not simply our deepened understanding that makes the world complex. It really is.

Additional References

Bendix, R. *Work and Authority in Industry,* chap. 7. New York: Harper Torchbook, 1963.

Bornstein, Morris. *Comparative Economic Systems, Models and Cases.* Homewood, Ill.: Richard D. Irwin, Inc., 1965.

Crozier, Michael. *The Bureaucratic Phenomenon.* Chicago: University of Chicago Press, 1964.

de Hevesy, P. *The Unification of the World.* New York: Pergamon Press, Inc., 1966.

Harbison, Frederick, and Myers, Charles A. *Management in the Industrial World,* chap. 6. New York: McGraw-Hill Book Co., Inc., 1959.

Jencks, A. E. "After Nationalization: Changes in the Attitudes of Management," *Management International Review,* Vol. 8, No. 1 (1968), pp. 55–64.

Kerr, Clark, *et al. Industrialism and Industrial Man.* New York: Oxford University Press, Inc., 1964.

Marko, Kurt. "Soviet Ideology and Sovietology," *Soviet Studies* (University of Glasgow) (UK), Vol. 19, No. 4 (April, 1968), pp. 465–81.

Moore, Wilbert E. "Global Sociology: The World as a Singular System," *American Journal of Sociology,* Vol. 69 (March, 1966), pp. 475–82.

Patch, Richard W. "New Techniques and Old Ideas—The Inertia of Attitudes as Observed in Peru," American Universities Field Staff Reports Service, West Coast South America Series, Vol. 11, No. 6 (August, 1964).

Pethybridge, Roger. "The Assessment of Ideological Influence on East Europeans," *Public Opinion Quarterly,* Vol. 31, No. 1 (September, 1967), pp. 38–50.

Rostow, W. W. *The Stages of Industrial Growth.* London: Cambridge University Press, 1960.

Tannenbaum, Frank. "The Survival of the Fittest," *Columbia Journal of World Business,* Vol. 3, No. 2 (March–April, 1968), pp. 13–20.

Terestchenko, V. "Advertisingwise, Here's Looking at You," *Industrial Marketing,* August, 1967, reprinted from *Literaturnaya Gazeta,* February 8, 1967.

"Trends in Management Until 1985," *Management International,* Vol. 2, No. 6, 1963.

chapter eleven

Conclusion: American Students and Foreign Management

So what? What does this survey of culture and management mean to the reader? This depends upon who the reader is. Among present and prospective American managers, three categories are pertinent:

1. The individual located overseas in a foreign subsidiary.
2. The individual with international responsibilities in the domestic office of a firm with foreign subsidiaries.
3. The individual in a domestic firm without foreign interests.

We shall address ourselves to categories one and two first, and then devote most of this final chapter to the last group.

A message to present and prospective managers in foreign lands is the burden of this volume: The premise and conclusion of the chapters and selected readings are that culture matters to the manager. If one is to organize, plan, control, and most important, motivate in a culture other than one's own, awareness of cultural variables is critical. Attitudes toward authority, willingness to communicate, legitimacy attached to economic activities, class structure, and so on—all these facets of a society will influence the philosophy and practice of management.

Experience suggests that the U.S. firm abroad has greater freedom from cultural restraints than the native organization. The American manager in Turkistan may be able to do things that the domestic manager cannot, because the people have different expectations about work in the American subsidiary than in the local firm.[1] However, the American is not free. He ignores local customs, attitudes, and values at his peril. I hope that this volume sensitizes the American

---

[1] C. Wickham Skinner, "Management of International Production," *Harvard Business Review,* September–October, 1964.

reader to these factors and provides some concepts to assist him in understanding management in whatever cultural setting he finds himself.

To the second category of U.S. managers (those at home with present or prospective international responsibilities), this argument is equally valid. As suggested in the first chapter, one may need a greater understanding of the interplay of cultural and managerial variables if one is to work with a foreign-managed subsidiary from a Manhattan office than if one is on the scene overseas. To be sure, the research by Haire, Ghiselli, and Porter [2] indicates that American managers and their foreign counterparts are relatively similar in their thinking. Hence, they should be able to communicate. Nonetheless, to facilitate co-operation, Americans must understand the cultural pressures on their overseas associates.

But what about the third category—those readers who neither have nor expect international responsibilities? Does this examination of culture and management have anything to offer to this group (which includes most U.S. managers)? Again, as suggested in the first chapter, the answer is yes. Study of foreign managerial philosophy and practice can contribute to American management—in spite of our apparent superiority. Unfortunately, what we can learn is less clear, for the flow of management personnel and managerial expertise in recent years has been out of the United States, not into.[3] And experienced executives have not been systematically surveyed to determine what we can learn from foreigners—indeed, many of them probably would reject the very premise of such a study.

PROMISING FOREIGN PRACTICES:
AS PERCEIVED BY AMERICAN STUDENTS

Lacking operating managers, what about managerial students? I have been impressed with the insights of students in comparative management courses. All have been graduate students in the Master of Business Administration program at the Wharton School; almost all have had business and/or military experience; many have traveled or lived abroad fairly extensively. From their experience, their study of American management, and their course survey of foreign management, what foreign practices impress them as potentially useful in the United States? Since they will be among the executives of the future, what these fledgling managers perceive as desirable in foreign management may have some implications for this country.

What the Students Say

The following question was asked of students after a course in Comparative Management: Indicate and discuss what foreign managerial philosophy or prac-

---

[2] Mason Haire, Edwin Ghiselli, and Lyman Porter, *Managerial Thinking* (New York: John Wiley & Sons, Inc., 1967).

[3] See J. J. Servan-Shreiber, *The American Challenge* (New York: Atheneum Publishers, 1968).

tice might be helpful to management in the United States. The most common responses were (in order of frequency mentioned):

1. Employment security (as in Japan).
2. Participation of subordinate managers and workers (as in Japan, Sweden, and eastern Europe).
3. Involvement in the community (as in some developing countries, Soviet Russia, and eastern Europe).
4. Less formal structure, more personalized management, and greater individuality (as in the United Kingdom and Latin America).
5. Personnel interchange between government and business (as in Japan, western and eastern Europe).

It is not suggested that all or any of these practices should be blindly adopted by American management. No, the central theme of this volume is that managerial practices and cultural values must be compatible. Foreign practices have developed for particular reasons relevant to their origins—origins that also have given birth to conditions undesirable in the United States. We would not want the wide class and work distinctions characterizing the Latin countries where manual labor is considered so degrading. Most of us would not want the authoritarian style characterizing German and some Scandinavian management, and so on. Even with the more attractive practices mentioned by our students, America's heritage of individualism, competitive enterprise, and mobility might prevent adoption of any—although some experimentation might be appropriate.

This experimentation, however, is not our concern here. Diagnosis, not prescription, is the subject of this chapter—diagnosis of what might be some of the problems of American management, rather than prescription of foreign practices as curatives. Of course, the student survey is not systematic and scientific, but the responses are suggestive: What characterizes them is not so much admiration for foreign management practices, but more a questioning of American values.

Interpreting What the Students Say

One must be cautious in interpreting the students' responses. What foreign policies are admired does imply certain criticisms of contemporary American management, but just what the criticisms are is not obvious.

Consider the most common response: The Japanese tradition of virtually guaranteed lifetime employment. American students' praise for this policy might suggest that they are sensitive about being discharged, that they see U.S. business as an uneasy jungle where at any time one is liable to lose one's livelihood. But such is emphatically not the view of these students. "I don't have to worry, I will be taken care of" is how one young man from New York put it to a group of senior managers at a Wharton Executive Development Program. These hard-driving and successful executives recoiled visibly; and they turned off the young student by not really listening to anything else he had to offer. Nonetheless, what the impertinent young man said was not that he is unwilling to strive. Rather, he meant to suggest that he would work hard, but not just to keep the wolf from the door or to avoid being fired. He is simply not worried about this. With his education and skills, and with economic conditions as they have been throughout his lifetime, this 22-year-old student is convinced he can always find a well-paying job; if ABC Corporation is not a satisfying place to work, XYZ Company might be. Depression-influenced, middle-aged managers may shudder at the student's naïvete and fear for his optimism, but such is the world the young graduate sees.

Insecurity about making a living, therefore, is not the explanation for our M.B.A. candidates' interest in the Japanese lifetime job. As we shall see, more complex values are involved. In listing promising foreign managerial policies and practices, the students say less about the advantages of these practices than about their perspectives on U.S. management—especially where future problems may lie. Somewhat like a Thematic Apperception Test or a Rorschach ink blot, the students project their values onto the subject they have studied.

VALUES IMPLICIT IN STUDENT OBSERVATIONS

Naïve or sophisticated, idealistic or realistic, what are the values that dominate the American students' attraction to certain foreign managerial practices? Can we bring meaning to the list of their responses? Commitment, participation, individualism, personalization, and involvement seem to be the ideals characterizing their observations. Some of the words sound oddly inconsistent.

Commitment

As indicated, our students are attracted to Japanese job permanency. Arguments are advanced that such security would encourage independence and creativity. Cited as example is the academic system whereby tenure supposedly guarantees academic freedom and promotes new ideas without the innovator fearing for his career. Some students also suggest that greater security might free the manager or specialist from organizational politics, thus allowing him to devote more time and energy to problems.

Still, more fundamental values are involved. There seems to be a search for a sense of belonging, or, more actively, for commitment. This concern apparently is widespread among young people. Professor Craig Lundberg at the University of Pennsylvania has been informally polling to find out whom people admire as heroes. Recently he polled a class of undergraduates and the business managers in the executive program referred to earlier. The questions were: What living figure do you most admire as a hero? What are his admirable characteristics? The executives concentrated on two men—Dwight D. Eisenhower and Harry S. Truman; well over half of the executives named these two former Presidents. Their reasons? Decisiveness first, and courage second.

The undergraduates' responses were very different. A similar number of students mentioned a much longer list of people (including Che Guevara, Ho Chi

Minh, "me," and "Dad"); there was less central tendency in their answers. Nonetheless, the most common name mentioned—by a wide margin—was Eugene McCarthy. They admired first his commitment to a cause, and second his courage.

One can make too much of the differences between these two groups, for, after all, years separate them and undergraduate students simply may be less familiar with Truman and Eisenhower. The basis for heroism would appear to be different, however. The executives admire decisive leadership, the unshirking use of power. The young people, in contrast, admire commitment to a cause— especially when the cause is in opposition to an established hierarchy or power structure. Both value courage. What the students seek, perhaps, is not to be in front leading personally, but to be submerged in a leading cause. As one of the activists who had occupied a building in the Columbia University student revolt put it, "It was the first time I had ever felt committed to anything."[4]

In collective commitment, many students reject the individual who is apparently committed to his own success, or even to hard work for its own sake. For example, in responding to Lundberg's poll, some undergraduates went out of their way to criticize the late Robert Kennedy as being too ambitious.

Now the typical clean-shaven and ivy-league-suited M.B.A. candidate at the Wharton School is not the bearded and blue-jeaned undergraduate revolting against the establishment; the former fundamentally are committed to the system. However, they apparently want the business organization to be a cause rather than simply a job, a setting for societal commitment rather than merely an opportunity for personal advancement. Consider these comments by two graduate students:

> I question the benefit of the growing trend of American managers to plan careers around job mobility.[5] Psychological costs are involved which are difficult to measure in terms of the individual and society. Management in Japan is currently a lifetime commitment for executives. This commitment encourages risk taking, self-expression, and enables company executives to devote less time to company politiking. I believe that a more committed approach is needed in American management.
>
> Our concept of employment, hiring, and firing must change. One step is the guarantee of employment. In my opinion, the corporation as a *society* is far more advanced in Japan than in any other nation. Teamwork, a sense of mutual obligation among all members of the society, represents a major step from purchase of laborers' time for money. It also avoids the degrading situation caused by employment—a word that should be used for things, not human beings.

Perhaps some students are inconsistent; they want a one-way street. They admire commitment to the organization, but they still want freedom to change jobs. In contrast, in the Japanese system the ties are just as strong from man to

---

4 "Special Report: Columbia at Bay," *Newsweek,* May 6, 1968.

5 For example, Eugene E. Jennings of Michigan State University recently wrote: "Mobilographic interviews and studies reveal a manager whose central concern is for mobility itself. Success is mobility; it is less position, title, salary, or exceptional performance. Success is moving and movement." E. E. Jennings, "Charting the Difficulties to the Top: A Study of Executive Mobility Patterns," *Management of Personnel Quarterly,* Summer, 1967, p. 21.

organization as from organization to man. There is little movement from firm to firm (at least until very recently). Our students share the American values of mobility, but they are critical of over-mobility (the I.B.M. "I've been moved" syndrome) and especially critical of the pervasive impermanency characterizing American interpersonal relations and geographic locations. "The nomadic trek of many American families," writes one student, "must be reduced. It must be a grand feeling for parents not to know just how many schools, in how many different cities, their children will attend before they are ready to enter college!" In short, they want to move when they want to, not when the company wants them to.

Participation

Greater participation is also desired. In some countries, national legislation has created formal representative bodies within private and public companies (even prescribing membership, frequency of meetings, subjects to be discussed, etc.). Whether these groups are really effective as influence devices is doubtful, but the idea is attractive to many young (and older) people. One student observes:

> What has evolved in Russia is a sense of participation in the business. I believe that American management should try to develop a greater sense of participation both on managerial and rank and file levels. Some workers feel alienated. What is needed, ironically, is a more soviet type of identification with the enterprise.

Many favorable comments are expressed regarding the Japanese "ringi" system of decision making and European employee representation through factory committees and works councils. Especially wanted is lower management involvement in upper executive problems. Our students admire the use of the "assistant to" in Japanese business, where early in a college graduate's career he gets involved in policy matters—not necessarily as the decision maker, but in a position to at least observe, and perhaps to influence. What they are looking for, apparently, is something like the well-known McCormick junior boards of directors whereby young men are involved meaningfully in analysis and discussion of actual top-level organizational problems early in their careers.[6] Perhaps there would be more willingness (and ability) after this exposure to take over responsibility in lower-level jobs with less sense of frustration and disillusion—such as Porter found in beginning specialists and managers in large organizations.[7]

In their comments, our M.B.A. candidates are concerned mainly with involvement of junior managers and staff specialists. But they do mention the desirability of more participation by all employees, including more formalized and institutionalized upward flow of communications and ideas.

---

[6] See Charles P. McCormick, *Multiple Management* (New York: Harper & Bros., 1938).

[7] Lyman Porter, "Where Is the Organization Man," *Harvard Business Review*, November-December, 1963; and "Job Attitudes in Management: Perceived Deficiencies in Need Fulfillment as a Function of Job Level," *Journal of Applied Psychology*, 46 (1962).

Paradoxically, with this awareness of mutual interdependence, and desire for participation and commitment, our students also want more individuality.

Individualism and Personalization in Management

The students are familiar with personality studies of successful executives describing their "impersonality" and ability to choose objectively.[8] Research on men and boys with high needs for achievement indicates that when faced with a task, they are likely to objectively choose helpers with high abilities.[9] In contrast, in similar situations, people with high needs for affiliation are more likely to choose by social criteria. For example, when picking sides for a sandlot ball game, the boy with high affiliation need may select his friends, the higher achiever might select the best players regardless of personal feelings.

Impersonality is helpful in a business executive's career; it facilitates changing positions, moving geographically and socially, the whole recurring cycle of arrivals and departures that characterize the climb up the hierarchy.[10] Yet many of our students call for more personalization. In managerial recruiting, hiring, and training, they want less patterned, less statistically based criteria, and more individually oriented judgment. A student writes:

The trend in this country should be toward more personalized interpersonal relations. We are dealing with a generation that places a high value on interpersonal relations. When one considers that today's college student will be tomorrow's leader, it seems likely that new personal styles eventually will emerge.

In short, students want more individuality. They are admirers of individualism and criticize American business for what they perceive, rightly or wrongly, as conformity. How ironic in a country where businessmen are the great preachers of individualism! Nonetheless, in dress, speech, even beard and hair, these M.B.A. candidates (none of whom has a beard or long hair) want greater freedom for the individual. To them, the possibility that General Motors might be upset with an executive wearing plaid trousers and Edwardian sideburns is ridiculous—and, as the following comment suggests, probably detrimental to business.

To reverse this trend requires overturning one of the sacred cows of American culture— the regular guy. Conformity to norms in dress, speech, thought, and social habits is extreme, and provokes the rebellion exemplified by the hippies. Surely, business and America would benefit if more individual freedom was encouraged.

Another student picks up the same theme:

Whereas human relations in European business lack the outer nonchalance and friendliness found in the United States, they do not seem to share the inner tensions which are

---

8 William E. Henry, "Psychodynamics of the Executive Role," *American Journal of Sociology*, Vol. 54, No. 4 (January, 1949).

9 See David M. McClelland, *The Achieving Society* (Princeton, N.J.: D. Van Nostrand Co., Inc., 1961) for many references to this.

10 Norman H. Martin and Anselm L. Strauss, "Patterns of Mobility Within Industrial Organizations," *Journal of Business*, Vol. 29, No. 2 (April, 1956), pp. 101–10.

often apparent in this country. American tensions stem largely from an unrealistic expectation that one must like everybody, or at least pretend to. We need to change from liking everyone to respecting them. For it is easier to respect people with differing views and styles than it is to like them.

Even career nepotism is mentioned as desirable. Perhaps what is being sought is some sense of stability, or feeling of certainty. Throughout most of the world, a father's occupation is a great source of security and stability to the son because it points the way—and also of course because it may ease the effort required. So life may be less hectic and serious. A mature student who has worked and lived in Latin America writes:

> At the risk of losing some efficiency, it would be interesting to watch American managers operate more informally. Everything is terribly serious in the United States. It seems to me that Latin managers, although I realize that they lag far behind in a professional approach to business, do enjoy life a great deal more than their American counterparts.

This desire for personalization and individualism also is reflected in comments about emulating the less structured organization of European firms—especially less elaborate staffs (again ironic because many, if not most, M.B.A. graduates go into staff positions).

> American management suffers from the disadvantage of being overstructured. At all levels managers are too constrained. While it is accepted that some sacrifice of individual autonomy must be made in the interest of the organization, it is submitted that it is going altogether too far. If the trend continues, U.S. management will consist mainly of men highly trained in narrow skills, all conforming, with little inspiration. By contrast, in the United Kingdom and some of Europe, the persistence of the "amateur" manager insures that many executives retain autonomy with less undue constraint by organizational pressures. There are more charismatic and nonconforming managers than in the United States. It is possible that what Europe lacks in managerial skills is compensated for by originality. American companies must learn that overstructuring may inhibit individuality and endanger the organization.

Our students are attracted to the generalist orientation of British and continental firms—their avoidance of over-specialization, emphasis on wisdom, and sense of history. With Hugh Parker, the chairman of McKinsey and Company's London office, and with Ernest Dale, recent president of the Academy of Management, they feel that European individualism, lack of structure, and broad perspectives contribute to greater creativity and risk taking than is apparent in the American concern.[11] For as Parker and Dale suggest, contrary to American prejudices, the top levels of European management may be more willing to undertake risk ventures than are American executives.

Community Involvement

Life within the organization has been our concern so far. In addition, our students maintain that this commitment and involvement should extend outside the business. Espoused is a modified syndicalism. The students want business to

---

11 Hugh Parker, "The Missing Urge of British Management," in *The Director* (London), April, 1967; Ernest Dale in a lecture at the University of Pennsylvania, April, 1968.

be a society of mutual commitments, duties, and responsibilities. Their call seems to be not only for business to extend its activities more into the community, but also for the boundaries between private business and public society to disappear—or at least to become more open. For example, a number of students praise the interchange of people between business and government as in France and Germany, and indeed in some of the socialist and communist countries. (A textile engineer, A. N. Kosygin started his career as a foreman in the Zhelyavov factory in Leningrad 33 years ago.) The greater respect for government service existing in these nations is admired, for such esteem might ease the latent business-government conflict existing in the United States. One former career military officer, now a graduate student, writes:

> One of the key areas where we could learn something from foreign philosophies and practices is in our attitudes toward management. When you consider how much of our wealth, health, and very existence depends on the programs and organizational structures managed at the federal level, it is shocking that we do not exert considerably more effort to upgrading careers in civil service.

By improving America's evaluation of careers in government service—and perhaps more important, by jointly educating government, business, and other institutional executives—ignorance about other's activities and misunderstanding of other's objectives might be reduced. Closing this gap might facilitate the community involvement that is thought desirable.

Described as promising is the direct involvement of foreign firms in urban development, housing, and education; the Soviet Union, Eastern Europe, and Japan are named.

> Ernest Dale[12] challenges American management to support its lofty contentions of social responsibility with tangible results. He suggests that we note the ways in which many foreign firms, notably Shell and Olivetti, have made concrete contributions to the communities in which they operate. Dale characterizes their contributions to small business and to better community living as far superior to the much publicized, but often dysfunctional, efforts in this country.

The students probably exaggerate what is being done in these countries. Their admiration for the firm's social activities in the U.S.S.R., Eastern Europe, and Sweden may not reflect its importance nor management's success. What is implicit is a recognition that these nations do not have the social problems we have—and a wistful wish that we didn't either. Nonetheless, what they suggest is not foreign to American history. They seem to call for a return to some aspects of old-fashioned paternalism.

> Foreign management practices might have their greatest application in handling minority problems in the United States. A paternalistic firm similar to a Japanese, German, or Latin-American enterprise might help to solve the race problems here. A firm could become a part of the ghetto community or reservation working directly on critical deficiencies in housing and education.

Emphasis is on the community; the call is for greater management participation in building homes and guiding schools—not just for employees, but for the

---

[12] The reference is to the lecture by Ernest Dale, *ibid.*

local populace. In a sense, the focus is narrowed from national to local. Most discussion of social responsibility has been in terms of national interest (wages, prices, competitive practices, and such). What the students admire in the social activities of foreign firms tends to be more their concern with the local community.

None seem to worry about the old problem of the firm's dominance of local affairs in its own economic interest. Again another irony, because since the 1920's and 1930's many American companies have attempted to maintain arm's-length relations with the local community—bending over backwards not to interfere in local decisions on taxation, housing, recreation, or what have you. Certainly, corporate managements have given to the Red Cross, Community Chest, and United Fund in their local communities, but many managers (and social critics) consider direct involvement by business in local problems a form of colonialism not suited to modern American pluralism.

CURRENT MANAGERIAL PRACTICE IN THE UNITED STATES

When commenting on foreign management, our M.B.A. students implicitly and explicitly state what they perceive to be philosophy and practice in American management. These perceptions are probably naïve and distorted—as more experienced readers undoubtedly believe at this point. Even if not entirely realistic, however, the students' observations are important, for they will act upon perception, not reality. Nevertheless, reality shapes the perception. Within space limits, therefore, we shall examine current U.S. conditions in relation to the students' listing of promising foreign practices.

1. Employment Security. Among professional and managerial employees, the differences among Soviet Russia, Japan, and the United States are not so great. Research indicates that departure from executive office in the U.S. increasingly is by promotion or retirement, not dismissal.[13] To be sure, involuntary resignations occur, but industries vary widely in this regard. Be that as it may, the U.S. manager probably has more security than the Russian. Finally, given prosperous economic conditions and scarce skills, job security for the manager or professional is not so important anymore.

Security has greater relevance to clerical and blue-collar employees, although even here it is lessened by economic prosperity. Unions such as the United Automobile Workers still call for a guaranteed annual wage and greater job security. Nonetheless, the gap between American practice and that cited elsewhere seems to be closing. The Soviet Union does have involuntary unemployment;[14] Japanese companies have been backing away from their absolute guarantees in the interest of flexibility;[15] court decisions in the United

---

13 W. Lloyd Warner and James Abegglen, *Big Business Leaders in America* (New York: Harper & Bros., 1955).

14 Theodore Schabad, "Soviet Says Lack of Jobs Confronts Nation's Young," *New York Times,* June 30, 1965.

15 Selwyn Feinstein, "Japan's Paternalistic System Is Changing in Face of Tight Labor Market," *Wall Street Journal,* April 5, 1967.

States point the way toward certain property rights in a job.[16] Much can still be done in this country—especially for low-income minority employees—but workers here have more security than most nations.

2. Participation of Subordinate Managers and Workers. Participation is less formalized and institutionalized in most American companies than in the works councils, factory committees, and joint boards in the United Kingdom and Europe. Many American companies administer elaborate suggestion systems that imply substantial worker participation in the generation of ideas and the sharing of rewards—although the participation is more apparent than real. In addition, some companies delegate specific decisions about meaningful production problems (methods, quality, design, and so on) to employee groups (as in the Scanlon plan), but frequently such groups consider only minor issues such as the location of the Coca-Cola machine, or the titles of lunch-hour movies.

I do not suggest that no upward influence exists in American business. It does. The union has been an important vehicle for democracy because of its strength at the local level. Such is not the case in most other countries where the national union is politically oriented and the local union is impotent. In most of the world—capitalist and socialist alike—at home, and in plant or office, management reigns supreme. Collective bargaining, union elections, and grievance procedures guaranteeing due process are vital means for worker involvement in the United States.

Whether equivalent participation by lower level managers and staff specialists exists is not clear. Organizing these people is difficult; they are resistant to the invitations of the teamsters as well as more professionally oriented unions. Several observers of the American scene voice concern about the lack of due process and the unilateral authority exercised over these employees who do not enjoy a union's protection.[17]

Nonetheless, influence does flow upward. As David Mechanic points out in his article "The Sources of Power of Lower Participants in Complex Organizations," power and influence extend up and down in all business organizations.[18] To the extent that the professional or lower manager has skills that are in demand, he is not helpless when individually bargaining with the organization. However, it is true that American corporate managerial and white-collar men are not characterized by the formal representation procedures found in blue-collar ranks—and in some foreign concerns.

Just the same, a revolution in authority relations is shaking contemporary America. The turmoil has not yet spread into business organizations, but as current students enter corporations, some dramatic changes in American management may emerge.

16 See William Gomberg, "The Job as a Property Right," *Nation,* Vol. 191, No. 18 (February 26, 1960); "Featherbedding: An Assertion of Property Rights," *Annals,* January, 1961; "The Job as a Property Right," *Current,* January, 1961.

17 William Gomberg, "Problems of Due Process in Management," *The Personnel Administrator,* Vol. 13, No. 3 (May/June, 1968).

18 *Administrative Science Quarterly,* Vol. 7 (1962/63), pp. 349–64.

3. Community Involvement. Social responsibility is, of course, one of the great public issues of the day. As government agent in some socialist and communist countries, business does play a critical role in housing, schooling, and recreation. American pluralism, however, traditionally has suggested that democracy and human freedom are best served by separating the activities of various kinds of organizations and confining them to their major objectives—profits for businesses; wages, hours, and working conditions for unions; education for school boards; public tranquility for governments; and so on.[19] Certainly, most of us are aware of an increasing need to expand cooperation among these institutions, even to blur some of the boundaries. U.S. business does participate in the community through gifts to educational institutions, United Funds, Red Cross, and so on.

This participation, however, has been confined mostly to money, although engineering skills and managerial expertise are also vital. In the Birmingham civil rights crisis of 1963, Roger Blough of U.S. Steel maintained that it is the responsibility of executives as private citizens, not as business officials, to follow their consciences in correcting social ills.[20] Our students would agree, but over and above this they maintain that their organizational roles should also include such involvement. Current activities of Ford, Chrysler, and General Electric executives, among others, who are involved in major efforts to develop Negro employment opportunities, indicate that some top companies feel the same way.[21]

4. Less Impersonal Organization, More Personalized Management. To summarize the state of American management in this area is probably impossible—mainly because it is difficult to imagine what U.S. management would be like if it were more personalized. Perhaps our young people are inconsistent on this. They complain about politics in business (and think Academia is different in this regard—how naïve!), but criticism of business politics implies that social relations, rather than purely objective criteria, influence decisions. Isn't this what personalized management encourages? In addition, we have had our share of nepotism reflected in family or old-school-tie advantages.

No, the students may be more concerned with the impersonality of bureaucratic ideology than with interpersonal reality. The predetermined, specialized organizational slot (which they have learned about in their studies) seems too drained of human variables—variables obviously present in less-structured, and perhaps more chaotic, European and Latin-American business.

What is ultimately involved is the desire for autonomy. Partly this reflects unrealistic expectations about life in any organization, but American business must plead guilty to inhibiting individuality. Pressures on dress, haircuts, and company image are real and students do not separate such matters from pressures to conform on ideas. Indeed, American management confirms the connection by allowing more freedom in appearance and behavior in research labora-

---

[19] Milton Freedman, *Capitalism and Freedom* (Chicago: University of Chicago, 1962).
[20] Letter to the *New York Times,* November 2, 1963.
[21] "Target: Negro Jobs," *Newsweek,* July 1, 1968.

tories where ideas are obviously critical. Too many practicing managers comment about adverse reaction to the checkered sport jacket, or to the striped shirt (much less the turtle neck!) to reject the reality of this pressure. In addition, stories about not admitting one's artistic interest on the personnel department's tests are all too true. Much improvement is needed in American business in defining legitimate organizational requirements and desirable human freedoms.

5. Personnel Interchange between Government and Business. Our business students share a cultural bias against the challenge and desirability of government work. They are the same age group that David McClelland in 1961 reported as rating government service very low in prestige.[22] Yet they differ from many older people in being aware that their bias is harmful. In the long run, this suggests that better people will be attracted to government and that freer interchange will develop between the so-called public and private sectors. Until now, the flow of managerial personnel has been mainly at upper levels—and from business to government. The exceptions have mainly been generals or admirals taking positions with defense-oriented manufacturers. The McNamara pattern is fine, but we need more joint education and more two-way flow at lower levels.

CONCLUSION

However superficially, we have journeyed through history and around the globe to view the interplay of culture and management. Our survey has not been that of the civilized anthropologist examining strange native practices. Rather, regardless of how economically advanced the United States may be, we have suggested that equal and better managerial practices may exist elsewhere. We have read articles describing things that look attractive: Commitment of workers in Japan; creativity at the top in Great Britain; individualism in Latin America; worker involvement in Eastern Europe, and so on. We have also summarized how some aspiring American managers respond to this exposure to foreign management. Their views tell us something about the immediate and future problems of U.S. management concerning commitment, participation, involvement, and individualism.

Readers who have made this journey with us may (as the late Robert F. Kennedy was fond of borrowing from George Bernard Shaw) "see things as they are, and wonder why." More important, fledgling and practicing managers may use some of these ideas to "dream of things that never were, and wonder how."

---

22 McClelland, *op. cit.,* pp. 240–56.

appendix

Suggested Topics for Independent Research

All these topics have been used successfully for written and verbal reports by individuals and/or small groups. Some of the selected readings in this volume obviously are pertinent and should be helpful to the researcher. In addition, the references listed at the end of each chapter are relevant. Finally, a few references are given with each topic below, but the student should be able to add to the list.

1. Why are minority groups so frequently associated with high achievement drives and business success (e.g., the Jews in America, Nisei Japanese, Pharsees in India, Lebanese in South America)?
    a) David McClelland. *The Achieving Society.* Princeton, N.J.: D. Van Nostrand Co., Inc., 1961.
    b) David McClelland *et al. The Achievement Motive.* New York: Appleton-Century-Crofts, 1953.
    c) James W. Vander Zander. *American Minority Relations: The Sociology of Race and Ethnic Group.* New York: The Ronald Press Co., 1966.
    d) B. C. Rosen. "Race, Ethnicity, and the Achievement Syndrome," *American Sociological Review,* Vol. 24 (1959), pp. 47-60.

2. What are the relationships of Catholicism, achievement motivation, and business?
    Above references plus:
    a) Amintore Fanfani. *Catholicism, Protestantism and Capitalism.* New York: Sheed & Ward, 1955.
    b) R. H. Tawney, *Religion and the Rise of Capitalism.* New York: New American Library, 1954.

587

c) Helen M. Robinson and Marion Monroe. Children's Reader Series. Chicago, Ill.: Scott, Foresman & Co.

3. What is the relationship of Islam, achievement motivation, and business? References to question 1 plus:
   a) Charles F. Gallagher. "Contemporary Islam: The Straits of Secularism—Power, Politics and Piety in Republican Turkey," American Universities Field Staff Reports Service, Southwest Asia Series, Vol. 15, No. 3 (October, 1966).
   b) Charles F. Gallagher. "Contemporary Islam: The Path of Pragmatism," American Universities Field Staff Reports Service, North Africa Series, Vol. 12, No. 3 (December, 1966).
   c) Charles F. Gallagher. "Contemporary Islam: The Plateau of Particularism," American Universities Field Staff Reports Service, Southwest Asia Series, Vol. 15, No. 2 (July, 1966).
   d) Sayyid Abol A'la Maududi. *Islamic Way of Life.* Lahore, Pakistan: Islamic Publication Ltd., 1965.

4. Why have the overseas Chinese (Chinese living outside the mainland of China) been so successful in business?
   a) "Achievement Motivation," *Asian Survey*, April, 1965.
   b) Toshio Hayese. "Overseas Chinese in Southeast Asia," *The Oriental Economist*, October, 1965.
   c) Victor Purcell. *The Chinese in Southeast Asia.* 2d ed.; New York: Oxford University Press, Inc., 1965.
   d) Albert Ravenholt. "The Ling Nam Wanton Parlor—A Chinese Restaurateur in Manila Copes with the Problems of Success," American Universities Field Staff Reports Service, Southeast Asia Series, Vol. 15, No. 3 (October, 1967).
   e) G. W. Skinner. *Leadership and Power in the Chinese Community of Thailand.* Ithaca, N.Y.: Cornell University Press, 1958.

5. Compare the achievement needs in various countries (as reported by McClelland) with their conceptions of management (as reported by Haire, Ghiselli, and Porter).
   a) David McClelland. *The Achieving Society.* Princeton, N.J.: D. Van Nostrand Co., Inc., 1961.
   b) Mason Haire, Edwin Ghiselli, and Lyman Porter. *Managerial Thinking.* New York: John Wiley & Sons, Inc., 1966.

6. How are European-owned companies managed in the United States (e.g., Shell Oil, Lever Brothers, Nestlé, Olivetti-Underwood, etc.)?
   a) Jean-Luc Rocour. "Management of European Subsidiaries in the United States," *European Business Review*, pp. 13–27.
   b) Charles H. Wilson. *The History of Unilever.* London: Cassell, 1954.

c) Kendall Beaton. *Enterprise in Oil.* New York: Appleton-Century-Crofts, 1957.

d) *Fortune* and *Business Week,* various issues.

7. How is the form of national government (e.g. dictatorship, socialistic, democratic) related to achievement motivation and business management?

   a) Eliczar B. Ayal. "Nationalist Ideology and Economic Development," *Human Organization,* Vol. 25, No. 3 (Fall, 1966), pp. 230–39.

   b) Roger W. Benjamin and John H. Kautsky. "Communism and Economic Development," *American Political Science Review,* Vol. 62, No. 1 (March, 1968), pp. 110–24.

   c) Mason Haire, Edwin Ghiselli, and Lyman Porter. *Managerial Thinking.* New York: John Wiley & Sons, Inc., 1966.

   d) Clark Kerr, John Dunlop, Frederick Harbison, and Charles Myers. *Industrialism and Industrial Man.* New York: Oxford University Press, Inc., 1964.

   e) David McClelland. *The Achieving Society.* Princeton, N.J.: D. Van Nostrand Co., Inc., 1961.

   f) Roland Sarti. "Facism and the Industrial Leadership in Italy Before the March on Rome," *Industrial and Labor Relations Review,* Vol. 21, No. 3 (April, 1968), pp. 400–417.

8. Do colleges and universities aid or hinder business development?

   a) R. Farmer and B. Richman. *Comparative Management and Economic Progress.* Homewood, Ill.: Richard D. Irwin, Inc., 1965.

   b) F. Harbison and C. Myers. *Management in the Industrial World.* New York: McGraw-Hill Book Co., Inc., 1959.

   c) F. Harbison and C. Myers. *Education, Manpower and Economic Growth.* New York: McGraw-Hill Book Co., Inc., 1964.

   d) H. Hartmann. "Industry and the Universities," *Progress—The Unilever Quarterly,* Vol. 52, No. 294 (4, 1967–68), pp. 116–20.

   e) Kenneth R. Schreider. "Development Universities: Special Institutions for the New Nations," *International Development Review* (Society for International Development), Vol. 10, No. 1 (March, 1968), pp. 17–22.

   f) Lyndall F. Urwick. "What Have the Universities Done for Business Management," *Management of Personnel Quarterly,* Vol. 6, No. 2 (Summer, 1967).

9. How do origin and education of British management affect their philosophy and practice?

   a) Acton Society Trust. *Management Succession.* London: The Trust, 1956.

   b) R. V. Clements. *Managers—A Study of Their Careers in Industry.* London: G. Allen & Unwin, Ltd., 1958.

   c) G. H. Copeman. *Leaders of British Industry.* London: Gee & Co., 1955.

d) R. Lewis and R. Stewart. *The Managers.* New York: New American Library, 1961.

e) David Granick. *The European Executive.* New York: Doubleday & Co., Inc., 1964.

f) P. W. Musgrave. "The Educational Profiles of Management in Two Iron and Steel Companies with Some Comparisons, National and International," *British Journal of Industrial Relations,* Vol. 4, No. 2 (July, 1966).

g) *20th Century,* Spring, 1965.

10. Discuss the challenges that face British management.
  a) A. Sampson. *The Anatomy of Britain Today.* New York: Harper & Row, Publishers, 1965.
  b) "The 1966 Battle of Britain," *Business Week,* November 19, 1966.
  c) Hugh Parker. "The Missing Urge of British Management," *The Director,* April, 1967.

11. Compare the origins and educations of managers in France and Germany.
  a) H. Hartmann. *Authority and Organization in German Management.* Princeton, N.J.: Princeton University Press, 1959.
  b) R. Lewis and R. Stewart. *The Managers.* New York: New American Library, 1961.
  c) D. Granick. *The European Executive.* New York: Doubleday & Co., Inc., 1964.
  d) W. Hahn. "Higher Education in West Germany: Reform Movements and Trends," *Comparative Education Review,* Vol. 7, No. 1 (June, 1963).
  e) A. Legendre. "L'École Polytechnique," *Arthur Anderson Chronicle,* Vol. 28, No. 2 (March, 1962), pp. 26–33.

12. Compare the philosophy and practice of management in France and Germany.
  Same references as question 11.

13. Discuss Russian attitudes toward authority and management under the czars before the Revolution in 1917.
  a) Reinhard Bendix. *Work and Authority in Industry.* New York: Harper & Row, Publishers, 1956.
  b) Arvid Brodersen. *The Soviet Worker.* New York: Random House, Inc., 1966.

14. Discuss the use of money as a motivational device in Soviet management.
  a) Barry Richman. *Soviet Management.* Englewood Cliffs, N.J.: Prentice-Hall, Inc., 1965.
  b) David Granick. *The Red Executive.* New York: Doubleday & Co., Inc., 1961.

- *c*) Joseph Berliner. "Managerial Incentives and Decision Making," in Prasad, *Management in International Perspective.* New York: Appleton-Century-Crofts, 1967.

15. What is "workers' management" in Europe? Has it worked?
    - *a*) Ken Coates and Anthony Topham. *Industrial Democracy in Great Britain.* London: MacGibbon & Kee, 1966.
    - *b*) Jiri Thomas Kolaja. *A Polish Factory: A Case Study of Worker's Participation in Decision Making.* Lexington: University of Kentucky Press, 1960.
    - *c*) Jiri Thomas Kolaja. *Worker's Councils: The Yugoslav Experience.* New York: Frederick A. Praeger, Inc., 1966.
    - *d*) Ian Rosner. "Management by the Workers in Poland," *International Labour Review,* Vol. 76, No. 3 (September, 1957).
    - *e*) Josip Zupanov. "The View from Zagreb," *Columbia Journal of World Business,* July–August, 1967.
    - *f*) Erland Waldenstrom. "Works Councils: The Need to be Involved," *Columbia Journal of World Business,* Vol. 3, No. 3 (May–June, 1968), pp. 59–66.

16. What is the relation of religion, achievement motivation, and business in Japan?
    - *a*) Edward Norbeck. *Changing Japan.* New York: Holt, Rinehart & Winston, Inc., 1965.
    - *b*) Alvan J. Obelsky. "Japan's Transition: A Socio-Economic Transition," *Kobe University Economic Review,* Vol. 9 (1963).
    - *c*) Shin-ichi Takezawa. "Socio-cultural Aspects of Management in Japan," *International Labour Review,* August, 1966.

17. Discuss the relation of Japanese personality, attitudes toward authority, and management.
    - *a*) Edward O. Reischauer. *Japan–Past and Present.* New York: Alfred A. Knopf, Inc., 1964.
    - *b*) Stanley S. Miller. "Management by Omikosi," *Management International,* Vol. 3, No. 1 (1963).

18. Discuss management in *any* country.
    See Chapter Nine for references.

19. Discuss how business ethics vary with the cultural setting.
    - *a*) Thomas M. Garrett. *Business Ethics.* New York: Appleton-Century-Crofts, 1966.
    - *b*) Edward Sanford. "The Impact of the 'New Morality' on Western Business," *Cost and Management* (Society of Industrial & Cost Accountants of Canada), Vol. 42, Nos. 3 and 4 (March–April, 1968), pp. 12–16, pp. 13–17.

    c) Joseph W. Towle (ed.). *Ethics and Standards in American Business.* Boston: Houghton Mifflin Co., 1964.

20. How is management's perception of purpose and social responsibility affected by cultural factors?
    a) M. Fogarty. "British Management: An Uneasy Legitimacy," *Columbia Journal of World Business,* July–August, 1967.
    b) P. Heymann and J. Schmidth. "French Business Probes Its Raison de'Être," *Columbia Journal of World Business,* July–August, 1967.
    c) C. Walton. *Corporate Social Responsibilities.* Belmont, Calif.: Wadsworth Publishing Co., Inc., 1967.

21. Pick two cultural variables (e.g., attitudes toward personal achievement, or class structures, etc.) and show how these factors affect the basic managerial functions. Use specific cross-cultural examples.

22. Pick three foreign management practices that might be usefully applied in the United States. How would cultural factors in the United States affect these practices?

Index

A

Abegglen, James, 38, 582
Achievement need, 21–22, 163–82, 286–94
Acton, Lord, 21
Acton Society Trust, 399, 410
Adler, Alfred, 20
Adorno, T. W., 70
Affiliation need, 17–18
Africa, 145, 509
Alexander, Franz, 77
Allport, Gordon W., 69, 72
Ansbacher, H. L., 20
Aquinas, Thomas, 95, 134
Argentina, 513
Aristotle, 130
Armytage, W. H. G., 276
Ashby, Eric, 277
Asia, 510
Attitudes
  affecting economic activities, 55, 286
  affecting industrialization, 189, 286
  of managers in more and less developed
    countries, 341
Autonomy need, 21
Aymara Indians, 73–76

B

Backwardness in
  population, 153
  productivity, 145
  social attitudes, 148
  workers, entrepreneurs, and bureaucrats,
    149
Baldwin, George, 264
Ballantine, Duncan, 265
Barnouw, Victor, 55, 67–81
Bates, Marston, 11
Bauman, Zygmunt, 462
Beals, Ralph, 68
Beard, Miriam, 42, 131
Behavior
  appointment punctuality, 12–14
  delays, 14–15
  managerial behavior and culture, 12–15,
    27–29

Belgium, 219
Bellah, Robert, 439
Bendix, Reinhard, 14, 374
Benedict, Ruth, 12, 24, 55, 56–66
Bennis, Warren, 525
Berg, Elliot J., 550
Berliner, Joseph S., 454, 553
Black, Eugene, 150
Blanksten, George, 271
Blitz, Rudolph, 272
Blomfield, J. M., 77
Boddewyn, Jean, vii
Bolivia, 73
Boston, Mary, 77
Bowlby, John, 77
Brandenburg, Frank, 237, 239
Braun, Robert, 247, 286
Brazeau, Jacques, 503, 506
Brazil, 241, 514
Brown, Wilfred B., 49
Brown, William, 394, 428
Burling, Temple, 23
Burns, Tom, 401
Business schools, 295

C

Calvin, John, 100
Campbell, Robert W., 562
Canada, 501
Capitalism
  the growth of, 89–91
  the spirit of, 91–112
Carmichael, Oliver C., 278
Carr, E. H., 2
Carroll, John J., 292
Catholicism, 99–108
Ceram, C. W., 11
Childhood determinism, 76
Chile, 240, 514
China, 120–24, 467
Chowdhry, Kamla, 394, 441
Cicero, 131
Clements, R. V., 399
Clocks, 83
Cochran, Thomas, 372
Cohen, Elie, 79
Communication, 36

593

Competence need, 19-20
Confucious, 120
Conrath, David, 9
Convergence, 517
  diversity, 522
  economics, 563
  the future, 524
  industrial societies, 567
  uniformity, 517, 530
Copeman, G. H., 398, 410
Corke, Helen, 129
Cotgrove, Stephen, 403
Councils, workers', 461, 481
Crosland, C. A. R., 549
Croy, Homer, 15
Cuba, 235
Culture
  Apollonian, 11
  and communication, 36
  Dionysian, 11
  and economic attitudes, 55
  Faustian, 12
  and human needs, 22-27
  and management development, 311
  and managerial behavior, 12-15, 325-41
  the meaning of, 10-12, 56-66, 67-69
  and personality, 67-81
  sub-cultural groups, 23
  and work, 31
Curtis, Mark H., 276
Czechoslovakia, 511, 521

D

Dale, Ernest, 580
Darwin, Charles, 143
Davis, Allison, 78
Davis, R. C., 367
Dawson, Christopher, 45
Dean, William Friske, 17
De Witt, Nicholas, 281
Diljias, Milovan, 19
Dollard, John, 78
Douglas, J. W. B., 77
Dunham, H. Warren, 79
Dunlop, John T., 519, 523, 528, 530
Dunning, John R., 142

E

Economic development
  and business managers, 127
  and higher education, 257, 286
  and need for achievement, 168
Economic growth, the stages of, 157
  age of high mass consumption, 161
  beyond consumption, 162

Economic growth—*Cont.*
  drive for maturity, 160
  preconditions for take-off, 158
  the take-off, 159
  the traditional society, 157
Education
  in advanced countries, 275
  in Canada, 504
  in developing nations, 248
  foreign business schools, 295
  heroes and industrial growth, 286
  higher education and economic development, 257
  and management, 247-308
  in partially developed countries, 261
  in semi-advanced nations, 267
  in underdeveloped countries, 257
  in the United Kingdom, 402
Eells, Richard, 127, 128
Egypt, 488
Elkins, Stanley, 79
Ethnocentralism, 2
Europe (early modern period)
  acceptance of the profit principle, 138
  theory of mercantilism, 139
Europe (medieval period), 132
  attitudes toward business, 133
  evolution of the capitalist, 136
  philosophy of trade, 133
Europe (modern period), 140
  business and class in, 218
  business schools, 299
  first industrial revolution, 141
  group management, 356
  management philosophy, 346
  new philosophy of business, 142
  references, 511
Evolving organizations, 538

F

Faris, Robert L. K., 79
Farmer, Richard, 518, 521, 528
Farouk, King, 490
Fayerweather, John, 363
Fayol, Henri, 49
Feldman, Arnold S., 529, 567
Fenichel, Otto, 77
Finland, 511
Flanders, Allan, 409
Flexner, Abraham, 282
Florence, P. Sargant, 398
Ford, Henry, 41
France, 219, 511
Frankel, Charles, 2
Franklin, Benjamin, 46, 96
Freedman, Milton, 584
Frenkel-Brunswik, Else, 70

Freud, Sigmund, 20, 77
Fusfeld, Daniel R., 377
Future of the industrial system, 554

G

Galbraith, John K., 164, 521, 529, 547
Gandhi, Mahatma, 56, 112
Garbutt, J. T., 13
Gellerman, Saul, 19
General Motors, 41
Germany, 218, 357, 512
Ghiselli, Edwin E., 24, 25, 26, 574
Goldman, Marshall, 559
Gomberg, William, 583
Granick, David, 51, 198, 218, 459, 553
Gras, N. S. B., 141
Greece, 129, 512
Grinker, Roy, 79
Guatemala, 317
Gunther, John, 147

H

Haberstroh, Chadwick, 528, 538
Hacker, Louis, 47
Hagan, Everett, 22, 292
Haider, Michael, 4
Haire, Mason, 24, 25, 26, 309, 325, 574
Hamilton, Alexander, 47
Hampton, David R., 527
Hamsun, Knut, 16
Hansen, Alvin, 148
Harbison, Frederick, 51, 247, 257, 519, 523, 528, 530
Harbron, John D., 198, 233
Harlow, Harry, 81
Harris, Seymour, 49
Hecksher, Eli F., 139
Heilbroner, Robert, 1, 13, 42, 127, 145
Henninger, G. Ross, 278
Henry, William E., 78, 579
Heredity, 64
Heroes, 286
Higgins, Benjamin, 146
Hirschman, Albert, 151, 387
Historical views on business, 42–44
Hobson, John A., 138
Hoebel, E. A., 68
Hofstadter, Richard, 278
Hoijer, Harry, 68
Holland, 357
Hollingshead, August B., 79
Hoselitz, Bert F., 374
Houghton, Arthur, 4
Hsu, Francis L. K., 67
Hsu, Immanuel, 265

Hu Shih, 56, 120
Hutchinson, John, 248, 299

I

Ideology, 82
Impersonality, 14
India, 441
Industrializing elites, 199
Inkeles, Alex, 284, 293
Israel, 510
Italy, 512

J

James, B. J., 78
Japan, 428, 510
Jefferson, Thomas, 47
Jennings, Eugene E., 577
Joyce, James, 10
Jucius, Michael J., 367
Juram, J. M., 314

K

Kahl, Joseph A., 293
Kantor, MacKinlay, 15
Kantorovich, L. V., 561
Kazuo, Noda, 429
Kennedy, John F., 42
Kerr, Clark, 198, 519, 523, 528, 530
Kettering, Charles F., 31
Kimble, George, 146
Kluckhohn, Clyde, 67
Knapp, R. H., 13
Kneller, George E., 279
Kolaja, Jiri, 461
Korean students, 9
Kornai, Janos, 455
Korol, Alexander, 283
Kosygin, A., 426, 525
Kroeber, A. L., 67

L

LaBarre, Weston, 73
Labor theory of value, 561
Laistner, M. L. W., 129
Landreth, Harry, 529, 557
Lange, Oscar, 566
Langenderfer, Harold Q., 394, 488
Latin America, 232, 366, 376, 513
Lauterbach, Albert, 310, 370
Lazarus, Emma, 45
Leadership, 327
Leavitt, Harold, 23
Lee, James, 12
Lenin, Nikolai, 13

Lentz, Edith, 23
Levinson, D. J., 70
Levy, D. M., 77
Lewis, Hilda, 77
Lewis, Oscar, 78, 151
Lewis, W. Arthur, 260
Liberman, E. G., 426, 557, 559
Linton, Ralph, 68
Lupton, T., 398
Luther, Martin, 99
Lynch, C., 470

M

de Madariaga, S., 368
Maillart, Ella, 76
Managerial philosophies and practice
  American, 346, 366, 582
  as an art, 366
  in China, 467
  cultural patterns, 325
  European, 346
  in French Canada, 501
  in Germany, 357
  in Guatemala, 309
  in Holland, 357
  in India, 441
  in Japan, 428
  in Latin America, 366, 370
  leadership, 327
  in Poland, 453
  promising foreign practices, 574
  science, 366
  in Soviet Union, 416
  in United Arab Republic, 488
  in United Kingdom, 395
Mantoux, Paul, 141
Marshall, Alfred, 277
Martin, Norman H., 579
Marx, Karl, 145, 558
Maslow, Abraham, 16
Mason, Edward S., 549
McCann, Eugene C., 310, 366
McClelland, David, 13, 21, 22, 46, 52, 70,
    128, 163, 199, 214, 292, 310, 341,
    503, 579
McCormick, Charles, 578
McLuhan, Marshall, 1
Mead, Margaret, 128, 182, 247, 248, 450,
    495
Mechanic, David, 518, 583
Medieval Europe, 132
  attitudes toward business, 133
  evolution of the capitalist, 138
  philosophy of trade, 133
Mercantilism, 139
Merton, Robert K., 78
Mexico, 238, 514

Miedzinska, Janina, 461
Money, 95, 172, 187
Montcheuil, Yves, 440
Montias, J. M., 455
Moore, Wilbert E., 316, 529, 567
Morison, Samuel Eliot, 46
Morris, C. J., 76
Motion, the concept of, 87
Mukerji, D. P., 56, 112
Mukerji, S. N., 271
Mumford, Lewis, 13, 56, 82
Murray, Henry, 67
Myers, Charles A., 51, 247, 257, 519, 523,
    528, 530

N

Nash, Manning, 309, 317
Nasser, A., 490
Needs
  achievement, 21
  affiliation, 17
  autonomy, 21
  competence, 19
  effect of culture on, 22
  hierarchy of, 15
  physiological, 16
  power, 20
  prestige, 18
  safety and security, 16
  self-actualization, 21
  self-esteem, 19
  social esteem, 18
  status, 18
  in various countries, 334, 341
Nelson, Benjamin, 134
Nepal, 76
Netherlands, 512
Nevins, Allan, 41
Niebuhr, Reinhold, 21
Nietzsche, Friedrich, 21
Nove, Alec, 559
Novozhilov, V. V., 561
Nowotny, Otto, 310, 346

O

Ong, Walter, 2
Organizations
  change, 545
  evolving, 538
  structural elements, 542
Origins of managers, 199
  business and class in Europe, 218
  colonial administrators, 209
  dynasts and paternalists, 201
  the industrialist in Latin America, 232
  industrializing elites, 200

Origins of managers—*Cont.*
  middle class and open market, 207
  nationalist leaders, 209
  revolutionary intellectuals, 207
  social class background, 214
  in United Kingdom, 398
Orleans, Leo A., 266
Orwell, George, 18
Osgood, Cornelius, 70

P

Parker, Hugh, 580
Parkinson, C. Northcote, 351
Parks, F. Newton, 310, 356
Payne, George L., 279
Pelletier, Gaston, 394, 501
Personality
  childhood determinism, 76
  consistency, 71
  and culture, 67
  internal conflicts, 72
  situational approach, 78
  world view, ethos, 79
Peru, 73
Physiological needs, 16
Pirenne, Henri, 43, 132, 138
Plato, 131
Pluralistic industrialism, 534
Poignant, Raymond, 280
Poland, 453, 512
Porter, Lyman, 24, 25, 26, 574, 578
Potter, David M., 78
Power need, 20
Prestige need, 18
Prince, Morton, 69
Prokofiev, M. A., 283
Protestant ethic, 31, 91
Provincialism, American, 2

Q

Quakers, 52

R

Ram, Charat, 497
Rawin, Solomon, 394, 453
Redlich, Frederick O., 79
Redlich, Fritz, 372
Research, suggested topics, 587
Reynolds, R. L., 136
Ribble, M., 77
Richman, Barry, 394, 467, 518, 521
Ridicule, 19
Riesman, David, 20, 78
Ringer, Fritz F. K., 277
Ringisho, 434

Rome, 130
Rosen, Bernard, 292
Rosenbluth, Dina, 77
Ross, Arthur, 518
Rossi, P. H., 284
Rostow, Walt W., 127, 157
Roudinesco, J., 77
Rudolph, Frederick, 278
Russell, Bertrand, 21
Ryapolov, Gregory, 393, 416

S

Safety, 16
Schachter, Stanley, 18
Schlesinger, Arthur M., 47, 49
Schumpeter, Joseph, 547
Schurz, W. L., 368
Security, 16
Self-actualization, 21
Self-esteem needs, 19
Servan-Shreiber, J. J., 574
Shapiro, Harry L., 68
Shonfield, A., 274
Situational approach, 78
Skinner, C. Wickham, 5, 28, 573
Slater, Philip, 525
Sloan, Alfred P., 41
Smith, Adam, 140
Smith, Dan Throop, 248, 295
Snow, C. P., 140
Social class background of managers, 214
Social esteem need, 18
Socialism, 548, 565
Sombart, Werner, 128
Soviet Union, 416, 472, 515, 557
Space, the concept of, 87
Spain, 512
Spiegel, John, 79
Spitz, Rene A., 77, 81
Stark, Harry, 367
Staub, Hugo, 77
Stewart, Rosemary, 393, 395
Strauss, Anselm L., 579
Students, 573
Sturmthal, Adolf, 461
Summer, Charles, 527
Sundaran, K., 479
Sweden, 513

T

Tannenbaum, Frank, 372, 522
Tawney, R. H., 138
Taylor, F. M., 566
Taylor, Harold, 283
Taylor, Walter W., 68

Technical change, 182
  attitudes affecting, 189
  effects on health and nutrition, 188
  industry and the social unit, 191
  introduction of new tools, 186
  money economy, 185
  solutions in process, 195
Technics, 82
Technostructure, 547
Tierney, Brian, 135
Tilgher, Adriano, 131
Time
  and the clock, 83
  the meaning of, 12
  utilization, 13
Tocqueville, de, Alexis, 50
Tschopik, Harry, 73
Tuchman, Barbara, 522
Turgeon, Lynn, 563
Tylor, Edward B., 68

U

United Arab Republic, 488
United Kingdom, 395, 515
United States
  business in, 44
  colonies and colonists, 45
  economic development, 47
  education, 49
  management professionalism, 49
  nobility, 46
  ownership and management, 50
  politics and business, 47
Urquidi, Victor L., 386
Urwick, Lyndall, 49

V

Vakil, Chandulal N., 386
Venables, P. F. R., 280
Venezuela, 244
Vernon, Raymond, 385

W

Waller, W., 78
Walton, Clarence C., 127, 128
Ward, Lewis, 507
Warner, W. Lloyd, 582
Watson, John B., 70
Webber, Ross A., 527
Weber, Max, 31, 46, 56, 91, 357
Wesley, John, 110
Western Europe, 128
Westfall, Ralph, 493, 498
Wharton School, 49, 52
White, Robert, 19
Whyte, William F., 30, 247, 286
Whyte, William H., 78, 410
Wiles, P. J. D., 455
Williams, L. K., 293
Williams, Maslyn, 19
Wilson, Robert, 23
Wolf, K. M., 81
Wolff, Werner, 71
Work, the meaning of, 31
Wright, D. M., 131

Y

Yugoslavia, 513

Z

Zaleznik, Abraham, 352
Zauberman, Alfred, 559

This book has been set in 10 point Press Roman, leaded 2 points, and 8 point Press Roman, leaded 1 point. Chapter numbers are in 18 point Times Roman italic; chapter titles are in 24 point Times Roman italic. The size of the type page is 27 by 45½ picas.